REMEMBERING ROOTES

REMEMBERING ROOTES is a compilation of extracts from magazines published by the company to encourage in many ways the interest and enthusiasm for their products.

This book will be of interest to the many enthusiasts of the Rootes products which include **Humber**, **Hillman**, **Sunbeam-Talbot**, and **Sunbeam** cars. It should recall many happy memories to those who are old enough, and enlighten those who are not to the great many varied activities that the company embarked upon.

JUNE	1951
NOVEMBER	1951
MARCH	1952
OCTOBER	1952
JANUARY	1953
FEBRUARY	1953
APRIL	1953
MAY	1953
JUNE	1953

This book has been published by   Mercian Manuals Ltd
353 Kenilworth Road
Balsall Common
Coventry
West Midlands
CV7 7DL
+44 (0) 1676 533304
www.mercianmanuals.co.uk

Forgotten anything?

"Hope not! Brief-case, keys, handkerchief — all present, I think."

Car all right?

"Yes, petrol, oil, tyres, radiator — everything checked."

But there's something else, something *vital*. Brakes need little attention, so they're apt to get none — for much too long. Modern linings wear down so very gradually, you may be deceived — you yourself don't notice you're pushing the pedal harder. *Yet, at any moment, lives may depend on full stopping-power.*

To be ready for that moment, have your brakes checked *regularly*. Adjustment, if needed, is simple. When at last they need relining, follow your repairer's advice to fit Ferodo linings — standard on most British vehicles, and supplied in correct grades for *every* make in the world.

Points to remember

For good control, brake action must be carefully balanced. Periodically, operating linkage should be lubricated, hydraulic systems checked, brake linings and drums inspected. Your repairer knows how, and how often, to attend to these points — get his advice.

Ask yourself now *the following safety questions:*

1. Does pedal go down nearly to floor?
2. Do brakes grab, chatter, or make grinding sound?
3. Do brakes fail to respond to increased pedal pressure?
4. When you brake, does steering pull to one side?

If the answer to any of these is "Yes," your brakes need attention — quickly. But even without such symptoms they may be dangerously below standard. *Regular* testing is your safeguard.

HERE'S A GOOD SAFETY RULE:

Test your brakes when you change your oil—every 2,000-3,000 miles

Published by the makers of

FERODO
BRAKE AND CLUTCH LININGS

as a contribution to safe and pleasant driving

FERODO LIMITED, CHAPEL-EN-LE-FRITH • A Member of the Turner & Newall Organization

A right royal welcome awaits you

at Devonshire House, Piccadilly, in the heart of London's West End. Here are displayed the world-famous products of the Rootes Group—Humber, Hillman, Sunbeam-Talbot Cars: Commer and Karrier Trucks. Here is a part of Britain on parade . . . an opportunity to inspect a fine array of Britain's fine cars, in ideal surroundings.

**HUMBER
HILLMAN
SUNBEAM - TALBOT** **ROOTES**

EXPORT DIVISION : DEVONSHIRE HOUSE, PICCADILLY, LONDON, W.1.

ROOTES GROUP
REGIONAL REPRESENTATIVES
located at
U.S.A. 505 Park Avenue, New York, 22, New York, and 403 North Foothill Road, Beverly Hills, California.
CANADA 170 Bay Street, Toronto.
AUSTRALIA & NEW ZEALAND Fishermen's Bend, Port Melbourne, Australia.
BELGIUM Shell Building, 47 Cantersteen, Brussels.
CENTRAL AFRICA Jackson Road, P.O. Box 5194, Nairobi, Kenya.
SOUTHERN AFRICA 750/2/4 Stuttaford's Buildings, St. George's St., Cape Town, South Africa.
EUROPE Devonshire House, Piccadilly, London, W.1.
FAR EAST Macdonald House, Orchard Rd., Singapore 9.
MIDDLE EAST 37, Kasr El Nil Street, Cairo, Egypt.
INDIA Agra Road, Bhandup, Bombay.
ARGENTINA Casilla de Correo 3478, Buenos Aires.
BRAZIL Av. Presidente Vargas 290 (S/1003), Rio de Janeiro.
CARIBBEAN 28 Duke St., Kingston, Jamaica, B.W.I.

Modern Motoring & Travel

PROMINENT PERSONALITIES & THEIR CARS—New Series, No. 63

His Excellency the Governor of Trinidad and Tobago

Humber Pullman Limousine

His Excellency Major-General Sir Hubert Elvin Rance, G.C.M.G., G.B.E., C.B., at Government House, Port of Spain, with Lady Rance and the Colonial Secretary, Hon. P. M. Renison, C.M.G.

MODERN MOTORING & TRAVEL

June, 1951

Conducted by E. D. O'BRIEN

Editor:

THOMAS R. MULCASTER

Festival Traffic

THE "Festival of Britain" South Bank Exhibition and the nearby pleasure gardens are now happily emerging from their protracted teething troubles.

The biggest ache since the opening has been the many thousands of would-be visitors who spent more time by hours in the long queues of approach (within the turnstiles as well as outside) than in the actual exhibition buildings.

There have also been those countless thousands interested only in seeing, at more convenient distance, the much advertised "Exhibition and other wonderful illuminations forming part of Festive London."

The combined pressure very nearly closed both Westminster and Waterloo Bridges, and certainly the full length of the Victoria Embankment, from Blackfriars to Lambeth, to all vehicle traffic.

In Battersea itself streaming masses queued for more than a mile across the park to the town beyond. Nearby Albert Bridge and its feeder thoroughfares have frequently been forbidden areas to all but pedestrian movement.

* * *

WE never once doubted the Festival's success from the attendance angle.

Our greatest concern always has been that in regard to full and adequate consideration being given to inevitable traffic problems attaching to large-scale gatherings of the kind. We remain thus concerned, for any half-hearted acceptance of the facts, or failure to keep developments constantly under review, may well cause a major calamity in local and nearby traffic co-ordination and flow which could seriously affect the entire Metropolitan area.

* * *

"All Out of Step but . . ."

SPEAKING at the annual dinner of the Institute of the Motor Industry, Lord Brabazon of Tara, pioneer motorist and aviator, is reported to have said : " Some of the products foisted upon the British public to-day are extremely unstable, almost death traps."

Lord Brabazon went on : "With the motor industry in the most unhealthy condition that we cannot compare our products with their foreign rivals, it is easy for anyone to prosper in it. . . . When pushed the U.K. motor industry could produce better vehicles than anyone in the world. . . . To-day the only thing it need produce really well is something for export, because everything first-class goes overseas, the people at home being left with the residue."

How odd that such a world-famous pioneer motorist should be so far out of touch with the motor industry of to-day, and of the difficult conditions under which it is forced to operate ! "All out of step but Lord Brabazon . . ." is a fair comment.

Mis-statements of this kind travel far and wide, unfortunately at a pace seldom caught up by the truth. By and large, Lord Brabazon's remarks are damaging to the U.K. motor industry, which has had one standard ever—one which is second to none for quality and performance. The manufacturer to-day cannot be blamed for the present price competition position, while sources of raw materials and of production are rigidly controlled by Government departments.

Lord Brabazon later criticised the industry as being " out of touch with the man-in-the-street's interests in motor sport : that it did not appreciate the enthusiasm existing : nor had it done anything to encourage it."

Here again Lord Brabazon is on the wrong track. In motor sport time and time again the industry has produced world beaters and could do so to-day. Having built a new world challenge, however, where is it possible within the British Isles to put it to tests which can compare with conditions in other countries ?

Where in these islands are there tracks suitable, or even adaptable, for either the maximum speeds which could be reached, or for accommodating the crowds of spectators ?

What encouragement does the Government give, at a time when our foreign rivals, almost without exception, are subsidised on grounds of the national prestige involved ?

Brooklands has been destroyed. The Government maintains a persistent hold on Donington, while at the same time they offer only a miserable short-term tenure, at a cost which, as the R.A.C.'s decision to give up Silverstone shows, is completely uneconomic, given the present rate of entertainment and other taxation.

We cannot help feeling that Lord Brabazon spoke in haste. If he wants a target for his powder and shot, let him choose that officialdom which is conspiring to prevent either him or the man-in-the-street enjoying what he so earnestly and innocently desires.

* * *

Dazzle that is not !

THE dazzle problem is once again in the limelight of public concern.

Complaints are spreading that motorists in ever-increasing numbers are refraining from dipping, or dimming their car's headlights when meeting other drivers.

Alternatively, if and when they do, that nearside headlamp beams are so badly focused and misdirected as to cause irritating glare to the oncoming road user.

The facts are these :

Firstly, with the majority of motor-cars in use to-day over 10 years of age, where anti-dazzle devices are fitted they are those of the old dip-and-switch system, i.e., cutting out the offside headlamp illumination and dipping the nearside beam.

Many vehicles are of even earlier manufacture, entirely without such courtesy device.

Such new motor-cars as leave the assembly lines to-day, however, are equipped with the more modern and highly efficient Lucas "double-dipping" mechanism whereby *neither headlamp beam is blacked out*, both dipping to the nearside, controlling all possible dazzle, at the same time providing vastly improved driving light where it is needed, on the road ahead ! It is this visual retention of double-headlamp-usage that is attracting this new public doubt.

It will take time, of course, before units are available—as ultimately they will be—for replacing old-type lighting systems, and until this is possible, or until new models are more freely available, there must continue to be this needless anxiety—in effect no more than an optical illusion and a mistaken belief that, because the normal one-headlamp-blackout is not apparent, the driver concerned is necessarily inconsiderate.

We hope this explanation will help to remove all doubt in the shortest possible time.

"IT'S NOT JUST FOR THE RECORD"

says JOHN COBB, holder of the World's Land Speed Record...

"that I drive on Dunlop"

❝ *On my record run at the Salt Flats, Utah, in 1947,*" says John Cobb "*I drove on Dunlop. On my ordinary business journeys here at home, I naturally use Dunlop, too.* ❞

Practical tests such as that carried out by John Cobb in his Napier-Railton have proved of direct value in the production of tyres for the ordinary user. This continual research, coupled with the Company's manufacturing experience — the longest in the world — ensures that Dunlop tyres remain in a class by themselves.

DUNLOP

THE WORLD'S MASTER TYRE

BY APPOINTMENT
MOTOR CAR TYRE
MANUFACTURERS
DUNLOP RUBBER
CO LTD.

1H/113

"LONDON to NEW ZEALAND" in the HUMBER HAWK

Progress according to schedule, but much fêting all along the route—says

JOSEPHINE WHITEHORN
leader of the crew

The scene was Kensington High Street, London, W.8. The date, March 5. The time, 10 o'clock.

SUITCASES, bedding, shovels, frying-pans and Thermos flasks, all piled on the footpath; reporters and photographers trying to get a story and pictures; finally a round of farewells, a mass of tangled streamers blowing over the car, and we were off on the first of 15,000 miles driving, only 20 minutes behind schedule!

The Hawk caused a great deal of amusement and much hand-waving and cheering as we drove out through London. We had allowed plenty of time to reach Dover, but just before Canterbury there was a strong smell of petrol.

The worst had happened. The top of one of the spare tanks had come off and petrol had been sloshing out over the equipment in the boot.

I really pushed the car after that, and found she held the road beautifully at 60, only to reach the dock gates just as the last hooter was blowing.

The guard was interested, sympathetic, vastly amused, but quite adamant. We could not get on the boat.

After numerous telephone calls arrangements were made to cross to Dunkirk that night.

* * *

Males offer help!

PASSENGERS and cars were disembarked at the horribly early hour of 4.30, to be greeted by a thick yellow fog, cold wind and slippery roads. After a number of false starts, we found the road to Ostend and pushed on for Brussels, where we contacted the Rootes Group representatives in Brussels. The courtesy and service here was most encouraging, and anyone travelling through Brussels who needs mechanical work done, and who has difficulty with the language, would be well advised to go to this garage, "Dimotor."

With Joan driving, we left Brussels and again found our sign, "London to New Zealand," causing a great deal of amusement. At the border came numerous offers of male company to assist with the mechanics, the driving, and general protection!

Just before reaching the main Cologne–Frankfurt autobahn, we pulled off the road, to catch up on a little sleep in the car. With the seats adjusted it was remarkably comfortable.

* * *

Well loaded

"RIEXIE," the Canadian girl who was to be the third member of the party, met us in Munich.

Although we cut down our personal clothing to one suitcase and one small grip each, the luggage boot was full, and so was the top and the inside. In fact, the car was rather low on the springs when we pulled out!

There was plenty of room, however, for the three of us to ride in front, and we found that it balanced the weight better.

Heavy snows

AT the German–Austrian border everyone was intrigued by the car and all proceeded to inform us that the road to Innsbruck would not be possible without chains. We had none and just waved cheerfully and pushed on.

The car, by this time named "Belinda," made it without any difficulty, keeping her lead in a long line of cars climbing the same hills.

The Brenner pass, which we climbed on March 12, was quite clear of snow until the top, where there was about six inches of packed snow and more coming down.

* * *

Into Italy

THE Italian Customs were pleasant and presented no difficulty, except for the fact that there was 242 lire to pay for the radio. We protested that the radio was entered in the carnet, but were told it was a "radio tax" and even the Italians had to pay it.

Our limited Italian, mostly supplied by me, caused a good deal of amusement at the hotel in Trento when we asked for baths. It appeared they had only one bathroom, and we had to wait a long, long time.

The petrol taken on in Germany was still lasting and, in fact, took us to Trieste, a matter of 389 miles. Petrol proved to be 3s. 6d. a gallon in Trieste, because we discovered that the nearest branch of the Italian Touring Club, where one can obtain special petrol tickets, was about 80 miles before the Trieste "border." There is no branch in Trieste.

* * *

Over the air!

THE "London to New Zealand" got us some Press contacts and a few minutes over the Trieste radio. Of course it was in Italian, but the next morning quite a crowd gathered to see us off, all very excited because they had heard about us on the radio, and here we were in the flesh! People were so pleased to be able to say, "I met those three girls who are driving to New Zealand."

The scenery, looking down from the road which climbs steeply out of Trieste, is magnificent. It was March 16, there was bright sun and Trieste was spread out below us.

* * *

Into Jugoslavia

THE road from Trieste into Jugoslavia is excellent, built rather like the autobahns in Germany.

The Trieste side of the border was not interested in what we were carrying, but checked all documents carefully. The Jugoslavian side of the border, on the other hand, had a field day with our baggage.

They opened every bag, looked at our magazines (upside-down), thumbed through our log-book, and then asked about cameras. We had five between three of us, which staggered them.

The country from Sezana to Zagreb is splendid, with high snow-capped mountains in the distance. The road is in excellent condition, tarred, for about 40 miles beyond the border, and then suddenly, without warning, we found we were on a gravel road, full of holes.

In Zagreb we stopped at the first policeman on point duty and asked where the British Consulate was. To our astonishment, a man walked over and spoke to us in perfectly good English.

* * *

Hospitality—and eggs!

MARCH 18 saw us leaving Zagreb on the autoput to Belgrade. At dusk we pulled off the road, along an open lane, and proceeded to set up camp—in the car.

Joan and Riexie took the watercan, a torch and the phrase book, and set off towards some village lights. They returned with a dozen eggs and the can of water carried by two amused young men.

Ten minutes later the car was surrounded by interested neighbours who would not hear of us camping in the car, but insisted we stay in one of their houses. We compromised by parking in a farmyard, but still proposed to sleep in the car.

It must have been an amusing sight with the car following the farmer who was carrying a red lantern to show us the way, followed by at least 40 people.

* * *

Embassy welcome

THAT evening we had our first introduction to the hospitality of the Jugoslavian peasants. Our host brought in a flask of Raki, and the next four hours were spent drinking with him, singing, and answering the many questions which were put to us by the crowd which squeezed themselves into the tiny room.

We eventually crawled into the car about 1 a.m.

We were welcomed in royal fashion by the Embassy, and were invited to a cocktail party, which we attended dressed in extremely grubby pullovers and baggy corduroy slacks!

* * *

We appear amusing!

IN Belgrade we experienced for the second time the somewhat overwhelming attentions of the populace.

While we were waiting for "Putnik," the Jugoslavian Travel Agency, to find accommodation for us, the car was surrounded by a mob of people, curious to see these weird creatures who were driving a privately owned automobile! By smiling and saying a few words to anyone who could speak English, I managed to keep them amused.

The crowd grew rapidly to about 250

or 300 people, and about that time the police thought they should take a hand.

The crowd resented this and it looked as though there might be some trouble, but a lad of about 14 who spoke English managed to translate to the policeman the fact that I had permission to wait there. The crowd then laughed at the discomfort of the policeman.

* * *

Friendly Jugoslavs

HOTELS in Jugoslavia, generally speaking, are cold, drab and expensive, though the people were friendly and helpful and did their best.

The countryside from Belgrade going south was quieter, still with rolling hills and good bitumenised roads.

After an over-night stop in Kragujevac, thanks to the help of an English-speaking member of the town, we got on the road towards Skoplje.

* * *

Cobbles and filigree

SKOPLJE is quite a mixture of East and West. Many of the women wear the baggy pantaloons of the Turkish peasants, and mosques with their slender minarets were to be seen.

The market quarter is also quite Eastern, and we thoroughly enjoyed ourselves poking into the tiny shops which open directly on to the cobbled streets, and where the workers can be seen doing their marvellously bright quilting, or putting together the tiny pieces of silver filigree jewellery.

Leaving Skoplje the road was a mixture of large rocks, clay and gravel, surfaced by the inevitable dust.

We made ourselves "nosebags" out of cheese cloth, so that we could breathe without inhaling clouds of fine white dust, and startled the local inhabitants, who pulled up short at the sight of three figures with white masks over their faces!

* * *

AT the first farmhouse where we had camped, between Zagreb and Belgrade, our host had written on a piece of paper a request for us to park our car in some farmyard, and to sleep in the car. It was of great assistance, being in Serbian, and saved a great deal of the energy we usually devoted to sign language!

When we pulled into a tiny village for the next stop, we drove up to the pump which is the centre of the village life, and produced this piece of paper. After much pondering, discussion and laughter, it was deciphered and we were made welcome at one of the houses.

The family insisted that we sleep in a spotless room, and we could not refuse.

The main room of the house had a beaten earth floor and the lady of the house wore no shoes, but their kindness and courtesy will be something to remember.

We took photographs of the whole clan, and then with their final gift of six eggs sitting precariously in our laps and escorted to the main road by the entire population of the village, we continued on our way to the border, 25 kilometres ahead.

It took about one and a half hours to clear the border control, barriers and road blocks, but we finally left Jugoslavian territory at 11.30 on Easter Sunday, March 25. *(To be continued)*

In Garmisch, while the weather was still well below zero, but where we pushed ahead well on schedule.

A welcome indeed, with generous entertainment for us all, including "Belinda," from a farming family near Zagreb, Jugoslavia.

The family in whose home we were welcome "staying guests" prior to reaching Djeodjelje.

Below: Actually our first picnic on the journey, at Veles, where our improvised yet efficient "kitchen service" intrigued, and amused apparently, the local peasantry.

Festivals of the Little Boats

Regattas on Sea and River provide that "Holiday Extra" for Motorists

By GEORGE HOWARD

The Tamesis Club's Thames sailing season opens at Teddington Reach.

BRITAIN isn't called a maritime nation for nothing. Water proves a stronger magnet to the people of this country than any other. And when there's some celebrating to do, or some prowess to exhibit, then for untold centuries the people have instinctively gone to the country's wealth of rivers or her thousands of miles of coastline.

No single article, or even a book, could describe the thousand or so regattas which take place in Britain every year.

There are close on a hundred of them on the Thames alone, and a list of the harbours, ports and havens of the British Isles is a schedule of the regattas as well, for no coastal town misses this chance for some aquatic fun and gaiety.

* * *

MANY of the regattas are purely local affairs not designed by an enterprising council to attract visitors; others are of world renown. Personally, I love the small regattas because of their spontaneous enthusiasm and the resourceful skill of the participants. It is a time to get to know the local inhabitants as they really are, for reserves disappear as young Jim pits his sailing skill against old Tom, whose fishing smack has beaten all comers for more years than he cares to remember. So my advice is: if you notice signs of a regatta at a tiny Cornish harbour or along the dour coast of Western Scotland, try to be there on the day.

Then there are the big regattas of international repute, providing scenes of real beauty and thrills which the converted say are no match for any other.

* * *

SOME will suggest that a hole in one, a goal in that five minutes of extra time, or a century at Lords, are *the* thrills of sport, but to the sailing men the sight of three or four sunlit yachts, every inch of canvas out, foaming into the Solent with not a quarter-mile between them, is the British sporting thrill without peer.

This Festival year is going to be a landmark in the history of regattas. Every town bordering a river or on the coast is arranging something special as part of the Festival celebrations.

And very appropriate this is, too, for it was on the occasion of the 1851 Exhibition that an extensive programme of regattas was arranged with an international flavour. One upshot was the beginning of the America's Cup Races between the New York Yacht Club and the Royal Yacht Squadron. The first race (won by America) took place on August 22, 1851, and the course was round the Isle of Wight.

ALTHOUGH the day of the big yachts seems to have passed, Cowes Regatta (July 30–August 14) is undoubtedly the biggest occasion of its kind in the world to-day. Notable this year will be the first race for a new challenge cup, the Britannia, presented by the King to the Yacht Racing Association to be competed for by yachts of any country.

This race will be held under the burgee of the Royal Yacht Squadron, formed in 1815. Old as the R.Y.S. is, the title of the oldest sailing club in the British Isles is easily held by the Royal Cork Yacht Club, formed in 1720.

* * *

THE Isle of Wight and the Hampshire resorts will be an excellent locale for anyone wishing to see plenty of sea racing and the illuminations which will follow at night.

In addition to the Cowes festivities for sailing ships, the Royal Motor Yacht Squadron are holding a special festival race for motor cruisers from Cowes on July 28, and regattas will take place in the Solent continuously from July 30 to August 14, entries coming from clubs in the Thames and along the South Coast.

* * *

FOR earlier holidaymakers—and those who live in the North—there is the Clyde Yachting Fortnight (June 29–July 11).

With the ability to judge this annual event without any bias of patriotism I would nevertheless agree with Scotsmen that the Clyde regattas are the best of all for onlookers. Cowes may be most fashionable and most famous, but on the Clyde there is the excuse for a day out for thousands of Glasgow's citizens.

Many of them spend their days building big ships and engines, but the tradition of sail is still in their blood, and for contagious excitement there is nothing better than to be with a great crowd of these folk watching the entrants coming round the pile of Ailsa Craig, maybe almost awash in a running sea.

* * *

A CAR is a necessity to enjoy the Clyde regatta to the full. It enables sight-seeing to be combined with the water events, and to become envious of the Glaswegians who have this perfect coastline within a short distance of their homes.

The Clyde is also the place to see some of the big races, such as the arduous one round the Isle of Arran to Dublin and back.

* * *

LONDONERS who know all too little of their Thames can atone for it by making a resolution to visit Royal Henley (July 4-7). It was the first Oxford and Cambridge boat race in 1829 which started Henley regatta. The course was between Hambleden Lock and Henley Bridge.

Henley is the perfect setting for a river regatta, with a broad straight stretch of water extending for nearly one and a half miles. It is the greatest amateur sporting event for boats in the world. The major events are the Grand Challenge Cup for eights, the Stewards' Challenge Cup for fours, the Silver Goblets for pairs, and the Diamond Challenge Sculls for scullers. All of these contests are more than a hundred years old.

Henley is, of course, an occasion for parties and parades as well as sport. For the ladies, indeed, the fashions, the teas on the sloping lawns, and the illuminations at night are doubtless of more interest than the races—so that everyone finds something to his taste.

* * *

IF Royal Henley has been given more space than the other Thames regattas it is only because of its international flavour. The regattas at Marlow, Staines, Kingston, Richmond, and Reading are just as charming. All Thames regattas are very old institutions—days of celebration for the river's watermen who for centuries have earned their living on the ferries, barges, and other craft which use this great artery.

The schools created the vogue for rowing races with four or eight in the crew. Eton had started them in 1812, and Westminster School in 1813. Other young men saw the attraction of the exercise, and small clubs sprang up all along the Thames. In 1818 two of them, the Star and the Arrow, combined to form the leading amateur club of to-day, the Leander.

* * *

HINTS on regattas to see this Festival year queue up in one's mind, and only space prevents the mention of some which will doubtless delight thousands of motoring holidaymakers who come across them more by luck than planning.

They range from Babbacombe (August 12-14) and the national dinghy championships at Falmouth (August 14-29), to the magnificent spectacle in Weymouth Bay during Weymouth Week (August 9-12) when the Royal Navy will be host to the visitors and will turn night into day with the ships' illuminations.

* * *

VISITORS may prefer the leisurely, lazy day watching the little sailing boats cavorting in the great neck of water at Fowey, Cornwall (August 29-31) or want to join the crowds at the big events which will take place at the big holiday resorts of North Wales and Lancashire.

Anyone who lives within motoring distance of the latter area should remember that Liverpool is planning big regattas on the Mersey, including a firework display which is claimed to be the greatest event of its kind the world has ever seen.

June, 1951 — Page 17 — MODERN MOTORING & TRAVEL

MILES AHEAD... *in performance comfort and safety*

The HUMBER Super Snipe

BY APPOINTMENT H.M. THE KING
MOTOR CAR MANUFACTURERS
HUMBER LTD. COVENTRY

HUMBER

Craftsman-built by

THE ROOTES GROUP

THE HUMBER SUPER SNIPE carries forward the great tradition of its famous predecessors. To already brilliant top-gear performance and impressive acceleration are now added important improvements to the suspension which give better riding qualities and increased stability when cornering at speed. Important new styling details add to traditional Humber grace and distinction. Wherever in the world your journey takes you, you'll be ahead in the Super Snipe.

PRICE £945 *plus purchase tax* · ALSO HAWK · PULLMAN · IMPERIAL

HUMBER LTD. RYTON-ON-DUNSMORE COVENTRY · LONDON SHOWROOMS & EXPORT DIVISION: ROOTES LTD. DEVONSHIRE HOUSE PICCADILLY LONDON W I

EVEN in 1951 I think it is very bad manners to walk without great care through woods and fields. For these are the homes of creatures who are important; some of them, perhaps all, are necessary to our life.

Flowers too; I hate to see them wantonly killed. They have feelings, some sense to follow the sun and, no doubt, a little instinct or thought.

The latest idea for increasing the seeding capacity of trees is quaint. The tree is "frightened," like a sensitive plant, by fastening a narrow steel band round its trunk. After a while, the tree senses that it may die and promptly tries to correct the result of such a calamity by producing a greatly increased crop of seedlings.

The method appears to have been successful in America where I hear that specialists in arboriculture have vouched for this explanation.

* * *

This sand is quick

I WAS asked the other day by someone who had very nearly been trapped in some quicksand what was the difference between this type and the ordinary kind which you find on the beach and bring home in your shoes.

Quicksand looks very much the same as the ordinary variety, and is merely loose, wet sand which is light in weight, its grains being worn very smooth by the action of water. It is moist because of an underlying layer of clay or other substance through which the water cannot drain away, and the smooth grains are separated by the water which acts as a lubricant.

Although quicksand is almost like a liquid, its mass is too dense to allow the quick movements used in swimming. It has no sucking power of itself, but if you try to lift a foot immersed in it, it tends to form a partial vacuum under your foot and gives you the impression of a downward pull or suction.

As a matter of fact, real quicksand is uncommon and much of the so-called quicksand is only soft mud covered by a layer of ordinary sand.

* * *

Not those Cycles!

YOU know that your alternating electric current supply changes its direction in accordance with the number of cycles, usually 50. Electric clocks keep time for this reason and by using transformers we can build up or break down a voltage without great loss.

In England we suffer from a multitude of forms—it is almost true to say that a house might be papered by the forms necessary before it can be built.

The story was told of a farmer who wrote to his Ministry applying for a permit to purchase a 2½ h.p. electric motor, giving as its details 10 amps., 240 volts, 50 cycles.

The reply came back, and I can well believe it, "Kindly complete the enclosed form before applying for the motor. Supply of motor is granted, but your application for cycles should be forwarded to the appropriate department."

"YOU CAN FRIGHTEN TREES... TO GET MORE SEEDS!"

says
Professor A. M. LOW

Fireside Reflections on Science

Wool-gathering

THIS is not about the dogs which collect sheep's wool in order to drive fleas from themselves. It is about myself at a Committee Meeting.

I attend many of them and, when I can keep awake, I learn a great deal.

At the end of a long table, last week, sat an indignant man who rapped gently to make his points in a rather excitable speech. Every time his fingers touched the table my pencil, several yards away from him, leapt into the air. It was, of course, quite clear that a loose board at one end of the table was transmitting the blow through the wood grain. Is it not quaint to think that if you stamp in a rage it rattles teacups the other side of the world? You may not hear the rattle and the cup may move so slightly that its tremor is invisible.

That is what science is often doing. It is making evident things which have been in existence without our observational senses being sufficiently keen to see, hear, smell or touch unaided.

King Charles I could have had radio and might easily have lit his palace with electric light if only a few little details had been noticed which would have enabled his workmen to produce the necessary spark and the simple crystal set for reception.

The world must be full of things which we have not yet seen and he who sees them first can make a fortune. That is how all fortunes are made.

* * *

How old?

WHEN considering problems of change, and change is all we can recognise, we seldom pause to consider how long are the time periods at stake. There was a time when a child in the form of our earth left its star in flames, slowly cooled down and became our home. This was a mere baby of about 3 trillion, trillion pounds.

The age of the earth has been discovered by aid of the astronomer, the geologist and the physicist with his "spectroscopic" instruments.

We have now a reasonable method of determining the world's birthday. A metal, such as our atomic bomb friend uranium, constantly disintegrates into radium, and the latter again into lead at a very definite rate.

By testing parts of rock and determining the percentage of uranium and lead content a fairly good estimate can be made of the time during which the process of radio-active disintegration has existed.

Geologists, knowing the age of rock in this way, guess, Mrs. Earth has been here since almost 2,000,000,000 B.C. It is by analysing the content of the sun from a knowledge of the light beams which it emits that we also opine with some certainty that the earth and the sun are daughter and mother.

* * *

Take a chance

ALTHOUGH true that we may be lucky in casting dice, it is quite inaccurate to say that we must be so in the future, or to imagine that there is such a thing as a lucky person. This is merely due to chance affecting a particular period of time of which we have knowledge.

With two dice the odds are 35 to 1 against double six and 1,679,615 to 1 against four consecutive throws of this kind. If two dice are thrown simultaneously four times by 10,000,000 people it is probable that a few will throw four double sixes. What appears to be extraordinary chance is merely that if such unusual occasions never occurred it would violate all known laws.

It is often said that in a battle a bullet will not strike the same place twice. Although true that two shots might hit exactly the same spot very seldom, it by no means follows that after one bullet has struck, the chance of another hitting the same place is any smaller than that it might hit any other previously chosen target.

* * *

Odds against!

PLAYING bridge you think it wonderful if you find 13 cards of the same suit, but it is equally wonderful every time you collect your cards for as you touch them the chance that your hand would contain the cards which are there is exactly equal to the chance of your holding 13 diamonds.

If you write down the characters of 13 cards or define 100 such hands you can easily note the number of games which you must play in the future for one of these hands to come up. The odds against it are in the neighbourhood of 635,013,559,599 to 1. Pretty hopeless, isn't it!

Some recent experiments after the style of Dr. Rhine were thought, not by me, to suggest that wishing could affect the turn of a coin. Psycho-kinesis is the word used and I suppose that the emanations of thought are not utterly free from material effect. Matter and energy, thought and radiation... I wonder. Shall we one day radiate a pot of jam across the Atlantic?

June, 1951

Road Trial Report:

The Humber Super Snipe gives convincing proof of British automobile engineering leadership

Quality motoring as symbolised in the Humber Super Snipe.

IT is thirteen years since I had the first Humber Super Snipe out on trial. I remember the occasion clearly for two reasons.

Firstly, it presented an entirely new conception then in really advanced automobile engineering design and performance; secondly, an incident during the trial, uncannily related in an abstract manner, proved unforgettable to this day.

* * *

DRIVING north on A.1 in the early morning hours the better to indulge more readily and safely in the car's higher speed range, I experienced a sudden and eerie outside interest in my preoccupation.

Within a foot of my face—and this while driving at near 60 m.p.h.—was a dark object, going my way, at even speed, giving off a distracting flapping sort of whirr!

A hurried glance revealed that it was a large bird, a thrush I thought at first, its wings not clearly visible in their rapid movement, but what intrigued me most was its long, long beak.

We sped along in company—I was making a test for acceleration up to 60 m.p.h.—and then, as I slowed down, the bird made a lightning dart across the front of the bonnet and disappeared out of sight.

Later, one hundred miles later, when inspecting the car in its garage, I discovered, laying dead between the bonnet and the offside wing, yes, a Snipe!

I can only repeat that my speed truthfully was between 50 m.p.h. and 60 m.p.h. and that Snipe flew at an even pace for an appreciable distance.

* * *

THE recollection came back vividly as I set off recently in the latest Humber Super Snipe, in the interim to become an even better motor-car by comparison, a car to-day in universal esteem. Indeed, for quiet running, masterly performance, high maximum speeds with easy variable ratio steering and dependable braking, it stands unchallenged on the roads of the world.

It is a big car in every way, a full six-seater trimmed throughout in leather, with abundant head, leg and shoulder room for all occupants, each to ride throughout the exceptionally elastic speed range—5 m.p.h. to 80 m.p.h. in top gear, for example—in complete, rather luxurious comfort. Of the incidental interior equipment details contributing to inclusive riding luxury, more anon.

* * *

LET me describe my trial run factually, as you, the reader, might appreciate were you in the pilot's seat and your friends as rear seat passengers.

A touch on the starter button and the engine is purring instantly and silently, the while giving an impression of unlimited potential robustness awaiting your demands.

The synchromatic four-speed gear change lever mounted beneath the steering wheel looks exactly what it is, neat but sturdy without being clumsy, giving in all its operations, with the Borg and Beck single dry plate clutch, easy and reliable synchromesh engagement in relation to all gear ratios.

Silently we move forward in bottom, a light change over to second, then to third and finally to top—doing now, shall we say, a modest 40 m.p.h. Traffic becoming denser, however, we must await the thrill of impressive speed.

A quick flick of the finger, down again to third, an opening and as quickly back to top. It is all that simple, and the least pressure on the accelerator pedal is like a touch of magic, instantly responsive in a surge of power that makes us impatient to put it to peak test.

"Doing 50 m.p.h.", you say, "but more like 20 m.p.h. because of its silence and smoothness."

* * *

AT this moment another motorist, or pedestrian perhaps, attempts "something foolish," to say the least. But the brakes, only lightly applied, slow us up evenly and rapidly—two notable impressions already of the Humber Super Snipe's refined performance.

It is the same all through. There is no fussiness, no awkward moments of doubt, no involuntary shifting of passengers—we all ride restfully and observant of all there is about us, so expansive is the forward arc of front seat vision through the wide screen and, for the rear passengers, maximum six-window left-to-right inclusive viewpoint.

* * *

DISCUSSING the general specification, I tell you that the six-cylinder engine is of 4,086 c.c., developing some 100 b.h.p. at 3,400 revs.

You are "Not surprised. Its feel is that of a thoroughbred."

How true! But later we will see the full measure of its stamina. Meantime we admire the neat facia board, all driving instruments clearly in line of view, the free upper half of the steering wheel giving unobstructed sight of ammeter, speedometer, water temperature and oil pressure gauges, etc. We have already noted, too, the convenient horn operator ring in the centre of the steering wheel and the nearby trafficator and headlamp dip-and-switch levers, the screen wipers that come into operation by a light turn of the knobs before us, sun visors easily lowered, window lifts ready to hand and the generous free leg space everywhere in the front compartment.

* * *

WE have noticed, also, that the front seat is adjustable for best leg reach, a simple lever movement combined with sliding the seat on its ball-bearing rollers giving what we want.

There are centre folding armrests to front and rear seats; and all this is standard equipment to include ashtrays, cigar lighter, interior roof light, pillar

Road Trial Report of Humber Super Snipe

(Concluded from page 19)

pulls, adjustable front quarter and rear window panels, roomy pockets in doors, etc.

Additionally, as an extra, there is the H.M.V. automobile radio and an efficient interior heating and ventilation control giving every desirable variation of interior atmosphere—hot, cold or medium, each lightly or pressure circulated, the rear-seat occupants enjoying identical conditions. Incidentally, a convenient rug rail can be fitted behind the front seat as an extra.

* * *

WITH a clearer road now ahead, let us indulge awhile in real "Super Sniping." For this purpose, I will take over the wheel and demonstrate while you hold the stop-watch. Firstly, we will take "stationary to 50 m.p.h., through all gears. Ready? Off! First, second, third, top—forty, fifty!"

"Fourteen seconds."

"Now stationary to 60 m.p.h. Ready? Go! First, second, third, top—forty, fifty, fifty-five, sixty!"

"Twenty-one seconds."

"Now 10 m.p.h. to 60 m.p.h. in top. Now! Ten, twenty, thirty, forty, fifty, fifty-five, sixty!"

"Thirty-two seconds. Extraordinary!"

"Now the quarter-mile at 60 m.p.h. to check the speed. We will turn round while all is clear and cover the measured distance A to B. When at 60 m.p.h. I will hold it steady. Ready? Now, thirty, forty, fifty, fifty-five, sixty—I am holding it—line A—line B."

SPECIFICATION

ENGINE. Six-cylinder monobloc, side by side valves, special design detachable alloy head. 4-bearing, counter-weighted crankshaft, full pressure lubrication and by-pass oil filter. Automatic choke for easy starting under all conditions. Cushioned Power engine mountings absorb any vibration. Bore and stroke: 85 mm. x 120 mm. (3.35 in. x 4.72 in.).
IGNITION. Coil and distributor, automatic advance and retard.
CLUTCH. Borg and Beck single dry plate. Chain linkage to pedal.
GEARBOX. Proved four-speed gearbox with control ring synchromesh on all four gears, and finger-tip lever on steering column.
OVERALL RATIOS. Top: 4.09:1; Third: 5.89:1; Second: 9.56:1; First: 15.95:1; Reverse: 16.91:1.
REAR AXLE. Semi-floating design with spiral bevel final drive. Ratio 4.09:1.
SUSPENSION. Evenkeel independent front springing, extra-long semi-elliptic rear springs fitted with plastic grease sleeves, anti-sway bar and transverse stabiliser, Armstrong double acting hydraulic shock absorbers.
WHEELS. Five "easy-clean" disc wheels with detachable chromium rimbellishers and attractive nave plates.
BRAKES. Latest Lockheed two-leading-shoe system, hydraulically operated.
STEERING. High efficiency, variable ratio, Burman worm and nut type.
ELECTRICAL SYSTEM. 12 volt. 64 amp. hours Lucas battery housed under bonnet. Lamps incorporating twin stop lamps operated by brake pedal pressure and twin reversing lamps operated by gear-change lever. Independent illumination for rear number plate. Separate boot lamp for luggage compartment. Self cancelling trafficators controlled by switch on steering wheel.
FOUR CORNER JACKING SYSTEM.
CHASSIS DIMENSIONS (approx.).
Front Track ... 57.92 in. 1471 mm.
Rear Track ... 61.00 in. 1549 mm.
Turning Circle ... 40 ft. 6 in. 12.4 m.
WEIGHTS (approx.).
Unladen (with petrol and water)
    34 cwt. 3 qr. 0 lb.
Laden (five occupants)
    41 cwt. 1 qr. 22 lb.

"Fifteen seconds, dead!"

"And you see how smoothly and squarely we draw up?"

"What is its maximum speed?"

"Let us try, without the stop-watch. We shall have to pick our road."

Later: "Here we are, we're off—fifty, sixty, seventy, eighty, eighty-five—that's the lot."

"I wouldn't have believed it—more like sixty, so smoothly all the way. But those brakes, what make are they?"

"Lockheed hydraulic two-leading-shoes, as easy and light in their application as in acceleration."

"A splendid motor-car. Small wonder it has a big following."

"Any discomfort at the rear?"

"None at all, a thrilling ride; we all enjoyed it."

"Where are they selling mostly overseas?"

"Everywhere, almost, Canada, Australia, South Africa, India, Europe and Scandinavia, as well as generally at home, not forgetting the many national services, newspaper transport, mobile police forces and the like, where speed and safety are the prime essentials."

"Which doesn't surprise me in the least."

* * *

"LET us finish off the trial then with a little rough going." For which purpose, with my companions observing on foot, I take the Super Snipe over typical colonial terrain, actually once a tank testing ground, to manœuvre in and about, up and down, over ruts, ditches, gravel and sand, steep gradients and shingled descents.

"If only you could have seen those front wheels," my companions say excitedly, "one up, one down, bobbing about fantastically."

"That is because of its Evenkeel independent front-wheel springing," I reply, "the body, in effect, is always on an even keel!"

"I noticed that especially, a remarkable demonstration."

* * *

NOTHING more one could do or say further to interest my companions, we meander slowly back home, proud to have enlightened others in the exceptional merits of the latest Humber Super Snipe, veritably the last word in British automobile engineering excellence, a product of the U.K. motor industry which, by its world-wide patronage, has made and continues to make so valuable a contribution to Britain's export drive.

T.R.M.

During the "colonial" section of the test course—demonstrating the car's exceptional "Evenkeel" performance, abundant power and steering precision.

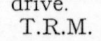

FIT and FORGET...

THE FINEST AND FASTEST PLUG ON EARTH

THE K·L·G RECOMMENDATIONS FOR ROOTES GROUP CARS

HILLMAN
All models requiring 18 m.m. Plugs..................M.50
All models requiring 14 m.m Plugs..................F.50

HUMBER
All models up to 1935..................M.50
All models 1936-51..................F.50

SUNBEAM-TALBOT
Ten, 3 litre and 4 litre 1938-9 and 2 litre 1946..................F.50
Ten 1945..................FE.50
Models "80" and "90" 1948-51..................FE.70

To ensure the best performance, it is vital, when fitting a new set of plugs, to see that the gaps are adjusted to the settings given in the engine manufacturer's handbook.

SMITHS K·L·G *sparking plugs*

 SMITHS MOTOR ACCESSORIES LIMITED, CRICKLEWOOD WORKS, LONDON, N.W.2.
THE MOTOR ACCESSORY DIVISION OF S. SMITH & SONS (ENGLAND) LIMITED

At the "FESTIVAL OF BRITAIN"
State Service of Dedication, St. Paul's Cathedral, May 3rd,
attended by Their Majesties The King and Queen and members of the Royal Family.

The Rt. Hon. Clement Attlee, Prime Minister, and Mrs. Attlee, leaving St. Paul's Cathedral at the close of the State Service of Dedication.

Below: The Rt. Hon. Viscount Jowitt, K.C., the Lord Chancellor, was accompanied by Viscountess Jowitt.

Above: The Rt. Hon. Winston Churchill, leader of the Opposition.

Below: The Rt. Hon. Tom Williams, Minister of Agriculture and Fisheries.

IMMEDIATELY following the State Service of Dedication, His Majesty the King declared open the Festival of Britain from the steps of St. Paul's.

On the steps of St. Paul's this splendid scene, impressive with dignity and colourful in its pageantry, passes into the pages of Britain's history as His Majesty the King performs the opening ceremony.

Visiting the South Bank Exhibition, London's centre-piece of the Festival, the Royal Family pass through the Transport and Communications Pavilion. Their Majesties the King and Queen pause in front of the Hillman engineering exhibit, the "Ghost Minx." Also in the picture are Queen Mary, Princess Elizabeth and the Duke of Edinburgh, Princess Margaret, the Princess Royal, the Duke and Duchess of Gloucester with Prince William and Prince Richard, and the Duchess of Kent.

I GO TO BATH—and dally along the 100 interesting miles from London

By VINCENT BRENNAN, M.B.E., F.R.G.S.
(Our Touring Adviser)

Bath Abbey and the Roman Baths—our final objectives.

WHATEVER you do, don't try and start from Hyde Park Corner about five o'clock in the afternoon to follow the normal route for the Great West Road, now the beginning of the Road to Bath.

If you do, you'll find that about 10,000 other motorists have the same idea in mind so that, practically speaking, it will be nigh on midnight before any of you get past Hammersmith Broadway.

Unless you can wait for Sunday morning, when all is comparatively clear, take my tip and, instead of making for Kensington High Street, plunge into the unknown along the Cromwell Road, the road of which J. M. Barrie said that nobody knew where it went!

You will benefit, first, by avoiding sight of the Albert Memorial, and second, by dodging most of the traffic you will come out all right in the end in Hammersmith.

I wish I could suggest a means of skirting the congestion here—sooner or later everything here will freeze into a solid jam—but I have concluded reluctantly that it cannot be done. You can evade subsequent nerve strain by turning left, to leave Chiswick High Road at Turnham Green, later to emerge at the entrance to the Great West Road.

* * *

WHEN I say that you will need to contend with some of the worst driving in the world along that phony speed track, Great West Road, you may begin to wonder why on earth anybody should want to travel the Bath Road at all.

Have no fear! Once you get past Slough it is worth all the trouble.

If you like, follow the old road through dismal Brentford. This is slower than Great West Road, but the actual distance is less and you will find the driving a lot more comfortable.

The first big sight to be seen along the Bath Road of to-day is London Airport, so huge that you could lose yourself in it in a car. Spend an hour in the Public Enclosure (tea and refreshments) and see gigantic aircraft taking off for, and arriving from, the farthest corners of the globe.

* * *

LEAVE Colnbrook's By-Pass on the right for the original road through the old-world Middlesex village itself, if only to stop at the Ostrich Inn, and what a story they can tell you here.

Out of the centuries of its history going back to 1106, I select the sixteenth when its clients were murdered on a huge scale. A wealthy traveller would be allotted the Blue Room. When he was abed and fast asleep mine host operated a trapdoor so that bed and traveller and all were flung into a vat of boiling liquid in the cellar!

Slough, the next place on the road is dull, crowded and seemingly unending. Trust the signpost which points to "Reading and the West," along unfrequented by-roads and you will come out safely, well on towards Maidenhead, with little more to fear from many others trying to use the road simultaneously for the remainder of the Road to Bath.

* * *

FIVE miles beyond Slough and 26 from London comes Maidenhead, "gayest of riverside resorts," whose bridge affords a view in both directions of Old Father Thames at his best. Skindle's Hotel, just short of the bridge, was the favourite haunt in Edwardian days of the gorgeous Gaiety Girls and their *beaux*.

Now comes Maidenhead Thicket, in former days the lair of highwaymen, which reminds me that, in the eighteenth century, the prosperous traveller by coach from London was indeed lucky if he got thus far without suffering the attention of gentry like Dick Turpin, Claud Duval and Captain Hawkes.

They used to say that the difference between English and French "gentlemen of the road" was that the former just robbed you, whereas the latter robbed and murdered you as well. The mammy of them all, in

(Continued on page 26)

Silbury Hill, the highest artificial hill in the country, its origin still a complete mystery.

Right: Noted landmark on the Bath Road—the old toll-gate near Longford.

I GO TO BATH—
(Continued from page 24)

my opinion, was the Berkshire Lady of the days of Queen Anne. For she armed and masked herself not to rob her chosen victim of his money or his life, but of his hand in marriage!

* * *

BUT of dozens of stories of ancient but now wealthy, industrial Reading I choose one about Henry VIII which has a topical touch. The Abbot of Reading of his day complained in the presence of a hungry stranger, who had sought his hospitality, that he himself "would give £100 if I could feed as lustily on beef as you do. Alas! My digestion is poor."

A few weeks later the Abbot found himself clapped in the Tower without knowing the reason why, and on a diet of bread and water. Then they put a sirloin of beef in front of him to which he did ample justice. Whereupon the "hungry stranger," who had been watching through the keyhole revealed himself as the King's Own Majesty, saying, "I'll trouble you for that £100 you were talking about."

* * *

IT is a fast, wide stretch along the 17 miles between Reading and Newbury, with the picturesque Kennet Valley on the left and later the comparatively little known Hampshire Downs which rise to nigh on 1,000 feet at Inkpen Beacon, an ideal spot for a picnic.

Theale Church, five miles along the main road, past Reading, was built in 1840, when British art was at its lowest point, after the style of Salisbury Cathedral. Very much after it.

They had fun and games with Woolhampton railway station years ago, because people would keep on confusing it with Wolverhampton, with disastrous results, so in the end they had to re-christen it Midgham. Of an inn which once stood a mile from the pleasant market town of Newbury, a poetaster wrote:—

> The famous inn at Speenhamland
> That stands beneath the hill,
> May well be called the Pelican
> From its enormous bill.

* * *

I LIVED for several years near Newbury, so I know it pretty well and I love it, for here you have almost the ideal country town. Stop for lunch on Thursday, which is market day, and you will see what I mean. There are lots of old inns including "The Chequers," for in the palmy days of the Road this was the natural stopping place for the night on the two-day journey by coach to Bath.

See the bridge over the Kennet, which might have been lifted stone by stone from Venice, and the ancient Cloth Hall, now a museum.

Henry VIII crops up again, for Jack of Newbury, the town's most notable citizen, once entertained his monarch here in lavish style. Two of the battles of the Civil War were fought in the near neighbourhood and their traces can still be found by the persistent enquirer.

* * *

AT Hungerford we leave Berkshire for still more truly rural Wilts, and now are in the midst of what may be called the "thatched cottage" country. Hocktide is the time to be here and see the so-called tutti-men exchange oranges for kisses with the coy but not so very reluctant local maidens.

If you have time, turn off here for Littlecote, a mile or two north of Froxfield, which is a really outstanding Tudor mansion, with legends of blood, treachery and murder calculated to freeze anybody's marrow, whatever that may be.

Then, back to the Road to traverse Savernake, one of the grandest forests in England, sadly damaged in the great frost of 1947, when the noise of branches cracking under the weight of snow and ice resembled machine-gun fire.

Marlborough, at the base of the ensuing hill, boasts of the widest High Street in the country, but something they don't brag so much about is that it can be one of the coldest places in the country.

* * *

SIX miles farther on Avebury should be explored, an entire village enclosed within the greatest stone circle in the world. Its stones, dating from about 1900 B.C., are older than those of Stonehenge and, in my opinion, Avebury is the more worth-while sight of the two.

When I add that we now pass Silbury, the highest artificial hill in Europe, my reader may agree with what I said earlier that the Bath Road, from the point of view of interest, fully justifies any bother entailed in reaching its beginning. I believe they have tried over and over again to find out what lies beneath Silbury, but without success.

* * *

THERE is not so much to see in the last 20 miles of our 106-mile journey to Bath. Calne used to be renowned for its Wiltshire bacon and Chippenham is the base for a visit to Lacock Abbey, among other things the scene of the discovery of photography.

There is ground for supposing that the village of Pickwick lent its name to the most popular of the works of Dickens. Hence onwards, one seems to enter a different world on the five-mile descent into Roman Bath, the landscape taking on a changed appearance owing to the increased use of Bath stone for walls and buildings.

* * *

IN the year 863 B.C. Prince Bladud, later as king to become the father of King Lear, contracted leprosy and was exiled from court. Becoming a swineherd, his pigs were infected. But one day they discovered some hot juicy mud on what is now the site of Bath and inevitably rolled in it. To the amazement of Bladud their leprosy disappeared so he did a bit of mud rolling himself, with the same happy result, whereupon he founded a city.

I will conclude with a reference to the modern Treatment Centre at Bath, now I understand, available to all under the National Health scheme. I should think it must be the most comprehensive in Europe. I counted 40 different things they can and will do to you with hot water, from the only natural Hot Springs in Britain— and electricity.

F. J. Camm's working model of the Blue Room "murder bed" to be seen in the Ostrich Inn, Colnbrook, near Slough. It was ceremoniously unveiled by the Marquis of Donegal on December 3rd last to commemorate the "sixty-first" murder perpetrated in this twelfth-century hostel.

FIT

"TripleX"
Regd.

AND BE SAFE

42 HECTIC HOURS IN FRANCE

RAYMOND BAXTER, B.B.C. Commentator, makes a speedy radio reconnaissance on the Sunbeam-Talbot 90—and admittedly " pushes it a bit."

ONE of the principal ingredients of the job of a B.B.C. commentator is the inexhaustible element of surprise.

The other week I found myself motoring fast down the familiar road to Folkestone and Dover; I had had just five days' notice of the brief and busy trip to the Continent which lay ahead. Consequently, though I confess it is nearly always the case, I was pushed for time to catch the night ferry to Dunkirk.

Now "time spent on reconnaissance is seldom wasted," but time is a precious commodity. Only three full days were available in this instance, and my job was to conduct a rather tricky reconnaissance in connection with a project I was planning for the Outside Broadcasts Department.

* * *

A new experience

MY own hard-worked car was booked for a servicing job at the time, but a trusty friend came to the rescue by offering to loan me his Sunbeam-Talbot 90 Coupé for the job.

I had not previously had experience of this car, and I accepted with alacrity.

* * *

Port formalities

IT was a dark, wet, and blustery night on the road to Dover, but proceedings were much enlivened when we overhauled a Daimler Sportsman's Coupé which appeared to have the same urgent appointment in Dover as ourselves!

Sped through the formalities at Dover by my friends of the A.A. Port Office, we had ample time to chat of this and that with that very human group of H.M. Officers—the Customs boys—then to seek our rather cramped cabin on the French boat with the English name of *Twickenham Ferry*.

Interesting motoring

DUNKIRK dock before dawn is not the most heart-warming spot in Europe, but the lofty cranes and jagged ruins of the town were showing starkly in "first light" as we threaded our way out on to the canal road for Berceus. A dull traveller it must be who doesn't feel a tingle in his veins as the roads of the Continent start to open up before him once again!

We were treated to a glorious sunrise of orange and gold as the rather naked-looking trees of the coastal plain poked their skinny fingers through the morning mists.

The main road Route Nationale 29 by-passes the ancient town of Cassel, and that, I think, is regrettable. The view from its hilltop is a favourite of mine: miles of water-meadow and dyke with the historic sand dunes of Dunkirk barely visible to the north, and there's no better time to enjoy this panorama than very early morning. (No additional hardship from the night ferry.) Furthermore, the winding pavé road up the hill affords a very interesting little section of motoring if one is in the mood for some controlled slides. I wonder how long it will be before this miniature hill-climb is included in a Rally?

* * *

Welcome breakfast

AT Arras we fancied some breakfast and decided to investigate a restaurant bearing the familiar R.A.C. sign. This led to one of those chance encounters which invariably enliven the unplanned tour. The "Restaurant Calaisien," in Rue Saint-Aubert, turned out to be the adopted home of an ex-R.A.F. man who "married into the country." His wife, however, has lost none of her Gallic skill, even in her treatment of so British a dish as ham and eggs!

The slag heaps and smoke of the northern coalfields were soon left behind along the varied scenery of N.25, and just before the little town of Ham there's a stretch of road on which I swear nary a cobble has been disturbed since the days of Louis Quatorze. The straight road is flanked by a lofty avenue of beech, and hard by, a graceful château sleeps by its ornamental lake.

Raymond Baxter giving a competitors' running commentary at Folkestone, on the occasion of the Monte Carlo Rally—for the B.B.C.'s Humber recording car. Time did not permit photography during the special trip described here.

Good road-holding

IN the forest of Compiegne the wood daffodils were in full flower, and the local lads and lasses lined the road with armfuls of yellow blossom for the traveller.

The traffic of Paris, in the throes of its transport strike, seemed to be even more closely packed and erratic than ever as we aimed for the Seine and lunch. This was a business appointment with technicians of Radiodiffusion Française. But French radio men, in common with the remainder of the population, have a mean eye for a restaurant, and the Trois Marronniers, on the Quay de Tokio, overlooking the river, has a menu worthy of the deepest consideration.

We headed out of Paris at 6 p.m.—a heartbreaking time to have to leave the city—but the serpentine charm of N.1 where it winds through the orchards and low hills to the north softened the blow.

Good road-holding is a "must" if one is to hurry on this section, but though she called for a deal of wheel-play, the little "90" never caused us anxiety, though we were admittedly "pushing it" a bit.

* * *

Proud history

SO to the ancient town of Beaumont on the Oise. There's none of the fairy-grace of Chârtres here, nor the somnolent charm of a Provençal town. But in this rather ugly and war-scarred little community, the visitor can find the real France, unspoilt by "la tourisme" and false civic pride.

Beaumont is a town which works for its living: its market seethes with activity, its factories hum. But in its narrow cobbled back streets, the ancient walls echo a proud history which reaches back beyond the twelfth century. A rugged Norman Abbey Church, a half-derelict château, and the many traces of the town's fortifications bear their silent testimony to the past. In a narrow street, named after his father, M. le Maire lives quietly in a spotless little house with a bust of Voltaire occupying a place of honour in the parlour.

* * *

The real France

BEAUVAIS, battered by both sides in the war, struggles back to life, but its surrounding countryside is surely amongst the loveliest regions of France.

The Easter fair which jammed the square of Gournay could well have inspired Tatti's riotous film "Le Jour de Fête"— the gaudily striped awnings of stalls and

(Continued on page 32)

You get so much more out of the Minx!

... and you get so much more into it!

More power when you need it most—at the start and on the hills. More reliability—because the Minx has been improved continuously for 19 years. More economy, too, than ever before. You get so much more out of the Minx.

In the Minx, every inch is used to good advantage—from the wide divan-type front seat to the spacious enclosed luggage accommodation. Yet no full-size family car was ever so easy to park or manoeuvre in traffic, **so economical to run.**

The HILLMAN **MINX MAGNIFICENT**

SALOON £425 *plus Purchase Tax*   *Also* CONVERTIBLE COUPE · ESTATE CAR

CRAFTSMAN-BUILT BY THE ROOTES GROUP

HILLMAN MOTOR CAR CO. LTD. COVENTRY   LONDON SHOWROOMS AND EXPORT DIVISION: ROOTES LIMITED DEVONSHIRE HOUSE PICCADILLY LONDON W.1

For the June bride: Elaborately embroidered satin wedding gown in old-world style, with panier skirt and shaped waist. V-shaped bodice and push-up sleeves are stitched with pearls and sequins, also matching halo head-dress featured by Greta Gynt, J. Arthur Rank star.

June Notes and Notions:

with many a faint echo of Aladdin!

By BRIGID de VINE

DID you know that there was a world shortage of SKELETONS?

Mr. Thomas Wood Fazakerley, of Croydon, does.

Two years ago he met a Sutton doctor who was busy producing experimental plastic models of feet. He learned that the international shortage of skeletons, needed for medical students, etc., was "absolutely fantastic." So together they opened a factory in Croydon and soon the first life-sized plastic skeleton was produced.

Mr. Fazakerley made his "product" as comfortable as possible in the back seat of his car and drove off to the London Headquarters of British Plastics to have the skeleton photographed. (When he parked his car the skeleton momentarily lost its travelling rug and Mr. Fazakerley was nearly arrested for causing a public nuisance.) Since then the production of skeletons has been stepped up from one to 40 a week, the price is "just half that of the real thing," and "delivery is 14 days as against up to nine months." The Company, the only one in the world in this field, now exports its products all over the world.

* * *

AT the British Industries Fair last month the Company introduced a new product—"the bouncing brain"—a model of the human brain made of a special rubber which can be separated to display each section for study.

All previous models had been in hard plaster material which chipped and broke when the models were passed round the laboratory or classroom. The rubber brain is likely to help Britain's export trade as successfully as the plastic skeleton has done.

Lovely Nadia Gray is a beautiful continental actress who has recently become an important addition to British pictures. During the war her "pro-Allies" attitude resulted in her being detained in concentration camps. England ultimately came her way, and to-day Nadia, of the flaming red hair and beautiful figure, is with the Rank Organisation.

ANOTHER success story concerns Mr. Robert Buckland who, 17 years ago, was an unknown London youth left jobless when the small firm he worked for closed down. He decided to put his life's savings, £20, into the only kind of work he knew, making lead-acid batteries. To-day at 36, he is already exporting to 10 countries and *has just bought his second £10,000 yacht*.

In the electrical section of the Castle Bromwich section of the Fair he showed a standard battery (claimed to be the heavy weight champion among British batteries), as an entry for world honours in the export field.

* * *

THE "Disease Detective" is the title given to a third inventor, Mr. Edward Gurr, who exports micro-biological stains needed for the study of disease in humans, animals and plants. Before the war the Germans had a monopoly in the matter of biological stains and reagents.

When the war ended and they were out of the business Mr. Gurr saw his chance.

Against all the warnings of his friends, he resigned his comfortable, safe and well-paid position and set out alone to accomplish what friends and competitors alike were convinced would require a lifetime. He used a cellar as works and warehouse, his London flat as a research and control laboratory and started business. Now he is world-famous, and to-day, spends a lot of his time running a free advisory bureau built up entirely spontaneously and used by scientists and research workers all over

Terry Moore's sun-ray pleated skirt is a deep blue; and the pleats allow plenty of movement. The sweater, of the same colour, has a deep ribbed band round the neck which can be pushed off the shoulders, and fits snugly at the waist into a stiffened belt. She wears a wide silver bangle, and small brooch on the jumper.

the world. Now 70 to 80 per cent. of the firm's production is being exported to help in the study of such scourges as tuberculosis, cancer, sleeping sickness, yellow fever and malaria.

* * *

"JOKES and Magical Tricks" are another of the odd things contributing to the success of Britain's export drive. Practical jokers' cabinets made by the London Magical Company and containing soap that fails to lather, exploding theatre tickets, a match box that falls to pieces, a gadget that closely imitates the noise of crashing crockery, etc., sell to customers all over the world.

One vigorous branch of the trade has been built up with the witch doctors in certain parts of Africa, who find the boxed sets of magic tricks useful as conjuring is a serious part of their business.

There was no magic trick, however, about the new dolls which could not only walk by themselves but could talk and sing to buyers in their own languages, including Chinese, Afrikaans, French, Spanish and Portuguese.

* * *

ALMOST "magical" in effect is the new British building system under which it is claimed 45 unskilled or semi-skilled men can build *a hundred houses in a hundred days*. The scaffolding consists of frames joined together by locking devices which slot into each other, no clamps, nuts or other moving parts being used.

Houses are built of concrete blocks, moulded by the machine on the site, the machine can turn out in one day concrete blocks equal to more than 1,500 bricks. The machine itself is simple to handle by a five-man team, weighs only between 30 to 40 lbs., and is 18 inches long, 10½ inches wide and 9 inches high.

The firm (Building Plant Hire (On Site), Ltd.), of St. Mary Cray, Kent, claims that houses can be built at a cost of £1,225 for a two-bedroom house, and £1,300 for a three-bedroom house.

* * *

OTHER new inventions seen during the month which may eventually come our way were :—

JUNE BEAUTY: *By Ann M. Capell*

HOWEVER tempted you may be in warm weather, don't go without make-up. The right foundation acts as a real protection against the weather as well as providing a matt base for powder. Women with fine skins especially, need good protection, otherwise the sun dries the complexion.

Oily creams and lotions help to encourage an even tan, if a tanned look is your choice. Dry or mature skin needs a vitamin cream, smoothed in with long upward strokes. There is also a "sun tonic"—a semi-liquid foundation that filters out the burning rays of the sun and can be used not only on the face but on the arms, legs and back, etc., to prevent burning. If yours is the type of skin that burns a horrid lobster-red, this lotion is invaluable.

Rose-gold is a lovely shade of foundation, and gives your skin a glamorous tan used with beach-tan powder. There is a new "top-tone" one that gives greater skin coverage and doesn't cake or streak when the face gets hot.

The *way* you powder is important. Press in generously from the throat upwards, doing the nose last.

Lovely Joan Bennett (Universal), one of America's loveliest and best-dressed women. Here she wears a broderie anglaise blouse with a smart printed linen skirt and chunky jewellery.

Jane Russell makes a charming picture in this unusual pose. Miss Russell will shortly be "seen" in this country co-starring with Frank Sinatra and Groucho Marx in "It's Only Money."

Barbara Hale (R.K.O.) really has beauty with talent and believes swimming and short period sun bathing to be essential keep-fit routine.

A silent refrigerator which will operate on electricity, gas, bottled gas or kerosene.

* * *

A teapot unit which plugs into the car circuit for freshly made tea on tour.

* * *

A portable battery booster which will charge car batteries without removal from vehicle, using ¼ unit an hour.

* * *

A domestic boiler in which the ash is emptied *only once every seven to fourteen days*.

* * *

The Cowfeteria—a mobile canteen for cows; and the Radio Ferret, an electrical device which allows immediate location of the ferret as soon as it makes contact with rabbit underground, "saves wastage of rabbits and steps up ferrets' results."

* * *

A mattress designed to give perfect sleep with one side specially prepared for winter weather and the other prepared for summer.

June Notes and Notions:

(Concluded from page 31)

A razor which fills with warm water like a fountain pen and uses any type of safety razor blade *without* soap, shaving cream, after shaving lotion.

* * *

A ball point pen *which lasts for twelve months without a refill.*

* * *

A double bed electric blanket which allows each half of the bed to be independently controlled at temperatures from blood heat up to 130 degrees.

* * *

A 35 mm. film strip projector which works off a kerosene pressure lantern, and is designed for use by missionaries—or salesmen opening up remote parts of the world.

* * *

THERE is a faint echo of Aladdin in the title " New Lamps from Old Bottles." The official description of the Pifco Adaptalite, an " ivory plastic push-bar switch lamp holder with an adjustable cork stop to fit the neck of the bottle or vase," together with two core flex and adaptor.

With one of these it is an easy matter to convert vases into lamps. I have seen quite a nice lamp made out of an empty VAT 69 bottle with labels from several bottles decorating a plain parchment lampshade on top.

* * *

A NEW blend in *beer* has been produced for the Festival Year. It is a new lager, the joint product of three brewers from three different countries. It was introduced at the B.I.F. in an amusing stand, a replica of " The Barrel Inn," a 700-year-old English pub situated at Bretton Clough in Derbyshire, and many visitors from overseas have decided to make a point of visiting the original while exploring England this year.

* * *

VISITORS to England are usually convinced that a raincoat is a necessary part of their luggage and sometimes, as during the last year, they are quite right. But now English raincoats are being styled with a French touch which makes them smart enough to wear anywhere.

The famous designer, Pierre Balmain, has been retained to style exclusive raincoats for an English firm of manufacturers. I met the designer at a party recently in the Orchid Room at the Dorchester when he was showing some of his luxury furs. And his suggestion that a short coat of white mink worn over a short black skirt might be a suitable costume for the English housewife's " shopping," shows that he brings a fresh mind to any subject (he admitted afterwards that the skirt was short because his time was short, and he had not included a long black skirt in the collection of garments flown over). One of his " tent style " new raincoats has been developed from a Paris designed mink coat.

Another model was inspired by a visit to New York's Chinatown on Balmain's recent American trip. He has also designed a mandarin pillbox in waterproof material as part of the Eastern inspired outfit and he shows octagonal shaped berets and jockey caps made of satin waterproof as gay alternatives to the usual wet-weather " hood."

* * *

STILL the sun may shine and this year holiday frocks are more charming than ever. One of Molyneux's former designers is now producing styles for Horrocks. And the show of Horrockses 1951 Fashions included many elegant models in dark poplins suitable for town wear and adaptable for day or evening. Some of these frocks will certainly be seen in the 51 luxury bar at the South Bank or in the Regatta Restaurant or the Restaurant of the Royal Festival Hall which all have riverside views of the loveliest part of the Thames, and are so gaily decorated that even Londoners will be able to feel themselves " abroad."

Cocktail dresses in cotton, " uncrushable " and " crease-resisting," will also be worn for parties in the " Wine Garden," which has been set up among the fantastic vistas and towers in the Festival Gardens in Battersea Park.

To keep one's hair tidy for open air dining there is the new gadget designed by Riche of Hay Hill. A spring composed entirely of light weight pearls fits over the top of the head and curves round to keep top and side curls in position. Or it can be reversed and worn backwards to hold in the hair at the nape of the neck when it is at the troublesome " growing " stage. The pearl spring comes in several designs, is self attaching, and can be put on and removed in a few seconds.

It is perfect for use as a bridal head-dress for the June bride because it can be used again and again after the wedding is over. Indeed, it is possible that many brides will choose London as a honeymoon spot this summer. There will be so much to do and see to make it a memorable occasion.

* * *

NOT least the experience of a visit to the Telecinema at the South Bank Division which shows the first examples of *completely three-dimensional films* incorporating stereoscopic vision and stereophonic sound.

Here for the first time we have pictures in the round and sound which moves with the object in the film. Sound can come from the depth of the screen or the back of a cinema.

In one experimental film a fanfare originating in the distance *behind* the screen builds out into the auditorium until it seems to envelop the audience, while at the same time, a row of columns springing up in the far distance builds out in diverging rows from the screen into the auditorium. It gave one an odd Alice through the Looking-Glass sensation; one was almost convinced that there was a complete world of sights and sounds behind the flat screen. The device will add enormously to the realism of films, for example, the roar of a bomber seen in the distance will increase in volume as it grows larger, until it seems to roar out of the screen and over the heads of the audience. Indeed, when the Telecinema showed a film of sea lions diving at the Zoo, it was so life-like that those in the front rows almost ducked to avoid being splashed!

* * *

IN spite of everything, this summer promises a number of enjoyable experiences. We will have to pay for the Festival anyway, so we may as well enjoy it—and forget if we can the new threat implicit in a new office gadget just introduced, " *which allows forms to be filled in with the feet at speeds of 2,000 an hour.*"

42 Hectic Hours : *from p. 28*

roundabouts, the panting Diesel power units, and the laughter and jostle of hard-working country folk on holiday.

But on the main Paris-Dieppe road one passes the village of Sérifontaine—and I'm sure that " passes " is the operative word for the vast majority of touring motorists. But here again is the real France.

In the village smithy we discovered an ancient and battered Citroën receiving attention, together with an astonishing assortment of agricultural machinery being prepared for the weeks of work ahead. Needless to say, there was not a tractor in the place. Then, in the tiny office cubicle in which we were received, a tricolour-bedecked portrait of General LeClerc looked out towards the spitting forge. " Mon Général, M'sieur ! "

At the estaminet there's one of those delightful football-playing machines (11 players a side, " push-rod " operated), which can reduce four fully grown and intelligent men to a state of nine-year-old excitement at the rate of 10 francs for nine balls.

Our own attempts to cope with this fearsome device, only " two-up," did not in any way meet with the approval of the rather dour proprietor.

* * *

THE château at Dieppe, familiar to every traveller who has ever used the port, is in process of renovation. And there we were treated to the somewhat startling spectacle of a central-heating radiator being installed in a perfect medieval room. But when the renovations are completed, in a few weeks' time, the château should be a " must " to every motorist embarking on a maiden tour from the port. I know of no finer introduction to the antiquities of France.

Incidentally, the new layout of the seafront would appear to offer a first-class " 500 " circuit if anyone's interested !

We took the coast road to Le Treport, and into Abbeville, across those " vasty fields of France." Thence, St. Omer, and the road by the newly widened canal back to Dunkirk. Finally, if you have time to spare before the night ferry home, try the " Restaurant Henry IV " for your last " rill mill." It provided us with an ideal rounding-off to our 42 hours' energetic but amply rewarded trip.

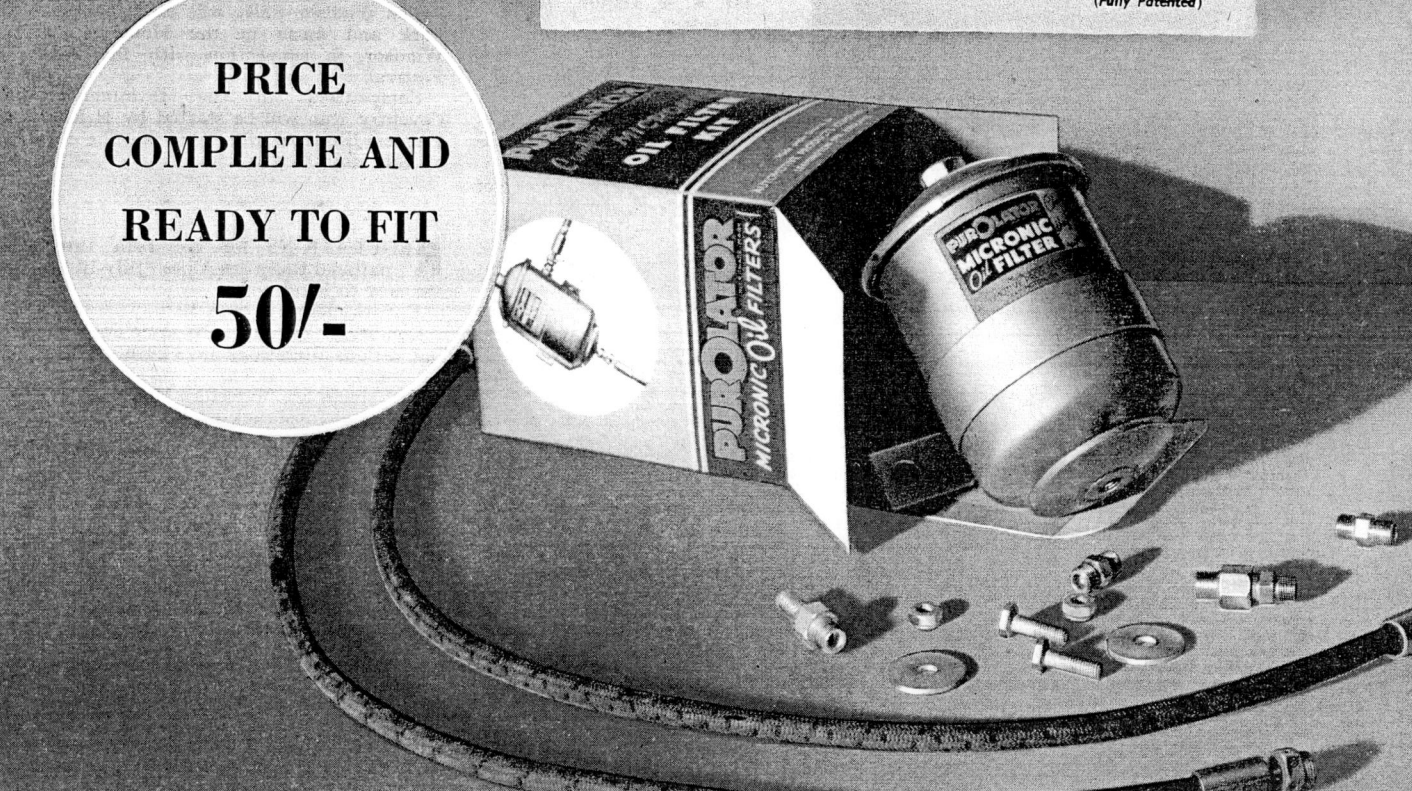

Easy to fit

and takes the harmful abrasives out of your oil.

PUROLATOR micronic
REGD. TRADE MARK
OIL FILTER KIT

Saves your engine EXPENSIVE OVERHAULS

Destructive micronic-sized abrasives in the oil can grind down the important working parts of your engine and impair its silence and efficiency.

The Purolator micronic filter arrests these minute abrasives—as small as 0·00004 in.—and greatly prolongs the life of your engine.

Neat, simple-to-fit element, easily changed without mess or trouble.

Available for Hillman Minx, for all models from 1934 to 1950, kit MF. 2399, price 50/- each.

Ask your agent for particulars.

AUTOMOTIVE PRODUCTS COMPANY LTD., LEAMINGTON SPA.

(Fully Patented)

PRICE COMPLETE AND READY TO FIT 50/-

SPORTING SPOTLIGHTS

ROUND THE CLUBS
by
JACK MASTERS

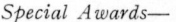

THE second Sunbeam-Talbot Owners' Club "Scottish Rally and Concours d'Elegance," held at Ayr and Turnberry over the week-end, May 5 and 6, was quite the most successful yet in the long series of the Club's localised fixtures.

Entries came from all parts of Scotland, with a goodly representation from south of the Border—to engage in a series of intriguing driving tests on the Esplanade at Ayr—in which the prowess of the northern members undoubtedly claimed the limelight of spectacular interest, and received all the recognition from fellow competitors it deserved.

Events were divided into three classes—for Sunbeam-Talbots up to 10 h.p., for those over 10 h.p., and an invitation class for Hillman entries.

In the latter section, the major interest was in the obvious contest going on between N. Hiskins, of Lichfield, and R. Walshaw, of Halifax, two drivers of international experience, split seconds, as well as sand flying in all directions as they manoeuvred their cars in and about the obstacles. R. Walshaw won by a narrow margin.

On the Saturday morning there was held a regularity test, four laps of a special circuit (lap one for practice, lap two for time, laps three and four for consistency), and all put up a commendable show.

In the afternoon there were tests for acceleration, braking, reversing and manoeuvring in and out of a set of "complicated driving jigsaws," and here again the driving was above reproach, making the task of the judges no light matter.

Prizes were presented at the Club's dinner held in the Turnberry Hotel—a delightful and luxuriously comfortable establishment, whose management did everything possible to ensure a successful sojourn—in the lovely gardens of which the Club's Concours was held under ideal conditions on the Sunday morning.

Everyone voted the week-end a memorable one—good weather, good sport and excellent company. Tribute to the courtesy of the Ayr Borough Council in making such admirable facilities available for the Club's second visit was made by Mr. Norman Garrad, Chairman of Committee, who took a keen personal interest in the week-end proceedings from the comfortable rear seat of a Humber Pullman; he continues to make rapid progress following his recent serious accident.

Results:

Class A (Sunbeam-Talbot 10 h.p.)—
 1st, T. K. Lawrie, of Edinburgh.
 2nd, G. Greaves, of St. Annes-on-Sea.

Class B (Sunbeam-Talbot over 10 h.p.)—
 1st, R. A. Dando, of Manchester.
 2nd, J. Gibson, of Bradford.

Class C (Hillman Cars)—
 1st, R. Walshaw, of Halifax.
 2nd, J. R. Williamson, of Edinburgh.

Special Awards—
 Sydney Latimer Trophy (for best performance on a Sunbeam-Talbot): T. K. Lawrie.
 Robert Anderson Award (for most meritorious performance on a Sunbeam-Talbot by entrant not connected with motor trade): C. K. Black, of Newton Mearns.

Concours Result—
 1st, G. F. Pye, of Lancaster (Sunbeam-Talbot).
 2nd, C. Orrell, of Preston (Sunbeam-Talbot).
 3rd, R. Walshaw, of Halifax (Hillman).

* * *

IN the special competition devised in connection with the Sunbeam-Talbot Owners' Club's Continental Rally to Spain, the lucky winner of the two free tickets was Mr. G. Hutchinson, of 6, Redewater Road, Fenham, Newcastle-on-Tyne.

* * *

MEMBERS of the Veteran Car Club are certainly getting value for their money.

From now to August 18, they have no fewer than 13 events scheduled, including rallies, speed trials and parades.

Outstanding events are the Windsor Rally on June 3, the Birmingham-Coventry Run on June 9, and the Paris Rally (August 18-25).

The Windsor Rally will start in Hyde Park and finish in the Home Park, Windsor, in connection with the local Festival.

Competitors in the Birmingham-Coventry Run will be started by H.R.H. Princess Elizabeth who is visiting the city on that day.

* * *

REGULATIONS for the 14th International Rally des Alpes (July 10-20) are now to hand.

Entries close on June 10.

Conditions are much the same as usual, but various alterations have been made to the route.

The stages are Marseilles-Milan-Cortina D'Ampezzo-Innsbruck-Chamonix-Cannes.

The third stage is a circuit of the Dolomites, a 180-mile route, starting and finishing at Cortina.

Average speeds vary from 32¼ m.p.h. for 750 c.c. cars to 37¼ m.p.h. for over 3,000 c.c. machines.

On the Dolomite circuit speeds are stepped up to 35½ m.p.h. (750 c.c.), to 42¾ m.p.h. (over 3,000 c.c.), whilst on the Asutotrade "blind" from Turin to Sesto San Giovanni the equivalent averages are 94.6 and 68.2 m.p.h., respectively.

IN the recent S.T.O.C. "Treasure Hunt" in the Bedfordshire district, attended by nearly 200 members and friends, the route embodied some of the most beautiful countryside in England, seen under ideal weather conditions. Our pictures show above Mr. K. G. Holland, of Bedford, the winner, with, right, close-up of the oddities in the treasure trove which included acorns, corks, screws, bottle tops, worms, dated pennies and newspapers! The occasion, mainly social, was a great success.

Above: H. A. C. Mackenzie, of Alness, Ross-shire, makes a smart "getaway" in the special obstacle test.

Centre: Competitor races to his car for the special "timed reversing and acceleration test" round the centre barrier.

Below: Contestant in the intricate "parking" test—

to finish within 9 inches of the kerb.

Above: A. Bicket, of Kilmarnock, makes good time in the complicated "manœuvre" test for acceleration and reversing.

Below: J. Gibson, of Bradford, tackles the "snake" test in fine style; he was second in his class.

SUNBEAM-TALBOT OWNERS' CLUB, SCOTTISH RALLY, May 5 and 6

IMPORTANT Trials Contests and Concours d'Elegance attract big entry of Scottish members at Ayr and Turnberry. Ayr Corporation and police authorities give the Club a cordial welcome to contribute generously to the success of the meeting.

T. K. Lawrie, of Edinburgh, winner of the Sydney Latimer Trophy and of the 10 h.p. class, Sunbeam-Talbots.

R. A. Dando, of Manchester, winner of the class for Sunbeam-Talbots over 10 h.p.

R. Walshaw, of Halifax, winner of the Hillman Class, with third place also in the Concours.

BUMPERS & OVER-RIDERS • IGNITION LOCKS

DOOR HANDLES & LOCKS • WINDOW WINDERS

STEERING WHEELS • LOCKING PETROL CAPS

ROOF LAMPS & SWITCHES • BADGES & MASCOTS

BONNET HINGES • BODY MOULDINGS • GRILLES

ASH TRAYS • HYDRAULIC ELECTRIC EQUIPMENT

WILMOT BREEDEN
LIMITED

COMPONENTS AND ACCESSORIES

Wilmot Breeden Ltd. are the leading designers and manufacturers of automobile accessory equipment in Britain. Virtually every British car embodies Wilmot Breeden components, a significant testimony to their quality and efficiency and to the high standing of this engineering organisation.

BIRMINGHAM • LONDON • MANCHESTER • BRISTOL • GLASGOW

June, 1951

BRITISH CARS IN ITALY, SIAM and the U.S.A.— OPERATION "EXPORT"

At the recent Turin Motor Exhibition; featuring the stands of the Saigarage and Autofomosa companies of Milan and Rome, respectively, distributors of products of the Rootes Group.

The President of the Italian Republic, Signor Einaudi, is received on the Rootes Group stand by His Excellency the British Ambassador, Sir Victor Mallet, K.C.M.G., C.V.O. Also in the picture are Signor Biscaretti, President of the Italian Motor Manufacturers' Association (Annfia) and Signor Bosio, Secretary; the visitors making a detailed inspection of the exhibits.

★ ★ ★

Right: The imposing Monument to Democracy in the Rajadamnern, Bangkok's main avenue, forms a striking background to the Humber Hawk.

Members of the M.C.C. touring team, when returning home via New York, toured the city in a fleet of Humber cars placed at their disposal by Rootes Motors Inc. Left to right can be seen: D. Wright, R. Tattersall, B. Statham, G. Parkhouse, C. Washbrook, A. J. McIntyre, D. S. Sheppard and A. V. Bedser.

Photograph taken on the occasion of Hillman Minx Convertible Coupé successes in the recent Palm Springs, California, Concours d'Elegance. Mr. T. D. Rootes, director, and son of Sir Reginald Rootes, Deputy Chairman of the Rootes Group, is seen with Mr. Peter Satori, the California distributor, who, incidentally, recently celebrated his 1,000th Hillman sale in under 12 months.

TEE-TIME TOPICS
By F. J. C. PIGNON

Why, when all seemed favourable, did we lose the Walker Cup?

THE Festival of Britain doubtless originated from the idea that this country should show the world that in spite of the tail-twisting which the younger nations find so amusing, this great Old Country of ours is not yet defunct.

Gladly we welcome overseas visitors to look at our shop window and hope they find the prospect pleasing.

Purely incidentally, I hope, there has been a great influx of golfers who have planned tours of the most famous courses in this country, to see for themselves the championship links of St. Andrews, Sandwich, Birkdale, Hoylake and several other courses which have figured prominently in Britain's golfing history.

If this should catch the eye of any such golfing enthusiast I would suggest to him or her, that Royal Blackheath (our oldest club so far as records go), Westward Ho! and Richmond Club in Sudbrook Park (which celebrates its 60th anniversary this year) would interest them.

They can also see the little shed which at one time was the clubhouse in the days when many great players were members of the Westward Ho! club.

They can spend a day in the lovely old mansions of the Royal Blackheath and Richmond golf clubs and still find something to interest them.

So far as I know, neither of the Clubs I have mentioned has put down its rather frayed red carpet to receive visitors.

As a matter of fact, the Blackheath clubhouse walls are still shored up to hide the scars of the Battle of Britain, because there are more important building undertakings to attend to.

Richmond, too, with its winding basement corridors, in which one can easily get lost, has not had a face lift for festival year. But in these and many other clubs I could mention, the overseas golfer will be able to realise how great is the influence of the game of golf in this country, and comprehend something of the game's historic associations.

* * *

The answer is obvious!

AS I write, our visitors are showing Britain how to play golf.

The United States won the Walker Cup once again and are busy winning also the Amateur Championship.

This championship is yet to be concluded but "I hope for the best but fear the worst," if worst means that the Cup will once more cross the Atlantic.

As everybody knows, Britain came near to wresting the Walker Cup from America at Birkdale.

Why did the British team at one stage in the match, in a seemingly invulnerable position, fade away so badly, is a question everybody is asking.

The answer is the obvious one that British golfers, less accustomed to big events than the Americans, found the strain of tight finishes too great for them.

* * *

Nerve and Stamina

THERE are not many amateur golfers in the British Isles who can afford the time or expense of playing in all the big tournaments as do most of the Americans, so that when it comes to summoning just that little extra call on nerve and stamina, the United States have a reserve.

To those who moan about British failures in these matches, I would point out that, for one reason or another, American amateurs are able to combine their business with their golf which gives them an advantage they always will enjoy.

After all, these internationals serve a very useful purpose. Nothing can bring us to a clearer understanding of our different points of view than golf matches of this kind.

* * *

More practice

WE see the American golfer playing golf as though his very life depended on it : working at the game by hours of practice and training strenuously.

I suppose, and hope, we shall always treat golf as a game ; a serious game, of course, requiring training and concentration and we must be grateful to the members of the British team who gave up much of their time in training for the recent Walker Cup match.

* * *

ONE outcome of this contest is that there is now some possibility that the Rules of Golf of the Royal and Ancient Club, and the United States Golf Association, will be brought closer into line.

Already two conferences between officials of these bodies have been held and I believe considerable progress has been made.

It was when the last Walker Cup match was played in the United States that some approach on this matter was made.

Obviously it was desirable to have one code of rules for the two great golfing countries of the world. But there has been a certain amount of stubbornness on both sides.

St. Andrews, whose authority had never been seriously questioned, produced a code of rules which, in many respects, was not acceptable to some other countries, including the United States.

Suggestions from America were not adopted by St. Andrews and, consequently, there was a spirit of "you go your way and I'll go mine" about the whole unfortunate business.

* * *

The Stymie

THE suggestion came that there should be a meeting between the two authorities to see whether it was possible to iron out the differences. And now it looks as though something really worthwhile will be done at last.

I know that St. Andrews is by no means satisfied about the out-of-bounds and unplayable ball ruling.

Neither is America, who consider the penalties too light.

A referendum was taken on the stymie rule and, as a result, St. Andrews decided to retain this without amendment.

The United States retain the stymie but in a modified form.

They maintain that a player should have some chance of holing out even though stymied, and if the intervening ball is within six inches of the hole (as well as six inches from the other ball) it is not a stymie.

After seeing Willie Turnesa, the American Walker Cup captain, laid a dead stymie at the 36th hole of his match with the intervening ball about half an inch from the hole and his own ball four feet away, I can imagine the Americans will be adamant about their stymie rule and could hardly have better evidence of its virtue.

June, 1951

BUILT IN 1914—
Good for 90 m.p.h.
to-day!

By K. NEVE

"All-out" at Silverstone last year in the Vintage types event—a vigorous performance despite its 37 years!

In the Bugatti Owners' Club's Prescott Hill climb, 1949, to win its special invitation class.

IF you were to ask 100 present-day owners of luxurious "Hawks" or "Pullmans" whether the firm of Humber made a racing car, it is long odds that in 99 cases out of the 100 the answer would be a negative shake of the head.

* * *

MEMORIES would flood back of a line of sturdy open tourers, wonderful, reliable cars, characterised more by longevity and refinement than by sheer speed; but out-and-out racing cars—No!

* * *

YET early in the year 1914 the Humber Company had just completed and were testing three of the most advanced racing cars in the world.

* * *

ONE pouring wet day in April of that year these three dark green, beautifully proportioned Humber racing cars stood on the starting line of the T.T. race then held in the Isle of Man. The drivers were W. A. Burgess, F. Tuck and Sam Wright, the first of these three being the designer of the cars, assisted incidentally by a young man named W. O. Bentley!

Historically these 1914 T.T. cars are of great importance. Until 1912, cars with gigantic engines of 15,000 c.c. or so capacity, but with a power output of perhaps 8 to 10 b.h.p. per litre, had reigned supreme in racing.

By 1914, 4,500 c.c. was an average size racing engine, and then came these new 3-litre Humbers which developed some 35 b.h.p. per litre and which were, with the Sunbeams, built for the same race, among the first examples of the small, or perhaps we should now say medium-sized, high efficiency racing cars.

THE Humber, as has been mentioned, was designed by W. A. Burgess. The engine has four cylinders of 82 bore × 156 mm. stroke, giving 3,295 c.c. capacity. The non-detachable head carries twin overhead camshafts operating four valves per cylinder set at 45 deg. If contemporary reports are to be believed the engine gave over 100 b.h.p. at 3,300 r.p.m. In fact, in a letter to the *Autocar* in 1920 Burgess claimed 113 b.h.p. at 3,900 r.p.m.—but, as its present owner, I am too fond of it to push a 156 mm. stroke 3-litre engine up to 3,900 r.p.m. just to prove this statement.

The engine drives through a large cone clutch to a four-speed close-ratio gear box and thence by open prop. shaft to the 3 : 1 back axle. This axle, with 820 × 120 mm. tyres, affords just over 30 m.p.h. per 1,000 revs.

The slim 2-seater bodywork, with its round "bolster" petrol tank behind the staggered seats and the 4-in. open exhaust pipe, may be recalled by some readers who saw the historic racing cars lapping the Silverstone circuit on the occasion of the Grand Prix race in August last year, and it will probably be familiar to those whose enjoyment takes them to watch an occasional hill-climb or Vintage Sports Car Club event, for one of those 1914 Humber racing cars is running to-day as well as it did 37 years ago

* * *

THE two sister cars of the team are gone: the last was scrapped in the early days of the last war.

Both had Brooklands careers, one a long history in the hands of C. O. Wallbank, whom the present owner was pleased to meet at Silverstone last year.

It was he who recalled that the wind passing through the radiator builds up into a whistle, and when you hear the whistle you know that you are going fast!

Sure enough on that very day a banshee howl started as we came down towards Stowe Corner at some 2,800 r.p.m. or getting on for 90 m.p.h.

* * *

THE car, which forms the subject of these notes, was bought by a Mr. Sgonina from the factory in 1916. It was used from 1920 to 1922 for Sprints and the Caerphilly Hill Climb; then it was put on blocks in a heated garage, where it stayed until 1938, when, after five years of entreaty, Mr. Sgonina, who had kept it since 1916, accepted a modest cheque and let me take it away.

Spare time during the war years gave an opportunity for overhaul, and when competitions started again after the war the only remaining racing Humber began a new career.

It is taxed and licensed and, running on petrol-benzole, offers a 60-70 m.p.h. cruising speed with a maximum of over 90 m.p.h.

The 1914 Humber weighs but 23 cwt.; the large rear wheel brakes, plus a 15-in. diameter transmission brake, permit a pull up in a manner more reassuring than nameless ill-conditioned "modern" cars I have driven.

Developing 110 b.h.p. in a car weighing just over a ton spells performance with a capital "P"; enough in fact to have enabled this early masterpiece of the House of Humber to lap the Silverstone club circuit at over 64 m.p.h. in its present owner's inept hands, to climb Prescott fast enough to win an odd class award and to startle motor-cars many years its junior in the matter of sprints.

* * *

THERE are older Humbers certainly, Humbers more luxurious, quieter, faster perhaps, but none will ever supplant in my affections the 1914 T.T. car whose performance in 1951 will command respect for many, many years to come.

Photograph taken during the two-lap event for historic racing cars, on the occasion of the Silverstone Grand Prix, 1950.

CALENDAR OF COMING EVENTS

JUNE

1 (to Aug. 31)	Festival: Ulster Farm and Factory Exhibition, Castlereagh, Belfast.
4-6-8.	International Tourist Trophy Motor Cycle Races, Isle of Man.
4-9.	R.A.C. International Motor Rally: Start, Cheltenham; finish, Bournemouth.
6-23.	The Royal Tournament, Earls Court, London (T.M. the King and Queen attend opening performance).
7.	H.M. the King's Official Birthday—Trooping of the Colour Ceremony, Horse Guards Parade, London.
7-9.	Richmond Royal Horse Show, Richmond, Surrey.
7-12.	Cricket: First Test Match (England v. South Africa), Trent Bridge, Nottingham.
14.	British Empire Trophy and Manx Cup Car Race, Isle of Man.
16.	Sunbeam-Talbot Owners' Club Continental "Rallye Espagnol".
19.	49th Annual Theatrical Garden Party, Chelsea.
20-30.	Festival Ship "Campania" (Travelling Exhibition), at Hull.
21.	International Tourist Trophy Bicycle Race, Isle of Man.
23.	Motor Hill-Climb, Shelsley Walsh, Worcestershire.
	National Air Races, Hatfield Aerodrome, Hertfordshire.
23 (to July 14)	Festival: Travelling Exhibition, at Leeds.
28.	Jersey Motor Road Race, Jersey, Channel Islands.
29-30.	British Automobile Racing Club Rally, Eastbourne, Sussex.

JULY

4.	T.M. the King and Queen and General Eisenhower will attend a service in memory of members of the United States Forces who lost their lives in the British Isles during the Second World War, St. Paul's Cathedral, London.

LIGHTING-UP TIMES THIS MONTH

	1st	9th	16th	22nd	30th
London	10.6	10.14	10.19	10.21	10.21
Bristol	10.6	10.24	10.29	10.31	10.31
Birmingham	10.20	10.28	10.33	10.35	10.35
Leeds	10.25	10.33	10.39	10.41	10.41
Manchester	10.26	10.34	10.41	10.42	10.42
Newcastle	10.32	10.40	10.47	10.49	10.49
Glasgow	10.49	10.57	11.5	11.7	11.7
Belfast	10.48	10.56	11.3	11.5	11.5

Cleaning Hood Cover

SIR,—I am the owner of a 1951 Hillman Minx Convertible. The top has become very dirty with soot from a chimney near my parking lot.

To add to my dismay, a grease monkey sprayed the top with a pressure gun while my car was being serviced.

The literature accompanying the car warned against gasoline to clean the top, but omitted to say what should be used to clean it. Would you please print, for the benefit of all Convertible users, the approved method of cleaning such a top?

(Sgd.) T. W. D. F.,
HAMILTON, ONTARIO.

Our recommendation is to use a soft brush, applying it lightly in one direction.

When the material has become stained, it is necessary to use neutral soap, applying the sides with a sponge and lukewarm water. To deal with small local stains, methylated spirit can be used judiciously.

Do not use petrol (gasoline) or other spirit. Volatile cleaning spirit, strong alkaline solutions should also be avoided.

While the above treatment is effective in normal conditions, it may not be possible for the grease contamination to be eliminated entirely without the rubber proofing having suffered.

* * *

Foreign Petrol

SIR,—I intend taking my 1950 Sunbeam-Talbot over to the Continent, and should like to take advantage of your Information Bureau to ask a few questions.

I understand that the use of the Super Carburant petrol is not advised after the use of Pool petrol. What do you recommend as a safe cruising speed for the Sunbeam-Talbot "80"?

(Sgd.) W. B. S.,
MACCLESFIELD.

There does not appear to be any likelihood of difficulty with the fuel you mention, but we would suggest it is beneficial to fit a petrol filter between the petrol tank and petrol pump.

Regarding a safe cruising speed for this model, the range of 55-60 m.p.h. is recommended, although, of course, this could be increased in "short bursts".

* * *

Towing Bar

SIR,—I am having some difficulty in obtaining a tow-bar to enable my 1948 Hillman Minx to draw a caravan.

I should be grateful if you would let me know whether you are able to suggest any suppliers, and also what is the maximum weight you consider safe for a car of this horse-power. For your information, the caravan in question is approximately 15 cwt. unladen.

(Sgd.) N. D.,
PRESTON.

We suggest you contact our Distributors, Castle's Motor Company (Leicester), Ltd., of Leicester, who will be able to provide you with the necessary equipment.

The maximum weight we advise for towing, without appreciably affecting the performance, is 10 cwt., although we have received reports from owners who have exceeded this figure without experiencing any difficulty. If the figure is exceeded, we would stress the importance of choosing a route which will avoid steep hills.

5-80 m.p.h. in Top Gear

SIR,—I should be much obliged if you would give me your opinion as to the maximum speed which it is possible to obtain from a 1950 Humber Super Snipe, and the maximum from the same model when fitted with a super-charger.

(Sgd.) J. B.,
SANWICK (Nr. Preston).

The maximum speed of the Super Snipe is approximately 80 m.p.h., but naturally this figure will vary in accordance with the general condition of the engine.

We have not carried out any experiments on this engine with a super-charger fitted, and regret we are unable to quote any figure.

* * *

Into Yugoslavia?

SIR,—My wife and I will be taking our holiday in Italy this year, and would like to run through to Trieste and along the coast road to Dubrunik. Unfortunately, so far I have not been able to obtain any information regarding Yugoslavia.

(Sgd.) U. B. D.,
YORK.

Messrs. Hickie, Borman & Grant, of Charles Street, Haymarket, London, S.W.1, act as agents for the Jugo-Slav. Express Agency, and no doubt will advise you.

* * *

Procedure

SIR,—I should appreciate any hints on the fitting of a new timing chain to my 1946 Hillman Minx.

(Sgd.) I. P. O.,
GLASGOW.

Remove the radiator by disconnecting the hose joints at the top and bottom.

Remove baffle from centre section in front of the radiator by removing the five screws and washers.

Release brackets between radiator and centre section, by removing two bolts, nuts and spring washers at each side.

Release two tab-washers and remove two nuts which secure the radiator to underframe brackets.

Remove fan belt by levering over crankshaft pulley and straighten tab of lock washer and unscrew starting handle jaw nut from the crankshaft.

Remove crankshaft pulley by means of two levers, taking care not to bend or damage either the pulley or timing cover.

Remove set screws and bolts securing timing cover and lift clear of the timing chain.

Release lock washer and remove set screws securing the camshaft timing wheel to camshaft.

Turn engine until crankshaft key is at top centre and timing marks are in line. Draw off the camshaft timing wheel forward from camshaft, at the same time levering forward the crankshaft timing wheel.

To avoid straining the chain, care should be taken to withdraw the timing wheels in line. This is important when refitting a new chain.

The replacement of a new chain is a direct reversal of the above, but care must be taken that the timing marks are in line, the dowel in position at the end of the camshaft and the hole in the camshaft wheel registering properly with the dowel.

OFFICIAL TECALEMIT SERVICE

INSTALLATION AT ROSS BROS. (BEN RHYDDING LTD.), ILKLEY, YORKSHIRE

The Service behind the Car

THE MAIN POINTS OF TECALEMIT SERVICE

1. Chassis Lubrication.
2. Springs sprayed.
3. Engine, Gear Box and Back Axle checked for oil.
4. Bodywork and Metalwork washed and polished.
5. Brakes and Steerings carefully inspected.
6. Tyres inspected and checked.
7. All work recorded.
8. Reminder sent you when car needs re-servicing.

LUBRICATION AND SERVICING EQUIPMENT
for every Industry
METERING AND FILTRATION

If you are the possessor of a new car you will naturally wish to maintain its performance and appearance. And knowing that so much now and in the future depends upon efficient maintenance, you will entrust its care to Tecalemit-trained operatives backed by all the facilities afforded by modern Tecalemit equipment. Recognising that "free" petrol encourages extra mileage you will, if wise, pay more frequent visits to your local Tecalemit Garage displaying the well known Target & Arrow Sign.

Specialised maintenance service from 500 to 10,000 miles.

TECALEMIT
The Authority on Specialised Maintenance
BRENTFORD · ENGLAND

T306

O.K. for SOUND

FILM SHORTS and STARLIGHTS

BRITAIN'S technical achievement in developing large screen television for cinemas is revealed to Festival of Britain visitors at London's South Bank Exhibition.

Cinema-Television Ltd. (of the J. Arthur Rank organisation) installed the equipment in the Exhibition's "Telecinema" which is winning high praise from audiences. After demonstrations in Italy and South Africa, these are the first ever in Britain.

The equipment used on the South Bank is of the instantaneous type—that is to say, the picture on the cinema screen is viewed at the exact moment that the action is taking place elsewhere.

* * *

ALSO demonstrated at the "Telecinema" are three-dimensional pictures and stereophonic sound.

For bringing stereoscopic projection into focus, special glasses are provided for the audience and collected by the usherettes after the performance.

* * *

IN "Huckleberry Finn," a Technicolor musical version of the Mark Twain classic, Danny Kaye has his first role for Metro-Goldwyn-Mayer.

He is co-starred with Gene Kelly.

"Huckleberry Finn" will reunite the team of producer, director and song writers that made "Wedding Bells," starring Fred Astaire and Jane Powell.

* * *

BIG chance for 21-year-old Barbara Murray, J. Arthur Rank actress, is the only other important female part in "Another Man's Poison," the film Bette Davis has come to England to star in.

Barbara, who recently completed "The Dark Man," is now finishing another picture entitled "Mystery Junction."

Also in "Another Man's Poison" will be Gary Merrill, Bette Davis's husband.

* * *

HOLLYWOOD'S first Technicolor ice rink is being constructed at the Metro-Goldwyn-Mayer studios for Fred Astaire and Vera-Ellen's new dance routine in "Belle of New York."

The rink will be made of frozen coloured water in varied shades of the rainbow and wired so that it can be lighted from underneath the ice.

* * *

TITLE of the new Somerset Maugham picture to follow "Quartet" and "Trio" will be "Encore."

Produced by Anthony Darnborough, it will comprise the three short stories, "Gigolo and Gigolette," "The Ant and the Grasshopper" and "Winter Cruise." Maugham is speaking the foreword in the grounds of his villa at Cap Ferrat.

* * *

GEORGE SANDERS has been signed by Metro-Goldwyn-Mayer in a three-picture deal, the first of which will be a top role in "The Light Touch."

This will be partially filmed in Italy with Pier Angeli and Stewart Granger as co-stars.

* * *

BRITAIN'S Stewart Granger follows "King Solomon's Mines" with another sound performance in "Soldiers Three."

"Soldiers Three," suggested by Rudyard Kipling stories, is set in India and describes the adventures of three rollicking daredevils who have served for 18 years as privates of the British Army in the 1890s. With Granger are Robert Newton and Cyril Cusack.

Heading the cast is Walter Pidgeon as the soft-hearted Colonel, about to be retired. The feminine lead is Greta Gynt, making her Hollywood screen début.

David Farrar, now appearing in "Night without Stars," is the owner of this 3½ litre Talbot tourer, which he purchased from Prince Bira, the racing motorist. It is finished in the blue of the Royal Household of Siam, and is one of David's proudest possessions.

IN the two years since Marjorie Main became "Ma Kettle" in Universal-International's "Kettle" family comedy series, she has received enough free samples of household appliances to equip several homes.

The gadgets, almost all of which Marjorie has given away to her friends, arrived at the studios with requests that she use them conspicuously in the "Kettle" films so that the manufacturers would derive free publicity. They have included gas and electric stoves and refrigerators; automatic window cleaners; push-button door openers; disappearing folding beds; armchair-control heating; electric table setters; eight kinds of automatic dishwasher; an automatic bed maker; and an electric head-and-back scratcher.

* * *

ONE of the most novel swimming routines ever devised will be presented by Esther Williams in "Texas Carnival."

For an underwater sequence in the new Technicolor musical, Metro-Goldwyn-Mayer has built an entire room on the bottom of the outdoor water tank usually used for waterfront scenes.

In the routine, Miss Williams will float through a window, sit down at a desk, move from chair to chair, and finally disappear out of the window again.

* * *

CLARK GABLE and Lionel Barrymore were both represented at the 1951 Hobby Show in Hollywood.

Gable, who has long made a collection of interesting guns, displayed seven of them, one dating back to the seventeenth century. Barrymore contributed three etchings, each made with a gramophone needle.

Also displayed: an exhibition of sculptures by Deborah Kerr, and several African trophies collected by Stewart Granger.

* * *

ELIZABETH TAYLOR, young M.-G.-M. star of "Father of the Bride" and its sequel "Father's Little Dividend," plans to step into the business world as a Palm Springs, California, shop owner.

If plans develop, Jane Powell will go into partnership with her, specialising in teen-age fashions.

* * *

THE present Paul Soskin production being made at Pinewood Studios, "Secret Plan X23," is to be re-titled "Sabotage."

"Sabotage," written by Roy Boulting and Frank Harvey, deals with large-scale sabotage in Britain.

Products of the ROOTES GROUP

For Good Service!

GEO. T. HILTON & CO. LTD.
NORTH STREET · RUGBY
Telephone: 2291

HUMBER · HILLMAN
SUNBEAM-TALBOT
CARS

COMMER · KARRIER
TRUCKS

BUILT FOR THE ROADS OF THE WORLD

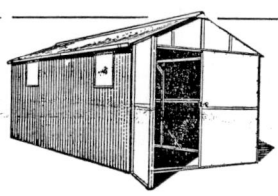

Neata

GARAGE
STEEL AND ASBESTOS

Size 14' × 7'
Price £41 - 10 - 0
Larger sizes and H.P. terms available.

Delivered FREE by our own transport.

NEATA PRODUCTS (CHELTENHAM) LTD.
Dept. M.M., ST. PAULS, CHELTENHAM, Glos.

Michelin MAPS & GUIDES

1951 EDITION MICHELIN GUIDE TO FRANCE
NOW ON SALE!
17/6d
(Packing and Postage 9d)

THROUGH YOUR USUAL BOOKSELLER

Also Regional Guides to France and Maps of France and Continental Countries

Price list from exclusive distributors:
ANGLO-FRENCH PERIODICALS LTD.
(Dept. M.40) 25, Villiers Street, W.C.2.

How to Dirt-Proof
YOUR ENGINE OIL

and prevent THIS

Dirty oil wastes your money. It clogs piston-ring slots, gums-up valve stem guides and constricts oil passages.

Your AC Oil Filter goes on filtering out the clogging sludge, dirt and grit which grind away engine efficiency — until the element is *packed solid*. A fresh A.C. Element at least *every 8,000 miles* means fewer repair bills ... greatly reduced engine wear ... less frequent oil changes.

Get your local Humber-Hillman Agent or any good garage to change your AC Filter Element at least every 8,000 miles.

REPLACEMENT ELEMENTS

Humber-Hawk 1948-9 L11—11/-	Sunbeam Talbot 2-Litre 1947-48-49 1948-50 "90" L11—11/-
Super-Snipe and Pullman 1948-50 K11—12/6	1948-50 10 HP & "80" L14—9/6

MINX OWNERS! Your agent can now fit the approved AC Oil Filter to your car.

AC Oil Filters

AC-SPHINX SPARK PLUG CO., DIVISION OF GENERAL MOTORS LTD., DUNSTABLE, ENGLAND

IN A FEW WORDS!

News Items of Modern Motoring and Travel Interest

THE FESTIVAL AND THE MOTORIST

THE South Bank Exhibition, London's centre-piece of the Festival of Britain, was opened by Their Majesties the King and Queen on Friday, May 4.

The King and Queen, who were accompanied by many members of the Royal Family, made an extensive tour of the Exhibition. In the Transport and Communications Pavilion the Royal visitors saw the fine Hillman engineering exhibit, the "Ghost Minx," which was recently shipped back to this country after exhibition in the United States.

Under the scheme to change exhibits at different periods, models of the Humber, Hillman and Sunbeam-Talbot ranges will have been displayed before the South Bank Exhibition closes in September. The same applies to Commer and Karrier trucks and the Tilling-Stevens Single Decker vehicle, all of Rootes Group manufacture.

* * *

In conjunction with the Festival, special exhibitions are staged at the Devonshire House showrooms of Rootes, Ltd., in Piccadilly, London, and at the various Rootes Depots in the South and Midlands.

At the Coventry and Luton factories of the Rootes Group detailed tours for visitors are being arranged.

* * *

Parking arrangements for a million vehicles throughout the Festival period have been made in London by National Car Parks, Ltd. There are 16 separate car parks catering for the South Bank Exhibition and Battersea Gardens.

Charges are: coaches, 5s.; motor-cars, 2s.; motor-cycles, 1s.; and bicycles, 6d.

The name and number of the car park is printed on the back of each ticket issued to avoid confusion. All users of National Car Parks also receive a site-map (by courtesy of Regent Oil Company, Ltd.) showing the quickest return route to the parking place.

* * *

Coventry's Celebrations

A feature of Coventry's Festival Week in June will be the Lady Godiva Historical and Industrial Pageant on Saturday, June 23.

Mrs. Franklin D. Roosevelt arrives at Broadcasting House, London, on her recent visit to this country. With Sir William Rootes, K.B.E., she made both radio and television recordings.

A colourful procession will portray in tableau form the history of the city, and after the figure of Lady Godiva follows the story of Coventry's industrial development.

A tableau by the Rootes Group of the 1895-1900 era will depict the penny-farthing bicycle leading to the first form of mechanised transport, a Humber "Quad" of 1897.

In the 1900-1920 era five veteran cars are entered by the Group, which is represented by models of different years throughout the decades up to the present day.

* * *

On Tuesday, June 26, a distinguished visitor to Coventry will be Field-Marshal Viscount Montgomery, Deputy Supreme Commander, S.H.A.P.E. He will tour the Ryton factory of the Rootes Group.

* * *

London Hotels Guide

The Automobile Association has just brought out the 1951 edition of its London Hotels List.

This concise booklet is of special value to visitors, for, besides giving full details of over 100 hotels in the London Postal Area, it includes short lists of cathedrals, churches, art galleries, museums and other important buildings as well as places of interest within easy reach.

* * *

Veteran Cavalcade

H.R.H. Princess Elizabeth is to visit Birmingham on Saturday, June 9, to start a Cavalcade of Veteran Cars on its run from Birmingham to Coventry.

Three of the veteran cars are entered by the Rootes Group from their "museum" at the Humber-Hillman factories.

The Cavalcade will be met at Coventry by the Mayor.

* * *

The Broads—by Road

Most holidaymakers think of the Norfolk Broads mainly

Refuelling in progress at the Bromma Airport, Stockholm, by a Commer 5-ton forward control petrol tanker belonging to Svenska Petroleum Aktiebolaget Standard.

in terms of boating expeditions, and it si probably news to many that a car can add greatly to the enjoyment of a tour of "Broadland."

The Automobile Association has prepared a suggested itinerary of this popular district, which includes many beauty spots often missed by those who go by boat. A special A.A. sketch-map outlines the tour, and contains detailed directions and mileages, together with descriptive notes on the scenery and places of interest.

* * *

New Eastbourne Showrooms

Speaking at the opening, on May 2 last, of the new Showrooms, in Cornfield Road, of Langney Motors, Ltd., Eastbourne, His Worship the Mayor (Alderman J. S. Croft, J.P.) paid high tribute to the vigorous enterprise of its directors, Mr. B. F. Bovill, chairman; Mrs. B. F. Bovill; Mr. Eric Edgerton, managing director, and all executives in developing "this great public service to citizens and visitors in defiance of economic problems, this day to present, from a very small beginning, an organisation of which the town is truly proud," which sentiment Mr. G. Lloyd Dixon, director of sales, Rootes Group, enthusiastically endorsed as "another example of foresight and courage in the face of difficult circumstances," i.e., heavy taxes, restrictive measures and, because of export priorities, manufacturers are unable to play their full part in meeting present-day demands for the home market.

The occasion was attended by a large gathering of leading citizens, representatives of associate industries, trade suppliers and the Press, all to express admiration for the marked efficiency and workmanlike atmosphere characterising the Company's servicing facilities and especially the dignity and resplendence of the new showrooms in which a full array of Humber, Hillman and Sunbeam-Talbot cars were attractively displayed.

The special Service-Show week which followed, with comprehensive displays of all modern automobile servicing facilities, supported by visiting equipment and repair specialists, and the obvious enthusiasm of the Company's factory trained service personnel, proved an outstanding success, many patrons touring the workshops, accessory and spares sections as well as the commendable welfare amenities of the employees.

(Continued on page 52)

PRESTCOLD REFRIGERATION

keeps good food good

•

PRESSED STEEL COMPANY LIMITED · COWLEY · OXFORD

FOR STYLE, ELEGANCE AND DURABILITY...

Rootes

LOOSE CAR SEAT COVERS

Rootes Loose Seat Covers improve your car in every way. Tailor-made from superfine felts of the highest quality, they fit like a glove and keep their good looks as well as their shape through a lifetime of hard wear. They are moth and shower proofed and can be dry-cleaned by the approved processes.

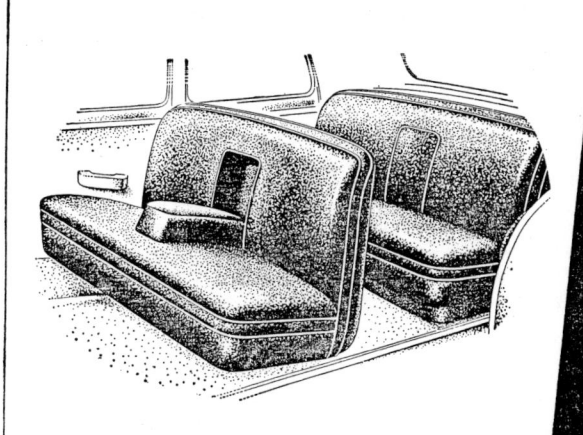

Patterns available on application to Dept. M.M.

ROOTES

LADBROKE HALL, BARLBY RD., LONDON, W.10
Tel. LADbroke 3232

London, Birmingham, Manchester, Maidstone, Rochester, Canterbury, Wrotham, Folkestone

Miss Judy Garland, the American film star, leaving a London hotel and entering the Humber Pullman Limousine put at her disposal by the Rootes Group during her visit to England.

This novel summer display in one of the main stores in the town of Randers, Jutland, centred round Britain's family car, the Hillman Minx Saloon. Rootes Group distributors for Denmark are British Motors A/S.

In a few Words! *from page 50*

Clothes and Cars

A new appeal in fashions—a Concours d'Elegance of clothes and cars—is being staged in London on Tuesday, June 5. Sponsored by the Chairman and Directors of the Rootes Group, and the Editor and Directors of British Vogue Export Book, it is arranged for overseas buyers and will be held at 7 p.m. at Devonshire House, Piccadilly, during the Fashion Fortnight.

With an eye on the dollar export market the show presents fashion in cars coupled with Haute Couture.

Humber, Hillman and Sunbeam-Talbot cars will be accompanied by mannequins dressed in the latest fashions, both cars and clothes bearing the same stamp of fine British workmanship.

* * *

Epicures in France

Cook's "Autotravel" Service has again been appointed by the organisers of the Gastronomic Rally in France to make all arrangements for British competitors entering the event.

The Rally starts at Rheims on Monday, June 11, and finishes on Monday, June 25, with a gala night at Versailles.

* * *

Straying Animals

Motorists travelling in open moorland or in mountainous districts are advised by the Automobile Association to be on the look-out for straying animals.

A.A. Patrols in the New Forest area have also reported instances of grazing cattle and the well-known ponies straying across the roads.

* * *

1,900-mile Week-end Trip

Driving through mist and rain, Mr. Austin Dabbs, the Cape Town racing driver, completed a 1,900-mile week-end motoring trip from Cape Town to Johannesburg and back in a 10 h.p. Hillman Minx in a total driving time of 33 hours 34 minutes.

The Minx was a standard model except for a specially fitted fuel tank, and Mr. Dabb's verdict on the car and the week-end was "Marvellous."

Mr. Dabbs left Cape Town at 3 o'clock on the Friday afternoon, reaching Johannesburg in the outstanding time of 16 hours 29 minutes. At 10 p.m. on the Saturday he left on his return drive and arrived back in Cape Town at 3.5 p.m. the following day after 17 hours 5 minutes on the road.

"Although there is no official speed record for the journey, Mr. Dabbs's time betters a previous record for the Cape-Johannesburg trip set up by Miss Pat McDonnell (now Mrs. Larkins) in 1937 by almost eight hours," reported the Johannesburg correspondent of the *Cape Argus*.

* * *

At Your Service

What surely is one of the most modern car selling and servicing establishments in the country was presented by the Phoenix Motor Company (Surrey), Ltd., to the general public at Sutton, on May 7 last; the opening date of a special service week.

Designed on entirely new and up-to-date lines, with new premises, giving every latter-day interpretation to motorists' car-servicing requirements, incorporating all the latest machinery and maintenance/repairs equipment, emergency lighting and power, staffed by factory-trained personnel, the keynote throughout is "quality service on time schedule, by dependable operatives"—a fact which is abundantly reflected in the scientific layout of maintenance and repair sections, electrical and mechanical testing bays, spare part and accessory stores—a picture of efficiency all its own—fuel and oil services, and in the general workshop cleanliness.

Nor should one overlook the good working conditions and welfare amenities certain to inspire operative enthusiasm and efficiency.

With a strikingly modern frontal appearance, embodying handsome showrooms and office facilities, with dignified after-dark illumination, all motorists residing within, or touring the district, would be well advised to pay a visit to these remarkable High Street premises.

* * *

Show Week

A Show Week from June 4 to 9, has been arranged by the Tower Service Garage (Epping), Ltd., the Rootes Group dealers at High Road, Epping, Essex.

* * *

S.M.M. and T. Appointments

Mr. G. E. Beharrell, Deputy-Chairman and Managing Director of the Dunlop Rubber Co., Ltd., has been elected President of the Society of Motor Manufacturers and Traders for the year 1951-52.

He succeeds Mr. W. Lyons, Chairman and Managing Director of Jaguar Cars, Ltd., who becomes Deputy-President.

Part of a Humber fleet operated by Middleton and Wood (1919), Ltd., of Wigan. In all, they have taken delivery through Rootes, Ltd., of Manchester, of nine Humber limousines and three Humber hearses.

Four Humber Super Snipe Touring Limousines are handed over to the Danish Army by British Motors A/S. More than 200 Rootes Group vehicles are now in use with the armed forces in Denmark.

WINTER COLD PLUS CARBON MAKES STARTING HARDER

Get rid of **Carbon** *for a start*

Drain and refill with Carbon-dispersing

Mobiloil Arctic

NOW IS THE TIME to change to free-flowing, carbon-dispersing Mobiloil and kill two motoring bogies for the winter:—

1. DIFFICULT STARTING. Mobiloil Arctic (or Mobiloil 'A' if recommended for your car) circulates freely when cold, minimises oil-drag, saves engine wear and helps your battery to turn the engine over quickly for easier starting.

2. CARBON. Mobiloil contains special carbon-dispersing and corrosion-preventing agents that clean away harmful power-stealing deposits; actually holds them harmlessly suspended in the oil, to be carried away when you drain and refill.

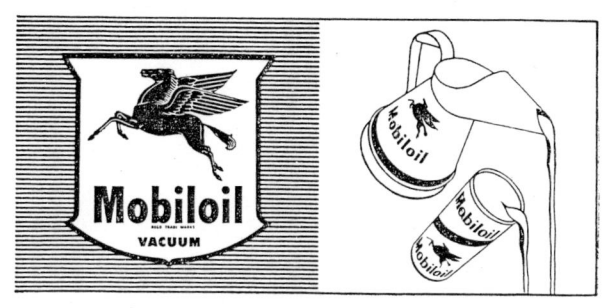

GET A FLYING START ON WINTER: CHANGE TO MOBILOIL ARCTIC NOW!

VACUUM OIL COMPANY LIMITED, LONDON, S.W.1

A CAR LOOKS AS NEW AS ITS CARPETS!

★

NEAT, PERFECT FITTING, LASTING.

Obtain complete car-interior cleanliness. Put into position or removed without fuss; design and finish in keeping with car's key-note of quality.

They are constructed of laminated rubberised cotton fabric, woven together on galvanised steel wires.
GUARANTEED FOR TEN YEARS.

FREE TRIAL OFFER

PRICES:

Humber Hawk 1950/51:	£ s. d.	Hillman Minx 1950/51 (Phase IV):	£ s. d.	Sunbeam-Talbot "80" and "90":	£ s. d.
Front Mats	2 2 0	Front Mats	2 3 10	Front Mats	1 16 7
Rear Mats	2 3 6	Rear Mats	1 18 5	Rear Mats	1 17 9
	4 5 6		4 2 3		3 14 4
Purchase Tax	1 1 4	Purchase Tax	1 0 7	Purchase Tax	0 18 7
	5 6 10		5 2 10		4 12 11

Fill in this coupon and post to The Universal Mat Co., Ltd., Tileyard Road, York Way, London, N.7.

Please send me on a week's free trial

Front pair mats................ ⎫
Back pair mats................. ⎬ Please mark here set
Complete set mats........... ⎭ required.

for............ h.p. Make................Year................

Signed (Name) ....

Address ....

Date.................... ....

I sign this coupon on the distinct understanding that I am at liberty to return the mats any time within one week of receipt. If retained, I undertake to pay for the mats within thirty days net.

THIS OFFER APPLIES TO U.K. ONLY

Protect Your Carpets with UNIVERSAL CAR MATS

NOW! In 20 minutes! COMPLETE WINTER PROTECTION

with the brightest, toughest wax polish of all!

Positively no rubbing!

Hundreds of thousands of motorists have proved this summer that Car-Plate gives a genuine wax finish, the brightest shine, the most lasting protection — in 20 minutes!

Now that winter is coming, all motorists are guaranteed that when they wax with Car-Plate their cars have the best-known protection against rain, sleet and snow. You can test this for yourself—just wipe off any surface dirt or dust and see how the raindrops "bead-up" on the clean waxed surface. Water just cannot begin to soak into the cellulose to do its hazing, dulling work.

And with Car-Plate complete winter protection is *so easy!* Just spread Car-Plate on a clean★ car, let dry — then wipe lightly. No rubbing with Car-Plate! Get a tin today!

5/- from all garages

★ The easy way to prepare the finish of your car for a Car-Plate waxing is to clean it super-clean with Johnson's Carnu — the quick, safe cleaner for cellulose and chromium.

JOHNSON'S CAR-PLATE
SPREAD...LET DRY...WIPE!
MADE BY THE MAKERS OF JOHNSON'S WAX

FOR MEN OF ENTERPRISE

Men who need their car for business, and enjoy it for family week-ends, select the Humber Hawk ... a comfortable six-seater, renowned for its effortless power, notably low running expenses ... and a price well within their range.

HUMBER

BY APPOINTMENT TO H.M. THE KING
MOTOR CAR MANUFACTURERS
HUMBER LTD.

Craftsman Built by the Rootes Group

Also Super Snipe, Pullman and Imperial

Humber Ltd. Coventry.   London Showrooms and Export Division: Rootes Ltd. Devonshire House Piccadilly London W.1

The NORWEGIAN—BRITISH—SWEDISH ANTARCTIC EXPEDITION 1949-52

A "Weasel" used by the Norwegian-British-Swedish Antarctic Expedition.

is using **KILFROST** Radiator Liquid (Anti-freeze)

Herewith is the actual report sent by the Expedition from Queen Maud Land in the South Polar Regions.

"Kilfrost Radiator Liquid

(1) Equipment on which used.
   Studebaker amphibious cargo carriers M29C ("Weasels").
   Petters Diesel Motors AV2 (coupled to Morrison generators).

(2) Lowest atmospheric temperature encountered.
   Cargo carriers, -40°C. while in operation, -45°C. when parked.
   Diesels, -20°C. at time of starting.

(3) Average atmospheric temperature.
   Cargo carriers — These machines were in nearly daily use, in temperatures ranging from -10°C. to -40°C.
   Diesels—in an unheated shed, usually at about -5°C.

(4) Percent strength of solution.
   A 50-50 solution of Radiator Liquid and water was used in all radiators. As the specific gravity of the solution checked well with the charts supplied by you, and the strength of the solution appeared to be maintained uniformly, no systematic record of specific gravity has been kept.

(5) Were internal surfaces free of scale before use? Yes.
   after use? Yes.

(6) Was it ever necessary to change radiator contents?
   No — except when the radiators became damaged by other agencies.

(7) Remarks.
   Highly satisfactory."

(By Courtesy of the Royal Geographical Society, London).

KILFROST MFG. CO. LTD. Albion Works, HALTWHISTLE,
Northumberland.
Telephone 332 & 357.

COLOURED fully-fitted CAR MATS
to tone with your car

Ask your local garage to show you the new and attractive coloured TYPROD fully-fitted CAR MATS.

Careful research in our dye works has enabled us to produce a standard range of 5 perfect colours to harmonise with your car interior.

TYPROD MATS
Guaranteed for ten years

TYPROD MATS are shaped to fit your car. There is a special mat to fit every make and model of car.

―――PLEASE SEND ME FULL PARTICULARS―――
TYRE PRODUCTS LTD., Palace of Engineering, WEMBLEY, Middx.
Telephone: WEMbley 1222 (10 lines).

NAME......................................
ADDRESS..................................
Make of my car..........................
H.P............Year............Model..........
Name and locality of usual garage..................
MMT

Fabram The ARISTOCRAT OF RADIATOR MUFFS

- For quick starting, petrol economy, reduction of starting-strain and engine wear.
- For prevention of damage by frost and for conserving engine heat.
- Triple material throughout, clean tailored lines, reinforced seams.
- ALSO THE FABRAM MINIMUF with Patented quick-action attachment.
- DELIVERY FROM STOCK FOR ALL POPULAR MODELS.

PRICES:

Hillman Minx 1940/48:
  Minimuf only supplied 35/-
Hillman Minx 1949:
  Minimuf only supplied 35/-
Humber 1946/48. 14, 18, 27 h.p.: Muff 57/6.
  Minimuf 40/-
Humber Pullman 27 h.p.:
Hawk 14 h.p.:
Snipe 21 h.p. 1948.
  Minimuf only supplied 40/-

Sunbeam-Talbot 1946/47
  10 h.p.: Muff 52/6.
  Minimuf 35/-
Sunbeam-Talbot 1946/47
  2 litre.
  Muff 55/- Minimuf 35/-
Sunbeam-Talbot "80" and "90"
  Minimuf only supplied 35/-

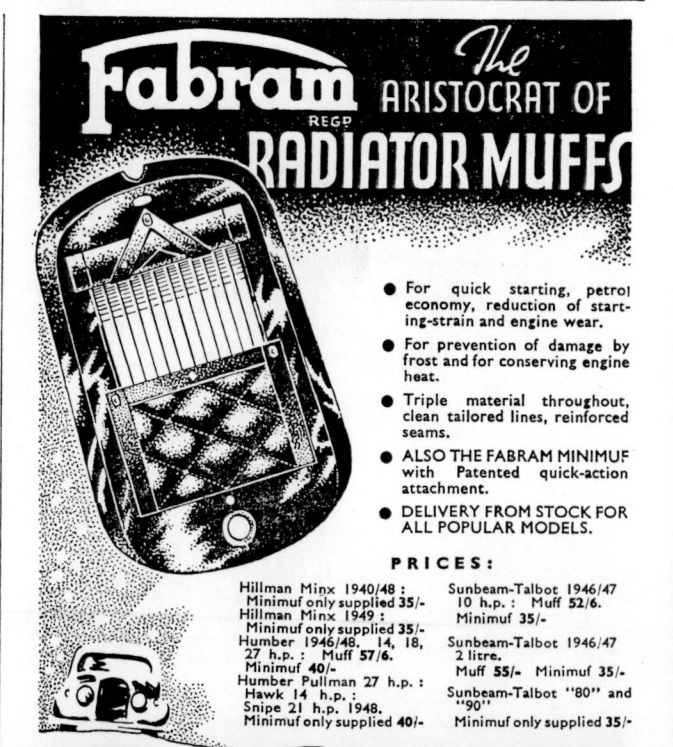

FAXALL PRODUCTS LTD., BLACKLEDGE WORKS · HALIFAX.
Telephone: Halifax 5208   Telegrams: FAXALL, Halifax

You won't get this at half the price

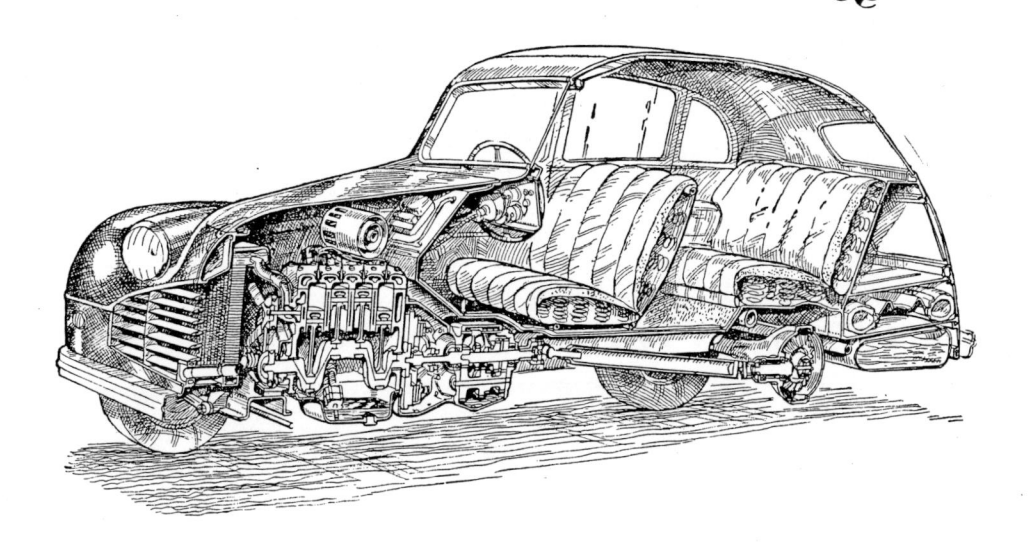

TYRESOLES give you new tyre mileage over again at approximately *half the cost* of new tyres

Before & After TYRESOLES

There are now 39 "TYRESOLES" factories in Great Britain to give you rapid local service.

There are also "TYRESOLES" factories in 43 Countries throughout the World.

Write for full details to:—

TYRESOLES LTD., PALACE OF ENGINEERING, WEMBLEY, MIDDX. Tel: WEMbley 1222 (10 lines)

We supply the pressing need!

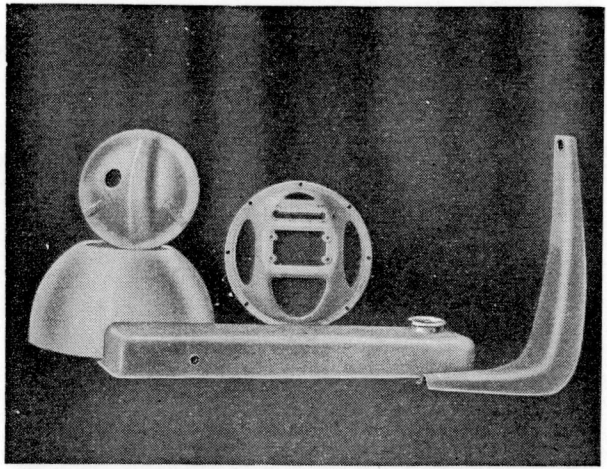

A. E. JENKS & CATTELL LTD
WEDNESFIELD near Wolverhampton
Telephone: FALLINGS PARK 31271

WILCOT
RADIATOR MUFFS & MUFFETTES

Don't wait

TILL THE COLD WEATHER SETS IN

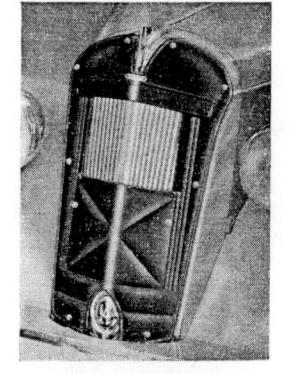

ORDER EARLY TO ENSURE PROMPT DELIVERIES

FROM YOUR GARAGE OR SEND FOR ILLUSTRATED LIST AND PRICES

WILCOT (PARENT) CO. LTD.
FISHPONDS, BRISTOL.

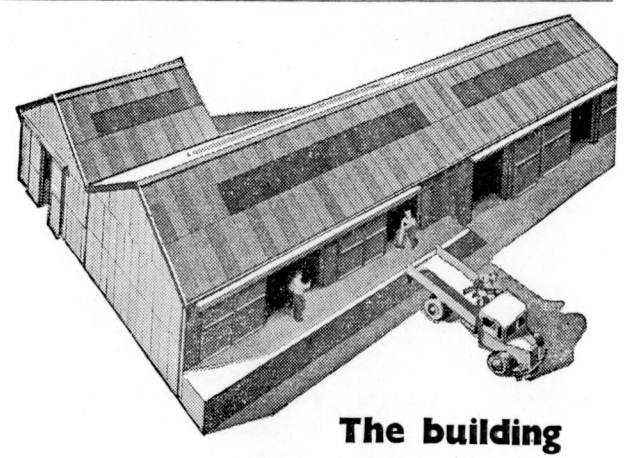

SUNBEAM-TALBOT OWNERS' CLUB

PLEASE send me full particulars regarding Membership. I was/was not* a member in pre-war days.

Post this to the Hon. Sec. Sunbeam-Talbot Owners' Club, Sunbeam-Talbot Ltd., Ryton-on-Dunsmore, Coventry, Warwickshire.

Name ....

Address ....

....

*Member { R.A.C. (Full) / R.A.C. (Associate) / A.A.

Type of Car ....

Date .... *Delete where necessary.

The building you need...

is very likely one of Thorns standard range of Industrial Buildings, which includes new steel structures for factories, stores, garages; timber and asbestos buildings for offices, canteens, halls, etc., and reconditioned Nissen type huts and 'Blister' hangars.

★ Write today, stating details of your requirements and requesting prices of suitable buildings.

THORNS J. THORN & SONS LTD

Box 67, BRAMPTON RD., BEXLEYHEATH, KENT   Bexleyheath 305

BD-F1

LEADING MOTOR
MANUFACTURERS

recommend

Essolube
MOTOR OIL

THE OIL FOR WISER DRIVERS

ESSO PETROLEUM COMPANY, LIMITED, 36 QUEEN ANNE'S GATE, LONDON, S.W.1

P&O

to
Australia
and
The East

For sailings and fares, apply:—
14/16 COCKSPUR ST., S.W.I.
9 KINGSWAY, W.C.2.
122 LEADENHALL ST., E.C.3.

Built like a BRIDGE

By using the "natural forces" of stress and strain, Watney's have made the DRAGOMAN supreme in its field.

This scientific approach, besides giving dynamic strength to the rack, also prevents strain to the roof and guttering. Strength is given to the rack by rigid steel tube, to take heavy luggage. The patent fixing gear, fitting neatly under the car door top sill, exerts vertical pressure.

FIT A 'WATMAC'
DRAGOMAN
★ detachable ROOF RACK

Patent No. 487,483

Fitted by anyone in a few minutes, without drilling or tools, the DRAGOMAN is available from good garages and dealers.
8 to 10 h.p. £6 17s. 6d.; over 10 h.p. £8 8s.
Or write for details, giving make, year and h.p.

WATNEY MOTOR ACCESSORIES CO. LTD.
Blaby Trading Estate · BLABY · Nr. LEICESTER
Tel.: Wigston 89601. 'Grams: Watmac, Blaby

DESMO
CLIP FITTING MIRROR
No. 200

RETAIL PRICE
18/6

Size of glass, 4 ins. Overall length, 8½ ins. Solid Brass, heavily Chrome Plated.

This mirror has a new type of fitting for attachment to the edge of the car door, thus obviating drilling the body, and is fixed in a few seconds. A new type of enclosed adjustment for the mirror head is also incorporated.

DESMO LTD
BIRMINGHAM · 7
Telephone - ASTon Cross 2831/2/3

London Showrooms
220, SHAFTESBURY AVENUE, W.C.2.
Telephone - - TEMple Bar 1994/5

HOLDENS

B. DIXON-BATE LTD.
CHESTER 12
Telephone : Chester 24034 (3 lines)
Towing brackets for most modern cars

TRUCK TRAILER
Model D12C
Capacity 12 cwts.
£77 . 0 . 0

wisely chosen from the famous range of
"D-B"
SUPER TRAILERS

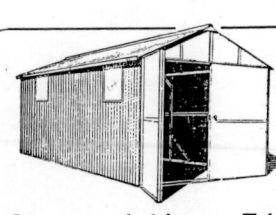

Neata
GARAGE
STEEL AND ASBESTOS

Size 14' × 7'
Price £49 - 15 - 0
Larger sizes and H.P. terms available.

Delivered FREE by our own transport.

NEATA PRODUCTS (CHELTENHAM) LTD.
Dept. M.M., ST. PAULS, CHELTENHAM, Glos.

This is the bulb for night driving

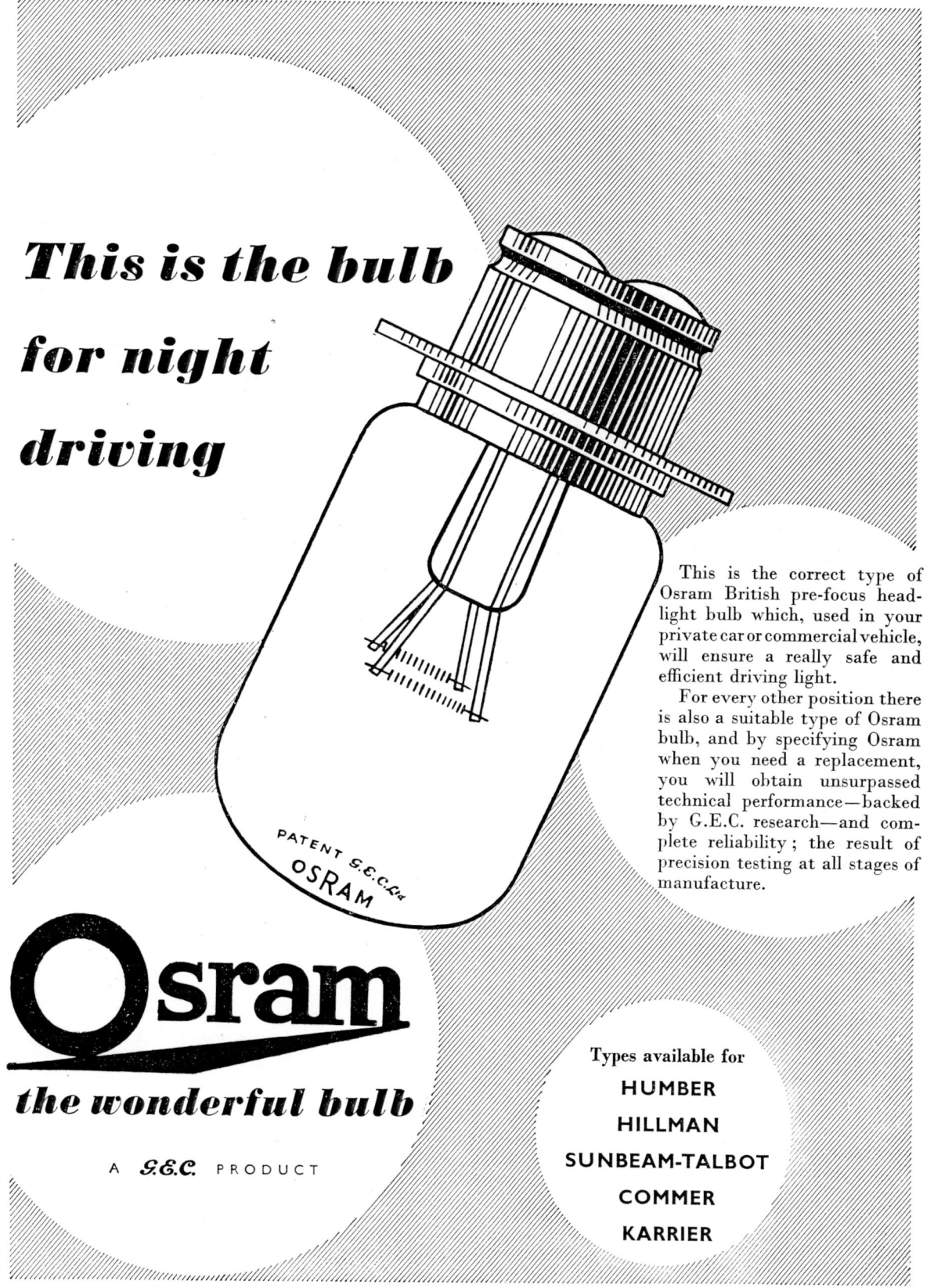

This is the correct type of Osram British pre-focus headlight bulb which, used in your private car or commercial vehicle, will ensure a really safe and efficient driving light.

For every other position there is also a suitable type of Osram bulb, and by specifying Osram when you need a replacement, you will obtain unsurpassed technical performance—backed by G.E.C. research—and complete reliability; the result of precision testing at all stages of manufacture.

Osram
the wonderful bulb

A *G.E.C.* PRODUCT

Types available for
HUMBER
HILLMAN
SUNBEAM-TALBOT
COMMER
KARRIER

THE GENERAL ELECTRIC CO. LTD.

You get the
best out of
your Rootes Group Car

because we put the best into it!

HUMBER · HILLMAN · SUNBEAM-TALBOT

Craftsman-built by the Rootes Group

EXPORT DIVISION

ROOTES

DEVONSHIRE HOUSE

Piccadilly, London W.1

ROOTES GROUP REGIONAL REPRESENTATIVES
Located at:
U.S.A. 505 PARK AVENUE, NEW YORK 22, N.Y. and 403 North Foothill Road, Beverly Hills, California
CANADA. 1849 EGLINTON AVENUE EAST, SCARBOROUGH, NR. TORONTO, ONTARIO

AUSTRALIA & NEW ZEALAND
Fishermen's Bend, Port Melbourne, Australia.

BELGIUM
Shell Building, 47, Cantersteen, Brussels.

SOUTHERN AFRICA 750/2/4
Stuttaford's Buildings, St. George's St., Cape Town, S.A.

CENTRAL AFRICA Jackson Road, P.O. Box 5194, Nairobi, Kenya.

EUROPE Devonshire House, Piccadilly, London, W.1.

FRANCE 6 Rond-Point des Champs Elysees, Paris 8

SWITZERLAND 1 Rue du Rhône, Geneva.

FAR EAST Macdonald House, Orchard Road, Singapore, 9

INDIA Agra Road, Bhandup, Bombay.

MIDDLE EAST
37 Kasr El Nil Street, Cairo, Egypt.

ARGENTINA
Casilla de Correo 3478, Buenos Aires.

BRAZIL Av. Presidente Vargas 290 (S/1003), Rio de Janeiro.

CARIBBEAN
28 Duke Street, Kingston, Jamaica, B.W.I.

Clouds over Buttermere:
Photo by Val Doone

I am the daughter of earth and water,
   And the nurseling of the sky;
I pass through the pores of the ocean and shores,
   I change but I cannot die.—*Shelley.*

Boston's crowded streets on the occasion of the opening of the British Exposition on September 10, which included a British motor-car section, when bands and bluejackets from H.M.S. "Snipe" and "Superb" participated in the official ceremonies.

One of a fleet of 30 Humber Super Snipe station wagons (fitted with two-way radio, etc.,) in the service of the Radio division of the Singapore police force.

Below : Photo depicting Mr. Anthony Eden, with Mr. Douglas Fairbanks, during his recent tour of the U.S.A.

Editorial Comment

EDITORIAL AND ADVERTISING
53 STRATTON STREET,
LONDON, W.1
Telephone: GRO 3401

Conducted by E. D. O'BRIEN
Editor : THOMAS R. MULCASTER

Progress

WITH the close of the 36th British International Motor Exhibition, we think it timely to examine the latest developments of the Industry, with comparisons of allied interests.

Firstly, with nearly 3,250,000 motor-cars in use on 183,000 miles of highways in Great Britain to-day, at 17.6 vehicles per mile this exceeds even the traffic density of the U.S.A. with 15 times as many motor-cars and 16 times the road mileage !

Secondly, the increase in motor fuel consumption, by which the full use of British roads is best assessed, provides this remarkable comparison—806 million gallons in 1928 ; 1,832 million gallons last year.

* * *

Inertia

WITH direct motor taxation in 1928 at £11,000,000 per annum and, for 1950, £187,000,000, over the past 40 years we have added only 8,334 miles to our highways system.

Road expenditure, at £72,000,000 in 1949, was, last year, only one-third of the total revenue. This year it may be considerably less ! Moreover, present-day accident costs to the community exceed the country's total road construction and maintenance bill.

What more can one expect with profound inertia on the one hand, and on the other, over 1,250 different highways authorities, each interpreting "ordered savings" in no common or purposeful pattern of economy ?

* * *

Brighter Outlook

THE disposal of trams, for example, those anachronisms of "fixed track" transportation by which immeasurable delay and confusion has been caused wherever they have been operated.

With nearly 15,000 in 1927, the figure of 4,000 for 1950 is dropping steadily. And it would drop quicker if reduction in the one metropolis did not mean, by transfer, increase in another !

In goods' vehicles—permitting door-to-door bulk delivery by the hour rather than by the week by rail—what are the statistics here ? Of A, B, C and D licence users the 1937 figure of 500,000 is to-day almost doubled !

Of diesel-engined units, also contributing to vastly improved road haulage economics, to-day's figure of 88,597 is 12 times that for 1934.

* * *

Achievement

OUR last point concerns truly unprecedented industrial achievement, that regarding our own Industry.

As Britain's Exporter No. I—and all praise to the 1,783,000 operatives—the value rise of its 1950 exports is 3,500 per cent on 1932. The respective figures are £6,000,000 and £216,000,000.

How to spend £30 on a dinner for two

Simply park your car without the protection of Bluecol anti-freeze in the radiator. Then when you've finished your meal you'll probably find £30's worth of frost damage on your plate.

Some cars without Bluecol may get through the winter, *but the odds are against it.* Last year many motorists found that a burst radiator, cracked block, or badly damaged cooling system is no joke. It was months before they could use their cars again. Even in a mild winter, frost strikes 45 times in the South, 110 in the North . . . so the risk of damage is real.

Why take a chance when you've nothing to gain and a car to lose? Fill with Bluecol and know you're 100% SAFE against 35 degrees of frost for the whole of the winter.

SMITHS BLUECOL

the SAFE anti-freeze

SMITHS MOTOR ACCESSORIES LIMITED, CRICKLEWOOD WORKS, LONDON, N.W.2
THE MOTOR ACCESSORY DIVISION OF S. SMITH & SONS (ENGLAND) LIMITED

My Hawk headed for the interior of the "Silver City" aeroplane, by which we made a rapid Channel crossing.

"I enjoyed my holiday in Spain— its beauties are almost inexhaustible, if not in the obvious places!"

By E. D. O'Brien

SOME months ago in an article in these pages I told readers of *Modern Motoring and Travel* that I had a particular hide-out on the Costa Brava in Spain to which I was going. I refused, however, to reveal its whereabouts.

Alas! I need not have been so cautious, as when I got there I found that the tiny little hotel in this beautiful setting was over-run.

However, so lovely is Aigua Blava, so clear the sea, and so perfect the bathing that it was a case, in the words of the hymn, "where every prospect pleases and only man is vile."

* * *

ONE of the joys, if you are a keen motorist, of a visit to Spain is the journey there, and I must say (having once experienced it) I shall never fail, if I can help it, to use the "Silver City" Air Ferry between Lympne and Le Touquet.

Below: Fishing nets and all that—a secluded spot by Aigua Blava.

We were a little late taking off (but that is a common experience with air transport), but from the moment of driving up to the British Customs to being waved away at Le Touquet we took no more than 55 minutes by my watch.

* * *

IT started to pour with rain after our lunch at Abbeville (by this time, via the surface route, we should have only been half-way across the Channel with all the long process of unloading and Customs before us) and the gloom of the afternoon's drive was only lightened by the cheerful spectacle of what seemed to me like 300, but I gathered subsequently was only 35, Sunbeam-Talbots in procession returning from the Sunbeam-Talbot Owners' Club's "Rallye San Sebastian."

Incidentally, while handing out bouquets, I must deliver two more. One is to the Motorists' Travel Club, an organisation of which I had not heard before, but who arranged at a moment's notice most satisfactory accommodation all along the route for six people.

The Hotel Gavina at S'Agaro—typical of the architecture of the place.

The other is to the designer of the boot of our faithful Humber Hawk. Six people, even if two of them are children, plus their luggage for a fortnight, present no small problem and while we can, I think, congratulate ourselves on the ingenuity with which luggage and passenger list were stored, we remained lost in admiration for the genius who enabled us to carry so much and drive so far in such comfort.

The Hawk itself, incidentally, took us tirelessly, smoothly and at a high average speed over the fine roads of France, and is so sprung that the pot-holes of the coast roads of the Costa Brava were apparent only to the shock-absorbers.

IN so short a space one can only record fleeting impressions. They include happily revisiting the long sweep of the vineyards of the Côte D'Or, the delicious " escargots " and " Jambon à la crème " at Joigny (the youngest member of the party, aged 10, thereafter demanded snails for every meal) and Avignon, as beautiful as ever, the romance of its moonlit streets marred only by the English girls looking like nothing on earth in what appeared, to my untutored male eye, to be their panties! (Why *will* people behave abroad in a way in which they would never think of doing at home ? The female English visitors who insist on going into Spanish or French churches in Bikinis have only themselves to blame if the natives resent it.)

Then there was the long climb up to the Franco-Spanish frontier at Le Perthus, the first glimpse of that incredibly blue sea and the friend who met us in Gerona with ices for the children and huge iced brandy and sodas (costing 1s. 8d. each) for the hot and tired grown-ups.

Not all our time was spent at Aigua Blava. By an incredible piece of amiable shoe-horning on the part of Senor Ensesa, the proprietor of the whole place, we managed to get in for four nights at S'Agaro, to my mind one of the most beautiful simple-sophisticated seaside resorts in the world.

* * *

INCIDENTALLY, one must issue a word or two of warning.

Firstly, do not expect, in the season, at any rate, to turn up in Spain and expect to get rooms unless you have booked.

A second is, if you do want to see a bull fight, do not go to one where novices are trying their hand as *matadores*. When first-class bull-fighters are performing the beauty of their movements and the cleanness of

The Author and the " snail fan " by the Pont d'Avignon.

the kills remove a large part of the distaste felt by the average Briton at his first *corrida*, but a novice's fight can be a messy business

A third is this. Don't be too upset by the apparent poverty of the beggars in the tourist quarters of such places as Barcelona. Begging is a hereditary profession in Spain, like smuggling. A true story is told of the Englishman who offered 5 pesetas (a day's subsistence) to a beggar in Seville to carry his bags. " Sir," replied the beggar, drawing himself up, " I am a beggar, not a porter." In fact, in 1934, there was a beggars' strike in Barcelona. Being a Catholic country there is an obligation on the part of the faithful to give alms. Previous to the strike the public satisfied their consciences, without unduly damaging their pockets, by giving 5 centimos— the smallest coin available. The beggars, however, banded themselves together and demanded a 10 centimos " minimum." Not getting it, they struck—refusing to beg for a month,

Waiting for Pedro's ferry—at Aigua Blava.

at the end of which time the population surrendered and 10 centimos became the basic alm.

A fourth is, if you haven't had your holiday, go to Spain out of the summer season. Go now, for instance, and you should find the sun and sea in the south as warm as in a fine English summer.

Finally, and this hardly needs saying to readers of *Modern Motoring and Travel*, go to Spain by car. The railways, with the exception of a few magnificent super-modern trains, are vastly out of date. Moreover, the beauties of Spain, and they are almost inexhaustible, are not for the most part in the obvious places or on the main routes.

* * *

Footnote

FOR those who collect specimens of " foreign English " I must add this notice on the beach at S'Agaro. It stands outside the little bar where we ate those delicious " sea foods " of all kinds for " elevenses," and where we danced the Sardana with the locals on our last night—to find to our embarrassment that the proprietor of the bar would not allow us to pay for the many drinks which we had ordered for the dancers and ourselves.

It runs :—

" Bathing Enclose—Advertisement.

" It is indispensable to the Mesars Bathers, to obtain the Bath-Ticket to have right to any one service of douches, screen-shadows, bathing houses, and urgent cures that this establishment has installed.

THE ENTERPRISE."

I am still wondering what an " urgent cure " could be.

" Elevenses " and the Hawk at S'Agaro.

TEE-TIME TOPICS

By F. J. C. PIGNON

It is 20 years since I took the Ryder Cup to the United States. This year, perhaps!

BY the time you read this the last and, in many ways, the most important fixture of the year—the match between professional golfers of Great Britain and the United States for the Ryder Cup will probably be concluded.

But it is rather fun for those who have scant respect for the feelings of sports writers to see how wrong we can sometimes be. So, with utter recklessness, I intend to discuss the prospects of the match, which will, at the time of writing (October 15), take place a week or two hence at Pinehurst in North Carolina.

* * *

FIRST of all, let me say that Britain has never won a Ryder Cup match in the United States.

As manager of the 1931 team, I took the little gold trophy, presented in 1927 by the late Samuel Ryder of St. Albans, to the United States.

It took me an hour or more to convince Customs' officials in New York that this was not imported manufactured gold, and that I had no intention of selling it. And having got it into the country, there it has remained except for one fleeting glance of it, though the match is played once every two years alternately in Great Britain and the United States, regardless of which side wins.

* * *

I SHALL be as surprised as delighted if the British return with the Cup this time, but it is some time since this country had such a good chance of winning it.

Apart from the confidence of the British players, they were not so heavily handicapped by climatic conditions as on previous occasions, the normal weather at Pinehurst in November being rather like a nice autumn day here.

Then most of the British professionals have mastered the shot with which Americans have in the past eclipsed them—the pitch to the holeside with a wedge. But the result may turn on the British players' ability to play this shot as well as do their rivals and whether they can putt accurately on soft luscious greens to which they are unaccustomed.

I DON'T think they will be able to do these things, but if they can, Britain has more than an even money chance of winning against a team composed almost entirely of American professionals who came near to defeat in the match at Ganton, Scarborough, two years ago.

I think it will be a close thing with the odds against Britain.

* * *

IT is obvious that the standard of play among professionals at least, was considerably higher in this season's big tournaments than it has been for many years.

I am not so sure that the same progress has been made in amateur golf during the past season, though a few young golfers have been "discovered" during the year.

The difficulties with which amateur golfers are faced these days is the lack of time and, to some extent, money.

Frequently those who have the time cannot afford the cost of competitive golf nowadays, when there is very little change of fifty pounds left after a week of championship golf.

Those who can afford such luxuries are usually working so hard in order to consolidate their financial position that many of them are little more than week-end golfers.

Send us your Golfing Problem

IF you encounter a set of circumstances likely to be of interest, the solution of which might aid also fellow golfers, why not submit the problem to our expert.

F. J. C. Pignon, the well-known golfing authority, will be pleased personally to examine readers' letters and to offer practical advice on all matters relative to the game.

ONE of the main reasons why scoring in professional tournaments is so much lower nowadays is, as I remarked earlier, because of their skilful approach play. Reading "Golf My Way," by Dai Rees (Heinemann, 10s. 6d.), I see that we are eye to eye in that "golf is simpler now with matched sets.". . . "One hears scornful references to the latest clubs like the wedge and sand-iron as 'buying shots in a shop' . . . these clubs obtain results which would not have been possible with the clubs of thirty years ago."

Whether one buys a shot or learns to play, it is a matter of personal taste, but there is no doubt that the wedge has revolutionised the game.

It is not an easy club to master, but it is a most effective club for approach play and can knock strokes off any player's handicap by effective use.

* * *

AT one time I was one of the scoffers who deprecated "Buying a shot" instead of learning to play it. Of course it can be done. The late Mr. John Ball, who won both the Open and Amateur Championships, never had a niblick in his bag during his brilliant golfing career.

A lady golfer, Gloria Minoprio, carried club economy to extremes and competed in the British championship, in which she won a few rounds, using only one club, a sort of mid-iron, with which she played every shot.

* * *

IT is quite obvious that if modern clubs make the game easier, they also make it more enjoyable.

Very few handicap golfers are willing to spend their week-ends at practice, and modern clubs cut out a lot of drudgery. And of these the wedge is one of the most valuable clubs in the bag.

When this club has been mastered it will get the ball out of any rough, the deepest bunker and also make the pitch and stop shot from anywhere up to about 90 yards within the scope of a week-end golfer.

It has reduced the scores in professional tournaments and can do the same for you. But don't think you can master the wedge in a few minutes. It can be a clumsy instrument until you get used to it, and half an hour with the club professional can at least start you right.

FIT

"TripleX"
Regd.

AND BE SAFE

FOR THE OWNER-DRIVER MECHANIC

You can attend to these simple, but important, maintenance points on your Hillman Minx:

Carburetter:
Fuel pump:
Lighting system:
Winter precautions

FUEL SYSTEM

THE A.C. Type "T" Air Silencer (Home Models) which is mounted on the carburetter intake, requires no service attention beyond the occasional checking of the fixing clip and support stay for tightness.

* * *

Carburetter

THE carburetter is easily dismantled for cleaning, the first operation being to empty the float chamber, by the removal of the drain plug at its base. This operation in itself should be sufficient to ensure a clean float chamber base. When cleaning any of the jets depicted on the illustration it is advisable that it be carried out simply by washing in fuel and blowing through. Under no circumstances prick out with wire.

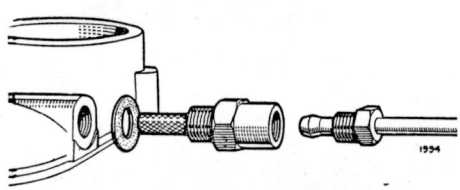

Filter at Main Fuel Union.

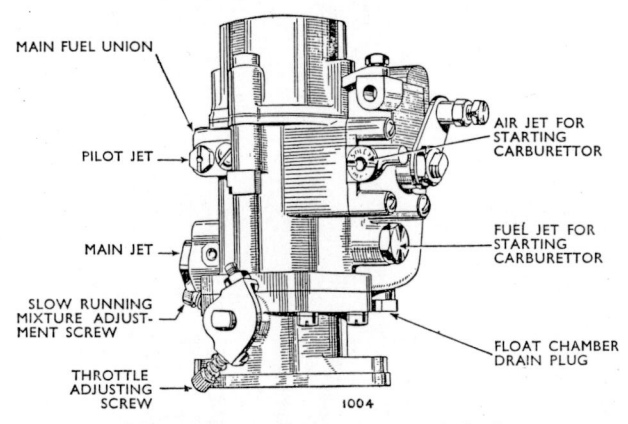

Solex Carburettor (30 F.A.I. Down-draught Type).

This carburetter has two external adjustments only:—
1. The throttle adjusting screw.
2. The slow-running mixture adjusting screw.

Both these controls are indicated in the illustration.

Adjustments to these controls must only be made when the engine is hot, and when symptoms such as engine "stalling" are occurring.

Adjustment No. 1 should be so set that a reasonable tick-over is attained. This controls the position of the throttle "butterfly" valve.

Adjustment No. 2 covers the slow-running mixture volume. Turning the screw clockwise restricts the volume; anti-clockwise increases the volume. Adjust the screw until the engine runs freely. A final setting may then be necessary to Adjustment No. 1.

NOTE.—Do not attempt to set the idling of the engine too slow, or "stalling" may occur when the clutch is disengaged.

* * *

Inlet manifold

IT is important that the manifold drain pipe is kept clear of obstruction. Fouling due to carbon or gum deposit from fuel will cause flooding of the manifold with consequent difficulty in starting.

Periodically the drain pipe should be removed and cleaned and refitted after checking for correct operation. (This work should also be carried out when reassembling the engine after decarbonising, etc.):—

Remove the drain-pipe from the manifold by unscrewing the brass union nut securing it. Clear the drilling in the manifold with a piece of wire.

Clear the small hole in the jet at the top end of the pipe by passing a piece of fine wire through it. If required, the jet may be removed from the pipe as it is a push fit.

See that the pipe is clear and rinse pipe and jet with petrol. Refit drain pipe assembly to engine, making sure that the brass union is fully tightened and making a good joint to the olive at the upper end of the pipe.

* * *

Fuel pump

THE cleaning of the gauze filter and sludge chamber, both of which are exposed when the top cap is removed, are the only two items of maintenance required on the fuel pump.

A drain plug is provided on the side of the pump for draining the sludge chamber before cleaning.

When replacing the top cap, care must

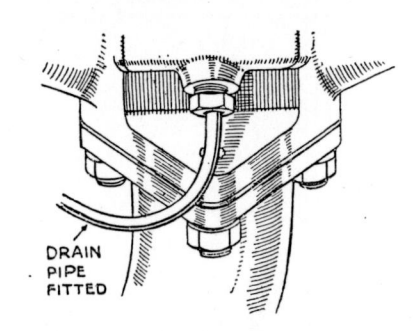

Inlet (Intake) Manifold Drain Pipe

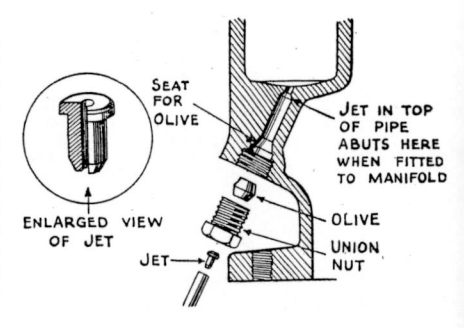

be taken to see that the cork gasket is intact and that it lies on its seat and that the fibre washer is replaced under the head of the retaining screw, or the pump will not operate.

* * *

Hand-priming lever

THE hand-priming lever shown in the illustration is for use when, for any reason, the carburetter float chamber or pump bowl has become empty. A few strokes of the hand-priming lever on these occasions will fill the float chamber with petrol and ensure easy starting without prolonged use of the starter and consequent excessive strain on the battery.

Owing to the special construction of the pump it is impossible to overfill the carburetter, as after several strokes with the hand-priming lever this will become free, indicating that the carburetter is full.

Should it be found that the hand-priming lever will not operate, turn the engine one revolution with the starting handle, thus freeing the fuel pump operating lever mechanism from the eccentric on the engine camshaft.

Fuel shortage

IF the pump should fail to deliver fuel to the carburetter the following points should be checked:—

1. That fuel is available in the tank and that the unions in the pipe connecting the tank to the pump are tight.
2. That the pump filter is clean and that the cork washer below the top cap is in good condition.
3. The action of the pump, proved by working the hand-priming lever with the delivery pipe (pump to carburetter) disconnected.

If, after extended service, trouble is experienced with the pump, no attempt should be made to remove it from the engine or to repair it. The services of the Hillman Distributor or Dealer should be sought as these pumps are of specialised manufacture and their overhaul and repair is not normally within the scope of the owner-driver.

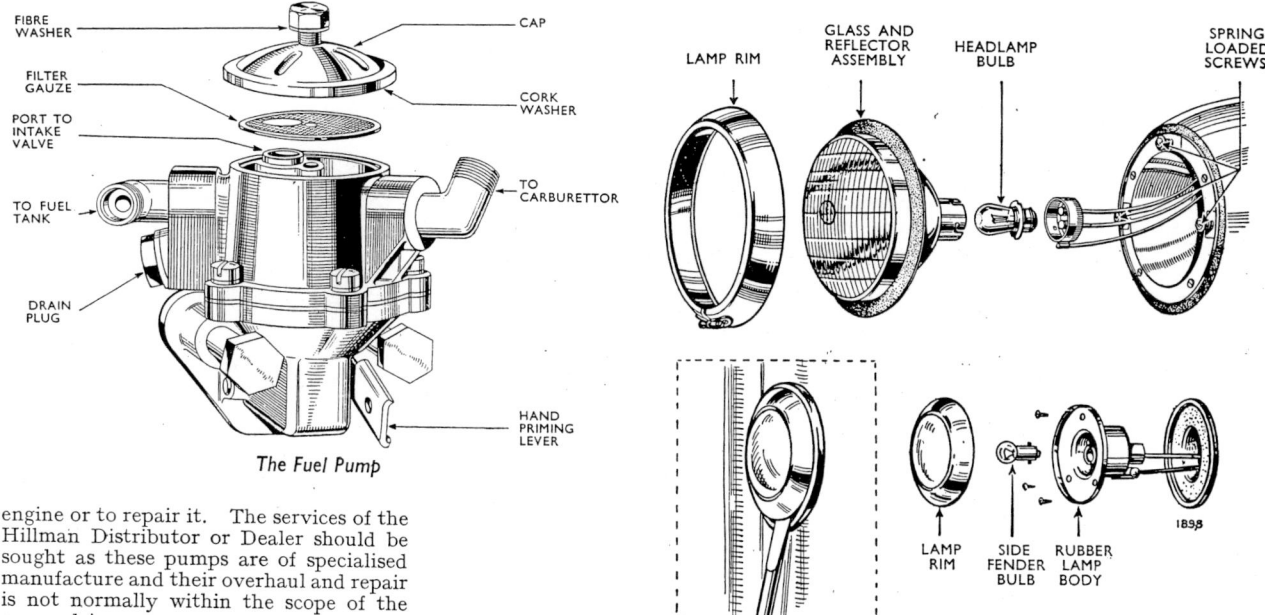

*   *   *

LAMPS

TO remove the lamp rim loosen the clamp screw at the base of the rim. The lamp rim can then be lifted off, leaving the glass and reflector, which are permanently sealed together as a unit, still in position. Reverse procedure to reassemble. (See illustration.)

To remove glass and reflector assembly, remove lamp rim as above. Grasp glass and reflector assembly with both hands, press rearwards and turn slightly in an anti-clockwise direction, which will release the three "key hole" apertures in its rear edge from the three spring-loaded screws.

Do not turn or remove these screws, as this will upset the alignment of the lamp. Reverse procedure to reassemble.

*   *   *

To renew headlamp bulbs

REMOVE lamp rim and glass and reflector assembly.

Press the adaptor inwards, meanwhile turn slightly to line up the two arrows, marked on the adaptor and reflector; the adaptor can then be withdrawn and the bulb taken out.

To reassemble adaptor to reflector, press on with arrows in line and turn to the right.

*   *   *

To renew side bulbs

THE rim is held by a location tag at the top, and by the shaped rubber flange surrounding the rim. Carefully insert a screwdriver under the lamp rim after raising the rubber flange and prise the rim off. Remove bulb. To refit rim, locate tag at top and press into place, making sure the rubber flange holds rim all around its periphery.

NOTE 1.—On Home Models, a single filament bulb is fitted to the right-hand side headlamp and a double filament bulb to the left-hand side headlamp.

On Export Models, double filament type bulbs are fitted to both headlamps.

NOTE 2.—In replacing headlamp bulbs with double filament types, there are two alternative positions. Replacement bulbs marked "TOP" must be fitted with this word uppermost, other types can be fitted in either position.

Do not attempt to remove the glass from the reflector assembly as this is a sealed unit, the bulbs being removable only from the rear of the reflector.

NOTE 3.—The double filament bulb is so designed that the filaments are exactly opposite to each other. Hence, if the filament responsible for the dipped beam should fail, remove the bulb and replace it the other way up in order to regain a dipped beam, but, of course, there will be no straight ahead beam from the lamp if the switch is in the non-dipped position.

Stop and tail lamp

A LAMP unit is fitted at the side of each rear wing.

To dismantle—remove the two screws with a coin or screwdriver and lift off the red glass and rim. Remove bulb.

When refitting the bulb, turn the main lighting switch to "side." Put the bulb into position. If the powerful filament lights up (very bright), remove the bulb and give it one half-turn.

When replacing the glass, make sure that this is the correct way round, or the bulb will be broken.

To adjust beam in vertical axis, turn top screw as shown in illustration below. To adjust beam in horizontal axis, turn side screws.

The Fuel Pump

Headlamp and Side (Fender) Lamp Details.

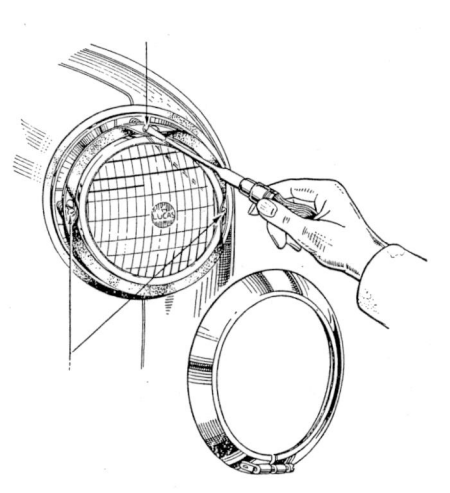

Beam Adjustment.

Maintenance:
(Concluded from page 23)

Headlamp alignment

IF the car can be parked on a flat space in front of a garage door or wall so that the headlamps are at least 25 feet (7.6 m.) away, the adjusting of alignment can be carried out very easily, without taking the car on the road. The lamps must *not* be dipped during the check.

It is essential that the car is square with the door or wall. The lamps should be aligned so that the horizontal axis of the oval light area is level with the centres of the lamps. The vertical axis should, of course, be central with the front of the car.

If a lamp appears to be out of adjustment, proceed as follows:

    Remove lamp front.
        Switch on headlamp.
        See that headlamps are not "dipped."

The reflector can be aligned to the required position by adjusting the three spring-loaded screws as indicated in the lower illustration, on page 23. The setting should then be cross checked on the road.

* * *

Rear number plate illumination

THIS contains two bulbs.
    To dismantle, remove one screw from the top of the lamp with a coin or screwdriver. Lift the cover downwards, this will disclose the bulbs.

When refitting the lamp cover, make quite sure that the fixing at the lower side of the cover is in position before tightening the fixing screw.

* * *

Instrument panel lamps

THERE are five single filament bulbs behind the instrument panel.
To replace the bulbs in the speedometer, oil, and ignition lights, no dismantling is necessary, the hand can be inserted to the rear of the instrument panel from the passenger side, and these three bulbs can easily be extracted from their cylindrical sockets. The connecting wire being of sufficient length for the bulb holder to be brought into view to facilitate replacement. These bulbs are all of screw-cap type.

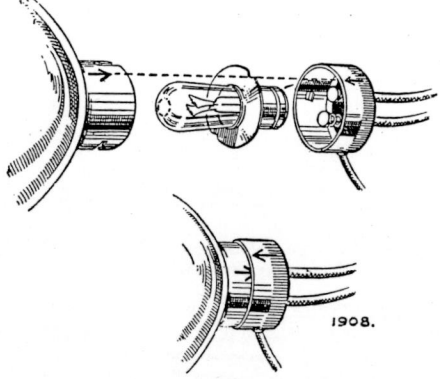

* * *

Renewal of Headlamp Bulbs.

WINTER PRECAUTIONS

TO avoid the possibility of the cooling system freezing whilst the vehicle is stationary, *or whilst being driven* in very cold weather it is recommended that an anti-freeze compound obtainable from any Hillman Distributor or Dealer should be used, and added in the quantities stipulated by the anti-freeze manufacturers.

Before putting anti-freeze compounds of any kind in the cooling system, it is imperative that the cylinder head and all hose connections should be checked for tightness, as these compounds have a very searching effect and should any leak into the sump, very serious damage could ensue owing to the possibility of engine seizure.

COMMERCIAL GLYCERINE MUST IN NO CIRCUMSTANCES BE USED

If the radiator has not been protected with anti-freeze compound when extreme conditions have been encountered it should be drained before being left standing for any length of time and refilled with warm water before moving off.

* * *

If there is no anti-freeze in the radiator and the atmospheric temperature is below freezing point, the radiator should be blanked right off with a rug or muff until the engine has reached its working temperature.

* * *

It is recommended that a portion of the bottom of the radiator is blanked off in very cold weather. Owners should consult the Hillman Dealer who will advise and carry out the work very simply.

* * *

Provision is made in the form of slots in the discs of the wheels, adjacent to the rims, to allow the fitting of non-skid chains. The use of such chains is recommended in heavy snow or icy conditions, also for use on soft and loose surfaces. Strap-on type chains only should be used of which there are many types available. Consult your Distributor or Dealer.

More maintenance points next month.

Distance between centre of headlamps.

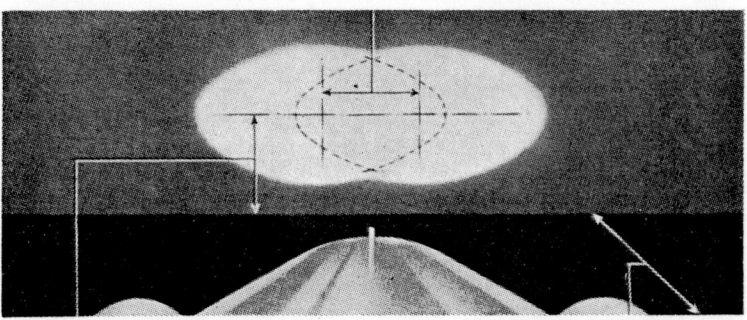

Height of headlamp-centres from ground.   **Distance not less than 25 feet.**

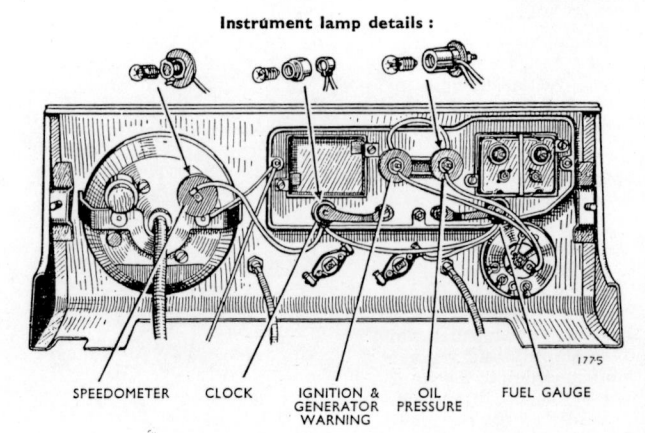

Instrument lamp details:

SPEEDOMETER   CLOCK   IGNITION & GENERATOR WARNING   OIL PRESSURE   FUEL GAUGE

INVITATION TO READERS

PAPER supplies restrict the number of copies of *Modern Motoring & Travel*. Supplies to newsagents and booksellers are quickly sold.

"Guarantee" a copy each month by becoming a regular subscriber. There are a few vacancies on the subscribers' list.

Send your subscription (11/6d., post free, per annum) to The Manager, *Modern Motoring & Travel*, 53, Stratton St., Piccadilly, London, W.1.

GOOD NEWS FOR THE PRIVATE MOTORIST

YOU'VE REACHED THE HEAD OF THE QUEUE

FOR TOO LONG NOW we've had to cut down on sales of "His Master's Voice" Car Radio to the private motorist. Almost every set we could squeeze out of the hard-working "H.M.V." factory at Hayes has either been going straight overseas (we earned some 100,000 dollars for Britain in the first 9 months of this year) or else has gone into the home and export models of some 20 famous British car manufacturers who exclusively fit and recommend our receivers. We are proud to have played so notable a part in making British cars so acceptable overseas. *But now it is the turn of the private motorist at home.* We have managed to step up production to meet both export and home requirements. Those of you who have waited so long and patiently for your "H.M.V." Car Radio can go along to your Accredited Smiths Radiomobile Dealer and ask him to fit it now. You will then become the proud owner of the set that has revolutionised car radio. Because of its unique "Electrical-Link" construction "H.M.V." Car Radio gives motorists the same high-fidelity reception they get at home, or even better. See your Smiths Radiomobile dealer today.*

* If you do not know who your nearest dealer is, drop us a line and we will send his name together with full details about "H.M.V." Car Radio.

"HIS MASTER'S VOICE" CAR RADIO

This is Model 4200 with push-button tuning for 5 pre-selected stations. The price with "A" type amplifier is £20.15.0 (fitting and purchase tax extra).

MARKETED BY

SMITHS RADIOMOBILE
S. SMITH & SONS (RADIOMOBILE) LIMITED

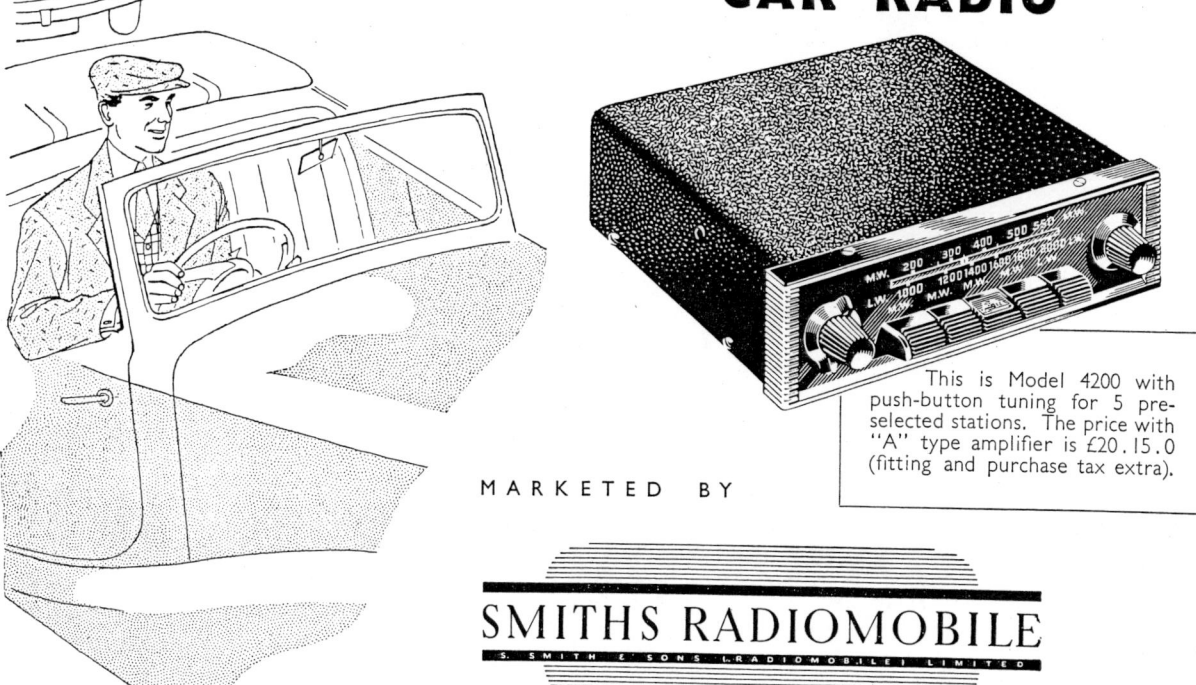

S. SMITH & SONS (RADIOMOBILE) LTD., 179-185 GT. PORTLAND STREET, LONDON, W.1

"We stood together on top of that terrific hill from Gudvangen to Stalheim, the worst hill in Europe——"

from Brussels, to do the air journey from over St. Pauls Cathedral to over Waterloo Bridge—two miles in 10 seconds. Altogether a marvellous sight."

M.: "What is your favourite country, other than England, of course?"

"The Editor and I"
(Continued from page 26)

I had expected it to be grey, like St. Paul's Cathedral. It turned out to be the colour of honey, wonderful glowing honey!"

M.: "What about particular views?"

B.: "I often wish I knew more about geology. When you come to think about it, geology is the science of scenery and, if you have even a smattering of it, it helps to explain how comes the scenery! As to views, you can have your grand ones, your high ones, your mountains and lakes, your deserts and forests, but of all those I have seen, one, quite close to London incidentally, always comes to my mind as the dearest, if not the most spectacular, of them all. I refer to the view over Surrey from Smithwood Common, in the neighbourhood of Cranleigh.

"I hold strongly that you often get a better view from half-way up a hill or mountain than you do at the top. This certainly applies to my Surrey favourite.

"However far you get in foreign parts, and whatever you see, I think it is when you get home again to the little fields of dear old England, its hedgerows, and the infinite variety in so small an area which brings tears to the eyes. Which reminds me, years ago I climbed a fearful height in the Alps, largely because 'Baedeker' described the scene as 'one of almost painful beauty.' A telling phrase, I thought."

M.: "Talking about heights, have you ever stood at the base of Cologne Cathedral and looked up, or on the top of the Eiffel Tower and looked down?"

B.: "Indeed I have. As regard the latter, it makes me feel what a pity

Halfway on the ascent of the Wasterngrat, in the Bernese Oberland; literally on top of the world."

it is that we have no one spot in London from which so comprehensive, a view can be enjoyed. The only time I have ever seen London as a whole was when I flew over it recently, timing the B.E.A. Viking in which I was returning

CAN WE HELP YOU?

"MODERN MOTORING AND TRAVEL"

Information Bureau

READERS are cordially invited to take full advantage of the facilities provided. The services of the "MODERN MOTORING & TRAVEL" Information Bureau (address, 53, Stratton Street, Piccadilly, W.1— Telephone, Gro. 3401), with its team of Expert advisers, are entirely free. Correspondents are requested, if a reply direct is desired, to enclose a stamped and addressed envelope for this purpose.

Readers are also offered the free use of the Magazine's correspondence columns. All letters submitted for inclusion therein are subject, of course, to the Editor's approval, and all letters must bear the sender's signature and full address—not necessarily for publication—as an indication of good faith. Readers' criticisms and/or suggestions are especially welcome.

B.: "I think the nicest people in Europe are the Danes, with the Norwegians running a close second. As regards countries, I have in recent years fallen for Spain, which interests me tremendously. In my opinion it is the cheapest country in Europe, bar our own, in which to travel to-day."

M.: "Look here, you and I could go on like this for ever, but space and time is running out. Let us have something good with which to end, at least for the time being. We should certainly continue our discussions, perhaps when you return."

B.: "All right, I give you 'the Hillman Minx.' I must have motored over 50,000 miles since the end of the war and, apart from the odd puncture, I cannot remember a single involuntary stop in mine. On all my foreign trips I have carried a box of spares with me, just in case! Only once was this opened, then by a Customs' official who wouldn't be satisfied with the supporting documents I carried, in English, French, German and Spanish, and insisted on checking them over himself."

M.: "A very deserved tribute. Well here's wishing you the best of luck on your journey, B., and—I am going to get this one in first—'A Merry Christmas to the Holy Land and to all good fellow travellers'."

November, 1951

"HOW TO STOP KILLING YOURSELF"

is the intriguing title of a new book just published by Dr. Peter J. Steincrohn (*World's Work*, 12s. 6d.).

* * *

"EACH of us, consciously or unconsciously, is killing himself in his own fashion," says Dr. Steincrohn. "*The methods of subtle suicide are legion. They include excesses . . . self-diagnosis, destructive fallacies, recklessness and poor judgment.*"

I can read the chapters on the poor people who insist on drinking and smoking and eating too much even when all these habits are fatal to them, with a fairly clear conscience.

I am not one of those who let dangerous symptoms progress dangerously while I adhere faithfully to some trick " cure " prescribed by a garage attendant—which may work for him but be death to me—but I am glad to have the book and to leave it lying about where my friends can see it *for the sake of two chapters*.

The first, *Too Much Visiting*, tells of the harm often done to a patient by too enthusiastic visitors—and how I *loathe* visitors when I am ill.

The second is headed, *Exercise Was All Right in Grandfather's Day*, and it has three excellent paragraphs :—

"Remember that your muscles get more exercise daily in your work, even if you are a desk sitter, than you realise."

"Remember that if you are a woman your work is never done. You need not find other ways to throw away energy. You use up enough of it doing your daily chores."

"Remember that exercise will not protect you from disease. The chances are it will make you tired and thus more susceptible."

* * *

I HAVE a marker at that page. Anyone who tells me that I ought to go for a nice walk on a nasty November day will have that piece read out aloud. And then I shall insist that we get out the car and drive.

If I *have* to walk then I shall make the exercise as brief as possible ; and be fussy about my shoes. I am glad that a new factory for Gold Cross Shoes has recently been opened in England for these shoes, made over the Limit lasts sent from Cincinnati, seem to combine American fitting with English finish. " K " shoes with heel fittings narrower than the forepart which give a

In palest blue and cyclamen, this Acquer silk tulle evening dress is reminiscent of gossamer dragon-fly wings. Delicate hand-made roses complete the picture.

Exercise was all right in Grandfather's day!

Some November Notions by **Brigid de Vine**

close fit round the heel and yet allow ample toe room are also a boon to a reluctant walker like myself.

Some of this year's " K " shoes have soles of Neolite, a new material evolved in America and now made here.

It is in very short supply but you will find " NEOLITE " stamped on the soles of about a dozen new " K " styles. Neolite is not a substitute but a new material—used here for the first time. In America it has been used very widely for about eight years and some millions of pairs of shoes are soled with it every year.

Neolite :

WEARS THREE TIMES AS LONG AS LEATHER.

REDUCES REPAIRS COSTS CORRESPONDINGLY.

IS WATERPROOF.

LOOKS LIKE LEATHER.

ALSO new in the footwear line this winter are little bootees warmly lined with a medium leather heel and buckle fastening, available in *black* as well as brown.

I loathe the suburban winter uniform of scarf on head, worn with clumping brown boots, indeterminate tweed coat, and ugly shopping bag. Little heeled bootees are much more elegant—and you *can* get shopping bags made of nylon thread which are colourful yet enormously light and strong.

Swan & Edgar's have supplies, knitted in Italy, from time to time, which sling over the shoulder and hold an enormous

"Let it snow," says lovely Hazel Court, J. Arthur Rank star, who adds a little holly to be really seasonable.

composed of items that were simple and wearable, the colours were mostly grey and black, the materials tweed, jersey and broadcloth.

* * *

EVENING dresses in wool are an innovation but there are now woollen materials so chiffon fine that 60 yards can be put into a single evening gown. And it will still have all the resistance to crush and easy-to-pack qualities that make wool the ideal material for the women who travels.

(Continued on page 50)

amount when needed, and fold into a handbag when not in use.

* * *

AS for "peasant style" scarves—it is a loathsome fashion. There are so many other types of warm practical headgear. Jaegers are selling trim little woollen hats to match their inexpensive woollen dresses this year; there are all kinds of neat little waterproof hats in corduroy velvet; and some of the smartest models shown in the recent Rhavis collection included little tweed hats made of the same material as the coats. Little mandarin caps, and Sherlock Holmes deerstalker caps, with a fall of tweed at the back to hide growing hair, were neat and practical and enormously becoming.

* * *

THERE was a wonderful new hat—*not* intended for shopping wear—shown among examples of La Couture Parisienne displayed recently at the Savoy Hotel by the International Wool Secretariat in co-operation with The Chambre Syndicale de la Couture Parisienne.

The grey velvet hat was flat and wide and it rested on a grey chiffon veil which fitted over the model's hair at the back and came forward to tie under the chin. It topped a grey ensemble of dress and cape designed by Pierre Balmain.

The cape was trimmed with mink and the model carried a most unusual grey umbrella. As she walked down the raised platform she negligently raised the handle of the umbrella to her lips and blew a concealed whistle! Useful for summoning taxis, perhaps?

* * *

BY a curious coincidence on the same day that the 20 models of the leading Paris couturiers were showing the most up-to-date use of wool fabrics at the Savoy, Mr. Norman Hartnell, the designer to the Royal Family, was giving a party to celebrate the despatch of a collection of Berkertex dresses to Paris. The Berkertex dresses, available at amazingly reasonable prices at shops all over England are designed by Norman Hartnell and then produced at the Berkertex factory in Plymouth, the largest dress factory in the world, which has intricate machines capable of working at 4,000 stitches a minute. It is now over three-and-a-half centuries since Francis Drake set out with his fireships from Plymouth to beard the King of Spain and the Berkertex people are most proud that dresses from their Plymouth factory should make the shorter trip to Paris and "set alight" the streets that have been so long ruled by Parisian fashion alone.

"*It is like delivering a million tons of coal to Newcastle*" was Mr. Norman Hartnell's own description of this unusually successful export feat.

* * *

PRINTEMPS, the famous shop in the Avenue Haussman in Paris, devoted a whole window display to the collection of Berkertex dresses and they have met with such success that orders have poured in from all over France.

Most of the dresses are in the classic styles which Norman Hartnell made famous when the link between the famous designer and the Berkertex team was forged 10 years ago, and there is no doubt that they will be appreciated by Parisiennes reared in the tradition of skilful simplicity which has been the mark of the best French designing.

I read recently the suggestions for an ideal winter wardrobe by several of the leading Parisian couturiers and they were all

NOVEMBER BEAUTY...

THE indoor season draws attention to the hands, and for those that are red and rough looking the new "hand treatment" cream helps considerably. First washed in soap and water, then "washed" with the cream (which is well worked in then wiped off) the hands are left beautifully smooth.

For pretty arms and necks: sweep a nourishing cream up and out, massaging well into the elbows and into the hollows of the neck and shoulders. Necks, like elbows, need a gentle scrubbing with a soft brush to soften the skin. A deep-pore cleansing cream soon improves colour and appearance.

For thin, falling hair: change the parting so that you have a brand-new section covering the thin parts and give yourself a two-minute daily scalp massage, using strong fingers in a rotary movement all over the head.

★ ★

NOVEMBER DRESS...

A NEW outfit is not the only answer to the problem of how to look fashionable and smartly dressed. A clever woman can create the illusion of an entirely new outfit by attracting attention to gaily coloured jewellery and accessories.

For example, a plain brown woollen frock can be high-lighted with a choker necklace and chinky bracelet of deep red coral ... or transformed with the delicate yet vivid blue of turquoises in an old gold setting.

With suits and dresses of red tones the blood-stone or dark green-and-red-flecked jasper is an excellent gem to choose.

Another favourite with reds is carved jet. Gems which bring added attraction to outfits in grey or smoky-blue are the rich purple amethysts or deep wine-red garnets, whereas cornelian, yellow, amber and milky agate team well with tweeds, fawns or beige woollens. And, of course, the plainest black dress can be made elegant with pearls or any of the gem stones.

HURRICANE IN JAMAICA

"We barred up the door – almost immediately the roof blew off!" –

Graphic eye-witness tribute to the magnificent efforts of the St. John Ambulance Brigade.

THE invaluable service of the St. John Ambulance Brigade in the widespread distress after the hurricane hit the island on Friday, August 17, was reported in the British West Indies newspaper, the *Daily Gleaner*.

"The Brigade," said the paper, "have been responsible for the provision and distribution of medical supplies to Relief Centres in the island, and its members are working day and night to succour the sick and injured.

* * *

1,500 rescues in two days

"THEY had treated 1,444 cases up to Sunday, and transported 50 cases to hospital in the Brigade's ambulance, which has also been used for the collection and conveyance of homeless people to the centres."

The *Daily Gleaner* also stated that Miss M. Stephens, District Superintendent of the Brigade in Jamaica, herself collected volunteers on the day of the hurricane and took them to the Red Cross Depot for posting to relief centres.

* * *

Alerting ambulance officers

MISS MARIE STEPHENS, who is on the staff of Rootes Motors (Caribbean) Limited, later submitted a detailed report to the Countess of Brecknock, Assistant Superintendent-in-Chief, St. John Ambulance Brigade, in London.

"We received notice from the Weather Office at 9 a.m. that the storm was due to strike Jamaica late in the evening," she wrote, "and I telephoned the Red Cross to check with them on the arrangements. I alerted all my Officers to stand by for orders."

It was decided to set up relief shelters in concrete buildings throughout Kingston and St. Andrew, and Miss Stephens set out in the Brigade's ambulance wagon, driven by Cpl. R. H. Williams, to round up members.

* * *

The storm strikes—

"THE wagon broke down several times and we had to carry out repairs in the pouring rain, with the result that I arrived at the Red Cross Depot very late with the last two members.

"Lady Foot (wife of the Governor) herself tried to take these to their posts but the storm broke too soon and the party had to take refuge in a house. Cpl. Williams endeavoured to drive the wagon to a place of shelter himself.

—its full fury!

"I TRIED to get home with the secretary of the Red Cross and her husband, but we could not even reach the car to drive away.

"Therefore we barred up the door of the Depot and prepared to stay the night. Almost immediately the roof of the building blew off and the water came pouring in."

When daylight came Miss Stephens was

AS reported in the October issue, a Commer ambulance presented by the Rootes Group for relief work in Jamaica following the disastrous hurricane, was despatched immediately to help in the rescue work.

* * *

A CRATE of clothing, given by employees, was also shipped to Jamaica by the Rootes Group to assist in relief work.

---

sent for by His Excellency (Sir Hugh Mackintosh Foot, K.C.M.G., O.B.E.) and asked to tour the area and report on conditions as affecting St. John. The Commissioner of Police put a vehicle and driver at her disposal.

* * *

Roads completely blocked

"WE managed to get through to all centres in the Corporate area," continued Miss Stephens in her report, "but the roads to those situated on higher ground were completely blocked.

"Everywhere I found utter devastation.

"Some of the Relief Centres were severely damaged and had to be evacuated during the night, and many others were under water and badly leaking roofs. I left medical supplies, gave instructions on arrangements for the day and provided relief staff.

* * *

Great personal risk!

"MANY of our girls did splendid work. They not only comforted and attended to the refugees, but had in some cases gone out in the storm to rescue people and had torn up their own clothing to wrap up the naked, wet babies."

A First Aid Post was set up and assistance for sickness and injuries rendered. Patients were conveyed to hospital in the ambulance wagon.

Inoculations were carried out throughout the week, and on Wednesday, August 29, the "cable arrived with the wonderful news re the ambulance" (referring to the Rootes Group relief donation).

* * *

Good news arrives!

MISS STEPHENS completed her report that day, a fortnight after the hurricane, during which time the Brigade had treated 2,035 cases and given hundreds of inoculations.

"I hope," she concluded, "this will give you some idea of what has been taking place and of our efforts. The ambulance gift has been a great pep up to our members, in fact, they can hardly believe it is true, they are so overwhelmed."

LET PRATT TRAILERS SOLVE YOUR TRANSPORT PROBLEMS

2 to 8 CWT. CARRYING CAPACITY

LEADERS IN THEIR CLASS!

THE PRATT ENGINEERING COMPANY NORTHALLERTON YORKS. TEL: 142

General view of the Exhibition.

AT THE 36th BRITISH INTERNATIONAL MOTOR EXHIBIT[ION]
Highlights at Earls Court—in exhibits and personalities

H.R.H. Princess Margaret visits Earls Court and is received on the Hillman Stand by Mr. Geoffrey Rootes. Below: Mr. G. R. Strauss chats with Sir William Rootes and Sir Reginald Rootes on the Group's important Continental marketing development.

Keen interest is taken in the "X-Ray" Hillman Minx exhibit [by] world-wide film units. Below: Sir William and Sir Regi[nald] Rootes discuss the Humber Pullman Limousine with Mr. H. L[?] of Thrupp and Maberly, Ltd.

The B.B.C. visits the Hillman stand and records impressions (with Daphne Padel at the wheel) of the Minx Convertible Coupé.

Competition stars, Norman Garrad and Stirling Moss, meet on the Sunbeam-Talbot Stand.

Spacious indeed is the luggage locker of the Humber Hawk—as these stars from the Windmill Theatre happily portray.

The "X-Ray" Minx gives an "at home" to the general and technical press.

PRODUCTS of the Rootes Group—Humber, Hillman and Sunbeam-Talbot—were impressively displayed, to attract keen interest from all visitors, with enquiries for overseas and Continental markets reaching new records.

Tribute was paid to the interesting variety of sectional engineering exhibits, permitting full view of mechanical operation, the "X-Ray" Minx securing marked popularity throughout the full period of the exhibition.

The "X-Ray" Minx in all its high-lighted engineering glory; undoubtedly the star attraction of the Exhibition

November, 1951

SPORTING—

S.T.O.C. Scarborough Rally

THE fourth annual Scarborough Rally of the Sunbeam-Talbot Owners' Club, held during the week-end, September 22–23, proved more successful than any of the three previous events—which is saying a lot!

Undoubtedly the weather, with one of the finest week-ends of the year, contributed primarily to the excellent sporting interest from both the competitors' and spectators' points of view. Indeed, the "gallery"—and the high banks of Albert Road Hill were thickly lined with onlookers—was given one of the finest sporting displays of the year, watching the numerous Club members, old and new, experienced and beginners, pit their driving skill, powers of judgment and correct timing in a series of even more intriguing driving tests for acceleration, braking, manœuvring and intricate distance-judging for the variety of fascinating obstacle tests.

Only split seconds separated the leaders from the runners-up, this despite the fact that among the 50-odd contestants were many accepted aces at the game who, surprisingly enough, found their Waterloo in the hands of not a few novices!

Scarborough, of course, has the ideal course with its Marine Drive and its Albert Road Hill, placed at the disposal of the Club by the courtesy of the Corporation authorities, and all events, under the co-operation and protection of the Chief Constable and his stalwarts, went off without incident and to the programme minute as planned by the organisers.

Entrants came from all parts of the country, from as far south as London, Gloucester, etc., as well as north to beyond the Border county.

Yorkshire was in full attendance, which fact was convincingly emphasised when, at the celebration dinner held in the Royal Hotel, the proposal that "all members of Yorkshire should rise to drink the health of fellow Club competitors and friends," the diners seemed to stand as the body complete!

Prizes were graciously presented by Mrs. H. Arundale, of Appleton & Arundale, Ltd., local Sunbeam-Talbot distributors.

Great crowds also attended the special Concours d'Elegance, held on the Sunday on the Marine Drive, the display of glittering cars here presenting almost a miniature "Earls Court" Motor Exhibition.

1.—Start of the Hill Test, on Albert Road.
2.—John Pearman gives his usual informative running commentary.
3.—F. J. Merritt, of Minchinhampton, makes a clean climb.
4.—J. C. Snell, of Barnsley, does the reversing test at speed.
5.—Bad luck for Norman Hiskins—a mid-way fault.
6.—F. W. Webster, of Leeds, at speed in the pylons test.
7.—Norman Garrad, chairman of committee, gives the "off" signal to C. Hardy, of Hull.
8.—Grandstand view for spectators on Royal Albert Drive.
9.—"Carobatics?"—Well, hardly a side-car!

RESULTS OF DRIVING TESTS:

Class "A": Sunbeam-Talbot 10 h.p.
  1st, E. N. Hiskins, Lichfield.
  2nd, G. Greaves, St. Annes-on-Sea.

Class "B": Sunbeam-Talbot over 10 h.p.
  1st, E. Elliott, York.
  2nd, J. Stamper, Penrith.

Class "C": Hillman Cars
  1st, R. Walshaw, Halifax.
  2nd, G. Robinson, Sheffield.

Result of Concours d'Elegance
  1st, A. A. Vandervieren, of Studham.
  2nd, Dr. W. C. Winterbottom, of Olney.
  3rd, G. Greaves, of St. Annes-on-Sea.

November, 1951

SPOTLIGHTS

S.T.O.C. Torquay Rally

THE same grand weather conditions favoured the Sunbeam - Talbot Owners' Club Torquay Rally, held on September 29–30.

The same massed crowds also found considerable excitement and sporting interest in the close contests between the many competitors, in driving tests held on the Meadfoot Sea Road and Marine Drive, where the cornering tactics on the acute hairpin bend surprised even the officials, not forgetting the police ! Indeed, one constable, despite the closed circuit and special arrangements made for ascertaining the fastest ascent of the hill, sent a message down to the starters suggesting that " competitors be advised to drive much slower on the hill, please."

He laughed, too, when he knew the true facts and was finally among the most thrilled of the many spectators.

Yet again the newcomers introduced real need for " looking to their laurels " by the experts, while among the latter, especially, the tussles for leading positions saw the seconds—and not a few sparks !—scattered to the winds.

Notwithstanding, tremendous tribute is due to the novice classes, their skilful handling of cars through the many difficult obstacles, the time-cum-speed judging tests and the complicated manœuvring tactics, being a prominent feature of the final awards.

Torquay inclusively took a keen interest in the entire proceedings with, notably, the generous collaboration of the town authorities, headed by the Mayor and Mayoress (Alderman and Mrs. E. G. Ely, J.P.), Town Clerk and police officials. The thanks of the Club are also due to Mr. Eric Perry, local Sunbeam-Talbot distributor, who placed his entire services and establishment at the disposal of Club members and their cars. Nor should we omit acknowledgment of the great help given by H. Berkeley Hollyer, Torquay Publicity Officer, and the local Press, by whose support the success of the occasion was assured.

Similar competitor and spectator enthusiasm was evident in the Concours d'Elegance, held on the promenade on the Sunday : a truly difficult task for the judges even under the ideal conditions obtaining.

RESULTS OF DRIVING TESTS:

Class " A " : Sunbeam-Talbot 10 h.p.
1st, J. Nott, Luton.
2nd, W. E. Ford, Wolverhampton.

Class " B " : Sunbeam-Talbot over 10 h.p.
1st, M. F. Orchard, Gloucester.
2nd, C. J. Woodrow, Plymouth.

Class " C " : Hillman Cars
1st, E. D. Barnfield, Gloucester.
2nd, J. D. Leavesley, Burton-on-Trent.

Ladies Prize
Miss M. Walker, Wooler.

Result of Concours d'Elegance
1st, G. Greaves, St. Annes-on-Sea.
2nd, R. Brown, of Hereford.
3rd, E. N. Hiskins, of Lichfield.

1.—R. A. Dando, of Manchester, in the Handicap test.
2.—Fast cornering on the Marine Drive hairpin corner.
3.—K. E. Nicholls, of Bedford, does well in the parking test.
4.—E. D. Barnfield, of Gloucester, makes a lively sprint in the obstacle test.
5.—The Mayor of Torquay (Alderman E. G. Ely, J.P.) officially welcomes the Club.
6.—The Lady Mayoress graciously presents the prizes.
7.—Miss Mary Walker, of Wooler, winning lady driver, receives her prize.
8.—Scene on the promenade during the successful Concours d'Elegance.
9.—Concours winner, G. Greaves, receives the coveted trophy.

British Aircraft over the Atlantic:

A missed opportunity!

By Major Oliver Stewart

AT the time of Princess Elizabeth's journey to Canada, one of our leading newspapers mentioned that it was a pity that the Royal Air Force Transport Command had no British aircraft in which she could travel.

Instead, the Royal party travelled in an American aircraft with American engines operated by B.O.A.C.

The point demands attention.

* * *

AMERICAN critics have been writing a great deal recently about British developments in gas turbine engined transport machines; but they have all emphasised what they believe to be the weakness of these machines, which is that their range is restricted if they are to carry a reasonable payload.

Thus these critics point out that the Series I Comet could not be used as an Atlantic airliner. With a good payload it would not have the range necessary to enable it to make the flight against a headwind and to have sufficient fuel left for the elaborate and usually lengthy holding procedures at the terminal airports.

* * *

IT is, therefore, evident that the criticism made by the British newspaper and the criticisms made by the Americans have justification.

With existing holding procedures, gas turbine engined aircraft, especially those with plain jet drive, are at a disadvantage. While they are on their way they are not using an excessive amount of fuel per mile covered. Their engines use vast quantities per hour but the aircraft have exceptionally high speed.

When a gas turbine engined transport is held prior to landing, however, it may have to orbit an airfield for a long time and then the fuel runs away rapidly.

* * *

THIS is merely a statement in transport terms of the already well-established fact that gas turbines are good prime movers for high speeds, but not for low speeds.

It follows that if the holding procedures at airports could be improved, and the orbiting time reduced, the turbine transport aircraft would be better able to work long-range routes.

If there were a 50 per cent. reduction in the time allowances that have to be given for holding diversion, the existing Comets could work the Atlantic with a reasonable payload.

* * *

WE must conclude, therefore, that it is the holding procedure that requires modification in order to fit it for up-to-date aeroplanes. This is the crux of the matter, as was understood by the Commonwealth Conference on Air Transport which was sitting in London during the latter part of September.

But the whole of the picture is not contained within this frame of aircraft range and transport holding procedures.

* * *

THERE has been during recent years an extraordinary neglect of the Royal Air Force Transport Command. And this neglect is difficult to explain.

All experience in the 1939-1945 war pointed to the value of air transport, not only for the conveyance of parachutists and supplies but also for reinforcing, for communications and for many other things. The lesson was always that the side with good military air transport facilities had an advantage. Moreover, the suggestion was clear that, in any future conflict, air transport would play a greater part than in the past.

It is astonishing that, in face of all this evidence, R.A.F. Transport Command has been allowed to dwindle.

* * *

IT has been allowed to continue using old aircraft of American origin and no attempt has been made to revivify it by supplying it with the latest turbine engined transports.

Had R.A.F. Transport Command been given these new machines, both British military and British civil aviation would have benefited.

* * *

WE come now to the great central fact to which all these matters point. It is this: Britain has obtained the lead in the design and construction of transport aircraft, both civil and military, by designing them round gas turbines. But Britain will not benefit from that lead unless there is a whole-hearted effort by the Government and by the State Corporations to cash in on it.

It has failed to make use of these new designs for R.A.F. Transport Command.

Had it done so, and done so right at the beginning, there would have been a reasonable chance that Princess Elizabeth and Prince Philip would have been able to travel across the Atlantic in a specially fitted Comet jet-driven airliner, and that would have been a tonic for British prestige.

* * *

IT is too late now to repair these past omissions, but at least they should be a warning for the future.

The striking Showrooms opened in the Rond Point des Champs Elysées, Paris, by Rootes Continental Motors, a new associated company of the Rootes Group. There is also a first-class Service Depot at Rue Pierret, Avenue de Madrid, Neuilly, staffed by mechanics trained in the Rootes Group. The premises cover 40,000 square feet of floor space, and Rootes Continental Motors are supported by 20 service points throughout France. This is the first entry of its kind into the French market by a British motor manufacturer. The opening coincided with the annual Paris Salon.

Cross country champion...

Instant acceleration, sure stability, sensitive control, and an almost casual 70 m.p.h. cruising speed—these fine qualities make the Sunbeam-Talbot 90 very safe, as well as very fast across country. Graceful in line, cushioned for comfort, and precision-built throughout, the Sunbeam-Talbot 90 has powers of endurance and reliability proved up to the hilt.

THE *Sunbeam-Talbot 90*

Winners in 1948, 1949 & 1950 International Alpine Trials

Craftsman Built by the Rootes Group

SMOOTH

SPEEDY

SAFE

SUPREME

SUNBEAM-TALBOT LTD RYTON-ON-DUNSMORE COVENTRY · *London Showrooms & Export Division:* ROOTES LTD DEVONSHIRE HOUSE PICCADILLY W.1

Capetown to Livingstone in the Hillman Minx —

"I was told it was 'a dependable light family car': now I am convinced!"

* * *

Tribute from South Africa

* * *

ON October 23 my wife, myself, my three children, plus one cabin trunk and three suitcases, left Cape Town for the Victoria Falls via coastal and mountain routes.

We traversed, loaded to the hilt, the toughest mountains, including the Zwartberg and Robinson Passes above Ouldtshoorn.

We went over the slippery passes to Mount Ayliff, through Basutoland, all through Natal, and eventually to the Limpopo River via that fearsome corrugated menace known as "The Ribs of Death" between Louis Trichard and Beitbridge.

After passing Messina, a copper mining town whose garages thrive on repair work to cars that "cannot take it," on the above-mentioned road, we hit Bulawayo and then went on to the famous Victoria Falls on the Zambesi.

* * *

IN all we did 2,881 miles at an all-in consumption of 33⅛ miles per gallon. Throughout the whole trip we carried out normal servicing, and we never lost a nut or bolt, nor a single trace of engine, brake, shock absorber, or ignition trouble. We never had a puncture even—Dunlop tyres !

Once we were loaded up there was not room for a box of matches in the boot. It was like this for the whole 2,881 miles.

My accounts to friends of the mountain passes we went over—rocks, shale and mud, with a 1,000 feet drop on an error of judgment awaiting you, have astounded them. In fact, I have already *sold* a Hillman from the record I have kept of my trip.

* * *

This is merely a brief story to tell you that I could not have had a better car, and I have been astounded at the performance given.

Quite frankly, when in England, I had misgivings about taking my wife and three daughters in a small car fully loaded over stretches of country where for many miles there is no trace of human habitation and where a breakdown or skid, or faulty braking on mountain roads, might result

Sans habitation, range after range.

Interested natives in the Basuto country.

ROUTE

Cape Town — Laingsberg — Prince Albert — Mossel Bay — Kryrna — Groot River Pass — Jeffries Bay — East London — Umtata (in the Transkei) — Mt. Ayliff — Bizana — Port Shepstone — Winkelsfruit — Durban — Maritzburg — Escourt — Newcastle — Ermelo — Middleburg — Petersburg — over the "Ribs of Death" to — Beitbridge on the Limpopo — West Nicolson — Bulawayo — Victoria Falls — Livingstone.

COMMENT

AVERAGE SPEED.—40-45 m.p.h. on 1st and 2nd class roads ; 10-20 m.p.h. on passes.

DISTANCE COVERED.—2,881 miles, Cape Town to Livingstone, on above route, including short tours to places of interest at various points.

ECONOMY.—33⅛ m.p.g. Mostly undulating and mountainous travel for first 2,000 miles.

in a feed for the vultures unnoticed by the odd passing traveller.

However, we did this trip by the routes not normally taken by those travellers who are content with the usual run, i.e., Cape Town to Johannesburg to Petersburg to Beitbridge, and we have never regretted it.

We went over the finest scenery I have seen in any part of the world—and I still have a damned good car !

* * *

Well done, Hillman ! Well done, private enterprise.

I was offered a new-ish French model in exchange for my car (now 8,700 miles) the other day. I still keep mine !

Yours faithfully,
H. G. WILTSHIRE
(Inspector of Police).

INVITATION TO OVERSEAS READERS :—

Why not write to the Editor about motoring in your country ? Short reports of interesting journeys, like that of Mr. Wiltshire's above, are always welcome, especially when accompanied by photographs taken on the way.

Address your contribution to the Editor, "Modern Motoring & Travel" 53, Stratton Street, Piccadilly, London, W.1.

INCREASE THE LIFE OF YOUR TYRES

The Schrader Gauge keeps down running costs

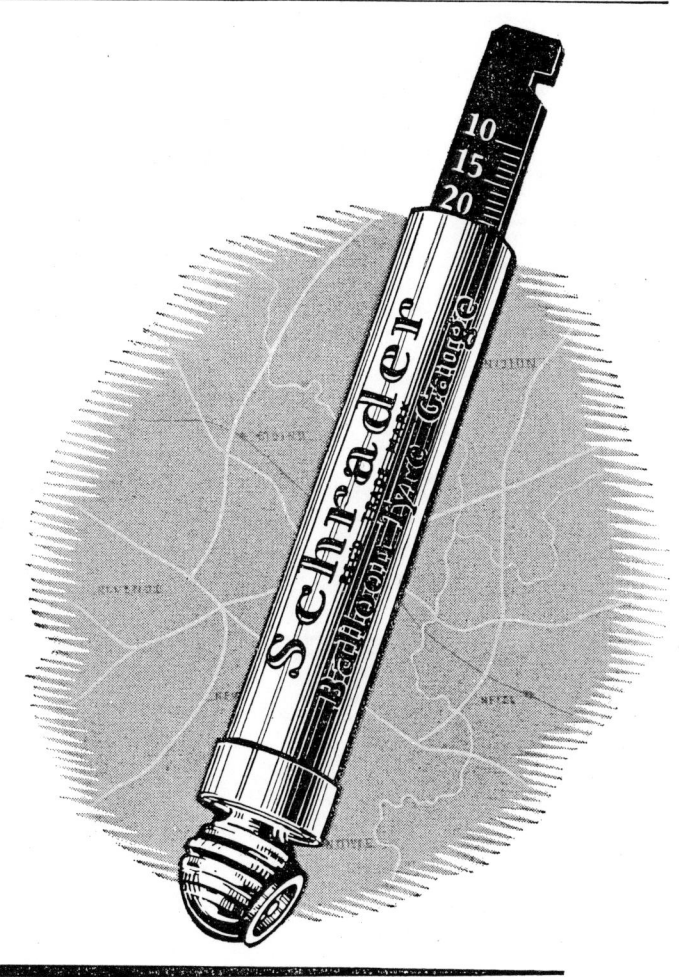

The accuracy of the tyre gauge reflects the accuracy of the tyre pressures. With a Schrader gauge, designed and built by the makers of the Schrader valve, it is easy to ensure the maintenance of correct pressures and so reduce unnecessary tyre wear. This, with the saving on petrol consumption, enables running costs to be kept down. Better motoring with comfort, braking and road-holding follows automatically.

TEST THE PRESSURES REGULARLY
WITH A
Schrader *Gauge*

A. SCHRADER'S SON · BIRMINGHAM · ENGLAND

"O.K. for SOUND!"

Film Shorts and Starlights

BEING made in Technicolor at Pinewood Studios is "The Importance of Being Earnest," with one of the greatest casts ever brought together for a British film.

It includes Michael Redgrave, Dame Edith Evans, Margaret Rutherford, Joan Greenwood, Miles Malleson and Michael Denison.

The producer, Teddy Baird, and director, Anthony Asquith, last made the record-breaking "The Browning Version."

* * *

THE film rights in the best-selling novel "The Cruel Sea," by Nicholas Monsarrat, have been acquired by Sir Michael Balcon for production at Ealing Studios.

The story of a corvette and a frigate during the Battle of the Atlantic, the book is receiving international acclaim.

"The Cruel Sea" will be directed by Charles Frend, who made "Scott of the Antarctic."

* * *

MRS. BRENDA CARSTAIRS, of Stanley Grove, Reading—she has never been further than the Isle of Wight—left with her husband, on October 12, on a 10,000-mile journey into Africa.

The trip was first prize in the cinema competition, sponsored by Metro-Goldwyn-Mayer and the East African Tourist Travel Association, for listing the 12 most thrilling scenes in "King Solomon's Mines."

Mr. and Mrs. Carstairs flew by B.O.A.C. to Nairobi, from where they are to go up country and set out on safari.

* * *

DEAN MILLER, personable young American television star, was in the club bar of a California-bound train. He was chatting to three strangers, unaware they were top film executives.

"Hollywood needs new faces," said Miller.

Hollywood has one—Dean Miller, tested, signed up and cast for the M.G.M. comedy "You For Me."

* * *

"EAGLE on his Cap," to be filmed by Metro-Goldwyn-Mayer, is the story of Colonel Paul Tibbetts, U.S. Air Force Commander and B-29 pilot.

Tibbetts's flying career culminated in his dropping the first atomic bomb on Hiroshima in 1945.

* * *

HOWARD KEEL, singing star of the film "Annie Get Your Gun," has been voted "Number One Star of To-morrow" in the "Motion Picture Herald's" 11th annual poll.

He was in "Show Boat," has just finished "Callaway Went Thataway," and is now making "Lovely to Look At," another Technicolor musical.

* * *

CALIFORNIAN-BORN Yolande Donlan, who had to come to England to make her name and fame, is to star in a Technicolor comedy entitled "The Penny Princess," which is to be made on location in Spain and at Pinewood Studios.

She first came to London to play the dumb blonde in "Born Yesterday," and followed this with three more stage shows, "Rocket to the Moon," "Cage me a Peacock" and "To Dorothy a Son."

Yolande's two British films have been "Traveller's Joy" and "Mr. Drake's Duck."

* * *

TWO-YEAR-OLD Benjie, son of Esther Williams, makes his film debut in "Skirts Ahoy."

The actress's son, who has been swimming since he was 14 months old, joins his mother in the pool for one of the musical water numbers in the Technicolor production.

* * *

FRED ASTAIRE has become a hero to bridegrooms.

Since news was printed that Astaire's bachelor dinner in "Belle of New York" is not held with his men chums but with his girl-friends, he has been deluged with letters from grateful bachelors who are about to become bridegrooms.

One from Indianapolis wrote, "You've taken the boredom out of a man's last night of freedom."

Northern Malaya Express Road Service

PHOTOGRAPH depicting the ceremony held in Kelantan (one of the states of Northern Malaya) of the opening of a new Express Service between the town of Kota Bahru and Kuala Trengganu. The Tengku Makhota (or Regent) of Kelantan cutting the tape with a pair of golden scissors in declaring the service opened. The coaches were supplied by the Vulcan distributors in Singapore, The Cycle and Carriage Co. (1926), Ltd.

> The life of your tyres is in your hands
>
> ② DON'T DRIVE ON YOUR BRAKES

INDIA TYRES are too much in demand to be "on demand". Treated with care they will give the longest service of any tyre made to-day.

INDIA "The Finest Tyres Made"

ERIC BRANDON, Ace of the "500s," is interviewed:

"The sport is good and worth all it involves, if mostly hard work and patience," he says

ERIC BRANDON and I had arranged to meet at the "Steering Wheel Club," Piccadilly.

That was a mistake.

The "Steering Wheel Club" is the popular rendezvous, of course, for everyone who is anyone at all in the motor-racing world, and as far as I could perceive, they all were there on this particular occasion.

In actual fact, Eric and I secured only 10 minutes' seclusion in a session that lasted two-and-a-half hours. The remaining two hours, 20 minutes were spent in "meeting the boys" and doing what comes naturally!

* * *

HOWEVER, I had heard that Eric had recently acquired a Commer Express Delivery Van as an auxiliary runabout for his stable of 500 c.c. Ecurie Richmonds, and knowing his top-line status in this intensely popular side of motor sport, I felt that readers of *Modern Motoring and Travel* would like to know more about his activities, about his cars and something of the background to his many successes throughout Europe.

Of the Van he said, "It is just the thing, a grand job!"

* * *

FEW phases in motor sport have witnessed a more meteoric rise to popularity than the 500 c.c. event; always the big "gate" and always the greatest enthusiasm and sportsmanship between respective competitors, which is why, no doubt, Eric suggested at the outset that in any comment about himself and the Ecurie Richmond, it would be unfair not to include reference to his friend and teammate, Alan Brown.

I agreed wholeheartedly; these two inseparable pioneers of the sport, between them, have achieved considerable successes in many leading International fixtures, with no less than 21 Firsts, 13 Seconds, 4 Thirds, 7 Course Records and 5 Championship wins, at Goodwood, Brands Hatch, Boreham and Silverstone, as well as in France, Luxemburg and Germany, all within the current season.

Not that there is no competition between them personally. To the contrary, indeed; their personal bouts are usually a major feature of all race meetings in which they are taking part, and have provided some of the greatest thrills for the masses of spectators which always assemble at events of this character. And Alan Brown, who had now joined us, did not dispute that, on points, Eric was well in the lead.

"Sure he is," said Alan. "At least, for the time being!"

* * *

I RECALL, too, many interesting moments watching them busy in the paddocks, tuning up and discussing respective components (with, more often than not, their heads buried so deep within the works the only views I got was of their posteriors!), discussing the *pros* and *cons* of modifications, the results of these developments and, best of all perhaps, the inevitable friendly chaffing at the finish of a contest.

Eric Brandon with his Commer Express Delivery Van and at the wheel of his Ecurie Richmond. Below, giving it that famous final "Brandon" tuning touch!

For both of them 500 c.c. racing with its practical and mechanical sides is their leading leisure pre-occupation, all detail, routine, administration, formality, keeping of books and records, travel arrangements and the like, being the concern of Mrs. Sheila Brandon upon whom they both depend to a very large extent; and as popular a figure at meetings as is her husband and his team-mates.

* * *

BOTH their Ecurie Richmond cars are based on the popular and successful Cooper Chassis, employing the Norton engine, the while there is essentially much that is of exclusive "Brandon/Brown" development—"Solely with the object of realising," as Eric put it, "our mutual hopes ultimately to win all that comes our way!

"And why not?" added Eric. "The sport is a costly business, something like £30 an event in direct expenses, I should say from experience, and, well, if we have been lucky, what about the other chaps, many of whom must be devoting entire resources to the sport with little, or at best, only occasional reward.

"Which inspires me to make this comment," went on Eric, "something ought to be done for these lads and for the sport in general in the way of reasonable appearance money. Not only would it encourage and help them and the sport directly—after all, the bigger the entry the bigger the 'gate,' the keener the contest and the more assured are track authorities of useful and regular patronage —but it would also do much in keeping the 'Aces,' if I might be permitted to use that term, continuously on their mettle.

"Everyone should get appearance money, we think, and then the losers—and these there will always be—would be at no personal loss for their participation. That is the real point; the large entry necessarily maintains the sport in first-class public appeal. Organisers should recognise this fact and give intending contestants encouragement in this practical manner."

* * *

"FINALLY, Eric, have you any words of advice to offer the novice or the newcomer to the sport?" I asked.

"Only this: the sport is good and worth all it involves, if mostly patience and hard work. It can be a thrilling hobby with a grand class of sportsman in the opposing ranks. It is well to remember, however, that the course can be hard and surfaced with much disappointment. It is in overcoming these things that secures the fun and generally leads to success. Both Alan and I, believe me, would be among the first to wish any competitor, whoever he may be, 'the best of good luck.'"

T. R. M.

Products of the ROOTES GROUP

For Good Service!
GEO. T. HILTON & CO. LTD.
NORTH STREET · RUGBY
Telephone: 2291

HUMBER · HILLMAN
SUNBEAM-TALBOT
CARS

COMMER · KARRIER
TRUCKS

BUILT FOR THE ROADS OF THE WORLD

WEATHERSHIELDS'
Centre Arm Rest
FOR USE WITH **BENCH-TYPE SEATS**

Easily fitted to front or rear seats, and adjustable to any required position.

This independent arm rest, originated by Weathershields Ltd., is simply hooked over the back of bench-type seats in any position to suit the convenience and comfort of driver and passengers. On long journeys it will be particularly appreciated for its additional comfort; also serves as a useful container for gloves, maps, etc.

It is strongly made, well upholstered and supplied in various standard colours to match the car upholstery.

Supplied by post, 35/- each

Weathershields Ltd.
BISHOP ST., BIRMINGHAM 5 · ENGLAND

THE TOOL OF UNLIMITED CAPABILITY

The Grebe
GARRINGTON

- Single Handed Adjustment
- Force is applied at the strongest point
- Teeth are not in shear
- All wear absorbed by the special cam snail
- Quick action return

THE "GREBE" (PATENT APPLIED FOR) **GETS A GRIP ON IT!**

Garrington HAND TOOLS

MAIN DISTRIBUTORS FOR GREAT BRITAIN AND EIRE:

Chas. Churchill & Co. Ltd., Coventry Road, Birmingham, 25 and Branches

L. J. Hydleman & Co. Ltd., 206-212, St. John Street, Clerkenwell, London, E.C.1

J. Thomson MacLeod, Ltd., 88, Cadogan Street, Glasgow, C.2

Nettlefold & Moser, Ltd., 170, Borough High Street, London, S.E.1 and Branches

Obtainable from all recognised Tool and Motor Accessory Stockists

WRITE FOR ILLUSTRATED LEAFLET

GARRINGTONS LIMITED
DARLASTON, STAFFS., AND BROMSGROVE, WORCS.

IN A FEW WORDS
Miscellaneous News Brevities

A master of illusion is Kalanag, and one of many extraordinary tricks of stage illusion in his Magical and Musical Revue, now touring the country, is this disappearance of a Hillman Minx. Kalanag's blonde partner is Gloria—or was!

R.A.C. roadside telephone boxes in the Lake District are being painted green, to harmonise with the surrounding countryside.

* * *

THE 22nd Monte Carlo Rallye is to take place from January 22 to 29 next. Values of prizes have been considerably increased, First Prize being raised to 1,000,000 francs.

* * *

THE National Caravan Council's new and revised list of approved manufacturers is now available from the Council offices, 8, Clarges Street, Piccadilly, W.1.

* * *

THE National Trust announce the gift, from Commander and Mrs. Walter Raleigh Gilbert, of Compton Castle, near Torquay. The gift includes 230 acres of farm land.

* * *

ESSENTIAL lubricating oil additives, formerly obtained from dollar resources, are now being produced on a large scale by the new Castrol plant at Stanlow, Cheshire.

* * *

TWO new and interesting Notek products, first shown at the Earls Court motor exhibition—the Glomaster heavy-duty red reflector and the Flaremaster self-contained emergency roadflare, are now on the market, price 10s. and 33s. respectively.

* * *

MANY applications have already been received from intending exhibitors in next year's Salon international de l'Automobile —Geneva's big international motor exhibition—to be held from March 20 to 30.

* * *

LATEST versions of the British Overseas Airways Corporation's *Comet* jet airliners are to have a radar device in the nose which will give the pilot a 40 miles' warning picture of approaching storm clouds.

* * *

B.E.A. announce price increases in its Continental air services; examples, return fare: Paris £15 6s., Rome £58 10s., Barcelona £43 8s., Berlin £42 6s., Geneva £29 9s., Milan £49 3s.

More than 160,000 people crowded into the 14-day Exhibition of British goods staged by the Jordan Marsh Company, of Boston, Mass., the largest department store in New England. The Humber, Hillman and Sunbeam-Talbot ranges were featured in the motor-car section, the largest single display. Beside the Hillman-Minx Coupé, on left, are Mr. H. Breckenridge, Mr. Brian Rootes (regional director of the Rootes Group), and Sir William Welsh, north American representative of the S.M.M. & T.

REVISED regulations covering changes in records kept by operators of public service vehicles used for private parties, come into operation on January 1. Copies are now available, on sale at H.M. Stationery Office.

* * *

A 26,000 MILES' Africa and India cruise by the 34,183-ton *Caronia* is the highlight of winter's programme of dollar-earning cruises from New York. For the motor-liner *Britannic* a 66-days' cruise in the Mediterranean is scheduled, and the *Mauretania* will again be making four sunshine voyages to the West Indies.

(Continued on page 58)

STYLE, ELEGANCE DURABILITY

ROOTES CAR SEAT COVERS

Tailor-made from highest quality materials, they offer the following advantages:

ADDED COMFORT

GOOD LOOKS AND SHAPE

PREVENTION OF SHINE TO PERSONAL CLOTHING

CAN BE DRY CLEANED BY APPROVED PROCESSES

AVAILABLE IN A VARIETY OF COLOURS

Patterns available on application to Dept. M.M.

ROOTES

LADBROKE HALL, BARLBY RD., LONDON, W.10.
Tel. LADbroke 3232

BIRMINGHAM	90/94 Charlotte Street	Central 8411
MANCHESTER	Olympia, Chester Road	Blackfriars 6677
MAIDSTONE	Mill Street	Maidstone 3333
ROCHESTER	High Street	Chatham 2231
CANTERBURY	The Pavilion	Canterbury 3232
WROTHAM	Wrotham Heath	Borough Green 4
FOLKESTONE	86/92 Tontine Street	Folkestone 3156

A *NEW* REFRIGERATOR *STAR IS BORN!*

Spangled with a galaxy of new features—starred for brilliance of design and finish

THE NEW L71 PRESTCOLD REFRIGERATOR

* 7 cu. ft. capacity in small floor space.
* Extra large frozen food locker (26 lbs. capacity).
* Glass-topped transparent Crispator.
* Trigger-type door latch.
* 2 new design ice trays—quick release cubes.
* Fold-down top shelf, adjustable middle shelf.
* Adjustable feet for levelling cabinet.
* 5 year guarantee on Presmetic sealed unit.
* Automatic interior light.

and a host of other starred features.

FULL LENGTH STORAGE

Prestcold have made many fine refrigerators—but here is the star of them all. Prestcold perfection of design and finish and construction are world-famous—but here is a refrigerator which shines with a new and brighter beauty. Greater in space, greater in grace, with full length storage, new features, new hold-everything design, new beauty, here is the refrigerator star which dims all others.

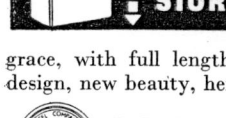

GREATER IN SPACE ★ GREATER IN GRACE

PRESTCOLD REFRIGERATION *keeps good food good*

PRESSED STEEL COMPANY LIMITED, COWLEY, OXFORD. London Office & Showrooms: Sceptre House, 169 Regent Street, W.1

Dr. Henry Edward Merritt, M.B.E., D.Sc.(Eng.), Chief Research Officer to the British Transport Commission since 1949, has been appointed Chief Administrative Engineer to the Rootes Group. He is 51. Dr. Merritt is an expert on gear design, and his contribution to the British war effort was recognised by the Royal Commission on Awards to Inventors for his Merritt-Brown Transmission, which was applied to the Churchill and all heavy tanks of later date.

In a Few Words
(Concluded from page 56)

B.O.A.C. made an operating profit of £108,000 during August, or a clear overall surplus of £10,000 for the month. This compares with an overall loss of £378,000 for August, 1950, and £732,000 for August, 1949.

* * *

ANOTHER major gift to the National Trust is that of Penrhyn Castle, Bangor, North Wales, together with some 40,000 acres of land, announced recently by Lord Crawford, Chairman of the Trust.

* * *

"SHROPSHIRE," by John Fife and John Betjeman, is the first Shell guide to be published since the war and the first of a new county series which will consist of new titles and complete revisions of old ones. Beautifully indexed and illustrated, and with clear contour map, it sells at 12s. 6d.

* * *

NATIONAL Benzole Co., Ltd., announce the retirement, owing to ill-health, of Mr. R. J. Smith, director and general manager, and the appointment of Mr. H. H. Bates, member of the executive committee, as managing director, as from October 1.

* * *

SPEAKING at a pre-motor show press conference, Mr. G. E. Beharrell, President of the Society of Motor Manufacturers and Traders, Ltd., stated that an additional 100,000 tons of steel for the motor industry would make all the difference to the industry's economy and its rate of production. Emphasising the industry as Britain's Exporter No. 1, he said the value of its exports were to-day at the rate of £300 million a year, or something like £570 for every minute of the day and night!

INDIA COMES TO COVENTRY

A DISTINGUISHED visitor to the Coventry, Warwickshire, factories of the Rootes Group recently was His Highness the Maharajah of Gwalior.

During a comprehensive tour, His Highness talked with a number of workers, and in the foundry at Humber Ltd. he tried his hand at pouring molten metal into moulds.

Of special interest to the Maharajah was the export packing department, where component parts are "completely knocked down" for shipment and assembly abroad. India is an important sterling market for car exports.

Above, Mr. E. W. Hancock, M.B.E., works director, shows the Maharajah a model replica of the Humber-Hillman factories. Below, component parts being crated in the export packing department.

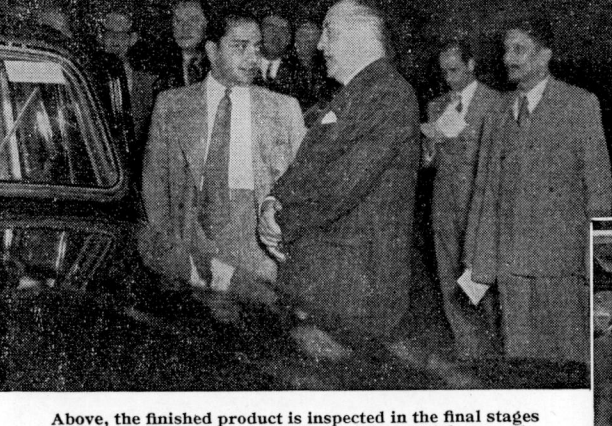

Above, the finished product is inspected in the final stages of the assembly lines. Below, the Maharajah sees the modern surgery with its up-to-date facilities for the care and well-being of factory employees.

IS YOUR CAR *really* SAFE

SAVE YOUR CAR

Let your Esso Dealer do these jobs now!

Change your oil
Grease the chassis
Inspect your tyres
Check your battery
Inspect your brakes

That depends on the care you take. Regular servicing and greasing, changing the engine oil at proper intervals, and, above all, skilled attention, *can* make even an older car last longer, and last with safety on the road.

Drive in regularly to your Esso Dealer, and let him check your car and keep it up to the mark with the famous Essolube motor oil and Esso greases.

FOR *happy safe motoring*

SEE YOUR ESSO DEALER

ESSO PETROLEUM COMPANY, LIMITED, 36 QUEEN ANNE'S GATE, LONDON, S.W.1

Modern Motoring & Travel

March, 1952

NOW! In 20 minutes! COMPLETE WINTER PROTECTION

with the brightest, toughest wax polish of all!

Positively no rubbing!

Hundreds of thousands of motorists have proved this summer that Car-Plate gives a genuine wax finish, the brightest shine, the most lasting protection—in 20 minutes!

Now that winter has come, all motorists are guaranteed that when they wax with Car-Plate their cars have the best-known protection against rain, sleet and snow. You can test this for yourself—just wipe off any surface dirt or dust and see how the raindrops "bead-up" on the clean waxed surface. Water just cannot begin to soak into the cellulose to do its hazing, dulling work.

And with Car-Plate complete winter protection is *so easy!* Just spread Car-Plate on a clean* car, let dry—then wipe lightly. No rubbing with Car-Plate! Get a tin today!

5/- from all garages

★ The easy way to prepare the finish of your car for a Car-Plate waxing is to clean it super-clean with Johnson's Carnu — the quick, safe cleaner for cellulose and chromium.

JOHNSON'S CAR-PLATE
SPREAD...LET DRY...WIPE!
MADE BY THE MAKERS OF JOHNSON'S WAX

Fabram Specialities

RADIATOR MUFFS
LOOSE SEAT COVERS
OVERALL CLOTHING

Manufactured by —

FAXALL PRODUCTS LTD.,
BLACKLEDGE WORKS · HALIFAX.
Telephone: Halifax 5208   Telegrams: FAXALL, Halifax

We supply the pressing need!

A. E. JENKS & CATTELL LTD.
WEDNESFIELD near Wolverhampton
Telephone: WOLVERHAMPTON 31271

Luxury Liner of the Road!

Greater prestige

The distinguished modern styling of the exterior, the smart fittings and unusual comfort of the interior, together with the cushioned ride—achieved by a co-ordinated suspension embodying shock-absorbers and low-pressure tyres—are the features the public notices, and warmly approves.

Greater safety

Apart from the advantages of full forward control which gives the driver a wide margin of safety in manœuvre, the "Avenger" embodies smooth and powerful hydraulic brakes, servo-assisted; a deep-section chassis frame; and high output dynamo for easier night driving.

> Unsurpassed both in performance and appearance, the Commer "Avenger", latest and proudest heir to a famous transport name, bears the Hallmark of Reliability throughout.

Lower costs

By constant reliability the Commer "Avenger" holds down operating costs. Designed specifically for a long life at non-stop working pressure—as witness its powerful six-cylinder engine with chrome finished bores which gives prolonged periods of trouble free service between overhauls—this craftsman-built coach can be trusted to put in maximum passenger carrying hours for minimum fuel and maintenance charges.

COMMER "AVENGER"

A 32-35 seater with o.h.v. 'under-floor' engine developing 109 b.h.p.

SILENT SAFE AND SPEEDY

A PRODUCT OF THE ROOTES GROUP COMMER CARS LTD. LUTON BEDFORDSHIRE

HILLMAN MINX BREAKS LONDON-TO-CAPE RECORD BY 2 DAYS 5 HOURS

You get so much more out of

THE HILLMAN MINX

Craftsman Built by the Rootes Group

ROOTES GROUP REGIONAL REPRESENTATIVES *located at:*

EXPORT DIVISION ROOTES
DEVONSHIRE HOUSE
PICCADILLY LONDON W1
Distributors throughout the World

U.S.A. 505 Park Avenue, New York 22, N.Y. and 403 North Foothill Road, Beverly Hills, California.
CANADA 2019 Eglinton Avenue East, Scarborough, Ontario.
AUSTRALIA & NEW ZEALAND Fishermen's Bend, Port Melbourne, Australia.
SOUTHERN AFRICA 750/2/4 Stuttaford's Buildings, St. George's St., Cape Town, S.A.

CENTRAL AFRICA Jackson Road, P.O. Box 5194, Nairobi, Kenya.
BELGIUM Shell Building, 47 Cantersteen, Brussels.
FRANCE 6 Rond-Point des Champs Elysees, Paris, 8.
SWITZERLAND 3 Jenatschstrasse, Zurich.
FAR EAST Macdonald House, Orchard Road, Singapore, 9.

INDIA Agra Road, Bhandup, Bombay.
MIDDLE EAST 37 Kasr El Nil Street, Cairo, Egypt.
ARGENTINA Casilla de Correo 3478, Buenos Aires.
BRAZIL Av. Presidente Vargas 290 (S/1003), Rio de Janeiro.
CARIBBEAN 28 Duke Street, Kingston, Jamaica, B.W.I.

Photograph by Dorothy Wilding.

The Nation and Commonwealth mourn their beloved and illustrious King, George VI. Born Dec. 14th 1895; died Feb. 6th 1952.

In Memoriam

MODERN MOTORING AND TRAVEL joins the nation in mourning King George VI.

His Late Majesty and his beloved Queen, during a reign of fifteen memorable years, gave their all generously and spontaneously in their devotion to duty, upholding all the many traditions of State as well as the sanctity of British family life in a manner that will be revered for generations to come.

✠ ✠ ✠

GRACIOUSLY accepting the destinies of this mighty Empire at short notice, His Late Majesty and his Queen from the beginning elevated the dignity of the British Crown while, at the same time, as the happy family head, he won the profound devotion of his peoples at home and in the Realms beyond the seas.

We mourn a King who was also a friend. Our deepest sympathies go out to the Queen Mother and to all members of the Royal Family.

✠ ✠ ✠

TO the new Queen Elizabeth II and to H.R.H. The Duke of Edinburgh, as well as to their children, Prince Charles and Princess Anne, we humbly submit assurances of heartfelt loyalty and affection, added to, as in the case of the Queen's illustrious father, by virtue of so much personal charm and grace and unselfish service to Nation and Empire.

Long Live the Queen.

Memorable Incidents in the reign of the late King George VI

1935—Scotland: Their Majesties (then T.R.H. The Duke and Duchess of York) are given a regal reception on the occasion of the Royal visit to Edinburgh.

1936—London: The then new King leaves his Piccadilly home (later destroyed by enemy action) to attend the Accession Council held at St. James's Palace, December 12.

1939—Weymouth: His Majesty King George VI on his way to review H.M. Reserve Fleet.

1946—Rhodesia: Their Majesties visit the Victoria Falls during the Royal South African tour.

1946—Scotland: Over 15,000 members of the British Legion greeted Their Majesties when they attended the special Drum-head service and march past, held to commemorate the 25th anniversary of the Scottish Division.

1947—Right: All Bulawayo turns out to greet the Royal visitors during the Royal South African tour.

I am not terribly interested in the Pyramids!

says Professor A. M. Low

Fireside Reflections on Science

The Pyramids

I MERELY believe that the Pyramids are enormous structures built by slaves who laboured under horrible conditions. Men were sometimes bricked up inside.

It is nonsense to say that they could not be constructed nowadays, and that we have "lost the art." Just as it is absurd to suggest that Japanese swords were marvellously made. No more marvellous than the mirrors which by surface etching give beautiful figures when placed in a certain light.

Yet there are people who argue that 40 times round the Pyramids divided by two and added to the weight of a piece of butter proves that the Old Testament is true. There are, of course, *some* interesting points and that I readily admit.

It is quaint to think of the planks they used as levers, or the huge number of employees which must have been required and maintained, or the accuracy with which the blocks were prepared for variation in the lengths of the long and short sides of the 750 ft. base is only a bare fraction of an inch.

Marks on the stone show that straight saws, jewelled drills and circular saws were used and you can guess that the blades were of bronze by noticing the green stains in the cuts of the stones. People will imagine the same fairy-tales about our buildings in a few thousand years and this should be a lesson to those who think that we are civilised.

* * *

Not necessarily a cold

JUST as a good automobile engineer realises that the out-of-balance armature of a dynamo may eventually cause a crack in the petrol tank at the other end of the chassis, so does a Doctor know that symptoms are often interconnected most mysteriously.

I know a most brilliant man of medicine who said that he and many others always sneezed when they went from a darkened room into sunshine.

Now, sneezing is clearly due to a slight irritation which so blows clear this trouble out of the delicate filaments. When we really have a cold a sneeze can propel moisture containing germs to a distance of some yards. It gets rid of the germs even if *you* pick them up and this has been tested by actual experiment.

Dare we say that the sunlight produces in the atmosphere or its content various chemical or ionising changes? We know that a thunderstorm brightens grass by virtue of the ozone contained in the air, and because it hands nourishment to the grass in a nascent sensitive condition.

But, as it were, a little piece of other air with a tang in it or even some actual material generated by the sunshine into your breathing apparatus and I think you have a simple explanation of this quaint phenomenon.

Small quantities

THE iodine which is found in sea-water and which has long been known to have medical value, exists in the human body.

A lack of iodine in your throat glands can possibly cause goitre, although the total of all the iodine in the human frame is only about one-tenth of a drop of the ordinary tinctures.

* * *

What would happen?

THERE is no doubt in my mind that each person is surrounded by some etheric influence. Something like that which enables colonies of flies to communicate with each other, something not quite so material as a plain smell.

People are strangely savage and when I once wrote a popular article under the title "Good secretaries are in love," I must have had hundreds of letters of both denial and affirmation.

What I mean, you will readily understand, is that the care and thought which makes a helpmeet is something far different from that which one can buy and something which avoids the competitive jealousy of men by substituting the feeling which results when flowers or creatures of opposite sex are not very far from each other in mind or body.

Surely a scientist ought to be able to use his own terms in describing these happy things? I would hate to say that a girl had eyes like a violet because she would surely be suffering from cataract or at least "argo" senilis. No, I shall tell her she has eyes like a cow, a figure like the glass connectors used when one is distilling hydrochloric acid and wishes to check the moment of reaction, together with a skin like the velvet which is used to line the compartments of an assay balance weight box.

I wonder what would happen!

* * *

What is a worm?

SOMEONE rudely called me a "worm" the other day which gave me furiously to think.

"What is a worm?"

Well, in olden days men used the word to describe dragons, the kind that Saint George, and others, killed with so much courage. But, to-day, broadly it may denote any kind of elongated, limbless creature from a lizard to a blindworm. At least so says my dictionary!

But though so lowly, earthworms, like boy scouts, do their good deeds every day. Indeed, if you removed every worm from your garden you would soon have to pack it up altogether, for the soil would deteriorate and no prize cabbages would result.

Worms not only live in the soil, but on it as well, for they literally devour tons and tons during their lifetime and throw out what they don't want in neatly piled castings that look like coiled-up ropes of agglutinated particles of mould.

They are mostly nocturnal creatures, and only come to the surface when the rest of the world are in bed (except those who frequent night clubs) but they work just the same during the day, only beneath the ground.

Naturalists call the poor worms hermaphrodites, which means that each individual can be both Mr. and Mrs. Worm according to circumstances. The young hatch out as fully formed worms and when grown can be about 10 inches long, or in tropical countries, nearly 4 ft.

* * *

In the fashion

I HAVE always noticed that women's hats which fascinated 50 years ago might almost land the wearer in the Courts to-day. Certainly this applies to bathing dresses.

But what is more serious is that fashions also apply to inventions. I was heartily laughed at for recommending television in 1914 and looked upon with grave suspicion when I gave a demonstration.

For countless years inventors have produced arc lamps and carburetters by the dozen, but more popular of all is the electric car which either runs by means of accumulators of astonishing lightness or is fed from some kind of wet battery into which one places a pennyworth of mixed chemicals.

Before long we shall have plenty of atom car flotations all of which will be useless, but I do not think this applies to cars run by induction.

The latest idea is a battery which occupies no more space than a large cigarette case. The inventor claims that it requires a small piece of silver renewed annually and one of the bi-chromates as a depolariser.

I strongly advise would-be investigators to rely upon technical rather than popular reports and to watch the depolariser in action, for in spite of its name it is a simple thing.

March, 1952   Page 13

Over desert, jungle, trackless wastes and swamps, in the Hillman Minx

The author (bearded) and his co-driver, Mr. J. Bulman, photographed immediately before the start at 6.15 a.m., on Monday, December 31st last, and left, arrival at Cape Town on the morning of January 22nd.

500 MILES A DAY FOR 21 DAYS!
London to Cape Town in record time.
By G. Hinchliffe, M.Inst.B.E., M.I.M.I.

A JOURNEY of 10,500 miles in just over 21 days means an average of between 400 and 500 miles daily—or 20 miles for every hour, day and night continuously, for the 21 days.

An interesting thought, and rather satisfying as a job well done as I recall many of the details of our recent London to Cape Town record overland journey. The actual time taken was 21 days, 19 hours, 45 minutes.

It is while my co-driver, Mr. James Bulman, and I try to relax aboard the *Caernarvon Castle* on its journey homewards to Southampton that we recount and re-live the many incidents and recollections of the journey across France, over the Mediterranean to Algiers, south across the Sahara Desert for Nigeria, French Equatorial Africa, the Belgian Congo, Uganda, Kenya, Tanganyika Territory and through Northern and Southern Rhodesia for the Union of South Africa, and our destination, Cape Town.

* * *

HOW quickly the route can be summarised in that way! But it is a long, long distance back to that early-morning start from London, Pall Mall, on December 31 last, headed for Lympne Airport to take the *Silver City* freighter for Le Touquet.

Here, I recall, commenced a sequence of courtesy and kindliness spread across the continents of Europe and Africa that played no small part indeed in the success of our trip.

I remember with gratitude especially the magnificent co-operation of the Airways and Customs' officials by whose courtesy I was on the road for Marseilles within three minutes of touching down.

* * *

MY promise to be at the Mediterranean French port by 8 a.m. the following morning, I was determined to keep. Which meant that we covered the 700-odd miles in under 21 hours, or the journey from London to Marseilles in under the 24 hours. Welcome, indeed, was the brief respite afloat after that not insignificant drive.

Off-loaded at Algiers our route was for Laghuat, El Golea, In Salah, Tamanrasset, In Guezzam, Agadez and Zinder, crossing the Sahara Desert from North to South for Kano, Nigeria, Forts Lamy, Archambault and Crampbel, for Bangassou in French Equatorial Africa, and thence for Stanleyville, in the Belgian Congo.

Pressing East for Kampala in Uganda, passing Mount Kenya, and on to Nairobi, we turned South, then in the wake of Mount Kilimanjaro (19,316 ft., and the highest mountain in Africa), for Arusha, Eringa, Mbeya, Mpika, and on to Broken Hill for Salisbury, Fort Victoria, Beitbridge, Pretoria, Johannesburg, Kroonstad, Kimberley, Paarl, and so to Cape Town.

DURING the daytime we made it a practice to take two-hour spells of driving, varying this to one-hour each during the hours of darkness. Bearing this in mind and the fact that on two occasions only in the 21 days did we have a complete night's rest, the months of preliminary work in ensuring real physical fitness, on those long-distance preparatory drives for special endurance training—with 12,000 miles (including 4,000 miles "running in") all over Europe before the start—were well rewarded. I had been told: "You have to be tough and be prepared to live rough" and, by goom, there was never a truer piece of advice.

At odd times, of course, we both experienced the urge to sleep. It was inevitable. When we would stop, take a brisk walk or have a dressing of Eau de Cologne to face and neck, to put us right for another hundred-odd miles.

It is easy enough, too, to say that in the first seven days we covered the journey from London to the southernmost tip of the Sahara, at Kano, and actually made the fastest-ever desert crossing, with a time of under five days, in spite of the intense heat and physical discomfort.

I recall this particular section only too well as I glance down at my broken finger nails and my still sore finger tips acquired in the never-ending battles with the heart-breaking sand into which we frequently sunk to axle level.

* * *

WITH all the usual outside aids, sand mats, picks and spades, there was always that final grovelling with our bare hands to clear inaccessible parts, and hot Sahara sand can be like blistering emery paper; we show the scars as proof.

Nor was it all that easy to maintain the straight-ahead course. Without land marks, certainly without signposts, so terribly alone, thirsty under the blazing sun, doubly alert and watchful at night, weary ever of the day's heat, small wonder that occasionally we went in circles. Those many occasions, too, when clearing the sand at one spot, laying down the sand mats, I or my colleague at the wheel, the other pushing to maintain progress, it mostly meant driving the car ahead for a considerable distance in order to reach more solid ground, when the one left behind would have to roll up and carry the heavy sand mats on bare and blistered shoulders.

I confess that on more than one occasion had I grievous doubts as to the sense of

March, 1952

pushing on. Indeed, I remember vowing to friend Bulman: "Not if all the sand of this ghastly desert were dust of gold would I attempt a second crossing." Which is amusing now, of course, as we lounge comfortably on the deck of the *Caernarvon Castle*.

I knew all the time that we must push on. We had to keep faith with our consciences, with our friends; we were out to do our best.

* * *

TO tell all the many stories of our fears—and we had them !— our hopes and, at times, necessarily modified plans, would occupy the space of volumes; the occasion particularly when out in that vast sea of loneliness, in a moment almost of complete and utter despair as to the correct route, as a last resort I clambered to the top of the car and peered anxiously through my binoculars. Were we glad to see, as mere spots on the distant horizon, a camel convoy, so weary were we of endeavouring again and again to retrace our tyre tracks in order to discover the point at which we erred, with no more success than simply adding to our gyrations.

However, we finally reached Kano at 10.55 p.m. and gladly pushed on for Fort Lamy, where there was more delay at the ferry crossing for French Equatorial Africa, one of many river crossings, mostly by primitive transportation, before we were to reach Stanleyville. If we enjoyed our overnight stop at In Guezzam, in the middle of the desert, we certainly did our halt at Bangassou.

* * *

RIVER crossings varied from ferries constructed of hollowed-out tree trunks, lashed together with ropes and planks, paddled across by the natives, by natives pulling wires stretched from the one bank to the other, to the more modern method of tow by a small auxiliary motor unit attached to the ferry craft, yet always that eerie, if not unpleasant, rhythmical motion inspired either by beats on the " Tom-tom " or the swaying of a loud voiced native, giving impressive illustration to leisurely team work, with time no object in all things.

My gifts of odd remnants of silks, or other textiles, samples of which I had brought with me from Bradford as possible aids in emergency, proved indescribably effective.

* * *

FURTHER South we drove along the Equator for two days on our way to Jinja to come to still more hazards, flooded countryside with the water some 2 ft. in places, literally oceans of mud, frequently delaying us for hours on end, and always when time was our main concern.

Often Mr. Bulman and I, in our turn, had to leg it ahead feeling and testing the nature of the surface below, pushing on this way to Kampala.

Here we were able to get a welcome routine service, and equally enjoyable wash and opportunity to eat in comfort, all in the course of two-and-a-half hours—a delay which called for a non-stop drive through that day and night in order to reach Nairobi on time.

Adding to our troubles here, we lost our way on a detour made necessary by major road repairs, followed by miles of back-breaking and machine-wrecking road and track corrugations of Tanganyika Territory and the Tsetse fly-infested country hereabouts, where we were subjected to repeated spraying of car and occupants on entering and leaving the areas concerned, as precaution against desease spread.

Top to bottom: Laying the sand mats, under the blazing sun, the only method, frequently, of maintaining any progress at all over the desert.

Fording one of the many deep and fast-flowing rivers in French Equatorial Africa.

A typical Uganda "road"—just a course of mud and twitch.

Right: Leaving the Congo ferry, the Minx again becomes amphibian.

AT the hotel where we stayed for a brief rest we were warned that it would be madness to continue.

We could not, of course, afford to delay, and pushed on for Broken Hill, the water now threatening the mechanical parts and, in actual fact, we lost much valuable time in drying out the affected pieces.

At this particular point, moreover, we were warned that our route for Bulawayo, via Livingstone, was definitely impracticable, that we would be lucky if we could get through any way at all.

We were directed, therefore, to make for Salisbury, and further advised, strangely enough, to drive as fast as possible in the mud and water, not to creep slowly through.

* * *

TROUBLE was inspired also by our " mobile " baggage, the large fuel and water tanks, now only partially full, causing the rear of the car to swerve most distractingly. Later, too, in ascending steeper sections of the muddy roads, it seemed there was to be no progress at all.

The native trick of cutting down branches and laying them carefully in the mud beneath the water, to give more stable wheel course, we found most helpful. Indeed, one section of over 80 yards had to be prepared in this manner. Then with Bulman driving, myself pushing to help maintain approximately upright progress, we managed once again to overcome what threatened to be the end of our plans.

* * *

AT Salisbury, I remember, we had the misfortune to break a shock absorber. Now all Salisbury closes down at midday on Saturday, and we were told that we would be very lucky if we could get servicing anywhere. As I had seen quite a number of Hillman Minx cars in use in this part of the country, however, I decided to stop the next owner in the hope that he might at least be able to direct me to a likely garage.

To say the owner was keenly interested is to put the facts mildly. He questioned us : " What is the idea ? Where are you going ? Why the hurry ? How far have you been ? "

When we told him of our plans, of some of our experiences, and of the narrow possibility of our breaking the London-Cape Town record by two or three days, he replied simply, " Come along, follow me," leading us to a small garage where we were truly astonished by his instructions : " Let these fellows have everything they want from my car. As long as you leave me sufficient to be reasonably mobile, they can have the rest."

In actual fact we borrowed a bolt from a rear shock-absorber, a complete front shock-absorber, and a nut from a third. How grateful we were it is hard to express. This delay, however, meant a drive now of nearly 400 miles for Beitbridge and entry into the Union.

* * *

IT was Sunday when we reached Johannesburg, minus any South African money, yet anxious to push on to Kroonstad.

The only sign of life at the early hour of 4 a.m. was a light in a shop opposite to the small garage outside which we had already jacked up the car, removed a wheel and a half axle-shaft, hoping for an early appearance of the garage hand.

We decided finally to knock up the shop in which the light appeared, and found the occupier, the local butcher, preparing

Top to bottom : For three whole days the outlook over the desert was as this—an ocean of sandy desolation.

The only variety of terrain over the desert—more sand of a different kind.

Natives of French Equatorial Africa give a friendly welcome.

Possibly the only really efficient ferry, of many, at Fort Lamy.

500 miles a day for 21 days! : *(Concluded from page 15)*

his joints. Appreciating our problem, he persuaded the proprietor of the garage to join us, in pyjamas and slippers, who in turn fetched the storesman, also in pyjamas and slippers, when we thankfully acquired the necessary part. Working together we completed the repair and were away in under three hours. It was at this moment when we realised fully how generously helpful everyone endeavoured to be.

* * *

HERE we cabled Cape Town, some 700 miles away, that we hoped to reach journey's end by midnight the same day. Despite a punctured spare, repaired inside the car while on the move, two further punctures on the way, the combination of our heavy load, the acute road camber and tyre pressures necessarily at 35 lbs. per square inch to take the strain, it meant a non-stop drive for 18 hours.

Ten of these we actually covered without once varying from our 55 to 60 m.p.h. average, and actually changed seats while the car was in motion.

Throughout the Karroo the heat was intolerable, and the nearer prospect of achieving our objective kept us going. As matters turned out we clocked in at Cape Town at 4 a.m. (G.M.T. 02.00 hrs.) on January 22—exactly 21 days, 19 hours and 45 minutes after leaving Pall Mall, London.

* * *

I RECALL with gratitude all the kindness and help we received from almost everyone with whom we came in contact—Customs officials, police, Europeans and natives; they all made us feel increasingly and morally bound, no matter the obstacle, the hazard, and the ever recurring difficulty, to keep faith with ourselves and our good Samaritans.

I am inspired especially, of course, to make all due acknowledgment to our brave little Hillman Minx which completed the journey against all odds without major mechanical failure or replacement, on a journey averaging nearly 500 miles a day, a journey over tracks, and roads, good, bad and indifferent, even non-existent, over sandy wastes, dried-up river beds, mountainous country, through floods and over thousands of miles of unmade roads.

It all convinced me that the Old Country does not build itself simply on the prestige of its peoples, but rather on the quality of its products.

It must be remembered, too, that we each had 200 lbs. of personal luggage as well as spare parts, emergency rations and water and petrol supplies.

Yes, we are proud of the little Minx, and proud to have achieved our objective, driving a privately owned British motorcar, unsponsored by its manufacturers, indeed without their knowledge of our plans, prepared for months past, until we were well on our journey. These facts make the success all the more satisfying.

* * *

THE Hillman Minx symbolises "proof positive British quality and reliability," and carried the message across the continents of Europe and Africa in record time.

My own personal reward, I feel, is that given to me by fellow passengers on the *Caernarvon Castle*, to 500 of whom I was invited to give a short account of the journey. Their silent interest for some one-and-a-half hours and their unspoken, yet apparent, tribute at the finish of my talk, cheered both my co-driver and myself with a measure of inward satisfaction that alone seemed to make the journey inclusively worth while.

* * *

SPACE permits only brief mention of the facts.

In our minds we carry many unforgettable memories—of the intense silence of the desert (when we could hear even the bones of our necks creak with every turn), the awful "silent fear," the utter loneliness of the desert and, on the other hand, the contrasting mystery of the jungles of the Belgian Congo and French Equatorial Africa when, in the darkness, even during the day when the trees blanked out all sun and daylight, the cries and screams of every variety of wild bird and animal life, curious at our presence, struck queer fears in our hearts. Indeed, Bulman when changing a tyre in the jungle, had to awaken me from my sleep to keep him company, so scared was he by the many peering eyes and piercing cries of prying wild life.

* * *

CENTRAL Africa can be mysterious indeed—an age still of pygmies with bows and arrows, of nature in the raw, even if civilisation is progressively creeping forward.

Yet there is indescribable beauty over all, the birds, beasts and the fruits of the forests, bananas nearly 2 ft. in length, passion fruit, etc., all within hand reach on the sides of those endless tracks.

These and many other memories have etched themselves on our minds, indelibly so!

I have tried to relax. I cannot! I shall live that fantastic journey for the rest of my life.

Mr. G. C. Hinchliffe describes his record-breaking run to an interested gathering at the showrooms of Carson & Co., Rootes Group distributors in Cape Town. A reception held in honour of the two drivers was attended by many prominent personalities of industry and press.

The Modern SUPER ★
puts INDIA miles ahead!

Developed in a modern factory, backed by the most up-to-date tyre research laboratory in the country, the improvements in mileage performance, cushioned resilience and wider area road traction built into the modern India SUPER make it

the tyre of tomorrow for the car of today

March, 1952

LOOKING BACK:
Reminiscences of the Monte Carlo Rally

By John A. Cooper (of the "Autocar") co-driver with Stirling Moss and Desmond Scannell on the successful Sunbeam-Talbot

Members of the Sunbeam-Talbot team are given a civic "Welcome home" to Coventry. L. to R.: Douglas Perring, W. Chipperton, John Cooper, Desmond Scannell, John Cutts, John Pearman. Front row: Mr. Geoffrey Rootes, managing director, Rootes Group, Car Manufacturing Co.'s, Norman Garrad (team captain), the Mayor of Coventry, Councillor Harry Weston, and Stirling Moss.

LOOKING back now to the Monte Carlo Rally, to those unbelievable days of celebration which followed it, to Stirling bursting through the revolving doors into the lounge of the Hotel Metropole in Monte Carlo, where I was drinking tea, to tell us that we had finished "Second," with Sydney Allard in "First" place, I remember how a few months ago Stirling Moss and I decided that it would be a good thing to enter together in the Rally.

Desmond Scannell, Secretary of the B.R.D.C., made up our team of three, and his skill at organisation propelled us through the preliminary arrangements.

* * *

WE were invited to join the official Sunbeam-Talbot team, driving a works-sponsored Sunbeam-Talbot 90, with Norman Garrad as our genial team captain.

For us—Stirling, Desmond, the Sunbeam-Talbot number 341, the luggage and I—the adventure really started at Paris before the Rally began.

We were to start from Monte Carlo; Stirling joined us at Paris, which we left at the same time in the evening as that scheduled for the start of the Rally.

We planned to maintain the required 50 k.p.h. average over the prescribed route, with an allowance of 24 hours in which to reconnoitre the various alternative routes around Clermont Ferrand and Valence.

* * *

CONDITIONS were almost friendly as far as Le Puy, where we breakfasted and changed the rear wheels of the Sunbeam-Talbot—for the two spares were fitted with special snow tyres. That day we found that the shortest route to Valence was not necessarily the quickest, and eventually decided that a course through Montfaucon and Bourg-Argental was probably the best one to follow.

After a night at Le Puy, we woke to find the sky full of snow. It looked as though the snow would fall for some days; and it was on this day that we lost a quantity of self-confidence and found—besides the impracticability of opening the passengers' window when buried in a snow-drift — the surprising unditching efficiency of two oxen, referred to by Stirling as "two thousand Chateaubriand-power," and a length of chain. It was, in fact, not easy to abandon the idea of having two oxen as part of our equipment! We reached Valence, but not within our time limit, and made Monte Carlo only after having been swept into another ditch—by a snow plough this time—from which we were extricated by an ex-U.S. lorry.

* * *

THE next few days were busy with arranging time schedules for the regularity test.

This was to be run over a 50-mile mountainous course just outside Monte Carlo, divided into four sections by three controls.

The scheduled average speed was 45 k.p.h., and this had to be maintained from one section to the other.

One of the controls was a secret check point. As it was impossible for competitors to ascertain where this might be, it was necessary for drivers to maintain the precise average as near as possible on the entire course.

We were relying mainly on visual check points, such as kilometre stones, road intersections and the like. The car's odometer was not used, for, although accurate, it would naturally be affected by wheelspin resulting from the icy conditions forecast.

* * *

ON Tuesday, January 22, with Desmond at the wheel—who afterwards confessed to an extreme nervousness—and snow tyres fitted, we left Monte Carlo at approaching 10 p.m.

Stirling took over at Grasse for the tricky run to Digne, but on the mountainous section, over the Alpes Maritime—which the Monte Carlo contingent has to cover twice—no one experienced much difficulty on the outward run.

There was a good deal of snow covering the surface, but none of it was recent. Then I took over, and urged the Sunbeam-Talbot over the Col de la Croix Haute, to Grenoble. By Megève the snow was very thick, but the special tyres were doing their job well. At Geneva we removed the snow tyres, but after Desmond had conducted us gingerly on a sheet of ice down to Berne, we replaced them, and used them for the rest of the journey.

* * *

LOOKING back now, three things persist more vividly than others in my memory.

The first was Stirling's grief at arriving too late at Berne to visit his favourite restaurant and eat a *banane flambée*; the second, Stirling's fantastic drive from Saint Flour to Le Puy, and the third was, of course, the regularity test—but the *banane flambée* cropped up at Berne, and the other two much later in the itinerary.

I was awakened from my sleep in the back of the car, which had been curtained off with black-out paper covering the windows (the latter to render Stirling a less nervous passenger) by hitting the roof several times in quick succession.

We were covering the road from Luxembourg to Liège; the surface was covered with ice, rutted sometimes as much as five inches deep, but it was all "good practice" to Stirling, who maintained his normal cruising speeds. We arrived, therefore, at Liège level with cars bearing numbers between 190 and 200. Through Amsterdam, Brussels and Rheims to Paris the going was easy. Incidentally, television cameras awaited us at Amsterdam, and Stirling and I in kapok-filled flying suits were made uncomfortably hot under the glare of those huge arc lights.

* * *

IT was lucky that our only puncture occurred on one of the easiest sections, between Paris and Bourges. Luckier still that a tyre depot was miraculously open at midnight at Montargis, where we were able to buy a snow tyre. True, it was of a different tread and make and extremely expensive, but it was a snow tyre, and we were still able to make up the time lost.

From Bourges the route lay to Mont Luçon, where I took over again. I had intended to hand over to Stirling at Le Puy, but when I arrived in a heavy snowstorm at the passage control at Saint Flour with not much time in hand, having passed half a dozen cars ditched on the Col de la Fageole, I decided that surely this was the time for Moss to drive.

He did!

It was still dark, there was a blizzard and low cloud restricted visibility to as little as 20 or 30 feet.

No one else could have avoided losing time.

The narrow road was rutted with ice beneath the snow, and the rear axle thumped and crashed between the bump and rebound stops. Yet, at one point, where a short straight stretch appeared, the speedometer registered 130 k.p.h. (over 75 m.p.h.), and neither Desmond or I were worried, either — a confidence borne of the fact that neither of us could have maintained Stirling's speed.

From Le Puy to Valence we had daylight, and the blizzard grew less fierce, and at Valence we were told that less than

(Continued on page 48)

Incidents in the Monte Carlo Rally

Top left: Indicative of the severe wintry conditions, snow, ice and fog, encountered over the Col du Braus, during the final regularity test.

Circle above: Stirling Moss, John Cooper (the author) and Desmond Scannell, at the Brussels Control, after the run North from Monte Carlo.

Left: Mrs. Nancy Mitchell, Miss Sheila Van Damm, and Mrs. "Bill" Wisdom, study the Continental section of the route before crossing the Channel from Folkestone. They were fourth in the Ladies' class, in the Sunbeam-Talbot.

Rootes Group products highly successful

Right: J. H. Kemsley, and his Hillman Minx, who, despite the gruelling nature of the trial, reached Monte Carlo among the earliest finishers.

Below, circle: Stirling Moss, with his co-drivers, receive their awards for second place in the entire classification, from the hands of Prince Rainier III at the Monte Carlo prize presentation.

Bottom, right: M. B. Anderson and R. M. Hastie, with their Hillman Minx, which gained First Prize for its class in the Concours de Confort, for the fourth successive time.

B.O.A.C. Comet jet airliner with one of the Corporation's new Commer "Avenger" passenger coaches—a 21 seater with bodywork by Harringtons, of Hove.

"Once we had to warm the pilot; now it seems we must refrigerate him!"

Says Major Oliver Stewart

JUST at the moment when we thought we were clearing the final obstacle to ultra-high speed flight, somebody has discovered another. The sonic barrier is behind us so far as technical knowledge is concerned; but now here is the thermal barrier.

With aircraft, as with other things, the faster they go the hotter they get. American youths, I am told, call their specially tinkered motor-cars "hot rods" and we speak of "hotting" up engines to give more power. So somebody will soon come along with a hot kite, or aircraft which flies so fast that it is heated by friction with the air.

* * *

AT a speed on Mach 1 (the speed of sound), when flying near the ground (say 760 miles an hour), existing aircraft would heat up considerably.

Pilots who have been test flying our new aircraft at speeds of over Mach 0.9, or nearly 700 miles an hour, tell me that the heating effect is noticeable in the cockpit although they are never sustaining these speeds for any length of time.

But designers are now visualising sustained speeds of over Mach 1. They are thinking in terms of Mach 2, or twice the speed of sound. And when that figure is reached the heating effects are extremely serious. In some conditions the pilot would be roasted and many of his instruments would fail to work correctly.

* * *

FORTUNATELY the circumstances of high speed flight may have a corrective effect. Much of it is done at great heights where the air temperature is low and this to some extent counters the heating of the machine. But it does not completely counter it, and if we intend to fly aircraft at speeds much in excess of 1,200 miles an hour, an entirely fresh study of their external surfaces will have to be undertaken and they will have to carry a large refrigerator into which pilot and instruments will be packed.

So to the addition of complication there is no end. We have had to warm the pilot; we have had to give him oxygen; we have had to keep him under pressure; we have had to protect him from centrifugal loads and now we are going to have to refrigerate him.

But it may be that refrigerating the pilot will be the least of the troubles faced by ultra-high speed machines. If ordinary materials were used for the structure and skinning of the aircraft and for the pilot's canopy, there would be risk of failure. The plastic canopy will probably reach its limit before the rest of the machine; but the metals now employed have their limits. As they heat up, so their characteristics change. They become, in some respects, weaker.

* * *

IT is a common feature to metals that their strength characteristics change with changes in temperature. The indications are that the outer skin of high speed aircraft will be heated excessively at speeds not very greatly above those now being attained. So we begin the search for new materials; for some kind of metal or alloy which will retain its strength characteristics when it is very hot.

It is the same kind of search that has been going on in the realm of the gas turbine since the beginning. Turbine blades have to be made of metals which will retain sufficient strength at high temperatures. All the talk one hears about "creep" strength is related to exactly this problem. But it is in some ways easier to find metals which will stand up to engine work than to aircraft work because there is greater latitude in weight. It does not matter so much if the metal out of which turbine blades are made is heavy; but one cannot use a heavy metal for skinning an aircraft.

* * *

ALL this has led to some extremely interesting speculation in papers read before the Royal Aeronautical Society and other learned bodies. Eminent metallurgists and engineers have been discussing what they are going to do about this trouble of over-heated aircraft. One suggestion is the use of titanium, and recently there has been a great deal of excitement about titanium.

It appears to have the qualities that are needed and elaborate tables have been presented in various papers showing its great strength and the way it retains that strength at high temperatures. Some people think that, aeronautically speaking, titanium is the metal of the future.

* * *

IN this country we are doing little about titanium. The ore is found in Russia, and it is also found in Canada and in Australia. The United States have been working on titanium for some time, and in that country it is already in small scale production. Here it is so far only in experimental production. It appears as if a considerably greater effort in the production of titanium is needed if we are to be in a position to continue the work that has been done on the development of ultra-high speed aircraft.

As for the cockpit canopy, this presents an even more difficult problem for the designers of aircraft intended to fly much beyond the speed of sound. The plastic transparencies now in use are already difficult to mount and hold in place without risk of failure. Glass would be no better and would have other defects. One speaker at the Royal Aeronautical Society described the aircraft designer's requirements for canopies as a "challenge to the organic chemist."

* * *

SOME people scoff at all these difficulties on the grounds that, when speeds of Mach 2 (say, 1,300 miles an hour at altitude) are contemplated, they will be done in the outer atmosphere where the density of the air is so low that the heating effect from friction will be reduced. But it will still be necessary to get through the thicker layers of the atmosphere and—for military purposes, at any rate—it will be necessary to fly fast in those thicker layers. So the problem of heating is a very real one. The "thermal barrier" is going to be just as troublesome as was the sonic barrier.

Titanium is not the only solution. There are other materials to which designers are directing their attention; but titanium seems at the moment the most hopeful. But for the transparencies there is as yet no material giving promise of a complete solution to the strength-at-high-temperature requirement.

* * *

THERE, then, is the continual fascination of aviation; there seems no end to the novel problems that have to be tackled, and each problem is a challenge to the intellect and a demand upon assembled information. When the difficulties of aircraft heating at high speeds have been overcome and we are reaching out into space with yet faster, higher flying machines, there is no doubt that other unforeseen obstacles will appear. The fact that fresh problems appear in such rapid succession is testimony to the rate of aeronautical progress.

March, 1952 Page 29

"Let there be Method in March Madness"
says
Brigid de Vine

"Get me a return ticket to Santander, leaving London on Friday. I want to travel by the 10.5 a.m. from Victoria to Newhaven, connecting at Dieppe with the Le Mans train to Irun. I want third class in England, second class in France and first in Spain. Book me a couchette on Friday night and ring me back reporting that all is O.K."

THAT is a suggested test for the secretaries of readers of *Modern Motoring and Travel*. It is taken from a book "The REAL Personal Secretary" by F. Addington Symonds (World's Work, 7s. 6d.), which everyone who is a secretary, has a secretary, or has daughters training to be secretaries, should read, for it is full of practical advice.

The paragraph above, for example, is a memory test.

It is supposed to be fired at the secretary by a busy boss at a moment when she has no means of making a note and must rely on memory only.

If, after hearing it read out, once only, you can repeat the orders verbally *and* in writing, without hesitation and without error, then "*you may congratulate yourself on possessing a keen memory and a good grasp of English, in the sense that you can express your chief's thoughts as clearly and concisely as he does himself.*"

* * *

SOME secretaries may, of course, give a hollow laugh at the thought of *their* chiefs ever being able to express themselves clearly on any subject. For them there is useful advice on how to "guess" what he *meant* to say when he paused "to chew his cigar"!

* * *

FOR "the Boss" himself there is a helpful booklet "The Health of Executives," published for 1s. by the Industrial Welfare Society.

Many breakdowns in business might be avoided and many useful business careers continued longer if people would only recognise some of the early signs of "breakdown."

One is the insistence on doing oneself trivial matters which could well be delegated.

The other is fear of taking time off for a "break."

A very successful managing director once told me that the most obvious sign that a man needed a holiday very badly was when he began to feel himself indispensable. "I cannot possibly be away" is often a sign of bad organisation due to fatigue; and the remedy lies *not* in taking more work home, but in taking a complete week-end "away from it all."

SPRINGTIME IS PERFUME TIME!

FRAGRANCE is an obvious necessity for beauty in Springtime—to echo the lovely note of the blossoms.

When planning your new Spring wardrobe, be practical as well as glamorous. Turn over a new leaf for the new season and resolve to get the utmost from every sweet-smelling product you buy. Buy tiny phials of new perfumes, so that you have one to suit every outfit, every mood . . . a light one for mornings, a spicy one for afternoons, and something really "sultry" for evenings! These will pep you up; and you will feel feminine and refreshed.

Toilet water or Cologne should be the basis of your fragrance make-up; you use perfume to accent it, just as you use your lipstick to accent your facial make-up. And remember, perfume needs re-touching every few hours, just like your lipstick.

Never put your perfume direct on to the fabric of a suit or dress. There is always the chance that it might mark or spot the material. Besides, your perfume belongs on you, not your clothes!

AWAY from the office, on the farm, new methods are still helping to speed up traditional processes, and one new "gadget" which serves to save time and labour, in both factory and farm, is the "Scale Scoop." *As the scoop lifts up food stuffs or chemicals, etc., it weighs them.*

A device at the back of the scoop automatically registers accurate weight.

It is calibrated to weigh from ¼ lb. to 5 lb. and there is nothing to go wrong. The Scale Scoop is made in rust proof aluminium—to last a lifetime—and costs only 39s. 11d. (plus 1s. postage) from the makers, Scoop, Ltd., Wood Street, near Guildford, Surrey.

* * *

FOR the kitchen there is a new timer, Smith's "Pinger," which looks rather like a clock.

You can set it to ring an alarum at the end of any period from one minute to an hour, and it is invaluable for cooking. You put your cake in the oven, set the "Pinger" to the correct time and you can then go away and do something else, knowing that you will hear a bell ring when the cake is "done."

The "Pinger" is a wonderful aid if you are, like myself, a Pressure cooker "fan," and I am told it is also most useful for the correct "timing" of "home perms."

I think it would make an excellent gift for a Spring bride, for so many meals are ruined by a new cook "forgetting there was something in the oven"; and it is "pretty enough for a present," in a variety of pastel shades.

* * *

A METHOD of cutting time and labour in painting and distempering walls and ceilings is a find nowadays, when even quite highly paid "executives" find the bills for household repairs quite staggeringly high.

With the new method you use not a brush but a roller. The device for "rolling" the paint on to walls has been a favourite with American handymen for some time, but it has only just reached London.

Now Selfridges offer the Victory

VEILED BEAUTY

Two models by Erik, Danish-born British designer. Below: a black patent sailor worn straight on the head with grosgrain trimming and coarse mesh face veil. Right: Spring goes to the head with this grey bonnet-style straw, the crown massed with spring blossoms and topped with a large white love-bird. A coarse face veil adds a trim.

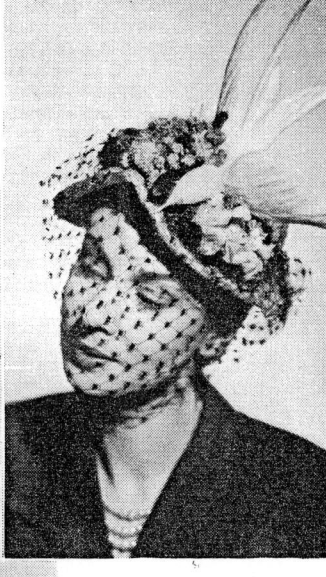

Page 30 — March, 1952

Left: Amusing Balenciaga overcoat in black and brown check on a beige ground; has bias yoke, funnel sleeves and straight front gathered above the bust-line.

Judy Breen, J. Arthur Rank star, certainly has selected a comfortable winter garment in this check hooded coat.

Method in March Madness:

(Continued from page 29)

"Decroller" set in a neat box containing: (1) the roller, covered in pure lambswool, and seven inches wide, with (2) a 1 in. paintbrush, for corners, skirting edges, etc., and (3) a paint tray.

The whole set for 49s. 6d.

You prepare your surface in the ordinary way, then fill the tray half full of paint, roll the Decroller into the edge of the paint, remove surplus paint by rolling to and fro on the shallow end of the tray, then roll it lightly over the surface to be covered. The lambswool gives a smoother finish, holds more paint so that it covers a larger area without redipping, and it does not drip down your sleeve as you work and spatter spots all over the floor. The demonstrator at Selfridges assured me that she could paint a ceiling, using the Decroller, without either putting on an overall or covering her hair—and I am anxious to try that test myself.

Over two million "rollers" are being used by home decorators in the U.S.A., and it is estimated that each roller will last "about ten years." They are easy to clean, and "refill rollers" are obtainable. I think the gadget makes a timely appearance here to help with Spring cleaning.

* * *

NEW furniture to meet new needs is already making its appearance, ready to take its place in our newly decorated rooms, and one piece which I saw first at Heal's is the Joel Television table, a useful small table which has *a revolving top* so that the television set can be moved to give the best viewing position with the minimum of trouble. It is a nicely made piece of furniture and makes a useful occasional table if you have a console model later on.

* * *

THE four-in-one cabinet is another novelty. From one supporting base you can draw out four different "drawers" fitted according to your needs as writing table, work box, or whatever you wish. It makes excellent use of small space.

* * *

"THE best furniture value since the *war*" is the title given to the new utility Put-u-up suites which have just become available. In order to meet the need for better design in furniture, two of the new settee-beds have beautifully moulded *wooden* arms, shaped by a process developed from the latest scientific technique for moulding woods, as used in modern aircraft construction. These curving wooden arms combine grace and strength—and make useful resting places for glasses, cups and ashtrays.

* * *

FOR those who prefer cloth to wood, there are two more designs in the range which have fully upholstered arms, without the "heavy" appearance which in the past has spoiled the look of "settee beds." Armchairs to match the new designs are also available and the prices are surprising.

* * *

A *fully stuffed "Put-u-up" for under £24 retail, £49 10s. with two armchairs*, is a very reasonable price for a three-piece suite, *plus* hidden bed for occasional guests.

An *expanding* bed, shown at Heal's, saves parents the cost of a cot plus bed for a child. The small bed, only 4 feet 6 inches long, has an extension piece which pulls out to adult length as the child grows up!

The problem of correct "sizing" has at last received the attention it deserved from the makers of English off-the-peg clothing for women. Mr. G. G. Herring, who drew up the demob clothing scheme for World War II soldiers is, I find, the man behind the drive being made by Peter Robinson, Ltd., to provide ready-made clothing for women to fit without expensive alterations. Mr. Herring who is 6 feet 4½ inches himself (with two daughters over the 6-foot mark), joined Peter Robinson's six years ago and as deputy managing director began to ask why, if it was possible for the men's clothing trade to provide 120 different fittings, the women's side of the trade could not do better than the existing *eight* fittings. Soon Peter Robinson's were advertising clothes in 38 different sizes.

Now they have increased this to 44 to take in women *under* 5 feet 2 inches.

* * *

I ATTENDED a recent party at the Savoy when Miss Anona Winn—who is herself 5 feet 2 inches, praised the manufacturers of "Eastex" clothes for

Attractive Audrey Long (Columbia) wears round draped ear-rings and matching medallions on her choker necklace in jewel shades to match her titian hair and sea-green embroidered gown.

March, 1952   Page 31

manufacturing outfits for the small woman who will remain *short* all her life but is not necessarily always slim.

"Eastex 52" clothes are made in seven hip sizes, *from* 30 *to* 44, to ensure that shorter women of all types are catered for in suits and coats as well as in dresses.

Since it has been estimated that one woman in every five is 5 feet 2 inches or under, it seems amazing that we have had to wait so long for clothes cut to smaller proportions.

* * *

NEW methods of *feeding* the human race are outlined in Dr. Josue de Castro's book, "Geography of Hunger" (Gollancz, 18s.).

He holds out hope of food from six new sources.

The first is already being tried in Jamaica, where a factory is turning out five tons of vital protein each day by "feeding yeast on molasses." The substance that results can be given any flavour, even that of meat! There is also hope of growing vast quantities of a sea plant—chlorella—in huge sea tanks; increasing the supply of fish; developing new plants in Brazil which yield calcium and vitamin A; and developing a Central African weed destroyer which would enable more crops to survive. There are also plans for making food grow in the Arctic by training plants to endure rigorous weather.

* * *

ON the "human relations" side there is also news of a new "Method." It is the recipe for a happy marriage given by Roy Campbell, bull fighter and winner of the W. A. Foyle Poetry Award for 1952.

In his autobiography, "Light on a Dark Horse," Mr. Campbell describes his belief that any marriage in which the wife "wears the pants" is a "farce."

In the early days of their marriage Mrs. Campbell sometimes fell short of his ideas of "wifely obedience." "So," he writes, "to shake up her illusions I hung her out of the fourth floor window of our room so that she should get some respect for me."

"This worked wonders."

Police on the other side of the street began yelling to Mr. Campbell to pull her back. He said, "We are only practising our act, aren't we, kid?" and she replied "Yes," as calmly "as if we did it every ten minutes." So the police left them alone, saying, "Well, don't practice it so high over other people's heads, please."

Mr. Campbell concludes:

"My wife was very proud of me after I had hung her out of the window and boasted of it to her girl friends. This infuriated them, as their young men always gave in to them, and they got no excitement...."

* * *

BUT I accept no responsibility if any reader of *Modern Motoring and Travel* wants to try *this* "March Method."

We women may grumble that we cannot see much of the world on £25—but I do not think any of us really want to see what it looks like upside down as a change from domestic routine.

Even if cuts and Budgets make us feel that we are living in a topsy turvy world, I do not really believe that any of us envy Mrs. Campbell her flying trip out of the window.

Perhaps the Chancellor's March Methods may yet result in a better outlook for us all. We can only "wait and see."

Meantime, I hope I have shown a few ways for "Method in March Madness."

Perfect for evening occasions, accentuating the elegance of black and white, this snow-white mink bolero features the soft look in contrast with the dark background; exclusive model of the National Fur Company.

"Let there be Method in March Madness"

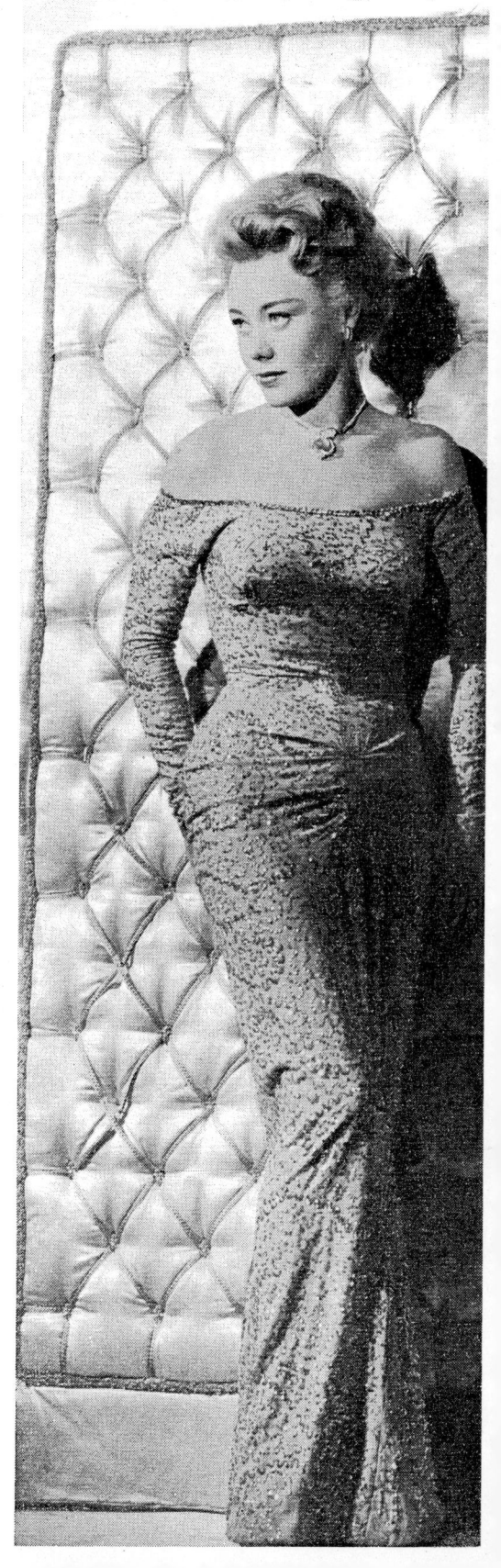

Glynis Johns, who wears this tight-fitting lime green gown covered with gold and silver sequins, is now one of the most sought after young women on the British screen. She scored a big hit in Somerset Maugham's "Gigolo and Gigolette." Recently married in the U.S.A.

MODERN MOTORING & TRAVEL

March, 1952

"O.K. for SOUND"

Film Shorts and Screen Gossip

Petula Clark has her first screen marriage—to Alec Guinness, who plays the title role in Arnold Bennett's comedy "The Card." See below.

EALING Studios have eight pictures in preparation, including Nevil Shute's "A Town Like Alice," and Nicholas Monserrat's "The Cruel Sea."

There will also be an original comedy, "Private Line," by ace script writer, T. E. B. Clarke. This concerns a small railway line which was overlooked when the railways were nationalised!

* * *

THE French Charlie Chaplin, "Bourvil," makes his English début in United Artists', "Mr. Peek-a-Boo."

A French comedy filmed in English, "Mr. Peek-a-Boo" is the story of a meek little government clerk who suddenly discovers that he can walk through walls.

Bourvil has a fly-away right eyebrow, a pixie-like smile and a droll Chaplinesque quality.

* * *

THE leading role in Betty Box's forthcoming picture, "Venetian Bird" will be played by Richard Todd, who has just completed the Technicolor version of "Robin Hood."

"Venetian Bird" is a post-war thriller set entirely in Venice.

* * *

ARTHUR KENNEDY has received the New York Critics Award for the Best Actor of the Year for his performance in the Universal-International film, "Lights Out."

He portrayed a soldier blinded in battle and undergoing the physical, mental and emotional processes of readjustment.

* * *

IN the film programme of Pinewood Studios is "To-night at 8.30," the tentative title for a trio of Noël Coward stories.

These are "Fumed Oak," "Red Peppers" and "Ways and Means."

* * *

ELEANOR PARKER has been called back by Metro-Goldwyn-Mayer to team with Robert Taylor in "Eagle on his Cap."

She will portray the wife of Colonel Paul Tibbetts, U.S. pilot who dropped the first atom bomb on Hiroshima.

ARNOLD BENNETT'S celebrated comedy, "The Card," in which Alec Guinness plays the title role, had a charity world première, in aid of the Animal Health Trust, on February 28, in London.

Mr. J. Arthur Rank was recently appointed chairman of the executive committee of the Animal Health Trust, the voluntary organisation benefiting from the première. The Trust is engaged in the urgent work of improving the health of British livestock.

Also starring in "The Card" are Glynis Johns, Valerie Hobson and Petula Clark.

* * *

AFTER nearly four years' absence, lovely Patricia Roc is returning to the British screen in a starring role in "Something Money Can't Buy."

Being made at Pinewood, this is a light-hearted story set in post-war England. Co-starring is Anthony ("Where No Vultures Fly") Steel.

Since her marriage to a French film cameraman in 1949, Pat has lived near Paris.

* * *

Linda Darnell, star of "Saturday Island," which was filmed in Jamaica, she portrays a Canadian nursing sister marooned with an American marine on an uninhabited island in the Pacific.

PAUL SOSKIN'S great sabotage thriller, "High Treason," has broken all records at Stockholm's Palladium cinema.

It looks like becoming one of the most successful British films ever shown in Sweden.

* * *

FOLLOWING the completion of the Technicolor comedy, "Penny Princess," Dirk Bogarde is cast in a stage production.

He is appearing in a revival of Noël Coward's play, "The Vortex."

* * *

WITH an eye on young flying enthusiasts, Robert Taylor is planning to become author of a book tentatively entitled, "On Your Own."

One of Hollywood's top private pilots, he aims to present aerial navigation in an easy, interesting form, avoiding the scientific wording which he feels frightens many youngsters away from flying.

* * *

DISCUSSING Press agents, Van Heflin recalls that the first agent he engaged wanted him to climb to the top of the Empire State Building flag-pole and thumb a ride from a helicopter.

"He said it would make front pages all over the world either way," says Van.

"When I asked him what he meant by 'either way,' he replied that he meant either if I succeeded in boarding the helicopter or if I fell from the flagpole!"

* * *

FREDERICK ASHTON, noted ballet dancer and choreographer of the Sadler's Wells troupe in London, has been signed by M.-G.-M. to do the choreography for the sequence in "Three Love Stories" to star ballerina Moira Shearer.

Ashton has been associated with many brilliant ballet productions in England and throughout the world.

Moira Shearer has starred in two top British films, "The Red Shoes" and "Tales of Hoffmann."

* * *

NORTHERN IRELAND will see the successful Somerset Maugham film, "Encore," for the first time when it opens in Belfast on March 31.

March, 1952   Page 41   **MODERN MOTORING & TRAVEL**

FIT
"*TripleX*" Regd.
AND BE SAFE

YOU CAN TAKE YOUR CAR ABROAD!

THIS *FREE* BOOKLET SOLVES CURRENCY PROBLEMS

When a little foreign money must go a long, long way it is more important than ever to read Autocheques' new booklet. Most motorists find the Autocheques system cuts £10 or even £20 *per person* off their budgets.

You will read, for instance, how a man and his wife can go on a 10-day tour, and yet still have as much as £17.10.0 in foreign currency to spend on lunches, drinks, souvenirs and petrol. The booklet tells you, too, how Autocheques let you budget *precisely* in advance yet leave you free to go where you like with no fixed route or time-table. Packed with all sorts of useful information it is a MUST for every motorist who longs to go abroad. Send the coupon for your copy NOW!

POST THIS COUPON TO-DAY

Please send me FREE Autocheques booklet.

NAME ....

ADDRESS ....

221F .... *Post in an unsealed envelope, using a 1½d. stamp*

Autocheques LTD

A DIVISION OF POLY WORLD TRAVEL SERVICE

221 (Dept. F), Regent St., London, W.1. Tel: GROsvenor 8901

AS the first item in the ambitious 1952 calendar of the Sunbeam-Talbot Owners' Club, the Club's recent fifth annual Dinner-Dance, held at the Royal Station Hotel, Newcastle-on-Tyne, went over in a really big way : a good omen, it was felt, for a further year of successful meetings if the general enthusiasm of the occasion was anything to go by.

Among the near-two-hundred members and friends who attended, despite the arctic conditions at the time, they came from near and far—from London, Edinburgh, Windermere, Durham and Dumfries.

Being held simultaneously with the results of the Monte Carlo Rally, and the success of Stirling Moss driving a Sunbeam-Talbot, the occasion found no difficulty in reasons for celebration ; they raised their glasses high, collectively and individually, in honour of added Sunbeam-Talbot glories and were profuse in their congratulations, especially to Mr. Cliff Wheeler, organiser, who, at very short notice, presented almost a complete photographic display of incidents in the Monte Carlo Rally for members' inspection.

But, there, Cliff Wheeler, whose associations with the Club go back to the early Talbot days, always does things well ; his great work in connection with the Club in the Newcastle area is reflected in no small measure indeed in the Club's present enviable position, with a membership around the 1,000 mark, as one of the leading one-make-car-clubs in the country.

A message of regret was received from Mr. Norman Garrad, chairman of committee, absent on the Monte Carlo Rally, the while the gathering was delighted to have Mrs. Norman Garrad as a very charming deputy.

Specially welcome, too, were Mr. and Mrs. Jack Nutt, member of committee, Mr. and Mrs. R. F. Moffat, Mr. and Mrs. Vincent Edwards, Mr. and Mrs. " Joe " Hedworth, Mr. and Mrs. Geo. Hutchinson, Mr. and Mrs. D. Rankin, Dr. and Mrs. J. R. Steadman,

SPORTING SPOTLIGHTS
Club Notes and News

and Mrs. N. Rankin. We hope, Mrs. Rankin, that Norman is now fully recovered.

After an excellent dinner, there was dancing to the popular " Joe Q. Atkinson " dance band, whose unbroken enthusiasm for keeping the party " on their toes " helped enormously in the success of the evening.

* * *

THE 1952 Monte Carlo Rally will long be remembered for its outstanding British successes. British drivers and cars 1st and 2nd and British cars 4th, 5th and 6th has made an enormous impression in Continental circles and similar sweeping successes in the Concours de Confort has rather shattered the idea that some of our Continental friends were unapproachable in this particular feature.

Nor could two more popular figures have headed the list than Sydney Allard and Stirling Moss, the former an experienced rally driver and the latter temporarily switching over from racing to rallies seems to have proved that fast driving on snow and ice is very akin to four-wheel drifts on corners at Silverstone. No fewer than ten Sunbeam-Talbot, four Minx and one Humber were included in the 162 finishers.

* * *

OPINIONS still differ, and somewhat increasingly, in Club circles as to whether the present trend of trials is, after all, the right policy. All the principal club trials, with the exception of the M.C.C. classics, are now of such a nature that the ordinary car has been practically eliminated therefrom. With the increasing use of almost impossible sections on private land it is doubtful whether many of these trials still qualify as " road " trials at all. It was certainly a wise move for the B.T.D.A. to institute a Rally Championship " Star " as a counterpart to their " Trials " Gold Star. It should extend the membership considerably amongst the very large number of motorists who enjoy the atmosphere and not too easy conditions of a long rally, but are not a bit interested in the type of event which produces photographs of " Breezy Bill climbing a tree good and hard on a Greasy Gully."

* * *

THE Land's End Trial at Easter promises to be the usual imposing cavalcade of motor-cycles and cars. An interesting feature this year will be the participation, by invitation, of the Vintage Sports Car Club and the Vintage M.C.C., who will stage a 25 years' Commemoration Trial by following the 1927 route.

It may surprise some present-day competitors to learn the Porlock and Lynmouth (then in a very rough state), Beggars Roost and Bluehills Mine were all included in the 1927 route. These M.C.C. " Classics " are nowadays about the only events for long-distance enthusiasts who

(Concluded on page 46)

With the S.T.O.C. at Newcastle. Left : The Editor recounts some of the incidents in the Monte Carlo Rally, illustrated by a special photographic display prepared by Mr. Cliff Wheeler ; also pictures of Club members and friends in happy mood.

ANOTHER

Sunbeam-Talbot

SUCCESS

2nd

IN MONTE CARLO RALLY

AGAINST ALL COMERS IRRESPECTIVE OF

PRICE OR HORSE POWER

Driven by Stirling Moss

WITH DESMOND SCANNELL AND JOHN COOPER

(subject to official confirmation)

"A NOTABLE ADDITION TO THE RECORD OF SUNBEAM-TALBOTS IN INTERNATIONAL RALLIES" — The Times.

A ROOTES GROUP PRODUCT

OUR CONTINENTAL HOLIDAY RALLY

RALLYE "BRUNNEN" NEED NOT BE CANCELLED !

It can be facilitated within the new currency regulations and without drastic modifications:

It is up to you !

BECAUSE of the recent modifications in the foreign travel allowance schedules, we have necessarily reviewed the entire proposals for Rallye "Brunnen" as originally announced in the January issue of this Journal.

What at first threatened to erase all prospects of any project of the kind this year, we now find need not be met with quite that feeling of total frustration.

In short, it can be done, if modified in what amounts to quite modest proportions.

* * *

BRIEFLY, the changes amount to this : the length of the tour is reduced by three days only—making the stay at Brunnen seven nights instead of nine and making the journey home the one day less running time.

Outwardly the original plans remain unaltered, i.e., as far as Brunnen. Then, instead of departing on the Wednesday, July 30, Rallye "Brunnen" will leave on the morning of Monday, July 28, for Nancy.

Next day there is unavoidably a long run—the 240 miles to Arras. Which leaves only the 75 or so miles to cover on the 30th (or the Wednesday) for Calais to be reached by midday, crossing to Dover early afternoon.

* * *

SO keen has been the demand for accommodation on this special *Modern Motoring and Travel* Continental excursion—that is, until the Chancellor of the Exchequer introduced his potential "knock-out" to the scheme,—we believe the new itinerary, published in detail on this page, should not be unworthy of acceptance. Indeed, it still comprises a unique opportunity of providing, in spite of restrictions, a thoroughly worthwhile and enjoyable Continental visit.

* * *

FOR this still possible and quite attractive, modified Rallye "Brunnen" we are indebted especially to the tremendous endeavours of the Motorists Travel Club. They, like we, have left no stone unturned in order to preserve the hopes of our readers in this matter. We are convinced beyond doubt that it can still be done, and done well!

WHILE thanking all those who made early reservations in regard to the original scheme, it is our earnest hope that they, and others, will now give their full blessing to the new proposals.

* * *

FINANCIALLY this is the picture. Apart from the revised costs of Rallye "Brunnen," which can be paid in sterling, the spending powers, taking three in party, are made up as follows :—

Travel allowance, £25 each	...	£75
Car allowance	...	15
Sterling reserve, £5 each	...	15
		£105
Required for "V" form, at £15 each	...	45
		£60

So there is still the total of £60 to cover petrol and oil and spending money, and putting car costs at £15-£20 maximum, there remains, therefore, foreign currency up to £45 for personal spending, £15 each for the 12 days.

So, you see, it can be done !

* * *

STUDY now the detailed itinerary, the respective costs, and when you compare them with the original scheme, you will find only limited new restrictions.

May we ask, however, for early confirmation by those who (a) have already requested reservations and (b) intimation by any other reader anxious to participate.

Reservations should be directed, in the first place, to the Editor, *Modern Motoring and Travel*, 53, Stratton Street, Piccadilly, London, W.1, all requests being accompanied by a deposit of £10 per person.

(Continued on page 46)

COST PER PERSON :

No. of Persons In Car	Cost per person according to wheelbase			
	Under 8' 6"	8' 6"—9' 0"	9' 0"—9' 6"	9' 6"—10' 0"
4	£40 8 9	£40 15 9	£41 15 9	£43 0 9
3	£41 11 0	£42 4 0	£43 11 0	£46 3 8
2	£43 19 6	£44 19 6	£46 19 6	£47 9 6

Supplement for single rooms £3 per person. The foreign currency required £15 per person (£18 for a person using a single room).

WHAT THE PRICES INCLUDE :

1. Outward transport of car at owner's risk in the Car Ferry from Dover to Calais.
2. Homeward transport of car at owner's risk in the Car Ferry from Calais to Dover.
3. Out and home passenger tickets by the above service.
4. A.A./R.A.C. Foreign Touring Documents for the car, customs insurance, etc.
5. G.B. Plate.
6. A.A./R.A.C. Port service charges outwards and homewards.
7. Landing and embarkation charges.
8. Dinner, room, continental breakfast at St. Quentin, Gerardmer, Nancy and Arras.
9. Dinner, room, continental breakfast and luncheon, or picnic lunch for seven nights at Brunnen.
10. All gratuities to hotel servants in respect of accommodation and meals provided.
11. All Government taxes and taxe de séjour.
12. Detailed itinerary for the entire tour.
13. Road maps, covering the whole route.
14. Services of a Courier from departure from Dover on the first day until arrival back at Dover on the last day.
15. A qualified mechanic and a spare part service will be provided throughout the entire tour.

SPECIAL NOTES

SINGLE ROOMS AND ROOMS WITH PRIVATE BATHROOMS

It is always possible to obtain a certain number of single rooms, but they are few compared with the number of rooms containing two beds or a large bed. You are, therefore, asked not to demand single rooms unless it is absolutely essential.

Although no guarantee can be given as to the numbers available, it is certain that some of the accommodation will consist of rooms with private bathroom. These will be distributed as fairly as possible. In most cases a private bathroom can usually be secured by the payment of a supplementary charge.

How to Dirt-Proof YOUR ENGINE OIL

and prevent THIS

Dirty oil wastes your money. It clogs piston-ring slots, gums-up valve stem guides and constricts oil passages.

Your AC Oil Filter goes on filtering out the clogging sludge, dirt and grit which grind away engine efficiency — until the element is *packed solid*. A fresh A.C. Element at least *every 8,000 miles* means fewer repair bills . . . greatly reduced engine wear . . . less frequent oil changes.

Get your local Humber-Hillman Agent or any good garage to change your AC Filter Element at least every 8,000 miles.

REPLACEMENT ELEMENTS

Humber-Hawk 1948-9 L11—11/-	Sunbeam Talbot 2-Litre 1947-48-49 1948-50 "90" L11—11/-
Super-Snipe and Pullman 1948-50 K11—12/6	1948-50 10 HP &"80" L14—9/6

MINX OWNERS! Your agent can now fit the approved AC Oil Filter to your car.

AC Oil Filters

AC-SPHINX SPARK PLUG CO., DIVISION OF GENERAL MOTORS LTD., DUNSTABLE, ENGLAND

The apple and the downfall!

It happened when he reached out too far for a large apple and came down from the tree with an almighty crash! He couldn't walk again for months, but the accident taught him something. Lying in bed while his business expenses mounted, he learned the true value of his 'General' Personal Accident Policy.

Peace of mind costs very little

£4 a year covers business and professional men for £10 a week accident benefit (and pro rata). Similar attractive rates for other occupations. It's worth while finding out more about this and other benefits of the 'General' Personal Accident Policies—just send the coupon.

General

ACCIDENT FIRE & LIFE ASSURANCE CORPORATION LTD

General Buildings, Perth, Scotland

PA/8

Please send me full particulars of 'General' Personal Accident Policies.

NAME

OCCUPATION

ADDRESS

M.M.

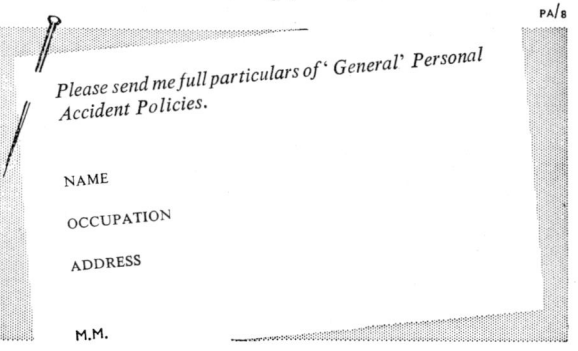

FAMOUS FOR ALL CLASSES OF INSURANCE

Our Modified, but still attractive, Continental Rally: *(Concluded from page 44)*

Official entry forms will be sent by return—this first approach being necessary in order to book hotel and other facilities *en route*.

* * *

WE shall, of necessity, have to decide early as to the ultimate going through with the Rallye in relation to the numbers of participants. You can help, therefore, in making all the emergency plans—and they will comprise to make a thoroughly enjoyable holiday.

* * *

AMENDED RALLYE "BRUNNEN"
Visiting France and Switzerland
12 days inclusive, from £40.8.9 per person

Saturday, July 19: Cross the channel in the car ferry and commence the road journey via St. Omer to spend the night at St. Quentin. 115 miles. Hotel Moderne et Commerce.

Sunday, July 20: A goodish day's run via the central city of Rheims, across the moors to Bar-le-Duc and thence via Neufchateau, Epinal and Remiremont to spend the night in the centre of the Vosges Mountains to Gerardmer. 225 miles. Hotel Beau Rivage.

Monday, July 21: Leave Gerardmer and descend to the plains thence via the Col du Bussang Pass through Mulhouse to cross the Swiss frontier at Basle. Continue via Leistal and Olten to Lucerne and thence follow the shore of the Lake via Kussnacht and Weggis to spend seven nights at Brunnen. 170 miles. Hotel Waldstatterhof.

Tuesday, July 22 to Sunday, July 27: At Leisure. Brunnen is a delightful holiday resort, situated on Lake Lucerne and is an excellent centre for local excursions such as:—

(1) A steamer trip to Lucerne returning either by steamer or train.
(2) The three passes—the new Susten; the Grimsel; the Furka with the Rhone.
(3) A day in Zürich shopping and sightseeing.
(4) Ascend by mountain railway to the summit of the Rigi.
(5) A day's run via the Susten Pass to Interlaken and Grindelwald returning via the Brunig Pass and Lucerne.

Monday, July 28: Leave Brunnen and proceed via Zürich and Baden to Basle and cross the frontier into France for Mulhouse and Epinal to spend the night at Nancy. 210 miles. Grand Hotel.

Tuesday, July 29: Leave Nancy and proceed via Verdun, Sedan and Cambrai to spend the night at Arras. 240 miles. Hotel Moderne.

Wednesday, July 30: Leave Arras and proceed via Bethune and St. Omer to embark on the car ferry at 12 noon for Dover. 75 miles.

Total mileage, approximately, and without tours while at Brunnen—1,035

Sporting Spotlights:
(Concluded from page 42)

like something a little more sporting than the average rally yet within the capabilities of ordinary standard vehicles. Entries close March 15th.

* * *

THE B.R.D.C. are getting on with the big job of replacing Silverstone track. This involves the re-siting of the grandstand and pits to a position near Woodcote Corner, the erection of various other semi-permanent structures, resurfacing of parts of the track and the hundred and one other items which are making the job one of some magnitude. A full programme of meetings has been booked—four public meetings and sixteen club events. The former consist of the *Daily Express* International Trophy, May 10th, the R.A.C. British Grand Prix, July 19, and two motor-cycle (B.M.C.R.C.) meetings will be seen over the full perimeter course. The club meetings will be run over a new course based on Woodcote Corner.

* * *

A GLANCE at the R.A.C. Calendar of events for 1952 shows the enormous popularity of motor sport. No less than 701 events are listed, including race meetings, rallies, trials, hill-climbs and driving tests. No wonder the R.A.C. view the promotion of new clubs and new events with concern.

MODERN MOTORING & TRAVEL

EVERY car owner and user, or travel-minded reader, should read "MODERN MOTORING & TRAVEL" regularly; a Journal devoted wholly to his, or her, interests.

To avoid delay and/or disappointment, make sure of your copy, month by month, by becoming a subscriber.

Subscription, per annum, post free, 11s. 6d. Fill in the form provided and post, together with your remittance, at once.

The Manager,
"MODERN MOTORING & TRAVEL,"
53, Stratton Street, Piccadilly,
London, W.1

Please enrol me as a subscriber for twelve months commencing with the next issue.

Name..

Address..

Date........................   Mar. '52

Products of the ROOTES GROUP

For Good Service!

GEO. T. HILTON & CO. LTD.
NORTH STREET · RUGBY
Telephone: 2291

HUMBER · HILLMAN
SUNBEAM-TALBOT
CARS

COMMER · KARRIER
TRUCKS

BUILT FOR THE ROADS OF THE WORLD

You can order by post —with confidence!

MUFFETTE
A winter necessity that promotes easy starting, smooth running and saves on petrol. With three-position adjustable flap. Neat, efficient, easy to fit. Supplied by post for all cars. When ordering, please state make, model, year and h.p.

Send for latest price list.

ARMREST
for bench-type seats

An independent accessory, simply hooked over bench-type seats to any desired position. Saves driving fatigue. Also acts as a useful container for gloves, maps, etc. In standard colours to match upholstery. 40/- each.

Send for illustrated leaflets.

Weathershields Ltd
BISHOP ST., BIRMINGHAM 5 · ENGLAND

Well sir ... ... there's no excuse for a speedometer not working ...when you can buy

Nobby
UNIVERSAL SPEEDOMETER ASSEMBLIES
at any up-to date **SERVICE STATION**

Nobby Flexible Pipes for Petrol and Oil Lines packed "5 in a box" offer maximum service from minimum stock. Full range — British and American vehicles.

Made for Nobby by The S.S. White Co. of Great Britain Ltd.—the world's largest manufacturers of speedometer assemblies for British and American cars.

Please write for details and full information.

WILLIAM CLARK (SPARE PARTS) LIMITED.
NOBBY WORKS · HEDLEY ROAD · St ALBANS · HERTS.

STYLE, ELEGANCE DURABILITY

ROOTES CAR SEAT COVERS

Tailor-made from highest quality materials, they offer the following advantages:

ADDED COMFORT

GOOD LOOKS AND SHAPE

PREVENTION OF SHINE TO PERSONAL CLOTHING

CAN BE DRY CLEANED BY APPROVED PROCESSES

AVAILABLE IN A VARIETY OF COLOURS

Patterns available on application to Dept. M.M.

ROOTES

LADBROKE HALL, BARLBY RD., LONDON, W.10.
Tel. LADbroke 3232

BIRMINGHAM	90/94 Charlotte Street	Central 8411
MANCHESTER	Olympia, Chester Road	Blackfriars 6677
MAIDSTONE	Mill Street	Maidstone 3333
ROCHESTER	High Street	Chatham 2231
CANTERBURY	The Pavilion	Canterbury 3232
WROTHAM	Wrotham Heath	Borough Green 4
FOLKESTONE	86/92 Tontine Street	Folkestone 3156

and from all Rootes Group Distributors and Dealers

LOOKING BACK

(Concluded from page 20)

---

20 of the 328 starters in the Rally were still unpenalised at this point. For the first time we realised that we were in the running.

* * *

AFTER the section from Valence to Digne, which Desmond and I shared between us, came the notorious passes between Digne and Grasse. But this time, although slippery, the surfaces were not especially difficult, and Stirling took them in his stride. The worst was now over.

After a brief stop at Nice to check over the car and refuel for the last time, we arrived at Monte Carlo. We learned that only 15 other competitors had finished the road section without penalisation; the regularity test loomed ahead.

The wait on the Sunday morning for the test to begin was the worst part of it all. The Sunbeam-Talbot had been inaccessible in the *parc fermé*, but we had managed to practice for a lap or two on a borrowed car, to find our timing schedule disrupted by the disappearance in the snow of many of our check points.

When we screamed away up La Turbie on the actual test, the course had been made even more difficult by a night snowfall.

* * *

TWO minutes ahead of us was Wisdom's Daimler, but when we caught up with him just before the first control on the dangerous Col de Braus, he pulled the huge car right over to let us through.

At this check we were within six seconds of our scheduled time. At the second fixed check, after reaching the top of the Col de Braus a little late and hurtling through the snow and slush to make up the deficit, we were dead on time; but owing to an error in the official chronometers this control was omitted from the final reckoning.

* * *

WHEN we reached the tunnel at the entrance to Castillon, we reckoned ourselves to be within three seconds of our correct time, so accurately had Stirling maintained his speed along the narrow stretch of snow-bound road, although the odometer had already gained one kilometre through wheelspin. But here the road was a sheet of ice, and the Sunbeam-Talbot's nose buried itself into the snowdrift at the entrance of the tunnel.

Spectators willingly pushed us out, while the wheels spun uselessly in reverse, and Desmond counted on his stop watch each second we were losing. Then Stirling was away again, hurtling down the Col de Castillon at a tremendous speed.

* * *

ALL depended now on the location of the secret check, for if this were after our mishap, there was no point—and in fact more penalty—in regaining the time we had lost.

We decided, therefore, to equalise as far as possible the amount of error by making up half of our lost time. As it turned out, the secret check was on this downhill run, and we finished 28 seconds early on the section therefrom to the finish.

There were then five hours of waiting for the result to be announced; five hours of endeavouring to appear unconcerned, until Stirling rushed through the revolving doors of the Hotel Metropole—but that is where I started, and the Monte Carlo Rally for 1952 is over.

IN A FEW WORDS:

News Items of Modern Motoring and Travel Interest

IN 1951 the exports of the British motor industry brought in overseas exchange to the value of £317 millions.

This sum, states the Society of Motor Manufacturers and Traders, was equal to the cost to this country of the million tons of meat, 300,000 tons of butter, and 1,400 million eggs imported for our daily rations for the year.

* * *

A NEW "low fare" daily air service between Canada and Europe will be introduced by Trans-Canada Air Lines on May 1. The London to Montreal return fare drops from £244 19s. to £170 7s., a saving of £74 12s.

* * *

THE "X-RAY MINX," show-piece of the International Motor Exhibition in London, last year, is being exhibited by the Rootes Group at the Los Angeles Motor Show this month.

* * *

FOR THE FOURTH successive year Silver City Airways have reduced their fares for flying motor-cars across the Channel.

The new rates cut up to 20 per cent. on the 47-mile route from Lympne to Le Touquet. Rates on the 92-mile Southampton/Cherbourg service, opened last month, are comparably low.

* * *

MR. KARL KOBELT, the new Swiss President, is to perform the opening ceremony at the Geneva Motor Show, which is being held from March 20 to 30.

The complete range of Humber, Hillman and Sunbeam-Talbot cars and Commer and Karrier commercial vehicles will be on show. The Rootes Group will also exhibit a working engineering model.

THE ROYAL AERO CLUB announces that the 1952 King's Cup Air Race is to be flown on July 12, from Newcastle-upon-Tyne municipal airport.

* * *

MOTORISTS are warned by the R.A.C. that frost strikes suddenly, and the results may well be costly.

Anti-freeze is recommended, and before the solution is put into the radiator the system should be well flushed out with clean water to remove any sediment. All cylinder nuts and hose connections should be checked for tightness.

* * *

LAST YEAR more than one in four British motorists who asked the A.A. for holiday routes abroad were destined for Spain.

The big expansion of State inns, which cost the tourist a little more than £1 a day full pension, will enable the British motorist to stay longer in Spain for his £25 than in any other Continental country.

* * *

OVERSEAS students attending the newly opened Rootes Group School, at Coventry, Warwickshire, took part in the Midlands' magazine programme, "Around and About," broadcast recently from the B.B.C. Midlands station.

The B.B.C. interviewer, Mr. "Bill" Hartley, spoke to students from Canada,

Miss Patricia Laffan, who plays the part of Poppaea in "Quo Vadis," attended the London premiere of the film. She travelled in a Humber Pullman Limousine.

Part of a fleet of Commer "forward control" brewers' lorries operated by Messrs. John Smith's Tadcaster Brewery, Ltd. The lorry on right has covered 110,000 miles and has not yet been decarbonised.

LET **PRATT TRAILERS** SOLVE YOUR TRANSPORT PROBLEMS

LEADERS IN THEIR CLASS!

2 to 5 CWT. CARRYING CAPACITY

THE PRATT ENGINEERING COMPANY NORTHALLERTON YORKS. TEL.: 142

INVITATION TO READERS

PAPER supplies restrict the number of copies of *Modern Motoring & Travel*. Supplies to newsagents and booksellers are quickly sold.

"Guarantee" a copy each month by becoming a regular subscriber. There are a few vacancies on the subscribers' list.

Send your subscription (11/6d., post free, per annum) to The Manager, *Modern Motoring & Travel*, 53, Stratton St., Piccadilly, London, W.1.

MODERN MOTORING & TRAVEL

IN A FEW WORDS:
(Concluded from page 49)

British West Indies, British West Africa, India and Pakistan.

Mr. S. H. Turner, Chief Instructor at the school, said the Parts and Service training given was important in relation to the export drive.

Since the school has been in operation, students have come from all over the world.

* * *

TOURIST earnings, including fare payments to British carriers, have risen from an estimated level of £40 million in 1938 to £104 million in 1951. There are indications that 1952 will prove the best year ever for American traffic.

* * *

"TEACH yourself Motoring," by Dudley Noble, explains clearly and simply all that an ordinary motorist needs to know about a car and its use on the road. For the novice and the inexperienced motorist, here is advice from a motoring journalist well qualified to advise.

English Universities Press, Ltd., price 6s.

* * *

A SECOND skilift has been constructed at Norefjell, Norway's latest winter resort. It climbs 215 metres up the mountain side.

* * *

THE eighth International Music Festival in Geneva will be held from September 22 to October 5. Last year 218 candidates from 29 countries took part.

* * *

ONE of the valuable but less known services of the R.A.C. is its constant endeavour to improve road conditions in the interests of the motoring community.

During 1951 satisfaction was obtained in 329 cases taken up with highway authorities. The majority of cases concerned signposting, obstructions and road surfaces.

* * *

MR. R. GRESHAM COOKE, Director of the Society of Motor Manufacturers and Traders, has been admitted to Fellowship of the Institute of Industrial Administration. This, in turn, conferred upon him Founder membership of the British Institution of Management.

* * *

MR. WILLIAM SIMPSON, O.B.E., D.F.C., acting Public Relations Officer for B.E.A., has been confirmed in that appointment with the new title of Chief Press and Information Officer.

Mr. Norman Ryder has been appointed to be his deputy, with the title of Senior Press Officer.

* * *

"CARBURETTERS and the Fuel System," by E. P. Willoughby, B.Sc., M.I.Mech.E., C.A.E., comprises part five of the series, "The Modern Car Easy Guide." Published by Temple Press, Ltd., price 2s.

* * *

SHELL-MEX and B.P., Ltd., have published a pictorial map of the Lake District, the Poets' Corner of England, illustrating some of the many interesting sights to be seen there.

* * *

THERE are still a few special *Modern Motoring & Travel* binder cases available. These hold up to twelve copies of this journal and permit all pages of respective issues to open flat—see full details as advertised on page 2 of this month's cover. Order now before too late: the opportunity will not be repeated.

Messrs. Brown, Muff & Co., Ltd., one of Bradford's largest departmental stores, employ this Commer 25 cwt. "forward control" van to give television demonstrations in the district. Collapsible 35 feet aerial equipment is carried on the roof. The van, which is tastefully fitted out inside with seats for four viewers, was supplied by the Thornton Engineering Co., Ltd., Rootes Group distributors, of Bradford.

Reception counter at the new Rootes Group Parts Service Division at N'Dabeni, Cape Town, South Africa. Below: Operators in the Stock Control office.

October, 1952   Page 3

KARRIER "BANTAM"

with phenomenal life chrome finished cylinder bores

A two-ton tipper that meets every short haul need

OPERATING EFFICIENCY. Low loading height saves handling time and energy. Full forward control, with cab over front springs and power unit forward of front axle, provides exceptional bodyspace and balanced load distribution.

STURDY AND POWERFUL. Chrome finished cylinder bores, simplicity of design, and precision finish give phenomenal engine life, whilst chassis, body and cab are all built to endure the most gruelling working conditions.

ECONOMICAL PERFORMANCE. The Karrier 'Bantam's' combination of strength, lightness and accessibility reduce both running and maintenance costs to a low level.

Salient Features

★ 48 b.h.p. engine embodies long life chrome finished bores.

★ Full forward control, with over 11 ft. bodyspace.

★ Bodywork cleared of obstructing wheel arches.

★ Low loading frame of pressed steel.

★ Exceptional manœuvrability; 30 ft. turning circle.

★ Powerful hydraulic brakes.

★ Comfortable all-steel cab.

A PRODUCT OF THE ROOTES GROUP

SEE THE KARRIERS ON STAND 75 AT EARLS COURT, SEPT. 26–OCT. 4.

A CAR LOOKS AS NEW AS ITS CARPETS!

★

NEAT, PERFECT FITTING, LASTING.

Obtain complete car-interior cleanliness. Put into position or removed without fuss; design and finish in keeping with car's key-note of quality.

They are constructed of laminated rubberised cotton fabric, woven together on galvanised steel wires,
GUARANTEED FOR TEN YEARS.

FREE TRIAL OFFER

PRICES:

Humber Hawk 1950/51:	£ s. d.	Hillman Minx 1950/51 (Phase IV):	£ s. d.	Sunbeam-Talbot "80" and "90":	£ s. d.
Front Mats	2 2 0	Front Mats	2 3 10	Front Mats	1 16 7
Rear Mats	2 3 6	Rear Mats	1 18 5	Rear Mats	1 17 9
	4 5 6		4 2 3		3 14 4
Purchase Tax	1 1 4	Purchase Tax	1 0 7	Purchase Tax	0 18 7
	5 6 10		5 2 10		4 12 11

Fill in this coupon and post to The Universal Mat Co., Ltd., Tileyard Road, York Way, London, N.7.

Please send me on a week's free trial

Front pair mats ....⎫ Please mark
Back pair mats ....⎬ here set
Complete set mats ....⎭ required.

for.........h.p. Make............Year............

Signed (Name) ....

Address ....

Date............... ....

sign this coupon on the distinct understanding that I am at liberty to return the mats any time within one week of receipt. If retained, I undertake to pay for mats within thirty days net.

THIS OFFER APPLIES TO U.K. ONLY

Protect Your Carpets with UNIVERSAL CAR MATS

Touch — and it goes!

No pumping, no pulling. Just a momentary touch of the button, and two jets of water give your screen a wash. Cuts out automatically. There's *nothing* so simple as a TRICO Windscreen Washer, for keeping your windscreen dirt-free, bright and safe. Cleans both left and right hand sides. Quickly installed in any car, old or new, and operated by free power from the induction pipe.

ONLY 49/6 COMPLETE

TRAVEL WITH

TRICO AUTOMATIC WINDSCREEN WASHER

and clean your windscreen on the move!

TRICO-FOLBERTH LTD., GREAT WEST ROAD, BRENTFORD, MIDDX.

Light and HEAVY PRESSINGS

OF ALL TYPES IN ALL METALS

A.E. JENKS & CATTELL Limited

PHOENIX WORKS, WEDNESFIELD, WOLVERHAMPTON.

You get so much more in the MINX

and you get so much more out of it

The Minx includes more headroom, 5-seater comfort, double-dipping headlamps, lighter steering and weatherproofed brake drums. Refinements in styling and attractive new colour schemes, added to outstanding Minx performance and economy, complete 20 years' continuous development.

THE HILLMAN MINX

SALOON · COUPE · ESTATE CAR *Craftsman Built by the Rootes Group*

HILLMAN MOTOR CAR CO. LTD. COVENTRY.   LONDON SHOWROOMS & EXPORT DIVISION ROOTES LTD. DEVONSHIRE HOUSE PICCADILLY W.1

Prepare for Winter NOW!

For more than a quarter of a century Desmo Anti-Freeze has protected motorists from expensive repairs. This high grade Anti-Freeze mixture will protect YOU. Desmo E.-G. Anti-Freeze is extensively used by H.M. Government Departments and is stocked by garages offering first class service facilities. Do not ask for Anti-Freeze.

INSIST on
DESMO ETHYLENE GLYCOL
and be safe

RETAIL PRICE **65/-** PER GALLON

DESMO LTD.
BIRMINGHAM 7
Telephone: ASTON CROSS 2831/2/3

London Showroom:
SHAFTESBURY AVENUE, W.C.2
(Adjacent to Princes Theatre)
Telephone: Temple Bar 1994/5

Quick-fitting grille attachment

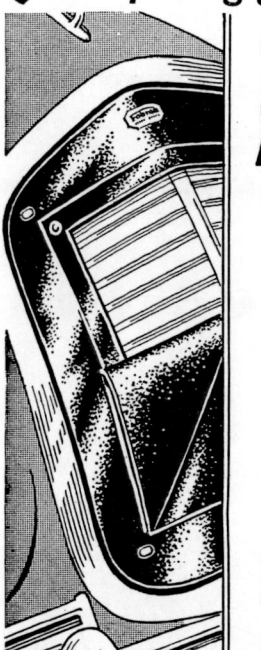

Fabram MINIMUFS
Patented

★ The Best winter safeguard against frost and engine damage.

★ Ensures quick starting and minimum of wear and strain.

★ Sturdily made; triple material throughout, clean tailored lines, reinforced seams; fixed in a few moments with patented quick-action attachment.

★ DELIVERY FROM STOCK FOR ALL POPULAR MODELS

PRICES (retail)

Humber (all models) 40/-
Hillman Minx (all models) .. 35/-
Sunbeam-Talbot (all models) .. 35/-

Also FABRAM RADIATOR MUFFS; all popular models at current prices from stock.

FAXALL PRODUCTS LTD.
BLACKLEDGE WORKS ·· HALIFAX
Telephone: Halifax 5208   Telegrams: FAXALL, Halifax

MODERN MOTORING & TRAVEL

EVERY car owner and user, or travel-minded reader, should read "MODERN MOTORING AND TRAVEL" regularly; a Journal devoted wholly to his, or her interests.

To avoid delay and/or disappointment, make sure of your copy, month by month, by becoming a subscriber.

Subscription, per annum, post free, 11s. 6d. Fill in the form provided and post, together with your remittance, at once.

The Manager,
"MODERN MOTORING & TRAVEL"
53, Stratton Street, Piccadilly,
London, W.1

Please enrol me as a subscriber for twelve months commencing with the next issue.

Name..

Address..

Date...............   ....

Oct. '52

Modern Motoring & Travel

Prominent Personalities and their Cars

At the International Court of Justice, The Hague.

Photographs show His Excellency, Mr. B. Winiarski, of the International Court, with his Humber Hawk Saloon at the Palace of Peace.

Supplied through the N.V. Internationale Automobiel Maatschappij.

Photograph taken on the occasion of the visit of H.R.H. Princess Margaret to Norwich recently, here seen leaving the City Hall with the Lord Mayor en route to Assembly House for luncheon. A fleet of Humber Pullman Limousines was provided by the Norwich Motor Co., Ltd., in arrangement with Humber, Ltd.

The new showrooms of Natal Motor Industries, Ltd., Rootes Group distributors in Durban. Supporting the former chairman and founder, Mr. Dave Campbell-Brown and Mrs. Campbell-Brown (seated) at the opening ceremony were S. Spiro, director; P. Fagin, of S.A. Motor Assemblies, Ltd.; J. B. McIntosh, general manager; M. S. Brookes, managing director, S.A. Motor Assemblies, Ltd.; F. T. Riley, director and general manager, Rootes (Pty.), Ltd.; and E. S. Mennell, chairman, Natal Motor Industries, Ltd.

Editorial Comment

EDITORIAL AND ADVERTISING
53 STRATTON STREET,
LONDON, W.1
Telephone: GRO 3401

Conducted by E. D. O'BRIEN

Editor: THOMAS R. MULCASTER

WE publish this month two well-deserved tributes. Number one goes to that team of intrepid trials' drivers, George Murray-Frame, Stirling Moss and Mike Hawthorn, who, handling their Sunbeam-Talbots so magnificently in the recent Rallye Internationale des Alpes, gained an unprecedented, all-in success for Great Britain.

The second bouquet goes to " Mr. and Mrs. Reader and family," who, taking part in " Rallye Brunnen " and handling production cars of similar design, over almost identical terrain and with admirable if less spectacular dexterity, gives the practical answer to the question, which is always cropping up, " What good do rallies, endurance tests and road racing do for the ordinary motorist and his car ? "

A 2,000 miles Alpine circuit, covered at high speed, down as well as up in a course varying from sea level to 10,000 feet above, will assuredly bring to light all physical shortcomings as well as quickly eliminate any but the soundest mechanical propositions. The Sunbeam-Talbots' triple achievement—First, Second and Third in its Class, securing also the coveted team trophies—is all the more commendable, therefore. The lessons learned, particularly those connected with engine power, steering, braking and shock-absorber efficiency and in mechanical reliability and safety are incorporated in the standard model. This is the interest the ordinary motorist has in Murray-Frame, Moss and Hawthorn and the cars they handled.

Both angles : (a) research applied in competitive effort, and (b) proof of the benefits to the ordinary motorist, are emphasised within these pages—in the epic story, (opening on page 19), of the official Alpine trials and, (commencing on page 42), that of the concerted "passstorming " experiences of private owners during " Rallye Brunnen," the Continental tour conducted by this Journal.

If Britain's success in the former impressed the world, " Rallye Brunnen "—made up of 20 first-time visitors to the Continent, who, at their very first attempt, made perfect, trouble-free crossings of the Furka, Grimsel, Susten and Klausen Passes, certainly took Switzerland by surprise.

The direct links between designer, manufacturer, competition driver and ordinary motorist could scarcely be better demonstrated.

BY APPOINTMENT
TO THE LATE KING GEORGE VI,
MOTOR CAR TYRE MANUFACTURERS

DUNLOP 'FORT'

In a class by itself

Archery is staging a spectacular "come-back," says

G. Bernard Wood

Twenty-five women archers from various parts of the country compete at Cheltenham, at a three-day meeting held by the Hereford Round of Archers.

ARCHERY provides a thrilling spectacle, whether one enjoys it retrospectively in such historic records as the Bayeux Tapestry—or in real life, to-day!

This Royal and Ancient Sport—which actually fostered golf!—has a great and an ever-growing number of devotees. All over the British Isles (and in the U.S.A.) the twang of the bow and the strange speech which the sport has promoted are being heard again.

Consider just a few of the archery societies now in existence. Their names fall on the ear like an echo from some bygone forest meet: Kingswood Bowmen, Scorton Archers, Dukeries Archers, Bowmen of Epping Forest, Archers of Taunton Deane, Ascham Bowmen, Archers of Bradford Dale.... A full list of Britain's archery societies would run to well over 150 names.

Some societies, such as the Royal Toxopholites and the Kilwinning Archery Society, can boast a great antiquity; others are the product of the remarkable post-war boom.

* * *

Usually a steel bow

VISITORS are generally welcomed at different meetings, these often being advertised in the local Press and also in *The British Archer* (published bi-monthly, from The Portals, Grove Road, Fareham, Hants.).

The ground itself may be part of a sports field. Some societies, however, enjoy a prouder setting. The Middlesbrough Archery Club shoots in the grounds of Ormesby Hall, while members of the Warwick Archery Club re-make history by assembling within a bow-shot of Warwick Castle.

Miss Joan Kite of Suttons Archers Club, takes aim. Note left wrist guarded by leather.

Probably equipped with steel bow and arrows (though some still favour bows of hickory or yew), many of the contestants will be garbed in Lincoln green. As procedure varies, it is always wise to make one's enquiries concerning "rounds" and other technical points from one of the scorers, or some other official on the ground.

Mastery of the archer's peculiar terminology only comes with time and experience, but one soon falls into the way of saying "loosing a shaft" rather than "shooting an arrow," and "piercing the gold" instead of "scoring a bull's-eye."

Even a straightforward contest, with the conventional butts of plaited straw in use, can yield almost as much pleasure to the informed spectator as to the archers themselves. Some societies, however, have their own peculiar "shoot" to heighten the interest.

There was a time when a society of West Essex Archers shot at effigies instead of ordinary targets, one of the favourite effigies being that of the Bishop of St. Andrews! The Kilwinning Archers (Scotland) recently revived their traditional Popinjay, or Papingo, Shoot, which originated in 1482. The popinjay is placed at the top of a 105-feet high tower at Kilwinning Abbey, and while shooting each archer has to rest one foot against the tower.

* * *

Striking trophies

MANY archers are now showing a greater interest in the history of the sport, and perhaps nothing is more likely to focus that interest than the beautiful, and sometimes singular trophies awarded by different societies.

Take the Kilwinning Trophy. This is a silver bow 3 feet long, to which are attached silver arrows and no fewer than

117 medals that trace the story of the society back to 1698.

At the Scorton Arrow Meeting (held at various places in Yorkshire during August or September) there are several highly coveted trophies. One is the Antient Silver Arrow itself, traditionally given by Elizabeth I as an archery prize to the Oxford Colleges, and later acquired by the Scorton Archers.

Another is the Thirsk Bugle, decorated with animals of the chase; and a third—really a booby prize awarded for the "worst white" (the white is the outer ring of the target)—is a horn spoon.

Then there is the Sheriff of Nottingham's Golden Arrow, competed for annually in the best Sherwood manner.

Amongst the newer trophies are the Wicker Arrow, awarded by the Abbeydale Archers of Sheffield to commemorate the old Wicker archery ground where wickerwork targets were the vogue; the Robin Hood Cup, awarded by the Exeter Company of Archers; and the Ascham Bugle, which reminds the Ascham Bowmen of Walthamstow that Roger Ascham —author of "Toxophilus" (1545), a famous treatise on archery—lived for a time at Walthamstow.

* * *

—and badge designs

THIS sense of history, inseparable from any study of archery, is increasingly being expressed in badge designs of the newer societies.

For example, the badge of the Archers of Theydon Bois incorporates a bow and arrow and two cattle-brands as used centuries ago in Epping Forest. The wild boar that once plagued Bradford folk, and for whose head the Government of the day offered a reward, has been chosen as their emblem by the Archers of Bradford Dale.

William of Normandy's all-conquering archers at the Battle of Hastings are recalled by the embattled ship, enclosed within a braced bow, adopted by the Cinque Port Archers. And the recently formed Company of Scorton Archers (distinct from the original Scorton Archers) summons the memory of Sir Hugh Calverley—first winner of the Scorton Arrow, in 1673—by portraying his coat-of-arms and the Thirsk Bugle on their badge.

Some novel developments

THE revival of archery has brought several novel developments. One is the Field Shoot, designed to reproduce as far as possible medieval archery conditions when deer provided the chief forest targets.

In May this year the Ulster Archery Association held a Field Shoot on the Dufferin Estate, where the obstacles to be negotiated before the targets came within range included bogs and lakes, cliffs and ditches, and thick undergrowth. Robin Hood conditions, no less!

Similar "shoots" are sometimes arranged, appropriately enough, in the New Forest. Even the sparsely wooded area around Hull staged a Field Shoot not long ago, the Bowmen of Holderness assembling on the site of Meaux Abbey to shoot from a variety of standpoints at stag heads mounted on poles.

"Roving" Archery is somewhat similar. Two or more archers rove through field or woodland choosing targets such as trees or shrubs as they go along. Only one arrow is allowed for each target, and he whose arrow comes nearest the mark chooses the next target. Clout shooting offers the archer further variety. Here the ring target is marked out in enlarged form on the ground, necessitating some accurate drop shots if one of those trophies is to be carried off.

Some societies provide an amusing interlude by releasing a number of balloons and then shooting at them as they career over the ground. Darts versus arrows is another diversion. The dartboard will be painted on a 4-feet diameter target, darts players shooting at the customary range of 8 feet and archers at 60 feet or more.

Other clubs are even experimenting with archery cricket, using a target showing wickets which the "bowler" tries to hit; meanwhile the opposing "batsman" scores on another target as quickly as possible until the first target registers his dismissal.

Contests between archers and golfers are now very popular. For each type of player the procedure is similar, arrow competing against ball, until the green is reached. Here, the archer, instead of trying to "hole" his arrow, takes aim at a fluffy ball, or a small cardboard disc, placed beside the golfer's hole.

* * *

Realistic in pageantry

HISTORIC pageants can be so much more realistic now that there are archers who can not only dress for the part, but who can really "loose an arrow" and find the target, thus making a forest glade or Tudor archery ground come to life. For the Festival of Britain members of several archery clubs found themselves in great demand.

One pageant, staged by the Borough of Surbiton and televised, depicted the visit of Queen Elizabeth I (Moira Lister) to an exhibition of archery in the grounds of Burnt Stub Hall. The Queen's known interest in archery was well expressed when the Master Bowman of England (Frank Bilson of the Harrow Bowmen) placed bow and arrow in her hands and showed her how to use them.

Another pageant, centring upon the luckless Lady Jane Grey and her father, the Duke of Northumberland, introduced a motley array of yokels who formed the local defence force. An inspection parade ending as a fiasco, the Duke calls for a demonstration of archery to stabilise the occasion. The three archers who step forward (all members of the Kirby Muxloe Archery Club) are welcomed by Roger Ascham, who expounds his five points for "fayre shootynge."

Roger concludes the episode by reciting the following prayer from his book, "Toxophilus":—

"*And thus I praye God that al fletchers (arrow makers) getting theyre lyvynge truly, and al archers usynge shootynge honestly, and al maner of men that favour artillery, maye lyve continuallye in healthe and merinesse, obeying theyr prince as they shulde, and loving God as they ought, to whom for al thinges be al honour and glorye for ever. Amen.*"

Lulla Lohmann, of Denmark, and Colette Beday (right), of France, inspect their marks at the 12th International Archery Tournament on the playing fields of Dulwich College, London.

In the archer's peculiar terminology, scoring a bull's-eye is "piercing the gold."

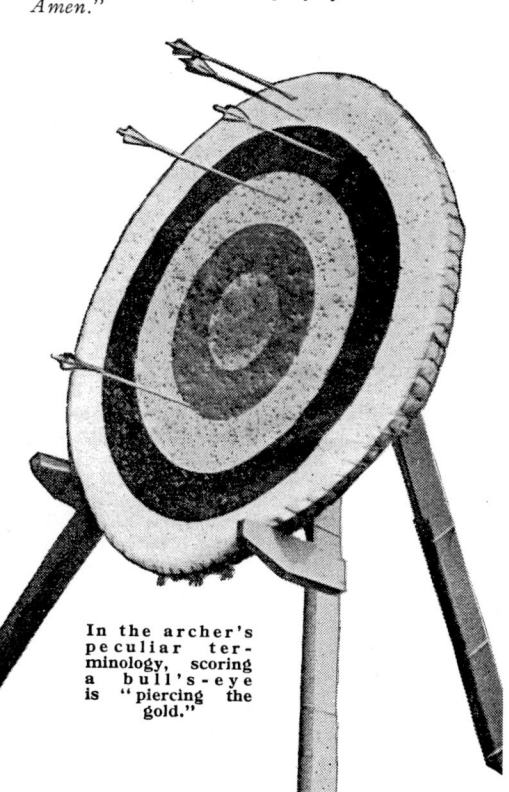

Try this joke

BORROW half a crown (or should I call it half a dollar?), press it firmly against the wallpaper of your expensive flat (or is it apartment), then draw it smartly down for a few inches and gently remove your hand.

The coin sticks, partly because friction has warmed the rough surface and allowed its frayed parts to adhere and partly because air is excluded so that the atmosphere can press upon it and hold it to the wall.

This is a good lesson as to the forces which hold back an aeroplane. Most of our engine power is devoted to overcoming air resistance. Air is quite sticky at high speeds and that is one reason why flying above the atmosphere is probably the only method that will appeal to our grand-children.

You would not think that this could lead to a household hint. But it does. When you clean the inside of a bottle it is not easy to scrape off the air which holds particles of dirt next to the surface. Chemists often tear up a few strips of soft paper, put them into the bottle with a little liquid and shake vigorously. You will be surprised how quickly a bottle can be cleaned in this way.

* * *

Food for breeding

IT is very obvious that all nature breeds —and requires, therefore, good nourishment. Plants are pollinated by insects, but the poor old flower needs food, and it obtains it from the soil.

This business of soil nitrates is interesting for sewage contains much of the necessary substances, yet in England we calmly throw most of it into the sea while importing nitrates at the same time.

We are really transferring a valuable material from one place to another and dumping it into the natural pool for the whole world.

On the Continent, even in Japan, people think we are very foolish and upon my word, I think they are right. It is an interesting point which science seems to have neglected to an astonishing degree. Here we have the mechanism of the body producing material which we want to grow more food, and except for a few attempts to manufacture tiles or bricks, very little attention has been given to the nitration of food by natural means. Here is a chance for a new kind of industry.

* * *

Flies

D. D.T. is a wonderful thing, but its action upon insects seems often to be delayed, and I hate to think that we are all cruel. A buzzing flypaper in a shop can make me not want to eat for quite a long time.

The London Brains Trust once argued for weeks whether a fly, landing upside down on the ceiling, looped the loop or did a half-roll. It should have been quite clear that the fly does not recognise "upside down" and merely flies on to the ceiling in the ordinary way.

A much more interesting thing is the reason why a blue-bottle zigzags all over the place when apparently he has a definite objective. I do not know the answer, but I suspect that the air is full of currents, attractive smells and above all that this kind of fly has enormous wing loading and finds it difficult to cope with draughts. Perhaps you can tell me?

* * *

Eyes are shockingly bad—from the instrument maker's point of view

says Prof. A. M. Low

Fireside Reflections on Science

Have you twins?

A FRIEND of mine the other day remarked feelingly, "Poor Agatha, she has had twins. I wonder how her husband manages to work with all that noise?"

This raises a highly technical subject, for sounds do not, as it were, accumulate, and the ear does not respond beyond a certain degree of internal oscillation. The conclusion is comforting, for quite clearly it is that two twins do not make so much noise as twice one twin. I hope I have made this clear.

* * *

Bad eggs

EGGS contain the cellular life of the embryo chicken and the goodness very often depends upon whether this life has been killed in any way. That is one reason why greasing eggs helps to keep them in passable condition by excluding air.

You often detect good from bad eggs by noting the position assumed by the baby chicken in its cradle. Also the change in the food around this embryo. If an egg is placed in water and it stands on end the position of the centre of gravity has changed as the result of badness. Good eggs commonly lie fairly flat while floating.

Another test is to put your hand round the egg and look through it at a candle or other bright flame. The small spots by the shell are not infrequently the beginning of badness, in other words, life in the cell which is not that of the hopeful chicken.

* * *

Spiders

SPIDERS are extremely delicate in their actions. They handle a web in a style far better than any jeweller can hope to imitate. Their web is stronger, weight for weight, than steel. But the point I want to make is that spiders do not carry parachutes as is so commonly believed.

Knock a spider gently off the table and she apparently unwinds a long piece of life-saving rope. So many people think that this is carried on a kind of endless drum in the spider's tummy that it may be worth while explaining what really happens.

Actually, the spider's thread is a sticky fluid secreted in one or two pairs of spinning knobs at the tail end of her body which flows out from numerous tiny tubes and hardens into thread.

The spider is not content with just one type of thread, but produces one kind to make her web, another for very sticky threads, sheet silk to wind round her large insect victims, and the very finest of all to make the cradles in which she lays her eggs.

It is the female spider who spins the strongest and most beautiful webs. The poor male is a feeble creature who lives in perpetual terror of his life and makes the quickest get-away possible after love-making.

The gossamer spiders whose webs are seen floating over the fields in autumn are small spinners who carry out a kind of Indian rope trick by fixing their thread to plant or stone, climbing up it, biting it free from its base and then sailing off into space.

* * *

Frying on ice

IF you are handy with a few simple tools you can astonish your friends by a sensational experiment. In the first place make an electro-magnet by winding 10 or 12 layers of ordinary bell wire round a bundle of soft iron nails.

The bobbin should be about 4 inches long by 2 inches diameter with the nail core, say, one half inch diameter. Connect this through a resistance such as a radiator to the alternating main.

Now obtain a nice copper frying pan and, on a table under which the coil is fixed, place a block of ice with the frying-pan on top.

The lines of force from this electro-magnet alternate very rapidly, passing easily through the ice, but setting up currents in the copper which eventually render the pan so hot that the eggs can fry.

If you put a thin sheet of aluminium on the ice it will possibly bounce in the air because the polarity of the induced current will correspond at each alternation to that of the coil. The poles repel each other and the aluminium dances mysteriously.

* * *

Television

IN these days of television and altered times everybody is going to be able to see everybody else. Only, I hasten to add, as a result of a complaint, when we want to; it is amusing to note that television depends upon a fault in your eyes.

They retain the impression of a light long after it has gone out and it is this which allows all the tiny parts of a picture to be signalled separately but to retain themselves on your retina as one image.

Eyes are shockingly bad—from the instrument maker's point of view.

Stop where you see Shell and BP

The Shell and BP Service sign means something new to motorists. Thousands of independent garages have joined forces with Britain's largest oil companies to raise the standard of garage service—and are sending their men to special Shell and BP Training Centres.

Expect speed, courtesy, efficiency wherever you see this sign. And when brands are back, every Shell and BP Service Station will offer motorists a *choice* of the most popular petrols.

Ask your Shell and BP Service Station about the new **SHELL X-100 MOTOR OIL** *It fights acid action—main cause of engine wear.*

GOLFING TOPICS

By F. J. C. PIGNON

What can a first class professional make in Britain?

WHY young men of the United States should go prospecting for uranium when there is a fortune awaiting them in sport I cannot imagine.

Take the game of golf as an example.

The leading exponents in this game in the United States count their winnings and earnings in thousands of pounds a year.

The winner of one tournament, claimed by Mr. George May of Chicago as the "World Championship," a misnomer since quite a number of champions, including Bobby Locke the holder of the British title were not competing, must have netted about £10,000.

* * *

THAT is, of course, exceptional, but nevertheless American professionals who follow the golden trail of tournaments from one end of the American continent to the other, count their season and their travels wasted if they fail to pick up less than £5,000 in tournaments and exhibitions, and are not unduly elated when their takings amount to £10,000 a year.

* * *

IN exhibitions alone Ben Hogan, America's number one professional, is making 4,500 dollars a week by playing only three—and is fully booked up for the summer months !

It is not surprising that Hogan has a comparatively minor place among the leading prize winners in the States, six of whom have already reached the 12,000 dollars mark during this season, which means approximately the last three or four months.

* * *

EVEN "Babe" Zaharias, who became a professional golfer after winning the British Women's Championship a few years ago, is in the dollar millionaire class.

Recently she declared, " I'm making about 80,000 dollars a year just in exhibitions, not counting the other little items." The other " little items " include interests in golf equipment and clothing concerns and women's professional tournaments which have caused a complete breakdown in the " Babe's " health.

In an interview with an American columnist, she declared it was " anything but pleasant living out of a suitcase, eating hamburgers on the run between engagements, interviews, luncheons and golf, golf, golf. It is not so bad playing for fun, but when the chips are down it is a terrific strain."

* * *

SO it is ! The American professional golfer's life as a top flighter is short compared with the competitive life of a British professional.

Fortunately for them, most of the United States professionals can make enough money in about ten years to invest in some golf or other business or live in " retirement " as a club professional.

* * *

BY comparison the British professional in top flight may appear to be a " poor man " unless his wealth be counted, not in pounds, but in the pleasure of his job.

I have frequently been asked what a first class professional in Britain can make.

It is a question nobody can answer with any degree of accuracy ; so much depends upon the man himself.

There is something wrong somewhere if the winner of the British Open cannot make at least £5,000 out of it, and the limit is certainly more than £10,000.

The prize fund in British tournaments totals approximately £30,000 a year, and there are exhibitions, tours, and lectures as well as profits on sales and lessons at the player's club. It depends to a great extent upon the man himself as to what he makes.

* * *

RECENTLY there was the case of Jimmy Adams who was bitterly disappointed with a job he accepted at the Royal Sydney Golf Club after selling up in Britain.

He had hardly arrived in Australia, at a club with an enormous membership, before he booked his return passage.

THIS bears testimony to the lot of the professional golfer in Britain. It is a hard life, of course, being always in training, constantly travelling and sometimes losing money on a tournament when, because of an off day, the prize does not cover the cost of the hotel bill and caddy fees.

Moreover, though there is no " closed shop " in professional golf, there are not many more than about a score of players who make any real money out of tournament golf—it would for the majority of the others yield a better dividend if they stayed at home.

* * *

THIS mundane reflection was conjured up after reading *James Braid*, a charming biography of one of the great British professionals, written by Bernard Darwin (Hodder and Stoughton, 12s. 6d.) and just published.

It was less than 50 years ago that the biggest prize in professional golf was £100—Braid won it in a tournament in which the total prize money was £200.

* * *

OF course golden sovereigns looked and were worth more than pound notes to-day, but even so it is surprising to learn that appointments for posts as professionals at clubs were often " sold to the highest bidder."

Even the great James Braid, who won five Open Championships, worked at the bench as a club-maker for eightpence an hour and made what he could in exhibition games and challenge matches in the little spare time at his disposal. Even so James Braid left a considerable sum of money when he died about two years ago.

* * *

PROBABLY Bernard Darwin is right when, in his delightful tribute to a great man and a grand golfer, he says, " Those were emphatically the days." Real hand-made golf clubs made by Braid cost 5s. 3d. " The novice could buy the game of golf complete in a box for 36s. 9d. all told. He could have four gents' clubs for 20s., a dozen balls for 10s. and a ' sling ' for 6s. 9d."

Most fellow golfers will agree with Darwin—those were the days !

October, 1952

THE ALPINE TRIALS—

or

*"Our Motoring Leap-frog,"
by George Murray-Frame,
leader of winning team:*

with "Comments by the
Team Manager"

George Murray-Frame and John Pearman have a "dizzy" time on the Col de Galibier.

The impressive showroom display in the Group's Devonshire House, Piccadilly, headquarters—the winning Sunbeam-Talbots with some of the trophies.

THE " Alpine " has for long been a favourite event with me, so I was naturally delighted to have the chance to go again this year, especially as I was able once again to get John Pearman as co-driver.

I joined the main Sunbeam-Talbot party at the quayside in Dover where John had taken our car. The other cars were being taken down by John Cutts, Bill Chipperton, Norman Garrad, Jack Kemsley, well known in rallies for his performances in a Minx, David Humphries and Count and Countess Kolaczkowski.

Leslie Johnson, Stirling Moss and Mike Hawthorn were flying down later, and John Fitch was also joining us at our headquarters in Bandol.

* * *

WE motored straight through from coast to coast in just under 24 hours without incident.

At Bandol we had a few days before the serious motoring started, but fortunately we had only routine maintenance and some headlight adjustment.

On Thursday we attended the usual formalities at the club in Marseilles, including scrutineering.

This year we were carrying two spare wheels plus two extra covers which ensured a change all round.

The regulations required the cars to be in the *parc fermé* before 5 p.m. on the Friday, which left us some six and a half hours to fill in before our starting time. However, the time soon slipped past and at 11.15 we were waiting our turn.

* * *

THE usual crowds lining the streets, engines and tyres screaming as competitors leave, give an atmosphere all of its own. Then the loud-speaker calling for Monsieur Stirling Moss—Monsieur Leslie Johnson and then our turn.

* * *

THE first section of 288 kilos is very easy going and we arrived at the control with nearly an hour on hand. We now had one of the difficult sections from Guillestre over the notorious Col d'Izoard and up to the frontier at Mont Genèvre.

As we left Guillestre the first signs of daylight were appearing in the east and we were glad indeed to see the dawn as we got to the top of the Izoard.

A crazy rush down and we clocked in with one minute to spare.

ON to Turin with time in hand to check and fill up with petrol, oil and water, then to Monza, on this section the average is raised to 105 k.p.h. (about 65 m.p.h.), but with the Sunbeam-Talbot cruising comfortably at 75 this was no hardship.

At Monza a timed kilo on the Autodrome and then a three-hour rest in which we shaved, had a frugal breakfast and a spot of " shut-eye."

An easy section to Bozzana and we were all set for the last mad dash of 170 km. into Cortina.

* * *

THERE are always lots of " Coupes " lost here and plenty of retirements. The roads are bad and, with the speed that cars are forced to do, this brings out the trouble.

It was here we lost the Sunbeam-Talbots of Leslie Johnson and George Hartwell; we pressed on, however, and made Cortina with three minutes in hand, but tired after 620 miles.

* * *

NEXT day was the circuit of the Dolomites, Cortina-Cortina via 300 kms. of mountain roads all at an average speed of 43 m.p.h.

The first 48 kms. over the Falzarego, Lana, and Pordoi are timed, and this along with Monza, Stelvio, Col de Frene and Col d'Izoard are used to decide final placings.

This circuit falls naturally into two sections; the first to Feltre is very difficult, the second has more main road and one can pick up time lost on the earlier part.

At Feltre we had a quick fill up with petrol and got away only eight minutes behind our schedule.

* * *

WE had just settled down to some fast motoring when the rain came down and turned the road into a good imitation of an ice rink.

Then the heavens really opened and visibility was down to a few yards.

Mike Hawthorn, with co-driver Bill Chipperton, maintains a penalty-free passage over the Col de Galibier.

Stirling Moss (co-driver John Cutts) openly admitted it was his most thrilling drive in international trials.

George Murray-Frame takes a hair-pin bend at speed, followed by Mrs. Nancy Mitchell, over the Italian section.

Mike Hawthorn loses no time in assailing the heights : speed with safety are his ingredients up or down.

The cloudburst didn't last long and on rapidly drying roads we welcomed the Sunbeam-Talbot's road-holding and soon made up time getting to Cortina with several minutes in hand.

By this time the results were taking shape : Perring's Sunbeam-Talbot was out. Tommy Wisdom's Aston had been late the night before at Cortina, the other Aston was out, both Healeys had dropped points, all four Morgans were gone.

In the 2-3 litre class only Moss, Hawthorn, Fitch and our car had clean sheets.

* * *

THE next day was steady motoring for about 500 miles from Italy into Austria, into Italy, into Switzerland, and back into Italy, including a timed climb of 14 kms. up the Stelvio.

It was after this climb and run down to the control at Bormio we made our usual check of petrol, oil and water, to find very little of the latter. We suspected a leaking radiator, but could find no sign of it, so we refilled and took along a can just to be safe.

On arrival at Menaggio we still had a full radiator, so we went to bed that night a little mystified. Then John Fitch retired with a broken rear wheel bearing, very bad luck.

THE battle for the team prize seemed to be boiling down to a straight fight between the "Jags," with Gatsonides, Appleyard and Herzet with clean sheets matched by the Sunbeam-Talbots of Stirling, Mike and myself.

Menaggio to Aix on the fourth day was the easiest of all and we were never really pressed for time.

Our water trouble was in not circulating the water properly, resulting in overheating and consequent loss of water on the mountain passes.

The last day's route to Cannes was almost the same as previous years and is the real *pièce de résistance* of the event.

We started in good heart and made the first control on top of the 9,000-ft. Iseran with time to snatch a cup of coffee and do our usual check, and then on to La Chambre where the real work began.

This is a "flat-out" drive up the Col de Glandon, down again and up over the Col de la Croix de Fer, six miles of main road and up to the check at the top of the 8,000-ft. Galibier. 103 kms. in all and only one minute to spare when we got there—and very little water left ! We made a quick check of the car, using our two minutes' latitude before clocking in.

OFF again over the Izoard in the reverse direction to the first night, a mad rush down the other side, up over the Col de Vars and a last dash up the Col D'allos to check in on time.

On the comparatively easy section down to Cannes we were suddenly startled by an infernal clatter. A hasty stop, fearing the worst after our overheating, we were relieved to find only the dynamo pulley had broken.

There was nothing for it but to take off the fan belt and hope we could cover the last twenty miles without too much overheating. Well, we checked in on time, much to the relief of our team mates who had also preserved their clean sheets.

* * *

WE afterwards learned that Herzet of the "Jag" team had dropped on the last day, so both team prizes and first, second and third in the 2-3 litre class, plus three Coupe des Alps, came our way— a magnificent proof of Sunbeam-Talbots' speed and reliability.

After winning my first Coupe in 1948, I said the main ingredients for success in the "Alpine" were good luck, a good co-driver and a good car. That is still true !

Another view of Stirling Moss at speed on the Col de Galibier—rising to over 2,500 metres.

Dust, pot-holes and sometimes concealed, sudden turns in the "roadway" kept all drivers fully occupied.

Leaving the Italian section for the French side of the Col de Petit St. Bernard: G. Murray-Frame gets a wave of "good luck."

The one highest sees most—Stirling Moss gets a fleeting glimpse of his ascending road on the Stelvio.

The Team Manager's point of view:

MANY people's conception of a Team Manager is that of an elderly gentleman who, in the evening of his days, acquires the job only because no other work can be found for him.

I can assure you, however, that "managing" the Sunbeam-Talbot Alpine Team, and a team such as we produced this year, was not a task for *any old gentleman*, but for someone who knew, from the hard school of experience, just that little more than the selected drivers.

The manager's job starts months before the actual event, of course, and the first important item is to get hold of the Regulations. These he must study in detail and know, in the very early stages, what is and what is not allowed by the organisers—so that he can advise the cars' preparation departments how far they can go in early assembly to save all last-minute rush.

The next thing is to secure practical appreciation of the entire route, on the best possible maps, and decisions made as to when and where the drivers and the cars will have to give of their best. As this particular event, to use a racing expression, is so profoundly "dicy," it may be that the manager, in company with one of the works' engineers, must go out over a particular section of the route and see if the running time as set down in the Regulations can in fact be achieved. On this run, too, decisions must be made as to best axle and gear ratios and, believe me, it must be a good guess, with minute degrees of accuracy attaching to it.

The next all-important factor lies in the choice of drivers. The number of applications a factory team manager receives from people who "could win the event outright" is indeed inspiring. In this respect, and with considerable modesty and knowledge of what is wanted in an Alpine driver, my opinion may be of interest to future would-be contestants :—

He must be absolutely fearless and mentally and physically suited, bearing in mind some sections incur up to 15 hours continuous driving in tropical heat—and his "reactions" must be as good at the end as at the start.

He must be able to drive the car really fast up a mountain and, what is more important, his judgment must be such that he can bring it down again equally as fast, if not faster !

This requirement may sound normal, but remember that on most Alpine climbs there is usually a considerable drop on one side or the other ; also, the road in most cases is made up of very loose surface.

He must be the type that will accept discipline without questioning and realise his responsibilities, i.e., in carrying a factory name and all it means once behind the wheel.

This year my choice of drivers was as follows :—

(a) GEORGE MURRAY-FRAME (co-driver, John Pearman) : here you have a combination of great skill and abundant experience of the " Alpine." Nothing in the world but mechanical trouble could stop George Murray-Frame gaining a Coupe des Alpes.

(b) STIRLING MOSS (co-driver, John Cutts) : a top line racing driver with an outstanding performance record and great driving ability, fearless and a wonderful " press on " outlock, supported by one of the soundest factory boys in this class of competition work.

(c) MIKE HAWTHORN (co-driver, W. Chipperton) : in this pair there is " Mike " the artist behind the wheel (and far better than his already impressive record) supported by " Chippy " who can never be accused of lacking in " urge," also with years

Modern Motoring & Travel

The Alpine Trials:
(Continued from page 21)

The successful Sunbeam-Talbots and drivers ready to be onloaded at Nice for Bristol transportation to Silverstone—here to be offered a special "Lap d'honneur" before the Grand Prix crowds.

of experience behind him of previous Alpines.

(d) LESLIE JOHNSON (co-driver David Humphrey): knocked out of the event by really cruel luck, but one of the most experienced "all-round" drivers in the business. Extremely fast, safe, knowledgeable and a great asset to any team manager fortunate to procure his services—supported by "young David," who knows all the answers and who learned his lessons the hard way.

* * *

WITH such drivers my worries as to how the cars would be driven were behind me. But the task of the manager is only beginning—he must attend to items of insurance, shipping, hotel accommodation, petrol and oil stops on the course, satisfy himself on the final testing of the cars, assembly of the drivers as well as take the cars to the official start at Marseilles. The anxiety alone of getting the cars there without a "prang" is more than enough at once a year. Then there is the movement of the luggage, etc., seeing the cars through their scrutineering, giving the drivers last moment instructions—which usually finishes up with some such words — "For Pete's sake, keep the ruddy thing on the road—don't miss a Control—and, most important of all, do not be late."

The manager usually leaves just prior to the official Start and transports himself somewhere near to the end of the first leg, and sweats it out there waiting for his "boys" to arrive.

The "tiddlers," as I call them, arrive first, then the next class, and at long last, the welcome sight of the Sunbeam-Talbots dashing up to the line.

Experience has taught me never to bother looking at the car. One look at the drivers' faces and I know immediately if they have made all the climbs and checking controls on time. Giving them the old Roman sign, a weary hand is raised in response—but it is enough!

We then meet at the *parc fermé*, take them to their hotel, see they get a bath and food, and, most important, get them off to bed, knowing they must be up and busy at 4 a.m. I, the manager mark you, rise at 2.45 a.m., dress, go down to the dining room, get the waiters cracking, and go into the hotel kitchen, to see that the drivers' breakfasts really are on the way. Then comes my round of the bedrooms, waking my precious young men and making sure they realise it is another day, not leaving their rooms until they are on their feet!

* * *

THE various reactions are interesting. "Mike" just gives a dirty look and makes some sharp remark. Under my breath I reply, "And you too!"

Stirling looks in a sad sort of way, but I know perfectly well what he is thinking—if later he tells me!

Murray-Frame is no trouble. Evidently his experiences as a prisoner of war (ex R.A.F.) have made him appreciate his liberty and, generally he is on his feet with a grin.

Then, when they have fed, we transport them to the *parc fermé*—and so it goes on for five days.

Eventually we reach the final control (the Finish).

Knowing already how our chaps were placed when they left early in the morning, this waiting is really hell in its worst form—if hell is like this! But imagine this is the end of the Trial. If they do not make it on time, all the months of preparation, the planning, the expense, become meaningless and purposeless, wasted effort. You cannot speak, you daren't, you just look up the road, waiting and waiting. Then, at long last, the Sunbeam-Talbots arrive.

The "boys" give the "sign," you pass then a drink and shake them by the hand, by which time, quite overcome by the effort you know they have made on your behalf, you watch them clock

(Concluded on page 24)

George Murray-Frame and John Pearman after the presentation of prizes at Cannes—with their Coupe des Alpes, 1st award in 2/3 litre class and the coveted team award.

Sir William Rootes, K.B.E., chairman of the Rootes Group, congratulates the successful competitors at the special celebration dinner given in their honour: right to left, John Fitch; G. Murray-Frame; Sir William Rootes; Mrs. Nancy Mitchell; Count Kolaczkowski; R. W. Hammond, C.B.E., financial director, Rootes Group; Dr. Marie Kelleher; Stirling Moss; Geoffrey Rootes, managing director; Countess Kolaczkowski; Mike Hawthorn and Harold Nockolds, "The Times" motor correspondent.

Hats off to Sunbeam-Talbot

for their outstanding performances in the Alpine Rally

ALPINE CUPS:
G. Murray-Frame
J. M. Hawthorn
Stirling Moss

and the MANUFACTURERS' TEAM PRIZE

using **SHELL X-100 MOTOR OIL**

The same high quality oil obtainable at your local garage. Ask them for the correct grade of Shell X-100 for your car

FUEL BY SHELL

The Team Manager's point of view: *from page 22*

in and drive away or, as in my case, feel so much relief, it literally hurts.

Well, that is what managing a successful Alpine team means, and in a flash goes the news to the four quarters of the globe—British supremacy, British guts. You almost hear the cheers of the lads at the factories thousands of miles away, those great boys who worked day and night to get things right, designers, engineers, mechanics, even the department's floor sweeper! My heartfelt thanks goes out to them all—with a thought or two for the losers, for I, too, have known the bitterness of failure and disappointment!

NORMAN GARRAD.

* * *

72 HOURS IN THE LIFE OF ALPINE DRIVERS

AT dawn on Monday, July 21, the victorious team of drivers of the Coventry-built Sunbeam-Talbot "90" saloon cars, which swept all before them in their class in the Alpine Rally, set out from Coventry for London to put their cars on view to the general public at Devonshire House, Piccadilly.

For the drivers, John Pearman, of Kenilworth, W. R. Chipperton, of Cheltenham, and John Cutts, of Coventry, the run to London was the end of a hectic and crowded 72 hours since the Sunbeam-Talbot team had won three Coupes des Alpes, and two team prizes in the 2,055-mile rally.

Early on the previous Friday, Mr. Norman Garrad, the team manager, had received an urgent signal that the Rootes Group in London, through Air Commodore G. J. Powell, Silver City Airways Managing Director, had chartered two Bristol freighters to fly out to Nice and back to bring back the cars and their drivers as they were wanted at the Silverstone, Northants, race meeting.

At midnight, still dressed in their tropical clothes, the drivers set out to fly over the French Alps at 10,000 feet for Blackbushe airport, near Camberley, Surrey. Arriving cold but happy to be back home again, the team then made a dawn start for Silverstone track, where Mr. Geoffrey Rootes, Managing Director, Humber, Ltd., was waiting to congratulate them.

Then followed a "lap of honour" drive of the cars with George Murray-Frame, the Glasgow tobacconist, and J. Pearman, in the leading car, followed by Mike Hawthorn, of Farnham, Surrey, and W. Chipperton, in the second car, and Stirling Moss and John Cutts in the third. The 100,000 spectators were told of the tremendous fillip which the British success at Cannes would give to the export of British cars.

PUT OUT MORE FLAGS!

SIR WILLIAM ROOTES, Chairman of the Rootes Group and of the Dollar Exports Council, made the confession that he was "an 'I.F.W.'—an 'Impenitent Flag-Wagger'" at the dinner which he gave to the drivers, mechanics and others who had contributed to the "wonderful success of the Sunbeam-Talbots in the Alpine Rally.

"The Sunbeam-Talbots, and the other British cars in the Alpine Trial, have shown by the fineness of their engineering, and the courage and endurance of their drivers that we can produce some of the best machines and men in the world."

The little Union Jack painted on their bonnets had once more become a symbol of the energy, skill and enterprise of this country.

"Some of you may remember the pompous gentleman who came down to the school speech day in Kipling's 'Stalky & Co.,' and whom the boys promptly nick-named ' the jelly-bellied flag-flapper.' In those days we were the strongest and richest nation on earth. We could afford, while we smugly said: 'Trade follows the flag,' to laugh at the flag itself. We could afford, in fact (to use a bridge term), to 'discard from strength.'

"Now, however, the situation is very different. We are far from being the richest or most powerful country in the world, and while we have much greater reserves of strength, resources and will-power than many people think, we are in a hole economically.

"I believe, therefore, that this is a time not merely for showing the flag, but giving it a damn good wag as well.

"London, for example, is still the great capital of a great Commonwealth. It has an immense number of flag-poles on its buildings. But look out over the roof-tops of London on any ordinary day. What do you see? Plenty of flag-poles—but hardly a flag flying.

"Over all the works and depots in the Rootes Group during the daylight hours you will see, and always have seen, our national flag, the Union Jack, flying.

"And the reason we have always insisted on having our national flag flying is this. A flag is a symbol—a symbol of a nation's belief in its past, its pride in its present, and its aspirations for its future.

"Far more sinister, to my mind, than any adverse trade reports on 'dollar gaps' for the true future of this country is the fact that many of us seem somehow to have lost faith in ourselves, and a belief in our country.

"For my part I have done no such thing."

Sir William urged others to follow the U.S. in one thing—the flying of the national flag, for he said: "it is no good talking about trade 'following the flag' when you never see a flag for trade to follow."

COMMENTS AT THE DINNER:

HIGH praise for the navigating of John Cutts, of Coventry, was paid by Stirling Moss.

"He knew the course like a book," Moss said. "When he said 'slow here' I went slow, and 'fast now,' I went as fast as I could go, however murderous the hairpins appeared as we approached them.

"'We stop here for petrol—there's nothing for miles afterwards,' and how right he was."

Moss said that most of the mountain passes were not roads at all, but just loose gravel surfaces.

* * *

GEORGE MURRAY-FRAME paid a tribute to the factory for the cars which they had produced.

"We appreciate cars which will stand up to motoring however tough the course.

"You may not realise the terrific strain on the cars that results."

He paid a "great tribute" to the Rootes Group for their confidence "in the men and the cars," and added his thanks to the mechanics.

* * *

JOHN FITCH said: "We have nothing like the Alpine back home. We have a hill course which with its six miles is about equivalent to 10 minutes of the Alpine."

* * *

HAROLD KNOCKOLDS, of *The Times*, described the results achieved by the Sunbeam-Talbots as "an outstanding event in the history of motoring in this country."

"I would stress the incredible treatment which the cars in this Rally received.

"It was quite unbelievable.

"We (with T. Wisdom) saw for ourselves what these cars (the Sunbeam-Talbots) did. We were in the same Section. Theirs was a phenomenal performance, day after day, from 6 a.m. to 9 p.m.

"Great courage was shown by the Rootes Group to submit their cars publicly to this Rally. No amount of testing in the ordinary way in the Alps could ever demonstrate the quality of the cars. No ordinary schedule could ever reveal the weaknesses—or the strength—of construction as this Rally does.

"Their performance was quite 'formidable.'

"The drivers did a fabulous job. But these drivers would not have had such a good run without their co-drivers. These co-drivers have to survive a sense of personal terror, which is only overcome by mental anguish. I know from personal experience."

Sunbeam-Talbot Successes in the Alpine Trials, 1952:—

"Coupe des Alpes" (for entrants completing the course without penalty): (Three)

George Murray-Frame; J. Mike Hawthorn; and Stirling Moss.

* * *

2/3 Litre Class:

1st, George Murray-Frame (co-driver, J. N. Pearman);
2nd, J. Mike Hawthorn, (W. R. ("Chips") Chipperton);
3rd, Stirling Moss, (John Cutts).

* * *

"Challenge Team de Marque" Trophy (manufacturers' team award for the best three cars of any make, irrespective of size, class or nationality).

* * *

"Challenge de l'Automobile de Marseille et Provence" (for the best team of three foreign cars (not French) irrespective of size and class).

"Coupe d'André Rey" (for the best performance of a team of ladies): Mrs. Nancy Mitchell (co-driver, Dr. Marie Kelleher).

* * *

"Coupe de Fidelite" (special cup, given at the discretion of the organisers, for an outstanding performance during the Rally): Count W. Kolaczkowski.

* * *

Final Acceleration and Braking Test at Cannes, 2/3 Litre Class: Stirling Moss, 33.4 secs.

* * *

In General Classification:

8, George Murray-Frame (no marks lost); 9, J. Mike Hawthorn (no marks lost); 10, Stirling Moss (no marks lost); 14, Alan Fraser (co-driver, F. W. Scott) (50 marks lost); and 21, Count W. Kolaczkowski (210 marks lost).

October, 1952

Extreme right: Dawn at the Summit of the Stelvio, highest mountain Pass in Europe. Photograph taken by "lightning" illumination.

Right: The author, with co-driver D. Young, at the Refuge Inn, on Stelvio, headquarters of the Alpine Club of Italy.

"Getting the Story" of the Alpine Trials — a trial itself!

by W. Paulson
Motoring Correspondent "Evening News"

THE road from Spondigna approaches Stelvio with deceptive ease. The car, having had two shock absorbers adjusted after a descent in which the tail was forever wagging the dog, now rode steadily, and the only cause for concern was the dark clouds which hung about the mountain tops.

We had been warned to be over the top in two hours, or take the consequences. We took the consequences. The road narrowed as the clouds came down, and the headlights shone out into space or sent the solid rock face hurtling in our direction as the wheel swung round. The driver, an enigmatic sailor who had made his trips around the Cape in a sailing ship while still in his 'teens took his hand off the wheel now and then to wipe the sweat from his brow, though we had left the summer heat in the valley below.

* * *

THE trick was to keep up the revs. so that the climb did not have to be made entirely in bottom gear. One approached along the cliff edge (it was now too dark to see whether it dropped sheer or merely graduated a few hundred feet) and then, locking the wheels as tightly as possible into the dip on the hairpin, swung the car round to miss the far wall by as many inches as one could; but not too many, because in that case the car would head back for the road below and the camber would conspire against its progress.

The hairpins following in quick succession seemed numberless. The mercy was that, as it was so late, no one else was on the road.

Came the rain, and with it the first few intermittent flashes of lightning. The scream from the outraged tyres diminished and instead came a more disturbing slide as the car keeled heavily over like a storm-tossed ship.

* * *

THERE was no way back, and anyway we had a rendezvous 200 miles further on at Menaggio with the other Alpine Rally cars, now at the end of the day's run.

Once a hiking party led by a priest passed by, and at another point, with not a house or a hut for miles, a coach or bus had been pulled in under the cliff and we wondered where the occupants could have gone.

The storm was now approaching its height and in the flashes it could be seen that we had reached the snowline. It was bottom gear now, overheat or not, and the family-model Humber Hawk at last pulled up triumphantly at the Stelvio resthouse at the top, where the doorkeeper shook his head sadly at the thought of such foolishness when we said we must press on, and induced us (with the aid of a coffee-cognac apiece) to stay at least until there was some light.

* * *

A SUMMER storm seen from below can be frightening. Sheet lightning at the same level as it travels round the snow-capped peaks is positively awe-inspiring. While the rain poured in through the open window, Ron Clayton, the photographer, sat happily sucking his pipe and changing the exposed slide of his camera until three o'clock in the morning. Doug Young, the driver, and I dashed from side to side trying to find the best view, but wishing all the time we could get some sleep before the next day's run brought new adventures.

Even when the dawn came and the valley lay sweating in the haze of another day, nothing could move the enthusiastic photographer until the sun had climbed lazily above the distant peaks and Stelvio had put on its glorious raiment for the benefit of his colour slides.

Below, the hairpins were all stacked one above the other, and the road wound round and round the sheer cliff, seemingly suspended in space. It was difficult to connect the one so distantly below with the road on which we were standing.

ON the way down it was evident that the crashes which had reverberated through the night were not all thunder. Great rocks lay across the road, and here and there the rainwater flowed in a torrential stream, washing away with it some of the muddy road. Wending our way through the debris, and at other times getting out to clear a navigable path, we reached the bottom at last and found cheerful Italian workmen already on their way to clear the road.

We never made Menaggio because the Passo del Gavia, which promised a short cut, turned out to be even more hazardous in daylight than the Stelvio at night. Here was no surfaced road at all, but only a track with hardly a stick or stone to delay the drop. Five miles an hour was a reckless speed, and it would have been a thoughtful precaution to have opened the nearside door as a ready exit had there been room against the cliff face.

* * *

A PERSONAL reminiscence of this kind would be a presumption if it did not point out some of the hazards which can be encountered even by those in a "ringside seat" at the Alpine Rally.

Through four days and a night the cars which enter this race—for it is a road race against time—are hurled through one mountain after another, along streets at times crowded with other traffic, and only the best and the luckiest arrive. At each stage one is agreed that the whole thing is crazy in conception and hazardous in execution.

But the French and the Italians and the Swiss and the Belgians who know these roads say that if a car can do this and survive then it is a good car and will stand up to years of normal fast motoring. That is why the British manufacturers send teams to compete, and in this year's event, at least, they have been well recompensed.

AVIATION TOPICS

Are aero-engines becoming too complex?: the question is extremely acute!

By Major Oliver Stewart

GAS turbines are tending to run away with us. I mean that so many kinds are tried that the basic differences are apt to elude us.

In motor cars there are certain fairly clearly defined and universally understood engine categories, usually based on the way in which the cylinders are mounted on the crankcase and, in aviation, piston engines were grouped in a similar manner.

No such simple grouping exists with gas turbines. In fact, nomenclature is such that it looks as if there is the makings of a first-class muddle. It may be useful, therefore, to look at the chief kinds of gas turbine for aircraft now being built in Britain.

* * *

FIRST of all there is the main division according to whether the air is compressed by being flung outwards centrifugally by the compressor or accelerated along a line about parallel to the axis of the engine.

The first kind of engines are centrifugal and the second kind are axial. The Ghost, Nene, Derwent and Dart are centrifugal engines; the Avon, Sapphire, Beryl, Proteus and Olympus are axial engines.

The quotation of those names shows immediately how inadequate is the simple description " axial " or " centrifugal." There could hardly be two more different engines than the Dart and the Ghos ; or the Olympus and the Proteus. So there has to be another main division, according to whether the engine is designed to deliver its thrust directly by means of a jet of hot gases, or indirectly through an airscrew.

The Dart is a gas turbine propeller unit, or " turboprop "; while the Avon is a plain gas turbine and jet or " turbojet." The Dart can be fairly fully described, therefore, by saying that it is a centrifugal flow, turboprop; while the Avon can be called an axial flow turbojet.

* * *

IF we could stick to these terms, turboprop, when there is an airscrew, and turbojet where there is not, and to the two kinds of flow, axial and centrifugal, there would be hope of a classification as simple as in motor-car engines.

But we cannot stick to those few, simple terms. The Olympus, for example, is a totally different kind of engine from the Avon though both are axial flow turbojets and the difference is defined by the term " two-spool." The Olympus is a two-spool axial flow turbojet.

* * *

A TWO-SPOOL gas turbine is a kind of compound engine, or more precisely an engine within an engine.

There are two separate compressors and they are each connected to their own separate turbines. The different stages of each compressor are, of course, connected to one another to make a single compressor.

It all sounds rather like the song about the bones being connected to one another. But with the engine the connections are contrived by the use of two concentric shafts, one inside the other.

* * *

TWO-SPOOL engines are a fairly recent development although several years ago there was an experimental design which was later abandoned. The object of the two-spool arrangement is to eliminate " surging "—another gas turbine term without its counterpart in piston-engine work.

Surging is a break down of the smooth flow of air through the engine and, when it happens, serious trouble can supervene.

It is claimed that with the two-spool engine surging cannot occur. And I have certainly tried hard to upset the air flow of the Olympus on the test bed without success.

One can slam the throttle open and the huge two-spool, axial engine roars up from idling speed to the full thrust figure of 4,400 kilograms without hesitation. It will soon be giving 4,500 kilograms thrust which is about 10,000 lb.

* * *

JUST when we were settling down to these different kinds of engine, Sir Frank Whittle came forward to remind us of another kind which may, in the future, become of supreme importance for very long range work : it is the " by-pass " engine.

In a by-pass engine the air which enters the intake can go either through the engine or round it ! It can go into the compressor in the ordinary way, be compressed, mixed with fuel, burnt and shot out through the turbine blades, or it can by-pass the main compressor, go through ducts round the engine and join the general flow aft of the turbine.

The claimed advantage of the by-pass engine is better fuel consumption than can be secured with the other kinds.

But the two-spool engine looks like giving excellent consumption figures. British by-pass engines are at present secret, but I can mention the small French Turboméca Aspin by-pass engine which has been flown successfully and has shown remarkably low consumption figures.

Next, just to confuse the issue, there is the " ducted fan."

Some engineers will tell you that the ducted fan is merely a particular kind of by-pass engine. Others will say that it is a different thing altogether.

I have been told one view by one great gas turbine engineer and the other view by another, equally eminent, gas turbine engineer !

I shall certainly not enter into the controversy.

Essentially the ducted fan consists in an airscrew completely enclosed in a duct, the duct being extended rearwards to enclose the whole of the ordinary gas turbine. Finally, there is the fully compounded type of engine like the Nomad where a two-stroke piston engine is compounded with a gas turbine.

* * *

LET me now tabulate the main engine types :

GAS TURBINE.—The generic term covering all engines.

TURBOJET.—A gas turbine exerting thrust by means of a plain jet.

TURBOPROP.—A gas turbine exerting thrust mainly through an airscrew.

AXIAL FLOW ENGINE.—A gas turbine in which the flow of air and gases is parallel to the engine axis.

CENTRIFUGAL FLOW ENGINE.—A gas turbine in which the flow of air is largely radial.

TWO-SPOOL ENGINE.—A gas turbine in which there are two paired compressors and turbines.

BY-PASS ENGINE.—A gas turbine in which some of the air flowing through the engine can be by-passed round the turbine.

DUCTED FAN.—A gas turbine driving an airscrew which is enclosed in a duct.

* * *

THERE are innumerable secondary distinctions—single-sided and double-sided compressors, " free " turbine engines and so on—but most of the engines now under construction in Britain can be clearly described by one or more of the main headings given. But they do show how the gas turbine, which started as an engine simpler than the piston-engine, has become more and more complex until it is fast approaching a point where it will leave the piston engine far behind in this respect.

Perhaps this is the inevitable course for most engineering products.

THE CRITICAL 00100 MILES...

The *first* hundred miles in a car's life can make or break it. So don't take chances with the delivery of *your* new car.

The CAR COLLECTION COMPANY protects your car in these important ways:

A SERVIS RECORDER is fitted to every car — an amazing "hidden eye" that makes a record of the entire journey for *you* to see.

EXPERT DRIVERS. Every one of them has passed a special test at the British School of Motoring. Paid extra to go slow, they get a bonus for *super*-safe driving.

DIRECT SUPERVISION. Our staff of Collection Supervisors backs the whole delivery system, from factory to you. And — a most important point — our trade plates bear our name, so that you can see for yourself how we handle cars!

Make sure your dealer arranges for delivery of *your* car via CAR COLLECTION. The extra cost is so small . . . it really is worth while.

THE CAR COLLECTION COMPANY LTD
Estd. 1926

7 Kendall Place, Baker Street, London, W.1

Britain to be Hosts to the World in CORONATION YEAR

★ ★ ★

Record number of overseas visitors expected

★ ★ ★

Advance details; a year of pageantry and rejoicing.

IF it would be an exaggeration to say that the whole world and his wife will be coming to Britain in Coronation year, it would not need a bold prophet to forecast that 1953 will be a record tourist year for this country.

Indications are that overseas visitors in far greater numbers than ever before will flow into Britain.

Shipping and air lines already report heavy bookings and travel agents in many countries, especially North America and the British Commonwealth, are being inundated with inquiries.

* * *

A crowded calendar

ALTHOUGH the glittering pageantry of the Coronation itself will be the main attraction, those whose job is to promote travel to Britain are stressing the idea that this country will have much to offer throughout the summer.

The Coronation will be a nation-wide celebration and most places in the country, large and small, are planning special events to mark this joyous occasion.

There will be the usual crowded calendar of national events with a wide appeal.

* * *

In Coronation Week itself there will be the greatest of all classic horse races, the Derby. The tens of thousands of tourists thronging London during that week will no doubt swell the colourful crowds on Epsom Downs.

* * *

On June 10 another annual event which has become a well-loved feature of English life, the Royal Tournament, will open at Earls Court.

* * *

Although the date has not yet been announced, it can be assumed that the Trooping the Colour ceremony, the most outstanding of all Britain's military spectacles, will take place on Horse Guards' Parade at about the same time in celebration of the Queen's Official Birthday.

* * *

Also opening on June 10 will be the Antique Dealers' Fair. London is the acknowledged world centre for antiques and art dealing, and the Antique Dealers' Fair, held at the Grosvenor House Hotel, Park Lane, attracts connoisseurs from many lands.

Some early dates

JUNE is an important month for agricultural shows, always a great feature of rural life.

Major shows to be held in June next year include the Bath and West (June 3–6), the Three Counties (June 9–11), the Royal Highland (June 23–26), and the Royal Counties (June 24–27). The Royal Agricultural Show, the greatest of them all, will be held in 1953 at Blackpool between July 7 and 10.

* * *

The Richmond Royal Horse Show, probably the finest outdoor horse show in England, will be staged in the Old Deer Park at Richmond next year between June 11 and 13. The unique charm and elegance of the Richmond Show make it the "Mecca" of horse lovers.

* * *

Notable events

SOON after the excitement of the Coronation has died down will come the flowering splendour of that great social and sporting event, the Royal Ascot Meeting, which is to be held next year from June 16 to 19.

At Ascot, Britain's visitors will be able to see the newly-crowned Queen taking part in the celebrated Royal Drive in an open carriage up the racecourse to her place in the Royal enclosure.

Another sporting event of international renown, the All-England Lawn Tennis Championships—"Wimbledon" for short—begins on June 22.

* * *

Many supporting attractions

THIS brief survey of events whose dates are already known indicates that there will be plenty to engage the attention of Britain's visitors in Coronation month.

A glance at the months to follow reveals that those who come to Britain after the Coronation, or who decide to prolong their stay, will still find many attractions besides the eternal beauty of the countryside and the perennial interest of historical associations.

* * *

July opens with another major social and sporting fixture, Henley Royal Regatta, which continues until July 4.

* * *

Throughout the Coronation summer the annual Royal Academy Exhibition at Burlington House will be attracting the plaudits of lovers of academic painting, and it is safe to predict that there will be a great profusion of exhibitions in the museums, art galleries, and smaller private galleries.

* * *

Leading Festivals

THE London theatre will doubtless play a worthy part in the Coronation festivities and London's musical life will see to it that the 1953 Coronation season will be in no way inferior to the splendid season of 1937, when King George VI was crowned.

It is too early yet to announce details, or even dates, of the well-established music and arts festivals which grace the provincial centres, but one can venture to predict that such fine festivals as Edinburgh, Glyndebourne, and Aldeburgh, as well as the Bath Assembly and the Welsh Eisteddfods, will strive to improve upon their already high standards.

* * *

A welcome for all

ALL in all, Britain's guests in Coronation year will find a host of attractions and special events to enjoy, whatever time they choose to come to Britain.

* * *

[Full details of all events to be held during Coronation year, together with a special supplement covering the Coronation itself, will be published in future issues. Look out for further advices.—ED.]

MOTOR HOW YOU WILL...

Mr. Mercury will give you more miles per gallon!

Some of the cars—well, vehicles—you see to-day are nearly as funny as this one. But every engine that runs on petrol runs better on National Benzole Mixture. In particular, it runs more economically. It does more miles per gallon. The day that National comes back into the pumps will be the day that the cost of motoring goes down. Roll on that day!

NATIONAL BENZOLE MIXTURE

National Benzole Company Limited, Wellington House, Buckingham Gate, London, S.W.1.
(The distributing organisation owned and entirely controlled by the producers of British Benzole)

Remember, Colour is Life!

It is always so easy to be dull

says Brigid de Vine

THE most widely read booklet in England to-day is non-fiction. It is quite short. It is issued free of charge.

The name of this popular publication is *Hints on Home Painting*.

It was written by W. P. Matthew, the expert of the B.B.C. Woman's Hour and Television, for the makers of Lifeguard Household Paints, who found that almost more paint was being sold to private customers than to the trade, and the demand has been so enormous that if you have not obtained a copy already you may have difficulty in getting one.

* * *

PAINTING THE HOUSE seems to have moved up to number one Home Hobby. First, I think, because professional help has been so expensive; secondly, because people found it fun to do once they had learned a few tricks on the right order to tackle a given job and so on.

HOLIDAY HINTS
By Ann M. Capell

WHATEVER holiday you are having, dusting powder or talcum is a "must," and it is a wise woman who buys these things beforehand so that once on holiday they will not have to come out of her spending money or, if she is abroad, out of her precious travel allowance. For after-swim freshness, for keeping the feet happy, they are invaluable.

If you are playing golf or tennis, remember that dusting your feet with talcum after a massage with Cologne will keep them cool and comfortable right through the game. Remember, too, that the best lightning quick reviver is a splash of some toilet water on temples and throat and on the wrists. . . .

When there is no chance of a wash-and-brush-up after the meal, freshen face and hands with a quick patting with Eau-de-Cologne (the sticks of solid Cologne are also useful for this purpose).

During the evenings put a drop of perfume on all your "pulse spots" and stroke it along the parting of your hair. If you're going dancing, spray the perfume round the hem of your gown . . . all simple tips and very effective.

Undoubtedly the invention of "roller" painting has given a fillip to the home decorator.

I first wrote of this transatlantic method in *Modern Motoring and Travel* some months ago.

Now it has become exceedingly popular. Especially with women who find they can paint a ceiling with so little "mess" that it is hardly necessary to cover their hair!

With a Rolakoton Outfit, costing about 55s., an average sized room can be given a "New Look" *in a matter of only four hours.* And the outfit will last for years and years.

No wonder I have heard so many people say, "*I'm saving a few days' leave to paint the house,*" when they were asked about holiday plans this year.

* * *

SPRING cleaning estimates were so large that many people decided they could not have redecoration *and* a holiday too.

Now they have had the holiday and coming back from brighter skies the house seems dingy.

Handy "Sky-Line" kitchen help with fruits and salads. Used like a knife, it peels, shreds or slices: price 1s. 6d.

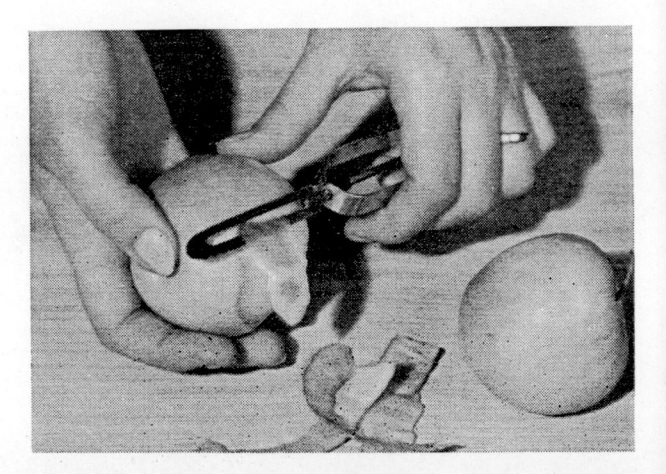

White bead necklace is the choice of exotic Dorothy Lamour for adorning her evening dress, in applique white lace. Did you see her big-hit appearance in the "Big-Top"?

The solution is to turn the family on to the job.

Schoolboy sons and daughters would find redecorating their rooms an ideal occupation for that gap—so wearisome to their parents and themselves—between returning from a tour and going back to school.

Mothers who might fear the resultant "mess" by other methods, will find that even the least tidy painter cannot make much work if the Rolakoton method is insisted on.

A Room of One's Own is every teenager's ambition, and *A Room Decorated by Oneself* is a very desirable goal.

* * *

IT is a little easier to get wood for carpentry now, and textiles for new curtains, etc., are certainly much easier to obtain so that schoolboy sons or daughters willing to provide the labour themselves can have a really attractive "den" for the cost of a few sessions at the cinema.

At a recent exhibition of modern furniture and furnishings in London, there was a most attractive room for a "Teenage" boy containing a work table topped with plastic sheeting, with an adjustable light above it, an oak bureau which was convertible into a dressing table, and a divan bed with a wall bracket above it.

Two of the walls were painted *primrose*, the other two dark blue; an idea that lends interest to a room that must be used a lot.

You can have a yellow wall to look at or a blue one according to where you sit and the change is refreshing.

Pale grey sisal matting on the floor was covered with a dark blue wool rug, the curtains were mustard on white, and the bedspread red and grey.

It was quite a small room, really, but the interesting colour scheme and the placing of the furniture took the "small" look away from it. There was ample room, too, for "doing things," and the working surface of the table could be wiped clean in a flash

* * *

WITH more contracted living-rooms the bedrooms of the older members of the family are best furnished as *bed-sitting-rooms*, where the occupants can read and work and write letters in most cherished privacy.

We may enjoy communal life in camp and school, but it is necessary for the healthy growth of the individual temperament to have some *place of one's own*.

October, 1952   Page 31

DUAL-PURPOSE has become a selling point in clothes as well as in furniture.

At the International Wool Secretariat party at the Savoy, attended by the Duchess of Gloucester and a distinguished company, as part of the Board of Trade's "Fashion Fortnight," we saw for the first time this year some of the fabulous fashions from the Couture trade in Italy.

They were vivid, colourful clothes, with some of the classical skill in drapery well displayed.

One dinner dress by Gabriellasport of Rome had a slim skirt wonderfully draped at the back in a bustle effect. It was made in fine red wool and worn with a short sleeved bolero in white corded wool.

I do not think it would be "easy to pack," but it *was* fun to see it.

One really practical travel suit by Antonelli of Rome showed the Italian skill in double-purpose clothes. It was a tailor-made suit in grey velour trimmed with mutation mink and named "London Fog!" The fur-edged basque came off to leave quite a different looking lighter suit with a battle jacket effect. That jacket in turn came off to reveal a knitted wool blouse exquisitely embroidered in silver thread matching the silver thread embroidery on the neat little hat by Canessa. You could meet any occasion at any hour of the day with this outfit; and it was beautifully made.

* * *

AT the Simon Massey display, also shown during "Fashion Fortnight," there was an unusually designed suit "Ecosse," which combined the effect of a loose box jacket at the back with a scarf and waistcoat effect in front. It was wonderful for travelling, for it was loose enough to add or subtract extra woollies underneath yet slim and trimly buttoned in front. Something quite new in travel suits.

* * *

DOUBLE-PURPOSE raincoats, designed primarily, I feel, to cope with our own changeable weather, won enormous applause at a recent Grosvenor House show.

There were raincoats of glinting satin, taffeta, velvet and even *glass*.

Many of them were made to sell at less than £10, and they were shown with a most captivating selection of rainproof hats, pull-on caps, deerstalkers or berets all charmingly styled.

One raincoat of pale gold looking like shining slipper satin, was designed by Pierre Balmain and we were told the material was *really* made from *finely pounded glass*.

It had a tiny matching cap and you will be able to buy it in West End shops for about 6½ guineas.

Another coat in black and white flecked cotton had a tiny fitted hat with wide halo brim trimmed with velvet. It will cost about £5.

* * *

FOR the really violent Canasta enthusiast there was a raincoat of pale lemon and black checked cotton printed with hearts, diamonds, clubs and spades and boasting a pointed collar of black velvet.

A different "Steiner" hair design—suggesting added hat from real hair, ornamented with decorative posy mounted on chiffon.

There was even an evening waterproof full length in black satin lined with white. So that if one has to "walk miles" after a show because it is so difficult to manœuvre the car right up to the theatre entrance at least one will not get wet, however much it may rain.

* * *

PERHAPS it is gloomy to talk of rain at present? It is often misty but rarely really wet. The midday sun is often hot still and the fruit we gather for bottling has a warm bloom on it.

Do you know that you can bottle fruit in a pressure cooker in record time?

The Hi-Dome Pressure cooker is specially made to take three 2 lb. Kilner jars or five 1 lb. jars.

"Prestige" Hi-dome pressure cooker with three-way control—15, 10 and 5 lbs.—for bottling fruit or vegetables.

This is how filmgoers will see lovely Linda Darnell in "Saturday Island," David Rose's Technicolor production.

Glamorous blonde Jan Sterling wears a plain white evening dress for holidays with swathed waist, the fullness caught to one side with a jewelled clip.

The Prestige people have added to their range of small gadgets a useful wire contrivance which fits round the neck of the preserving jars and makes it easier to lift them out when they are hot.

If you do not want to buy special jars for preserving you can use the "Porosan Way" which is very inexpensive. The Porosan fruit caps are 3s. a dozen (lb. size), 3s. 6d. for 2 lb. sizes, and they fit quite simply and easily on the tops of jam jars.

The caps are fitted with special "skin" rings which soften under intense heat and all that is needed to fix them firmly is a slight pressure from the palm of the hand.

It is a useful method, too, for those who may have stiff rheumaticky fingers and find screwing and unscrewing caps rather difficult. You can also buy rolls of Porosan fruit preserving "skin" and cut it to fit the top of any container. I like it for the re-use of unusual shaped bottles for the preserves that will eventually be given away as Christmas gifts.

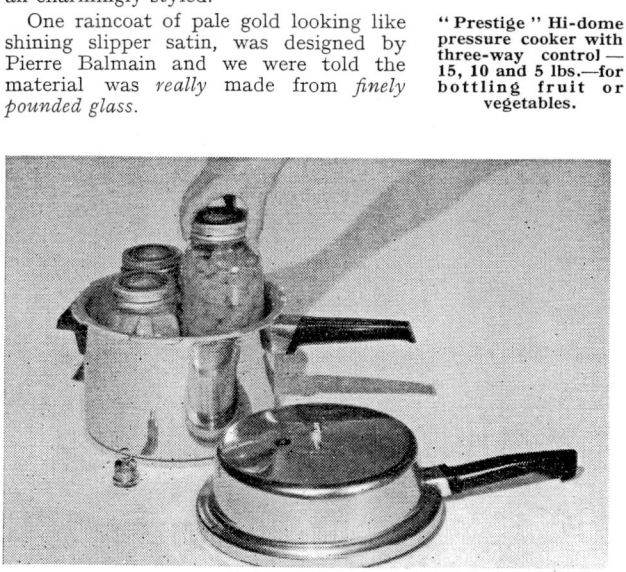

Freely cut "Hershelle" travelling coat, with wide deep-notched collar. Note giant raked pockets and pebble buttons grouped in page-boy fashion.

Remember, Colour is Life!: from p. 31

BUT it is dreary thinking of Christmas before all our holidays are over. It seems only yesterday that we unpacked and walked down Regent Street to see what was new in the shops and many people have not been a way at all yet.

Incidentally, one new thing I did spot on my "first-day-home" walk round Regent Street was—after the displays of decorated china now freely on sale—the new premises for the Scrivens Contact Lens Centre.

I have heard vaguely of the possibilities of the "invisible spectacles" as some people call contact lenses, for years, but this visit to the centre was my first opportunity to learn about them.

I actually met a girl who was wearing contact lenses.

They were quite undetectable and she showed me the pair of glasses it would be necessary to wear if she had not the lenses. They were very thick indeed and would certainly have been rather disfiguring.

Now that the wearing of glasses has become so common and as I have reported in recent numbers of *Modern Motoring and Travel*, rims are now matched to nail varnish and lipstick colours as a colourful accessory they are less likely to give the wearer an inferiority complex.

But some necessarily thick lenses *can* have a depressing effect on their wearers and it sometimes happens that a girl who has every other qualification for a career, on the stage for example, is handicapped by the need to wear such glasses.

These contact lenses fit over the eyes under the lid so closely that they are invisible.

Most people learn to put them in and out as easily as others cope with artificial teeth and find them perfectly comfortable to wear. If glasses are a real bar to the choice of a profession it is worth while examining the possibilities of wearing contact lenses instead. Nowadays the lenses are made in unbreakable light-weight plastic material and many boxers, divers and swimmers find them very useful indeed.

* * *

WE all have odd fears. Some people who wear glasses develop a morbid fear of accidents because they are afraid of getting their spectacles smashed.

For many others the great fear is of *Fire*.

They wake up in the night and "sniff," imagining they have detected the scent of smoke. They worry about coals popping out on hearthrugs, about gas left on; even about the effect of hot sun shining through glass!

I met the fire escape that is "Instant" both in name and action at this year's Chelsea Flower Show. It was among a display of ladders with an excellent "packaway" ladder that folds up flat, concertina-wise, and can be easily carried by hand or by cycle.

It is excellent applied to lofts for no structural alterations are needed and the ladder folds away in the loft so that when not in use only the control cord is visible below.

The steel fire escape ladder is made to fit under a bedroom window ledge as a permanent fixture.

If it *has* to be used, a child, or even an invalid can operate it.

Just a push and the ladder is fully extended: it does not sway and even the very old can descend without difficulty.

It is always ready for action and if you have a victim of fire "phobia" in your family it is better to invest in one. Then if you are wakened in the night by someone who smells smoke or hears a crackling sound, you can just say, "*Well, when the flames reach the door we'll go out by the window*"—and turn over.

* * *

SURROUND yourself with Happy Colours—and look forward to wearing the new "Coronation Red."

Already one enterprising maker of handbag mirrors is advertising his folding mirror in a lightweight coloured aluminium expanding frame as a "long-felt want."

See yourself from the back and top and sides as well as face to face—and remember it can also be used as a periscope to see the Coronation procession.

I call that forethought.

The price of mirror, incidentally, is 8s. 9d. The gadget is called the Stuart handbag folding mirror and you can buy it at most stores.

Addresses:

Rolakoton painting outfit. Stephenson Bros., Ltd., Listerhills Road, Bradford. Price, 55s. 6d. postage 1s. extra.

"Hints on Home Painting," free booklet. Lifeguard Household Paints, Ltd., 38, Berkeley Square, London, W.1.

Scrivens Contact-Lens Centre. 121, Regent Street, London, W.1.

Instant steel fire escape and folding ladders. Angel Truck Co., Ltd., Meteor Works, 218-219, Albion Road, London, N.16

Prestige Hi-dome pressure cooker, lifting tongs, etc., from the "Prestige" shop in most big stores—Selfridges, Barkers, Bentalls and Jackson's of Piccadilly—hardware department.

Stuart handbag folding mirror. From gift stores everywhere and made by Anodised Products, Ltd., 91, Upper Thames Street, London, E.C.4.

Left: Bright holiday smile comes from attractive British star, Barbara Murray, in Dorville sweater with white embroidery on shoulders.

Mink marmot is another reasonably priced and hard-wearing fur. This cape—by the National Fur Co.—is useful for day or evening wear. Double fronts cunningly conceal useful pockets.

O.K. FOR SOUND:

Film Shorts and Screen Gossip

WALTER PIDGEON and Greer Garson will be reunited on the screen as husband and wife in Metro-Goldwyn-Mayer's "My Mother and Mr. McChesney."
It will be their eighth picture together.

* * *

FAVOURITE sport of film star John Mills, who lives at Richmond, Surrey, is polo, and he is a member of the nearby Ham Polo Club.
He was in the Surrey team which beat Essex by 5 goals to 4.

* * *

THE Broadway musical "Kiss Me Kate," has been purchased for film production by Metro-Goldwyn-Mayer.
Cole Porter, who wrote the music for the original production, will add more songs for the screen presentation.

* * *

PATRICIA ROC, harassed mother of the Pinewood film, "Something Money Can't Buy," is expecting a baby in December. She has arranged to enter a London nursing home.
Pat's husband is André Thomás, a French film cameraman.

* * *

JAMES STEWART is to star in Universal-International's Technicolor production, "Thunder Bay."
The picture will team for the third time the star, producer and director of the Studio's highly successful "Winchester '73" and "Where the River Bends."

* * *

DAVID TOMLINSON, comedy actor of stage and screen, is to marry 22-year-old Jill Clifford. They have just finished films at Pinewood Studios—Tomlinson in the Technicolor comedy, "Made in Heaven," and Jill in the Betty Box thriller, "Venetian Bird."
A war-time Flight Lieutenant, Tomlinson is still appearing in the successful West End play, "The Little Hut."

* * *

AN unpublished Jerome Kern melody, recently discovered, is to be heard in the lavish Technicolor musical, "Lovely to Look At." It is entitled, "The Most Exciting Night."
Stars of the film are Kathryn Grayson, Howard Keel and Red Skelton, and old favourites by the late Jerome Kern will include "Smoke Gets in Your Eyes," "The Touch of Your Hand," and "Lovely to Look At."

* * *

EIGHTEEN-YEAR-OLD Armi Helena Kuusela, who, as Miss Finland, won the "Miss Universe" title, has been signed to a seven-year film contract by Universal-International, joint sponsor of the contest with Pan American World Airways and Catalina Swim Suits.
Other prizes for Miss Kuusela, physical training student from the Arctic Circle village of Muttos, were an ivory Sunbeam-Talbot "90" Sports Convertible Coupé and an £850 wrist watch.

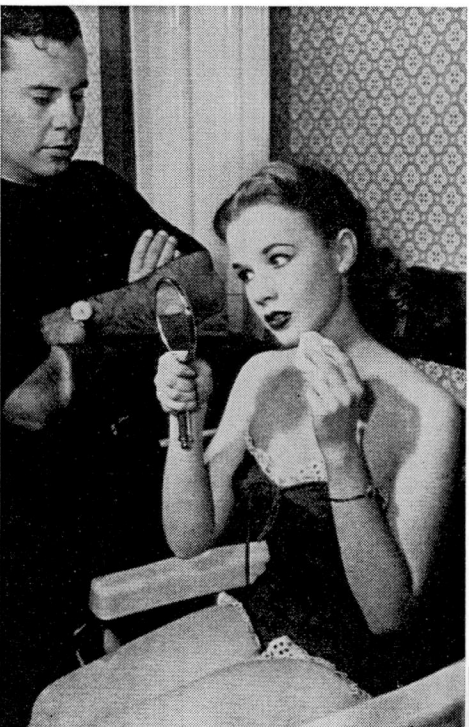

Lovely Piper Laurie who is teamed with Tony Curtis in Universal-International's "No Room for the Groom," a marriage comedy, and again in "Son of Ali Baba," a swashbuckling Technicolor production.

Mary Menzies (right), one of the seven Can-Can girls appearing in R.K.O. Radio's Technicolor film, "The Half-Breed," starring Robert Young and Janis Carter.

With blue eyes, blonde hair, she is 5 ft. 5 in. tall, weighs 110 lb., and has a 34-in. bust, 23 in. waist and 34 in. hips.

* * *

FOLLOWING her dancing hit opposite Gene Kelly in "Singing in the Rain," Cyd Charisse has been chosen to co-star with Fred Astaire in "I Love Louisa."
She will complete her romantic and dancing role in "Sombrero" before going to "I Love Louisa," a Technicolor musical.

* * *

THE mystery of the disappearance of Colonel Fawcett in the jungles of Brazil is recalled by United Artists' forthcoming "Strange World," filmed in the uncharted Matto Grosso interior.
This intrepid piece of picture-making is outstanding for its photography.

* * *

THANKS to Greer Garson, a small newspaper, previously devoted to society chatter and livestock weights, is winning a reputation in the American Southwest.
It is the *Santa Fe News*, recently acquired by Miss Garson and her husband, Colonel E. E. Fogelson.
Miss Garson filled all vacancies on the staff with ex-soldiers, and they have revitalised the paper, exposing local scandals and promoting civic interest in matters affecting the community.

* * *

GINGER ROGERS has signed a three-picture contract with Paramount.
First of the trio is "Topsy and Eva" a story based on the life of the Duncan Sisters of musical comedy fame. It is likely the other films will be "Rosalind" and "The New Haven Story."

* * *

JOHN HARDY, 13-year-old son of the British Consulate-General's commercial attaché in Los Angeles, has won the single juvenile role in M.G.M.'s "Julius Caesar." He will play Lucius, servant boy to James Mason as Brutus.

* * *

DURING the filming of "Pat and Mike," Spencer Tracy confided to Katharine Hepburn : "Sometimes it takes as long as 30 years to become a star overnight!"

Page 38   October, 1952

SPORTING SPOTLIGHTS

Round the Clubs

John Panks, winner of the Over-1,500 c.c. Class, in a One Hour Production car race in Toronto: see foot of column three.

Gold medal winners in the recent Austrian Alpine trials: Dr. Rolf Gurtler and co-driver Franz Marsch with their successful Sunbeam-Talbot.

THE Sunbeam-Talbot Owners' Club's lengthy fixture list finds members enthusiastically supporting the events all over the country — and asking for still more, between now and the end of the season and especially in regard to next year. All of which must be most encouraging, of course, to the committee and organisers who, considering the great amount of work involved, have, as we know, never lagged a moment.

* * *

SINCE our last notes there has been the Northumberland Rally, July 13, starting and finishing at the Royal Hotel, Hexham, when scores of northern members contested in a 35 miles fascinating mystery drive and treasure hunt—when R. F. Moffat, of Newcastle-on-Tyne, Dr. J. R. Steadman, of Monkseaton, and T. A. Boothroyd, of Bishop Auckland, proved first, second and third prize-winners, to receive attractive trophies presented and donated by Mr. Cliff Wheeler and Mr. Norman Rankin, both of Newcastle, and stalwart supporters of the club.

* * *

NEXT, on July 27, S.T.O.C. activities were transferred to the Chilterns for an intriguing, if short, reliability trial starting and finishing at Commonwood House Country Club, near Chipperfield, at which two competitive highlights proved to be F. Downs, of Andover; A. J. M. Milner, of Tolworth—first and second respectively, in the Sunbeam-Talbot class and P. Harper, of Stevenage and E. A. Lloyd-Davies, of Wolverhampton, first and second in the invitation Hillman section. Prizes were presented at the end of the trial by Mrs. Norman Garrad, wife of the Chairman of the General Committee.

* * *

FOLLOWING, came a popular diversion at Staverton aerodrome, near Gloucester, on August 10, in the form of a motor gymkhana attracting an enthusiastic entry with over 100 members competing in the fun and games. Fun there was—in the "thread-the-needle" race; the find the way "blindfold" test; the "wiggle-woggle," obstacle, etc., etc., with, as an appropriate finale, a more serious regularity contest for which there was equally keen competition.

Prizes were presented by Mrs. Mary Taylor, of Gloucester, immediately following tea in the Irving Hotel, Cheltenham—to, first, L. Tanner, of Minchinhampton; second, E. D. Barnfield, of Gloucester; and third, M. Orchard, also of Gloucester.

* * *

AS these notes go to press, the Club will be well into its annual Continental Rally to France, Austria, Germany and returning through Switzerland—in which nearly 100 members, travelling in some 25 to 30 Sunbeam-Talbots, are taking part. We hope to be able to publish an illustrated report in a later edition of this Journal.

* * *

HOWEVER, the dates go by and continue to come forward—for September 27-28 and October 11-12, two red-letter fixtures on the S.T.O.C. calendar. In short, regulations are now available for two autumn week-end rallies, the Scarborough Rally, September 27-28; the Torquay Rally, October 11-12.

* * *

IN view of the great success of the club's Southport Rally in April, which included a road section and a number of separate starting controls, this year's Scarborough Rally will be run on similar lines, with a road section of 220 miles, and with starting points at Manchester, Newcastle-on-Tyne, Birmingham, Luton and Scarborough. Rally Headquarters will be the Royal Hotel, Scarborough, where the usual dinner and dance will be held on the Saturday evening. This will be the Club's fifth consecutive annual visit to Scarborough, and promises to be the best yet.

* * *

FOR members who prefer the type of week-end rally which enables them to travel down to the rendezvous in their own time the previous day, the Torquay Rally has been arranged without a road section. It will consist of a very interesting hill test and a number of driving tests on the Meadfoot Sea Road in Torquay; followed, of course, by the usual Concours d'Elegance competition on the Sunday morning.

Once again the club has received the greatest co-operation from the Corporation of Torquay, and everything promises an outstanding occasion. This year Headquarters are the Imperial Hotel, where a dinner-dance will be held on the Saturday evening.

* * *

ENTRY forms, with details of hotel requirements should be forwarded to the Organising Secretary, S.T.O.C., Sunbeam-Talbot, Ltd., Ryton-on-Dunsmore, Warwickshire, as early as possible.

* * *

MEANTIME, a Scottish rally of members will be held on Saturday, September 13.

The rally will take the form of a treasure hunt, starting at 2.15 p.m., at Dunblane, and finishing at the Buchanan Arms Hotel, Drymen.

Cars will assemble in Dunblane (in the lane leading off the main Stirling-Perth road, opposite the entrance to the Dunblane Hydro).

The entry fee will be 7s. 6d. per car, and prizes will be awarded to the three competitors obtaining the highest number of points.

Entries should be submitted by not later than Wednesday, September 10, 1952.

* * *

NOR is that all!
In view of the club's rapid growth in membership, a London Branch is to be formed, to operate in the Home Counties. Steps have been taken to form a local committee which will work in conjunction with the General Committee.

Headquarters of the new branch will be at Ladbroke Hall, Barlby Road, London, W.10; Chairman of Committee, Mr. G. W. Rossiter.

The Honorary Secretary-Treasurer is Miss Marjorie Tinckham, whom pre-war members of the T.O.C. or the S.T.O.C. will remember as a leading light in Club affairs.

As soon as preliminary arrangements have been settled, full information is to be circulated.

* * *

FROM information received from Toronto recently, British cars are figuring prominently in the rapidly expanding world of motor sport in Canada.

(Continued on page 40)

THE SUNBEAM-TALBOT 90

In traffic or on the open road, the supreme Sunbeam-Talbot 90 seldom meets its match. Impressive acceleration, safe and sure stability, and needle-eye accuracy of steering, ensure high cruising speeds with effortless ease and comfort.

SMOOTH

SPEEDY

SAFE

SUPREME

SENSATIONAL SUCCESSES IN INTERNATIONAL ALPINE RALLY 1952
Three Coupes des Alpes — 1st 2nd 3rd — Manufacturers Team Prize
(2-3 LITRE CLASS)

Sunbeam-Talbot Ltd. Ryton-on-Dunsmore, Coventry. *London Showrooms and Export Division:* Rootes Ltd. Devonshire House Piccadilly W.1

Sporting Spotlights:

(Concluded from page 38)

At a meeting held by the Sports Car Club of Toronto at Edenvale Airport, in the vacation lake district 78 miles north of the city, John Panks on a Sunbeam-Talbot "90" saloon won the over 1,500 c.c. class in the One Hour Production Car Race with a Nash Rambler second and a 2½-litre Riley third. In the open, up to 3,000 c.c., race Panks on his Sunbeam-Talbot was second to an Aston Martin.

* * *

JOHN Panks, well known in motor sport circles over here before going to Canada two or three years ago, is a nephew of the late A. L. Ebblewhite, the famous R.A.C. international timekeeper.

* * *

IN the under 1,500 c.c. Production Car Race, Ian Garrad finished in second place in a Hillman saloon. Ian, by the way, is the son of Norman Garrad, Sales Manager of Sunbeam-Talbot, Ltd., and chairman of committee, S.T.O.C., and is attached to the Rootes Group Concessionaires in Toronto.

* * *

AUGUST Bank Holiday week-end provided a splendid assemblage of motor sport accompanied in most cases with that particular type of foul weather known as "uncertain, with bright intervals."

* * *

THE International meeting at Boreham with a 200 miles race for Formula 1 and Formula 2 cars running concurrently, two 100 miles races for Big Sports Cars and Small Sports Cars respectively and a 30 miles race for Formula III gave everyone value for money.

The 200 miles demonstrated how narrow is the margin of performance between Formulas 1 and 2, particularly in bad weather.

Although Villoresi (Ferrari) in winning the Formula 1 event put up fastest time in 2 hrs. 25 mins. 36 secs. (82·83 m.p.h.) Mike Hawthorn won Formula 2 in 2 hrs. 26 mins. 42 secs. (82·21 m.p.h.). Not only this, but for 22 laps Hawthorn actually led the entire field by some 20 seconds—a truly remarkable performance for the Cooper-Bristol with its 2-litre engine against the 1½-litre Ferraris and Talbots.

* * *

STIRLING Moss collected the unlimited Sports Car class in the 100 miles in his Jaguar XK 120C, Reg Parnell (Aston Martin D.B.3) doing the same in the 2,000/3,000 c.c. class and in the 1,500/2,000 c.c. class Ken Wharton (1,971 c.c. Frazer Nash) won from Salvadori's 2½-litre Ferrari.

The two BRMs, by the way, ran true to form, neither of them finishing. Repeating their Silverstone performance, one ran out of road and the other had gearbox trouble.

* * *

THE Brands Hatch International meeting produced quite a good foreign entry, but British drivers and cars proved quite equal to the occasion. D. Parker (Kieft-Norton) won both the International Trophy Race and the August Sprint, Stirling Moss (Kieft-Norton) being second in the latter event, breaking the lap record but retiring with engine trouble later in the Trophy Race.

Another piece of news from overseas is that in the recent International Austrian Alpine Rally, Dr. Rolf Guertler won a gold medal for a clean performance on his Sunbeam-Talbot "90."

* * *

THE next big rally on the calendar is the Tour de France which starts on September 9 from Nice and finishes at the same place on the 16th after a route which takes competitors practically round France. Schedule speeds, yet to be announced, are not likely to be any easier than the other continental rallies and the seven days "race" will be a tough conglomeration of long distances, hill climbs, sprints, racing (over the Rheims circuit) and a variety of tests *en route*.

* * *

REGULATIONS are also just out for the *Daily Express* Rally organised by the M.C.C. which takes place from November 12 to 15. For the past two years this has been the largest British rally and the indications are that it will again hold this position.

The road section will total approximately 1,200 miles, the finishing point being Brighton. General arrangements will be on similar lines to previously, but new routes have been planned from all starting controls.

* * *

THERE will be tests *en route* and at the finish and one point the M.C.C. emphasise is that although time will be a factor in the various tests, there will be no premium put on all-out speed. In other words, the average driver need not think himself outclassed, although naturally an expert on a good car is a combination which always takes some beating.

* * *

LIGHTHEARTED efforts of the map-reading, navigational or treasure hunt variety are very popular as a form of mild competitive work and certain go-ahead motor distributors, recognising the value of these events as a means of forming their customers into a "happy circle" are joining in the fray as organisers. Moorewell Motors, Ltd., of Cardiff, through their sports and social committee, have planned a series of events and recently held a very successful treasure hunt for the benefit of their Humber, Hillman and Sunbeam-Talbot clientele, some 70 of whom turned out. Mr. Hubert Johnson, chairman of the Cardiff Rugby Club, proved that football is not his only interest by winning the first prize in the rally.

* * *

SILVERSTONE finishes the season on September 20 with the Peterborough Club's meeting, following the Sunbac meeting on September 6 and the M.C.C.'s High Speed Trials and five-lap races on September 13. A novelty at the latter meeting will be a chicane in the runway down to Woodcote corner, designed to curb the enthusiasm of those who reduce responsible officials to nervous wrecks by cheerfully taking a dangerously blind corner "flat out."

* * *

SEPTEMBER 6 is also the date for the International High Speed Trials on the Madiera Drive at Brighton. This is now one of the oldest established events in the calendar, the first meeting having been held exactly 40 years ago. The writer "journeyed" down from London to Brighton on that occasion on a four-wheeled single seater, JAP-engined, belt-driven cyclecar known as the D.E.W. Monocar, but all thoughts of competing were washed out by an attack of overheating so severe that the bonnet had to be taken off and left at the George Hotel, Crawley, on the way down in order to reach Brighton at all!

* * *

ALTHOUGH the R.A.C. regulations for vehicles taking part in Trials and Rallies, which were introduced in 1949, will remain in force until December 31 of this year, the amendments which the R.A.C. have had under consideration for some time are due to be announced at the beginning of September.

One important point—the regulations will refer to vehicles taking part in Trials only.

This is certainly a step in the right direction. The application of the same regulations, for vehicles in both trials and rallies has not been satisfactory.

It is difficult to see that vehicle constructional regulations have ever been really necessary in rallies at all, particularly as most supplementary rally regulations relegate "specials" to a class of their own.

LET **PRATT TRAILERS** SOLVE YOUR TRANSPORT PROBLEMS

LEADERS IN THEIR CLASS!

2 TO 8 CWT CARRYING CAPACITY

THE PRATT ENGINEERING COMPANY — NORTHALLERTON, YORKS. ENGLAND

October, 1952 — Page 41 — MODERN MOTORING & TRAVEL

WHAT happens when YOU SPEAK

DO YOU hum-and-har and stumble in search of words?

DO YOU gape and gulp and become tongue-tied with embarrassment?

DO YOU shout (or whisper) all the time without tonal variety or interest?

DO YOU lose your point and miss your climax?

DO YOU get worse and worse as you feel your listeners getting more and more bored?

DO YOU forget what you meant to say, as soon as you're on your feet?

or

DO YOU marshal your arguments logically and convincingly?

DO YOU impress your listeners by forceful, calm reasonableness, punctuated by the right emphasis at the right place?

DO YOU reply to critics or enquirers without losing your self-possession—*or* your temper?

DO YOU feel that your audience is *with* you?

DO YOU *want* to be able to wield those most powerful of all weapons—*words*—to your own personal advantage and to your own advancement in any sphere you may choose? If so, this offer is specially addressed to you.

THE SPEAKERS' CLUB
(Dept. MMT/ES14), MARPLE, CHESHIRE

Speakers' Club (Dept. MMT/ES14)
Marple, Cheshire

Please send me your book, *How To Work Wonders With Words*. I enclose 2½d. stamp for postage.

Name ....
(Please Use Block Letters)

Address ....

....

SPEECH is the key to SUCCESS

WHATEVER your walk in life, the gift of speaking convincingly and forcefully will bring you immeasurable advantages—socially, commercially, financially. The ability to express your thoughts and convictions with tact, vigour and persuasiveness, opens all doors, breaks down all barriers, and leads you inevitably to the big things in life.

FREE ... This fascinating book "How to Work Wonders With Words," explains a new amazingly easy method of acquiring the gift of speaking efficiently, developing poise and personality, banishing timidity and self-consciousness. One hundred thousand men and women in all walks of life—including business executives, salesmen, factory workers, clerks and those in the Services—have found in this remarkable book a key that has opened a veritable floodgate of natural speaking ability. Send for a copy of this unique book today. It will show you how to develop this power of speech—easy—quick, sure.

WHAT THIS BOOK WILL SHOW YOU
- How to address meetings.
- How to speak before your lodge or club.
- How to train your memory.
- How to make the right impression.
- How to propose and respond to toasts.
- How to make an announcement.
- How to write better letters.
- How to enlarge your vocabulary.
- How to develop self-confidence.
- How to acquire a winning personality.

October, 1952

Northern France in its golden 1952 summer cloak—of endless acres of rich and record corn harvests.

Brunnen in all its holiday glory—in the private gardens of the Waldstatterhoff Hotel, where "Rallye Brunnen" spent a wonderful week.

The Story of "Rallye Brunnen":

Our most successful Continental Venture

"RALLYE Brunnen" first met in its entirety on the quayside at Dover on the morning of July 19—a party of 56 persons travelling in 18 Humber, Hillman and Sunbeam-Talbot cars.

For most participants it was a first-time venture on the Continent—which, to me as leader, was a comforting factor. I knew they would be ready to accept advice and guidance, the better to maintain perfect Rallye control.

There was to be nothing in the nature of a convoy journey—all were free to follow simple itineraries and routes provided.

Passed experience has proved, however, that with changed conditions generally—driving on the right of the road, unfamiliar road and traffic signs, problematical road surfaces, and everywhere an atmosphere entirely un-English—the novice to Continental touring at least welcomes brief initiation into local ways and means.

* * *

SO it was, therefore, that "Rallye Brunnen" was convoyed out of the dock area, through the cobbled thoroughfares of Calais (the first condition to inspire concern as to shock-absorber efficiency), South then for St. Omer (an even worsely cobbled congestion) and on to Bethune, a journey in which the most pleasant impression, perhaps, was the vast areas of richly golden harvests, stretching for miles on end.

It was not surprising, of course, to observe the carefully maintained distances between the cars, none daring to lose sight of its predecessor, all keeping well to the right of the road and ever on the alert for that " entry from the right " with its accompanying right of way.

If they had been well briefed and were willing to be guided, by the time "Rallye Brunnen" had reached St. Quentin (including visits to those famous battlefields of two world wars—Souchez, Vimy, Arras, Cambrai, Bapaume and Peronne) for their first overnight stop *en route* to the Swiss border, all drivers might well have been Continental die-hards.

DINNER that evening was understandably an exciting affair—new dishes, new drinks, the new experiences to be exchanged, and especially the new currency problems :—

"How much is 100 French francs ? "
" Oh, that's a lot of money ! "
" How much, then ? "
" Two shillings," I broke in.
" Oh, dear, is that all ? "
" Yes, but handle them carefully. Francs may be ' four a penny,' but you can waste pounds if you are incautious."

Small bottles of local " champagne " were on the dining tables, at 350 francs each, and very nice, too ; though some thought they were far too cheap to be good !

* * *

THE most interesting incident that first evening was the Rallye's visit to the local dance hall, when the young folk of St. Quentin really let themselves go, jitterbugging, jiving, reeling, gay in brilliant frocks, smocks and dungarees, with not an inch of floor space to spare. And each of our lassies was invited to dance, with a gesture of politeness that apparently was irresistible, the while there were a few blushes as their male partners bowed and shook hands at the end of the number. Appeal as I would, nothing could persuade that band to put on an old-time waltz for the elder members of the party, who finally elected to sip beer, beer that tasted extremely good, and watch the antics of the dancers.

Off again next morning, our way lay via Laon and Rheims, to visit the cathedral (being Sunday, the wine vaults were closed) and Bar le Duc, *en route* for the Vosges mountains and our second night's halt, at Gerardmer,

Lunch halt at Gletsch, in the wake of the spectacular Rhone Glacier, still a memorable sight though it recedes year by year.

October, 1952

nestling beside the beautiful lake, with all France, it seemed, on its banks and on and in those clear blue waters.

It was a long and memorable drive, and if the variety of picnic lunches, obtained more by barter and bewilderment than by knowledgeable choice, was the main topic at dinner, the evening meal was now generally accepted as a major affair, to be enjoyed in leisurely comfort with no thoughts now of a quick bite preparatory to going places.

Arrival at Bourgfelden, the Swiss frontier at Basle, where "Rallye Brunnen" was welcomed officially by the Automobile Club de Suisse.

Herren E. Mathis (right), and E. Ulli, of the A.C.S., meets the Rallye at the frontier to offer apéritifs as guests of the Club. They are seen with their "Rallye Brunnen" presentation souvenirs — smokers' companion sets.

The only late sitters that evening were the party who ran out of petrol some 15 miles from Gerardmer, rescued by "Freddy," our service mechanic, later to be the recipients of much good-natured chaff from those well into the third course.

We all would like to have seen more of Gerardmer, a delightful spot, but our morrow was to be another big day, the biggest in fact, our entry into Switzerland *en route* for Brunnen, the Rallye's destination.

* * *

RESPECTIVE routes (A.A. and R.A.C.) divided at Gerardmer, the majority headed for the Col de Bussang and Colmar, the few for Belfort and Cernay. Colmar, however, was the unanimous choice, the Col de Bussang rewarding with really magnificent views of almost the entire Vosges mountain range, all routes converging on Mulhouse and so for the frontier at Bourgfelden, Basle.

Here we planned a rendezvous at 12 noon. Precisely to the tick, "Rallye Brunnen" presented its invasion, accepted by Herren E. Mathis and E. Ulli, committee member and secretary, respectively, of the Automobile Club de Suisse, officially to be welcomed to Switzerland and to be invited, as guests of the club, to the Zoological Gardens' restaurant for apéritifs and refreshment—a gesture appreciated by all and reciprocated in a modest presentation from the Rallye to the Club of small souvenirs, in the form of engraved communal smokers' companion sets for use in the Club's committee rooms.

This little ceremony over, we were then led out of Basle for the road to Lucerne and Brunnen, now travelling countryside which, for the old-timer as well as the newcomer, never fails to thrill by its beauty, those emerald and steeply banked orchards, the cordial hand waves, the colourful hamlets and picturesque chalets, perfect roads, with, everywhere, the white crossed pennant or flag of the country seeming to endorse "Welcome to Switzerland."

Impressive, too, was the drive from Basle, through Olten and on to Lucerne, here to see the approaching peaks in vivid outline, all under a brilliant sun, round the lake then by way of Kussnacht, Weggis, Vitznau and Gersau and so to Brunnen and the Waldstatterhof Hotel, where our arrival was the signal, it seemed, for St. Gotthard to let loose one frightening tempestuous blast that whipped the lake almost to boiling point.

For a moment I was really anxious. Was this a warning, a change in the weather, a change for the worse?

Brunnen I had heard had been bathed in sunshine for days past—and Brunnen wet can be like drowning in the upright position!

No! The joke was soon over. The skies cleared, the peaks became silhouetted in blue against the golden sky, the stars emerged, the lakeside illuminations glittered increasingly, and we eventually retired happy, much comforted within, to appealing bedrooms that overlooked the lake, or, for the few, a later sitting in the hotel's attractive private bar or in wayside cafés, for choice night caps, beers or liqueurs at 90 cents a time or coffee *avec* cream, real cream, at 1 F. 20 c. for four!

* * *

NONE will forget dawn next morning— warm, cloudless, the mirror-like lake reflecting the mountains in perfect "topsy-turvey" outline, the sun-tipped peaks gaining in brilliance every second and, at our very windows, swallows and swifts greeting the daylight with all the promise of settled good weather. And that "opera of scenic grandeur" was presented five times in our seven days' stay.

* * *

OUR first full day in Brunnen was spent each our separate ways, resting, bathing, shopping, sight-seeing and, of course, dining and drinking upon the choicest of dishes and wines—the first day at least!

For the third day "Rallye Brunnen" went afloat, in two motor yachts, for an

"Rallye Brunnen" takes a brief rest between the Grimsel and Susten Passes, in a grand "triple pass-storming" expedition. All cars made a faultless crossing.

October, 1952

Herr K. R. Müller, past president of the A.C.S., Brunnen, supervises the judging of the Rallye's Concours d'Elégance. The Club presented valuable silver trophies to the winners.

extended tour of the lake and a special visit to Burgenstock for lunch and, later, a trip in the mountain lift rising perpendicularly over the face of the rock to some 3,500 feet above lake level. To those who ventured, the ascent was something never to be forgotten, the whole of Switzerland lay bare and awe-inspiring before us. Nor could we have had a better day, with a glowing sun throughout the eight hours on the water, and seldom has anyone enjoyed a more pleasant lunch, perched in a delectable garden 2,000 feet up, the vast Alpine panorama, from the Mythens to the Bernese Oberland, at eye-level and, below us, all Lucerne spread out like a bejewelled carpet as it glistened under the sun.

Followed next a day of rest, preparatory to the Rallye's storming of the Alps, the *pièce de résistance* of the trip, the occasion which we all considered to be the main objective of the tour.

* * *

PASS-storming is not to be taken lightly. Accordingly, drivers were carefully briefed on all necessary caution, rules to be observed, running schedules to be maintained, action in case of emergency, etc., the discussion closing with unanimous agreement that, knowing every inch of the way, I should take the lead,

Townfolk of Brunnen turn out to inspect the cars on display — an occasion which attracted much valuable press publicity for products of the Rootes Group.

decide according to the weather, select suitable stopping places and have full control.

The morning dawned cloudy and dull, to give some anxiety whether to proceed or to postpone.

I knew those clouds were too low to be really deep, that with a little luck, we might drive into and above them. So at Andermatt, at the end of the Axenstrasse, I decided to press on despite the mist, not very dense, with here and there brighter spreads confirming my belief that, somewhere above, the sun was ready to greet our reaching the higher regions.

That is exactly what happened!

Cautiously we pressed on to ascend the Furka Pass, wriggling our way over the countless hairpin bends, many undergoing repair, cars some 100 feet between, until at the Furka Hotel (7,500 feet) we emerged into brilliant sunshine, the clouds dropping and disappearing every second to reveal vaster and vaster areas of precipitous slopes and snow-capped peaks, now crystal clear against a blue sky, points below still heavily snow-bound,

Left: G. Griffiths, of Shropshire, winner of the Concours d'Elégance, receives the Silver Goblet of the A.C.S. from Mrs. Müller.
Below: L. Taylor, of Hayes, Kent, 2nd prize winner, was also presented with a silver goblet. A similar trophy was awarded to S. Winter, of Ceylon, the 3rd prize winner.

while, in turn, we proceeded to park until the tail-end of the pass-stormers signalled, "All up and no mishaps!"

If I had had any doubts previously, they had now vanished, especially when, at the hotel, I learned that the far sides of the passes were all bathed in sunshine.

Returning to our cars, we descended carefully, pausing a while by the Rhone glacier—it is receding increasingly every year, though still a spectacle to thrill!—for Gletsch and lunch by the roaring Rhone waters as they gather in force and speed from the glacier's continuously melting ice and snow. It is difficult indeed to realise that the Rhone river, thus created, presses on through the Brig and Martigny valleys for Lake Geneva, later to emerge and continue south for entry into the Mediterranean at Marseilles.

Lunch over, we began the ascent of the Grimsel Pass, rising in step-like gradients on its endless hairpin corners, to the higher dams and upper lakes, over a surface much improved on previous years, to reach its impressive road summit, at 6,572 feet, almost on top of the world, windless by an amazing chance, warmer still under a blazing sun, with all cars maintaining steady progress notwithstanding the inexperience in Alpine climbing by motor-car of most of the drivers.

* * *

OUR descent of the Grimsel was even more impressive. It seems to drop thousands of feet every 100 yards, with the verdant valley spread out before one and inviting, as a lusciously soft bed, upon which to lay and rest. Which, when we reached the base, we all did, having some 20 minutes to spare and coming as a welcome respite before tackling the more truly spectacular and precipitous, though magnificently engineered, Susten Pass (6,962 feet upper road), the last built of all Switzerland's great Alpine passes.

Hard it was to believe, indeed, that those mighty heights before us were actually on our course, that those fascinating blotches of white brickwork seen, from below, only as white spots on the upper mountain slopes, were actually the walls of hairpin corners awaiting our arrival and easy manœuvres.

* * *

THERE were no hesitant stragglers. They all linked up, 25 yards apart, and proceeded—up, up, up, engines

(Concluded on page 46)

"FOR MY HILLMAN **Give me CASTROL every time**"

Castrol

Every British car manufacturer approves Castrol

"Rallye Brunnen":

(Continued from page 44)

humming contentedly (with, perhaps, one or two exceptions)—2,000, 3,000, 4,000, 5,000, 6,000 feet, ears burbling with every 2,000-foot phase in the climb, the scene increasing in unbelievable grandeur, of lakes, valleys and peaks, the latter needle sharp against the azure sky, the ascent the continuous job in hand, and every hairpin turn presenting newer and more breathtaking views.

A perfect surface, corners well banked, our passed road dropping lower and lower every moment, here and there glimpses of the last of the line, thousands of feet below, like beetles on an endless white and trailing ribbon, we continuing up and up until, at long last, the summit is reached in an open and convenient parking place, with welcome refreshment available for those who would dally for the purpose.

* * *

AT the summit we stood around in silence, in awed amazement at the grandeur of the scene, as captains of our respective "ships," monarchs of all about us, proud of the achievement and grateful for such reward for our efforts.

My own thoughts were concerned, in convincing contrast, with other times, when the views, completely blanketed out by fiercesome storm clouds and heavy shadows, offered no such reward.

Of course we all dallied above, to take due fill of the scene, quite beyond description, with, ahead now, only the ever descending road, mile after mile, lower and still lower, in its rapid depth-dropping contours for Wassen—and tea! And eventually we glided down in unison, mostly in third gear, dropping wave after wave, corner following corner, then as on some giant shelf with the mountain edge at right angles to the depths below, easier now, and smoother, finally to enter picturesque Wassen and our return road for Brunnen.

Few of us will forget that tea, thrilled in conversation upon a wonderful drive. Never was I more proud of a brilliant set of drivers and cars, bearing in mind the newness of the experience, and such an experience for all of them; the initial experience, impressive as the passes always can be no matter how well one is acquainted with their ever-changing moods, never to be forgotten.

For days the main conversation was about that "triple-pass" drive, those towering peaks at the summit of the Furka as well as those on the ascent of the Susten. One just cannot grasp their full reality, in height and magnificence, even when seen, as we saw them, green, gold and blue-grey under a glorious sun, etched every inch against a cloudless sky.

* * *

ON the Saturday restful leisure in Brunnen, on the lake, the lidos and in mild local excursions was the general order, for the big reason that on the Sunday was to be the Rallye's special Concours d'Elegance, the first of its kind ever seen in Brunnen, to be judged by high officials of the Automobile Club de Suisse.

The local press, too, took an encouraging interest in the event, appealing to all Brunnen to patronise "this great display of British quality cars."

What a display! Their drivers had spent hours in cleaning and polishing—to look as if directly from the motor showroom, spread out in a wide arc in the town centre with the Rallye service van, in scarlet and gloss, acting as the centre sentinel.

* * *

THE panel of judges, headed by Herr K. R. Müller, past-President of the A.C.S., Brunnen, included Herr A. Dettling (A.C.S.), Herrens Boegeli and Deffinger of the Brunnen Kuverein and Herr Kuhliman (A.C.S.) who, between them, "judged" the cars as scrupulously as I have seen in any event of the kind anywhere—bodywork, upholstery, carpets, wings, chromium, touring aids, accessories, assessing points also in relation both to age and mileages covered.

The result found Geoffrey Griffiths, of Whitchurch, Shropshire; L. Taylor, of Hayes, Kent, and S. Winter, from Ceylon, holders of first, second and third places, in close contest. Moreover, to our great surprise, the Automobile Club de Suisse presented to the winners, in addition to their official Rallye awards, handsome solid silver goblets bearing the A.C.S. Club crest, while from the Rootes Group's headquarters in Zürich came welcome support, in the practical form of a cash prize of 100 Swiss francs. Additionally, all cars were decorated with a beautiful A.C.S. club pennant bearing, on one side the white cross of Switzerland and, on the reverse, the club's decorative badge design.

Here, too, the Rallye was favoured with ideal weather conditions, and small wonder drivers and crews made quickly for the lidos following those two hours awaiting the judges' decision under that blazing sun.

* * *

AT long last came the moment for our return, a moment of universal regret, headed on the Monday via Zürich, Baden and Basle for the Nancy night stop prior to staying at Arras before our final departure for Calais and our return cross-channel trip.

Our last evening in France was spent in a final get-together—to discuss the highlights of the Rallye, to plan for next time, but certainly to offer tributes to those to whom so much of the success of "Rallye Brunnen, 1952" was due—in particular to the Motorists' Travel Club (in the person of Mrs. S. W. Mason, who accompanied the Rallye) through which organisation all routine matters were facilitated; our courier, Norman Webb, and last, but certainly not least, Freddy Austin, the service mechanic, who, by his diligent observations throughout the near 2,000 miles route, ensured the successful and trouble-free passage of all vehicles from Dover back to Dover.

* * *

THAT, as briefly as space permits, is the story of "Rallye Brunnen, 1952."

The many incidents of interest, the members themselves, and the grand party spirit which revealed itself in the early stages and continued to the end, would make worth-while reading for continuous volumes of this Journal.

For example, people who met as strangers ('though perhaps fellow owner-drivers) only 12 days later dispersed as bosom friends. No longer "Mr. This," "Mrs. That," etc., but each his or her own pet nickname—in "Tweety-pie," "Chunky," "Phoebee," the "Doc!," "Sylvester," "Fancy Pants," "Cream Crackers," with, for me, an affectionate "Chiefy."

Such things may not, of course, be of great interest to the general reader, but the facts do show that "Rallye Brunnen, 1952" was not only wholly successful but a thoroughly enjoyable and friendly affair!

T. R. M.

Added Comfort for your Hillman Minx

ARM REST for Bench Type Seats
Saves driving fatigue, and serves as a useful container. Well upholstered in various colours. Can be fitted in any desired position. 40/- each.

SLIDING ROOF
Fixed-head saloons converted to sunshine opening roof. Send for full particulars and name of your nearest fitting agent.

"COOLRIDE" CUSHION
Provides cool, softly-sprung comfort by allowing free circulation of air between rider and upholstery. One size for all cars. 35/- each.

*You can order by post with confidence.
Send for illustrated leaflets.*

Weathershields Ltd
BISHOP ST., BIRMINGHAM 5 · ENGLAND

FIT "TripleX" AND BE SAFE

Regd.

COMMERCIAL MOTOR EXHIBITION, STAND 318

IT'S FUNNY!

that despite competing claims—"APOLLO" IS STILL THE ONLY CAR POLISH IN THE WORLD"—to carry the endorsement of *Leading* Car-Makers including Humber—Hillman—Sunbeam-Talbot—Morris—Wolseley—M.G.—Riley—Renault—Alvis—Allard—Singer—Standard—Triumph (five *others* use it)—*Leading* overseas assemblies such as Ashok Motors (India)—Peninsular Motors (Calcutta)—Dominion Motors (New Zealand)—*Leading* Motor-Cycle Makers including B.S.A.—Douglas-Vespa—U.K. Lambretta & Canterbury—Saxon & Viking Side-Cars—*Leading* Coachbuilders, Public, Commercial, Official Transport.

TOUGHER THAN WAX—See it demonstrated at the Motor Show (Stand 10).

"Apollo" is NEVER "in short supply"—we have NO "sole distributors" in the U.K.—and will send Post-Paid 3/9 tin against remittance (3/9 only), in case of difficulty.

Sole Manufacturers :

BERNARD J. ELLIS, LTD.

"Apollo" Polish Works, EPSOM ROAD, LEYTON, E.10

October, 1952

IN A FEW WORDS

The Humber Pullman Limousine belonging to His Highness Sheikh Sulman Bin Hamad Al Khalifa, J.C.V.O., outside the Palace gates at Bahrein on the Persian Gulf. On right of picture, the daily delivery of water is seen arriving, carried in goat skins on the camel's back.

THE Postmaster-General hopes to make a regulation, early in the next session of Parliament, concerning the fitting of suppressors to new motor-cars to prevent interference with television reception. Voluntary fittings proceed at the rate of 300,000 a month.

* * *

FIELD MARSHAL EARL ALEXANDER, Minister of Defence, will perform the opening ceremony at the Motor Show at Earls Court, London, on Wednesday, October 22.

* * *

ANTICIPATING a record demand for qualified guides to popular tourist centres in Coronation year, the British Travel and Holiday Association is planning a special training course for guide-lecturers. There are at present 242 guides on the Association's register, 48 of them women.

* * *

A COMET jetliner service between London and Colombo, Ceylon, was introduced by B.O.A.C. on August 11. Flying time is 16 hours 35 minutes, with stops at Rome, Beirut, Bahrain, Karachi and Bombay.

* * *

THE CROSS-CHANNEL air ferry, operated by Silver City Airways, has completed an accident-free record of 10,000 flights. In the past 12 months the service has carried 15,000 vehicles across the Channel.

A Hillman Minx passes through a giant Redwood tree on the Pacific coast of the United States.

BY 1954 the Pernis (Rotterdam) refinery of the Royal Dutch-Shell Group will have an output of 9,000,000 tons a year, thus becoming the largest refinery in Europe, including the United Kingdom.

* * *

FROM OCTOBER 26 the "Golden Arrow" all-Pullman service will leave Victoria at 1 p.m. during the winter months. A comprehensive ticket includes the cost of meals and dining car gratuities. Time of departure from Paris remains at 12.30 p.m.

* * *

ROADSIDE breakdowns are increasing, according to the figures of the R.A.C.

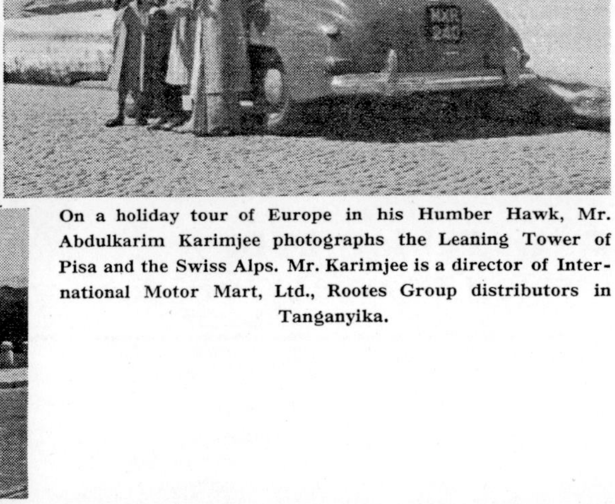

On a holiday tour of Europe in his Humber Hawk, Mr. Abdulkarim Karimjee photographs the Leaning Tower of Pisa and the Swiss Alps. Mr. Karimjee is a director of International Motor Mart, Ltd., Rootes Group distributors in Tanganyika.

"Get-you-Home" Service. In the first six months of 1952 the R.A.C. handled 13,146 cases, compared with 11,198 in the same period last year.

* * *

OF THE 18,200 motor vehicles registered in South Africa between January and May this year, 9,300 came from Britain. Vehicles from the United States, Canada and Germany totalled about 7,400.

* * *

THE FIRST petrol refinery in Chile, at Cerro Manantiales, Tierra del Fuego, will shortly be in operation. It cost 100 million pesos.

* * *

MR. H. BURROUGHES, Deputy Managing Director of the Hawker Siddeley Group, has been elected President of the Society of British Aircraft Constructors for 1952-53.

* * *

MR. F. E. ROKISON, Shipping Controller of the Rootes Group, has been elected Chairman of the Shipping Committee of the Society of Motor Manufacturers and Traders. He was previously Vice-Chairman.

The Committee, which represents all sections of the motor industry, deals with shipping and transport problems, especially with regard to exports. The vast traffic of the industry's products to overseas markets requires close liaison with shipping and port authorities, road haulage and the railways.

Mr. Rokison has been a member of the Shipping Committee since its inception in 1947, when it was set up by the British Manufacturers Section of the Society of which Sir William Rootes, K.B.E., was then Chairman.

Mr. F. E. Rokison

* * *

THERE WERE 518 entries in the architectural competition for designing petrol service stations, sponsored by Shell-Mex and B.P., Ltd. Two architects practising in London, one an Australian, shared the top prizes.

* * *

WHILE THE number of British passengers travelling to the Continent between February and May was 22 per cent. less than in the same period last year, British European Airways carried 7 per cent. more passengers on its international services.

* * *

IN MAY and June, with the start of B.O.A.C.'s "Mayflower" and "Beaver" Constellation tourist flights between Britain and North America, the Corporation carried 13,567 passengers across the North Atlantic.

(Continued on page 52)

October, 1952　　　　Page 51　　　　MODERN MOTORING & TRAVEL

How to Dirt-Proof
YOUR ENGINE OIL

and prevent THIS

Dirty oil wastes your money. It clogs piston-ring slots, gums-up valve stem guides and constricts oil passages.

Your AC Oil Filter goes on filtering out the clogging sludge, dirt and grit which grind away engine efficiency — until the element is *packed solid*. A fresh A.C. Element at least *every 8,000 miles* means fewer repair bills . . . greatly reduced engine wear . . . less frequent oil changes.

Get your local Humber-Hillman Agent or any good garage to change your AC Filter Element at least every 8,000 miles.

REPLACEMENT ELEMENTS

Humber-Hawk 1948-9　L11—11/-	Sunbeam Talbot 2-Litre 1947-48-49 1948-50 "90" L11—11/-
Super-Snipe and Pullman 1948-50　K11—12/6	1948-50 10 HP & "80"　L14—9/6

MINX OWNERS! Your agent can now fit the approved AC Oil Filter to your car.

AC Oil Filters

AC-SPHINX SPARK PLUG CO., DIVISION OF GENERAL MOTORS LTD., DUNSTABLE, ENGLAND and Southampton, Hants.

Yes, it's insured—but I'm not paying anything this year!

"I get the benefit of the 'General's' excellent idea of giving you free household insurance if you hold a Policy for five years without having had to make a claim. It's sensible that —and the saving is especially welcome in these days when economy is so necessary." 'General' Householder's policies cover your home against fire, burglary, storm, burst pipes and many other risks for 2/3% on buildings, 5/-% on contents. Send off the coupon for particulars.

.... *Peace of mind costs very little* ....

General ACCIDENT FIRE AND LIFE ASSURANCE CORPORATION LTD

Please send full particulars of Household Insurance

Name _____

Address _____

_____

_____

Send coupon to H.C. Dept., General Buildings, Perth, Scotland, or to nearest office (see Telephone Directory)

M.M. HC/16

Members of the British Olympic Equestrian Team, which gained three gold medals for Britain in the last contest of the Olympic Sports, photographed with their mounts alongside the Hillman Estate Car which the team used in Helsinki. From left, Foxhunter with Col. H. M. Llewellyn, Nizefella and Mr. W. H. White, Col. D. N. Stewart and Monarch, and Mr. G. B. Robeson.

The late Mr. B. F. Bovill ; obituary below.

IN A FEW WORDS:

(Continued from page 50)

MR. D. B. COLLETT, a son of the late Sir Charles Collett, Bart., Lord Mayor of London in 1933-34, is returning to England from Canada to join the Dunlop main board as an executive director. He has been vice-president and general manager of Dunlop Tyre and Rubber Goods Co. in Toronto.

* * *

A NEW chairlift reaching into the heart of the Alps has been inaugurated at Champex, well-known resort in the Canton of Valais. In 20 minutes the chairlift takes passengers to a height of more than 7,200 ft. to the mouth of the great Trient glacier, near to the 8,800 ft. Orny Hut and the Mont-Blanc Massif.

* * *

" Sir,—IN THE Royal Scottish Automobile Rally . . . the Minx's performance was superb. She was driven literally up and down some of the roughest mountain roads I have ever seen, and was put through some quite gruelling driving tests. We covered the 1,058 miles without even a puncture ; no mechanical trouble whatsoever. We gained the highest marks for the Braking Test *down* " Rest And Be Thankful " with high praise from the Marshal over the Minx's brakes. She was the only Minx entry in the Rally. . . . She well and truly lived up to her name, ' Minx Magnificent.' (Sgd.) M. D. P., Bournemouth."

SHELL-MEX AND B.P. LTD. have issued an illustrated booklet recording the triumphs of British motor cyclists in the international competitions of 1951.

* * *

" INNS TO Hunt Out," a booklet on selected Ind Coope inns in the Home Counties, follows the first booklet by Ind Coope and Allsopp, Ltd., dealing with the Midlands.

The honorary officers and officials of the Society of Motor Manufacturers and Traders for 1952-53 : Back row (left to right) : Mr. R. Gresham Cooke, M.A. (Director), Mr. A. B. Waring (Vice-President), Dr. F. Llewellyn Smith (Vice-President), Mr. S. E. Clark, O.B.E., A.C.A. (Secretary) ; front row : Mr. G. E. Beharrell (Deputy President), Mr. H. Spurrier (President), and Mr. W. B. Black (Hon. Treasurer).

WITH REGRET the death is recorded of Mr. B. F. Bovill, founder and chairman of Langney Motors, Ltd., of Eastbourne and Hastings, Sussex, in the Royal Masonic Hospital, London. He was aged 70.

Mr. Bovill began his motor business at Eastbourne in 1909, following 10 years in engineering in the Midlands, renting part of a small livery stableyard. He engaged one mechanic.

In 1949 Mr. Bovill saw the Mayor of Eastbourne open the handsome new showrooms and offices of Langney Motors at premises in Langney Road, Eastbourne. The staff by this time numbered about 100. There was also a successful branch at Hastings.

Mr. Bovill, who leaves a widow, was a Fellow of the Institute of the Motor Industry, and was also connected with the East Sussex section of the Motor Agents' Association. He was President of the Eastbourne and District Chamber of Commerce in 1949 and 1950.

* * *

THE DEATH is also recorded with regret of Mr. A. J. Bagley, at the age of 60, London Manager for Smiths Motor Accessories, Ltd. He had been with the company since 1919, and had held the managership for over 25 years.

* * *

IN a letter to the Editor, reproduced in the last issue, " N.B., of Surrey," referred to C.M.C. (Croydon), Ltd., of Croydon Road, Caterham, Surrey. Our correspondent was in error, of course, as the organisation concerned is C.M.C. (Caterham), Ltd., of Croydon Road, Caterham, Surrey.

The fleet of Commer vehicles operated by the Workington Brewery Co., Ltd., in Westmorland and Cumberland—the " John Peel " country—has a novel method of identification. Each vehicle bears a portrait of the head of a foxhound from the Melbreak Pack, the M.F.H. of the Melbreak Hunt being Major Iadele, Chairman and Managing Director of Workington Brewery. The vehicles were supplied through Messrs. Myers & Bowman, Ltd., of Distington.

January, 1953 — Page 1 — Modern Motoring & Travel

Don't wait till it's too late
PROTECT YOUR CAR NOW
with Esso
ANTI-FREEZE

Don't leave your car at the mercy of the first hard frost. Don't risk big bills for replacing a cracked cylinder block or a ruined engine. Take the simple precaution of driving round to your garage now for one swift easy treatment with non-corrosive, non-inflammable engine-protecting Esso anti-freeze. This will keep your car absolutely safe throughout the winter months.

**DON'T DELAY
call at your Garage
TODAY**

It pays to say **Esso ANTI-FREEZE**

THE ESSO PETROLEUM COMPANY, LTD., 36 QUEEN ANNE'S GATE, LONDON, S.W.1

A CAR LOOKS AS NEW AS ITS CARPETS!

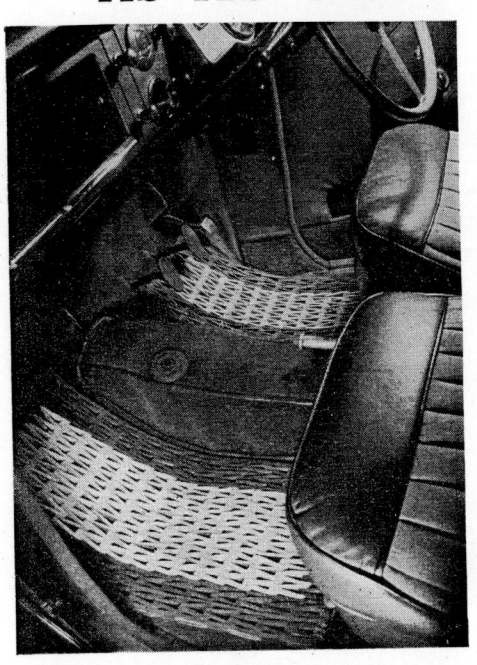

★

NEAT, PERFECT FITTING, LASTING.

Obtain complete car-interior cleanliness. Put into position or removed without fuss; design and finish in keeping with car's key-note of quality.

They are constructed of laminated rubberised cotton fabric, woven together on galvanised steel wires,
GUARANTEED FOR TEN YEARS.

FREE TRIAL OFFER

PRICES:

Humber Hawk and Snipe 1953:	£ s. d.	Hillman Minx 1950/53 (Phase IV):	£ s. d.	Sunbeam-Talbot "90":	£ s. d.
Front Mats	1 19 4	Front Mats	2 3 10	Front Mats	1 16 7
Rear Mats	2 12 10	Rear Mats	1 18 5	Rear Mats	1 17 9
	4 12 2		4 2 3		3 14 4
Purchase Tax	1 3 1	Purchase Tax	1 0 7	Purchase Tax	0 18 7
	5 15 3		5 2 10		4 12 11

Fill in this coupon and post to the The Universal Mat Co., Ltd., Tileyard Road, York Way, London, N.7.

Please send me on a week's free trial

Front pair mats .... ⎫
Back pair mats .... ⎬ Please mark here set
Complete set mats .... ⎭ required.

for.........h.p. Make............Year............

Signed (Name) ....

Address ....

Date...............

I sign this coupon on the distinct understanding that I am at liberty to return the mats any time within one week of receipt. If retained, I undertake to pay for mats within thirty days net.

THIS OFFER APPLIES TO U.K. ONLY

Protect Your Carpets with UNIVERSAL CAR MATS

Britain's best number plate

Ace "Silver Peak"

This is the number plate with the attractive silver-anodised characters — the number plate which actually adds to the appearance of a car. Fit a new set to your old car and see what a difference they make, and remember to specify "Silver Peak" for your new car when it comes along. We have a nation-wide service but if you have any difficulty please write direct to us.

N.C. 52

CORNERCROFT LTD
ACE WORKS COVENTRY PHONE COVENTRY 64123
32 CLARGES ST LONDON W 1 PHONE GROSVENOR 1646

Quick-fitting grille attachment

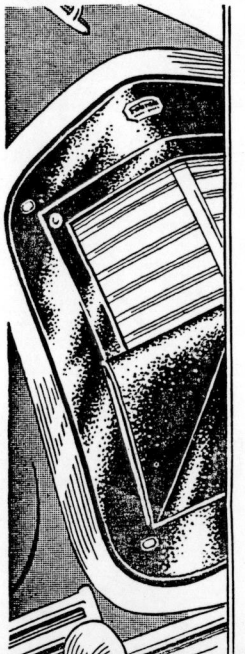

Fabram MINIMUFS *Patented*

★ The Best winter safeguard against frost and engine damage.

★ Ensures quick starting and minimum of wear and strain.

★ Sturdily made; triple material throughout, clean tailored lines, reinforced seams; fixed in a few moments with patented quick-action attachment.

★ DELIVERY FROM STOCK FOR ALL POPULAR MODELS

PRICES (retail)

Humber (all models) **40/-**
Hillman Minx (all models) .. **35/-**
Sunbeam-Talbot (all models) .. **35/-**

Also FABRAM RADIATOR MUFFS; all popular models at current prices from stock.

FAXALL PRODUCTS LTD.
BLACKLEDGE WORKS -- HALIFAX
Telephone: Halifax 5208   Telegrams: FAXALL, Halifax

for all round quality

G.K.N. 'R' high tensile bolts conform to the tolerances and physical requirements laid down in B.S.1083. They are precision bolts of first-class finish, owing their quality to careful selection of material, skilful tool design, correct heat treatment and constant inspection during production. G.K.N. supply these bolts, nuts and set screws with special protective coatings if required.

GKN 'R' HIGH TENSILE BOLTS AND SET SCREWS

if it's a matter of how to fasten one thing to another—get in touch with ...

GUEST KEEN & NETTLEFOLDS (MIDLANDS) LIMITED

Bolt and Nut Division: Atlas Works, Darlaston, South Staffs.   Telephone: Darlaston 28

P&O
to Australia and The East

For Sailings and Fares Apply:—
14/16 Cockspur St., S.W.1 · 9 Kingsway, W.C.2
122 Leadenhall St., E.C.3

Lis-tergent Autofoam SHAMPOO
with FLEXY CAR WASHERS

A NEW ERA IN CAR CLEANING

★ Removes dirt, oil and road film.
★ Restores and preserves cellulose and chrome.

The Secrets in the Suds

As easy as washing...

AUTO-FOAMED CARS AWARDED THREE FIRSTS in CONCOURS D'ELEGANCE

A MEDIUM CAR TAKES 20 MINUTES

Obtainable from your Garage, **HALFORD'S and GAMAGES.**
Ask for Catalogue L.A.S.1. from:

LISTER EQUIPMENT LTD · 3 CHARLOTTE ST · MANCHESTER 1

PROTECT YOUR CAR AGAINST FROST with DESMO HEATERS

DESMO RADILAMP No. 58
A well designed paraffin Heater which will burn for 250 hours with one filling.
Built on the miner's lamp principle and can therefore be used in close proximity to petrol vapour. Fitted with an outside flame regulator and a double-ended hook for hanging purposes - - *Retail Price* **17/6**

DESMO UNIVERSAL HEATER No. 126
The finest Car Heater ever produced. Only 6¾ in. high and will go underneath any car. Keeps oil in sump warm and facilitates easy starting on the coldest morning. Saves engine wear. Built on the miner's lamp principle, it can be used in close proximity to petrol vapour.
One filling of paraffin (4 pints) gives 250 hours of burning. Fitted with outside flame regulator - *Retail Price* **23/-**

Obtainable from all good garages and motor agents.

DESMO LTD.
BIRMINGHAM, 7 · Telephone: ASTON CROSS 2831-2-3
London Showrooms: 220 Shaftesbury Avenue, W.C.2. Tel.: Temple Bar 1994-5

Holdens

---

for Industrial Buildings..

...Consult THORNS

We have supplied many buildings to the motor industry and this may be just the building *you* want; but even if it is not, Thorns method of construction permits speedy adaptation. Basically the design is particularly suitable for:

OFFICE . CANTEEN . LIGHT INDUSTRY . STORAGE
15', 20', 25', 30' SPANS   7', 8', 10' EAVES

Or any design and size to your specification

Thorns also make
Commercial Garages, Coach Stations, Repair Shops, Spraying Shops, etc., in steel and concrete.

We shall be pleased to send details and prices.

J. THORN & SONS LTD. (DEPT. 67)
BRAMPTON ROAD, BEXLEYHEATH, KENT
Telephone: Bexleyheath 305   Established 1896

BD435

Light AND **HEAVY** PRESSINGS

As supplied to many of the leading Motor Car Manufacturers

OF ALL TYPES & IN ALL METALS

A. E. JENKS & CATTELL LTD.
PHOENIX WORKS, WEDNESFIELD
WOLVERHAMPTON

BIND YOUR
"Modern Motoring and Travel"

★

"EASIBIND" Covers to hold twelve copies, or one full volume, now available; strongly made, steel reinforced.

Price 15s. post free.

★

Orders, with remittances, to—
The Manager, "Modern Motoring & Travel,"
53 Stratton Street, Piccadilly, W.1.

AND NOW!
"AS USED BY THE DAIMLER CO., LTD."

WE ARE PROUD to be associated in the production of these Distinguished cars — as also the fine range of

HUMBER	HILLMAN
SUNBEAM-TALBOT	TRIUMPH
MORRIS	WOLSELEY
M.G.	RILEY
STANDARD	SINGER
RENAULT	ALVIS
ALLARD	JENSEN cars

B.S.A. — DOUGLAS-VESPA and LAMBRETTA U.K. motor-cycles

CANTERBURY—SAXON—VIKING and GARRARD side-cars,

for whom "Nothing but the best" is a grand old English tradition.

14-oz. TIN 3/9,—POST-PAID IF DIFFICULTY ANYWHERE IN THE WORLD UPON REMITTING 3/9 TO SOLE MAKERS

BERNARD J. ELLIS, LTD.
"Apollo" Polish Works,
EPSOM ROAD, LEYTON, E.10

"APOLLO" FOR ALL FINISHES without pre-cleaning—for all climates—on heated or wet surfaces and in shimmering sunshine.

"Apollo" CAR POLISH SUPREME!

"The MINX makes my whole family happy!"

" 35,000 miles of magnificent performance from my Minx—and not a spot of trouble!" reports Mr. Carl Storm, of Goteborg, Sweden. "In below-zero snowstorms and rough dusty roads in summer, its reliability, comfort and economy are unfailing. We often sit 3 in the front, and its handiness in traffic, leisurely 60 m.p.h. cruising, and perfect balance, make us happy with our Minx."

THE HILLMAN MINX

EXPORT DIVISION
ROOTES
DEVONSHIRE HOUSE
PICCADILLY LONDON W1
Distributors throughout the World

ROOTES GROUP REGIONAL REPRESENTATIVES *located at:*

U.S.A. 505 Park Avenue, New York 22, N.Y. and 403 North Foothill Road, Beverly Hills, California.
CANADA 2019 Eglinton Avenue East, Scarborough, Ontario.
AUSTRALIA & NEW ZEALAND Fishermen's Bend, Port Melbourne, Australia.
SOUTHERN AFRICA 750/2/4 Stuttaford's Buildings, St. George's St., Cape Town, S.A.
CENTRAL AFRICA Jackson Road, P.O. Box 5194, Nairobi, Kenya.
BELGIUM Shell Building, 47, Cantersteen, Brussels.
FRANCE 6 Rond-Point des Champs Elysees, Paris, 8.
SWITZERLAND 3 Jenatschstrasse, Zurich.
FAR EAST Macdonald House, Orchard Road, Singapore, 9
INDIA Agra Road, Bhandup, Bombay.
NEAR EAST 37 Kasr El Nil Street, Cairo, Egypt.
MIDDLE EAST & PAKISTAN Esseily Building, Assour Beirut, Lebanon.
JAPAN Strongs Building, No. 204 Yamashita-cho, Naka-Ku, Yokohama.
ARGENTINA Cassilla de Correo, 3478., Buenos Aires
BRAZIL Av. Presidente Vargas 290 (S/1003), Rio de Janeiro.
CARIBBEAN 28 Duke Street, Kingston, Jamaica, B.W.I.

Sunrise on Conway : N. Wales
Photo by Harry Fox

But yonder comes the powerful king of day
Rejoicing in the East. The lessening cloud,
The kindly azure, and the mountain's brow,
Illumed with fluid gold, his near approach
Betoken glad.

Thompson —*The Seasons.*

H.M. Queen Elizabeth, the Queen Mother, is received on the Hillman stand at Earls Court by Sir William Rootes, K.B.E., chairman of the Rootes Group.

H.R.H. Princess Margaret also visited the Exhibition and is here seen with Mr. Geoffrey Rootes, managing director, Humber, Hillman and Sunbeam-Talbot, examining the working "Blue Riband" engine of the new Humber Super Snipe.

Below: After officially declaring the Exhibition open, Field-Marshal Viscount Alexander of Tunis, K.G., G.C.B., G.C.M.G., C.S.I., D.S.O., M.C., Minister of Defence, toured the stands—here seen viewing the Hillman exhibits with Sir William Rootes.

Left: Field-Marshal Viscount Montgomery of Alamein, K.G., G.C.B., D.S.O., receives from Sir William Rootes a silver statuette of an "Officer of the Royal Warwickshire Regiment, 1908," as a memento of his visit recently, to the Group's factories at Coventry.

Editorial Comment

EDITORIAL AND ADVERTISING
53 STRATTON STREET, LONDON, W.1
Telephone: GRO 3401

Conducted by E. D. O'BRIEN

Editor: THOMAS R. MULCASTER

IN assessing the balance sheet for 1952 where the motor industry and associate interests are concerned, there comes to light a fantastic state of affairs.

Here are the facts ; judge for yourself !

* * *

The Credit Side

OPERATIVES directly employed total 1,827,000. Indirectly concerned, however, but dependent primarily upon the industry's well-being is a further 3,000,000 ; grand total, nearer 5,000,000.

Motor taxation—in licence duties, fuel tax and purchase tax—is expected to yield £350,000,000 for the year, making £1,250,000,000 for the six years ending March 31 next.

The value of the industry's exports—quoting the 1950 figure at £269,000,000, beaten in 1951 by over £40,000,000, may easily show improvement. As the third largest industry in the land, it still is Exporter No. 1.

On the credit side, therefore, we have only achievement and more achievement.

* * *

The Debit Side

NOTHING but frustration all the way.

For our rapidly deteriorating road system, allocation from the £350,000,000 revenue is but £20,000,000 !

To alleviate the " black-spot " scandal we are promised— " in appreciation of the urgency obtaining," admits the Government—£2,250,000 during the next three years !

The annual accident rate remains obstinately at the appalling figure of 5,000 killed and 250,000 injured year after year.

In the total of 4,245,398 casualties since 1928, the post war aggregate, at 1,076,647, challenges all British Service killed and wounded during World War II.

The Nation's " accident cost," moreover, reliably computed at £146,000,000 annually, looks like being an inflexible quantity.

Inferior road surfaces, acute bottle-necks, indifferent street lighting, growing street congestion, cuts in road maintenance personnel, all are leading factors in this inanity of our time.

Committee after committee, specially appointed to study the problem, submitting carefully considered recommendations, approved in principle officially, find no material backing.

* * *

What Should be Done?

USE the money acquired in licence fees and originally subscribed for the roads, for *that* purpose—if not exclusively, then in greater, if reasonable proportion.

Illuminate all roads efficiently and uniformly, not leave the task to countless local authorities, each to approach in its own particular manner.

Clear away all black-spots and bottle-necks now and *at all cost*, not in two-pennyworth portions spread over the years.

In short, let 1953 witness a genuine Safety-first drive, and the end to a generation of inertia. What more fitting dedication for Coronation Year than the crowning of the problem with its effectual solution.

WINTER'S HERE!

Here's the sign of WINTER WISDOM

IT MEANS

Greatest Safety – Greatest Strength
Greatest Service – Greatest Saving

Get ready now to meet and master treacherous winter road conditions. Fit the tyres that give you greatest winter safety—the tyres with the Gold Seal ...'Dunlop' and Dunlop 'Fort'. The safety secret is in the unique patented tread which, with its scientifically disposed knife-cuts, squeegees the water-film away so that the thousands of staggered 'teeth' can get a powerful grip on the road... *and go on* gripping through the long life of the tyre because the tread pattern goes to full depth. Yet another great feature is the rubber liner moulded to the *inside* of Gold Seal tyres. It greatly reduces risk of damage from chance under-inflation, deflation and kerb impact.

DUNLOP

THEY'RE FIRST IN SAFETY AND LONG LIFE

—yet they cost no more!

WINTER SPORTS:

Looking back to 2500 B.C.

By Kenneth D. Foster
(President of the Downhill Only Club)

Taking to the air in good style in a recent ski-jumping contest at Wengen, Switzerland.

SIR ARNOLD LUNN'S recently published *The Story of Ski-ing* traces the sport back to the year 2500 B.C. It seems that a pair of skis were dug up from a bog in Sweden and the backroom boys, in one of those *ex cathedra* announcements so inexplicable to laymen, unhesitatingly dated them as 2500 B.C. Then—inevitably—came the Chinese, who seem to have butted into every invention up to (but not including) Radar.

Chinese historians report that tribes of Turkish origin were in the habit of teasing the Frontier Guards on their far Western frontier by sliding rapidly over the snow in " wooden shoes " while the Chinese guards floundered crossly after them, knee deep in snow and presumably flourishing those cards listing articles that have to be declared.

* * *

BRITISH ski-ing does not date back quite so far. The first record is of miners in Cumberland who are said to have gone to work on " shees " made from barrel staves back in the 1860's.

This information will comfort those who claim that, whatever the Meteorological Office may say, winters *were* harder in the old days, there being no reports of the modern Cumberland miner having to ski to work. Were he to do so it would open up all sorts of fascinating possibilities. Would the Factory Inspector, for example, be charged with the duty of supervising the skis and ski-ing technique ?

* * *

THE British first took to ski-ing as a sport, rather than as a means of getting to work, in 1899 when Sir Arthur Conan Doyle and Dame Kathleen Furze started to ski at Davos. In the course of time they made many converts and the Ski Club of Great Britain (which now has over 14,000 members) was founded in May, 1903.

It is said that ski-ing now has more *active* supporters throughout the world than any other sport.

This claim may seem extravagant at first sight but a little thought shows that there is a good deal to support it.

The sport next in importance, from the point of view of active participation, is undoubtedly golf and British golfers

Sundown finalists in a curling match at the famous Swiss winter-sports' resort—St. Moritz.

would of course outnumber the 14,000 British skiers, but it must be remembered that the ski-ing world is one on which the sun never sets, like the British Empire before 1945 !

Ski-ing is practised in countries where golf is almost, if not quite, unknown (Norway, Sweden, Russia, Poland, Cyprus and Alaska, to name only a few), but it would be difficult to find a country where there are golfers but no skiers.

* * *

BRITISH ski-ing was confined to Switzerland in the early days due—oddly enough—to religious reasons. Sir Henry Lunn (father of Sir Arnold Lunn) was a Free Churchman who cherished a lifelong ambition to bring about a Union of the Churches. To this end he managed, in the early part of the century, to assemble at the Bear Hotel, Grindelwald, quite a collection of Church dignitaries of all denominations, his hope being that the rarefied air and almost cataleptic atmosphere of the Bernese Oberland might further his project but, in the event, it was proved that differences in dogma do not decrease with altitude.

However, Sir Henry was much struck by the ease with which he had transported all these old gentlemen across six-hundred miles of Europe and he decided to go into this transportation business from a more secular angle and so founded the famous Travel Agency that bears his name. He himself never put on a pair of skis in his life but the influence of his two sons led him to take active steps to popularise ski-ing and his efforts were a major factor in the growth of the sport in this country.

Competitors assemble by chair lift at the summit of the 6,600 feet Jochpass for the ski-descent. Champions knock off eight minutes of the 10-minute chair lift in their downward journey.

SWITZERLAND held its own as the home of ski-ing until the early thirties, when Austria entered the field as a competitor.

No two people can ever agree as to the relative merits of Switzerland or Austria. It is probably fair to say that when snow conditions are bad the chances of getting good ski-ing are better in Austria than in Switzerland and that, as regards cost, you may find that the total cost of a holiday in Switzerland is a little more than in Austria but that the Swiss hotelier, having been in the business for some two-hundred years, is apt to give you much better value for your money.

* * *

SCOTTISH ski-ing has developed rapidly of recent years but, unlike some of their other products, it does not lend itself to consumption beyond the Border.

The Scottish Ski Club will always oblige the Sassenach with weather reports, but the odds are that conditions will have changed completely by the time he arrives.

The season 1950-1951 was an outstanding exception, and it is claimed that ski-ing was possible in the high corries continuously from November 1950 through to October 1951.

* * *

AS THE Ski Club of Great Britain was founded in May, 1903, it is entering into its Jubilee Year and so skiers felt that it was particularly felicitous that the Queen, in the first Honours List of her reign, should have conferred a Knighthood on Mr. Arnold Lunn " for services to British ski-ing and to Anglo-Swiss relations."

It is not often that a Knighthood is bestowed for services to a sport, particularly if the sport is one that is practised outside this country for the most part, but the distinction has been well-earned.

* * *

WHEN Mr. Lunn (as he then was) first rolled up his sleeves and started on the job of establishing ski-ing the odds against him were formidable. The sport is controlled internationally by the *Fédération Internationale du Ski* (F.I.S. for short) which was established in Norway and which took no cognisance of any form of ski-ing other than Ski Jumping and *langlauf* (ski-ing along the level or uphill), neither of which were suited to British training or temperament.

After a battle that raged over a period of years he persuaded them, in 1931, to recognise downhill racing and the slalom race, thus securing a victory that can be compared with a successful attempt by Norway to get the M.C.C. to alter the rules of cricket.

* * *

THIS recognition of downhill racing was followed by what has been called the " Golden Age " of British ski-racing.

For the next eight years British skiers led the world in forming a code for ski-racing and were able to distinguish themselves in international events.

Those days have, alas! gone for ever. Ski-ing, like every other modern activity, has undergone a process of intensive development and the British skier, only able to spend a few brief weeks on the snows, cannot hope to compete with the highly-trained continental specialist who spends half the year on skis.

However, it is likely that Britain's contribution to the sport will always be remembered, and evidence of this is to be found in an article published in *Ski*, the Journal of the Swiss Ski Association, in 1947. The article was written by Dr. Zahnd of Wengen, who is prominent in Swiss ski-ing circles, and dealt with the early history of the Wengen Ski Club, which is one of the leading clubs in Switzerland. In it Dr. Zahnd says :—

" To Waghorn and his comrades of

(Please turn to page 24)

All for the summit of the Suveretta by ski-lift—to experience the thrill of rapid descent in split-second competition.

"Nature knew the answers millions of years ago – we are still probing"

says Prof. A. M. Low

UNDOUBTEDLY water is a very important part of our lives. Three quarters of the earth's surface is covered with water. Your body is about 80 per cent. water and a lettuce well over 90 per cent. ordinary water. So now you know what you are paying for.

Pure water is unknown in nature. Even country rain is not pure for it dissolves a certain amount of carbon dioxide as it falls and in this way is able to dissolve limestone more quickly to form various gullies and streams.

* * *

WHEN salts dissolve in this way they sometimes drip into caves. The water evaporates and the salts are left in the form of stalactites coming down and stalagmites going up.

The fur in your kettle is dissolved minerals and on an industrial scale causes enormous waste of heat in boilers. For this reason water is commonly softened which means that the minerals are removed.

The quantity of soft water obtained in this way would be far from good to drink because the minerals help to form the bones and teeth in your body. Drinking soft water might eventually give us rather flexible bones.

* * *

THE world of nature may be said to give us good drinking water in most cases, but it has not yet learned to produce water for boilers.

I often think how amusing it is that nature turns the vast forest into coal and oil with the help of the sea, but can hardly be expected to turn out an exact kind of oil such as we need for our automobiles.

We must not expect *too* much!

* * *

Talking of rennet

THE other day, like Little Miss Muffet, I was eating some "curds and whey" when my hostess asked me what made milk curdle and immediately my mind (always of the versatile variety) thought of rennet.

Now rennet is a slightly mysterious substance, at least I have been told recently that it is a plant, a chemical, and a sweet, none of which is correct, so I will try to explain where it comes from.

As a matter of stern fact, rennet is extracted from the lining of the fourth stomach of a calf! The linings used in the preparation of rennet are called "veils" and the curdling action they produce in milk is due to a ferment known as rennin which causes the casein to coagulate. Rennet also contains another ferment, pepsin, which helps in the ripening of cheese.

I am afraid that history does not relate who first discovered these strange properties of rennet; perhaps it was Miss Muffet's spider!

* * *

Does it shock you?

IN the marshes of Brazil (where the nuts come from) and in Guiana there is found a strange creature known as the electric eel, and in case you should ever think of visiting these salubrious places I want to warn you not to attempt to fondle this fish.

Nature has armed many of her offspring with very potent weapons and the electric eel is well capable of looking after itself.

By the way, it is no relation at all to the eels we all know, in spite of its outward likeness, but belongs to an order which includes carp and catfish. It is the only brand of the family which possesses electric "fittings," besides being 3 feet long and thick as a man's thigh.

The tail of the electric eel is four-fifths of its whole body and its electric parts extend the length of the tail. They are made up of longitudinal column composed of numbers of electric plates and the eel is able to give a full strength shock when head and tail are in contact with different points on the surface of some other animal.

So powerful is the shock of this natural battery that it is sufficient to stun the largest animal. The Indians, with great cleverness, render the electric eel fit for eating by forcing them to exhaust their electric power by driving horses into the ponds first and thereby making the eels discharge their "batteries."

* * *

Delicate conversation

IT must be very trying for the over-refined to find themselves surrounded by such coarse things as aviation engines, or even engineers, and I am wondering how long it will be before someone devises the conversation filter.

A radio technician knows very well that it is possible to filter or grid out certain unwanted oscillations and it is not at all difficult to make an apparatus which cuts out all voice frequencies over and above, say, 2,000 per second. Indeed, such a result is achieved much too effectively at every bad cinema theatre where the audience listens quite happily to voices which are far from natural.

* * *

THAT suggests the great invention of the future where the boxes at a theatre, speedway, or boxing match are enclosed in glass frames. But it would not be ordinary glass, it would be of special material; or the occupants might also close their ears with specially prepared headphones.

Then all would be well, these fortunate people could listen to the crowd if they wanted to and even to the commentary if they felt strong enough. Or, like the participants in that unhappy Nuremberg Trial, each could be provided with an apparatus so that they could discuss the weather with each other and never listen to the coarse sounds made by others who were outside their particular caste.

* * *

The kitchen workshop

I FIND it very difficult to distinguish between the kitchen as a chemical factory and the same place as the home of fairy tales. We all know that certain bleaching liquids use chlorine, we realise that sodium carbonate and acetic acid make flour rise, but there are other things which require more explanation.

From some household hints I gather that common salt can be used for many purposes, such as cleaning brass or even improving the brightness of an oil lamp flame.

For the cleaning of metals it seems to me that an acid which can produce electro-chemical action is of doubtful value, because no one wishes to use up their metal objects in order that these may be clean. But salt in the paraffin of an ordinary lamp is more mysterious.

Salt does not dissolve readily in paraffin but doubtless very small quantities are soluble and if there is any water in the paraffin included amid the oily particles some of the salt might be carried to the flame.

This will mean that the base of the light, ordinarily blue because of its incomplete combustion, will become yellow and thus give the effect of good lighting.

* * *

MUCH the same argument, strangely enough, applies to cows which are given water to drink in which sulphur is resting. Now, sulphur has three well-known allotropic modifications. In short, it can be rock sulphur, flowers of sulphur, or plastic sulphur. The latter being produced when the molten material is poured into water.

Probably, I imagine, the "flowers" should be sprinkled on the cows; food for the animals would absorb very little if they relied upon the quantity of sulphur which dissolves in ordinary water. Maybe it alters the colour of "combustion" taking place in their many stomachs.

* * *

QUITE a number of well-known medicaments rely upon these secondary effects. There are, for example, cold cures which make the user say, "Why, now I can smell; before, my nose felt absolutely useless." The fact sometimes is that the material is so powerful that it actually affects mucous membrane round the smell organs thus causing the user to believe that this sense has duly returned.

On this subject it is a commonly held idea that smells can bring disease. Children used to be told to hold their noses while passing a bad smell. Germs cannot be carried in this way unless the smell happens to indicate the presence of a fairly strong wind. A smell shows that microbes are feeding and causing what we call decomposition. Microbes cannot work without nourishment so remember that a bad smell is not only the fault of the microbe. You should not have left their food ready for them to eat.

January, 1953   Page 17

Mummy says are you ready, Daddy?

No, I'm afraid she'll have to walk.

Will she like that?

Not much. But tell her to look on the bright side—BP Super will soon be here.

What difference will that make?

All the difference between pinking and pulling—in fact it will make for better performance all round.

What will BP Super do, Daddy?

It will put paid to pinking and give us more miles per shilling. You can tell Mummy it's going to be a super season for motoring when BP Super comes.

(BP) is the trade-mark of ANGLO-IRANIAN OIL COMPANY, LTD., whose world-wide resources are behind it.

BP SUPER

TO BANISH PINKING

January, 1953

IF ONLY THESE WALLS COULD SPEAK!

What transpired when the Editor tried to make them:

The picturesque Plough House, Eaton Socon, Bedfordshire — of Twelfth Century origin and to-day a "museum" of Great North Road associations.

You'll find a "warmth of welcome" second to none here—and much of fascinating interest in the many rare antique adornments.

I HAVE just laid down a highly confidential document relating to the defence of England against an impending invasion by France, from Dunkirk!

No, there is no mistake: the document is dated December 13, 1745, and outlines in detail the Admiralty's plans for the protection of Sheerness, Chatham, Woolwich and Deptford as well as His Majesty's stores and magazines; instructions covering the replenishment and supply of the said stores with powder, shot, paper for cartridges, flints, etc., plus cutlasses, braces of pistols, pikes and the like for the defenders, including the depots' labourers.

* * *

THIS remarkable document, still in my possession, is one of several score discovered in an upper room of the 800 years' old "Plough House" at Eaton Socon (Eaton Slocomb of "Nicholas Nickleby") near St. Neots on the Great North Road. Its enormous timbers, steel hard and mostly cut from service-worn ships of an early-day navy, house countless additional relics of a long-passed age.

Low of ceiling, the interior is strikingly impressive in its overall North-South layout, as are the many adornments of rare antiquity and fascinating interest.

Here, indeed, is a veritable museum of the Great North Road throughout the ages, with visible links with the men of Oliver Cromwell, the Crusaders of Richard the Lion Heart, with the days of the stage coach and of the highwaymen who prospered thereupon—all pulsatingly real to the mind in the presence of blunderbuss, flint lock, cross-bow, jail-locks, leg irons and other legacies of the days when, so we are told, "men were men and women were proud of it."

* * *

IN timbers alone, beams pointed and pegged-out, stayed with oak still bearing their Roman numerals, reaching in the one piece from end to end of the building, wattle walls, the huge fireplace still bearing traces of the feet marks of early-day juvenile chimney sweeps—who climbed the inner chimney—its Twelfth Century origin, though proved, is hard indeed to believe in the light of present-time preservation.

Behind the main building are traces of the one-time drill-maker's shop, later a forge, so frequently used by Cromwell's men-at-arms. There are spy-holes set at eye level and used, in turn, by marauder or fugitive; an excellent Priest hole, and a wonderfully preserved studded door (excavated in the garden a short time ago) all as evidence of the good, or bad, old days of the Great North Road.

* * *

TIME and time again, too, when exploring the rough in the garden, there come to light curious examples of old iron forgings or the wrought iron decorative piece, to give still further proof to the legends surrounding its origin and passage of time.

It is known, of course, that in 1838 there lived here one Pinney, gentleman of his time and a celebrated wheelwright, who is credited with making the first-ever iron plough in the world. He also made an organ for the nearby church and played it regularly.

* * *

I HAD stopped at the Plough Tea House many times during my travels north and south, but seldom had time for more than a glimpsed inspection, always promising myself one day to do the thing well. I kept my promise recently.

By the kind invitation of its custodians, Mr. and Mrs. George Kemp, I stayed a long week-end—board residence is not normally possible—so that I was a privileged person; doubly so, in fact, for in George Kemp I found a most pleasant companion, with whom, the more we talked, I became the more attached. His theories of the house, his arguments on respective points, all tallied with my own; his outlook generally found endorsement almost without exception. We discovered, too, that in our time, we had done the same crazy and serious things, been to the same places, met the same people and, unknowingly, in World War I served in the same regiment of artillery!

* * *

WE realised these mutualities for the first time during our tour of investigation—which partnership in thought, when we fell upon the before-mentioned ages-old documents, we agreed, on his suggestion, to clinch for all time!

However, the manner in which George Kemp has restored the amenities of the house is beyond praise. His appreciation of its historic associations and of the value to the modern age of all it contains is a tonic of good British spirit.

* * *

IF perchance you call, after your welcome and your meal—and I can guarantee your pleasure in both respects!

January, 1953

—ask to see his replica of the *Mayflower*, a gem of modelling which he calls his "proudest symbol of England and of the English-speaking peoples," to see the carved headpiece of King Canute found at Winchester; the copy of Durer's "St. George," once the property of William Makepiece Thackeray; the trivet with handle; the old ship's bell, dug up in Wiltshire; the witch balls (beloved by Mrs. Kemp); the warming pans, roasting jacks, fire spits; horse brasses, the original "thimble-full" measure; his iron dogs fashioned as wheatsheafs; and his variety of Tudor iron plaques.

Right: Upper passage: the rare timbers as sturdy as the day they were first used.

Extreme right: Lower passage, showing original tile flooring, enormous timbers and, in places, sections of original wattle walls.

See also the original 10-inch padlock of Cambridge jail, those awful leg-irons, his collection of stained and leaded glass, his Tudor brasses from Hampton Court, his pewter (glass-bottomed, to the task of attacker or intended victim); his balancing ship's candlesticks, or his rare *brass* rush-light holder; finally, gracefully ask to see the beautifully timbered staircase and tiled passages similarly adorned with galleons, brasses, etchings and arms of all ages, not normally coming within the view of the visitor.

Right: Adornments of great historical interest are carefully displayed about the timbered staircase.

Extreme right: Original timbers of the unique sloping walls, with some of the custodian's treasured galleons and other relics of past ages.

Without these special items, however, there is ample to interest and please at the Plough Tea House. Best of all, perhaps, and one, while costing no more than good breeding, is more priceless these days even than the rarest antiques, is the Kemps' sincere warmth of welcome. Their subsequent table pleasantries are equally surprising.

T. R. M.

SITUATE on the Great North Road at Eaton Socon, Bedfordshire, the Plough House has defied the ravages of time and the perpetual roar and rumble of traffic over the ages. It stands to-day a beautifully preserved symbol of the Twelfth Century and houses many remarkable antiques. You should call one day; you will be welcome and agreeably surprised!

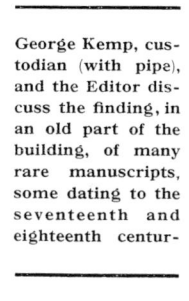

George Kemp, custodian (with pipe), and the Editor discuss the finding, in an old part of the building, of many rare manuscripts, some dating to the seventeenth and eighteenth centuries, and revealing important new interpretations upon notable historic events. The documents, fully protected, are being submitted for official scrutiny.

Comet jet-liner over the Himalaya mountains.

Flying Clubs and Civil air lines should preserve their independence!

says Major Oliver Stewart

AVIATION has been conspicuous for its advocacy of the principle of independence, but less notable for its application of that principle. Both the clubs and the air lines which are not within the ambit of B.O.A.C. or B.E.A., have proclaimed their desire to be rid of Government interference.

Government interference has been blamed for almost all the ills that have beset civil aviation. But the fact is that the case against Government interference would be more convincing if those who inveighed against it, were not so keen at the same time to receive Government assistance.

* * *

THE clubs, it will be recalled, pleaded that they played a part in the country's defences by increasing the number of people who knew how to fly and thus enlarging the reservoir of partly skilled men who might be called upon in time of war. The clubs said that it was disgraceful that they should be subjected to Government interference when they were in reality a basic part in the defence system.

It sounded well, until it became clear that the clubs wanted some financial return from the Government for their work. They wanted tax remissions not given to an ordinary private owner, or other kinds of subsidy. One would have thought that they would have seen from the outset that the moment they received subsidies, open or concealed, they would be bound to submit to controls of one kind or another.

* * *

THE truth is that it is not the business of the clubs to be part of the defence system although it sounds very patriotic of them if they are. But their purpose— as I feel—should be to offer civilians opportunities to do civil flying without any after thoughts about whether they might be able to join one of the Services in time of war. I have always longed to see aviation throw off the war shackles and pay its own way as motoring does— that is to say, because people want it enough to pay the price for it.

Imagine the situation if every private motorist asked to be let off petrol tax or given a Government subsidy because the ability to drive is useful in time of war. Aviation has no justification for its calls on the Government for financial help and those who really believe in it dislike to see subsidies granted. It is one of the most cheering things of recent months that B.O.A.C. have contrived to operate without being subsidised by the taxpayer. That is real civil aviation.

* * *

BECAUSE I do not believe that the clubs or the independent operators should ask for subsidies, it does not mean that I am the less convinced of the evils of Government interference. I believe that Government interference—sometimes encouraged by organisations like the International Civil Aviation Organisation—is one of aviation's most serious handicaps.

Freeing flying would help flying. To obtain a Certificate of Airworthiness for a new aircraft to-day, costs ten or twenty times what it cost a few years ago because of the increased complication of the regulations. If the regulations were reduced and simplified, I do not believe that it would have any effect on safety; but I am sure that it would have a big effect on reducing the cost of aviation.

Perhaps now my point of view is clear. Government interference is an unmitigated evil. But if Government help is asked for, there will inevitably be some kind of control going with it. So those who ask the Government for financial assistance in any form, are, in effect, also asking for more Government interference.

AIRCRAFT operators, whether of small machines like the clubs, or of large machines like the companies in the British Independent Air Transport Association, ought to learn to fend for themselves. We can recall Winston Churchill's words, said many years ago: " Civil aviation must fly by itself." It must fly by itself not so much in order to make a profit, as to keep it out of the clutches of the controllers and regulators.

Complication is a disease of the decade and it is most difficult to avoid it. Every machine becomes more complicated; every process of Government and of regulation becomes more complicated. The words of William Stout (often attributed to Henry Ford) are sometimes quoted: " Simplicate and add more lightness," but the facts of the time are that the tendency is usually to complicate and add more weight.

We look to those who retain their independence to fight the battle for simplicity, for direct dealing, for freedom from complication and from regulation. But they can only fight that battle while they remain truly independent and do not rely upon Government money in order to continue their operations.

* * *

MANY of the companies in the British Independent Air Transport Association do fine work. They are as efficient as carriers as any companies in the world. But there are one or two good companies not within the Association and they also deserve high praise for the work they do. The stronger all these independent companies the better for aviation in general. They provide the element of competition which is so important if efficiency is to be high. A great responsibility rests upon them therefore. It is not too much to say that what they do colours the whole of British aeronautical progress. Let us hope, therefore, that they will firmly remain independent in the fullest sense. That is the source of their strength.

This word Genuine...

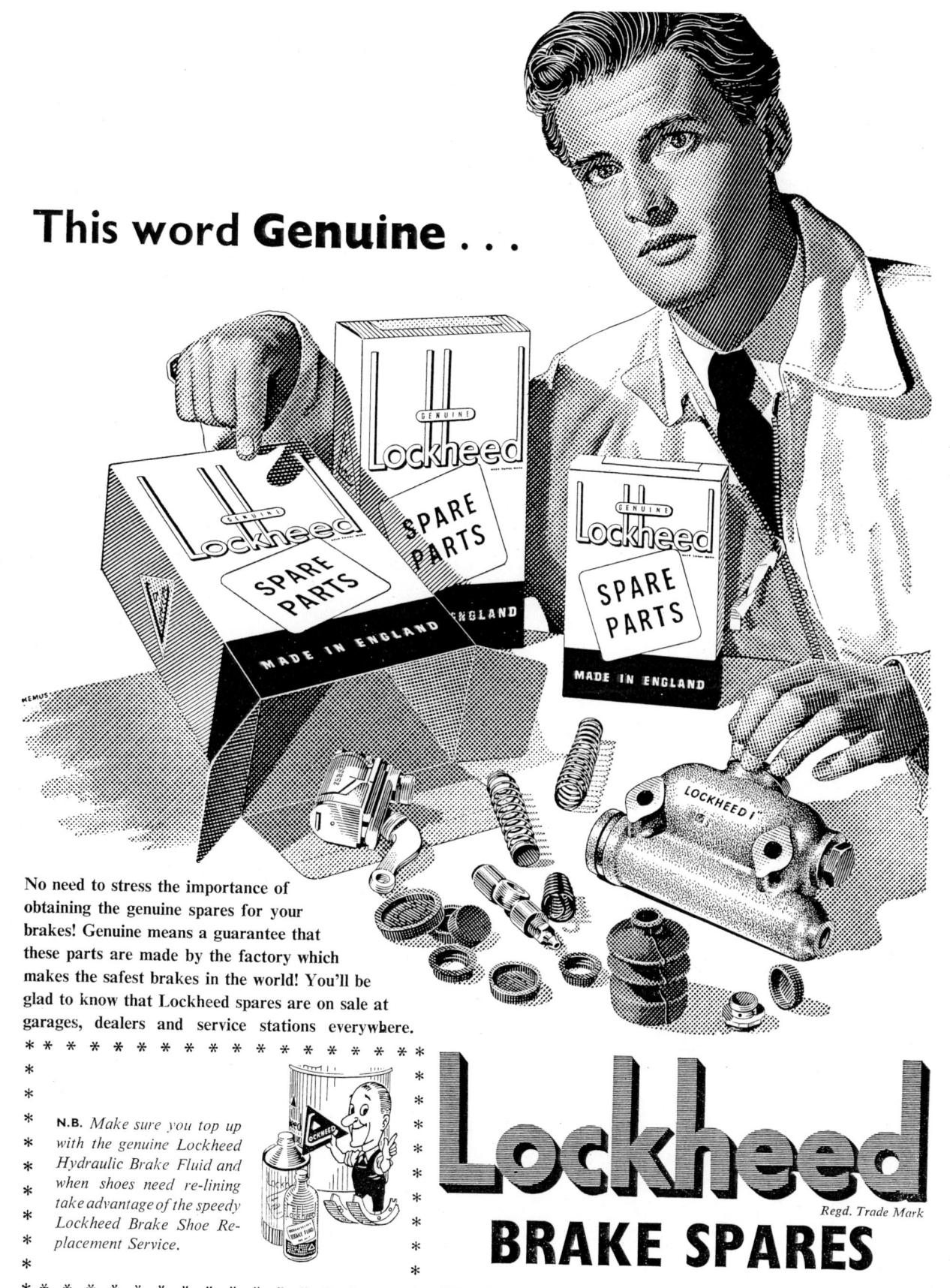

No need to stress the importance of obtaining the genuine spares for your brakes! Genuine means a guarantee that these parts are made by the factory which makes the safest brakes in the world! You'll be glad to know that Lockheed spares are on sale at garages, dealers and service stations everywhere.

N.B. *Make sure you top up with the genuine Lockheed Hydraulic Brake Fluid and when shoes need re-lining take advantage of the speedy Lockheed Brake Shoe Replacement Service.*

Lockheed
BRAKE SPARES
Regd. Trade Mark

AUTOMOTIVE PRODUCTS CO. LTD., TACHBROOK ROAD, LEAMINGTON SPA.

January, 1953

The Sierra Nevada, with its everlasting snow, seen from the Generalife, Granada.

In Sunny Southern Spain—

"the ideal holiday centre"

says

Vincent Brennan, M.B.E., F.R.G.S.

(Our Touring Adviser)

I HAVE never, in all my wanderings, had a finer subject to write about than Southern Spain.

Prior to visiting Andalusia, of cities in all Europe I had put Venice in a class by herself.

Andalusia has several such gems of historic and scenic splendour—Seville, Cordova, Malaga, Granada, and, of course, Jerez (pronounced " Hereth ") whence the sherry comes.

I have often been asked, " What is Spain like for a holiday ? "

One could justly reply that Spain is a large country (compare it with France on the map) of vast open spaces, studded at intervals with cities of astonishing interest and attraction—rich plums, in fact, in an appetising cake : especially to that portion of Spain which lies south of Madrid.

* * *

FOR the record it should be stated that my Minx covered the distance between Calais and the Spanish capital quite comfortably in four days (a hustler could make it three). Another three days' driving would see one in the farthest south.

If time be limited, and if Madrid has already been visited, the drill is to stay the night at the Albergue Nacional at Arandá de Duero, 100 miles short of Madrid, which enables one to lunch the day following in the city of the much maligned climate (" Wait for May 40th," says the proverb, " before you lay aside your cloak "), pop into the Prado for yet another look at Goya and Velasquez, and get well beyond by nightfall.

* * *

ARANJUEZ, not well known to us at home, is the first " plum," with a Royal Palace vieing in grandeur with the Château of Versailles. It has, for example, one room composed entirely of porcelain and another of mirrors. The gardens and park maintain an equally high standard and since Aranjuez is also renowned for its asparagus and strawberries, it is not a place through which to rush.

Away from its neighbourhood the countryside is bare and grim but, withal, starkly picturesque when there is the odd windmill on the horizon— " Don Quixote" country, I call it—until New Castille gives way to gay Andalusia. What music there is in the very names !

Here are countless millions of olive trees and, as one gets further south, the richest vegetation which could possibly be imagined—grapes, cotton, sugar-cane, oranges, lemons, melons, even bananas, everything most luscious.

But beware ! There may be many miles between petrol pumps.

* * *

ON the credit side, the roads you will traverse are excellent. Don't believe ill-informed people who tell you the roads of Spain are bad. The main roads, almost all of them, are first class.

* * *

CORDOVA (or, in Spanish, " Cordoba ") was the ancient capital of the Moors who held it for 500 years, until 1236.

Its cathedral will live in my memory, long after that of others has faded, because it was once the Chief Mosque of the Moors.

The original mosque was intended to compete with that of Mecca itself, and it was colossal, covering the same area as St. Peter's in Rome. Upon this magnificence sixteenth century Spain superimposed the splendour of the Church, giving rise to the famous saying of Charles V, " You have built me what you, or others, might have built anywhere, but you have destroyed something which was unique in the world."

Anyhow, La Mesquita, as they call it, is worth going a long way to see.

I liked the Hotel Simon in Cordova, very eastern in character.

It was in Cordova that I parked my car in a main street, despite the gesticulations of a policeman, saying, airily, I should only be a moment.

When I returned there were three of them waiting for me ! They were quite nice, but very firm. I decided I would not again risk collision with authority in this way.

What did stagger me between here and Seville was to receive the Grand National quite clearly on my Radiomobile—an astonishing feat considering I was a thousand miles away !

* * *

I AM not going to dwell on the guidebook stuff where Seville is concerned. I prefer to relate one or two personal experiences.

Beggars are super-persistent, and I am putting it mildly. To one, in sudden desperation, I said " Why should I give you alms ? Why don't you give me a penny ? " To my amazement he produced a copper coin from his pocket and handed it to me. My defences collapsed !

Then I was conducted to the " gipsy quarter " of Triana, where I was introduced to the famous horse-trainer, El Guajiro, referred to in Tschiffely's " Round and About Spain."

Above : Inside the sherry producing establishment of Pedro Domecq, of Jerez.

Left : The best-known corner of the Alhambra, the " Court of the Lions."

Left: The famous and lovely "Court of the Fountains" in the Alhambra, Granada.

Right: "Awaiting the alms of the faithful"; outside a church in Ubeda.

It was in El Guajiro's inn, and I also met "The Sleeper"—alleged to sleep night and day but never to miss a free drink—and the one-legged "champion swimmer of Spain" whose ambition it is to conquer the Channel, all this in a truly Southern Spanish atmosphere, with the odd castanet clicking and occasional fiery outburst of gipsy music.

* * *

NOR must I omit reference to the framed "Horse's Address to His Master" on the wall of the inn, of part of which this is my translation: "Forgive me for asking but after the work of the day give me shelter in a clean stable. Feed me and quench my thirst. If I am well looked after, I can serve you for I am strong. If I leave my fodder untouched, examine my teeth. Leave me my tail for it is my defence against tormenting flies. When you work me, speak, for your voice means more than reins or whip. Don't hurry me uphill, don't pull on my bit downhill. . . .

When old age weakens me and makes me useless, don't neglect me or let me die of hunger. Destroy me yourself, so that my sufferings be less."

The full text is most inspiring and would make wonderful propaganda for the R.S.P.C.A.

Here, too, was the gipsy who initiated me into the art of fortune-telling: "You have only one fortune and that is your own. I am going to get hold of it only if I am clever enough to rob you and you are foolish enough to part with it." It is as simple as that!

* * *

I CANNOT leave Seville without a mention of the all-pervasive scent of the orange-blossom in springtime.

Jerez is a different proposition, having its own special attraction referred to earlier.

Here I added my name to the long line of visitors to the House of Domecq, a line in which names like Napoleon and Ruskin are two a penny.

Of all the cracks in the Visitors' Book, I liked best that of Sir Alexander Fleming who wrote "Sherry is the superior of penicillin (which, of course, he discovered), for Sherry enables you to enjoy life whereas penicillin only preserves it."

Cadiz—quite all right for anyone who wants a day or two's rest from both motoring and sight-seeing, with plenty of sunshine and sea-breezes at the Hotel Atlantico, but nothing really very much to write home about. But the coastal road hence, through Algeciras and on to Malaga, is the finest in Europe.

Malaga—marvellous gardens and vegetation, wonderful food at the Gibralflora Restaurant, with magnificent views.

* * *

NEXT, Granada!

I have wanted to visit Granada more than anywhere else in the world, and the Alhambra was the principal "sight" in the civilised world I had not previously enjoyed.

With what delight did I find on my arrival, therefore, that the rooms booked for me in the ancient Convent of San Francisco—now converted into a *parador* or hotel and one of a number controlled by the Director-General of Spanish Tourism—was actually within the walls of the Alhambra. I was to linger there in the midst of its exotic gardens, its singing fountains, its birds, the innumerable nightingales, its views of the ever-lasting snows of the distant Sierra Nevada, and, of course, the glories of the Moorish Palace.

To cap it all, I encountered Marguerite Steen, the well-known authoress, lunching at the next table on the terrace and actually reading *Modern Motoring and Travel*.

Granada was indeed good! And I think I broke a record there, for I claim to be the first ever to have taken two bishops to a bullfight in my Hillman Minx.

By the way, if anyone wants to know something more practical about Spain and will drop me a line through the Information Bureau (enclosing stamped addressed envelope), I shall be glad to help. I have, in fact, just completed a small guide, "Motoring in Spain," for the Spanish Government. For obvious reasons they are unable to pay me in sterling; I have to go out there again and eat it!

Left: El Guajiro, the celebrated horse-breaker, outside his fonda in the gipsy quarter of Seville.

Below: Senor de Guzman as an escort round the Alhambra.

TEE-TIME TOPICS

By F. J. C. PIGNON

Golfing by electric chair! — need for special "Coronation" events — prospects for youth in 1953

IT was bound to come. Motoring and golf are so closely allied it was inevitable that somebody would combine both sports; speeding up the the one and slowing down the other.

It usually takes fully four hours to play a round of golf on American courses, partly because of congestion, but more likely because, smart as they may be in many ways, United States golfers like to sit down and think about any shot before playing it. Even then hustle does not enter into American golf—it is the most leisurely game in the world. So why the hurry?

* * *

HOWEVER, some bright firm in the transport business has decided that golfers can get more play for their big subscriptions by speeding up the game.

He has invented an electric car, chair or trolley—call it what you will—that will transport players and clubs round the links in double quick time.

The famous Babe Zaharias former British woman Champion, now a professional, and another woman golfer, Betty Dodd, recently went round an American course of full length, 6,400 yards, in 45 minutes and 75 strokes. They save nearly three hours by employing one of these electric chariots between playing their shots.

* * *

ONE hesitates to think of what might happen if Sunday morning golfers all employed such means of transport.

It opens a wide vista for the motor manufacturers of course, but imagine any suburban course at the week-end when a hundred or so gay old golfers go careering round the course in their motor chairs.

It might be necessary to employ traffic "cops," lights and zebra crossings and penalise impatient members for speeding.

But let us not worry. The caddy-cart may have become a part of golfer's equipment in this country, but that form of economy, which caddies forced upon players by heavy charges for inadequate service, is about as far as we are likely to go in the speeding-up of golf.

WE, like everybody else, are looking ahead at this season of the year but not so much for golfing evolution as for those things which are likely to happen. It is unfortunate to my mind that in 1953, a truly historic year, no great Coronation Tournament has been fixed in men's golf.

The Ladies' Golf Union—bless them for once again giving the men a lead —have already fixed one Coronation event, a Commonwealth Tournament, at Fromby, Lancs., next July, and I hear rumours of other similar events they have in mind.

So far as I can see from the official fixture list, one of the annual professional tournaments will be held at about the time of the Coronation itself while not a single national tournament in which our numerous and welcome visitors might compete, has been fixed for 1953.

The Lucifer Golfing Society has for many years sponsored one of the most important amateur events in the game and will doubtless have a record entry this year.

It is a stroke play competition open to amateur golfers who happen to be visiting Britain, from any part of the Empire. That tournament has done more to cement friendly relations between Britain and her outposts than all the propaganda in the world.

But it should not be left to the generosity of a Golfing Society to entertain ordinary overseas golfers at an occasion of this kind.

* * *

LOOKING at the forthcoming season from a purely domestic angle one sees the customary big list of professional golf tournaments already fixed.

It is noted that once again lack of imagination on somebody's part shows that the interminable 72 holes stroke play tournaments prevail.

I wonder when it will dawn upon those responsible that the golfing public is getting rather bored with numerous events of this kind.

However, there it is, and the British professionals will have approximately £30,000 in prize money to play for.

* * *

AMERICAN professionals are beginning to think of challenging for some of this money and Bobby Locke the Open Champion declares that he will be back here next April and will doubtless claim his share.

In any event, the United States professionals will be here in force next autumn to defend their title to the Ryder Cup.

The match which will be played at Wentworth, Virginia Water, Surrey, at the beginning of October is one of the two international contests this year between Great Britain and the United States, the other being the Walker Cup match between amateurs which will be played at Marion, Mass., in September.

* * *

BRITISH women won the Curtis Cup from the United States in 1952, but I dare to say that as things stand at present in British golf, the men are unlikely to emulate them.

For one thing, no new players have actually "arrived."

In professional golf Harry Weetman, Match Play Champion and Master golfer, confirmed his earlier promise. Another young man who made a mark during his first year in professional tournament golf is Eric Brown, a former Scottish Champion.

There are also several promising youngsters coming along—but that is the point, they have not yet established themselves.

So it looks as though we may have to depend upon the services of most of those who played in the last Ryder Cup match, and some who have seen service in this match for some years.

* * *

UNFORTUNATELY, it is much the same in Amateur golf and I do not envy the task of those who will have to select the Walker Cup team to go to America.

Each year one sees players in the Boys' Championship who are champions in the making but most of them seem to drop out of the game; perhaps that is not surprising when business careers and National Service are prime considerations.

However, it would be wrong to start this great British year on a note of pessimism for after all some new players must break through before long and why not this year?

Let us hope for the best.

Here's one car that won't be <u>overdriven</u> on delivery

make sure your car <u>benefits</u> from its first run!

Here are three ways in which we ensure that vehicles delivered by us get "cotton-wool" treatment:—

A Servis Recorder is fitted to every car — an amazing "hidden eye" that makes a record of the entire journey for *you* to see.

Expert Drivers. Every one of them has passed a special test at the British School of Motoring. Paid extra to go slow, they get a bonus for *super*-safe driving.

Direct Supervision. Our staff of Collection Supervisors backs the whole delivery system, from factory to *you*. Every car we handle bears our name on the trade plates. We like people to see for themselves how careful our drivers are!

Make sure your dealer arranges for delivery of *your* car via CAR COLLECTION. The extra cost is so small . . . . it really is worth while.

THE CAR COLLECTION COMPANY LTD.

Established 1926. 7 Kendall Place, Baker Street, London, W.1.

In winning the "Ladies' Cup" may we say "Thank you, boys!"—says Sheila Van Damm on Sunbeam-Talbot 317

Miss Sheila Van Damm, winner of the Ladies' Class in the "Daily Express" Motor Rally, receives the coveted award from the Mayor of Brighton (Alderman Miss D. E. Stringer.)

ONE of the first things that happened to me after we had heard the good news that we had won the Ladies' Prize in the *Daily Express* M.C.C. Rally, was the sight of my very good friend the Editor advancing towards me with a gleam in his eye and the request that I should write my impressions of the Rally : " Just a mere 1,500 words, and have it in the post in the morning—or else ! ! ! "

Not only was he pleased with our success, but it saves him having to write the article himself !

Actually, it gives me great pleasure to do anything he asks me because it is through him that I am driving a Rootes' car to-day, as he gave me my first introduction and recommendation to the Team Captain, Norman Garrad, just two years ago.

* * *

MY co-driver was Mrs. Françoise Clarke—well-known, I believe, to members of the S.T.O.C. We had driven together for the first time on the London Motor Club's Rally.

It was a lucky day for me when I met her, as she is all a co-driver should be—a magnificent navigator, an excellent driver and she puts up with me—I would even go so far as to say she spoils me ! I hope we will drive together for many years to come as it would be difficult to find anyone to better her.

Françoise had entered her own car in this event, but had cancelled it to co-drive with me. These events are seldom won by one person—in my case it is always a team job, and it is due to team work that we won through.

* * *

WE set off from Glasgow on Wednesday, November 12—George Murray-Frame and Malcolm Rennie in Sunbeam-Talbot No. 314, Ernest Sneath and John Pearman in S.-T. 315 and us in S.-T. 317.

Norman Garrad was unable to compete at the last moment due to pressure of work and so John Pearman became the skipper.

On this event the average speed was only 26⅔ m.p.h., which is not difficult to maintain if the conditions are good, and this time the weather was wonderful, except for a little fog round about dawn on the Thursday morning.

We had tea in Carlisle before reporting to Control—dinner at Weatherby before reporting in at Doncaster and, in fact, for us it looked like becoming a Rally Gastronique ! All agreed, I think, that half the enjoyment of the rally was the laughs we all had when we got together at each stop.

At Doncaster we saw a car pulling out with " Travelling Marshal " written on the screen. Françoise said : " I believe that man is operating the secret check."

We all said " Nonsense " ; but have since apologised, as she was right. I told you she was good !

It appears he reported several people, who were subsequently excluded from the rally and were to be seen at the party on Saturday night with lapel badges reading " Road Hogs' Union."

So on to Swindon, where we had over one hour to wait, round about 3 a.m., and 28 cars were to be seen parked with 56 or more snoring bodies, lying in various positions sound asleep.

I got a little worried when, from my " bed " on the back seat, I awoke to find Françoise's feet practically in my face, with the rest of her on the front seat. We woke in time to have a coffee and, shivering with cold, we got back into the warmth and comfort of our Sunbeam-Talbot and set off anew. How those open car chaps survived I will never know !

* * *

THE next section went through Warrington, Wigan, Preston and Lancaster ; the trial and tribulations of trying to keep up one's average through these towns is rather wearying, and to add to the difficulties the London starters were booking in at Warrington and adding to the problem.

In one of the towns a motor-cycle policeman pulled out in front of me and signalled me to follow him. Malcolm, who was behind me, thought I had gone quite mad and kept to his 30 m.p.h. It was a surprise to find a policeman in this country giving help in this way, and was greatly appreciated. It brought back memories of the Monte Carlo Rally, when one of the greatest thrills is to be led through Paris in the middle of the day by a police escort travelling at 60 m.p.h. !

As we neared Kendal we met the early starters coming down the other way, and Nancy Mitchell and I had time to salute each other as she flashed by. I won't say what form the salute took, but I will say we are very good friends, and I have a very great admiration for her as a driver.

At Penrith we had a quick lunch—you will notice that we are still busy keeping up our strength—and then on to the first test, a regularity test in the Lake district.

This went off successfully as the results show, which test proved that if you lose marks on it you would not make the results sheet.

It was obviously our lucky day, but we did not know the results till we reached Brighton. Our clocks showed we were one fifth of a second out, and we had a one second margin either way, but as was proved last year, and again this year, so many of our clocks disagreed with the official's, due to the fact that although we tried to start and stop our watches at the same time as did the officials, we must have been a fraction out. Only about a third of the entry got through without loss of marks. Yes, it was our lucky day !

* * *

ON again then and back once more through Lancaster, Preston, Wigan, Warrington to Chester. Here we only had about half an hour in hand, and I wanted my lights re-adjusted, so I went into our very good friends, the Anchor Motor Company, who were wonderfully kind. They fixed our lights, filled up the car, gave us bacon and eggs and coffee, and put us back in the car exactly 15 minutes later. To Bill Leaman and his boys, " Very grateful thanks. Your kindness and efficiency takes some beating."

We now come to the Welsh section, where we had to sit up and take full notice as there were about six short sections and Wales takes careful navigating.

(Continued on page 49)

Sheila Van Damm and co-driver, Mrs. F. V. Clarke, with their successful Sunbeam-Talbot "90".

Right: C. Oldbury and co-driver, G. H. Smith, Third year Concours d'Elegance winners of Class A1 (cars made prior to 1947).

"Thank you, boys!"
(Continued from page 26)

Here Françoise came into her own and navigated us right through without a hitch, and, later, when she had proved her ability the boys tucked in behind and followed us. I know they give "Full marks" to Françoise for her efficiency.

They were quite capable of navigating themselves, but she proved she could do it, and so they were happy to follow. That, you will agree, was a great compliment to her. I would explain here that on a long trip such as this we all take it in turn to lead the team, thus enabling the non-drivers to sleep.

* * *

IN Hereford we stopped at a garage, and a man rushed out with a bottle of champagne, tied to which was a note of good wishes from May Brown.

Whenever we pass through, Mrs. Brown carries on the hospitality her husband, the late Reg Brown, always showed to Norman Garrad and his team. Last year on the Monte Carlo Rally, she waited till 2 a.m. to hand each member of the team a bottle of champagne and some sandwiches, and again, on this occasion, she remembered. Bless you, Mrs. Brown; you are one in a million, and we were all very touched by your kindness.

At the Stockbridge Control, we had time for a bath and breakfast, the boys to shave, and soon three Sunbeam-Talbots, with six washed and scrubbed drivers, motored on to Brighton and the final tests.

We completed these, and again it was our lucky day. Everything went just right—we signed off at the end of the final test, Françoise holding my right hand to stop it shaking—that's how tests affect me.

We parked the cars, and stayed around awhile watching some of the other competitors arrive.

I saw Eleanor Allard and her sister in their very attractive Palm Beach Allard. We had a chat and decided that we would all get together and practice on a skid pan before we set off on the Monte Carlo Rally. This, we hope, will give us help when we have to motor on sheet ice.

I then talked with Hazel Dunham, who I had not seen since her great success in the Tulip Rally.

We then wandered off to our hotel, and crawled into bed for a couple of hours' sleep. Later at the official hotel we were greeted with the wonderful news that, "third time lucky," we had won the Ladies' Cup and registered third in the Class.

* * *

BEFORE I conclude, I want to thank John, Ernest, George and Malcolm for all they did for us. They were a tower of strength, and we were honoured to be with them.

I cannot finish this article without paying tribute to the one person to whom I owe my success—to the Team Captain—Norman Garrad.

Since he asked me two years ago, after the *Daily Express* Rally of 1950, if I would drive for Rootes, he has taken infinite time and trouble, and has shown incredible patience.

I know to-day how to handle a Sunbeam-Talbot. His faith in my ability as a driver is at last rewarded. "My very grateful thanks to you, Skipper!"

SPORTING & OTHER PHOTOGRAPHS

COPIES of photographs reproduced in these pages are mostly available to readers at the following prices:

    Size 8" × 6" - - 3s.
    Size 10" × 8" - - 4s.
    Size 12" × 10" - - 5s. 6d.

Orders, in writing, should be clearly identified and directed to The Manager, *MODERN MOTORING & TRAVEL*, 53 Stratton Street, Piccadilly, London, W.1.

How to Dirt-Proof
YOUR ENGINE OIL
and prevent THIS

Dirty oil wastes your money. It clogs piston-ring slots, gums-up valve stem guides and constricts oil passages.

Your AC Oil Filter goes on filtering out the clogging sludge, dirt and grit which grind away engine efficiency — until the element is *packed solid*. A fresh A.C. Element at least *every 8,000 miles* means fewer repair bills ... greatly reduced engine wear ... less frequent oil changes.

Get your local Humber-Hillman Agent or any good garage to change your AC Filter Element at least every 8,000 miles.

REPLACEMENT ELEMENTS

| Humber-Hawk 1948-9 L11—11/- | Sunbeam Talbot 2-Litre 1947-48-49 1948-50 "90" L11—11/- |
| Super-Snipe and Pullman 1948-50 K11—12/6 | 1948-50 10 HP & "80" L14—9/6 |

MINX OWNERS! Your agent can now fit the approved AC Oil Filter to your car.

AC Oil Filters

AC-DELCO DIVISION OF GENERAL MOTORS LTD.
DUNSTABLE, ENGLAND and Southampton, Hants.

A 1902 Humberette was driven in the Parade during Azalea Week at Pietermaritzburg, Natal. At the wheel was Mr. Hands, son of Mr. George Hands, manager of the local branch of Natal Motor Industries, distributors under Rootes (Pty.) Limited, of Cape Town.

IN A FEW WORDS:

MANUFACTURING COMPANIES in the Rootes Group obtained a number of awards in the Private Coachwork Competition, arranged by the Institute of British Carriage and Automobile Manufacturers in conjunction with the International Motor Exhibition.

First Prize for standard convertible coachwork on cars under £1,550 went to Thrupp and Maberly for the Sunbeam-Talbot "90" Sports Convertible Coupé. First prize for utility coachwork, again under £1,550, was won by the Hillman Motor Car Co., with the Hillman Estate Car.

The Institute's bronze medals were awarded to Humber Limited for the Humber Super Snipe (under £1,550) and the Humber Pullman Limousine (under £3,000).

* * *

WITH PROFOUND regret we record the death, after a short illness, on November 15, of Mrs. Brennan, wife of Mr. Vincent Brennan, M.B.E., F.R.G.S., Touring Adviser to this journal, of Dean Farm, East Farleigh, Kent. The Editor represented the staff at the funeral at East Farleigh on November 18.

* * *

WITHIN a few months all the available registration marks for motor vehicle number plates in some parts of Great Britain will have been exhausted. When this happens, it is proposed to introduce a new system of marks under which the letters will be placed after the numbers instead of in front.

* * *

SINCE HER introduction on the Dover-Boulogne route in June last, the s.s. *Lord Warden*, the Southern Region's newest and largest car-carrying vessel, has carried more than 16,000 motor-cars, nearly 500 coaches and 2,000 motor-cycles across the Channel.

* * *

THREE WHITE Dutch swans, named "Ka", "El" and "Em", were carried in the freight compartment on the opening flight of the new K.L.M. service from Amsterdam to Santiago de Chile in November. The swans, a gift to the city from the airline, were placed in the Santiago lake.

* * *

THE SOCIETY of British Aircraft Constructors announces that its Coronation Year Flying Display and Exhibition will take place from September 7th to 13th, at Farnborough, Hampshire.

(Continued on page 52)

In Bermuda, this Hillman Minx Convertible Coupé is operated as a taxi. The sun-shade was formerly used on a horse-drawn carriage.

A Commer breakdown wagon in the service of Agnew & Graham, Ltd., of Belfast, distributors for Sunbeam-Talbot in Northern Ireland. On left, Mr. Charles Agnew.

THE first Malta Trade Fair opened by H.E. Sir Gerald Creasy, K.C.M.G., O.B.E., Governor and Commander-in-Chief, proved so successful that it is to become an annual event.

Picture, left, shows Sir Gerald and Lady Creasy (centre) visiting the stand of the Industrial Motor Co., Ltd., which displayed Rootes Group products. Next to Sir Gerald is the Hon. Dr. G. Borg Olivier, Ll.D., Prime Minister of Malta. With rosette, Mr. John Mizzi, managing director of the Industrial Motor Co. Ltd. Mannequin Parades were held, while wax models gave added effect to the Hillman Minx Convertible Coupé mounted on an electrically operated turntable.

I keep it safe

says Mr. Coolie

From the farm to the front door step, says Mr. Coolie... at every stage from the churn to the children's mugs, I am at work guarding and protecting the Nation's milk. In the farmer's milk cooling equipment, in the dairies and bottling plants and in homes throughout the world, the coldness I provide keeps good food good. I am the cooling coil in every Prestcold refrigerator; I am Mr. Coolie, symbol of Britain's finest refrigeration equipment. Day in, day out I serve Commerce and Industry, Science and Medicine.

MR. COOLIE IS THE SYMBOL OF

PRESTCOLD REFRIGERATION

Prestcold refrigeration keeps good food good AND SERVES INDUSTRY, SCIENCE AND MEDICINE

PRESSED STEEL COMPANY LIMITED, COWLEY, OXFORD

EIGHT SOUND REASONS WHY THIS COIL IS *Better!*

1. Hermetically sealed against moisture — the major cause of ignition failure
2. Oil-filled for permanent insulation and better heat dissipation
3. Balanced windings for maximum performance and longer contact life
4. Improved top gear acceleration and flexibility
5. Reliable engine starting and low-speed performance
6. Smooth and steady tick-over
7. Guaranteed for 2 years
8. Backed by 40 years' experience of the world's largest ignition manufacturers

The Better coil for ANY CAR!

Delco-Remy OIL-FILLED IGNITION COILS

LIST PRICE 36/- 6 AND 12 VOLT

Consult your local garage or write for descriptive leaflet.

DELCO-REMY-HYATT DIVISION OF GENERAL MOTORS LTD · GROSVENOR ROAD · LONDON · S·W·1

The Rt. Hon. J. P. L. Thomas, First Lord of the Admiralty, receiving the gift of a Humber Super Snipe to mark his representation of the Hereford Division in Parliament for the past 21 years. The presentation was subscribed by local Conservative organisations and private individuals.

AMERICAN motorists are making a record payment this year of about £982,000,000 in petrol taxes.

* * *

IT IS with regret that the death is recorded of Mr. A. H. Glasspole, Sales Engineer at Commer Cars, Ltd., Luton, on November 15. He had been associated with the company for over 26 years and his technical knowledge led to many important appointments additional to his work with the Rootes Group. Among these, he was a representative of Light Commercial Vehicle Manufacturers on the panel which meets the Ministry of Transport on matters relating to "construction and use" regulations.

* * *

SPEAKING at the annual dinner of the Society of Motor Manufacturers and Traders, held in London on the eve of the International Motor Exhibition, Mr. Duncan Sandys, Minister of Supply, said that in recent years the British motor industry had been responsible for about 10 per cent. of our total visible exports.

He was sure the industry would intensify its efforts, under the stimulus of competition, and would not only maintain but further improve its position in the markets of the world.

* * *

THE NEW air terminal at the Royal Exchange, Manchester, was opened by Mr. Lennox-Boyd, Minister of Transport. Ringway, the city's airport lying 11 miles away, now operates extensive services on domestic and international routes.

* * *

TREETOPS, a delightful miniature hotel with three bedrooms built 50 feet above the ground in the branches of a giant fig tree, is situated in the Aberdare National Park about 10 miles from Nyeri town, in Kenya. It is organised and run under the excellent management of the well-known Outspan Hotel of Nyeri. A special Kenya feature will appear in an early future edition.

* * *

WE ARE advised by the British Pioneer Tobacco Growers' Association that their subscription is now 10s. 6d. per annum, and that there are now 15,000 active members. The Association points out that the £1 1s. subscription, when in force, covered the supply of a quantity of free plants, which is, however, not the case with the standard 10s. 6d. subscription.

The Mayor and Mayoress of Hereford, Alderman and Mrs. A. E. Farr, alight from a Humber Pullman Limousine during the recent Show Week of Brook Bros. (Hereford), Ltd.

A refuse collector and a gully emptier each on the new "Gamecock" municipal low-load chassis were among the exhibits on the Karrier stand at the Public Works Exhibition at Olympia, in London.

In a Few Words: *from page 50*

INADEQUATE rear lights are responsible for 3,400 after-dark casualties each year. The R.A.C. urges all car and motor-cycle owners to examine their lighting systems carefully, and strongly recommend twin rear lamps.

* * *

MR. J. PATERSON, M.A., Ll.B., C.A., Manager of Rootes Acceptances, Limited, has been appointed Director and General Manager of the Company.

The thirteenth century Mohun Gateway at the historic Torre Abbey, which forms part of the Borough Arms of Torquay, provides an imposing background for the Humber Hawk.

LET PRATT TRAILERS SOLVE YOUR TRANSPORT PROBLEMS

LEADERS IN THEIR CLASS!

2 TO 8 CWT CARRYING CAPACITY

THE PRATT ENGINEERING COMPANY   NORTHALLERTON YORKS. ENGLAND

January, 1953 — Page 29 — Modern Motoring & Travel

Making the SUNBEAM-TALBOT body

By a succession of carefully planned operations, the flat sheets of high quality steel are pressed into beautifully shaped panels, in huge presses such as this, by the British Light Steel Pressing Co., at Acton.

Right: at the R.T.B. Steelworks at Ebbw Vale; teeming steel into ingot moulds.

When the steel is 'set', the moulds are lifted off, the ingots go to the soaking pits, where they are reheated, are then rolled down into slabs, and again into a long strip of sheet steel, which leaves the famous continuous strip mill at twenty miles an hour. It is then cold-reduced in other mills, until it has the required qualities for panel pressing, and is then cut up and sent to the customer.

RICHARD THOMAS & BALDWINS LTD.
47, PARK STREET, LONDON, W.1

Seasonable Suggestions:

Beauty for the party — gifts for the family — aids for the home

By Brigid de Vine

January, 1953

Men, too, like beauty in the packet as well as in the figure!

Evening beauty personified in three attractive screen stars. British favourite Jane Hylton (left) wears a figure fitting satin gown, the strapless decollete edged with a collar of gold fringe to match her gold jewellery; youthful Mona Freeman (above) wears a gown in two tones of satin, the draped corsage being worked symmetrically on the bodice and continuing as a trim for the hips; and, (right), Suzan Ball has a strapless gown of pink satin with an accordion-pleated bodice in black net and matching stole.

"MUSICAL" greeting cards are the latest gadget for those who like to be up to the minute in their choice of gifts.

The cards are to be seen in Selfridges and cost 5s. 11d. each.

Inside each card is a small musical box which plays appropriate tunes: "Jingle Bells" for a Christmas card, and "Happy Birthday to You" for a Birthday greeting.

Unfortunate children whose birthdays fall near Christmas might score for once by qualifying for *both* cards!

Individual greetings can again be recorded in gramophone studios in various parts of the country, and the records can be safely packed and posted to relatives who cannot join the family circle for Christmas.

* * *

AIR travel has brought the whole world within easier visiting distance, but there is still the question of expense which makes very frequent visits "home" something of a problem.

Greetings spoken on to a record, or a record of a child's "party piece," can bring enormous pleasure to grandparents who cannot see their children and grandchildren as often as they would wish.

* * *

PRESENTS that are correct in their aim of pleasing the recipient are not really difficult to find. Even the most difficult person can be pleased by one of the three "Unbeatables": "Food," "Flowers" or "Money."

"*Men are such a nuisance,*" said a lady in Harrods the other day. "*Especially when they do not smoke or play anything.*"

She was standing in the Book Department looking doubtfully at a pile of books recommended as suitable gifts for men.

"But would he have read it already?" she wondered.

"How was one to know?"

Book Tokens always seemed "rather like sending a Postal Order," she thought.

I think she might have been happier if someone had suggested that she went instead to the Food Department, or to the Perfumery.

All men like things to eat, and most men like things to use in the bathroom. Any wife can tell you how menfolk habitually raid her favourite bath luxuries. They will not buy them for themselves, but they love luxuriously packed toilet things just as much as do their wives.

* * *

THIS year the beauty people have developed a line of "Gifts for Men" which are ideal for the man who "doesn't smoke or play anything."

He will surely use a huge tablet of bath soap and sponge packed together with a very "good" looking gold seal and sold by "Charles of the Ritz" counters for only 8s. 6d.

Yardleys solid brilliantine is so popular with men everywhere that "a Yardleys

(*Continued on page 32*)

Lovely Ann Todd, star in the London Film production "The Sound Barrier," directed by David Lean. Here she wears a full skirted pink-and-blue striped dressing gown in quilted satin.

WINTER BEAUTY... by ANN M. CAPELL

TREAT your skin carefully in the winter months; if it's the sensitive type give it a good massage every night with a lanoline cream, and during the day use an oily-type foundation.

Between times clean up the face with cleansing milk or cream, followed by a good skin freshener.

Coarse skin needs a weekly pack and the use of a refining lotion. It also improves with frequent cleansing with a whitening milk; and that goes, too, for sallow complexions.

For hands, a hand-lotion or jelly keeps them from getting red and rough in bad weather.

For lips likely to chap, use a trace of cream or oil beneath the lipstick, or a lip salve.

Bring back the sparkle to tired eyes by relaxing for ten minutes after the day's work, with pads soaked in witch hazel eye-tonic on your closed lids.

January, 1953　　　　　Page 31　　　　　MODERN MOTORING & TRAVEL

Seasonable Gift Suggestions:　　　　　By Brigid de Vine

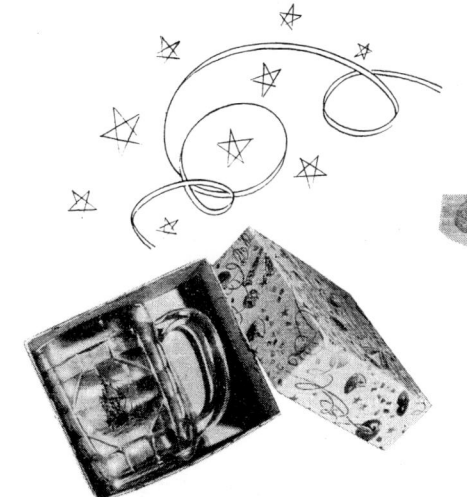

Above: Attractive coloured and expandable wire candle holders by Platers & Stampers, Ltd.—**2s. 6d.** set of four.

Left: Chance Lancer Tankard—in variety of sizes and gift boxes—from **1s. 6d.** to **16s. 6d.**

Right: Coty Cinderella slipper and perfume in box—**27s. 6d.**

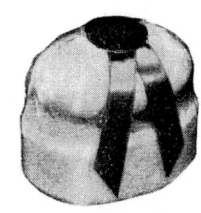

Above: "Charles of the Ritz" bath soap and sponge—a welcome gift—**8s. 6d.**

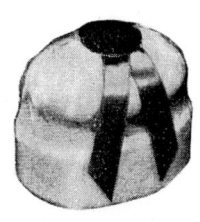

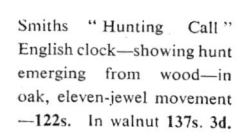

Right: "Airport" luggage sets—strong and distinctive—for the discriminating traveller, from all leading stores.

Coty morocco wallet containing lipstick, perfume and small purse—**47s. 6d.**

Neat desk set, scissors and paper knife, in velvet presentation case, by Champion (Scissors), Ltd.—**34s. 6d.**

Smiths "Hunting Call" English clock—showing hunt emerging from wood—in oak, eleven-jewel movement—**122s.** In walnut **137s. 3d.**

"Innoxa" hand lotion and three tablets of fragrant toilet soap—in neat case—**10s. 2d.**

Home radio—hear the "Pilot" Mariner—is always a welcome gift: available in a variety of sizes and finishes.

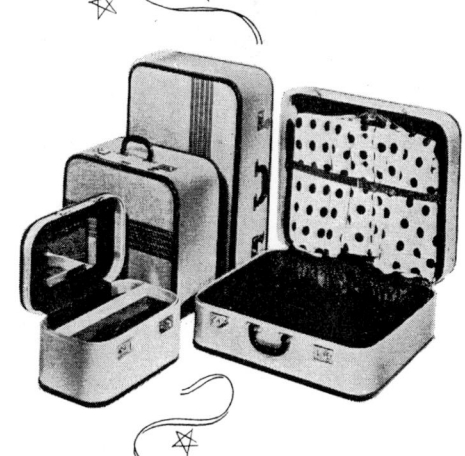

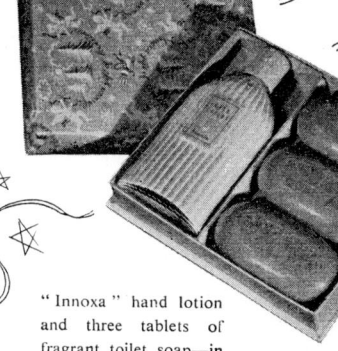

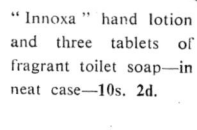

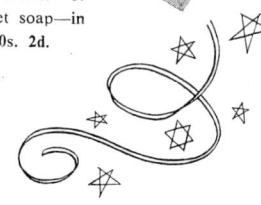

Captivating and carefree is this endearing hat, chosen by Columbia Pictures' beautiful young star, Donna Reed, who will soon be seen in a new Technicolor adventure for Columbia Pictures' "Hangman's Knot." Known as one of Hollywood's best dressed young stars, Donna has an impeccable taste when it comes to clothes ; she chooses them to suit herself. This particular hat has a tiny black velvet crown covered with veiling and is daringly decorated with eye catching ostrich feathers. With it she wears this smartly tailored black suit—untrimmed except for a pair of beautiful antique earrings.

Seasonable Suggestions:

(Continued from page 30)

please" has become the phrase for ordering any solid brilliantine in many non-English-speaking countries.

Yardleys have also brought back their famous wooden bowls of shaving soap this year, and they have a special talc and after-shaving lotion with a masculine "Cologne" scent that many women will find refreshing also.

Men might, also, like the latest Yardley novelty for the bath. It should remind them of happy days sailing model yachts on the Round Pond, or holidays in the South of France, for it not only softens and scents the water, but it turns it the colour of the Mediterranean, that intense "bathing-pool blue" that one sees on picture postcards. (And I am assured that it leaves no mark on the bath after use.)

Goya do a whole masculine range called *Corvette*. Mr. D. R. Collins thought of the range when he was serving in a corvette during the war. Both the shaving bowl and bottles have a raised decoration of "Turk's Head" knots.

Ships seem to be the most popular decoration on men's gifts, just as "a crinoline lady in an English garden" appeals to many women.

* * *

FOR Christmas gifts to hang on the tree *Bells* seem to be the most popular packing.

Elizabeth Arden suggests that you "ring in a Happy Christmas" for your women friends with a sparkling ribboned bell which has a bottle of the famous Blue Grass Perfume as its clapper.

Demuth fold bottles of their perfume, "Contraband," "Memento," etc., in a bell-shaped package with a loop to hang on the Christmas tree and each "bell" is supplied in a decorated box ready for posting. The bottles are the standard 7s. 6d. size, so that all the packaging is a "gift" to customers from Demuth.

* * *

BRONNLEYS have been making soap since 1888, the year after Queen Victoria's Golden Jubilee, and their goods, which met the approval of the Victorian demand for "the best" are still as popular as ever to-day. For this Christmas they are selling beautifully packed presentation boxes of their Bath and toilet soaps to offer "a fragrant compliment" to romantic ladies.

The tablets of soap are *heart shaped* with a flower decoration and the box of dusting powder is also heart shaped with a heart shaped puff.

* * *

COTY have used a real glass slipper as a novelty pack for their famous perfumes and the slipper like most of their other Christmas lines this year comes in a nicely decorated box which can be used afterwards for trinkets, etc. It is so made that the cardboard or satin-covered divisions can easily be removed without damaging the box.

A novel Coty gift this year, which would be ideal for the daughter about to start on her career, is a season ticket case with a Red Ribbon lipstick and a purser of L'Aimant perfume attached. It is made of red morocco, and on the back there is a little purse with a snap fastener for coins.

* * *

SHEEPSKIN is the basis of many practical Christmas gifts this year, and it turns up in all guises. It lines slippers and overshoes for men, women and children. It makes a comfortable fireside rug for an elderly relative's sitting room—or a bedside rug for anyone of any age who appreciates warmth.

Sheared white sheepskin makes an attractive evening bolero for a young girl—you would be warm wearing it even over a strapless gown on a December night.

* * *

FOR babies there is the double-fleece pram rug made by Morlands with appliqued decoration of rabbits or birds.

For warmth in the bathroom where sheepskin would not be suitable you can now get wonderfully deep piled bath mats by Osman with a design of stately swans sailing round the edge to match the border on the new Osman towels and bath sheets.

* * *

FOR *inner* warmth, by the way, there is, of course, nothing like RUM.

The United Rum Merchants, Ltd., of 40, Eastcheap, E.C.3, published earlier this year an enchanting booklet "Rum in the kitchen." It was offered free of charge, and if you write to them quickly they might have some copies left. It comes in a gay red cover and would be a nice thing to tuck into any grown-up Christmas stocking.

In order to be sure of getting the best results for the money you have set aside for Christmas gifts, there is, I am afraid, no substitute for Time and Effort. Each shop has its own special "novelty" and you can only be sure of getting the best

(Concluded on page 48)

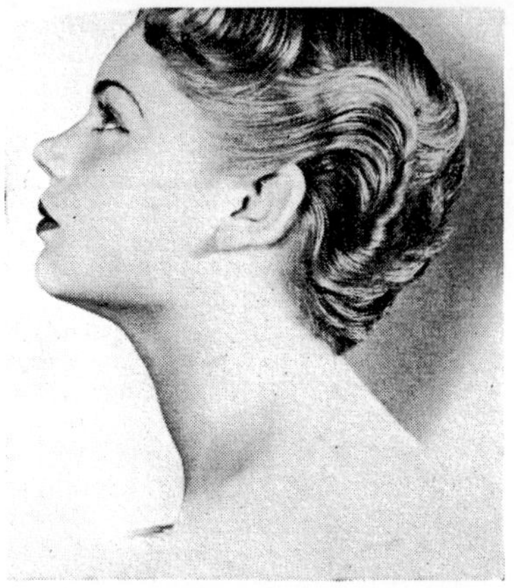

Raymond, of Mayfair, coins a new name for this, his newest creation—the "Millionairess."

The foundation of successful hair-styles lies in the cutting. When this is done by a master of the art, shampoo and setting at home then present no difficulties to the budget-conscious housewife or career girl.

The neat, simple style and the pure line of this attractive coiffure is achieved by the perfection and precision of cutting. Centre parted, the hair is gently waved back over the ears into a close-to-the-head dressing of half curls. The short top locks are combed forward either side into softly curled fringes on the brow. "A simple comb-through," says Raymond, "will bring the style into line even months after the original cut."

THE FINISHING TOUCH. Perfume is the finishing touch to beauty, to your whole personality. It is not enough to look nice ; you must smell nice-to-be-near ! Carry with you an atomiser in your handbag ; you can then be sure of moving in a fresh aura the whole day through.

Now that the long, social evenings are here again, with dance and dinner dates to the fore, you should start the evening really fresh by giving your body a perfumed body friction. Remember, lavish dusting powder, or talc, will give a coolness that is comforting.

Dressed for your evening out, create your own aura of feminine loveliness. Put a drop of perfume on all pulse spots and stroke it along the partings of your hair. If you are to dance the hours away, spray it round the hem of your gown, every twist and turn will waft a breath of fragrance near you.

Lastly, use your perfume to stroke away surplus make-up.

"Your perfume should echo your personality," says actress Dawn Addams, seen in our picture. Choose carefully the scent that evokes for you your favourite colours ... study your kind of life ... your moods ... your new clothes. "Smart Party" is the title of a new sophisticated perfume ... "Dual Control" is a lighter, more lingering fragrance, "Evergreen," light and cool with a spicy smell of pines and ferns.

If you like floral perfumes and prefer one like Lily-of-the-Valley or Honeysuckle or Violet or dashing Gardenia, then remember to sport a spray of matching flowers on your corsage, either real or artificial !

CAN WE HELP YOU?

Lights and Fuses

SIR,—I note that on the 1952 Sunbeam-Talbot there are fuses for the accessories, but no fuse for the head lights and side lights. I find this omission difficult to understand, and wonder what happens when there is a short in the wiring to the lights.

I am a new reader of your magazine and enjoy it very much indeed.

(Sgd.) F. A. H.,
RIPON.

The omission of a fuse in the side- and head-lamp circuits of the Sunbeam-Talbot is deliberate. The manufacturers feel that were a fuse fitted and a minor short developed, all lights would be immediately extinguished.

If this occurred while the car was at speed, it might possibly result in an accident.

* * *

On Ireland

SIR,—After reading Vincent Brennan's article on Ireland, I feel it is a very desirable " holiday country."

Would you please give me all the information you have on Ireland, Northern or Southern, places to stay and to visit in the summer months.

(Sgd.) M. H.,
BARRY.

The Irish Travel Association of Lower Regent Street, London, S.W.1, will provide full details regarding the Republic, and the Ulster Tourist Development Association, of Royal Avenue, Belfast, will do the same concerning Northern Ireland.

From such detailed information, you could plan a holiday suited to your own special tastes.

* * *

Treating Hoods

SIR,—I would be grateful if you could recommend any preparation that I could apply to the canvas top of my 1951 Sunbeam-Talbot " 90 " that would preserve the fabric without altering the original colour.

(Sgd.) J. W. J.,
KIRKBY STEPHEN.

In our opinion, the only treatment which

LIGHTING-UP TIMES THIS MONTH

	2nd	9th	16th	23rd	31st
London	4.31	4.40	4.50	5.1	5.16
Bristol	4.41	4.50	5.0	5.11	5.26
Birmingham	4.34	4.43	4.54	5.5	5.20
Leeds	4.25	4.34	4.46	4.57	5.12
Manchester	4.30	4.39	4.50	5.1	5.16
Newcastle	4.18	4.27	4.40	4.51	5.6
Glasgow	4.26	4.33	4.46	4.57	5.12
Belfast	4.38	4.47	5.0	5.11	5.26

Calendar of Coming Events

DECEMBER

10. Grouse Shooting Begins.
19 (to Jan. 31) Bertram Mills Circus, Olympia, London.
23 (to Feb. 7) Tom Arnold's Annual Christmas Circus, Harringay Arena, London.
31. Chelsea Arts Ball, Royal Albert Hall, London.

JANUARY

2-3. Car and Motor-Cycle Test Run, London — Stratford - upon - Avon — Penzance, Cornwall.
3. Rugby League Football : England v. The Rest, Twickenham, London.
17. Rugby League Football : Wales v. England, Cardiff, Glamorganshire.
25. Burns Day Celebrations.
26. Australia Day Service, St. Martin-in-the-Fields, London.
India Day.

---

should be given the hood topping is that outlined in the Owner's Handbook.

* * *

Safety Belts !

SIR,—In order to lessen the danger of injury to my small son while riding in a car, I wish to purchase, or have made for him, a safety belt, similar to that used by passengers in aircraft.

I do not wish to have that type of " safety " seat which clips over the seat back.

(Sgd.) D. W. M.,
INVERNESS.

Suitable clips could be fitted on the back of the rear seat squab, such that two leather straps could be attached at these points and led out between the joint of the squab and the seat cushion. A buckle or other quick release fastener could then be fitted to the ends of these straps securely to hold your passenger in position.

When this safety device is not required, the straps could be left permanently attached to the squab, but hidden under the seat cushion.

We are sure that your Hillman distributors, Messrs. Rossleigh, Ltd., Glenalbyn Garage, Young Street, Inverness, would assist in fabricating such a device for your son's use.

* * *

Still Chromium

SIR,—I notice that new cars being delivered have their bright parts " silver enamelled " instead of chromium plated.

Could you tell me if one can get some of this enamel and also if it is possible to use it on metal parts where the chromium plating has worn away, leaving smooth unrusted metal of a dull grey appearance.

(Sgd.) E. J. B.,
LINCOLN.

There is no " silver enamel " used on any of the Rootes Group range of cars.

Where, due to Government restrictions, the chromium plating has had to conform to an alternative specification, the final deposit is still of chromium, and this is protected by a clear lacquer varnish.

This process, like the original method of chrome deposition, is by electrolysis, and it will not be possible, therefore, for you yourself to treat any metal parts which are now devoid of chromium plating.

* * *

Out of Gear

SIR,—I should be glad of your advice on the trouble I am experiencing with my 1949 Hillman Minx.

When descending hills and using second gear to help the brakes, the car slips out of gear. When hill climbing no trouble is experienced, only the selection of gears between second and third is not positive.

(Sgd.) A. E. C.,
NEWPORT, MON.

It may be that the selector spring tension has weakened during service, or, alternatively, slight wear may have developed between the inner and outer members of the second speed synchro-hub.

You are advised to approach your local Hillman distributor, who will make a thorough investigation.

Rootes " Old Boys' " Association

IN the historic St. Mary's Hall, Coventry —enshrined with six centuries of the city's traditions and the spirit of craftsmanship covering inclusive phases of industrial effort over the ages—there sat recently some 200 present-day artisans in a memorable reunion of one-time pupils and apprentices for the inaugural dinner of the Rootes Group Pupils and Apprentices Old Boys' Association.

A more dignified and fitting venue it would be hard to conceive ; a more enthusiastic gathering never took place.

Following a cordial welcome to all present, Sir Reginald Rootes, deputy chairman Rootes Group, in his opening remarks left no doubt in the minds of his listeners as to the importance of the association to the Group, to the members themselves and—through the objects of social, cultural, scientific, sporting and other interests engendering good fellowship among former trainees of the Group—to Coventry and British industrial interests generally.

The Group's belief in sound administrative and technical training and the opportunity available within the organisation for those who extol themselves is well known, of course ; the calibre of those present fully endorsed the point ; which sentiment, as well as the profound dignity of the occasion and of the historic walls of the assembly was also stressed in the toast " The City of Coventry," ably presented by Mr. Geoffrey Rootes, managing-director, Humber, Hillman and Sunbeam-Talbot.

If the response by His Worship the Mayor (Alderman B. H. Gardner) understandably touched similarly upon the age-old traditions of the city and particularly those of St. Mary's Hall, his patronage was especially welcome and received in warm appreciation of the honour he bestowed.

Yes, the newly formed Rootes Group Pupils and Apprentices Old Boys' Association had a wonderful send-off, among those present included Mr. Rowland Smith, chairman of the Ford Motor Co., Mr. Alan Botwood, managing director of Harry Ferguson, Ltd., Mr. W. M. Heynes, director and chief engineer of Jaguar Cars, Ltd., and Mr. C. M. Simpson, chief engineer of the Daimler Co.—all " old boys "—not forgetting Mr. C. J. Banks, production manager at Rootes, Ryton, and Mr. F. G. Banks, his son, Ryton roller test, both " old boys " enrolled together, if some 32 years separates their joining the company.

The hon. secretary is Mr. R. M. Webb, reception manager, Ryton—himself an " old boy "—who invites all ex-pupils and apprentices to get in touch. A committee is now being formulated specially to further the objects and activities of the Association.

NEARLY 500 members and friends of the Sunbeam-Talbot Owners' Club attended the Club's annual dinner-dance held at the Dorchester Hotel, London, on October 24.

The traditional informality appealed to all present and the occasion was voted the best ever in the long series, always popular in the sporting calendar even in pre-war years.

Among those present, in addition to the President (Mr. W. G. Rootes), vice-presidents and officers of the Club, were many highlights of the sporting world—G. Murray-Frame, Stirling Moss, Mike Hawthorn, Leslie Johnson, George Hartwell, etc., etc., all of Monte Carlo, Alpine Trials and other famous sporting classics; almost the entire force of British motoring correspondents, and numerous Club friends from overseas. A good time was had by all!

* * *

YEAR by year the demand for tickets increases in leaps and bounds; who knows, perhaps the Royal Albert Hall may one day be the venue?

Undoubtedly, arranging the date for the first Friday during the Earls Court Motor Exhibition proved a very wise move: members were in town from all parts of the country and from overseas and thoroughly enjoyed the double London attraction.

* * *

CONSIDERABLE interest was expressed incidentally, in the comprehensive display of "blown-up" photographs taken by members at Club events during the year. These were supported by other pictures featuring the many Club continental rallies in France, Germany, Austria, Switzerland and Spain. Photographs taken on the occasion of the dinner are reproduced on the facing page.

* * *

Mid-winter Rally

ARRANGEMENTS have now been made by the S.T.O.C. for a mid-winter week-end Rally on December 6, with Bournemouth as the objective.

The Rally will be run on the lines of the Club's popular Southport and Scarborough Rallies and will incorporate a road section of some 200 miles, followed by a test on Ibsley Airfield, Hampshire, as well as the usual elimination tests on the promenade at Bournemouth.

In order that intending competitors will not have far to travel to any starting point, no less than 24 separate starting points will be included, which means that almost every large town south of Manchester will be given a Starting Control and no-one living south of Lancashire and Yorkshire will be involved in a journey of any length prior to the start.

A dinner-dance for members and friends will be held in the Bournemouth Pavilion. Tickets for this function will be available to Club members and their friends whether or not they take active part in the Rally. Rally Headquarters will be the Royal Bath Hotel, Bournemouth.

SPORTING SPOTLIGHTS

Events, personalities, records and regulations

1952 A RECORD YEAR:

660 Competitions,

205 Promoting Clubs,

10,000 Competitors—

and

still growing!

---

* * *

Record year of motor sport

THE year 1952 has been a record one in the history of British motor sport.

With over 660 events held under R.A.C. permits (138 being of the speed category) organised by some 205 promoting clubs, competition licence-holders (local) fell a few short only of the 10,000 mark.

What will 1953 bring?—certainly no dropping off in Club competitive enthusiasm.

* * *

Monte Carlo Rally

THERE is a record British entry, too, for the 23rd Internationale Rallye de l'Automobile Monte Carlo, to be held from January 20 to 27 next.

Rootes Group products are prominently represented—with 29 Sunbeam-Talbots; three Hillmans and two Humber Super Snipes. Featured in the imposing list of star trials' drivers are Norman Garrad (his 16th "Monte"), Stirling Moss, Mike Hawthorn, George Hartwell, Leslie Johnson, R. S. Henson, A. G. Imhof, J. H. Kemsley, D. H. Perring; E. W. Quero, J. R. Skeggs, P. C. E. Harper and Miss Sheila Van Damm (all on Sunbeam-Talbots); with M. B. Anderson, oft-repeated "Monte" winner of the "Touring Comfort" class, again on the Hillman Minx, and R. A. Dando and E. D. Maguire, also on the Minx.

Starting points will be Glasgow, Lisbon, Munich, Oslo, Palermo, Stockholm and Monte Carlo itself, in this instance, after a special circuitous route, joining the other competitors for the final trial sections.

* * *

Gas turbine speed record

GREAT BRITAIN becomes the first country officially to establish a speed record for gas engined turbine cars.

At its meeting in Paris recently the Federation Internationale de l'Automobile decided to establish classes for turbine engined cars and to recognise the performance of the Rover car (which timed a mean speed of 151·965 m.p.h. over the flying kilometre in Belgium in June last) as the first officially recognised performance in this category.

Other decisions taken by the F.I.A. concern International Racing Formulae. It was ruled that all Grand Prix races after January 1, 1954, must be for cars of a cylinder capacity up to 2,500 c.c. without supercharger and 750 c.c. with supercharger, providing at least three manufacturers make cars to this formula, which becomes Formula 1.

Formula 111 for 500 c.c. unsupercharged cars, in which class British cars are at present supreme, will continue, at least until the end of 1954.

* * *

International Fixtures

THE R.A.C. British Grand Prix continues to be one of 10 events counting towards the World's Racing Drivers Championship.

The R.A.C. Rally of Great Britain will be one of 10 events counting towards the European Touring Championship of Drivers, which will be awarded for the first time in 1953.

In conjunction with the Touring Championship, a definition of standard touring cars was agreed to, as were also definitions of sports cars on sale to the public and special prototype models—full details will be available from the R.A.C. later.

* * *

"Retreads" in sport

AFTER full consideration, the Royal Automobile Club has agreed to lift the ban on the use of retreaded, or remoulded, tyres. There is now no restriction on their use in the following circumstances :—

(a) On sports and touring cars taking part in races, hill-climbs or speed events of not more than one hour's duration.

(b) That retreaded, or remoulded, tyres so permitted be processed by the original tyre manufacturers or by firms who are members of the Retread Manufacturers Association and bear the identifying mark of the processer.

In events where cars may be expected to exceed 100 m.p.h., retreaded or remoulded tyres are forbidden.

The amendments come into force immediately and will be reviewed at the end of 1953.

SUNBEAM-TALBOT

Photo Nos. 1, 2, 5 and 6: Among those present were many leading motoring correspondents — too numerous to name—representing the national and overseas Press. Heads of tables, respectively, were Mr. E. D. O'Brien, Rootes' Public Relations Counsel; Mr. W. Martin, Public Relations Officer; Mr. A. D.

OWNERS' CLUB
Annual dinner-dance
(See facing page)

Rootes, Committee Member, and Mr. J. A. Masters.

Photo No. 3: The President's table, with the President (Mr. W. G. Rootes) extreme right.

Photo No. 4: Table of trials' aces, with G. Murray-Frame, John Pearman, John Cutts and Ken Wharton, and partners.

Photo No. 7: Members from "across the border," with, at table head, Mr. G. Lloyd Dixon, Vice-President.

Photo No. 8: Mr. and Mrs. Norman Rankin and friends, of Newcastle, "sit out" (new style) during the dancing.

Photo No. 9: "Happy birthday to you"—Mr. R. W. Lambert, cutting his birthday cake, has every reason to be happy with this bevy of attractive well-wishers.

O.K. FOR SOUND

Film Shorts and Starlights

Alluring Peggy Dow, of Universal-International shows her liking for unusual coin-shaped jewellery.

Marilyn Monroe, newcomer with 20th Century Fox, is causing quite a stir with her shapely figure.

A FIVE-STAR bill is planned for "Malta Story," Pinewood's screen tribute to the courage and endurance of the George Cross Island during the six-month siege of 1942.

Alec Guinness takes the role of a reconnaissance pilot, with Anthony Steel as his C.O. and Jack Hawkins the Air Officer in charge of the Island's air defences. Muriel Pavlow (wife of Derek Farr) plays a Maltese girl, and Renee Asherson a W.A.A.F. officer.

* * *

AFTER 40 years in show business, William Powell is planning to retire. His current role as Elizabeth Taylor's father in "The Girl Who Had Everything," is his last under contract at Metro-Goldwyn-Mayer.

Blonde American actress Yolande Donlan, currently seen in the British comedy "Penny Princess."

He will do one more film for 20th Century Fox, and then relax at his Palm Springs, California, home.

* * *

JACK WARNER and Robert Morley are starring with some of England's most famous cricketers in a screen version of Terence Rattigan's television play, "The Final Test."

Len Hutton plays the role he has played so well in real life—captain of England. Other cricketers include Jim Laker, Alec Bedser and Godfrey Evans.

* * *

WITH "The Prisoner of Zenda" and "Scaramouche" completed, Stewart Granger is in the midst of one of the most ambitious schedules ever undertaken by a star in Hollywood.

After "Young Bess," with his wife, Jean Simmons, Deborah Kerr and Charles Laughton, he will co-star with Robert Taylor and Elizabeth Taylor in "All the Brothers were Valiant." Then comes "Beau Brummel" and "Robinson Crusoe."

Mary Murphy, of Paramount, who plays the role of Laurence Olivier's daughter in the William Wyler production "Carrie."

IN Hamburg for his star role in George Brown's man-on-the-run thriller, "Desperate Moment," Dirk Bogarde met his own voice—face to face.

Dirk was taken to a German cinema for a showing of a dubbed version of his film, "Hunted." Afterwards, German actor, Wolfgang Rottspieper, introduced himself as "Deutsche Dirk." He had spoken Dirk's lines in the film.

* * *

PLAYING opposite Dirk Bogarde in "Desperate Moment," Mai Zetterling is being called Mai Splutterling.

A non-smoker, she has to smoke incessantly in the film!

* * *

MICHAEL WILDING'S first assignment under his new M-G-M starring contract will be in "Latin Lovers," with Lana Turner, Fernando Lamas and Louis Calhern.

Wilding will be seen as a wealthy suitor for Miss Turner's hand.

* * *

MAUREEN O'SULLIVAN has not only the distinction of having had more children—seven—than any other star in Hollywood, she is also the only star who has had three screen careers.

After retiring twice, she is back with Universal-International in a comedy, "Bonzo Goes to College." Bonzo is a chimpanzee.

* * *

RONALD HOWARD, son of the late Leslie Howard, joins the cast of London Independent Producer's film tentatively entitled, "The Policewomen."

Hyde Park Corner, Chelsea, Kensington, Fulham, Camden Town, Charing Cross Road and Piccadilly, are included in the location sequences.

* * *

ABBOTT and Costello get around. In their last picture they were on Mars, and their next comedy, "Abbott and Costello Meet Dr. Jekyll and Mr. Hyde," has an English setting.

* * *

PINEWOOD carpenters are superstitious about having to make coffins for a film sequence. When they were asked to provide one for the new spy thriller, "The Net," they were relieved to find a left-over from "Oliver Twist"!

Our Twenty days' care-free continental holiday;

very comfortable, too!

By A. E. Titchmarsh

MY wife and I have always had a liking for travel on the Continent, and when the Government reduced the travel allowance last year to £25 we were reluctant to abandon our plans.

"Where there's a will there's a way" we argued, and we decided to think it out.

The big expense abroad is, after all, the cost of a room in which to sleep and if that could be cut out we might manage a trip in spite of the restrictions.

We are a bit advanced in years for camping in a tent, but what about a good sized shooting brake? That seemed to offer possibilities.

* * *

AFTER a look round the second-hand dealers we found a grand bus in an ex-W.D. Humber Brake of 1940 vintage, and as it was first registered in 1947 the tax was only £10 per year. A good stout job with plenty of power and ample room.

We removed the rear seats for the time being and the local caravan builder very quickly fitted it with locker space and sponge rubber mattresses, each of which gave the full 6 ft. by 2 ft. usually fitted in caravans. Here was our hotel on wheels and under its own power, and very comfortable it proved to be.

* * *

WE shipped on the Dover-Dunkirk night ferry service and drove the first day to a spot near Dijon and thence to Lausanne and Brigue into northern Italy.

Here we crossed the Simplon Pass, the Humber making light work of the job.

Near the summit of the Simplon Pass, looking back to Brigue —a good stout climb essayed with ease on our Humber brake.

The only place we couldn't take our car —on the canals in Venice — where we spent many delightful hours.

In our opinion this is the most beautiful pass of them all and we saw it in ideal weather.

* * *

HAVING spent some time on the shores of the Italian Lakes we next pushed on along the Autostrada to Padua and Venice. The latter is, of course, delightful.

Now at the end of our outward journey, we retraced our steps in a leisurely manner into Switzerland where we spent some days, then making our way back to the port and England.

In all we travelled some 2,700 miles without the slightest trouble and without even a puncture.

The round trip took 20 days and we dined well every evening usually taking our midday meal in the brake.

In this way we were able to see the countryside in detail, which most of us find so much more attractive than the larger towns, and were able to manage quite well on the currency allowed and the whole holiday was a great success. We strongly recommend this to those who like to see new and exciting country in a novel yet satisfactory method.

January, 1953

OUR PHOTOGRAPHIC COMPETITION

Result of First Contest — a record entry

Still time for you to participate

FIRST PRIZE : "Toward the Pike"—Derwentwater, by D. Procter, of 10, Primrose Hill Road, Huddersfield, Yorks.

WHILE we expected the usual enthusiastic entry for our new series of photographic competitions, the response, at least for the first contest, has exceeded all expectations.

Consequentially, too, the task of judging has been unusually difficult, the merit of all pictures revealing the considerable thought and artistic consideration employed.

We should like to have given greater visual evidence of the remarkable quality and variety of the photographs submitted, in the number of reproductions published. As it is, over and above the premier entries, we reproduce six "Consolation" winners which are being awarded a special prize, each of half a guinea.

*   *   *

So concludes the First Contest. Now for the Second—which, of course, is open to all amateurs, whether or not they competed and/or won a prize in Event No. 1. The same photograph must not be submitted a second time, however, each contest being in relation to inclusively new subjects.

*   *   *

Entries for the Second Event should have been received by not later than November 30. Result will be published on January 1, 1953.

There is also the Third and last contest, open up to December 31, the result of which will be announced on February 1, 1953.

Prizes offered for each event are : 1st, Three Guineas ; 2nd, Two Guineas ; 3rd, One Guinea. Additionally, there is a special "Aggregate Award" of Five Guineas for the entry adjudicated the best of all three competitions. It is possible, therefore, for someone to win a total of Eight Guineas for only one picture.

SECOND PRIZE : "On Top of the World"—Summit of Susten Pass, Switzerland, by P. B. Booth, of 507, Idle Road, Bradford, Yorks.

Below : **THIRD PRIZE :** "Proud Parents"—scene on Dabton Loch, Thornhill, by E. G. Sykes, of "Drumshell," Thornhill, Dumfriesshire.

CONSOLATION: "Stonyhurst College, near Preston," by J. Stevenson, of 66, Lindsay Avenue, Marton, Blackpool, Lancs.

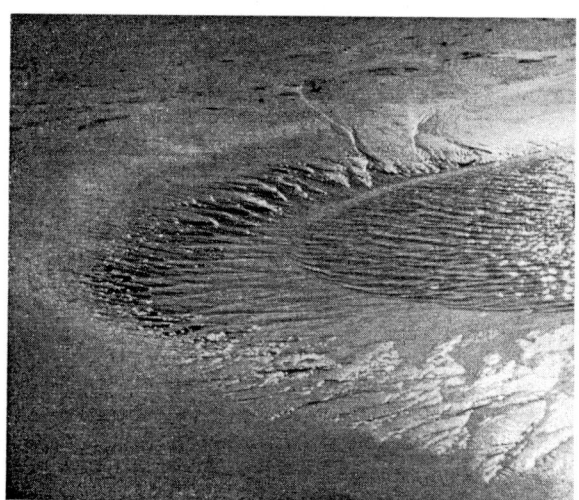

CONSOLATION: "Sun, Sea and Sand," by R. C. Yarnold, of 48, West End Road, Bitterne, Southampton.

If space and quality of photographs, relative to the Second and Third competitions, permit, further series of "Consolation" awards will be considered.

We look forward now to receiving many more entries for this popular annual event. Do not be discouraged by failure in Contest No. 1: you may still have just the subject that will bring you double success.

Address your entries: Photo Competition, "Modern Motoring and Travel," 53, Stratton Street, Piccadilly, London, W.1. All photographs must be endorsed: "Amateur and unpublished photograph by —(name)—of—(address)—after January 1, 1952," and be given a suitable description or title.

Selected subjects:—

(a) Lake or waterway settings.
(b) Architectural—old or new.
(c) Novelty or new angle.
(d) Beauty of countryside, home or overseas.
(e) Still life and portraiture.
(f) Direct motoring interest.

CONSOLATION: "The Stellisee"—near Zermatt, with Matterhorn in distance, by E. C. Ive, of "Green Willows," 218, Upper Woodcote Road, Caversham, Reading.

Below: CONSOLATION: "Mevagissey," by K. Mayne, also of 48, West End Road, Bitterne, Southampton.

CONSOLATION: "Corpus Christi," Sitges, Spain, by D. A. Bull, of "Oakdene," Wraxall, near Bristol.

CONSOLATION: "Flower Girl"—Funchal, Madeira, by H. J. Smeaton, of 97, Uxbridge Road, Ealing, London, W.5.

Seasonable Suggestions:

(Concluded from page 32)

for everyone if you make a point of getting all the catalogues and walking round a good many departments.

* * *

IN one day's shopping round London's West End I have found several gifts that could double for several names on one's list.

Harrods insulated food bag to keep food or drinks hot or cold is a good gift for any traveller or for those who watch winter sports, but it would also be useful to a young mother for trips with baby.

Druces have miniature vacuum cleaners, with a 6-inch bag, which are operated by a battery and meant to pick up ash or crumbs. They are meant for the careful hostess, but they would appeal to many children, and at 20s. 3d. are less expensive than many items in Toy Departments. Lilley and Skinner sell children's fluffy "rabbit" slippers with *moving* eyes in the rabbit-heads on the toes, that would please any number of children—if you remember to check their sizes carefully first.

* * *

A CASE of cider would please those who are on an anti-rheumatic diet, teen-age party-givers who enjoy the ceremony of a huge cider cup bowl as the centre on a buffet table, and also the thrifty young housewife who has found how well cider may often substitute for white wine in cooking. (You might give her, also, the *Cooking in Cider* recipe book, published by World's Work, Ltd., which is dedicated to those who like food that tastes "different.")

Long silk milanese evening gloves from Jay's or Marshall & Snelgroves might be bought in several different colours, and sizes, for half the feminine names on your list, and they are light and easy to pack, and cost less than a pound.

If you simply cannot tie up parcels, incidentally, Harrods have once again opened a Gift Package Counter, where you may take parcels to be tied up in such pretty paper and with such a wealth of ribbons that one can hardly imagine anyone having the heart to undo them.

* * *

FOR children who *love* "undoing" things, Harrods have a novel card for half a crown. It is a large picture of a winter scene, and it shows in the various parts of the scene no less than 20 little doors.

You present the card 20 days *before* Christmas, and each day the child can open up one of the cardboard doors and see a fresh scene underneath until by Christmas there are 20 new little pictures showing as part of the main scene.

There are always some unfortunate children who must miss the joy of a tour round the Toy Fairs because they must have tonsils out, or some other tiresome business that keeps them in bed away from all the fun. For them, especially, this card is an excellent idea. The child could look forward to opening a new little door each morning for 20 days.

* * *

YOU might, if you are clever, make an enormous Christmas card scene on one wall of a nursery, and arrange little presents to be found behind little doors instead of round the traditional Christmas tree as a novel idea for a children's party.

If you simply must give a children's Christmas party as usual this year, and the expense is really a consideration, *do* copy the inspiration of the wise mother who gave an Arab party to her little son's friends. The room was simply draped with white sheets to make a large "tent." A supply of white towels provided Arab "robes" for the children to dress up. The refreshments were mostly dates and sherbert. And each child received a present of a small "camel," from Woolworth's, from around a "date palm" contrived ingeniously out of a broom handle and some green paper.

It was the most successful party in the district, and the small guests enjoyed it more than many more expensive parties complete with "tree," conjurer, etc.

* * *

IF you remember to use your imagination, *all* your Christmas presents and parties will be a success—even if you have not much money. And on your tour round the shops you will see lots of delightful gifts to buy yourself with the Christmas cheques I hope you will receive.

"*No one was ever insulted by a present of money—provided it was big enough.*" That is a piece of wisdom you might start quoting now—whenever you find yourself within ear-shot of a cheque-bearing relative. I hope you do get a good cheque. In the next edition of *Modern Motoring and Travel*," I will tell you how to spend it.

Garringtons are pleased to announce **THE NEW UNIFIED HEXAGON SPANNERS and RING WRENCHES**

(B.S. 1768 1769
B.S. 192/43
(TABLE 1A))

NOW AVAILABLE

GARRINGTONS LIMITED, DARLASTON, STAFFS, BROMSGROVE, WORCS.

A MEMBER OF THE GKN GROUP OF COMPANIES

CONNOLLY *connotations*

The connotation of a word or phrase is what it implies in a particular connection.

"*mind your p's and q's*"

THERE are many possible explanations as to the origin of minding your p's and q's—perhaps the most likely is that it was originally the writing master's warning that a carelessly formed "p" could easily be confused with an "h" and a "q" with a "g". Happily, when it comes to leather there is no possible confusion—Connolly's is the best and no other is quite like it.

IN LEATHER

Connolly

CONNOTES **QUALITY**

CONNOLLY BROS. (CURRIERS) LTD., CHALTON STREET, EUSTON ROAD, LONDON, N.W.1   PHONE: EUSTON 1661

"The MINX makes my whole family happy!"

" 35,000 miles of magnificent performance from my Minx—and not a spot of trouble!" reports Mr. Carl Storm, of Goteborg, Sweden. "In below-zero snowstorms and rough dusty roads in summer, its reliability, comfort and economy are unfailing. We often sit 3 in the front, and its handiness in traffic, leisurely 60 m.p.h. cruising, and perfect balance, make us happy with our Minx."

THE HILLMAN MINX

EXPORT DIVISION ROOTES
DEVONSHIRE HOUSE
PICCADILLY LONDON W1
Distributors throughout the World

ROOTES GROUP REGIONAL REPRESENTATIVES *located at:*

U.S.A. 505 Park Avenue, New York 22, N.Y. and 403 North Foothill Road, Beverly Hills, California.
CANADA 2019 Eglinton Avenue East, Scarborough, Ontario.
AUSTRALIA & NEW ZEALAND Fishermen's Bend, Port Melbourne, Australia.
SOUTHERN AFRICA 750/2/4 Stuttaford's Buildings, St. George's St., Cape Town, S A.
CENTRAL AFRICA Jackson Road, P O. Box 5194, Nairobi, Kenya.
BELGIUM Shell Building, 47, Cantersteen, Brussels.
FRANCE 6 Rond-Point des Champs Elysees, Paris, 8.
SWITZERLAND 3 Jenatschstrasse, Zurich.
FAR EAST Macdonald House, Orchard Road, Singapore, 9
INDIA Agra Road, Bhandup, Bombay.
NEAR EAST 37 Kasr El Nil Street, Cairo, Egypt.
MIDDLE EAST & PAKISTAN Esseily Building, Assour Beirut, Lebanon.
JAPAN Strongs Building, No. 204 Yamashita-cho, Naka-Ku, Yokohama.
ARGENTINA Cassilla de Correo, 3478, Buenos Aires.
BRAZIL Av. Presidente Vargas 290 (S/1003), Rio de Janeiro.
CARIBBEAN: P.O. Box 1479, Nassau, Bahamas.

Loch Laggan, by Inverness.
Photo by Hugh Sibley.

                    Till the Moon,
Rising in clouded majesty, at length
Apparent queen, unveiled her peerless light,
And o'er the dark her silver mantle threw.—*Milton*

At the invitation of Sir William Rootes, K.B.E., chairman of the Rootes Group, some 50 Swiss automobile distributors and leading members of the Swiss Press recently made an extended tour of the Group's manufacturing and exporting establishments in Coventry and London—to leave "very considerably impressed." Our photographs show the eve-of-departure dinner given by Sir William and, on left, H. E. The Swiss Minister, M. Henry de Torrenté, in conversation with Sir William Rootes, and in centre, Mr. J. G. Chaldecott, managing director, Export Division.

Among other distinguished visitors to the Group's Coventry factories recently were Sir Lewis Hutchinson, K.B.E., C.B., deputy secretary of the Ministry of Supply and General H. E. Pyman, C.B., C.B.E., D.S.O., director-general of Fighting Services—here seen with Mr. Geoffrey Rootes, managing director, car manufacturing division, extreme left, and Mr. E. W. Hancock, M.B.E., director and general manager (Works), second from right.

Departure from Oslo of Stirling Moss and the Humber Super Snipe on its 3,280 miles epic drive, over 15 countries to Portugal, in under four days—see page 12.

Editorial Comment

EDITORIAL AND ADVERTISING
53 STRATTON STREET,
LONDON, W.1
Telephone: GRO 3401

Conducted by E. D. O'BRIEN

Editor: **THOMAS R. MULCASTER**

THE motor industry as a whole can take pride in two recent achievements.

In the first, a new Humber Super Snipe travelled nearly 3,500 miles across 15 European countries in a minute under 90 hours, and in the second, another new Humber Super Snipe knocked eight days—repeat eight days—off the London to Cape Town record.

In both cases, a standard production line car was used, with the exception, in the case of the London-Cape Town run, of the addition of extra petrol tanks for remote sections of the route where no petrol would be available.

* * *

GEORGE HINCHLIFFE left London un-noticed on the morning of November 26, and headed south like any ordinary motorist.

At 2 a.m. G.M.T. on December 2, Stirling Moss and his team left Oslo, Norway, on their long drive south to Lisbon.

* * *

ONCE across France and on African soil, George Hinchliffe proceeded to put up the fastest time ever recorded across the Sahara, through the Belgian Congo, across Kenya and the Rhodesias, and so to Cape Town, beating the previous best time, for any car, of 21 days—which he set up himself, incidentally, in January last in a Hillman Minx—by no fewer than eight days!

At the same time the Stirling Moss team was engaged in clipping off the miles, under some of the most appalling wintry conditions which Europe has experienced in recent years—through Sweden, Denmark, Germany, Holland, Belgium, Luxemburg, France, Switzerland, Italy, Austria, Yugoslavia, Spain and Portugal, in an attempt to cover the 3,280 miles between Oslo and Villar Formoso in five days. Their actual running time was one minute under 90 hours—30 hours better than their best hopes.

* * *

ELSEWHERE in these pages will be found a full description of their remarkable feat. It was not merely, as Sir William Rootes said, a great achievement on the part of the car, but also a tribute to "the type of young man which this country is now producing—and a very good type it is." (Newspapers which specialise in gloomy views on juvenile crime, please copy.)

However, men and machines have done a splendid job for Britain. As each frontier was passed, a new national flag was displayed in front of the bonnet until there were 15 in all, and flown from the wireless aerial was the Union Flag, dirty and tattered almost beyond recognition by the end of this epic run, but still a symbol of the reasons for which it was run—to no small purpose at this time when the British motor industry is facing greater difficulties, but greater opportunities, than ever before.

Here's the sign of WINTER WISDOM

it means Greatest Winter SAFETY

Fit the tyres designed to meet and master treacherous winter road conditions — the tyres with the Gold Seal... 'Dunlop' and Dunlop 'Fort'. The safety secret is in the unique patented tread which, with its scientifically disposed knife-cuts, squeegees the water-film away so that the thousands of staggered "teeth" can get a powerful grip on the road... a grip that lasts throughout the long life of the tread pattern, which retains its initial design right to the end. Yet another great feature is the rubber liner moulded to the *inside* of Gold Seal tyres. It greatly reduces risk of damage from chance under-inflation, deflation and kerb impact.

DUNLOP

THEY'RE FIRST IN SAFETY AND LONG LIFE

—yet they cost no more!

"Fifteen Countries in Five days" was bettered by 30 hours! Epic Oslo-Lisbon non-stop drive

THE object? To give proof positive, if any be necessary, to the all-round road worthiness of the new Humber Super Snipe with its remarkable "Blue Riband" power unit.

As Sir Reginald Rootes said at a Press Conference prior to the start, "There are those who would question the purpose, even the sanity, of an exploit of the kind, particularly at this time of the year.

"To these I would reply, it is to give practical demonstration, beyond all possible doubt, of our faith in the product, our confidence in a car designed and built for world-wide usage and this in relation to every variety of terrain and under all climatic conditions, as well as our trust in the drivers."

* * *

SO it was—at Oslo, at below freezing point, the start was made at 02.00 hours on Tuesday, December 2.

Conditions worsened all the way through Sweden and Denmark and Germany—icy and fogbound roads, even blizzards—yet the set average of 40 m.p.h. was rigidly maintained.

Not until they reached Holland and Belgium did conditions show any improvement—if sheet ice and crystallised *pavé* is any improvement!—to press on across France for Switzerland (the half-way point) and Italy, where progress was still maintained in spite of the now appalling conditions in the snow-covered passes, and so on for Trieste and Yugoslavia.

Due west again the prospects of sunnier climes did perhaps inspire brighter thoughts, though eating up the miles was necessarily the more imperative condition of mind. For still arduous going was ahead, the mountains and dust of Southern France, the endless snake-like, rise-and-fall going in the valleys of the Pyrenees *en route* to Spain, the last leg to the Portuguese border at Villar Formoso and thence to Lisbon.

* * *

FIFTEEN countries in five days was the target set, or 3,280 miles at an average speed of just under 40 m.p.h.

Well, something attempted something done, and done well, with no fewer than 30 hours knocked off the basic time schedule—actual

Sir Reginald Rootes discusses the route with the drivers, Stirling Moss, Leslie Johnson, John Cutts and David Humphrey at a goodwill send off.

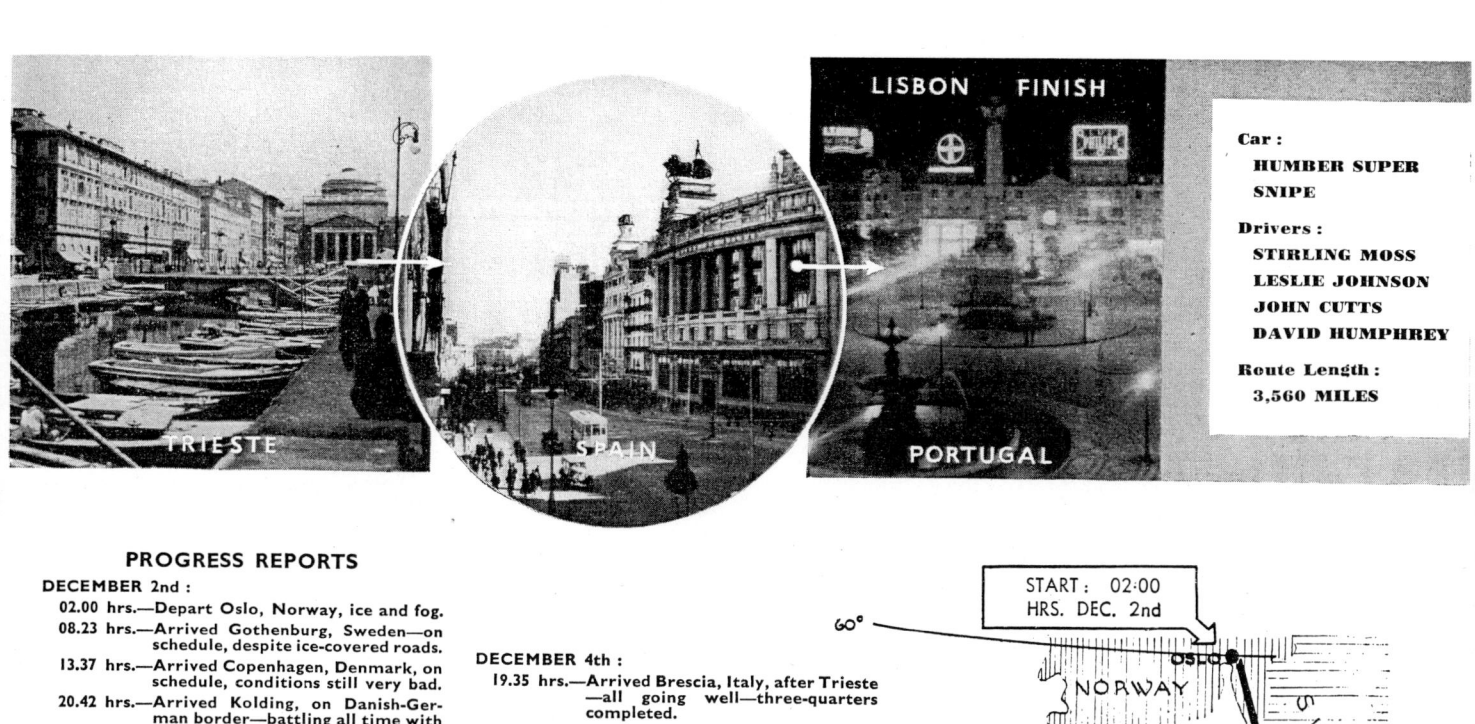

TRIESTE — **SPAIN** — **LISBON FINISH** — **PORTUGAL**

Car: **HUMBER SUPER SNIPE**

Drivers:
**STIRLING MOSS
LESLIE JOHNSON
JOHN CUTTS
DAVID HUMPHREY**

Route Length:
3,560 MILES

PROGRESS REPORTS

DECEMBER 2nd:
02.00 hrs.—Depart Oslo, Norway, ice and fog.
08.23 hrs.—Arrived Gothenburg, Sweden—on schedule, despite ice-covered roads.
13.37 hrs.—Arrived Copenhagen, Denmark, on schedule, conditions still very bad.
20.42 hrs.—Arrived Kolding, on Danish-German border—battling all time with ice and blizzards—still on schedule.

DECEMBER 3rd:
09.40 hrs.—Arrived Dusseldorf, Germany—completed first 1,000 miles, car running fine, still icy roads, poor visibility all way from Oslo. German motor clubs present pennants as "mark of esteem" for maintaining schedule.
15.55 hrs.—Arrived Luxembourg—on schedule—conditions improving through Holland and Belgium.
20.45 hrs.—Arrived Swiss frontier.
22.40 hrs.—Arrived Zürich, on schedule—1,656 miles—half-way point.

DECEMBER 4th:
19.35 hrs.—Arrived Brescia, Italy, after Trieste—all going well—three-quarters completed.

DECEMBER 5th:
08.30 hrs.—Arrived Monte Carlo, on schedule, despite new and more appalling conditions.
19.59 hrs.—Arrived Villar Formoso, Portuguese objective reached—15 countries in 1 minute under 90 hours. Distance now 3,280 miles—heading for Lisbon. Covered last 1,200 miles in 24 hours including all stops for frontier and other formalities, averaging 50 m.p.h. Lisbon 271 further on—"all well—but very sleepy."

running time being one minute under 90 hours —plus a faultless performance throughout.

A grand show, and one deserving the highest possible commendation.

The best of congratulations, therefore, to the drivers—Stirling Moss, Leslie Johnson, John Cutts and David Humphrey in upholding, in determined and outstanding manner, the sponsors' convictions placed both in them and the new Humber Super Snipe.

Stirling Moss and his crew fix the final flag as they enter Portugal, at Villar Formoso.

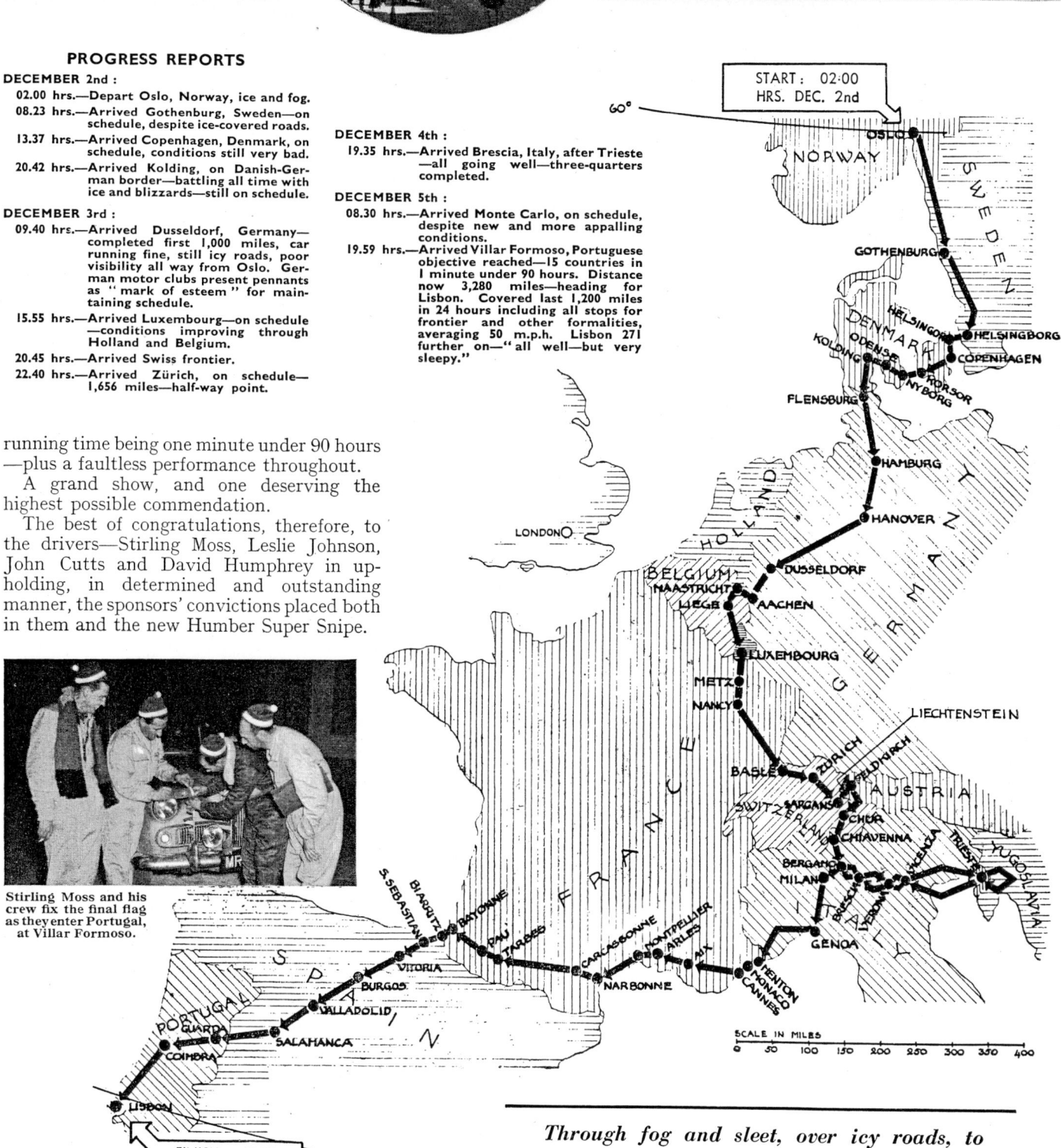

START: 02.00 HRS. DEC. 2nd

FINISH: 19.59 HRS. DEC. 5th

Through fog and sleet, over icy roads, to mountain passes and the Sunnier South

"Your body is no more than living character"

says Prof. A. M. Low

FIRESIDE REFLECTIONS ON SCIENCE

Everything is character

EYES have been worshipped by poets for centuries, but it is only the characteristic setting, or indeed the character, which we should admire.

The assertion that everyone has blue eyes seems to be absurd. But as a matter of fact this is the case. If eyes do appear of another colour it is because the blue is masked or shaded in some way.

The exquisite blue colour of some human eyes is due to the scattering of light and this blue is quite common in nature and goes by the name of "Tyndall Blue." It is produced by white light passing through a turbid media which causes dispersal of the blue rays and lends the lovely blue shade to the media.

This is what goes on in the eye. In the liquid of the iris are very fine solid particles in a state of dispersion. These particles are too small to be visible but they are able to effect the blue light rays.

If eyes seem to be brown, or green, or grey, it is due to a masking effect of the uvea, which is a screen frequently coloured so that it tones down the blue of the iris. So often things are not really what they seem. I believe that the body is no more than living character after all!

* * *

I don't think much of us

HAVE you ever noticed how many things seem still to be done by sheer grinding labour? I, for example, always want to apologise to the postman who drags round a big bag which seems to contain mostly income tax papers and Government forms. I admit there is an occasional letter worth reading.

Surely, in the far future, houses will be laid on for milk, letters, fuel, hot water and other things which have become necessities so that our brains can have time to develop without bothering about bodies?

It is very bad that just because I want to see some letters and write replies I should have to make a journey in an evil-smelling carriage at great expense and discomfort. Will it be many centuries I wonder before television and accurate telephony makes minds matter more?

Would it not be possible for us all to have a token-mark consisting of an arrangement of dots on a piece of card? If this were done a photo-cell sorting machine could quite easily sort every letter at the Post Office, and when once that was accomplished quickly, better transport would be easy.

In many works such a system has been adopted, and I think that some modern office proceedings are on a par with a man licking his thumb and slowly turning over each sheet to see if it begins "Dear Sir," and ends "Yours faithfully."

* * *

Is it cruel?

IT is probably very stale, not to say scientific, for me to remind you that all nature fights. A good definition of something living is, in my opinion, something which fights. Sometimes we can only just see the struggle amongst bacteria, virus or even crystals. But I think it is there.

You will remember my old suggestion that if a cinema picture is taken from a forest and run off too quickly, creepers can be seen tearing trees to pieces. Plants are, in a way, sentient beings even if they are not so "sentient" as ourselves. Quite a number of denizens of the vegetable world are sensitive to the touch and, still more, close up with a snap when an insect gets inside.

My point is, are they cruel? When a thrush smashes a snail, which should we save? And when we admire bird life in its gentle beauty do we always remember the Shrike which impales a bee and even nestling birds upon a thorn bush, using the spikes as a larder until this "butcher bird" feels hungry?

Some sparrows are notoriously immoral. One sees Mrs. Sparrow flirting desperately, but she must know that her husband has many wives and that he will kill other birds without hesitation. It is not unknown for a thrush to smash nestlings on a stone or to fly away with one of these little creatures as if it were a worm.

There are also certain insects which habitually stun others so that they may keep fresh for quite a long time till their captors want to eat them.

My friends always argue that a cat is not cruel. It is the "nature of the beast," they say, and therefore it cannot be blamed. For my part I do not like things with such a nature very dearly, be they fish, flesh or feline.

What I would like you to tell me is whether I can say all these are nature's ways, reminding myself that men are quite as cruel to each other through all the ages, or if we can rest assured that we have the right to kill animals by virtue of our rare and noble brains?

I never hesitate to give away my own idea, for if it is wrong I am anxious to learn. Would you agree with me that human nature is exactly the same as *all* nature and that the principle of life is the survival of the fittest whether this be by force, cunning, or in rare cases even a little intelligence?

* * *

Robots

IT worries me to explain so often to my friends that robots do not obtain their power from the station which directs them. Machines which answer questions are only gramophones with switches actuated from relays. In turn, the relay is made sensitive to a definite frequency so that a tone of voice will "set off" the right answer.

It also irritated me during the London bombing, when I had to stop dictating every now and then so that my secretary could make a bolt for the dugout, to hear how "clever were these German atrocities."

Whether they are atrocities or not is a matter of the direction in which they travel, but I do know that I and the late Sir Henry Segrave, who held the world's speed record, flew a robot round about 1916 in the presence of the allied staff. The machine was even launched by compressed air.

None of these instruments is powered by wireless. They have their own power plant on the spot—in our case the horizontally opposed engine; in the German machine, a jet. All the control does is to alter the setting of a gyroscope which, in turn, calls up the local power to move the rudder or whatever it may be.

While talking about myself I cannot resist pointing out that with Commander Brook I designed an anti-aircraft steerable rocket in 1917, television in 1914, and an electric engine indicator about 1912. It is awfully difficult to think of anything new, but, for the same reason as I have already mentioned, the idea that Germany first fired rockets from aeroplanes was too funny for words.

The Germans were, and still are, magnificent copyists. In actual origination they are far less skilled.

* * *

Evidence before you!

AT the Science Museum in London is a wonderful collection of old and new apparatus, although I would almost give the palm to the German rocket and to some other radio-controlled weapons which are now exhibited.

It is quite unfair to attribute the invention of these things to Germany. Development, if you like.

Within a biscuit's throw of these unnecessary war devices, for war would be unnecessary if it were less profitable, is an early model of the Foucault pendulum, and if you have not seen it in operation you must demand to have this principle demonstrated to you at your local Home of Science.

The world goes round. That you have noticed, but if it goes round and a pendulum is suspended over a point on its circumference why does not the pendulum swing as if it were out of truth?

As it happens, it does. And to me it is a most thrilling thing to stand a few yards from a London street and to watch this slowly travelling pendulum moving across a scale of degrees as the world swings on its course.

How the mind can wander! It is better than standing on top of a hill and looking at the stars. Far more thrilling than any film, far more wonderful to think of our origin in the sun, or that this little globe is passing along through endless space for what we call for ever and with no-one knowing or caring a row of beans.

"Swears by TECALEMIT!! The moment the Service Reminder Card arrives — *wham!* — he's in!"

The Tecalemit "Reminder" Card sent you by your Garage will advise you when your car needs Tecalemit Specialised Maintenance. It is part of the Tecalemit Service.

THERE ARE OVER 4,000 OFFICIAL TECALEMIT EQUIPPED SERVICE STATIONS

T358

TEE-TIME TOPICS

By F. J. C. PIGNON

Rules of Golf—few know them, and still fewer observe their requirements!

ST. ANDREWS has announced that there will be no change in the code of Rules of Golf, as amended in January, 1952, during the current year.

The United States code of rules, which is substantially the same, will also stand as they do at present without modification.

This probably is just as well, for having tried them out for a year the authorities cannot have failed to realise that a great number of golfers do not observe the rules, obviously through lack of knowledge of them.

* * *

IT is quite understandable that the golfer who confines his play to not much more than week-ends, should have only a sketchy knowledge of a code of rules which occasionally baffle Club officials, who have to seek guidance of the Rules of Golf Committee.

This committee issue from time to time Decisions of the Rules of Golf which form volumes of " case law " in golf, and very valuable these are, too, to those in charge of important events.

But it is remarkable that club officials should sometimes display such ignorance of elementary rules. Members may think that the Club secretary is the overriding power in the interpretation of the rules and consequently sometimes get an entirely erroneous impression about them.

* * *

ONE golfer who wrote to me recently, told of being penalised two strokes during the course of a 36 holes stroke play competition *because he had returned a very low score in the morning round.*

In spite of the two strokes penalty, he tied for the first prize. Even then nobody could tell the result of the competition.

The Committee had made no provision for a tie, but hurriedly decided that the two competitors must play off.

One wonders what would have happened if either had refused to do so.

* * *

SINCE the conditions of the tournament did not lay it down that ties would be decided by a play off, neither player was obliged to replay. I have no idea of how this matter ended, but I do know that the unfortunate player whose handicap was reduced in the middle of a 36 holes stroke competition actually won, although he was not given the trophy.

This is just one example of what can happen when those whose business it is to know the rules of golf handle or mishandle a competition.

* * *

IN several Alliance competitions, those delightful happy-go-lucky affairs which enliven the winter days for amateur-professional partnerships, one can hardly expect that the letter of the law should be obeyed in every respect.

" Winter Rules " are frequently introduced—very wisely, too !

Rolling the ball out of a cupped lie in the fairway, which is one of the concessions of winter golf on some courses, is wise from every standpoint. This not only adds to the pleasure but preserves the course.

But I am not so sure that it is asking rather a lot from competitors to rule that some play over a different course to fellow competitors with whom their scores are compared for the purpose of determining the winner.

The Committee in charge may, according to the Rules of Golf, lay down almost any conditions they wish, but it is doubtful whether it goes as far as this.

* * *

THE competitions I have in mind are those 27 holes events in which, to save time, one half of the competitors play their afternoon nine holes over the first nine holes and the other half over the second nine.

Obviously, all competitors are not playing the same course. But there it is, nobody seems to mind very much and it would be a pity to make these Alliance tournaments rigid for the sake of the letter of the rules—the spirit is very much in evidence.

* * *

NOW that we are on the eve of another tournament season, those in charge of important events might clear up a few points which might make them more enjoyable for everybody.

Golf, especially competitive golf, is becoming slow to the point of tediousness. But, so far as I know, no golfer has been penalised for slow play.

Warnings have been posted to the effect that there are rules which allows the committee to penalise or even disqualify a player for slow play. In fact, individual players have, I know, been warned. But nobody has been penalised and the rule is, of course, held in contempt.

* * *

THE abolition of the stymie from the rules has made for slow play.

The everlasting lifting of balls on the putting green is the principal time waster.

In a stroke competition the player whose ball is nearer the hole may either hole it or lift it, but rarely is the nearer ball holed ; it is lifted and replaced after his partner has putted.

Then, more often than not, the partner lifts his ball while the other man putts. This is exasperating to spectators who pay to watch professional tournaments.

It might be better if the word " must " was substituted for " may " in this rule, so that the ball nearer the hole must be holed first if it interferes with the partner's putt.

* * *

ON this question of lifting, I have seen scores of first-class professionals technically disqualified in tournaments without their knowledge.

Markers, and some of them can be very officious, sometimes lift the player's ball and meticulously replace it when it is his turn to putt. But the player who allows the marker to do this incurs a penalty of two strokes and, unless his card shows the penalty, he is obviously disqualified.

The rules are quite clear on this point—a marker may not touch a ball and should he do so the player must replace it for the marker is an " outside agency."

However, this is a technical breach of the rules, but it serves to show how necessary it might be for those competing in major tournaments and officials in charge to know the rules.

Perhaps the Rules of Golf Committee have similar views—it is no time to alter rules when many golfers do not know them in their present form !

February, 1953 — Page 19 — MODERN MOTORING & TRAVEL

The story of
the air you ride on

NUMBER FIVE OF A SERIES

Just as pneumatic bicycle tyres were introduced to America from England — so it was from Europe that the idea of applying pneumatics to the fledgling automobile first came. Production of the new tyres was immediately started in the United States, and the responsibility for making their valves fell to August Schrader.

This was not by chance, for Schrader had been closely associated with the young rubber industry. He had developed valves for air pillows, life belts and diving equipment, and his experience carried him automatically to the pneumatic tyre. Schrader produced his first tyre valve in 1891. From it, by 1898, had been developed the valve with the core replaceable in one unit. Construction and materials have been repeatedly improved, but today this basic design is still the keeper of the air you ride on.

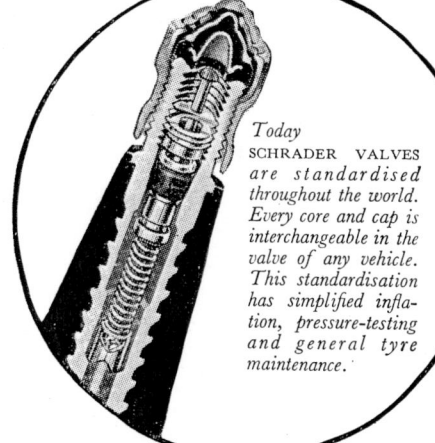

Today SCHRADER VALVES *are standardised throughout the world. Every core and cap is interchangeable in the valve of any vehicle. This standardisation has simplified inflation, pressure-testing and general tyre maintenance.*

Schrader
STANDARD TYRE VALVE
Keeper of the Air you ride on

A. SCHRADER'S SON · BIRMINGHAM · ENGLAND

CAN WE HELP YOU?

Question of Balance

SIR,—I have a Sunbeam-Talbot 90 Coupé which, during the last few weeks, has developed a most marked vibration when the speed reaches 65 m.p.h. or so. If I keep going this disappears at about 70 m.p.h.

At about the same time as this started I introduced one new type of tyre to the car, a Michelin. The other three are Dunlop, but I cannot believe this could possibly be the cause.

(Sgd.) T. A. B.,
BISHOP AUCKLAND.

From the information provided, we feel that the vibration experienced on your Sunbeam-Talbot "90" Coupé is, in fact, due to an unbalanced wheel, in all probability the fitment of an odd cover having destroyed the original adjustment.

We would, therefore, suggest that you contact your local distributors, Minories Garages, Ltd., of Northgate, Darlington, who will be only too pleased to carry out a careful inspection on your behalf, and, at the same time, check and adjust the wheels for balance.

* * *

Windscreen Washer

SIR,—I recently purchased a Trico windscreen automatic washer for fitting to my Humber Hawk. I find that the instructions included with the equipment make no provision for fixing to a car without the normal scuttle.

I should be glad if you could advise me as to the most suitable means of adapting this equipment. It appears that it may be possible to fix the jets to the hinged bonnet as the connections to these jets are made of rubber tube, but the inlet connections of the jets would need to be made at right angles in order not to kink the tubing when the bonnet is closed.

(Sgd.) T. L. T.,
TRURO.

When fitting a screen washer to the Humber Hawk, the absence of an externally visible scuttle pressing need cause no undue concern. The jets may be fitted into the bonnet panel.

While it will be found that the bulkhead underneath the bonnet prevents the location of the jets at the normal recommended distance from the windscreen, it is necessary only to move the jets slightly forward, i.e., away from the windscreen, and at such a position that there is just sufficient clearance for the jet and its union and pipe to clear the bulkhead. Sufficient slack in the connecting rubber tube should be allowed to permit the full opening of the bonnet and, providing a small loop in the rubber tube is allowed, we feel that specially manufactured jets will be unnecessary.

* * *

Seat Changing

SIR,—The driving seat of my Sunbeam-Talbot 1946 car has collapsed; what can I do? Are the seats interchangeable or must I have a new seat?

(Sgd.) G. F. D.,
LONDON, N.16.

Without being able to inspect the driving seat on your 1946 Sunbeam-Talbot, we are unable to assess the degree of damage, and consequently cannot advise you whether local repair is practicable or whether the complete seat frame be replaced.

The two seats are not directly interchangeable, although it may be possible temporarily to replace the driving seat with the existing passenger seat to minimise inconvenience. We strongly suggest you get in touch with our Distributors, Messrs. Rootes, Ltd., Ladbroke Hall, Barlby Road, North Kensington, W.10.

* * *

Sparking Plugs

SIR,—I have a Humber Super Snipe Staff Saloon (ex-W.D.) which left the works (new) February, 1946.

The plugs fitted when I bought it were Champion N 8 which is a long reach plug, yet a short reach plug is listed as being the correct plug. Can you please explain this?

The threads of the plugs are perfectly clean when extracted, which seems to point to the fact that they do not protrude into the combustion chamber.

(Sgd.) E. J. D.,
UFFCULME.

The correct sparking plug for an aluminium cylinder head is ½-inch reach "Champion L 10," whilst for a cast iron head a ¾-inch reach "Champion N 8" should be used.

* * *

Eire Tour

SIR,—I realise that the Irish Tourist Association publish a brochure giving details of the hotels in Eire in so far as grades, terms, etc., are concerned, but I am anxious to obtain leaflets or booklets which would, by illustration and a brief description, give me some idea of the type of seaside resorts in Donegal as well as places of interest to visit while there.

Can you recommend any Donegal seaside resorts which are not too large and crowded, but with comfortable, friendly hotels.

(Sgd.) MRS. M. E.,
MAIDSTONE.

There is not actually a great deal of choice between seaside resorts in Donegal. We can vouch for Bundoran, which is one of the principal resorts in Ireland. There is a golf course and an ample selection of hotels of various grades. It is in the very south of Donegal, but distances are not so great as to prevent exploration by car.

Another place very well spoken of is Buncrana, situated on the eastern shore of Lough Swilly.

If you want a luxury hotel then that at Rosapenna is one of the best. This is also in the north.

If you write to the Irish Travel Association for information we are sure they will send you plenty. We wouldn't call *any* Irish resort, except perhaps Bray, large and crowded.

LIGHTING-UP TIMES THIS MONTH

	1st	9th	16th	23rd	28th
London	5.19	5.33	5.45	5.58	6.7
Bristol	5.29	5.43	5.55	6.8	6.17
Birmingham	5.23	5.37	5.51	6.4	6.13
Leeds	5.18	5.32	5.45	5.58	6.7
Manchester	5.21	5.35	5.49	6.2	6.11
Newcastle	5.12	5.26	5.42	5.55	6.4
Glasgow	5.19	5.33	5.50	6.3	6.12
Belfast	5.32	5.46	6.1	6.14	6.23

Decarbonising and Grinding

SIR,—Can you give me full instructions for decarbonising and grinding in the valves on my 1936 Hillman Minx?

Shall I need any special tools?

(Sgd.) K. R. J.,
DORSET.

We assume you are familiar with the basic principles involved, and therefore we do not feel it necessary to give detailed procedure of the operations. The decarbonisation procedure for a 1936 Hillman Minx is fully covered, incidentally, in the Workshop Manual for the 1936 to 1939 Hillman Minx cars. This publication, Reference IB.209, may be obtained from any Hillman Dealer or Distributor, or by direct application to "The Parts Department," Humber, Ltd., Stoke, Coventry, at a price of 8s. including postage.

The special tools required will be a short offset $\frac{5}{16}$-inch ring spanner for the manifold nuts, a "C" type, or other universal valve spring compressor and a suction cap tool for rotating the valves.

When removing the valve cotters, a piece of rag should be placed round the tappets to prevent items being dropped into the sump.

All carbon should, of course, be removed from the cylinder head, valveports, etc., and we would suggest that a ring of carbon be left on the edge of each piston, since this will maintain an efficient oil seal. The best way to do this is to place the old piston ring on the top of the piston and then carefully scrape away all visible carbon.

At the time of decarbonisation the sump should be removed and all filters carefully cleaned. Reassembly should present no difficulty, but when adjusting the tappets care should be taken to ensure that the tappet is resting on the heel of the cam. The actual adjustment can be performed by suitably sized spanners, although you will no doubt find it more convenient to use a set of tappet adjustment spanners as supplied by any Hillman Distributor.

* * *

Handbook

SIR,—Can you please let me know where I can obtain a handbook for a 1938 Talbot 10?

(Sgd.) J. E. B.,
LINCOLN.

If you will communicate direct with the undermentioned, we think you will find they will be able to help you: Parts Department, Humber, Ltd., Stoke, Coventry.

* * *

Lubricant

SIR,—I have a 1948 Hillman Minx. The oil recommended for the engine and gearbox is Double Shell, but I have been contemplating changing to Shell X.100.

I should be grateful if you could let me know whether you would recommend the change suggested, and, if so, whether any special precautions should be taken when changing to Shell X.100.

(Sgd.) B. G. G.,
HORSHAM.

The equivalent of Double Shell, as originally recommended for your model, will be Shell X.100, S.A.E. 30.

No particular precautions need be taken when changing over to this lubricant. You may care to have the sump removed and cleaned out after the first 1,000 miles running, after which oil changes and sump cleaning should be carried out in accordance with the instructions in the Owners' Handbook.

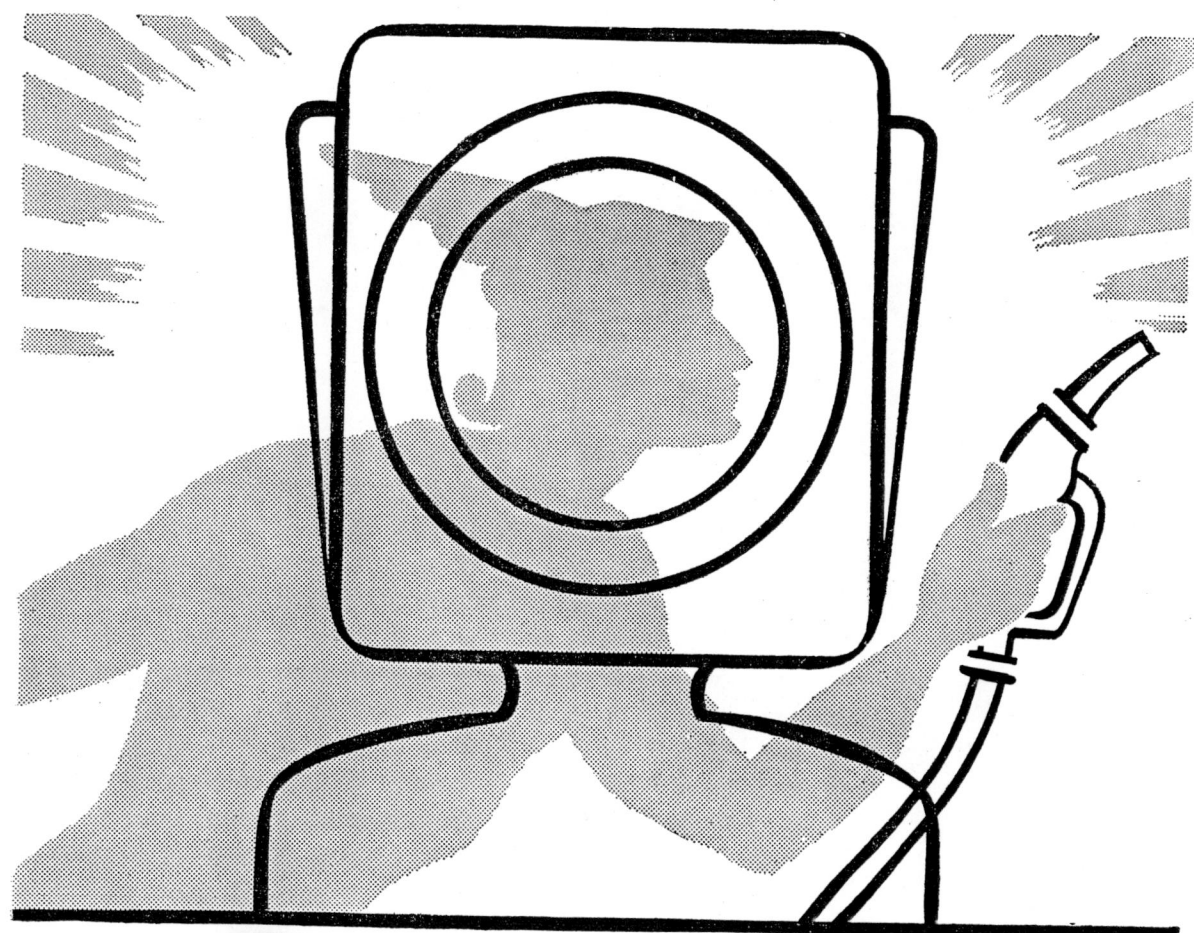

Benzole is coming back!

ON 1st FEBRUARY

However good petrol may be, adding Benzole to it makes it better for your car. *Better for starting*, because Benzole so very easily turns into a dry, easily-ignited vapour even on icy days. *Better for smooth, quiet running*, because Benzole is a fine anti-knock agent as well as a fuel, giving the piston a powerful shove in place of a harsh, hefty wallop. And best of all—*Benzole is better for more miles per gallon* because Nature herself has packed into every drop of Benzole more power—more energy —than she has packed into petrol.

NATIONAL BENZOLE MIXTURE

National Benzole Company Limited, Wellington House, Buckingham Gate, S.W.1
(The distributing organisation owned and entirely controlled by the producers of British Benzole)

15 Countries in 90 hours

VIVID PROOF OF THE ENDURANCE, RELIABILITY AND SPEED OF THE NEW

HUMBER SUPER SNIPE

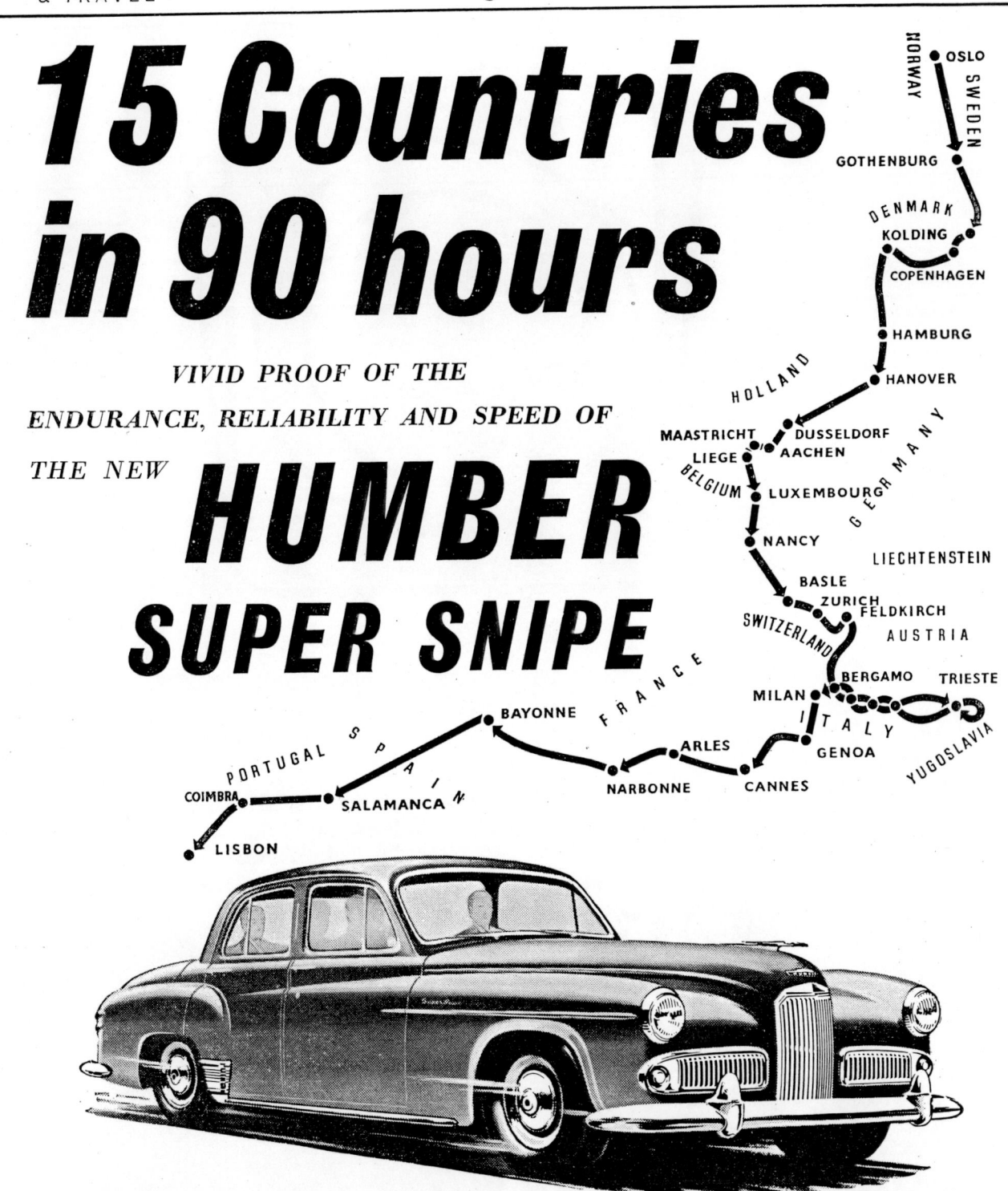

In a dash across Europe, a new HUMBER SUPER SNIPE, straight off the production line, has proved its qualities of absolute reliability, rugged stamina and dynamic power. Driven by British racing drivers Stirling Moss and Leslie Johnson through 15 countries in midwinter, through blizzards, over snow and ice-covered roads and six major mountain passes, it achieved this 3,280 mile journey in 3 days 18 hours.

An unprecedented performance . . .

BLAZING A TRAIL INTO A NEW ERA OF FINER MOTORING

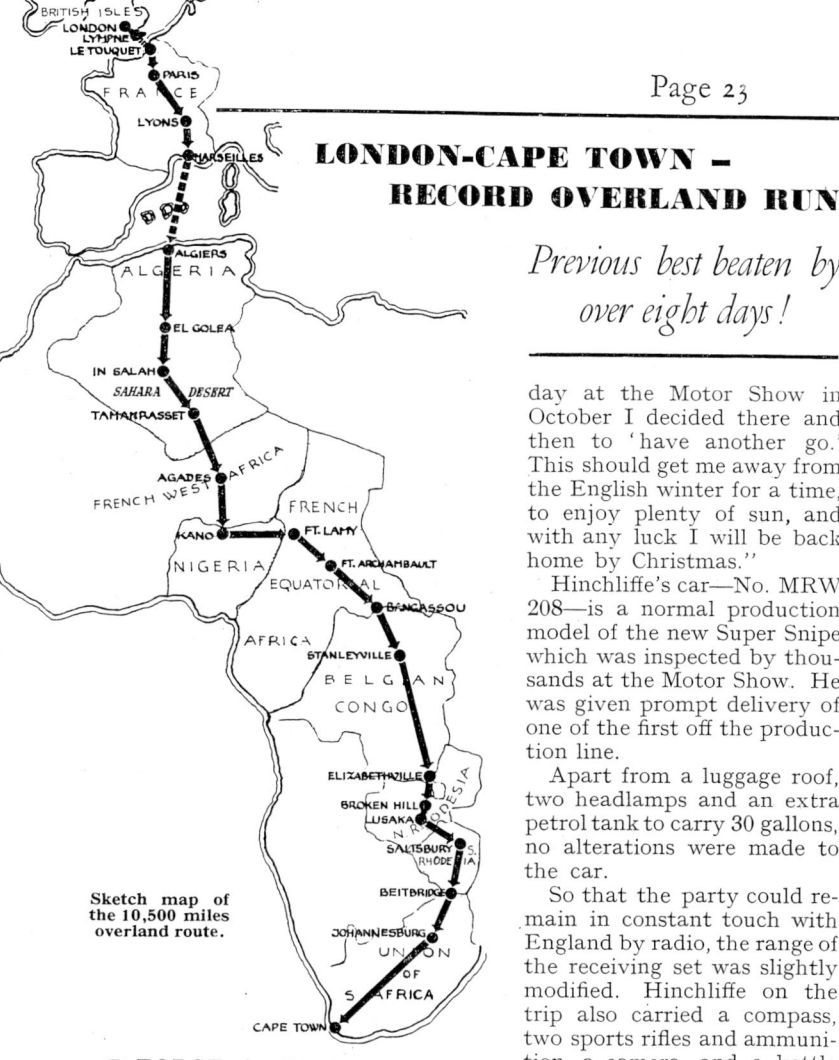

LONDON-CAPE TOWN – RECORD OVERLAND RUN

Previous best beaten by over eight days!

Sketch map of the 10,500 miles overland route.

"No parking, Sir," says the constable, as Hinchliffe prepares to leave Hyde Park Corner, London, for Cape Town!

If Hinchliffe was the only bearded member of the team at the start, he certainly had two rivals at the finish.

GEORGE C. HINCHLIFFE, the 41-year-old Bradford garage owner, who, in January last, established the fastest overland time (21 days) in a Hillman Minx car from London to the Cape, has done it again.

Covering 10,500 miles in 13 days 9 hours 6 minutes, he has knocked 8 days 10 hours 39 minutes off his January time, according to a cable received from Cape Town.

Hinchliffe, driving a new Humber Super Snipe, reached Cape Town on December 9 at 7.21 p.m. G.M.T. He had left Hyde Park Corner, London, at 10.15 a.m. G.M.T. on Wednesday, November 26th.

* * *

WITH Hinchliffe were R. Walshaw, aged 38, of Leyburn Avenue, Lightcliffe, near Halifax, Yorkshire, as co-driver, and Charles Arthur Longman, 39, of Haycliffe Road, Bradford, as fitter and mechanic.

Walshaw is an experienced international Rally driver. He drove a Hillman Minx in the 1952 Monte Carlo Rally from Glasgow, and in the 1951 *Daily Express* National Motor Rally he won a class award.

Before leaving London, Hinchliffe said: "If they ask, 'Where's George?' say 'He's gone to lunch in Cape Town.'"

"I was getting restless again," said Hinchliffe, who is a bachelor, "and one day at the Motor Show in October I decided there and then to 'have another go.' This should get me away from the English winter for a time, to enjoy plenty of sun, and with any luck I will be back home by Christmas."

Hinchliffe's car—No. MRW 208—is a normal production model of the new Super Snipe which was inspected by thousands at the Motor Show. He was given prompt delivery of one of the first off the production line.

Apart from a luggage roof, two headlamps and an extra petrol tank to carry 30 gallons, no alterations were made to the car.

So that the party could remain in constant touch with England by radio, the range of the receiving set was slightly modified. Hinchliffe on the trip also carried a compass, two sports rifles and ammunition, a camera, and a kettle "in order to make tea at any time of the day or night."

The Super Snipe had the normal United Kingdom lower-axle ratio of 3.9 : 1. Hinchliffe considered this more suitable for getting out of "the rough" while traversing North Africa. Incidentally, from Algiers on, Hinchliffe had donned the burnous dress of the Arab, with sandals, to keep as cool as possible.

As some example of the arduous going, Hinchliffe and his co-drivers completed over 1,200 miles in the last 24 hours, which means the remarkable average of 50 m.p.h.

* * *

IT is authoritatively reported, as we go to press, that Hinchliffe and his co-drivers are attempting an even better performance on the return journey.

In our next issue we hope to give a more detailed and illustrated account of both the outward and homeward journeys.

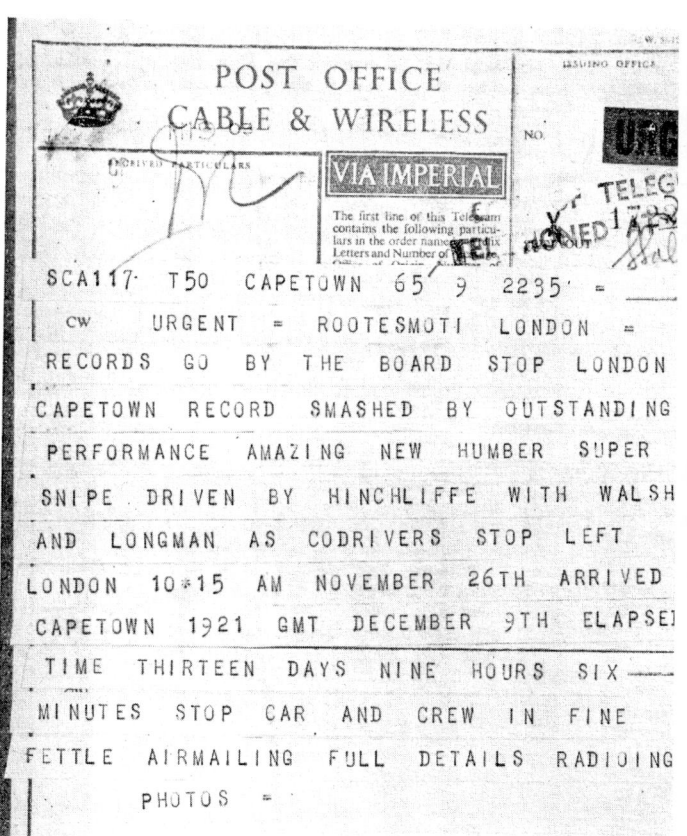

```
POST OFFICE
CABLE & WIRELESS
VIA IMPERIAL

SCA117  T50  CAPETOWN  65  9  2235 =
CW  URGENT = ROOTESMOTI  LONDON =
RECORDS  GO  BY  THE  BOARD  STOP  LONDON
CAPETOWN  RECORD  SMASHED  BY  OUTSTANDING
PERFORMANCE  AMAZING  NEW  HUMBER  SUPER
SNIPE  DRIVEN  BY  HINCHLIFFE  WITH  WALSH
AND  LONGMAN  AS  CODRIVERS  STOP  LEFT
LONDON  10*15  AM  NOVEMBER  26TH  ARRIVED
CAPETOWN  1921  GMT  DECEMBER  9TH  ELAPSED
TIME  THIRTEEN  DAYS  NINE  HOURS  SIX
MINUTES  STOP  CAR  AND  CREW  IN  FINE
FETTLE  AIRMAILING  FULL  DETAILS  RADIOING
PHOTOS  =
                    ROOTESMOTI  CAPETOWN
```

MODERN MOTORING & TRAVEL

February, 1953

Car park de luxe—in the grounds of the Hotel Baren on Lake Brienz.

One of the seven cascades of the Giessbach, waterfall on Lake Brienz.

Top, centre: Market day in Lugano—always a fascinating attraction.

Above: Morcote, the most picturesque village on Lake Lugano.

Pass-storming – then and now!

By Vincent Brennan
M.B.E., F.R.G.S.
(Our Touring Adviser)

WITH apologies, as regards "rambling" to the late Mr. Whympers's "Scrambles Among the Alps." I mean "rambling" in the widest sense, what I am doing being to yarn about my wanderings in that delectable part of Europe.

* * *

The first time I crossed the Alps, not long before World War I, was on a pedal bicycle.

Taking the Grimsel as a "typical" Alpine Pass, it has a maximum gradient of 9 per cent.—none of your 1 in 3 or 4, such as you may get on our freak hills at home. But there is 20 miles of it, from bottom to top, to a height of 7,100 feet above sea level, and down the other side.

What this meant when touring on, or rather *with* a bicycle, was that the loaded machine had literally to be pushed all way up, the process occupying the best part of a day. Afterwards came the reward—miles and miles of glorious free-wheeling, carefree-wheeling, if your brakes were sound!

* * *

In the case of the Stelvio Pass, which in those days was the loftiest of them all, it took the inside of two days to toil up the 18 miles from Spondigna, at the base, to the Stilfserjoch (or top), no less than 9,055 feet above sea level, or nearly thrice the height of Snowdon.

At any rate, it gave one plenty of time to admire the magnificent scenery, far finer, in my opinion, than several other passes since built which perhaps exceed the Stelvio in actual height. And this *per ardua ad montes* could be followed by anything up to 120 miles of coasting, for it was then downhill practically all the way to Milan.

* * *

YES, with its vistas of stupendous snow mountains and glaciers, with its sensational design (I believe there are 48 hairpin bends on the way up), with its thrills (including all-the-year-round snowballing at the summit), the Stelvio is, I think, still the parent of them all.

* * *

In the 1920s I tackled the Alps again with a motor-bicycle and sidecar and later with one of the earlier "popular" English baby cars.

With the welcome aid of petrol (once poured into the tank out of a teapot, in Italy, and charged for by weight), pass-storming became a matter perhaps of hours, rather than days, for the main difficulty—I write now mainly of the pre-war British car—was the tendency to boil.

* * *

I SHALL never forget one occasion when, halfway up the Great St. Bernard and quite a tough climb, I stopped with an ominous feeling that all was not well with my radiator. When I lifted the bonnet there was a rumbling noise which I thought was the engine running. It was not—it was the water boiling! When I lifted the radiator cap a column of boiling steam shot 20 feet into the air, very nearly taking the front of my face with it. I learned my lesson fortunately without personal harm.

* * *

I must make an exception, however, in favour of the Sunbeam-Talbot. In June, 1939, while returning from Southern Italy in a *coupé* I climbed the Simplon (6,600 feet) non-stop, so fast, and rounded the corners so speedily that my passenger complained at the top, for the one and only time in our experience, that my driving had made her dizzy!

Not very long ago the Rootes Group agent in Klagenfurt, Austria, told me he could make any car boil in the mountains while, on the other hand, with the same car he could climb any Pass without boiling. What he meant was, it is all so very much a matter of how you drive.

All the same, I think he would find it hard to make the present-day Minx misbehave, however long and stiff the gradient, always provided it was properly tuned beforehand.

During a recent visit to Switzerland I crossed three of the main passes, the St. Gotthard (7,000 feet), the Furka (8,000 feet) and the Grimsel—almost non-stop. One could almost reckon the time taken in traversing the 80 miles in minutes rather than the hours, still less the days, referred to earlier.

* * *

My fitted thermometer showed that the radiator water never even approached boiling point (well below 212 deg. F. at those heights). True, the weather was wet and cold, vile and filthy in fact, while at the summit of the St. Gotthard it was snowing hard, an excellent test for my screen-wiper but not conducive to loitering. Photographically it was impossible owing to the thick fog.

Hence, on this occasion, my one and only object was to get the journey over.

(Continued on page 26)

Here's one car that won't be overdriven on delivery

make sure your car benefits from its first run!

Here are three ways in which we ensure that vehicles delivered by us get "cotton-wool" treatment :—

A Servis Recorder is fitted to every car — an amazing "hidden eye" that makes a record of the entire journey for *you* to see.

Expert Drivers. Every one of them has passed a special test at the British School of Motoring. Paid extra to go slow, they get a bonus for *super*-safe driving.

Direct Supervision. Our staff of Collection Supervisors backs the whole delivery system, from factory to *you*. Every car we handle bears our name on the trade plates. We like people to see for themselves how careful our drivers are!

Make sure your dealer arranges for delivery of *your* car via CAR COLLECTION. The extra cost is so small .... it really is worth while.

THE CAR COLLECTION COMPANY LTD.

Established 1926. 7 Kendall Place, Baker Street, London, W.1.

Pass-storming – then and now! : *(Continued from page 24)*

WE were on our way home after a week of glorious sunshine, enjoyed from a balcony room overlooking Lake Lugano.

Lugano makes an admirable centre for you can pop in and out of closely adjoining Italy with a minimum of formality at the frontier.

The Italians just glance at your passport and bang yet another stamp on your *triptyque*, followed by " Next, please."

The Swiss do not even look at your passport, nor worry about your baggage or your money. This doesn't mean that I am criticising our own Customs authorities; indeed, I always feel they are the only officials in Europe who do their job *properly*, yet yielding in courtesy to none.

* * *

OUR most interesting excursion was to Tremezzo, on Lake Como, where Mussolini was finally disposed of by the Italian partisans. Further along the lake, at Dongo, some of the locals showed me the spot where, said they, 16 of his ministers were stood against an iron railing and shot.

Italy I found just a little more expensive than Switzerland, but both much less than in France, especially Paris where life on the simplest scale costs the earth.

* * *

JUST a few words on the Swiss Passes generally.

My favourite, scenically, is the Splugen, the southern half of which is in Italy.

The highest pass in Switzerland is the Furka, the view from whose apex Baedeker, in his earlier editions, used to describe as commanding a spectacle " almost of painful beauty." A commanding phrase and, to me, unforgettable.

The Col de la Forclaz, although a mere 5,000 feet up, is one of the most difficult up which to drive. Its maximum gradient is 20 per cent.

Switzerland's latest pride, the Susten, although a marvel both from a scenic and an engineering point of view, strikes me as lacking much of the air of mystery, of wildness, even savagery, of the older Passes.

The Umbrail is actually higher at the top than the Furka but, like the Splugen, it is only " half " a Swiss Pass since, a few hundred yards beyond the last of its 36 bends up from Santa Maria, at the far end of the Engadine (a valley itself 6,000 feet above the sea), it joins the Stelvio, in Italy, near the peak of the latter.

* * *

I FEAR that, having already mentioned the Great St. Bernard, I overlooked the fact that it, too, is rather a greater eminence than the Furka, being 8,130 feet up. It is easily the most historical of the Alpine Passes, dating back far beyond the dawn of the Christian Era.

At one time free accommodation for one night could be enjoyed at the Hospice founded by St. Bernard in the tenth or eleventh century, but no one who wants to make first-hand acquaintance with the famous St. Bernard dogs to-day would quibble about paying the reasonable charge now asked for a night's lodging.

* * *

NOW for a few hints about mountain driving—and I do hope Stirling Moss won't be too amused if he reads these words of one who has done every kind of motoring except actual racing—offered by one who used to think pass-storming the finest sport on wheels until he tasted the adventure and delight of desert motoring in the Middle East in peace time.

Some Swiss passes can be climbed in third gear in the Minx with an occasional change down to second just before tackling a hairpin bend. Occasionally, for third, read " second " ; for second read " first."

Don't push your foot hard down, other than momentarily. In fact, the aim should be to use as little throttle as possible so long as the engine is running comfortably. This is the secret of successful climbing thousands of feet without boiling.

Don't take risks.

See that your radiator is full at the bottom of the pass.

Even if you don't carry a spare can of water, you are almost certain, thanks to the Swiss Auto Club, to be able to get supplies at strategic points.

I never hesitate to top up with cold water but, naturally, avoid sloshing it over a hot engine.

Stop, if in any doubt, to admire the scenery for a while sufficiently to allow things to cool down. If it is a very hot day, open up the bonnet.

The best precaution of all, of course, is to get your Rootes Group agent to see that your car is in good order before you leave home. If you do this, I don't think you will have to worry at all.

When ascending, or descending, keep a lookout well above or below you, as the case may be, to avoid meeting with another car, still less a coach, while turning a hairpin.

I don't need to tell an experienced driver to approach as widely as is practicable so that, having rounded the bend, you can hug your own (right) side of the road closely.

Well,

" GOOD CLIMBING."

Below : Citizens of Dongo by the railings where the executions took place.

Centre: Crosses on the garden wall near Tremezzo, Lake Como, where Mussolini and Clara Petacci are alleged to have been shot.

Below: Bullet marks in the railings at Dongo—a close up.

Which of these Doctors takes his own advice?

—and how can you tell?

WHEN MOTORING, says the Doctor here seen adjusting his scarf, boredom and monotony are just as much of a distraction to the driver as a pack of children skirmishing on the back seat. What is his remedy? Radio—as you can see from the aerial on his car. On his professional trips, which are often long and always lonely, radio's pleasant, undemanding company keeps him interested and alert. At weekends, with the family in the car, it acts as a firm but friendly disciplinarian, holding the children's attention long after the novelty of the scenery has worn off. Like hundreds of thousands of motorists he has never regretted the day he had "H.M.V." Car Radio installed. Neither will you.

The Rootes Group exclusively fit and recommend "H.M.V." Car Radio on Hillman, Humber and Sunbeam-Talbot Cars

"HIS MASTER'S VOICE" CAR RADIO

MARKETED BY

SMITHS Radiomobile

S. SMITH & SONS (RADIOMOBILE) LTD., GOODWOOD WORKS, NORTH CIRCULAR ROAD, LONDON, N.W.2

London gets going!

IF success at the word "Go" means anything, it certainly means that the committee and organisers of the new London branch of the S.T.O.C., are to be deservedly congratulated upon one of the best local turnouts in the history of the Club.

What was to be basically London's opening social event, with subtle introduction of the competitive interest, the response exceeded all expectations. Nearly 50 cars, representing some 150 club members and friends, thus endorsed the long held belief that, given the opportunity, London would turn up trumps.

Novelty, too, played a big part in the success of the meeting—each entrant being given a carefully prepared group-photograph of some of London's best known landmarks, each to be identified and visited within a set time schedule.

Once the picture clues were distributed, you could have heard a pin drop as competitors went into conference. Not only had they to solve the picture problems, but the complete circuit had specially to be covered with economic mileage. Such points as the Hyde Park "Magazine"; the gates of the Oval cricket ground; Bishop's Palace, Lambeth; the Old Kent Road; Fleet Street; Roosevelt Memorial, Grosvenor Square, to name a few, required precise routing in this connection.

Encouragingly too, several of the City's stalwarts of police apparently found welcome diversion to their otherwise monotonous Sunday routine and, after a while actually advanced directed *all approaching Sunbeam-Talbots* the same way, competitor or not!

It was all interesting good fun, of course, endorsed in no uncertain terms when, at the Page Street, Westminster finish, the successful entrants proved to be: First, G. T. Lewis; Second, F. Willinger; and Third, J. Paterson.

Good luck London and more power to your elbows. Mr. E. W. Rossiter, chairman, and Miss Tinkham, hon. sec., and other officers in devising the new season's

SPORTING SPOTLIGHTS

Club News and Personalities

programme are determined, we know, to retain this splendid initial goodwill.

* * *

Fog to sunshine

FOR a long time members of the S.T.O.C. have been asking for a Mid-winter rally—to some place at journey's end where we could find a "spot of sunshine."

A tall order, but the organisers actually did all that, Saturday, December 6 finding Bournemouth under a blaze of sunny conditions, ready to receive competitors from their several starting points, Evesham, Oxford, Maidenhead and Minehead, with sub-starts as far removed as Manchester and Torquay, giving each section approximately a 200-mile approach route.

"Mid-winter" it was, reports reaching Bournemouth during the day of fog, ice and snow being encountered almost all the way. London, in particular, laid on things too generously, to prevent some contestants even reaching their starting point at Ladbroke Hall. Moreover, of the stalwarts who braved the start officially, but few only reached their southern destination.

A few miles out of Bournemouth conditions improved considerably, to permit the regularity test at Ibsley being conducted with proficiency and competitor eagerness. The West Dorset and Hants M.C. certainly did a magnificent job in taking over this test on behalf of the Club.

Onward then for the sea front at Bournemouth for a further series of driving tests, run under a friendly sun which warmed up competitors' efforts, in many cases to inspire them to effect flying finishes instead of stopping " astride the line." Indeed several excellent times were thus penalised; such a pity after so complex a journey.

Again, too, many newcomers to the sport gave very commendable showings in driving skill and judgment. If one bright star of the club roped in a "triple success," several others this time proved to be prominent back markers!

As always, however, everyone accepted conditions in good sporting spirit—reflected again during the dinner-dance held in the Bournemouth Pavilion Ballroom—which, by the way, has quite one of the loveliest dance floors in the country —with Hadyn Powell and his Pavilion Dance Orchestra giving delightful support for the near 300 club members and friends who eventually took to the floor.

In his official welcome to Bournemouth, His Worship the Mayor (Alderman H. A. Benwell, M.C., B.E.M., J.P.), expressed the hope that the Club would return next year, when the Corporation would be prepared again to co-operate in every possible manner.

The thanks of the Club are due, in any case, for the generous measure of support given this year; also to the Chief Constable and the Bournemouth Constabulary for their capable assistance in marshalling and control, as well as to the Mayoress for graciously presenting the prizes which included, incidentally, a handsome trophy presented by George Hartwell, of Bournemouth, offered for the best performance in the rally.

Results:—

Class A. Sunbeam-Talbots—
First: P. C. Harper, Stevenage.
Second: E. Elliott, York.

Class B. Hillmans—
First: G. R. Lindsay, Whetstone.
Second: G. W. Shingler, Salisbury.

Novices Award—
J. R. Beardall, Whatton in the Vale.

Ladies Prize—
Miss F. Howell, Lewes.

George Hartwell Trophy for best performance in Rally—
P. C. Harper, Stevenage.

Route Winners—
Minehead—S. B. Southcombe, Sherbourne.
Maidenhead—M. F. Orchard, Gloucester.
Oxford—M. Milner, Tolworth.
Evesham—P. C. Harper, Stevenage.

* * *

Novel Concours

FOR the special Club Concours d'Elegance, arranged at Matlock, by R. S. Beard and Co., Ltd., distributors of Mansfield, and open to members whose cars were supplied by them, some 25 entries faced the judges at the Lilybank Hydro, in what looked more like a display of models directly out of the showroom!

In the close finish, the eventual winners were T. Spalding of Edwinstowe (First), and W. H. Briggs, of Mansfield (Second).

Competitors' cars lined up for the Concours d'Elegance held at the Lilybank Hydro, Matlock, Derbyshire.

NOVEL CONCOURS
Mr. Norman Garrad, Chairman of Committee, S.T.O.C., congratulates Mr. T. Spalding, of Edwinstowe, first prize winner. The occasion included a special showing of the films, "Journey to the Snows" and "Conquest of the Alps."

Sunbeam-Talbot Owners' Club's successful "mid-winter" Rally to Bournemouth

W. F. Day, of Cambridge, puts up a good show during the special "Regularity" driving test on the Ibsley circuit.

Below: Miss M. Stamp, of Topsham, handles her Sunbeam-Talbot "Ten" in good style through the obstacle tests on the Undercliff Drive, at Bournemouth.

Despite severe wintry conditions encountered on the 200 miles approach routes, remarkably few failed to reach the concluding tests.

Below: George Hartwell, of Bournemouth, gave his usual expert showing in the series of manœuvrability tests at the Bournemouth finish.

Officials of the West Hants and Dorset Car Club did a grand co-operative job at Ibsley. Thank you, Dudley Ship.

Right: G. R. Lindsay, of Whetstone, winner of the Hillman invitation class, receives his prize from the Mayoress of Bournemouth.

The Club's sincere thanks are expressed to the Mayor of Bournemouth (Alderman H. A. Benwell, M.C., B.E.M.) and Corporation for the generous facilities extended to the Club during its visit.

P. C. Harper, of Stevenage, receives part of his "triple awards" —as winner of the Rally, winner of his class, and of his starting control. He was the recipient of course of the "George Hartwell" Cup, for the best performance in a Sunbeam-Talbot car.

P. C. Harper, with co-driver and friends, cannot be blamed for celebrating after so commendable a performance. Prizes were presented at the dinner-dance held in the Bournemouth Pavilion Ballroom.

If a little off the beaten track, few competitors missed Dr. Johnson's House, off Fleet Street.

Right: Competitors' cars carefully parked in Page Street, Westminster, during the luncheon break and prize presentation. Even the police complimented the Club on its efficient marshalling and control.

LONDON'S S.T.O.C. makes successful start

Mr. T. Lewis, winner of London's opening event—a mystery tour—receives his prize from Mr. F. J. Nutt, hon. organising secretary. Clues were in the form of untitled pictures, to be identified and visited in the shortest and safest possible time.

Left: Quite a family conference—with Mr. and Mrs. J. Kemsley hoping the children would know a thing or two.

Stanley Mason and partner, Miss V. Taylor, seek expert aid in solving the picture clues. "No, Sir," said the constable, "that's not Lords, it's the Oval!" But time was up!

Prizes were in the form of vouchers to the value of £5 and £3, respectively.

After a pleasant tea, there was a special showing of those much admired films, featuring Sunbeam-Talbots in international competition, "Journey to the Snows" and "Conquest of the Alps." Congratulations to the organisers, and what an idea for further local application!

* * *

All set for "MONTE CARLO"

OF Rootes Group products taking part in the Monte Carlo Rally, which is to be held from January 20-27 next, there will be some 30 Sunbeam-Talbots, three Hillman Minxes and two Humber Super Snipes.

Stirling Moss will again be driving a Sunbeam-Talbot, as will also George Hartwell, Leslie Johnson, John Fitch (U.S.A.); Sgts. John Skeggs, Ted Tear and Tom Cranfield, A. G. Imhof, J. H. Kemsley, Miss Sheila Van Dam and, of course, Norman Garrad, Captain of the Sunbeam-Talbot teams, this being his sixteenth "Monte."

Stirling Moss, it will be remembered, was a close "second" in the 1952 event —only 4 seconds behind the winner—his first-time participation in long distance international trials as distinct from out and out motor-racing.

M. B. Anderson, of Newton Kearns, will for the fifth time be out for the Concours d'Elegance in his Hillman Minx, having already four successive wins to his credit, while R. A. Dando, of Manchester, also on the Hillman Minx, will be another familiar Monte Carlo contestant.

However, with over 100 British competitors taking part this year, and all determined to secure yet another "all-British victory," the keenness of the contest as a whole and that sure to be witnessed within the British contingent especially, promises to make this year's "Monte" even more competitive than ever.

Whether or not the weather will contribute to the hazards of the 2,000 miles official route—with starting points at Glasgow, Stockholm, Lisbon, Palermo, Oslo, Munich and Monte Carlo itself, remains to be seen. Come what may, however, fog, ice, snow, even blizzards, competitors will certainly not be found to be unprepared! Besides which, the more aggressive become conditions one year, the succeeding event only finds the same faces determined to have another shot, the better equipped and experienced from past failures.

February, 1953 — Page 31 — MODERN MOTORING & TRAVEL

The New 90 m.p.h SUNBEAM-TALBOT 90

with powers of endurance proved by repeated international successes

...an exciting car Effortless high speed; brilliant acceleration, stability and accuracy of control; superb comfort and luxurious appointments... these qualities make the lovely new Sunbeam-Talbot 90 the sportsman's car of the year.

Arrange for an exhilarating trial run TODAY!

'THE TIMES' said of the 1952 Alpine Rally results:-
"In winning three cups, the Sunbeam-Talbots can be said to have made the best performance by one make of car in the Rally, a fact acknowledged by their being awarded the Team Prize... those that can survive this ordeal are very fine cars indeed."

A PRODUCT OF THE ROOTES GROUP

SUNBEAM-TALBOT LTD. RYTON-ON-DUNSMORE COVENTRY   LONDON SHOWROOMS AND EXPORT DIVISION: ROOTES LTD. DEVONSHIRE HOUSE PICCADILLY W.1

To Lapland, via France and Spain, in 14,000 trouble-free miles.

By F. Aspinall

WE landed in France on the Ides of March. It was a miserable, cold, rainy morning as we drove our Hillman Minx convertible coupé off the ferry at Dunkirk. Such a miserable morning was certain insurance that somewhere in the fourteen thousand miles ahead of us lay better weather.

Our week in Paris was all too short, and it was no time before the Louvre, the Tour Effeil, the Champs Elysées and the Arc de Triomphe were all a wonderful memory. We saw the famous Lascaux caves with their 22 thousand year old cave paintings, the Chateaux of the Loire and the Pyrenees.

Soon we were over the border into Spain. As we climbed up to the Puerta del Escudo there was no one to tell us, nor any sign to indicate, that the way ahead had over a foot of snow, and our Hillman had no idea either that it was going to charge through where other cars, even trucks, had failed.

We rose up and up until, finally, the snow lay all around " deep and crisp and even," and, at last, just before the summit of the pass we skidded to a halt.

Finally, I had to take off the front licence plate now acting as a miniature snow plough and, with a renewed charge we were on our way.

* * *

OUR trip through Spain led past Burgos to Avila, a lovely walled town with many narrow, winding streets crowded with quaint old houses.

The " calles " were nothing more than a driver's nightmare and often as not served as the local footpath as well as the main thoroughfare. Because of its excellent manœuvrability our Hillman made progress where other, larger cars and trucks were parked outside the city walls.

Roadside snaps in Austria and the Italian Dolomites.

From Avila we drove to the Escorial, the Palace of Philip II, claimed to be the eighth Wonder of the World.

* * *

AFTER Madrid, the Spanish capital, we passed many oxcarts and donkeys on our way south to Toledo, and, after spending a few days of " Semana Santa," with its colourful religious processions, in Sevilla, we drove via Ronda to Granada.

* * *

THE weather warmed up for our trip through the French Riviera to the Italian lakes, and the car gave us a steady 35 miles to the gallon, even under the hardest conditions.

In the mountains, surrounding Lake Garda and Como, we pulled back the roof to the "Coupé de Ville" position to give us a lovely view of the green covered mountains rising majestically from the water's edge.

" Sunny Italy " lived up to its name.

In our six weeks we never saw a rain cloud and the sun beat down on us continuously.

In Rome the best entertainment was given by the ballet-dancing policemen. Just stop on any corner and you will get the best free performance of your life, the policemen going through an intricate dance accompanied by much arm-waving.

We found that our Hillman Minx could pull away from the fastest of the cars in Rome and at the rate the cars travel in Rome that is quite a statement.

* * *

FURTHER south, in Naples, we parked our car in a volcano crater to see the bubbling, boiling, exploding mud in Pozzuoli.

After a visit to Ischia and Capri we drove on, past the ruins of Pompeii and Herculium, through Cantanzaro with its colourful Sunday market, to the furthermost tip of Italy—Sicily. To us, Sicily was the most interesting island we have seen.

The tremendous Greek ruins in Agrigento, Syracuse and Seluntite are wonders to behold. Those immense ruins and temples made us feel very unimportant.

Later we drove some 6,000 feet up the sides of Mount Etna. The black lava streaks like old gnarled fingers from the red smoking crater of the volcano and touches the very edges of the road.

* * *

GARAGES and service are a thing of the future in Sicily, and we were glad that servicing our own Hillman was such an easy job.

Apart from cleaning the petrol filters, due to dirty petrol, and washing out the air filter, we never once touched the engine. I did all my own lubricating according to the book and never had a spot of trouble.

Up Italy's Adriatic coast, with a few days in Venice, through the Dolomites, over the Brenner Pass and into Austria; the Austrian lakes we enjoyed better than the Swiss. The Tyrol costumes, the wooden farmhouses with their intricately carved balconies and the quaint churches are really worth seeing.

* * *

ON the Autobahns of Germany we had our first chance to give the car its head as we shot along to Holland and Belgium.

The windmills of Holland overlook flat agricultural land, 37 feet on the average below the level of the sea.

It was in Denmark that we got our flat tyre; indeed, three in succession, all due to nails. In Denmark we noticed how very similar the general appearance of the country is to that of England. Many of the people spoke English and all were extremely friendly.

Later we crossed from the land of Canute to Sweden, where the scenery, with pine-covered hills and wild lakes surrounded by cold, barren rocks, was a double to that of northern Canada.

In Stockholm, or the " Venice of the North," modern apartment buildings overlook beautiful fjords and pine forests crush the very outskirts of the city.

* * *

NEXT, into Lapland and up to the fringe of the Arctic circle, with the Midnight Sun watching over us.

Our car must have had as many restless, or sleepless, nights as we did with the long, bright nights that are never dark.

While we kept careful watch over that scarcely populated land with its rolling snow-capped hills for reindeer, the only specimens we saw were in a Zoo !

* * *

FINALLY, we drove south along Norway's beautiful coast to the old Norwegian capital of Trondheim which has one of the most interesting cathedrals of Scandinavia, later winding our way along the majestic fjords and by narrow gravel roads to Oslo.

Oslo, beautiful in many respects, has a number of " musts " for the tourist—the Viking ships, discovered in old burial grounds, the " Kon-Tiki " raft as well as the famous Vineland Park.

At Bergen we caught the ferry for England, to bring our trip on the Continent to a close. The Hillman, if dirty and dust covered, all the while behaved as when " new and shiny," and never any mechanical troubles in the four months to do the trip.

Three lovely film stars of to-morrow. Left to right: Blonde and pretty Dorothy Patrick (Republic), Piper Laurie (Universal) and petite Shelley Winters, already popular with film fans.

1953 should be a year to remember!—
Prepare now to enjoy it says Brigid de Vine

A NEW Year is always exciting but a Coronation Year is something that many may never see again.

Although June is still months away, the New Year is already lit by a royal gleam.

They have begun work on the stands in the Mall. Coronation souvenirs of approved design are already on view. London hotels are already "booked out."

* * *

I HAVE seen my first Coronation "novelty."

A stocking with a little jewelled crown most exquisitely embroidered on the instep.

"*To special order* only," by the makers of Plaza stockings, and to be kept in tissue paper, as an example of fine handwork, after perhaps one wearing, for I cannot think how it would ever be washed—but there it is.

* * *

THE Coronation influence goes from top to toe.

Otto Lucas has just designed a Coronation collection of hats which are on sale simultaneously in the finest stores in the United States, Canada and Australia—and, also, in the most exclusive shops in Great Britain. After years of seeing our finest goods going overseas, I am glad to be able to report that we, too, this Coronation year, will have a chance to buy Britain's best.

* * *

I HAD a preview of these hats before Christmas, on a horrid, dark, wet day, and they were a tonic to see.

Hats based on the design of a peeress's coronet or an Elizabethan man's bonnet might, in less skilful hands, come dangerously near clumsy "fancy dress," but these shapes were extremely chic, with brilliant jewel embroideries demonstrating a standard of workmanship unequalled anywhere in the world.

"Robe Red, Miniver White, Sceptre Gold, Garter Blue, all the Imperial Violets paling down to a tender lilac," were among the colours shown, and, in addition to satin and velvet, with, in one model, a touch of white angora recalling the base of a coronet, there were metallic straws, *actually woven from metal,* yet light as a moth's wing.

* * *

WOMEN everywhere from Kansas City to Hong Kong are asking: "What is London going to do for Coronation Year?"

This collection of model hats will show them that London intends to be gay with historical brilliance and colour.

The Coronation influence has affected even mackintoshes.

At the preview of the Aquascutum spring collection, there were magnificently cut travel coats in tweeds with the most discreet blend of red, white and blue in the material, appropriate for 1953—and for years to come an inconspicuous reminder of a great event.

* * *

THERE are Coronation cottons too. Lovely crisp blends of red, white and blue in fine gingham, made by Osman, will be on sale soon for only 4s. 11d. a yard and the clever dressmaker will be able to use these for all kinds of carefree frocks and accessories. You could make a crisp "Coronation cotton dress," for about 25s. Only you will have to watch the shops and buy as soon as these ginghams appear for there is sure to be an enormous demand for them.

* * *

IT is not too early to begin planning the new things you propose to have done in the house and garden for, as June approaches, labour and all materials are sure to be difficult.

Three useful accessories by Froys, of Hammersmith: Television viewer's lamp with three-phase light strength — price £3 15s. complete.

Any romantic "teenager" will love this tiny cupid-figure table lamp, at £1 19s. 6d., complete with shade.

Right: Portable heater with fan, giving ample heat in winter and cool air circulation in summer—price £9 11s. 7d. Below: The Coronation embroidered stocking referred to in the text.

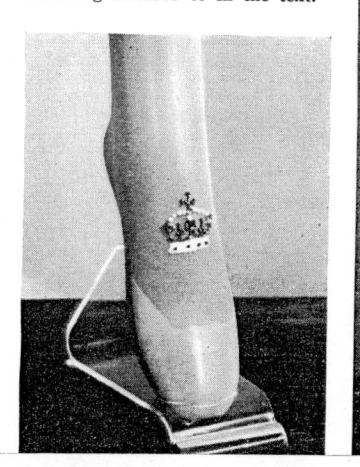

1953 should be a year to remember: *(Concluded from page 33)*

Think what you will need and buy it NOW. Flags, bunting, lights—many people will plan floodlit window-boxes for the front of their houses.

There has been a suggestion in gardening columns that we may become tired, before summer is done, of red geraniums, white alyssum and blue lobelia.

Many people have suggested that it would be better to plant a tree in commemoration of Coronation year, or some shrubs, instead of flowers, but most of us will look for an immediate show, and there *is* something about the geranium, as Lady Margaret Sackville says in her poem in Floral Symphony.

" I thought I heard the roll of drums.
 But no, it was Geranium's
 Deep-voiced, reiterated call . . ."

It *is* a " bombastic " flower, yet our gardens and window boxes would be sadder without it, and I hope London will be full of geraniums as scarlet as the Guardsmen's tunics all this coming summer.

* * *

IF it rains of course the spectators who are wearing " Warmlite " coats will have the best of it. These coats made by the famous Bradford firm of Robert Hirst in 100 per cent. wool gaberdine are now on sale with a new quilted Tropaline lining.

Tropaline, as you may know, is the latest and best lining material.

Three times as warm as wool, it has for its basic material Tropal—a damp-resisting hygienic product which comes from Indonesia, and is made on a new scientific principle. It acts as a special protection against rheumatism and other ailments arising from exposure, is completely rot- and insect-proof—and, reassuring note from the advertisement for visitors who have heard dreadful things about the English summer—it will " *keep you afloat in water.*"

Tropaline floats 32 times its own weight in water and it was used by the R.A.F. during the war.

The new Warmlite Weathercoat for men is offered as " supremely suitable " for every occasion and in every climate.

The quilted Tropaline " warmer " can be zipped in or out of the coat at will.

A man with a Warmlite can forget about buying a heavy winter overcoat altogether, and it is ideal for the business man, who must travel from one climate to another with the lightest possible luggage, as it is so readily adaptable to the quickest changes of temperature.

Many sportsmen wear Warmlite coats : I have seen Mr. Len Hutton wearing one, and many spectators watching him on a damp June day will be glad to be wearing one also !

Snow or rain, what matters ?—seems to picturise the thoughts, respectively, of vivacious Jill Clifford (Rank star) and glamorous Joan Caulfield, of Columbia, whose plastic mackintosh gives a delightful touch of fashion.

* * *

THE zip-in-and-out quilted lining is really a very old fashion. For 3,000 years the Chinese have worn quilted, padded clothing as a lightweight protection against varied weather conditions.

It was known to the Greeks and Romans. There is even a mention of a " quilted doublet " in the Æneid. In the first Elizabethan Age both men and women wore quilted cloaks, doublets and skirts.

Matching hats ; one for heavy rainwear, the other a new style called the Deerstalker for all sporting occasions are also available.

* * *

IF you fear that even the excitement of a Coronation New Year may not dispel that feeling of tiredness that has come to be known as " The English Disease," start now and take the new " food supplement " Vita-Yeast.

High grade brewer's yeast, which is known to be the richest natural source of the important B vitamins, has been unpleasant to take in the past because of its bitter taste. The new process used in producing the Vita-Yeast powder removes the bitter element while retaining all the important factors that make it valuable to those suffering from nervous fatigue and tensions. Much of the " forgetfulness" we all experience to-day has been put down to a deficiency in Vitamin B in our diet. Vita-Yeast which comes in packets for 3s. or 5s. 6d. can be taken in any way you please—and it combines very well with many savoury dishes. Here is a recipe for a Health Savoury.

 1 dessertspoonful picalilli.
 2 ozs. peanuts.
 1–2 ozs. watercress.
 1 small tin spaghetti in tomato sauce.
 4 rounded dessertspoonfuls Vita-Yeast.
 Fried bread.

Chop the picalilli, peanuts and watercress and add to the heated spaghetti. Add the Vita-Yeast and serve hot on fried bread or with watercress. It will give four people a healthful snack.

* * *

IF you have a baby in the house aged between three and 16 months, and you are naturally being very careful about diet, then I have a Coronation Year free gift for you.

It is a most charmingly illustrated booklet entitled " From Milk to Mixed Diet " and gives each development that may be looked for as the baby progresses.

There is also a useful chapter on Safety in the Home—and even a page of Hints for Fathers.

You can obtain your free copy if you write *mentioning Modern Motoring and Travel*, to Heinz Advisory Service, Heinz, Ltd., London, N.W.10.

* * *

HEALTH of both children and adults should be good in 1953 for the Coronation will stir our blood and make us feel full of vigour for the new age beginning.

British prestige in cars and clothes, already high, will mount even higher this year. One small straw already shows the direction of the wind. Chief feature of the wonderful ski-ing outfit offered by Paris designer Maggy Rouff's latest collection is *a British Boot*.

Made by Morlands of Glastonbury, it costs 7 gns. in this country.

We have worn Morlands boots for our sports, *and* for the weary shopping of rationed days. Now the Boot is high fashion *in Paris*.

We have endured our hardships and rationing ; this year we can turn our energies to pleasure and play.

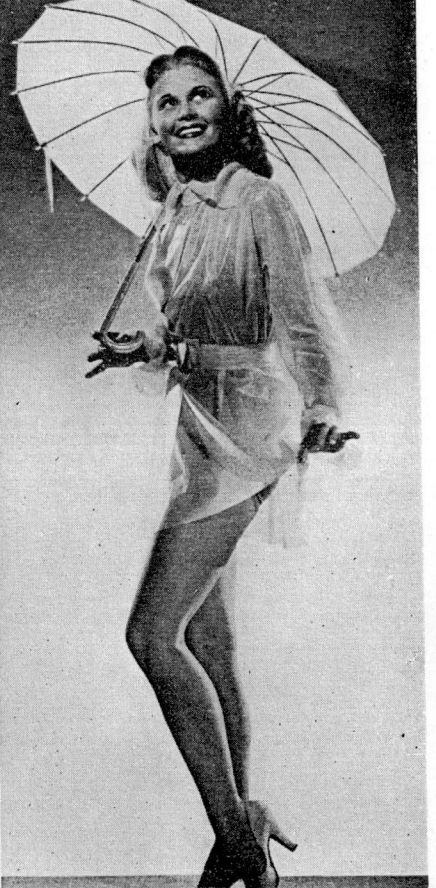

RUNS WITH AN OBJECTIVE— No. 1 CHESTER

Panorama of the River Dee and suspension bridge, with the popular Groves Walk on the left.

YOU want an excuse for a pleasant drive, with something to see at the end? What better first example than lovely medieval Chester, with its picturesque centuries-old houses, the several City gates and all their historic interest; also, of course, the lovely River Dee. Here is material, indeed, for the architect, artist, photographer and historian in abundance.

Below: Another of the exquisitely decorative half-timbered buildings—here, the Cross—in the old centre of Chester.

King Charles Tower, on the old wall. Legend records that the King stood here on September 24, 1646, and saw his army defeated on Rowton Moor.

Below: Picturesque beyond words—featuring the famous "Rows" and every contrasting decorative style.

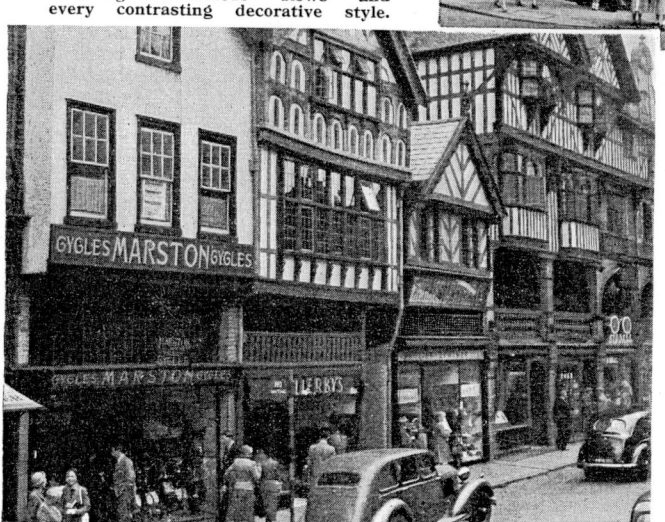

Built in 1503 (during the reign of Henry VII) and still in an excellent state of preservation; seen in Lower Bridge Street.

Below: Ancient and modern harmonise with seldom, it seems, time to pause to admire this setting by Eastgate.

February, 1953

"RALLYE OBERLAND" –
our 1953, and best ever,
Continental Holiday

The subject of our front cover: Lovely Lake Geneve, between Lausanne and Montreux—included in the routeing of Rallye Oberland.

SPECIALLY devised by the Editor, and carrying his personal assurances of opportunities for maximum enjoyment and satisfaction, our 1953 Continental holiday arranged exclusively for owners of Humber, Hillman and Sunbeam-Talbot cars embodies the pick of the plums from all previous excursions of the kind.

* * *

"Rallye Oberland" is dated for Saturday, July 18, to Saturday, August 1 —visiting France, Switzerland (Germany an optional free addition) in a near-perfect itinerary : (*a*) through the Champagne district and Jura Mountains of France ; (*b*) to Lake Geneva ; (*c*) up and over the Bernese Oberland ; (*d*) on to Lake Lucerne—returning via Alsace-Lorraine to the Pas de Calais.

Much research has gone into its compilation and planning, purposely to include the best of scenic interest, the most comfortable hotels, the easiest routes, the simplest formalities and, considering the generous holiday programme—everything laid on in first-class style—all at very reasonable cost.

* * *

We are satisfied ourselves that those who participate in this year's event, even bearing in mind the highlights of previous occasions, will still be very agreeably surprised. Even at this early date we know that all Switzerland is preparing to give " Rallye Oberland " a warm welcome.

Returning from one of the offered mountain rambles near Gstaad, with the snow-capped Wildhorn in the background.

The joy of visiting the Continent, and especially Switzerland, under the auspices of this journal is that, from the outset, those who take part are relieved of all irritating routine (shipping and Customs formalities, car and passenger documents, route maps, hotel reservations, etc.), being left only to indulge the pleasures of the tour. The fact that this journal has friends in " every town and port " is a further guarantee of complete enjoyment.

For example, invitations are already coming in for " Rallye Oberland " to be received officially in Geneva, Gstaad, Brunnen and Basle, but if the nightmare of formality looms up in this connection, let it be brushed aside immediately. The generous, if simple, greetings we are promised will give only added delight to the trip.

Ample leisure time will be available everywhere, of course, with much variety of pastime from which to make appealing choice.

* * *

There is to be nothing in the nature of convoy travel. Once away from the port, and for each day's run, the simple routes to the next stopping places can be followed freely and in one's own time, aiming only to book in at journey's end in nice time for refreshers and dinner. Your rooms will, of course, be ready for your arrival.

* * *

For those wishing for some assistance in the initial stages of " driving on the right of the road," the Rallye will be led out of the dock area and be headed by the leader for Arras and Péronne at moderate speed—an arrangement welcomed by most first-timers to Continental touring, but concerning a new practice which, in remarkably short time, becomes an accomplished art.

No one need lose his way and, knowing that there follows behind a qualified mechanic, with all appropriate equipment, this should alleviate any anxiety on this score. The only requirement is that each car maintains progress ahead of the mechanic's running schedule, copies of which are issued to all drivers—and usually it all goes as smoothly as that.

Now study the brief itinerary outlined on facing page. But let us emphasise that its brevity conceals innumerable pleasant surprises, full details of which are being reserved for a later announcement—in the interests of those who actually take part !

First things first, however. Get in your requests for accommodation on the Rallye as soon as possible. " House Full " will operate just as soon as 25 cars, the maximum number proposed, are booked and confirmed.

* * *

Approaches for reservations should be directed in the first place to the Editor, *Modern Motoring and Travel*, 53, Stratton Street, Piccadilly, London, W.1, and be accompanied by a deposit of £10 per person, cheques being made payable to the Motorists' Travel Club, through which agency, as in previous years, all routine matters are being facilitated on our behalf.

Warning words : cars other than those named will not be accepted ; requests for reservations will be dealt with strictly in order of receipt.

* * *

The dates have been chosen purposely to facilitate two important requirements— (*a*) to gain maximum hours of daylight the better to indulge the call of the alpine passes—and they will be within reasonable distance of several centres on the route— either solely or as one of a conducted party, i.e., being led by one who is familiar with local ways and conditions. First-timers to the Swiss passes will thus be assured of reliable routeing and timing to embody the grandest views with opportunity for rests and picnics.

* * *

During the Rallye abundant opportunity will be provided also for all the usual holiday attractions—boating, bathing, tennis, golf, etc., all under ideal conditions and in perfect surroundings. Providing the weather (*b*) is good— and it should be in mid-July—one can make added choice between wonderful mountain walks, the use of chair lifts or the funicular rail route (to points where the car is out of the question) ; alternatively steamer trips on Lakes Geneve and Lucerne, relaxing at the wonderful lidos, with always plenty of appealing evening entertainment.

* * *

WELCOME, too, is the incorporation of rest periods at Vevey, Gstaad, Brunnen and Basle. These should please everyone, but especially the feminine members for sunbathing or visiting the marvellous shops. At these places also are certain other special items reserved for participants.

February, 1953

"RALLYE OBERLAND"
Detailed Itinerary

A VERY attractive itinerary through the Champagne District and Jura Mountains of France, to Lake Geneva, Bernese Oberland and Lake Lucerne in Switzerland, returning via Alsace-Lorraine to the Pas de Calais.

Saturday, July 18.—Rendezvous Dover Harbour 9 a.m., board car ferry for Calais. Following clearance of Customs, road section via St. Omer, Arras and Péronne, to spend the night at RHEIMS. Mileage 170.

Sunday, July 19.—Continue south through the Champagne country via Châlons-sur-Marne, St. Dizier, Chaumont, and Langres to spend the night at DIJON. Mileage 175.

Monday, July 20.—Continue through the foothills of the Jura Mountains to Dole, Poligny and Champagnole, to cross the Swiss Frontier for Lake Geneva, and following the shore proceed via Lausanne-Ouchy to spend the next two nights at VEVEY. Mileage 135.

Tuesday, July 21.—At leisure. Opportunity to visit Geneva, steamer trips on Lake, boating, sailing, bathing, or just lazing; with other optional items.

Wednesday, July 22.—Follow the Lake shore via Montreux to the Castle of Chillon, and thence over the Col du Pillon to spend three nights at the delightful mountain village of GSTAAD; special programme at choice. Mileage 45.

Thursday and Friday, July 23 and 24.—At leisure. Either mountain walks, swimming, "sunning," or trips in the funicular.

Saturday, July 25.—Continue through the Bernese Oberland via Interlaken, Brienz to Lucerne, and thence along the shores of the Lake for three nights at BRUNNEN; special items. Mileage 115.

Sunday and Monday, July 26 and 27.—At leisure. Opportunity to cover the Swiss passes, Grimsel, Susten, Gotthard; steamer or boat trip on the Lake; mountain railway to summit of Rigi; bathing or just lazing.

Tuesday, July 28.—Leave Brunnen and proceed via Zürich and Baden for the Rhine Falls to spend the night at BASLE; special items. Mileage 90.

Wednesday, July 29.—At leisure. Excellent facilities for shopping, an excursion into Germany, a day on the Rhine, or just lazing.

Thursday, July 30.—Cross the French Frontier and proceed via Belfort, Epinal and Nancy to spend the night at VERDUN. Mileage 220.

Friday, July 31.—Continue via Sédan, Charleville, Cambrai, St. Pol and Boulogne to spend the night at WIMEREUX. Mileage 240.

Saturday, August 1.—Leave Wimereux to cover the 22 miles to Calais to arrive at noon to board the car ferry for DOVER.

FACILITIES PROVIDED

1. Advice Bulletins covering all matters concerning currency, passports, clothing, cameras, food, petrol, etc.
2. Foreign Touring Documents and G.B. Plate, for your car.
3. Return freight of car across the Channel at Owner's Risk.
4. Return passenger tickets.
5. Port and Harbour dues.
6. Hotel accommodation comprising dinner, room and Continental breakfast at Rheims, Dijon, Verdun and Wimereux.
7. Hotel accommodation comprising dinner, room, Continental breakfast, luncheon (or picnic lunch), including day of departure at Vevey, Gstaad, Brunnen and Basle.
8. Gratuities to hotel servants, taxe de séjour and local taxes, covering above accommodation and meals.
9. Detailed itinerary and town plans and maps, covering the entire tour.
10. Service of experienced courier throughout the tour.
11. Services of Rootes technician and service vehicle throughout the tour.
12. Freedom from any anxiety.

The Bernese Oberland in all its exclusive grandeur—as seen from the near summit of the Wasterngrat, 8,000 feet, reached by chair lift—with our road as a white ribbon in the valley below.

COST PER PERSON

No. of Persons in car	ACCORDING TO WHEELBASE			
	Under 8 ft. 6 in.	8 ft. 6 in.—9 ft. 0 in.	9 ft. 0 in.—9 ft. 6 in.	9 ft. 6 in.—10 ft. 6 in.
4	£63 7s. 6d.	£63 17s. 6d.	£64 17s. 6d.	£66 2s. 6d.
3	£64 12s. 6d.	£65 5s. 6d.	£66 12s. 6d	£68 5s. 6d.
2	£67 2s. 0d.	£68 2s. 0d.	£70 2s. 0d.	£72 12s. 0d.

Extra for single rooms, £5 per person. Extra for private bathroom (double rooms only), £3 10s. 0d. per person. Amount required from foreign currency allowance, £15 per person.

Finance—Example:

Three persons, each £25 personal travel allowance	£75
Car allowance to driver	10
Sterling, permissable, each £5	15
	100
Required for "V" form (3 at £15)	45
Balance for car expenses and personal spending	£55

DON'T worry too much on the side of finance. We know it can be done and done well—if perhaps limiting expenditure on the best wines all the time.

Taking three in party, from the schedule above it will be seen there remains over £50 spending money, petrol and oil being estimated at roughly £20, which still leaves £35 for "extras." In any case, "Rallye Brunnen" last year proved the point beyond doubt! Remember, the entire cost is paid in sterling before departure.

So there it is! We look forward to your response and to your company on what promises to be the best ever continental holiday tour.

Lovely Pantomime Queen, stage and screen actress, Hy Hazell takes a leading role in the Associated British-Marble Arch production, "The Yellow Balloon." She is shown here with her pet whippet, Judy.

"O.K. for SOUND"
Film Shorts and Starlights

JUST finishing the Technicolor musical, "The Band Wagon," Fred Astaire is to co-star with Bing Crosby in Paramount's "White Christmas."

"The Band Wagon" has 12 spectacular musical numbers, and also stars Cyd Charisse and Jack Buchanan.

* * *

NORMAN WISDOM'S first screen appearance since he signed a contract with the Rank Organisation will be in "Meet Mr. Lucifer," a Michael Balcon production now filming at Ealing studios.

He will appear only briefly—as himself—in this topical comedy about the impact of television upon several households.

* * *

LONDON Independent Producers' salute to the policewomen of Britain has been given the title, "Street Corner."

The picture stars Anne Crawford, Peggy Cummins, Ronald Howard, Rosamund John, Terence Morgan and Barbara Murray.

* * *

HOWARD KEEL'S booming baritone singing voice is silent for the third time in a row in M-G-M.'s "Fast Company." He played dramatic roles in "Desperate Search" and "Vaquero."

Next, Howard Keel is to take the lead in "The Marauders," an action-romance in Arizona following the American Civil War.

* * *

HAROLD SIDDONS plays a Wellington bomber pilot in "Malta Story," Pinewood's picture about the 1942 siege of the George Cross Island. Siddons appears as a squadron leader with the D.F.C. and bar.

In 1942 Harold Siddons was flying Wellington bombers based in Malta. He was a squadron leader with the D.F.C. and bar.

* * *

A WELCOME fit for a Queen was received by Jean Simmons when she began work at Metro-Goldwyn-Mayer on the Technicolor production, "Young Bess."

The young actress's dressing room overflowed with flowers, fruit, gifts and telegrams to an extent which old-timers at the studio said they hadn't seen in years.

* * *

BRITISH actor Guy Rolfe, who played King John in "Ivanhoe," which M-G-M. made in Britain, went to Hollywood for a part in M-G-M.'s "Young Bess."

Now Universal-International have signed him to play the villain in their new Technicolor production, "Prince of Bagdad."

* * *

THE news that Len Hutton, Alec Bedser, Jim Laker, Godfrey Evans and Cyril Washbrook were to appear in the screen version of "The Final Test" caused some raised eyebrows in cricketing circles. "What about Denis Compton?"

But this photogenic cricketer had not been left out. Pinewood studios sent their invitation to the wrong address.

Another invitation was sent, and Compton accepted at once.

* * *

ON location in the Old Kent Road for the new Pinewood Technicolor comedy "Genevieve," star John Gregson was mobbed by young autograph hunters.

Said one small girl of about 11: "Say, Mister, was you in 'Venetian Bird'?"

"I was," John beamed.

"And was it you who swiped Richard Todd on the back of the head?"

"That's right," agreed John.

The girl scowled. "Then I'll never see one of your pictures again as long as I live."

In a black négligée is Marie Windsor, who plays a vital witness trapped by gangsters aboard a train in the R.K.O. Radio drama, "The Narrow Margin."

JOAN COLLINS, whose bad girl in "I Believe in You" set the critics talking, stars in "Turn the Key Softly," now being made for the Rank Organisation.

The film is set in that part of London sometimes called "The square mile of vice." It tells a powerful story of 12 hours in the lives of three women, all outcasts of society, immediately after their release from Holloway prison.

* * *

ORIGINALLY published in *Collier's Magazine*, "Flight to the Islands" has been chosen as a starring vehicle for Spencer Tracy.

The plot revolves around a bored husband and family man who runs away from his responsibilities—to find his happiness is not in strange places, but back at home.

* * *

JOHN MILLS is to star in a new Michael Balcon production at Ealing studios, "The Square Ring."

One of the most hard-hitting plays of recent years, this strips boxing of its glamour and bares the pathos and heartbreak behind the scenes.

1. The remains of an old post type windmill at Billericay, Essex. The mill house, with its sails, were mounted on the central timber pivot.

2. Part of a collection of curious models in the front garden of a Potter Street house, near Epping, all made by Mr. Scott, village baker.

CURIOSITIES BY THE ROADSIDE

3. This pillar, a few miles out of Llandovery, Wales, commemorates a fatal accident in 1835, and is inscribed, "A Caution to Mail-Coach Drivers to keep from Intoxication."

4. This milestone at Trumpington, Cambridge, bearing the crescent of Trinity Hall, Cambridge, is 14 feet in height, nine feet having been buried in the ground when the adjacent bridge was constructed.

5. In the churchyard at Tongham, near Guildford, Surrey, is the narrowest detached church belfry in the country. A tall wooden structure, it houses the church bells acquired after the completion of the church.

6. A painting now displayed outside the "Rose and Crown Inn" at Hempstead, Essex, where Dick Turpin is reputed to have been born in 1705. The highwayman and "Black Bess" are shown on the road to York.

7. This is said to be the only "pivot" type lychgate in the country, which closes automatically. It is at Yateley, near Camberley, and is operated by the weight near left-hand roof beam.

From the Mediterranean to the Persian Gulf; and back!

2,400 miles across Arabia in the Hillman Minx

By Harry B. Ellis

NO Hillman Minx, perhaps, has gone through more rugged paces than the Mark V which I drove last summer from the Mediterranean Sea to the Persian Gulf, and return.

Sixteen hundred of those 2,400 miles lay across the burning and nearly trackless sands of the Arabian Desert, through heat reaching to well over 100 degrees Fahrenheit—in a Hillman Minx with no special equipment, other than a five-bladed cooling fan!

* * *

DESERT heat, said those who knew Arabia, plus lava ridges overlain by soft and treacherous sand, plus sandstorms that " would bury us axle deep," would be too much for this " civilian " car. Average life even of desert-equipped cars in this barren waste, I was told, was two years.

Everyone was against the trip; that is everyone except the Rootes Group people in Beirut, Lebanon, starting point of our minor odyssey. These Lebanese representatives of Rootes remained supremely confident that " Prince Charlie," for so the car had been named, would make the trip as easily as a run to nearby Sidon on the Lebanese coast.

It was they who fitted the five-bladed fan, placed two extra tyres and tubes in the boot, a jerry can of petrol and one of water in the rear seat, and told me my car was ready. Apart from these points, the car was no different from any other Hillman to be seen running daily about the streets of London, Manchester, New York, or Montreal.

* * *

WITHOUT the Arabian-American Oil Company and the Trans-Arabian Pipeline Company—American firms extracting oil from these desert sands—the trip would have been impossible, for there would have been no respites from the scorching shamal winds, no guides to smooth the way with the Saudi Arabs, and—most important—no place to restock petrol, food and water.

What was the purpose of the trip?

First, as a journalist, to study and report on the impact of Americans and oil in an ancient land. But, secondly, as a traveller, to visit Arabia, goal of travellers since Roman days and before, where life still belonged to the nomad, as it had thousands of years ago.

* * *

CRADLE of the Semites, Arabia had been alluring to Westerners since history began—traditional home of the Queen of Sheba, and of Job; of Hagar, the bondwoman, and of Ishmael, her son; the land where Abraham is said to have sojourned; where Moses and his people, the nomads of their day, toiled through the wilderness in their passage up from Egypt; the home, if not of the Wise Men themselves, then of the gifts they brought to Jesus—gold, and frankincense, and myrrh. And, finally, the land where Mohammed was born, and the religion of Islam, the heart of the Arabic Empire.

By the time the trip was done the colour of the car had been changed to that of sand; the windscreen had been " frosted " by stinging particles of sand, and headlamps and chrome had been similarly roughly handled. Yet these were, if anything, compliments to the stamina of the Hillman Minx, for, despite this mute testimony to the ruggedness of the trip, there was not one sign internally—from engine, springs, or transmission—that the car had been on anything more than a casual pleasure jaunt!

To-day, five thousand miles later, my car still purrs over Lebanese and Syrian roads, as sweetly as though it never had seen the desert, nor nosed over a dune into soft sand below.

* * *

MY companion on the trip was Joe Alex Morris, Jnr., young Harvard graduate loaned by Aramco as fellow-driver and guide.

Our route lay from Beirut over the Lebanon and Anti-Lebanon Mountains to Damascus, then south to Mafraq in the Hashemite Kingdom of Jordan, and east along the Baghdad road. It was along this road, between stations H-4 and H-3 of the Iraq Petroleum Company's pipeline, that we left " civilisation " and struck south through the desert, into Saudi Arabia, to pick up the route of Tapline to the Persian Gulf.

There was no road, in the proper sense, running beside Tapline, 30 in. to 31 in.

(Continued on page 42)

Veiled and shrouded Bedouin women outside Aramco pump station, Saudi Arabia.

The author, back to camera, greets a Bedouin family in the desert.

" Prince Charlie " tanks up at a desert fuel station—

—and continues unperturbed across the seeming limitless Arab sand.

The Car the world has chosen for its own

"Minx FOR RELIABILITY"
—SAYS EIRE
"Smooth running, perfect balance, exceptional comfort, and power and reliability under all tests!" *Hugh P. O'Neill, Eire.*

"Minx FOR ECONOMY"
—SAYS HOLLAND
"Four of us—with luggage—went over the Simplon and St. Gothard 'cols' at 31 miles to the gallon!" *H. F. A. Margadant, Amsterdam.*

"Minx FOR PERFORMANCE"
—SAYS SWITZERLAND
"Our good and faithful Minx performs beautifully and climbs hills like mad!" *A. Fischer, Zurich.*

You get so much more in the

Hillman Minx

and you get so much more out of it

A PRODUCT OF THE ROOTES GROUP

Hillman Motor Car Co. Ltd. Coventry.   London Showrooms & Export Division: Rootes Ltd. Devonshire House Piccadilly London W.1

Mediterranean to Persian Gulf: (Concluded from page 40)

pipeline snaking more than 1,000 miles from Dhahran on the Persian Gulf, across the north Arabian Desert, to Sidon on the Mediterranean coast. There was, however, the rolled sand track used by Tapline vehicles and the refrigerator trucks which carry fruits, meats and vegetables to the American families living at the pump stations built across the desert.

This sand track, for the most part, afforded hard-surfaced and excellent going, though necessarily it had become "washboarded" from constant pounding by heavy tyres. We discovered, however, that at high speeds the Minx fled over this type of road as smoothly as Tapline cars with balloon tyres and longer wheelbases.

Not once during this portion of the trip did the engine overheat, though when we stopped occasionally to chat with Bedouins or watch a herd of camels file slowly past, the heat would beat down upon us in a way that made a hundred-yard walk from the car something to be thought about deliberately and performed slowly, before easing oneself back against the burning leather of the seats.

* * *

FIVE Tapline pump stations—Turaif, Badanah, Rafha, Qaisumah and Nariya—are strung across the desert, roughly 200 miles apart, and the distance between each one we covered at an average speed of 45 miles per hour. From Qaisumah we struck due east, by-passing the station of Nariya, aiming at Ras el Mishaab on the Persian Gulf.

Here it was that the Minx proved its mettle, for the last 100 miles of this stretch is heavy sand dune country, over which the sand marches—deep, soft and treacherous—urged on by the shamal winds from the north. We could not, dared not, slow down, though just a few inches below the surface of this soft sand were clay-like ridges hard as iron.

Sometimes we would burst through a clinging patch of sand on to a windswept stretch of ridges that bounced us, time and again, against the roof of the car. Yet just ahead would loom drifted sand which only high speed would push us through, and we would be forced to gun the car despite the threat to springs and axles.

Once, indeed, we became stuck in soft sand, one shadeless noon, and that served to show us what the desert in summer must mean to a Bedouin and his camel, with the shamal blowing down as though over hot coals, and with no place the Bedouin could reach to-morrow, or next week, that would be any different from the spot he now stood.

Slowly, laboriously, we dug our way out with bare hands, clearing a path for the tyres, and then putting "Prince Charlie" in low speed forward while one man leaned against the boot and pushed. It took nearly one hour of this before we reached hard earth that gave us a footing—and still the Minx had not boiled over!

Finally, during this stretch, we left the sand track and struck out through the dunes themselves, seeking the spots where the sand had drifted least. Ahead of us, but too late to avoid, loomed the crest of a dune. In we plunged, until sand burst over the bonnet like a wave over a ship's bow. We dared not stop to seek out damage, for, once badly stuck in this country of dunes, there would be no telling how long before an Aramco search plane could pick us out.

And then, when we reached the Persian Gulf, we discovered that there was no damage! Despite the gruelling test of that last 100 miles, against which even Tapline drivers had warned us, the Minx had come through and "wet its wheels" in the blue and limpid waters of the Persian Gulf, 1,200 miles away from its "home port" of Beirut on the Mediterranean Sea.

* * *

THE return trip was equally hard. It could not help but be. One stretch of 50 miles, just before we reached the Baghdad road—this time with Mike Cheney, a new Aramco friend, at the wheel—was toughest perhaps of all. Along that stretch we crossed hard and rutted wadis that should have left our springs in the sand behind. And yet, when the trip was done, total damage for the 2,400 miles was one flat tyre.

Once again the Rootes people in Beirut took over, dismantled the car, even to doors and seats, to clean out the sand that had drifted into every nook and cranny, greased her, oiled her, polished her, and handed her back—apparently as good as new.

(I cannot explain my tendency to call "Prince Charlie" by the feminine "she," except that my post-Arabian affection for her has grown to such a point!)

There are American mechanics in Arabia who profess still to remember the little grey car that crossed the desert in summer heat. They regarded her with great respect, they told me. And so do I. She has given me memories of Bedouin and desert life rich enough to fill a book.

To-day the car's tasks are more prosaic, and yet, as I drive about on placid jobs, the thought keeps recurring—there must be other wilds this car and I can conquer!

Motor Industry's unique Research Centre

Sir Reginald Rootes, President of M.I.R.A., speaking at the annual luncheon of the Association.

THE Motor Industry Research Association's testing ground at Lindley, near Nuneaton, Warwickshire, is to be doubled in size. M.I.R.A. is, of course, a Co-operative Research Association backed by the Government and all sections of the industry.

By mid-1953 it will embrace, as well as existing testing and proving grounds, together with the extensive and comprehensively equipped laboratories and experimental establishments covering some 600 acres, a new high speed test track where speeds greatly in excess of 100 m.p.h. will be feasible.

M.I.R.A. now provides, almost at the industry's doorstep, operating conditions parallel with those obtaining in any part of the world; sections of *pavé*; water and mud-logged tracks; deep water splashes; dust and corrugations, to near identical areas of desert sand. The addition of the new high speed testing track will effect, therefore, what might well be claimed "the finest automobile research centre in the world."

All this and more was emphasised by Sir Reginald Rootes, President of M.I.R.A., at the annual luncheon of the Association held recently at the Dorchester Hotel. "The new test track," said Sir Reginald, "would not be confined to motor cars but be available for the testing of trucks and passenger vehicles at speeds quite impracticable with safety anywhere on our national network."

The problem of accommodating existing and supplementary research staffs and personnel is to be solved by the construction of a special housing estate. Inclusive development costs are estimated at over £500,000.

Proposing the toast of the Association, Lord Brabazon of Tara, extreme left in our photograph, stated that some 70 to 80 leading manufacturers were already making highly advantageous use of M.I.R.A.'s unique experimental facilities, with up to 1,000 vehicles being handled every quarter.

Incidentally, it may be of added interest to readers to know that Mr. B. B. Winter, director of engineering, Rootes Group, has played an important part both in the conception and in the planning of M.I.R.A.'s new high speed test track. He is deputy chairman to-day and has been chairman in past years.

BIND YOUR "MODERN MOTORING & TRAVEL"

MONTH BY MONTH
in the

"EASIBINDER"

SIMPLE—EFFECTIVE—PROTECTIVE

HERE is the ideal, instantaneous binder in which to preserve your copies of "Modern Motoring and Travel."

Each binder holds 12 copies, or one full volume series.

Copies of "Modern Motoring & Travel" can be inserted as received—a two-minute operation—when you secure the same ready service and all-time protection as with ordinary binding but without waiting for the full number of issues and without, in the meantime, separate copies becoming damaged or mislaid.

The "Easibinder" opens flat at any page of any separate edition, gives quick reference facilities and makes an excellent addition to any bookshelf.

It is strongly made with a stiff board foundation, metal reinforced and is capable of withstanding constant hard usage.

Price **15s.** *post free*

The binder holds 12 copies, readily inserted. It is embossed in bright lettering on a green background.

Address your order to-day, together with your remittance of **15s.** *to :—*

The Manager,

"MODERN MOTORING & TRAVEL,"

53, STRATTON STREET,

PICCADILLY, LONDON, W.1.

Each copy is secured by a steel bar, held at each end of the binder case.

All pages open flat and effect secure binding from the first to the last copy of the monthly editions.

February, 1953

Our Photo Competition
Result of Second Contest

FOR the second contest in this special series of three events there was an even keener entry, making the task of judging an unenviable one, indeed.

However, the results published reflect the high merit of all subjects and surely deserve the highest commendation.

As well as winners, there must, of course, be losers, yet there must be no small consolation in participating in an event of this kind which has attracted practical interest, not only from home readers, but from many parts of the world.

From the results of the third and last contest we shall be able to adjudicate the aggregate winner, i.e., the entrant submitting the photograph judged the best of all three events, which means success to the total amount of 8 guineas. The winner will be announced in the next edition.

Later in the year we will be announcing another contest—for pictures taken on or after January 1, 1953. To be forewarned, therefore, is to be forearmed, so keep a good eye open and your camera at hand—one of the special features of the next competition being "exceptional novelty of subject." The contest, as usual, will be open only to amateur photographers, endorsed as such on all entries.

First Prize: "The Torrent." By N. K. Stout, of 12, Warwick Road, Bishop's Stortford, Herts.

Second Prize: "The Parting of the Mists"—overlooking the Grindelvald valley. By E. C. Ive, of "Green Willows," 218, Upper Woodcote Road, Caversham, Reading.

Third Prize: "Lake Lucerne in Silent Serenity." By G. E. Lobb, of 16, Penrose Road, Falmouth, Cornwall.

Consolation Award: "Dolomite Chapel." By Marsh Gabriel, of 45, Southbrook Road, Lee, S.E.12.

Consolation Award: "Chateau D'Azay-le-Rideau." by R. J. J. Westlake, of 16, Grosvenor Road, Crownhill, Plymouth.

Consolation Award: "Flower Market, Brussels." By Berkeley Hollyer, of The Lawn, Lower Woodfield Road, Torquay.

Consolation Award: "The Close." By J. H. Parker, of 79, Grange Road, Woodthorpe, Nottingham.

Consolation Award: "Down Thataway is Home." By Stephen H. Excell, Avenue Spokane, Washington, B.C.

Consolation Award: "Picturesque Elm Hill, Norwich." By Michael Panton, of 7, Beverley Close, Barnes, S.W.13.

The results of the third, last, and aggregate contest will be announced next month

Page 46   February, 1953

IN A FEW WORDS

News Items of Modern Motoring and Travel

Miss Lana Baschana, with a Hillman Minx Convertible Coupé, the "girl and the car" the delegates to the ASTA Convention, Miami, elected they would like to travel with! By courtesy of Rootes Motors Inc.

One of two Tower Wagons supplied to the Highways Dept., Manchester Corporation, by Rootes, Ltd., Manchester distributors. On a Commer "CK 3" chassis, the Rawlinson tower, 13 ft. 6 ins. when closed, extends to 25 ft. 6 ins.

H.R.H. the Duke of Edinburgh has graciously consented to extend his Patronage to the Royal Scottish Automobile Club.

* * *

SIR WILLIAM ROOTES, K.B.E., announces an all-time record for exports of Rootes Group products in his statement to shareholders.

"I believe that the solid organisation and ground work on which our overseas business has been built will stand us in good stead in the more trying times ahead," he states.

Referring to the burden of direct taxation, Sir William suggests the time has now come when greater freedom and greater incentives are necessary if enterprise is to be allowed its proper scope.

* * *

THE PRICE OF PETROL and diesel oil in Switzerland has been cut by two centimes a litre, through a reduction in freight costs. Filling station prices are now: petrol, 61 centimes (1s.) a litre; diesel oil, 52 centimes (10d.) a litre.

LORD NUFFIELD'S RETIREMENT—TRIBUTE BY SIR WILLIAM ROOTES

Broadcasting recently in the B.B.C.'s Midland News Programme, Sir William Rootes, K.B.E., Chairman of the Rootes Group, in an interview with Godfrey Talbot, said:—

"LORD NUFFIELD is more than an industrial genius of the 20th century. His name is an institution, and therefore the news of his retirement must inevitably cast a shadow over the whole of the Motor Car Industry.

"It was when I was an apprentice in Coventry that I first met Mr. W. R. Morris, as he then was. He was one of the most enthusiastic distributors in Oxford.

"The passing years have brought a growing respect for the way in which he has given his whole life to public service. It needs no word from me to remind listeners of his wonderful benevolence in the relief of suffering humanity. It is known to many of his intimates that from boyhood he wanted to be a surgeon. And I have not the least doubt that had he taken up his first love, he would have achieved outstanding work, as he has done in industry.

"To him goes much of the credit for making the British Public motor-car-minded, while he was also one of the pioneers in selling British products abroad. In fact, he has always been Commonwealth-minded in word and deed.

"If any man deserves a rest, it is Lord Nuffield. He may step down from day-to-day active participation in the industry of which he was the undoubted leader, but his influence and his counsels will for ever remain with us. We all wish him many happy birthdays to come."

Sir William Rootes (then Mr. W. E. Rootes) was apprenticed to Singer Motors, Coventry, at the time when Mr. W. R. Morris was a Singer Motors distributor in Oxford.

THE DERBYSHIRE and Lancashire Gliding Club is offering its site for the International Gliding Championships due to be held in 1954.

* * *

MOTORISTS RESIDENT or travelling in the Metropolitan Police District will be interested in a list, published by the R.A.C., of places authorised by the Commissioner of Police where vehicles may be parked without lights.

(Continued on page 48)

Commer Tankers in the service of the Shell Company in Brazil and around Rio de Janeiro.

Fleet of Commer vehicles in use at the Atco Service Depot, Reading, to provide for the servicing and maintenance of over 17,000 Atco motor mowers operating in the area.

February, 1953 — Page 47 — MODERN MOTORING & TRAVEL

'I play for safety!'

'I can't afford to take chances with sports gear! That's why I have a 'General' Pastimes Policy. It covers me against accidents, too, and includes third party risks. It isn't expensive and lets me enjoy my week-ends with an easy mind!'

There are special policies for golf, tennis, and badminton, bowls, cricket, fishing, cycling and sporting guns or one policy covering all these pastimes. Send off the coupon below, naming your sport.

Peace of mind costs very little

General
ACCIDENT FIRE AND LIFE ASSURANCE CORPORATION LIMITED

General Buildings, Perth, Scotland
General Buildings, Aldwych, WC2

Please send particulars of insurance for
.... *or all pastimes.*
Name ....
Address ....
....
.... M.M.

Wilcot Loose Seat Covers

Tailor made in Tygan Woven Fabric, Felt and Cotton Duck. Send make, year and model of car for prices and patterns.

WILCOT (PARENT) CO. LTD.
FISHPONDS • • • BRISTOL

A WILCOT PRODUCT

How to Dirt-Proof YOUR ENGINE OIL

and prevent THIS

Dirty oil wastes your money. It clogs piston-ring slots, gums-up valve stem guides and constricts oil passages.

Your AC Oil Filter goes on filtering out the clogging sludge, dirt and grit which grind away engine efficiency — until the element is *packed solid*. A fresh A.C. Element at least *every 8,000 miles* means fewer repair bills . . . greatly reduced engine wear . . . less frequent oil changes.

Get your local Humber-Hillman Agent or any good garage to change your AC Filter Element at least every 8,000 miles.

REPLACEMENT ELEMENTS

Humber-Hawk 1948-9 L11—11/-	Sunbeam Talbot 2-Litre 1947-48-49 1948-50 "90" L11—11/-
Super-Snipe and Pullman 1948-50 K11—12/6	1948-50 10 HP & "80" L14—9/6

MINX OWNERS! Your agent can now fit the approved AC Oil Filter to your car.

AC Oil Filters

AC-DELCO DIVISION OF GENERAL MOTORS LTD.
DUNSTABLE, ENGLAND and Southampton, Hants.

MODERN MOTORING & TRAVEL — Page 48 — February, 1953

The impressive Rootes Group stand in the S.M.M. & T. marquee at the recent Canadian National Exhibition.

Mr. E. Hall, President of Ernie Hall, Ltd., of Galt, Ontario, Rootes Group distributors of Commer vehicles, with Mr. Mahlen Fisher, president of the Fisher's Bakery.

In a Few Words: *(from page 46)*

OPENING THE new Stores Department of Wolverhampton Motor Services, Ltd., in November, Sir Reginald Rootes, Deputy Chairman of the Rootes Group, congratulated the firm on their continued expansion.

This new stores development, he said, evidenced the importance which the Wolverhampton Motor Services, Ltd., attached to efficient after-sales service.

Sir Reginald, who had been welcomed and introduced by the Mayor of Wolverhampton (Councillor H. T. Fullwood), was of

Speke's popular 1952 Flower Queen rides high, with her Maids of Honour, on the Sunbeam-Talbot "90" Convertible Coupé. Photo by courtesy of John F. O. S. Graham.

the opinion that the capacity to develop continually and progressively was going to be a pre-requisite in the motor trade to survive in the more competitive times ahead.

* * *

"SPAIN is the cheapest tourist country in the world, and we want British visitors to help us to keep it so," said Don Mariano de Urzaiz, Duke of Luna, the new Director-General of the Spanish State Tourist Department in London.

"Overcharging by hoteliers and shops is the only possible threat to Spain's cheapness for the tourist. That is why we want any British tourist who feels he has been over-charged to let us have his bill."

Every hotel has in it a book called the "libro de reclamaciones," which gives the official maximum price for each room in that hotel.

Assembly plant of Buckleys Motors, Ltd., of Dublin, Rootes Group distributors for the whole of Eire, with a network of dealers covering the entire country. The plant assembles Rootes Group cars and trucks shipped in C.K.D.—completely knocked down—form.

* * *

NEGOTIATIONS ARE proceeding to make members of the American Credit Card Organisation temporary members of the equivalent British organisation while staying in this country. Members would then sign instead of paying at hotels and restaurants co-operating in the scheme, the Credit Card Facility organisation paying the account on demand. Each month the member settles up with the organisation.

* * *

THE HEAD office Marketing Departments of Shell-Mex and B.P., Ltd., have been divided into two groups, retail and industrial. Mr. R. D. Gibbs becomes Secretary and Law Officer of the Company.

* * *

"OFF THE RECORD," a 23-minute film made for the Vacuum Oil Company by Verity Films Limited, shows the way in which closer co-operation with garages can give better business to the garage and better service to the public. The close connection between good lubrication and economical motoring is an underlying theme, and the film will be shown to garage owners, managers and staffs throughout the country.

LET PRATT TRAILERS SOLVE YOUR TRANSPORT PROBLEMS

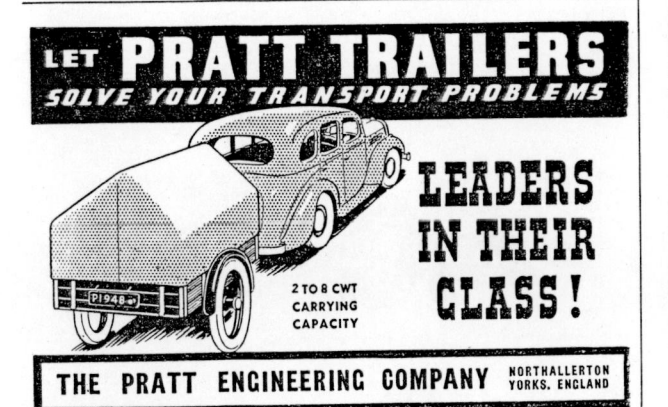

LEADERS IN THEIR CLASS!

2 TO 8 CWT CARRYING CAPACITY

THE PRATT ENGINEERING COMPANY — NORTHALLERTON, YORKS. ENGLAND

April, 1953   Page 17

O~~SLOW~~ 2 LIS *fire*

LON 2 the

done

Through 15 countries in 90 hours ... across Europe and Africa in 13 days, 9 hours, 6 minutes ... two remarkable cars, one remarkable oil ... no wonder Humber recommend Shell X-100 Motor Oil exclusively.

& **SHELL X-100 MOTOR OIL**

April, 1953

R.A.F. formation—not quite perfect!—above the R.A.F. Memorial, on Thames-side.

FLY-PASTS should be representative— and orderly!

says Major Oliver Stewart

DURING this year we shall have a surfeit of fly-pasts. Excluding the Coronation ceremonies themselves, we find a fly-past at the Naval review, a fly-past at the R.A.F. Review at Odiham in July, and a fly-past at the Battle of Britain anniversary celebrations in September.

For each of these events large numbers of aircraft will be marshalled in formation and will then fly past a selected point.

Without in any way wishing to detract from the spectacular effects of these ceremonies, I would like to ask whether the fly-past is really the best kind of parade demonstration for an air force.

It can be, without question, impressive.

In recent years, however, the formation keeping has been poor. The aircrafts tend to straggle.

It is not the fault of the pilots. It is the consequence of the extremely wide speed range between the slow and the fast machines. Moreover, safety considerations have forced these aerial processions higher and therefore farther away from the spectators.

* * *

WHEN a fly-past is done high it can be effective only if the formation is elaborate and perfectly kept.

We have to ask ourselves whether we want our air services—the Royal Air Force and naval aviation—to spend a great deal of time in perfecting their ceremonial flying.

Clearly the air services, like the other services, must have some means of parading before their commanders. The ordinary march-past of foot soldiers has its value from many points of view, disciplinary and psychological. But it is a more intimate affair than can be arranged with aircrafts.

Troops march past close to the person taking the salute and can see him as he responds to their "eyes right." The whole thing takes place in a relatively small arena and can be decked out with colours and flags and all the trappings of a ceremonial occasion.

In effect, the fly-past is nothing more than a transfer into the air of the ceremonial technique of the infantry soldier. And the question which has to be asked is whether it fits the different circumstances.

* * *

THE difficulties of accurate formation keeping in the air with modern machines have been noted, and so has the tendency to increase the height at which the aircrafts pass the saluting base. So the intimacy of the foot soldiers parade is lost.

Senior officers of the Royal Air Force have long known of the shortcomings of the fly-past; but nobody has as yet contrived to suggest anything better.

Attempts have been made.

At the first Sovereign's review of the Royal Air Force—by King George V —the attempt was made to make the best of both worlds.

A big static parade was organised at Mildenhall, with three or four hundred aircrafts picketed out on the airfield.

Here the King drove past the aircrafts and their attendant crews to inspect them. This arrangement had the merit that it brought in the ground crews as well as the air crews.

Then the King drove to Duxford where the fly-past took place. It was not particularly impressive and had the defects of all fly-pasts. But there had already been the inspection at Mildenhall, so that the review gave a full-bodied impression.

* * *

AS I write the details of how the review at Odiham in July is going to be arranged have yet to be fixed.

There was a suggestion that the fly-past should be a token affair by a comparatively small number of aircraft, specially drilled for the purpose. By this means the fly-past itself could be made highly spectacular. The aircrafts could keep much closer formation and could fly past at low level in full view of all those present. The risks always attending the assembly of large numbers of machines would be avoided.

On the other hand, a token fly-past, even by as many as 30 or 40 machines, would not be representative of the Royal Air Force. So the problem remains and it will be exceedingly interesting to see what official solutions are provided at Odiham.

* * *

IT must be remembered that it has taken time to evolve the best kind of air display. I imagine that most people would agree that the S.B.A.C. Display at Farnborough is the best thing of its kind in the world.

The basic idea is that people want to look at the aircrafts and engines at close range on the ground as well as to see them fly. Now other countries are attempting to copy Farnborough.

The Paris Salon, in June, is for the first time to be held entirely at an aerodrome, Le Bourget, and the method of running it is almost exactly the same as that employed at Farnborough.

In the United States plans are being made for running an American version of the S.B.A.C. Display. The formula is a complete success. As yet, however, no comparable formula has been evolved for the Services.

* * *

CEREMONIAL occasions are comparatively infrequent for the Royal Air Force. But when they do occur there should be a sound means of parading the air service in a spectacular and also appropriate manner. Flying itself can be a great and thrilling spectacle; but a ragged formation, however large, is never satisfactory.

My own view is that we ought not to devote the time and energy to enable us to put in the sky big formations capable of accurate ceremonial drill.

I believe that some other solution must be found.

The first Royal review had a promising idea, though it did not work out as well as had been hoped.

Perhaps this year, on the occasion of the Queen's first review of the Royal Air Force at Odiham in mid-July, the right formula will be found. At any rate this event will raise interest and expectation to the highest pitch.

IT IS MY 21st BIRTHDAY ANNIVERSARY –
let me tell my own story!

Autobiography of the Minx

ONE'S 21st birthday is an occasion of pride and rejoicing, it is said, in everyone's lifetime.

It certainly is in mine, and if I must necessarily talk a lot about myself, I feel I might be excused.

You would speak in terms of years, of course. May I be different and give expression to my story in figures of miles? Which allows me at once to say I first saw the light of day something like 21,000,000,000 miles back, a thousand-million miles, or more, for every year of my existence.

But that is putting the cart before the horse!

* * *

IT was in October, 1931, that the first news of my impending arrival was broadcast and received with excited anticipation. When I duly appeared, in early 1932, I was truly embarrassed at the world-wide accord to my virtues as a promising young thoroughbred, with all the signs of a perky future.

I am told that they sat continuously for hours on end, purposely to evolve my ultimate name. It had to be something synonymous of good breeding (I come from that long-established and highly respected family, the "Hillmans of Coventry"), my bonnie proportions, my apparent dramatic appeal to all who would claim acquaintanceship, at the same time to provide a happy, even affectionate, nickname by which I should not only be acclaimed on sight but also be a symbol of dependability in general conversation.

As you know, they called me "Minx," a name which, I hope and believe, has gained added esteem and trust over the miles.

* * *

I WAS brought up in no spoon-fed nursery! From the outset they planned to send me, both directly and in response to invitations, to all corners of the world.

I shall never, never forget the day I was first introduced to my thousands of would-be adoptors at Olympia in 1931. They pawed and petted, stepped back in adoration as if I was something quite unreal, something too, too desirable for words, and if they did not actually submit the usual "goo, goo" and "umpsey, wumpsey," they certainly ejected equally admiring expletives.

Soon, of course, I was admitted into the homes of increasing thousands of admirers—the "apple of the eye," so to speak, of father, mother, sister and brother, all over the country and in the lands beyond the seas.

Many of the latter, by the way, felt me to be the first of my kind ever to reach their shores, but the secret could be held no longer. Months before I was publicly announced, I had completed long, long periods of probationary service in their actual countries and localities. I was, in fact, no experiment at all, but a fully tried and tested member of the family, having proved my worthiness in all things on my own showing.

* * *

WELL, where have I been and what have I accomplished over the past 21 years—sorry, 21,000,000,000 miles?

I have encircled the globe innumerable times, accepted the all-in challenges in ever increasing internationally competitive markets, gained my degrees at home, my diplomas abroad, my colours everywhere, yet am I still entirely unconceited by the encouraging measure of accomplishment attributed to me and to those who conceived my entry into a discriminating and problematical world.

Which reminds me: in World War II, I also shared the tests and trials of service endurance, the long and endless hours of duty and the ever changing destinies of world-wide armageddon with the British Tommy and Jack and their Air Force pals, together with their allies, in all theatres of war. On demobilisation I, too, faced the many and urgent problems of resettlement, the while aiding in the repair of the vast ravages of war not, by any stretch of imagination, without their marks on the home front!

* * *

BUT let me now wind back the miles of recollection to the year 1932.

Already I was on the lists of countless would-be patrons, but one person who, perhaps, was specially intrigued with my capabilities in those early days was my old friend Captain T. Yates Benyon, late of the Indian Army.

He had a great idea!

Due for a return visit to the Far East at the time, he thought it would be an excellent notion to take me with him, or rather I to take him, on the 6,800 miles overland journey all the way—France, Belgium, Germany, Austria, Iraq, Persia, Turkey, Afghanistan, Baluchistan and India and on then to Calcutta.

That in itself was a pretty ambitious undertaking but, just to give useful incentive and interest, he conceived the added idea of setting out, as well as to save money on the trip, to beat the popular mail boat service, on time, by racing the S.S. *Manora* between London and Calcutta.

Did we? No!

But we could have done! I say "we" pointedly, because at one time Captain Benyon was long prostrate with malaria due to exposure to the sun in the deserts and plains, plus other physical stresses as well as unexpected official delays on the journey, while I, unperturbed by these mortal problems, continued to press on for just so long as my head was set in the required direction. As we entered Quetta, Baluchistan, the *Manora* slipped silently into Calcutta. But for the "unexpected," we should have reached journey's end with time to spare.

I recall, too, another epic dual performance, that in 1932, when, with William Hatfield, novelist and explorer, we covered the 8,000 miles circuit of Australia, through bush and arid plain, barren waste and jungle swamp, against all manner of hazards, setting up a record for the journey as yet unbeaten.

Then, in South Africa in 1933, this time with H. C. Leon, of Johannesburg, we succeeded, against many teams of intrepid contestants, in the notorious 1,500 miles R.A.C. Cape Town motor race, in claiming the coveted Premier Award.

Back home again in the same year, I

Autobiography of the Minx: (Continued from page 23)

remember, there was my "brilliant performance," as they said, in the special R.A.C. observed "running-costs" trial, "How far for Five Guineas?"

How far?

Exactly 2,364 miles, averaging 36·5 m.p.g. around Great Britain and Scotland.

* * *

ABOUT this time, I remember, there was that other notable step of mine—to lead the fashion in automobile radio, a development being handled by the majority of my friends only as an afterthought. I refer, of course, to my more intensely musical counterpart, the "Melody Minx," a model which had a marked following and which at least proved the principle of radio in the car. To-day automobile radio equipment is available for ready incorporation in all my kith and kin.

* * *

NOR must I forget that other unique guise of mine about this stage of my story, truly a sensation of the day, i.e., when I appeared as an "Aero" enthusiast employing all the then known aerodynamics in the aim for a still higher turn of speed on the basis of super streamlining, low centre of gravity and high-efficiency safety-performance. The lessons we learned in those early years have stood us all in good stead ever since.

* * *

LATER still, there was that other unforgettable journey, at the behest of Captain E. O. Kellett (who, sad to recall, was killed in the North Africa campaign) and Mrs. Kellett, when we conducted a six months' intensive survey of the entire Africa routes between Algiers and the Cape.

* * *

MY stay in Africa seemed extended at this stage, for it was in 1935 that, with E. E. James, we also secured the Premier Award in the 1,000 miles Africa Reliability Trial, to be followed, later that year, by our successful performance in the "2,000 miles Cape Town to Johannesburg and return," in just under 48 hours!

Then, in 1936, I met young Dick Slabber and Harry Zahn, when they chose me as the third in the trio to enter that arduous 2,000 miles day-and-night Cape-Rand-Cape trial, to bring off, just as they planned, one more of the much contested Premier Awards.

Yes, we collected the trophies in Africa in plenty, and it was about this time that I was told my reputation was "truly golden"—showing a return, to 1936 end, of £8,500,000 in world patronage.

The figure to-day? It must be of astronomical proportions!

* * *

WHILE minded of Africa, I hasten to refer to another stalwart champion of mine, none other, of course, than George Hinchliffe who, in early 1952 with James Bulman and I, smashed all existing records for the London-Cape Town journey—a distance of 10,500 miles—by blazing over desert and jungle in the amazing time of 21 days. No mean endurance effort, this, considering my modest proportions, nor when considering, and George will bear me out, his more recent and terrific achievement on the Humber Super Snipe, when he knocked no fewer than eight days off our time! "Uncle Humber" is a much bigger chap, of course, than I, and there is no animosity on either side.

* * *

SIMILARLY, the U.S.A., Canada, Argentina, the Caribbean, the Middle East— every country under the sun, in fact—are included in those of my endless miles. And in every country, too, my younger brothers have gone continuously over the years, in small numbers and in large ships crammed full, fully to uphold the prestige I created in my pioneering journeys.

* * *

NOR should I omit the many, and equally remarkable, competition successes nearer and within home shores. The "Circuit of Ireland" trials of 1950, for example. We won the Team Prize on that occasion. The Monte Carlo Rally in which, among other shining tributes, Maurice Anderson, of Newton Mearns, Scotland, has on five successive occasions inspired me to receive the Premier Award for the best entry in my class for Rally-touring-comfort. The Mexican road race, too, in which they awarded me 2nd, 6th and 7th places, losing first honours only to the big Alfa Romeo. Good luck to the winner; but we certainly forced the pace!

* * *

WHY shouldn't I be proud, then, of past achievements? Why should I not rejoice on gaining my majority?

* * *

MY pride includes, too, my great respect for the courage and prowess of all my companions, good, solid team work all the time. And not only in the world of competition, but in everyday conditions, in running my master and mistress to the office, the shops, for the week-end jaunt, the annual touring holiday, to the theatre, the golf club and on those many journeys, business bent, when questions of time and dependable service have been— always are, in fact—of major importance.

* * *

YES, 21,000,000,000 miles is a long, long journey, and I have enjoyed every yard of the way. Sharing many of these, I feel I should add, is the writer of my story; he, as well as being at my christening, has been among my most ardent admirers throughout the years; he who will be celebrating my 21st birthday, both officially and in his own manner by browsing over his maps and records of our countless journeys together, through nearly all Europe and Scandinavia, with never once a word of complaint on either side—and only I know to what merciless tasks he has so often subjected me—he whom I affectionately call "Uncle Tom" and he, of me, "Minxie."

Way back in 1931 he openly prophesied that I had "come to stay," as the best possible answer to the far-reaching demand for a reliable, economical and competent travel companion for the whole family, individually or collectively, at home or abroad. And he still thinks as kindly of me to-day. Of course, I am proud!

* * *

THAT, then, is my story, with every mile in the 21,000,000,000— which figure, incidentally, I consider an under-statement! —its happy and pleasurable memory.

May I be privileged to serve my patrons, present and potential inclusively, for millions of miles to come. T.R.M.

April, 1953

AND NOW THE "ANNIVERSARY" MINX

Elegance, Comfort, Refined Performance

Leader of light cars

FEW British cars can lay claim to such continuity of success as that attaching to the Hillman range, and particularly to the Hillman Minx.

In the 21 years since it was first introduced—even in 1932 when it launched "Cushioned Power" it was acclaimed a great and unique advance in quality light-car development—the Hillman Minx has gone from strength to strength.

To-day it represents one of the most popular cars of its class anywhere in the world. It has sold in its thousands week after week and its scores of thousands year after year. You see it everywhere, at home and abroad, with models almost of every vintage since the first still going strong. In short, the Hillman Minx by its own appearance and behaviour on the road has been its own advertisement, each for beauty of line with high tone finish; robust, safety performance in relation to family motoring needs and for long and dependable service. Its economic operating costs have been a theme song, composed by its owners in the earliest years, and still a favourite overture in the pride of ownership.

The Anniversary Minx Saloon—new, smart, beautifully styled, combined with dependable performance and low operating costs.

The Minx Convertible Coupé—three cars in one, Saloon style when closed, Coupé de Ville, and Open Tourer, as depicted.

Left: Rear screen of the Californian Hard Top Model — corner pillars dispensed with, full range rear vision to rigid but light weight hard top.

Bottom left: Depicting the commodious and more rigid luggage locker, flat flooring over all. Spare wheel and tools housed in special compartment below luggage level.

Below: The Hillman Estate car—an old favourite in a new guise. Has two double loading doors at back; front seats are of separate bucket type; rear occasional seats entirely concealed when not in use.

The new Californian Hard Top Model—fashionable compromise between Saloon and Coupé. Note clear view all-round vision; windows drop down into body panels.

HOWEVER, to mark the commemoration of the 21st birthday celebration of the smallest in the Hillman range, we now see a new star—the "Anniversary" Minx—itself a fully fledged adult with all the mature strength, vitality, ease of movement and commonsense application of power, roominess and speed acquired in first hand, long experience over the years.

In its new form it is brimful of up-to-date and fully tried features—more refined appearance, greater power, added riding comfort, greater all-round safety, increased driving simplicity and still more impressive performance.

* * *

STUDY the new styling of the front end, attractive, bold, practical. Observe, too, the neat continuity of line through to the graceful rear end combining inbuilt twin tail lamps with

April, 1953

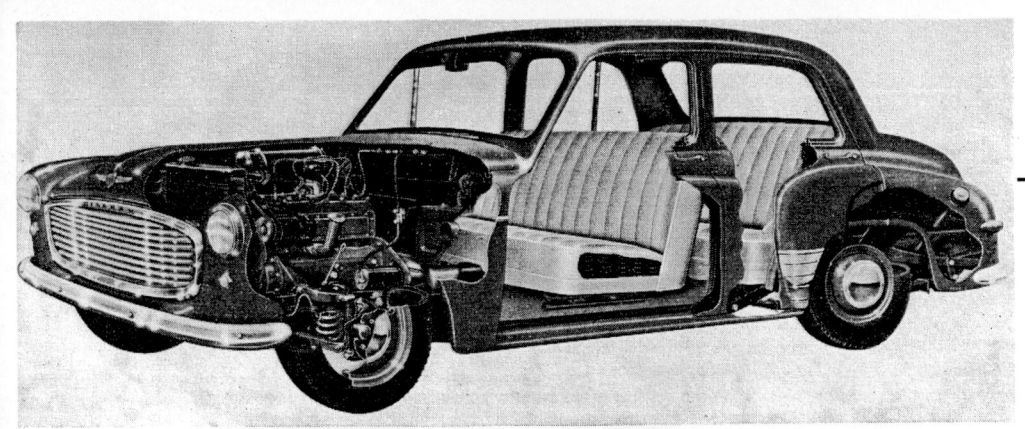

Sectioned view, featuring the all-steel unitary construction, well balanced deeply sprung upholstery, generous overall leg, head and shoulder room and marked comfort/safety design throughout.

Left: All-steel unitary construction in detail—permitting maximum strength with minimum weight. Absence of rattle, great rigidity, freedom from distortion under load and fine body styling are characteristics of the Anniversary Minx.

Below: New, highly efficient ventilation system permits greater selectivity of fresh air entering the car. Volume of air is directed to car interior by independent control on facia. The second duct can be fitted, as extra, for use in climatic extremes.

twin stop-lights operated by brake pedal lever; the generous clear view advantages to driver and passengers (large front and rear screens and side windows), the "quality comfort" seating, adequate head, leg and shoulder room for all occupants, the appealing new style facia with neatly grouped driving instruments, the smart two-spoke steering wheel with natural rake steering column, flooring free of all obstruction, unusually wide doors, the large capacity luggage locker blending tidily with the car's overall balance of line; in short, its pre-eminent craftsmanship throughout.

Under the bonnet, too, are more agreeable developments—easier accessibility still to all engine features, for chassis and engine lubrication and battery maintenance; an engine of still greater efficiency resulting from the redesigned combustion chamber contributing to smoother running qualities and, notably, the thermostatic heat-controlled manifold system making for easy starting and maximum power build-up with minimum fuel consumption. These, with the new pattern cast-iron detachable cylinder head, efficient side-valve design, together introduce a newer interpretation entirely in sturdy power co-related with economical operating costs: the family man's problem is thus solved while retaining all desirable quality and efficiency.

* * *

EVERYTHING for the driver is at the finger tips—gear lever mounted beneath the steering wheel linking full control-ring synchromesh top, third and second gear ratios, hand brake lever within easy reach of the right hand, neatly grouped and softly illuminated instrument panel, with ready-to-hand control knobs for starter switch, wipers, lights and choke, the dipswitch headlight control being pedal effected.

Add to these: sun visor, quick-action door levers, window lifts, ash trays, driving mirror, adjustable bench type front seat, press-button door handles (door wedges giving rigid hold over all surfaces), adjustable ventilation front window panels, interior ventilation system, roof light, side armrests to rear seat, with, as optional extras, H.M.V. automobile radio, heating and ventilating equipment, over-riders and Rootes Group rimfinishers and you will begin to appreciate the practical as well as the comprehensive approach that is embodied regarding driving and riding ease and comfort.

Take now the new suspension system—independent coil springs (in silico manganese) to front end, long semi-elliptic rear springs, Armstrong hydraulic double-acting "R" piston type shock absorbers all round (with steel and rubber bushes generally eliminating superfluous lubrication points) retaining maximum resiliency at all speeds over all road surfaces. In effect, road shocks are "ironed out" as soon as encountered, contributing with the improved Burman worm and peg steering mechanism, to notably light yet positive manoeuvrability, accurate to the fraction, reliable in regard to varying speeds and loads.

Braking, too, of Lockheed hydraulic two-leading-shoe pattern, is refined in design and operation, giving effectual retarding powers at all rates of travel—smoothly, evenly, with minimum physical effort.

* * *

NOT only are all those features that matter most to the discriminating motorist—roominess, comfort, performance, safety and reliability – the fundamental basis of the new "Anniversary" Minx, but in performance they reflect what the superior quality body design and finish compels in outward general appearance.

More than this, its advantageous economics—in outlay and operating costs—is not the least of its main attractions. Nor is the mine of successful experience acquired in 21 years of world-wide usage to be casually overlooked: it is the foundation on which the "Anniversary" Minx is lifted to a new high plane of engineering excellence.

* * *

CONSIDER now the choice of the three attractive models available—(a), the Minx Saloon; (b) the Minx Convertible Coupé and (c), an entirely new style, the Californian Hard Top, a fashionable compromise between (a) and (b). There is also the Hillman Estate Car. We illustrate the full range.

The new Californian Hard Top is certain to have a keen following: it is smart, eminently practical with fixed head yet providing most of the advantages of an open car—wide panoramic front and rear screens (the latter being cornerless), windows that lie concealed, when lowered within the body panels, elimination of side pillars the while preserving rigidity of construction and

BRIEF SPECIFICATION
ENGINE: Four cylinder, monobloc, side by side valves, three-bearing crankshaft, three-bearing camshaft, downdraught carburetter with special cold starting device and thermostatic heat controlled manifold system. Air silencer: "cushioned-power" engine mounting.
Bore, 65 m.m.; stroke, 95 m.m.; 1,265 c.c. engine develops 37.5 b.h.p. at 4,200 r.p.m.
IGNITION: Coil and distributor.
COOLING: Centrifugal pump and four-leaded fan.
CLUTCH: Borg and Beck, single dry-plate type.
GEARBOX: Four speeds, control ring synchromesh top, third and second. Ratios: Top, 5.22—1; second, 12.89—1; first, 16.64—1.
UNITARY construction of chassis and body.
FRONT SUSPENSION: Independent, silico manganese coil springs.
REAR SUSPENSION: Semi-elliptics. Armstrong "R" hydraulic shock-absorbers all round.
WHEELS: Fine "Easi-Clean" disc. Tyres: Dunlop 5.00 x 16.
BRAKES: Lockheed two-leading-shoes system, hydraulic operation.
STEERING: Worm and peg.
ELECTRICAL: Lucas 12 volt 38 amp. hrs.
FOUR CORNER jacking system.
WHEEL BASE: 93 ins. **Width** 62 ins.
FRONT TRACK: 48⅝ ins.
REAR TRACK: 48½ ins.
GROUND CLEARANCE: 7 ins.
WEIGHT: Saloon, unladen, 2,107 lb.

April, 1953

Below: Functional beauty describes the new instrument panel, with neatly grouped instrumentation. Note neat two-spoke steering wheel and synchromatic gear-change lever, steering column mounted.

Right: The beautifully appointed interior of the "Anniversary" Minx Saloon—light, roomy, comfortable, with maximum attention to detail. Front bench type seat is adjustable to suit any driver.

Right: Provision is made for optional fitting of H.M.V. automobile radio, heating and ventilation equipment.

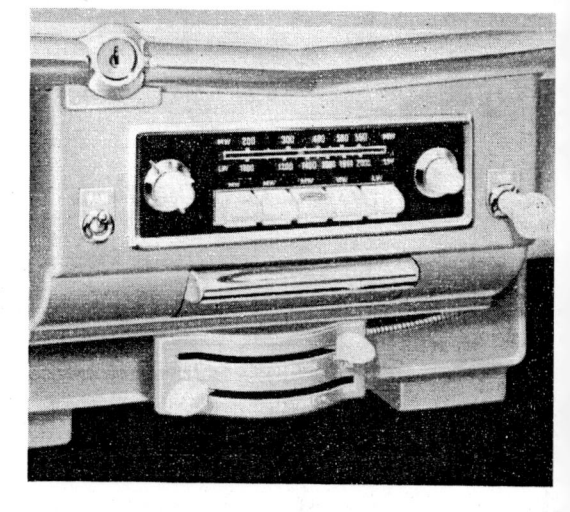

Press button door locks are fitted to Minx Saloon and Hillman Estate Car, eliminating rattle and giving long durable service.

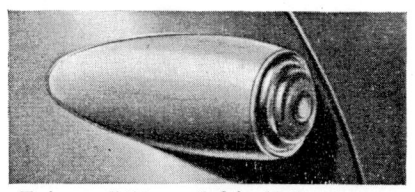

Twin rear lights, neatly faired into a streamlined housing, indicate car's full width, also incorporate twin "stop" lighting.

Specially designed thermostatically operated induction heat control gives easy starting and getaway, improved engine performance with less fuel consumption. A valve in the exhaust manifold deflects hot gases back over the induction system, assuring quicker and more efficient vaporisation.

Below: The power unit of the Hillman range is a compact, highly efficient unit bristling with advanced engineering features —vigorous performance, running silence, greater flexibility and more economical fuel consumption.

Independent front coil suspension with improved shock absorbers contribute to smoother riding, more precise steering and exceptional manoeuvrability.

notably clear all round vision. A thing of beauty and distinction from wing tip to wing tip, the new Californian Hard Top is destined to be a leading topic for a long time between motorists everywhere.

* * *

MODERN, too, is the choice of colour schemes available:

Minx Saloon and Convertible Coupé—Mid-green, light-fawn upholstery; golden sand, red upholstery; quartz blue, light fawn upholstery; black, red upholstery; black, light-fawn upholstery; claret, light-fawn upholstery.

Hillman Californian Hard Top—Ivory, black top, red upholstery; Balmoral grey, quartz blue top, red upholstery; pastel green, bottle green top, light-fawn upholstery; Limestone green, claret top, red upholstery.

Hillman Estate Car—Beech green, red or brown upholstery; cruiser grey, red or brown upholstery.

* * *

THE Hillman Estate car is an old favourite, of course, with its unique passenger-cum-bulk loading facilities whether for club, hotel or station use with passengers and luggage, transportation of goods or produce, or in Estate routine operation.

Three persons can be accommodated on the folding and disappearing occasional rear seat. Conversion is effected in a few seconds.

* * *

SO now, gentlemen, we introduce the Hillman "Anniversary" range for 1953 coupled with a welcome newcomer, the Californian Hard Top, a model that will do honour indeed to a highly respected marque.

April, 1953

The successful drivers in the 1952 International Alpine Trials, with their intrepid team manager, and, below, the coveted Dewar Trophy.

Sporting Spotlights:

Club News and Personalities

Sunbeam-Talbot is awarded premier status for 1952.

THE award of the Dewar Trophy for the most outstanding engineering and technical achievement during 1952 has been made by the Royal Automobile Club to Sunbeam-Talbot, Ltd., for the outstanding performance of Sunbeam-Talbot cars in the 1952 International Alpine Rally.

In this most arduous of motor competitions, the Sunbeam-Talbot cars obtained three Coupes des Alpes, out of a total of 10 only awarded in 1952; were awarded the manufacturers' team prize for the best team performance irrespective of size, class, or nationality; won a further team prize for the best team performance by foreign cars; occupied first, second, and third places in the 2-3-litre class of the complete event; were awarded a special cup for the outstanding performance during the 1952 event.

The cars were Sunbeam-Talbot Model "90," and the No. I drivers were G. Murray-Frame, J. M. Hawthorn, and Stirling Moss.

THE Sunbeam-Talbot Owners' Club is able to report a most satisfactory 1952 season in every way. Membership at 1,200 shows an increase of 300; programme of events for 1952 was bigger than ever; finances have never been more sound. Attendance at most functions was excellent. There was a first class turnout, particularly for the Southport Rally in April, which attracted over 100 cars with 350 members and their friends taking part.

The Club looks forward to the continued interest and co-operation of all members.

Week-end Rallies

Once again the most successful meetings in 1952 were the week-end rallies at popular seaside resorts. Arrangements have already been made to pay return visits this year to Southport, Eastbourne, Scarborough and Bournemouth. It has been proved during the past year that these rallies are very much more popular when they incorporate a competitive road section as well as the usual driving tests at the rallying point. Each week-end rally this year will include a road section of at least 200 miles.

Afternoon Trials

A number of afternoon "trials" is to be arranged in different parts of the country.

Continental Rallies

Last year's Continental Rally to Germany and Austria ("Rallye Tyrol") was voted a great success by all the 64 members who took part.

Arrangements have now been made for the coming summer, and in response to many requests there will be two Continental rallies this year, one in June ("Rallye Portofino") and one in August ("Rallye des Lacs").

Harold Eldred and Harold Cundall Trophy Winners, 1952

The Harold Eldred trophy is awarded each year to the Club member who has obtained the most marks in competitive events throughout the year. The Harold Cundall trophy is a similar award intended for the Club member *living in Yorkshire* who has obtained the most marks throughout the year.

The winners of these two aggregate trophies for 1952 are as follows:—

The Harold Eldred Trophy: Gordon Greaves (St. Annes-on-Sea).

The Harold Cundall Trophy: P. Rawlin (Keighley).

Final placings in these competitions were as follows:—

1st—G. Greaves, St. Annes-on-Sea, 60 points.
2nd—P. Rawlin, Keighley, 43 points.
3rd—P. C. Harper, Stevenage, 35 points.
4th—J. Nott, Luton, 33 points.
5th—A. H. George, Farnham Common, 30 points.
6th—L. Tanner, Minchinhampton, 29 points.

Marks for both trophies were awarded as follows:—

For *attendance* at any S.T.O.C. function (excluding dinner-dances, Continental rallies and the annual general meeting), 1 mark awarded.
For *competing* in any S.T.O.C. trial, rally, treasure hunt, gymkhana, concours d'elegance, etc., 1 mark awarded.
For every 1st place gained, 5 marks awarded.
For every 2nd place gained, 4 marks awarded.
For every 3rd place gained, 3 marks awarded.
For every 4th place gained, 2 marks awarded.
For finishing in any of above, 1 mark awarded.

A complete list of all prize winners in 1952 events is published.

Perpetual Challenge Trophies

1952 holders of the Club's perpetual challenge trophies are as follows:—

The Harold Eldred Trophy—G. Greaves, St. Annes-on-Sea; The Harold Cundall Trophy—P. Rawlin, Keighley; The Stanley Gambles Trophy—R. D. Lodge, Stockport; The H. T. Kirby Trophy—R. Clark, Berkhamsted; The Sydney Latimer Trophy—G. Greaves, St. Annes-on-Sea; The Eastbourne Trophy—P. Slatter, Kingswood; The Sunbeam-Talbot Yorkshire Distributor's Trophy—M. G. Briggs, Horsforth.

London Branch of the S.T.O.C.

A London Branch of the Club was formed in November last under the chairmanship of Mr. G. W. Rossiter and with Miss Marjorie Tinckham as the organising secretary.

Miss Tinckham will be remembered by all pre-war members of the Club as a

MONTE CARLO RALLY
ROOTES GROUP SUCCESSES

Sunbeam-Talbot
wins
TEAM PRIZE

for best performance nominated team of 3 cars

DRIVERS: S. MOSS · L. JOHNSON · G. IMHOF

GRAND PRIX d'HONNEUR

DU CONCOURS DU CONFORT

DRIVER: B. PROOS HOOGENDIJK

Hillman Minx

wins its class in comfort competition for fifth successive year

DRIVER: M. B. ANDERSON

(*Subject to official confirmation*)

ROOTES GROUP CARS BUILT FOR THE ROADS OF THE WORLD

April, 1953

leading light in T.O.C. and S.T.O.C. affairs and the Club is delighted to have her once more taking an active part in club matters.

The opening meeting of the London branch took place on November 23 and was an outstanding success. It will be noted from the calendar for 1953 that a number of events are being arranged by the branch committee.

Annual General Meeting

The Club's annual general meeting took place on Friday, February 27, at Gunter's Restaurant, 6, Stanhope Gate, London, W.1. The meeting was followed by a cocktail party and buffet and film show featuring excellent colour films of last year's Monte Carlo and Alpine Rallies as well as one or two other short films of motoring interest.

Suggestions and Criticisms

The Club welcomes members' criticisms and suggestions. If you have any ideas for future events which you think the Club might be able to use, please write to the Organising Secretary, F. J. Nutt, Sunbeam-Talbot Owners' Club, Ryton-on-Dunsmore, near Coventry, Warwickshire.

* * *

THE R.A.C. Calendar of national and club events for 1953 shows no sign of diminution, over 700 events being listed on the provisional calendar.

With a view to sorting things out the London M.C. are taking the lead in forming an Association of Southern Clubs. The Association of Northern Clubs has been operating for some time with a good measure of success in avoiding clashing of dates and other internal arrangements.

The position in the South, however, is somewhat complicated by the very large number of clubs involved as compared with the North, and the only obvious solution to the over-crowding of the calendar is for the clubs to agree to a weeding out of certain events for the common good.

The team of Sunbeam-Talbots at their Monte Carlo headquarters.

THE Sunbeam-Talbot was awarded the manufacturers' team prize, the coveted Charles Faroux Cup, in the Monte Carlo Rally for the "best performance of three cars nominated as a team." It was the first time a British make of car had secured this success in 21 years. The drivers were Stirling Moss (who finished sixth in the general classification), Leslie Johnson and Godfrey Imhof.

Miss Sheila Van Damm, also driving a Sunbeam-Talbot, narrowly missed winning the Ladies' Cup. Miss Van Damm and a Frenchwoman were the only two to reach the final regularity test, where the Sunbeam-Talbot lost vital minutes over a puncture (left) and so took second place.

In the comfort competition the Grand Prix d'Honneur for the car best equipped for winter motoring went to a Sunbeam-Talbot driven by a Dutchman, B. Proos Hoogendyk.

For the fifth successive year M. B. Anderson, of Newton Mearns, Renfrewshire, won the 1,500 c.c. class for the best equipped Rally car with his Hillman Minx Saloon.

THE London Branch of the Sunbeam-Talbot Owners' Club is opening its 1953 season with a dinner-dance to be held on March 27, at the Berkeley Rooms, Zeeta House, Putney High Street, S.W.15. Tickets (25s.) can be obtained from the Hon. Secretary at Ladbroke Hall, Barlby Road, London, W.10. Applications will be in strict rotation.

THE Club's annual Newcastle dinner-dance which took place at the Station Hotel fully rewarded by a large and enthusiastic attendance the excellent arrangements and organisation of those popular Club leaders, Mr. Cliff Wheeler and his son Derek. It was Northumberland's night out according to all reports; they made the most of it!

SUNBEAM-TALBOT OWNERS' CLUB

SUMMARY OF PRIZE WINNERS 1952 SEASON

COTSWOLD TRIAL—March 9
Class A:
  1st. W. E. Ford, Wolverhampton
  2nd. G. Greaves, St. Annes-on-Sea
Class B:
  1st. P. C. E. Harper, Stevenage
  2nd. J. D. Parsonage, Ludlow

YORKSHIRE TRIAL—March 23
Class A:
  1st. R. D. Lodge, Stockport
  2nd G. Greaves, St. Annes-on-Sea
Class B:
  1st. J. D. Leavesley, Burton-on-Trent
  2nd. R. Walshaw, Halifax

SOUTHPORT RALLY—April 19-20
Class A:
  1st. R. Clark, Berkhamsted
  2nd. L. Tanner, Minchinhampton
Class B:
  1st. R. Walshaw, Halifax
  2nd. K. Gregory, London
Class C:
  1st. G. C. Simon, Gloucester
  2nd. B. Campbell, Manchester
Novices award: I. J. Phillips, Rochester
Ladies' award: Miss M. Walker, Wooler

CONCOURS d'ELEGANCE
  1st. P. Rawlin, Keighley
  2nd. G. Greaves, St. Annes-on-Sea
  3rd. L. Tanner, Minchinhampton
  4th. S. Woolf, Manchester

SOUTH WALES TREASURE HUNT—April 26
  1st. A. S. Brooks, Brecon
  2nd. G. F. Grizelle, Dinas Powis
  3rd. F. B. Proudfoot, Barry

BEDFORD GYMKHANA—May 18
  1st. G. Greaves, St. Annes-on-Sea
  2nd. A. G. Goodwin, Harrow
  3rd. P. Rawlin, Keighley

EASTBOURNE RALLY—May 24-25
Class A:
  1st. P. Slatter, Kingswood
  2nd. J. Nott, Luton
Class B:
  1st. P. C. E. Harper, Stevenage
  2nd. G. W. Rossiter, London
Novices Award: A. S. Lusty, London
Concours d'Elegance:
  1st. L. Tanner, Minchinhampton
  2nd. P. Rawlin, Keighley
  3rd. R. H. Austin, London
  4th. H. J. Budd, London

SCOTTISH RALLY, TURNBERRY—June 14-15
Class A:
  1st. G. Greaves, St. Annes-on-Sea
  2nd. D. Norbury, Malton
Class B:
  1st. R. Walshaw, Halifax
  2nd. R. A. Dando, Manchester
Concours d'Elegance:
  1st. Miss M. Walker, Wooler
  2nd. P. Rawlin, Keighley
  3rd. G. Greaves, St. Annes-on-Sea

NORTHUMBERLAND TREASURE HUNT—July 13
  1st. R. F. Moffat, Newcastle-on-Tyne
  2nd. J. R. Steadman, Monkseaton
  3rd. T. A. Boothroyd, Bishop Auckland

CHILTERNS TRIAL—July 27
Class A:
  1st. F. Downs, Andover
  2nd. A. J. M. Milner, Tolworth
Class B:
  1st. P. C. E. Harper, Stevenage
  2nd. E. A. Lloyd Davies, Wolverhampton

GLOUCESTERSHIRE GYMKHANA—August 10
  1st. L. Tanner, Minchinhampton
  2nd. E. Barnfield, Gloucester
  3rd. M. F. Orchard, Gloucester

SCOTTISH TREASURE HUNT—September 13
  1st. R. L. Sharp, Edinburgh
  2nd. H. R. Anderson, Glasgow
  3rd. A. Martin, Glasgow

SURREY TREASURE HUNT—September 21
  1st. G. T. Lewis, Sutton
  2nd. A. R. Corner, Carshalton
  3rd. A. H. George, Farnham Common

SCARBOROUGH RALLY—September 27-28
Class A:
  1st. M. G. Briggs, Horsforth
  2nd. R. Clark, Berkhamsted
Class B:
  1st. P. C. E. Harper, Stevenage
  2nd. R. A. Dando, Manchester
Novices Award: R. B. Brydon, Wetheral
Concours d'Elegance:
  1st. P. Rawlin, Keighley
  2nd. J. Nott, Luton
  3rd. G. Greaves, St. Annes-on-Sea

LONDON "PICTURE HUNT"—November 23
  1st. G. T. Lewis, Sutton
  2nd. F. Willinger, London
  3rd. J. Paterson, London

BOURNEMOUTH RALLY—December 6
Class A:
  1st. P. C. E. Harper, Stevenage
  2nd. E. Elliott, York
Class B:
  1st. G. R. Lindsay, Whetstone
  2nd. G. W. Shingler, Salisbury
Novices Award: J. R. Beardall, Whatton-in-the-Vale
Ladies' Award: Miss F. Howell, Lewes

THE New 21ST ANNIVERSAR[Y]

* Completely new appearance
* All round increased economy
* More comfort
* Still gr[eater value] in every detail

Yes, it really [is 21 years since the Hi]llman Minx made its first po[pular] appearance! A fine car even in 1932, the Minx has been progressivel[y de]veloped and improved ever since; and to-day, with well over 21,000 m[illion] miles of happy family motoring to its credit, the Minx is part of the fab[ric of] life in almost every country in the world. To celebrate this great occa[sion,] here is the 21st Anniversary Minx . . . the most brilliant, the thri[ftiest,] the most reliable family car of all time!

21 years, and 21,000 MILLION MIL[ES]

HILLMAN MOTOR CAR CO. LIMITED COVENTRY · LONDON SHOWROOM[S]

Three - piece relaxation outfit by Tizzoni-Milano in red woven trousers with high-necked, fully sleeved, black jersey sweater. Outside is sleeveless coat worn also as sun dress.

Plaid skirt, by Deréta, with pointed pocket banded in jersey to match Elizabethan jester-cap. Above right: Anne Gunning wears a Dorville wasp-striped off-shoulder singlet, a new note in country casual clothes.

999 is the significant number for 1953– Spring Suggestions by Brigid de Vine

ALREADY 555, 33, 57 and even 1212, have special significance for the public.

This Spring 999 stands for the number of colours available in easy form for the redecoration of your home in Coronation Year.

In March, Jenson and Nicholson, Ltd., makers of Robbialac paints, introduce into this country the most revolutionary development in the history of the paint industry. It is an adaptation of the famous " Colorizer " system already known on the other side of the Atlantic.

You will simply go to your stockist and select the colour you want from a magnificent album. Then you buy a tin of white or grey base paint and with it a tube of colourant numbered according to the shade you have selected. Add the tube of colourant to your tin of base—it is as easy as putting milk in tea—stir once or twice and you have a perfectly blended tin of paint guaranteed to give the precise colour you have seen in the book.

To begin with, this new system will be available only in London and the Home Counties, but it will gradually be extended all over the country. Meantime out-of-town enthusiasts will be able to sample the system through the large London stores, Harrods, Selfridges, etc.,

The tubes come in various sizes for various quantities of base paint. You can try out a small tube in a small tin of paint, and if you like the test panel then you can order larger tubes and larger quantities of base in the absolute certainty that the shade produced will be exactly the same as the panel. And no matter how exotic a shade is wanted, not more than two tubes of colourant are ever required to obtain a " dead-on " match!

Can you imagine what this means to the enthusiastic home decorator as well as to architects and other professionals? With a choice of 999 colours you can pick out exactly the shade you want for ceilings, walls and paintwork and to fit in with your colour scheme for curtains and carpets. The strips of colour in the wonderful Colorizer album are made to detach so that you can actually try them against samples of wallpaper, upholstery materials, carpets, and so on, in the shop *or at home*.

I have always admired the ambitious colour schemes of American home decorators : I can see that with the Colorizer system they are quite easy. The whole exciting world of colour is wide open now to us also.

* * *

ANOTHER system of saving trouble which has come to us across the seas is the new Wastemaster.

For many years American and Canadian homes have had a sink fitment for disposing of waste which cuts out the unpleasant sink tidy and those frequent trips to the dust bin.

The ordinary sink opening is enlarged slightly and a pulverising machine fitted underneath. All your vegetable peelings, tea leaves, etc., are just dropped into the sink opening, then you turn on the cold water tap, flick a switch to start the Wastemaster, and all the waste disappears down the drain into the sewer in a mass of tiny pulverised particles which in turn scour your drain pipes from those accumulations of soapy, greasy matter which often cause stoppages.

I saw bits of bone which had been through the machine and had been ground to powder—and something which looked like powdered toffee *had* been, I was assured, *a beer bottle!* Normally metal or crockery would not be put through the machine but everything else, rinds, ashtray ends, are all rinsed away in a moment.

Deréta skirt and stole combined; the stole can be knotted round the hips or tied casually around the shoulders. Has a tiny pocket in one corner.

Sheered white lambskin is used for this attractive bolero with its flattering roll collar and deep cuffs; price 26 gns., from the Sheepskin Shop.

Indian Lamb, three-quarter length coat, modelled on swing lines, with small roll collar, wide sleeves. Available in brown or black, lined with coloured silk. National Fur Co.

The Wastemaster which I saw demonstrated in one of the marvellous "planned kitchens" in the showrooms of Froy's at Hammersmith comes from New Zealand, from the firm which already produces the famous Dishmaster washing-up machine which, it is claimed, is better even than many American makes.

You can have a Dishmaster and a sink with the Wastemaster device fitted together in a 4 ft. unit for your kitchen and end the washing-up drudgery forever.

Unfortunately purchase tax makes the unit expensive, but think of the hours you spend washing-up every week.

Think how nice after a party just to stack the dishes into the machine and have them perfectly washed and sterilised in about three minutes, ready to drain themselves dry without using the tea cloth!

* * *

MENDING is another job which manufacturers are trying to lighten.

If you have a son whose shirts, you feel, should really be made of chain mail to stand up to the treatment they get, then do look out for another ingenious novelty in the "Plusmore" shirt.

Each shirt is supplied with spare buttons, an *extra* collar, *one size larger to allow for growth*, and a piece of material to allow for patching.

There are senior Plusmore shirts as well as the junior Plusmore models, and since husbands invariably find that one good quality shirt will outwear *three* collars and *two* pairs of cuffs, the men's shirts are supplied with an *extra* collar and a pair of cuffs.

For the Spring Bride, unversed in mending method as applied to men's shirts, there is even a *Plusmore Service* which, for the sum of 2s. 6d., enables you to send shirts back to the makers, via your retailer, for the collar and cuffs to be expertly attached.

I do not think that even American standards of "service" could go further than that. Plusmore shirts in both men's and boys' sizes should soon be available in most good stores.

* * *

OVER 500 shops are already stocking the newest idea for growing *daughters*, the new Judy Two-Size dresses.

Extra buttons and an extra piece of fabric for the tears that even the best behaved daughters may get are attached to a card given with each Judy dress, but the card bears, in addition, illustrated instructions *for making the dress one size larger when needed*. In fact your little daughter's favourite dress can "grow with her."

I saw Margot Lovell, of TV fame, demonstrating recently how easily the enlarging operation could be carried out— and in only half an hour. One snip with a scissors through three threads on the hem of the skirt and the hem can be dropped to its new length with a new hem already in place.

Unpicking an extra inside row of machining down each side seam enlarges the bodice. Then the bodice is lengthened as the waist drops, and if a larger neck and back are required it is simply a matter of moving a few buttons.

The whole dress becomes one size larger.

Yet the extra material is so cleverly arranged that the dress does not seem at all bulky at the seams when you first buy it.

Beauty of the finger tips

BEAUTY can be yours, at your fingertips, if you give your nails daily care. Wash the hands in warm, soapy water, to which you have added a few spots of lemon juice. Dry thoroughly.

While still warm, rub in vaseline or almond oil, or a good nail cream. Relaxing them from the wrist, shake the hands loosely a dozen times to stimulate circulation and keep wrists supple.

Hands which suffer from chilblains need additional exercise. Curl the fingers into the palm; with the fingers of the hand strike briskly downwards until the hands glow. Then pull and stroke each finger between first finger and thumb of opposite hand to keep the joints slim.

Wash now with warm soap-and-water to remove greasiness. Dry again, and ease back the cuticles very gently with a soft towel. Finally, sprinkle a rich hand cream, or skinfood, over the hands until the cream disappears.

* * *

Shape nails from side to centre with an emery board (they should just tip over the end of the finger itself). It's best not to file them too closely at the sides, or point them. If the tips are not attractive, whiten beneath them with an orange stick wound in cotton wool moistened in liquid shampoo, warm water, and a spot of peroxide.

When applying varnish, brush the first coat *across* the nails so that the sides get covered, too. When that is dry, apply the second *down* the nail. Run the tip of your thumb round the extreme edge to get a smooth line.

Don't forget; if you have any beauty troubles in Coronation Year, write to me, I'll be pleased to help you.

ANN M. CAPELL.

AFTER letting out you simply rinse it through and iron damp to remove any needle marks and if you have one of the new Falk Stadelman Featherlight irons that is a *very* light job.

The new iron weighs only 3 lb. instead of the usual 5 lb., is ready for use within 60 seconds of switching-on instead of five minutes, has a special groove for ironing buttons, and a heat-selector for different types of fabric.

It is now becoming available through stores and branches of the local Electricity Authority and means a great deal to housewives for it reduces both her fatigue and her current consumption.

Indeed, with all the savings now possible in time and money even a busy Mother may find herself "In the Mink."

Steiner, who uses a mink pom-pom to decorate one of his newest hair styles, has just introduced a new perfume named "Mink." It comes in a case like a barred cage with a real mink tail protruding between the bars and is labelled:

THIS PERFUME IS DANGEROUS!

It is recommended "*For interesting women, and men who adore being interested.*" If you wish to try it, "Mink"—"*as wild as can be*"—costs £5 15s.

Some are haughty — others are sporty

but all motorists agree...

Benzole makes good petrol better

NATIONAL BENZOLE MIXTURE

National Benzole Co. Ltd., Wellington House, Buckingham Gate, London, S.W.1.
(The distributing organisation owned & entirely controlled by the producers of British Benzole)

AN INVITATION –   – to Overseas Readers

ARE YOU COMING TO EUROPE THIS YEAR?

Let your visit, and your tour of the British Isles and neighbouring countries, be pleasurable throughout: a unique opportunity for Coronation Year

IF you are coming to Europe this year you will be thinking seriously, of course, on matters concerning the best and most interesting places to visit, the easiest routes to follow, the nicest hotels in which to stay and, quite naturally, how ideal it all could be if only these questions could be answered readily to your satisfaction.

* * *

NEXT, you may be troubled by the thought of the many irritating yet essential formalities covering your journey to England and/or to the Continent (including Scandinavia) alone maybe, or as one of a party, with your own car, or with the idea of obtaining one on arrival in the United Kingdom.

* * *

THEN you will remember that it is Coronation Year for the United Kingdom and have thoughts of being in town, in London or in the provinces—for they all will be celebrating this great National occasion—and the more you ponder you may wonder " how can you possibly do it ? "—especially as you will have considered also the possibility of visits to the Continent (France, Switzerland, Italy, Spain) or to Scandinavia ; all of which would mean a lot of planning, a lot of mathematics as to dates, times, costs, etc., not forgetting the many routine matters covering customs, visas where necessary, car and passenger shipment, currency problems and many other items which flow to your mind in a proposition otherwise as attractive as this.

* * *

LET us say at once it can be done and done well—comfortably, easily and systematically from start to finish, to take in every conceivable aspect embodied in either a short or protracted tour of the United Kingdom and/or its neighbouring Continental and Scandinavian countries.

The scheme to which we refer provides comprehensiveness and completeness to the smallest detail, also that while the organisers carry the entire burden of formality and routine you have only the pleasures to indulge.

* * *

THE itinerary is unique in all respects. It can last from May to September inclusive, taking the full programme in its stride, or arrangements can be effected for your joining and leaving the main and continuously running programme at a number of pre-determined stages.

What more would you wish in an organised European holiday of the kind—organised, perhaps in so far as routes, maps, hotels, excursions, etc., are concerned, but with freedom to motor according to personal mood and moment.

Would you wish for courier service, for mechanic aid in emergency, for interpreter service, for reliable touring guides and information, for qualified and expert leadership in planning the best objectives anywhere en route ; are these among your foremost needs ? Then rest assured that no angle in regard to these and many other facilities has been overlooked—they are, in fact, part and parcel of the structure of the scheme, a scheme that has packed experience of years of successful personal survey and application, leaving nothing to chance and nothing missed.

* * *

STARTING from London on May 6th, the opening stages make a complete tour of England, Scotland and Wales, terminating with a free period in London from May 30th to June 7th, purposely to include Coronation Week and all it means in colour, movement, pageantry and tradition.

On Monday, June 8th, the itinerary takes one across the English Channel for France, Spain, the Rivieras, Switzerland, Italy, Germany, Austria, returning via Switzerland, Belgium, Holland, Denmark, Sweden, Norway and so back to Scotland and South then through England and Wales again for London, reached on Monday September 6th.

Naturally, the pre-eminent of all beauty spots are included throughout the full programme, from the Pennines to the Apennines, Lochs to the Lakes, mountain chalet to Royal palace, road-side shrine to renowned cathedral, etc.—nothing barred.

* * *

THOSE who can accommodate the full programme would be fortunate indeed, each in regard to outstanding itinerary and the overall moderate cost considering the first class amenities and facilities provided inclusively.

Then there are those—no doubt in the majority—who must necessarily limit the duration of their visits to Europe.

These, too, are adequately catered for and in appealing style. For example, anyone can join the main itinerary at any one in a given series of dates and similarly break away at clearly defined points anywhere along the route. All it means is the selection of both starting and leaving centres and the dates that are best suited to individual requirements.

From this schedule also can be ascertained the inclusive charges as well as those appertaining to respective sections. Generally speaking, however, the full route, and those in regard to the shorter divisions, averages approximately £6 per day per person, plus car running expenses. It might help to suggest that the latter, covering, say, a 14-day period of the tour, would amount to something around £25.

Place this £6 per day in close focus with the opportunities for maximum holiday comfort and pleasures, minus all annoying formalities embodied in the routine essentials referred to, and the unique values offered will be appreciated.

* * *

YOU may now ask, " How does one go about securing reservations and, in this connection, how does one finalise matters in regard to the car—be it one's own, or the car to be purchased or hired—and other relative matters ? "

The answer is simple: make known your wishes to your local Rootes Group distributor or dealer who, you will find, will have copies of the full itinerary and schedules, and be fully conversant with the inclusive reaches of the scheme.

Don't be hesitant on account of personal doubts upon any point whatsoever. The scheme is applicable and adaptable to any set of conditions. It is as flexible as anything can be in affairs of this kind, and, as the direct result of long research, no set of circumstances have as yet been found to be outside the province of the scheme.

* * *

WHEN you study the full itinerary, the main and continuous programme or the outward and inward sub-sections, you will observe that there are seven occasions on which one can leave London and converge with the main programme and a like number of departures heading back to the Metropolis.

This grand " Coronation Tour " is water-tight in all respects. Because of attaching administrative essentials, however, all dates shown are rigid in relation to phases of joining and leaving, as also are the terms quoted. Coverage outside stipulated requirements can only be considered on respective merits and quoted for accordingly, the while one is assured, of course, of identically expert handling with equally reasonable costing.

* * *

DO not miss this unique opportunity—presented exclusively for consideration by owners and users of Humber, Hillman and Sunbeam-Talbot cars—endorsed in principle by the Rootes Group Export Division but facilitated through the Motorists' Travel Club of 109, Piccadilly, London, W.1. Enquiries must be referred in the first place, however, to your local Rootes Group distributor or dealer.

SUCCESS!

..."MARKED ABSENCE OF PINKING"

..."THREE OR FOUR MILES PER HOUR BETTER"

..."NOTHING BUT PRAISE"

..."QUICKER AND BETTER ACCELERATION"

—these are typical user reactions to the Delco-Remy Oil-Filled Coil. In fact, *all* the claims made for this remarkable coil have been confirmed by the high sales figures and unstinted praise accorded by public opinion. *Now* is the time to fit a Delco-Remy Oil-Filled Coil and ensure that your engine gets the best out of its branded petrol. Hermetically sealed against moisture and oil-filled for permanent insulation, it carries a two-year guarantee from Delco-Remy, the world's largest ignition equipment manufacturers with more than 40 years experience.

Consult your local garage or write for descriptive leaflet.

Delco-Remy
OIL-FILLED COIL

IS a better coil for ANY CAR!

LIST PRICE 36/- 6 AND 12 VOLT

DELCO-REMY-HYATT DIVISION OF GENERAL MOTORS LTD.
GROSVENOR ROAD · LONDON · S.W.1

"RALLYE OBERLAND":

our Continental holiday. There is still time — if you hurry!

Salines Park Hotel, Rhinefelden, Switzerland, popular rendezvous on this and previous Continental Rallies arranged by this journal.

MAKE no mistake, you will need to be fast if you are hopeful of joining fellow readers of this Journal on our annual Continental touring holiday.

As reservations are at the moment of going to press, we look like closing the list any day. Only a few vacancies remain and they will go, as far as possible, in the order of application.

Leaving Dover on July 18, we set off for a 15-day ideal tour of France and Switzerland — everything arranged en route covering hotels, cross-channel shipment, routine documents, maps, in regard to an itinerary quite the most appealing in all the post-war tours we have as yet facilitated.

Formality is eliminated almost entirely for participants, the organisers attending to all routine matters inseparable from overseas travel. You have only the pleasures of the trip and these are bountiful.

Off-loading at Calais, we proceed for the first night halt at Rheims. Convoy driving? Only in the early stages for newcomers to Continental touring; we know this opportunity is welcomed always by the few. Otherwise, with maps and clear instructions issued to all drivers, each party is free to make separate progress—providing always that they maintain a schedule ahead of that of the service mechanic who accompanies the Rallye throughout. To lag behind relieves the Rallye of all attaching emergency responsibilities.

From Rheims the way lies through the lovely Champagne country to spend the second night at Dijon, but, actually, the third day out is the star turn, that by entering Switzerland at Geneva and driving along the lake for delightful Montreux and the Palace Hotel, where we abide for two nights.

Montreux has all the interest and beauty you would expect, and if you are sorry to leave we press on, notwithstanding, over the Col du Pillon, one of the most picturesque motoring roads in all Europe, for Gstaad, settled so cosily in the Bernese Oberland, high in the mountains, offering comfort and holiday attractions in full measure.

You can take your choice from lazing on the lidos, trips by chair lift to the upper peaks, swimming, rambling, motoring excursions to unlimited points of scenic interest with always good comradeship about you.

* * *

OFF again on the morning of Saturday, July 25, we head for the mountains and later by Lake Lucerne aim for picturesque Brunnen and the homely, though majestic, Waldstattehof, already planning to welcome Rallye Oberland.

At Brunnen there is much of holiday atmosphere, boating, swimming, mountaineering, visits to Bourgenstock, Rigi, Seelisberg, excursions over the passes—the Furka, Grimsel, Susten, St. Gotthard—even the famous Simplon is within easy reach—with hotel conditions at day's end giving full opportunity to congratulate yourself on joining the party!

* * *

ROOMS, cuisine and comfort are ideal—and in end July the weather should be kindly, of course, our guarantee cannot embody this assurance. Anyhow, we have never in all post-war years had occasion to be disappointed.

On Tuesday, July 28th, we make the 100-odd miles for Basle, via Zurich and Baden (here to see the Rhine Falls), where our arrival is to be given perhaps official recognition. But, while at several points along the route little ceremonies of welcome will be offered—and offered with irresistible courtesy and warmth of greeting—these occasions are at the option of participants, which is what we always say, but which, invariably, no one elects to miss.

After the second night in Basle we start northwards, through Belfort, Epinal and Nancy, for Verdun, an interesting town deserving more time than we can offer. Next we head nearer to the Channel port through Charleville, Cambrai, St. Pol, Boulogne and Wimereux for our grand evening finale in France.

* * *

HOWEVER, in this short summary of the Rallye programme, it is quite impossible, of course, to give illustration to the delights of the tour—the many wayside attractions, atmosphere, new surroundings, friendly peoples, scenic grandeur, exquisite dishes and wines—and even limited currency will permit some choice in this matter! Never a worry, all laid on in first-class style and always our mechanic friend ready to rope in the unlucky ones. Here, too, our experience with the good cars and drivers of other years has witnessed little but the odd puncture and other minor delays.

The point now, of course, is to make up your mind early. Study the summary in detail, the costs schedule, and send in your applications to the Editor, Modern Motoring and Travel, 53, Stratton Street, Piccadilly, London, W.1, accompanied by deposit of £10 per person, cheques being made payable to The Motorists' Travel Club, which agency is conducting all formalities on our behalf. This is probably your last chance—don't miss it!

" RALLYE OBERLAND "—INCLUSIVE COSTS:

These include all permissible travel allowances and are exampled on the " under 8 ft. 6 ins. wheelbase " of car: larger cars subject to scheduled extras.

	Four Persons	Three Persons	Two Persons
1. Cost of Rally, including car and passenger shipment, maps, hotels, service aid (not spare parts), etc., paid in Sterling ..	At £63 7s. 6d. each: (four in party) £253 10 0	At £64 12s. 6d. each: (three in party) £193 17 6	At £67 2s. 6d. each: (two in party) £134 5 0
2. Travel allowance: Each at £25	£100 0 0	£75 0 0	£50 0 0
Car allowance to driver	15 0 0	15 0 0	15 0 0
Sterling permissible, each £5	20 0 0	15 0 0	10 0 0
	£135 0 0	£105 0 0	£75 0 0
3. Required for "V" Forms, each at £15, to cover export of currency included in Item 1	£60 0 0 (*)£75 0 0	£45 0 0 (*)£60 0 0	£30 0 0 (*)£45 0 0
	£328 10 0	£253 17 6	£179 5 0
4. Inclusive divisible cost per person	(four in party) £82 2 6	(three in party) £84 9 6	(two in party) £89 12 6

NOTES: (*) This is the total amount of party spending money remaining, after the Rally costs in Sterling (Item 1) are paid, and must include car running expenses, estimated at £20–£25.

" V " forms are not paid for, being bankers' certificates only—but they do reduce the travel allowance by these amounts per person.

"P-sst! A courtesy tip — TECALEMIT regularly!!"

It's a good tip at any time to have your car regularly serviced at a Tecalemit Garage.

THERE ARE OVER 4,000 OFFICIAL TECALEMIT EQUIPPED SERVICE STATIONS

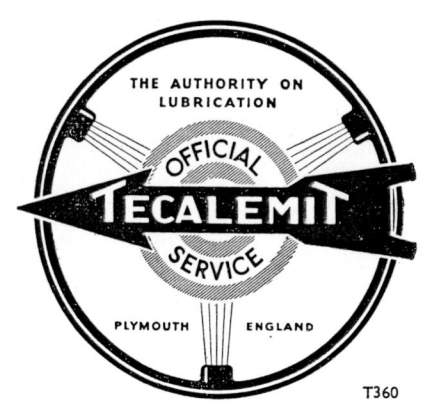

A wink from Ann Sheridan is worth having. Ann, whose latest picture is "Good Sam" for R.K.O., is one of the friendliest red-heads in Hollywood.

O.K. FOR SOUND

Film Shorts and Starlights

A TWIN-engined Anson has been supplying the M.-G.-M. unit filming "Mogambo" in Africa, the unit keeping in touch with Nairobi headquarters by portable radio transmitter.

Stars of the film are Clark Gable and Ava Gardner.

* * *

ANTHONY STEEL has flown to Africa to start work on Ealing's "West of Zanzibar," the sequel to "Where No Vultures Fly." Once again he will play the game warden.

He recently completed his role in Pinewood's Coronation picture, "Malta Story."

* * *

IN "Malta Story," Alec Guinness plays the straight role of an R.A.F. Spitfire pilot.

He has not given up playing comedy parts—"I had begun to think I was doing too many of the kind of roles usually associated with me."

* * *

JACKIE COOGAN, child star of 30 years ago, has been cast as a New England business man in "Fame and Fortune," a domestic comedy in production at Hollywood.

Other stars are Spencer Tracy, Jean Simmons and Teresa Wright.

* * *

JACK WARNER, who plays an English cricketer in Pinewood's "The Final Test," reported at Ealing Studios for his new role as an ex-boxer in "The Square Ring."

He had his arm in a sling, suffering from writer's cramp brought on by signing autographs!

* * *

M.-G.-M. have purchased an original story of inter-planetary adventures, "Fatal Planet." It is the studios' first venture in the science-fiction field.

The story deals with people from the earth on an expedition to Mercury, where they rescue a man and his daughter who were members of an expedition 20 years earlier.

* * *

TERENCE MORGAN and Peggy Cummins, Britain's new romantic team, are to co-star in "Always a Bride," a sparkling comedy in the Mediterranean setting of Monaco.

It is Morgan's sixth picture in 12 months and his first comedy part—a Treasury official whose job is to see that holidaymakers keep within the £25 allowance.

Morgan and Peggy Cummins recently finished making "Street Corner."

* * *

JOHN LUND is cast five times in Hollywood's "Latin Lovers"—once in a starring role and four times in plaster-of-Paris.

In the film he meets with the same bad breaks on the polo field as he does in romancing with Lana Turner.

* * *

SELECTED to play Romeo in the forthcoming Anglo-Italian Technicolor production of "Romeo and Juliet" is 25-year-old Lawrence Harvey, who was acclaimed by the critics in his first season at Stratford in 1952. He has never played Romeo before.

Born in South Africa, Harvey came to Britain in 1946 to study at the Royal Academy of Dramatic Art.

* * *

MEL FERRER has been signed by M.-G.-M. for the title role in "King Arthur and the Round Table," which is to be made at Elstree. The film will be directed and produced by the team responsible for last year's big success, "Ivanhoe."

Mel Ferrer will come to England from Morocco where he is filming "Saadia," in the part of a French doctor.

* * *

REPORTS filtering out of Hollywood about the filming of "Julius Caesar" indicate that Marlon Brando is giving a great performance in his Shakesperian role.

Brando's casting as Mark Antony took Hollywood by surprise, and comedians parodied Mark Antony in a torn toga—ripped up the back mimicking Brando's famous scene in "A Streetcar Named Desire".

* * *

THE 'bus started off down Charing Cross Road.

The girl on the pavement waved goodbye to the conductor. Then a woman brushed past her, grabbed the handrail and swung aboard.

But she had caught the wrong 'bus, as she soon found out when it turned down a side-street and stopped. "Hey!" she said indignantly, "this isn't the way to Victoria."

It wasn't. The 'bus, on hire from London Transport, was being used for a street scene in the new Pinewood picture, "Turn the Key Softly." The girl on the pavement was actress Joan Collins, and the conductor Glyn Houston.

Three Stars of 1953: London-born Elizabeth Taylor (left) who married Michael Wilding in February 1952 and is now at the height of her screen career at 21 years of age; centre, Shelley Winters who, now a top-flight star, is also likely to add to her laurels this year and, right, Canadian-born Yvonne de Carlo, star of some recent British and American pictures.

MODERN MOTORING & TRAVEL

"You will relax in contentment, drink deeply from your glass and watch the tranquil Thames slide softly by."

There is a fashion touch also—for men—featuring the S.B. belted Mattamac worn over a National fleece detachable lining ; also the neat windcheater by Masters (Fashions), Ltd. Has fleece backing, and washes well.

Pull-over by Cox, Moore and Co., Ltd., in the finest Geelong lambswool in a variety of colours.

RUNS WITH AN OBJECTIVE—
The Charms of Thames-side Taverns

By Joe Hollander

WITHIN a short ride of Central London, yet coyly tucked away in quiet, secluded spots, lie some of the lesser-known enticements of the Thames—its old, riverside taverns.

Day-trippers by steamboat or overseas sightseers transported in streamlined motor-coaches to the customary tourist resorts of Hampton Court or Windsor see little of these hidden jewels.

* * *

ONLY if you are genuinely nostalgic for the quiet pleasure of a cool glass of beer, enjoyed on the wooden balcony of a centuries old inn or on the time-worn timbers of an ancient landing stage, will you take the trouble to seek out these delectable places.

When you have found them, at Strand-on-the-Green, in old Isleworth, or by Twickenham Ferry, at Thames Ditton near historic Hampton Court, at sleepy Sunbury or somnolent Shepperton, you will relax in contentment, drink deeply from your glass and watch the tranquil Thames slide softly by.

* * *

HERE are some names for your notebook : the "City Barge" and the "Bull's Head" at Strand-on-the-Green in Chiswick (the first named tavern was granted a charter by Queen Elizabeth) ; the "London Apprentice" at Isleworth, Middlesex, where there is a ceiling dating back to the days of Henry VIII (when the apprentice lads of London Town rowed their girl friends up-river to this hostelry on their Sundays off) ; the "White Swan" hard by Twickenham Ferry and Eel Pie Island ; and the ancient, thirteenth century tavern called the "Old Swan" at Thames Ditton where to-day cocktails are drunk in Tudor surroundings.

Then there's the "Magpie" at Sunbury, venue of the first meeting of the Grand Order of Water Rats, way back in Victoria's golden days ; and the "Ship" at Shepperton with its gay umbrella-shielded tables outside and its inviting oak panelling inside.

You can reach them all by road or river. Each has its own landing stage for row-boats which call for refreshment and, without a car, a London Transport 'bus will take you very near to any one of them. A car, of course, will take you right to the door.

* * *

IN these days of restricted long-distance touring—the high cost of petrol, and those now nearly impossible plans for Continental holidays—we shall need more than ever to seek the lesser-known interests of "local" attractions, hidden off-the-beaten-track beauty spots, when, frequently to our surprise, we shall find much that is of unsuspecting beauty and charm, and enjoyed all the more for existing enforced limitations.

Please address your queries to :
INFORMATION BUREAU
"Modern Motoring & Travel,"
53, Stratton St., Piccadilly, London, W.1, and a stamped and addressed envelope should be enclosed if a reply direct is needed.

THEY WROTE TO US!

Unsolicited Testimonials

Home Tribute

I HAVE been prompted to write these notes of praise after driving a Mark IV Minx since June last year.

We admire its lines, enjoy its comfort in both the front seat and the back, its performance, economy, and, from the driving position, the easy and well-placed gear change.

The dashboard is bettered by none approaching its price. It has been quite surprising how much satisfaction is derived from this detail of design. The parcel shelf and the instrument panel are most pleasing. I would, however, prefer black dials with luminous hands and figures.

* * *

THE windscreen is broad and deep. In many cars I have sat in, my eye level seems to be far too near the top line of the windscreen, but in the Minx I can actually look up and through the screen. Headroom, too, is adequate. The main feature about the brakes is the hand brake —not one of those lunging contraptions that hit the knee when pulled out of the scuttle, but a businesslike pull-up lever. This is, however, about 3 inches short of the leverage I would like.

The car heater and Trico windscreen spray have proved to be most valuable accessories. The Smiths heater is a revelation for winter motoring, and the Trico screen spray ensures a clear view in all weathers. Misting-up of the rear window has been eliminated by GNOMIST—a transparent cellophane-like sheet (obtained from Rootes, Ltd., Manchester) stuck to the glass.

* * *

I AM a 16-stone, 6-foot male species. I travel at 60 m.p.h. whenever opportunity offers, and often use full throttle for full acceleration through the gears. My engine and gearbox oils are very thin, and the petrol consumption to date, at 15,125 miles, works out at 35 m.p.g. I lowered the main jet to 100 and fitted a 220 correction jet.

The fan has been removed and never used winter or summer; a thermometer has been added in the space provided for it on the dashboard. This has shown that my thermostat is not effective, and I have had half my radiator blanked off in the winter.

* * *

MY journeys include a run of eight miles to the office and trips from Manchester to Liverpool, Blackpool, Stoke-on-Trent, Rotherham and Chesterfield. A tendency to jerkiness when taking up the drive for the over-run on the standard or my own carburettor setting was eliminated by adjusting the slow running to a fast tick over.

I have had some trouble with a mildly creaking dash related, I think, to the heater and/or the scuttle ventilator. The chromium plating is no better than any other comparable models available at home to-day. Certain parts under the mudwings have started to rust and I am disappointed these parts have to be treated after only 10 months.

STARTING is instantaneous. I find 40 m.p.h. is no strain to the car in third gear which I use frequently for snappy acceleration when overtaking slow-moving traffic. In top I rarely wish to exceed 60, but the car passes a speedometer reading of 70 quite easily if I wish to show off to a friend. May I suspect some optimism?

The engine has not yet been decarbonised, nor does it seem to need it as the compression on the weakest cylinder is 100 lb. per sq. in. at starter speed. Absence of pinking in this engine under all conditions is a most pleasing quality, found in few motors of to-day.

* * *

IT is so roomy in the front. I am pretty hefty, of course, and my wife is not small, and yet we can fit in our five-year-old nipper between us, that leaves the back seat free for luggage which overflows from the boot on holidays. The boot is useful, but our cases are not tailored to it and a roof rack would have to be used if we wanted the back seat for passengers.

With four up the performance tails off somewhat, but with only my family aboard it is invigorating and I do not particularly want more.

Road holding on fast corners at speed is not quite as good as the best, and is my most serious criticism. The suspension, however, is most comfortable under most conditions.

* * *

TO sum up, this car lives up to its title —the "Minx Magnificent." On my present income I would not change it for any other make of car on the market to-day. No car made can satisfy all tastes, and I feel that this account would not be worth much attention if the praise was all unqualified.

(Sgd.) C. D. H. S.,
Heald Green, Cheshire.

From Australia

I HAVE been in Australia for the past two years, during which time I have had excellent service from a Sunbeam-Talbot "90" which I purchased from John McGrath, Ltd., Sydney, on my arrival.

Before returning to England I made enquiries from these people regarding the possibility of taking the car back with me, but found that with the various taxes and duties this would not be a good proposition.

* * *

COMBINING business with pleasure during my stay in Australia, I used the car for many journeys which are usually undertaken by plane. Travelling from Sydney to Melbourne on both the Hume Highway and the Princess Highway (approximately 580 and 680 miles respectively) we had many bad roads to traverse—the heavy transport and floods are jointly responsible for the tarmac breaking up—and the roads from Sydney to Brisbane had to be seen to be believed, the surface for 200-odd miles of the 700-mile journey being nothing but potholes and dirt roads.

WE took the car over to New Zealand where five of us—somewhat cramped, admittedly—toured all the North Island from Wellington to Auckland for nearly three weeks. In all these trips and with over 15,000 miles clocked on the speedometer I can honestly say the Sunbeam has never given a moment's trouble, the only service necessary being the usual 500-mile service and two decokes.

From the foregoing, you will realise that I am a very satisfied car owner—in spite of the fact that many Australians say that the Sunbeam-Talbot is too low for their roads.

(Sgd.) A. H.,
Prenton, Cheshire.

From Denmark

I AM the owner of a Hillman Minx car, model 1951, delivered through British Motors, of Copenhagen, and it is a great pleasure to me to express my satisfaction.

The speedometer is now at 50,000 km. There have been no repairs on the car, neither on the motor, the gear-box, the rear axle or the steering. The motor, however, has been decarbonised twice, partly due to the fact that the petrol we have to use in this country has a rather low octane figure and is not of the best quality.

You will understand that the car has been in use to a very high degree.

I have made several journeys abroad; journeys both North through Sweden, and South to the South European countries.

Working conditions, therefore, have been greatly exchanging. For instance, the temperature has varied between — 25 degrees and + 50 degrees C.

Roads have often been extremely bad, but the motor is still working irreproachably, with no perceptible wear and tear.

* * *

I AM a technical engineer and rather critically disposed.

The oil consumption at normal driving is rather insignificant, and at great speeds it does not surpass 1 litre per 800-1,000 km. On good roads, e.g., the German autobahn, it can easily manage a speed of 110 k.p.h.

The longest tour I have taken with the car is a trip of 7,000 km., from Copenhagen to Spain and back. On this tour we were four persons, with luggage for all of us. The route was as follows:—

Copenhagen – the Danish/German frontier Krusaa – Hamburg – Hanover – Kassel – Frankfurt – Strassbourg – Lyon – Nimes – Mont Pellier – the French/Spanish frontier la Junquerra – Barcelona – Valencia – Madrid – Toledo – Segovia – Santander San-Sebastian – Biaritz – Bordeaux – Paris – Bryssel – Køln – Hamburg – Copenhagen.

The tour of 7,000 km. was carried through, including rests in different places, within the three weeks. This included a trip by boat to Majorca. With no bad luck at all, some of the day's marches have been 650 km. The petrol consumption on this tour has been 8 litre per 100 km.

(Signed) H. C. CHRISTENSEN,
Copenhagen.

IN A FEW WORDS

News Items of Modern Motoring and Travel Interest

"Miss World" (May-Louise Flodin, of Gothenburg, Sweden) adorns a Humber for Press and magazine photographs.

The Temple Area (Al Haram al-Sherif) of Jerusalem provides a contrasting background to the modern lines of the Hillman Estate Car : photo by courtesy of Stewart Perowne.

"Snapping the Snapper"—a novelty picture by Peter Espe, of Oxford, reflecting in the nave plate the historic Canterbury Square.

CORONATION BOOKINGS for B.O.A.C.'s air routes are already heavy, and the Corporation is to put extra aircraft and extra services into operation.

* * *

THREE COMET SERVICES now link some 14 countries with the U.K., over 13,000 passengers flying by B.O.A.C. Comet last year. A fourth service between London and Tokyo is due to start within the next few months.

* * *

BRITISH RAILWAYS, Southern Region, have produced a booklet, "Sands Across the Sea," which deals with resorts in Normandy and Brittany and how to get there by surface routes of British Railways. Cost of the publication is 1s.

* * *

THE ROOTES GROUP companies in Coventry, Warwickshire, their staff and works employees subscribed £866 5s. 1d. to Coventry's East Coast Flood Relief Fund. A cheque for that amount was handed to the Mayor (Alderman B. H. Gardner) by Mr. R. G. Leaf, Secretary of the Group's manufacturing division.

* * *

DESPITE the increased price of petrol, the total mileage of routes provided by the R.A.C. for its members touring in the British Isles last year was greater than ever before.

* * *

SILVER CITY AIRWAYS, which operates the Cross-Channel Air Ferry, has begun operations in Libya with a company known as Libyan Airways. Services to Egypt and Tunisia are now contemplated.

* * *

SPEAKING at Leeds, at the annual dinner of the Yorkshire Division of the Motor Agents' Association, Mr. H. Spurrier, President of the Society of Motor Manufacturers and Traders, complained that on our eighteenth century road system we had over four million motor vehicles jostling with 10 million cyclists and over 40 million pedestrians. "Although an Act for the building of special motorways (the Special Roads Act 1949) reached the Statute Book in 1949, not an inch of these roads has been started," he said.

* * *

A REPRESENTATIVE GUIDE to the hotel accommodation in this country is provided in the 1953 edition of "Hotels in the British Isles," published by the British Travel and Holidays Association, of 64-65, St. James's Street, London, S.W.1. This should be particularly useful to visitors from overseas.

* * *

THE SOLE U.K. representation for the well-known Michelin Maps and Guides has been taken over by Seymour Press, Ltd., of 282, Vauxhall Bridge Road, London, S.W.1. Maps are 2s. 6d., Guides 7s. 6d., and the annual Guide to France is 20s.

* * *

A NEW road atlas of Switzerland has been published by Kummerly & Frey, of Berne, which divides the country into 17 sections. It includes maps of all the main towns and a list of 29 Alpine passes and a distances table.

* * *

THE LEGEND, "Finder will be rewarded by the R.A.C.," which is stamped on members' telephone box keys,

Photograph taken on the occasion of the recent Dealer Convention held by Buckleys Motors, Ltd., Rootes Group distributors for the whole of Eire with a dealer network covering the entire country. In centre—Mr. A. F. Buckley, director of Buckleys Motors; on his left : Mr. O. D. Horton, Rootes Group service manager.

Three smart 33-seater Commer "Avenger" coaches (coachwork by Plaxtons) supplied to Wallace Arnold Tours, Ltd., by Appleton and Arundale, Ltd., Commer distributors of Scarborough.

*

A new Rootes Group showroom has now been opened in Panama—photograph shows some leading guests attracted by the Minx convertible coupé at the recent official opening.

In a Few Words:

led to 662 lost keys being returned during 1952.

* * *

CITING a traffic increase of no less than 155 per cent. on the London–Glasgow and London–Edinburgh routes during the first nine weeks' operation of the £8 weekly winter fare, British European Airways say that by reducing the domestic air fares below the cost of first-class surface travel they have, for the first time, tapped the mass travel business. With the new "tourist fares" from April 1, the Corporation hopes to do the same on Continental routes.

* * *

DURING 1952 nearly 28,000 R.A.C. members made use of the Club's "Get-You-Home" Service—an increase of 16 per cent. over 1951. Ignition defects still constitute the main source of breakdowns.

* * *

SIR,—I wish to convey my congratulations on the Hillman Minx car and its performance.

A few weeks ago I started away from Phoenix, Arizona, making my way to Boston in Massachusetts. Quite a number of my friends said I wouldn't make it, but I did, and the total mileage was 3,325.

The car ran most satisfactorily and gave me no trouble on the road whatsoever; in fact, the whole journey was most comfortable and I have been able to enjoy driving it with ease.

(Sgd.) S. D.,
Medfield, Massachusetts.

* * *

COPIES of the Register of the Motor Industry (Red Book), 1953 edition, are now available at 32s. 6d. each, from the Registers Department of the Society of Motor Manufacturers and Traders, 148, Piccadilly, London, W.1. This is the fourth post-war edition of the Register, and lists some 25,000 companies, firms and persons engaged in the motor industry.

* * *

AGRICULTURAL SHOWS have been arranged as follows:—April: 29-30, Ayrshire, at Ayr.

May: 12-13, Oxfordshire, at Oxford Airport; 12-14, Devon County, at South Molton; 20-21, Shropshire and West Midland, at Shrewsbury; 27-28, Warwickshire, at Coventry.

June: 3-6, Bath and West, at Bath; 5-6, Suffolk, at Shrubland Park, near Ipswich; 9-11, Three Counties, at Hereford; 10-11, Essex, at Chelmsford; 10-11, Royal Cornwall, at Launceston; 17-18, Cheshire, at Chester; 17-18, Lincolnshire, at Brigg; 19-20, Leicestershire, at Market Harborough; 24-27, Royal Counties, at Portsmouth.

July: 1-2, Kent, at Maidstone; 1-2, Sussex, at Hassocks; 1-2, Royal Norfolk, at Swaffham; 14-16, Great Yorkshire, at Harrogate; 21-22, Tunbridge Wells and S.E. Counties, at Tunbridge Wells; 22-23, Staffordshire, at Burton-on-Trent; 31-Aug. 1, Durham, at Chester-le-Street.

August: 13-14, United Counties, at Carmarthen.

Attending by representatives of the Commonwealth Government departments, of the Army, Navy and Air Force, the Commer "4×4" gives its first public demonstration in Australia at the Royal Park, Melbourne—seen making light of gradients of up to 1 in 2½ and of the worst possible surface conditions.

THIS SPRING
Set your horsepower free

with carbon-dispersing

Mobiloil
REGD. TRADE MARK

Mobilgas
REGD. TRADE MARK

Britain's newest petrol — for flying horsepower

If Mobilgas is not yet sold in your area, have your tank filled up whenever you see a Mobilgas pump on your travels.

VACUUM OIL COMPANY LIMITED, LONDON, S.W.1

MODERN MOTORING & TRAVEL

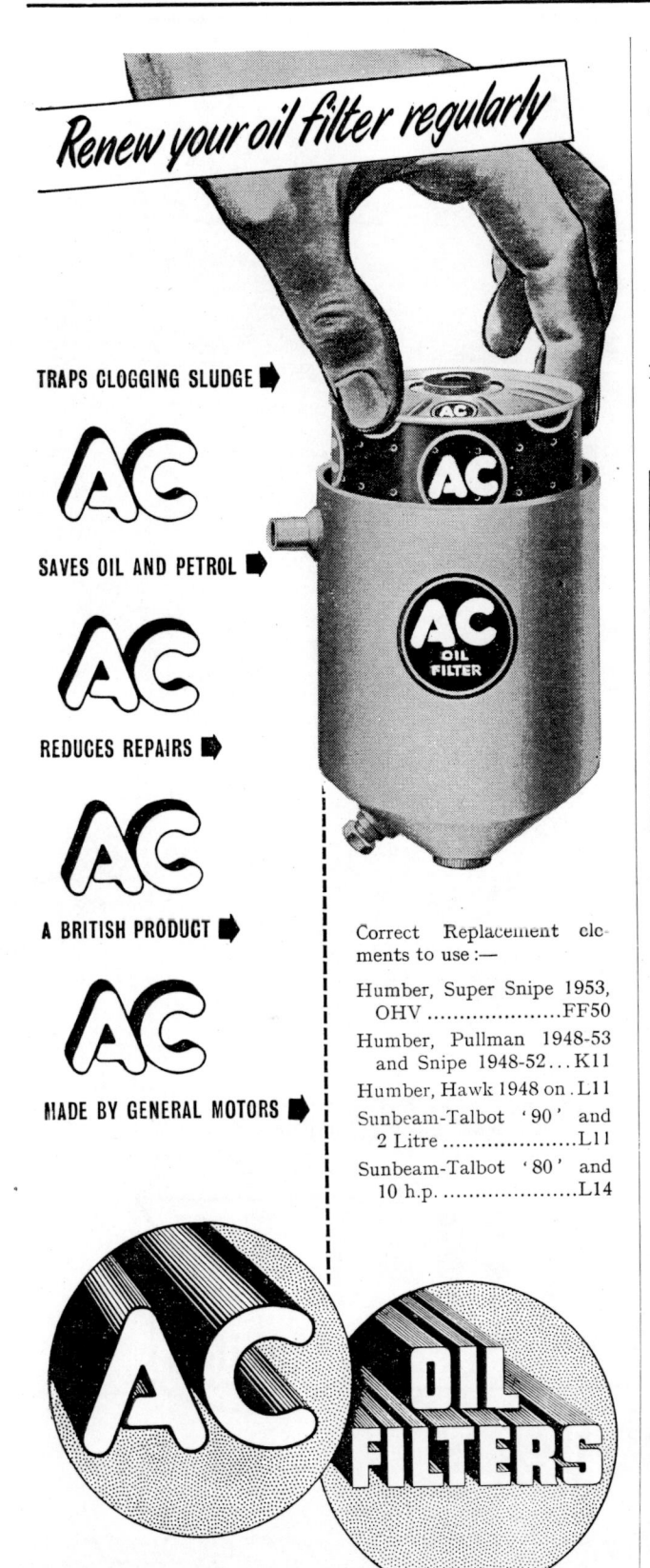

Page 2 — May, 1953

Renew your oil filter regularly

- TRAPS CLOGGING SLUDGE ➡ **AC**
- SAVES OIL AND PETROL ➡ **AC**
- REDUCES REPAIRS ➡ **AC**
- A BRITISH PRODUCT ➡ **AC**
- MADE BY GENERAL MOTORS ➡ **AC**

Correct Replacement elements to use:—

Humber, Super Snipe 1953, OHV FF50
Humber, Pullman 1948-53 and Snipe 1948-52 ... K11
Humber, Hawk 1948 on . L11
Sunbeam-Talbot '90' and 2 Litre L11
Sunbeam-Talbot '80' and 10 h.p. L14

AC OIL FILTERS

AC-Delco, Division of General Motors Ltd., Dunstable, Beds., and Southampton, Hants.

The "RESTAWILE"
No. 88 (Patent applied for, No. 3001/53)

A comfortable portable chair suitable for the garden, caravan, seaside, etc. Can also be used as a picnic table. Fitted with tubular legs and complete with high-grade canvas, in fast-colour gay stripes. Chair back is adaptable to two positions.

Folds to 16″ × 17½″, and weighs only 7 lbs.

PRICE **29/4** inc. P. tax

DESMO "PIC-PAC"
No. 77 (Patent No. 572757)
HOLD-ALL FOLDING CHAIR

Anodised Green finish. Compact, portable, rustproof. Folds to 21″ × 18½″ × 3″. Weight 6 lbs. Zip fasteners fitted to 14 oz. canvas form a useful hold-all.
PRICE, inc. P. tax **£3.19.4**
Canopy, if desired, £1 extra.

These first-class products are fully guaranteed to give years of service

DESMO LTD.
BIRMINGHAM, 7
Telephone: ASTon Cross 2831
LONDON SHOWROOMS:
220 Shaftesbury Ave., London, W.C.1
Telephone: Temple Bar 1994/5

ECCLES — design for Comfortable holidays

CORONATION
Produced specially for the small car owner. Compact, manoeuvrable, light in weight yet giving ideal touring accommodation for four.

NEW IMPERIAL
The finest living-touring caravan in existence. Every detail designed for complete comfort and providing the most luxurious mobile home.

ALERT Mk IV
Another edition of one of the most popular models ever produced, revised and improved to make the utmost use of a compact and comfortable interior.
Write for illustrated literature.

ECCLES (BIRMINGHAM) LTD.
145 HAZELWELL LANE, BIRMINGHAM 30
ECCLES — *the First name in Caravans!*

MAXIMUM BENEFIT FROM TOP GRADE PETROL

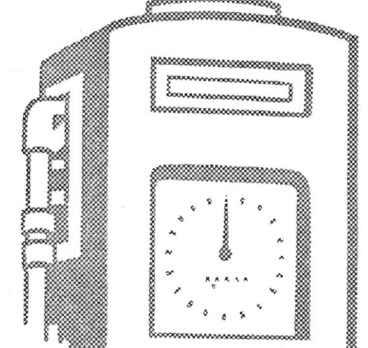

can only be obtained if CARBURATION is perfect

EXTRA miles per gallon and Supremacy in performance will certainly be yours if you fit

SOLEX
THE SERVICE CARBURETTOR

There is a SOLEX for every make of car. **Fill in the coupon,** and let us send you a quotation and list of Solex Service Stations.

If your engine is already fitted with Solex, we can offer you a guaranteed-equal-to-new RECONDITIONED SOLEX of the **latest type,** at a specially reduced price, taking your old carburettor in part exchange. Our pamphlet "Your Carburettor" will convince you that your investment will be well worth while.

SOLEX LTD

223-231 MARYLEBONE ROAD · LONDON · N.W.1

POST THIS COUPON TODAY   MM/5/53
NAME
ADDRESS
My car is a: .... make: .... Date: .... HP.
(Carb. now fitted)

SUCCESS!

"MARKED ABSENCE OF PINKING"
"...THREE OR FOUR MILES PER HOUR BETTER"
"...NOTHING BUT PRAISE"
"...QUICKER AND BETTER ACCELERATION"

Delco-Remy OIL-FILLED COIL

—these are typical user reactions. *All* claims made for this remarkable coil have been confirmed by the sales figures and unstinted public praise. *Now* is the time to fit a Delco-Remy Oil-Filled Coil and ensure you get the best results from branded petrol. Hermetically sealed against moisture and oil-filled for permanent insulation, this coil carries a two-year guarantee.

Consult your local garage or write for descriptive leaflet.

Is a better coil for ANY CAR!

DELCO-REMY-HYATT
DIVISION OF GENERAL MOTORS LTD.
GROSVENOR ROAD · LONDON · S·W·I

LIST PRICE 36/- 6 AND 12 VOLT

ROOTES *Car Seat Covers*

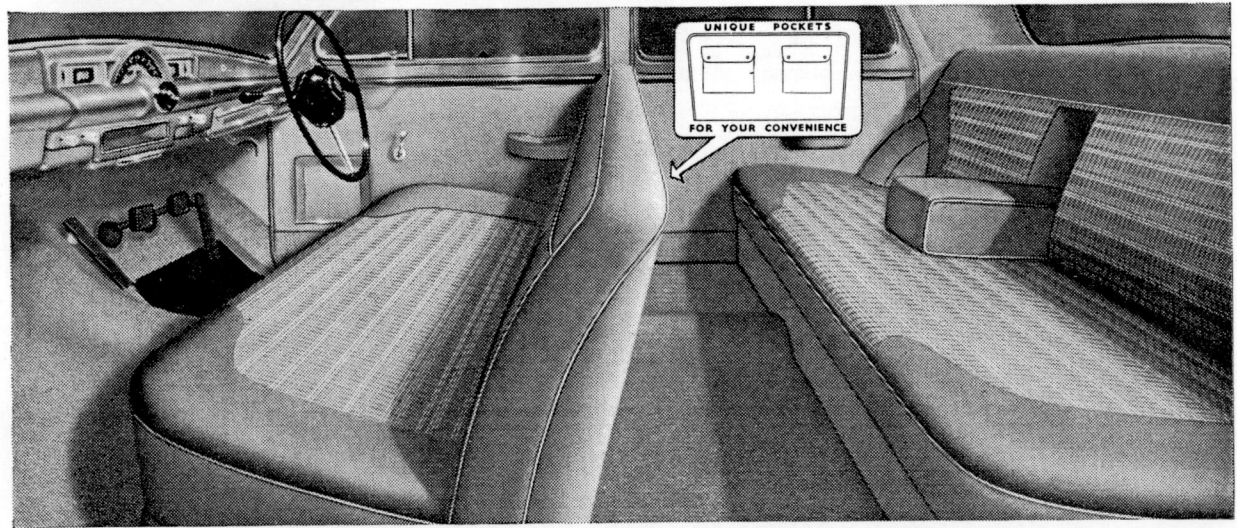

UNIQUE POCKETS FOR YOUR CONVENIENCE

Tailor-made from high quality materials for all car makes, they offer the following advantages:

ADDED COMFORT
GOOD LOOKS AND SHAPE
PREVENTION OF SHINE TO PERSONAL CLOTHING

A VARIETY OF COLOURS IN FELT OR TYGAN AND FELT
Patterns and prices available on application to Dept. A.C.

ROOTES LTD., LADBROKE HALL, BARLBY RD., LONDON, W.10
Tel. LADbroke 3232

BIRMINGHAM	90/94 Charlotte Street	Central 8411
MANCHESTER	Olympia, Chester Road	Blackfriars 6677
MAIDSTONE	Mill Street	Maidstone 3333
ROCHESTER	High Street	Chatham 2231
CANTERBURY	The Pavilion	Canterbury 3232
WROTHAM	Wrotham Heath	Borough Green 4
FOLKESTONE	86/92 Tontine Street	Folkestone 3156

and from all Rootes Group Distributors and Dealers

fill up and feel the difference

Burn it

THOSE of us who like to apply mild scientific reasoning to everyday affairs can often bring home the way in which such effects as heat can be tested. Heat travels by radiation, mostly infra-red rays, by convection as when hot air rises to the top of a room, or conduction which helps you to burn your hand when the maker has not provided saucepans with a heat insulator between the handle and the pot.

Now combustion usually requires oxygen, and there are three amusing experiments by which you can demonstrate some of the peculiarities of heat.

Obtain a glass tube slightly larger than a cigarette in diameter and about 1 inch long or less. You can stand this up on a good tablecloth and drop a lighted cigarette down in it without ill effects because combustion is quickly put out by carbon dioxide accumulated in the tube and the ash acts as a beautiful insulator to prevent burning of the cloth.

Take a handkerchief with a silver coin underneath it and casually put the burning cigarette against it. Still no burning because heat is conducted away so quickly by the good conductivity of the silver. It is time that you made these experiments pay, so give your friend a cigarette paper and challenge him to put it in such a position that it cannot be lit by a match.

Just wrap it closely round a glass tumbler and no match flame can do it harm. Air cannot get behind it and the paper temperature never rises sufficiently to cause a burn.

* * *

Fire! Fire!

INSURANCE Companies do not regard only such things as wood, paper and petrol as combustible. Given a sufficiently high temperature, many other things will flash violently.

Fine steel wire burns beautifully if there is nothing to conduct away the heat. Metallic dust makes quite a good explosive, so do many other finely divided substances which otherwise would be harmless.

Every time you scratch optimistically with your cigarette lighter you merely scrape off small pieces of a bismuth alloy and trust the heat of friction will start them burning in the air.

Visit a speedway and you will notice that sparks often fly from the riders' boots. This is commonly due to steel catching fire. The particles of steel are scraped off by the silicious cinders, raised to a high temperature by the action of scraping and then thrown into the air where they burn like miniature meteorites. Everything is interconnected in this world if only we could understand the reason.

* * *

Too late

IT was once said to me that " waiting " was the saddest word in the English language. I will try to be more hopeful and point out that if we had the mental skill we could save ourselves a great deal

All a matter of common sense, not of science!
says
Prof. A. M. Low

of trouble by never doing anything that is too late.

It is well known to anyone who sees a picture taken by flashlight that the flash is over before the eyes have blinked. So it is with many human sensations. If you examine the records of automobiles running into each other you will often find that where a driver says " I braked," he had not, in fact, allowed sufficient time to put on the brake let alone stopping before danger was reached.

He may have remembered that with wheels skidding, stopping effort is reduced, but he forgot the time taken in seeing the other vehicle and for his signal to pass from his brain via his muscular system to hands and feet.

It is natural for us to duck when we hear the whistle of a bullet, but it is far too late. When people jerk at a lightning flash they are doing it long after the danger has passed. They are wasting time and wearing themselves out.

You may have seen those amusing pictures of a lighted cigarette being placed against a man's hand. The high-speed cinema shows the hand being snatched away so long after the cigarette had touched it that the effect, shown at normal speed, was quite ludicrous.

* * *

An easy sensation

SOME years ago it used to be very popular for conjurors to blow fire in a flaming stream from their mouths. With a little courage this is not difficult.

Some magicians wrapped a fire producing material in a small asbestos pouch, but the real key is that breath is blown quite hard through the mouth so that flame cannot strike back to the lips.

This is very similar to what happens when the air-gas flame in an ordinary stove " lights back." The reason is that the mixture burns comparatively slowly when cool and in consequence the flame-rate of combustion is not sufficient to overcome the speed of the outward rushing combustible mixture.

* * *

What is the time?

I REMEMBER listening to a talk to Boy Scouts in which they were told how to tell their position by pointing the hand of a watch at the sun and dividing by two. That of course, is not quite right, but you will be familiar with this sort of thing, I feel sure.

Perhaps it will surprise you to hear that you can set your watch by the stars in the northern sky within a quarter of an hour of the proper time.

Take the Pole Star as the centre of your clock and the pointers of the " Plough " as the hour hand. Six is below the Pole Star and twelve above. Now take the time as shown by the pointers and add to that figure the number of months which have elapsed since January 1st. Be accurate to the nearest quarter month.

The figure so found is then doubled and subtracted from $16\frac{1}{4}$; if the result is more than $16\frac{1}{4}$ subtract it from $40\frac{1}{4}$ when the answer gives the time in hours after noon. My secretary asks me to add that the weather ought to be better by then!

* * *

Chemical marriage

THE popularity of plastics and the possibility of turning an increasing proportion of coal into oil has brought me many questions on the subject of catalysts . . . those queer bodies which affect chemical combinations without themselves suffering any great change.

Perhaps the best known example is the platinum cigarette lighter in which spongy platinum becomes hot in a stream of suitable gas or vapour. In the hydrogenation process, where oil is made to take up additional hydrogen, some types of nickel compounds have to be used in very small quantities, for without their presence in the mixture no proper chemical reaction occurs.

Another example is that of coal, which if it is completely dry can be made white hot without burning. An infinitesimal amount of moisture provides the electrons with a bridge across which they can march to allow of combustion. I always tell students that catalysts are rather like the parson at a wedding who produces changes in the couple concerned without, we hope, altering himself very greatly in the process.

You can demonstrate these interesting subjects (they suggest the presence of life in all matter) by endeavouring to light pieces of sugar with a match. The sugar will seldom burn, but if you casually touch it with the butt of a cigarette, the " bridge substance " is provided and the sugar burns quite fiercely in the air.

* * *

What a boy

IN London there was a boy who "ponked." I really mean it. He made a noise when shaken like a lead weight dropping into a china bowl.

He was examined by all kinds of medical people, I am told, but except for talking learnedly about poltergeists and mesmerism, no one bothered to use common sense.

The cause was quite simple. He had some slight deformation of a rather arthritic joint and the noise of jarring bone travelled to a still larger bone which acted as a diaphragm.

Being very thin the sound was reasonably pure and therefore sounded quite metallic. I gather that he has been cured (*a*) of rheumatism, and (*b*) of " ponking."

When I get my New MINX I shall use CASTROL — as always

Castrol WAKEFIELD MOTOR OIL

THE MASTERPIECE IN OILS

May, 1953

Holidays at Home, this year?

You could do worse than follow the advice of

Vincent Brennan, M.B.E., F.R.G.S.

(Our Touring Adviser)

Six giant Tunny, with total weight of 3,666 lb.—featuring a recent catch off Scarborough and Flamborough Head.

AS a rule, in the course of preparation of my monthly contributions to this journal, I tend to move around somewhat! On this occasion, just for a change, I want to try and interest what I will call the "family" motorist who seeks relaxation, annual or otherwise, somewhere attractive, not only to himself and madam, but also to the younger generation.

For this purpose I have chosen Scarborough.

* * *

THE local claim is that this world-famous Yorkshire holiday resort appeals in the main to three separate types.

There is the prosperous manufacturer who takes his luxury hotel, with its dancing and cocktails and golf at Ganton as a matter of course, and he will indeed find plenty of choice at Scarborough, from the massive Grand Hotel downwards.

Then there are what I will term the "executive" grades, who go for the superior guest houses, with amusements to match—and of these there are plenty —a full list is obtainable from the Information Bureau, Scarborough.

Thirdly, come mum, dad and offspring who, for their annual fortnight, want cosy "rooms" and ice-cream on the sands.

Scarborough has all these together, for added value, with a picturesque harbour into which the kids can be stopped from falling.

To these three kinds of holidaymakers, however, I will add a fourth, in the shape of the motorist who seeks a good centre with magnificent country all around, to be savoured in daytime trips coupled with loads to do in the evenings if so disposed.

* * *

YOU can learn all about such things from the absorbing booklet which a real live Publicity Department supplies to interested enquirers. After perusing this I was so impressed that the thought flickered through my mind, "By Jove, I believe something readable could be knocked together about Yorkshire's North Riding without even visiting it." However, I have never yet written about a place I haven't seen, and I do not propose to start now. So I made the 200-odd miles journey north from London along the awful Great North Road, and I am jolly glad I went.

THE first thing I did on arrival in Scarborough from the wintry south, was to doff my overcoat, never really to need it again in daytime throughout my stay: not bad for February!

When I mentioned this to Scarborough's dynamic Town Clerk, he said "You've hit it! Of course, Yorkshire people know all about us. It is the people from other parts who do not know us whom we have difficulty in persuading we are not *cold*. The fact is our weather comes mostly from the Atlantic, but there is little or no sting left in its tail by the time it reaches us moreover, the Gulf Stream keeps us snug."

* * *

IN further support of his claim, Scarborough proudly possesses an open-air theatre with the largest outdoor stage in the world—yes, it is bigger even than the Hollywood Bowl. You buy your ticket, say, for Monday, with the option of using it on Tuesday if Monday be wet, and if Tuesday is wet also, you get your money back. And so on for certain other days of the week.

Naturally, all this applies only to summer, but it does uphold the claim that Scarborough has a climatic appeal additional to other attractions.

* * *

AS for my welcome, nothing could have been warmer. It made me, a southerner with a slight tendency towards aloofness until I know how I stand, feel almost a foreigner. But this didn't last long. I wonder, is there such a thing as an ill-tempered Yorkshireman?

* * *

LET us deal now with some of Scarborough's outdoor features.

The colossal Open Air Theatre I have already mentioned. I have seen no other resort which has so cleverly manoeuvred, managed and developed its resources, natural and artificial, to such advantage.

The place is full of cosy nooks, of wide vistas, of parks and gardens, great and small, but all of them lovely. I even saw a bunch of bananas coming on very nicely in Wood End, the former home of the Sitwell Family (now a Natural History Museum), a grand place in which to spend a wet morning if you *should* happen to get one.

From the Sports angle we will begin with the Annual Cricket Week in September. I am told that the Hastings Cricket Week, which we in the south know well, drew 17,000 spectators last season. The corresponding figure quoted me for Scarborough is 80,000. Indeed, Yorkshire takes its cricket seriously. Incidentally, the Grand Hotel has a room containing one of the finest collections of Cricketers' Portraits in the world.

Also in the world class is the Centre Court at Scarborough, second only to that of Wimbledon. And in my personal opinion, until Wimbledon wakes up to the fact that tennis is no longer the exclusive preserve of the "amateur," Scarborough will continue to present the finest tennis in the world in the £1,000 Slazenger Professional Tournament

(Concluded on page 28)

Scarborough's mighty open air stage, the largest, it is claimed, in the world.

We're all for youth having its fling — but not in the vehicles we deliver. Our drivers must have at least ten years' driving experience and pass a strict British School of Motoring test. Other features of the world's largest 'on wheels' delivery organisation include:

NO OVER-DRIVING . . . drivers paid to go slow.
PROMPT COLLECTION . . . eight strategically placed depots.
IDENTITY PLATES . . . every vehicle driven carries our name—for all to see.
100% SUPERVISION . . . vehicles checked at the factory, drivers supervised on road.
SERVIS RECORDER . . . 'hidden eye' checks delivery journey.

THE CAR COLLECTION COMPANY LTD

THE WORLD'S LARGEST 'ON WHEELS' DELIVERY ORGANISATION

For prompt collection and careful delivery, wire your orders to:—

LONDON: KARKOLLECT, TELEX, LONDON
BRADFORD: KARKOLLECT, TELEX, APPERLEY BRIDGE
COVENTRY: KARKOLLECT, TELEX, COVENTRY
BIRMINGHAM: KARKOLLECT, BIRMINGHAM
OXFORD: KARKOLLECT, TELEX, OXFORD
BIRKENHEAD: KARKOLLECT, BIRKENHEAD
LUTON: KARKOLLECT, TELEX, LUTON
SOLIHULL: CAR COLLECTION, SHELDON 2668

REGISTERED OFFICES: 7, KENDALL PLACE, BAKER STREET, LONDON, W.I · TELEPHONE: WELbeck 4062

The Sunbeam - Talbot belonging to Mr. Colin Croft, Press officer of Scarborough, beside the pirate "Hispaniola," a favourite exhibit alike with old and young.

Holidays at Home: *from p. 26*

FOR "golf-wolfs" (try this for pronunciation on your foreign friends) there are two 18-hole courses by the sea, as well as the famous championship course at Ganton. What a tonic it is to breath the air of this last on a fine spring morning.

The Information Bureau produce a comprehensive booklet for the guidance of anglers, which makes no secret of the fact that Scarborough is Headquarters of the British Tunny Club. This, it appears, is not exactly a poor man's game.

Then there is a motor-cycle road-racing circuit on Oliver's Mount. I gather they've nibbled at the idea of fitting this out for car racing, but that the cost was prohibitive.

* * *

JUST a few more snippets. Scarborough claims to be the *oldest* seaside resort in Britain. I should think it must be, for Richard III had a house on the front, still to be seen, and they were sea-bathing here 20 years before Doctor Brighton thought of it.

The pirate ship *Hispaniola*, used in the film of "Treasure Island," attracts a myriad of excited young visitors in its present resting place in the harbour.

Lord Leighton was born in Brunswick Terrace and Anne Brontë ("The Tenant of Wildfell Hall"), whom I always confuse with Jane Austin, probably because sister Charlotte Brontë wrote "Jane Eyre," is buried in St. Mary's Churchyard.

In the gardens of Reighton Manor, smothered with snowdrops when the photograph was taken.

NOW I come to the surrounding country and one of the things I like about the resort is that beautiful scenery, such as that of Forge Valley, is accessible within minutes of leaving Scarborough by car. The Manor of Northstead is of political interest, in that Members of Parliament who wish to vacate their seats are reduced to applying for its Stewardship, as being an " office of profit " under the Crown, when the better-known Stewardship of the Chiltern Hundreds is already occupied.

* * *

NORTH-WEST of Scarborough lie mile upon mile of the glorious Yorkshire Moors, now translated into one of Britain's National Parks, but not, I believe, without some local opposition. Anyhow, the change, which is little more than one of name, does assure its natural features will remain a national heritage.

Nearby is twisty Whitby with its Abbey, Thornton-le-Dale, acclaimed as the prettiest village in Yorkshire, and a whole series of other abbeys, Rievaulx and the like, while peerless York itself is in easy reach for the motorist.

I referred to the journey up from the south which I had along the "awful" Great North Road.

I was more fortunate in my return, for I was advised to follow a much better route via Market Weighton and Thorne to Bawtry. Then, after only a few yards of the North Road, a fork to the right for Nottingham is taken after which one proceeds along A50 via Leicester, *Masons Bosworth* (italicised because it is the key to the whole route), Northampton,

The war memorial on Oliver's Mount with, in the foreground, the Mayor of Scarborough's Humber Pullman Limousine.

Woburn Sands and so on to Fenny Stratford and Dunstable.

This is a tricky bit to follow when leaving Leicester for the south, but otherwise there is the great advantage that this quite magnificent road is relatively free from traffic, until Fenny Stratford is reached, which in any case is a small distance only from town.

Appropriate tail-piece—return of the fisher fleet from sparkling and yielding waters.

May, 1953 — Page 29 — MODERN MOTORING & TRAVEL

Announcing the NEW COMMER EXPRESS DELIVERY VAN

Lively, Roomy and Super Smart!

Here are features that help to make this new Commer Express Delivery Van the smartest, fastest and sturdiest light van on the road

New attractive modern styling. 37.5 b.h.p. cushion-mounted 4-cyl. engine, water pump cooled, with **thermo**statically heat-controlled manifold for 'stop-start' economy.

All-steel body, integral with frame. Independent front-coil suspension with rubber seals doubling the periods between which lubricating attention is necessary.

BODY CAPACITY 100 CU. FT.

A PRODUCT OF THE ROOTES GROUP

COMMER CARS LTD. LUTON BEDS.   EXPORT DIVISION: ROOTES LTD. DEVONSHIRE HOUSE PICCADILLY LONDON W.1

May, 1953

Sunbeam Alpine Sports Roadster gives proof of Exceptional Capabilities:

THIS new Sunbeam Alpine Sports model has already given proof of its unique capabilities. On March 17, at Jabbeke, Belgium, timed officially by the Royal Belgium Automobile Club, Miss Sheila Van Damm, driving this new model, covered the flying kilometre at 120.135 m.p.h. and the flying mile at 119.402 m.p.h. Both speeds were the mean of two runs and constitute Belgian records and Women's records in the 2/3 litre class. Miss Van Damm is to be congratulated on being the first lady driver to exceed 120 m.p.h. on a production sports car.

IMMEDIATELY after Miss Van Damm's record-making drives, the car was taken to the Montlhéry track where Leslie Johnson covered 110.56 miles in the hour from a standing start and 111.20 miles in the hour from a flying start. Then Stirling Moss took over and completed several laps at 115.85 m.p.h. The latter performances were timed officially by the Automobile Club de France.

The new model will not be available for the home market for some considerable time, initial production being exclusively for North America.

MODERN MOTORING & TRAVEL

EVERY car owner and user, or travel-minded reader, should read "MODERN MOTORING AND TRAVEL" regularly; a Journal devoted wholly to his, or her interests.

To avoid delay and/or disappointment, make sure of your copy, month by month, by becoming a subscriber.

Subscription, per annum, post free, 11s. 6d. Fill in the form provided and post, together with your remittance, at once.

The Manager,
"MODERN MOTORING & TRAVEL"
53, Stratton Street, Piccadilly,
London, W.1

Please enrol me as a subscriber for twelve months commencing with the next issue.

Name..

Address..

Date................

May '53

May, 1953

For the Sports Car Enthusiast Overseas –

the new

SUNBEAM ALPINE SPORTS ROADSTER

The new Sunbeam Alpine Sports Roadster—sleek in line, inclusive quality-finish, impressive performance. Initially for export only (we feature specially left-hand drive), this new model is assured a marked patronage throughout the Western Hemisphere.

The neatly styled facia—with conveniently group instruments, and ready to hand controls. Note finger-tip steering column positioned gear-shift lever, and large size rev. counter.

IN the world of motor competition and sport, whether in relation to national club sprints and reliability trials or the more extended, certainly more arduous, world-contested sporting classics of the nature of the International Alpine trials, the Monte Carlo Rally and the variety of other major competitive events at home and abroad, the Sunbeam-Talbot has secured world-wide esteem solely on account of its consistently commendable and successful performance—to which statement the award by the R.A.C. to the Sunbeam-Talbot of its coveted Dewar Trophy (offered for the most outstanding technical and engineering development of the year) gives indisputable endorsement.

* * *

THE background of an age of applied and successful competition and racing experience is keenly reflected in the car's sporting lines and in its sound power-to-weight ratio, permitting high maximum speed derivatives well within all desirable safety limits: a thoroughbred in conception, design, workmanship and distinctive performance.

* * *

THAT special advantage should be taken of this unit of maintained front rank achievement is but a logical development. The outcome, in effect, is the introduction of the new Sunbeam Alpine Sports Roadster, initially for export only, which embodies the accumulated experience of the makers in a body styling which itself is the development of massed research in practical stream styling allied to speed potentialities: the finest and most convincing answer yet to that oft-repeated question, "Does competition and motor racing really improve the breed?" Here, indeed, is proof positive!

In this latest and vigorous example there is a mint of experience practically applied—up to the minute design, masterful performance, fractional re-reliability, maximum driver and passenger comfort, and generous marginal safety—each apparent in sharply defined focus in the car's sleek, sporting lines and exhilarating power.

* * *

HERE is a unique dual-purpose model, a first-rate competition car ideally suited also to high speed, long distance touring conditions, while for the sports car enthusiast seeking that dependable, sparkling performance so essential in split-second time reckoning—instantaneously responsive in things mechanical, precision steering and braking, peak acceleration and, withal, a notably high turn of speed—it has inclusive appeal. At the same time it offers maximum comfort in all weather conditions.

In the superbly fashioned two-seater coachwork there are top quality features throughout—distinctive sporting lines, generous seating roominess, rich detail finish, attractive colour schemes, not the

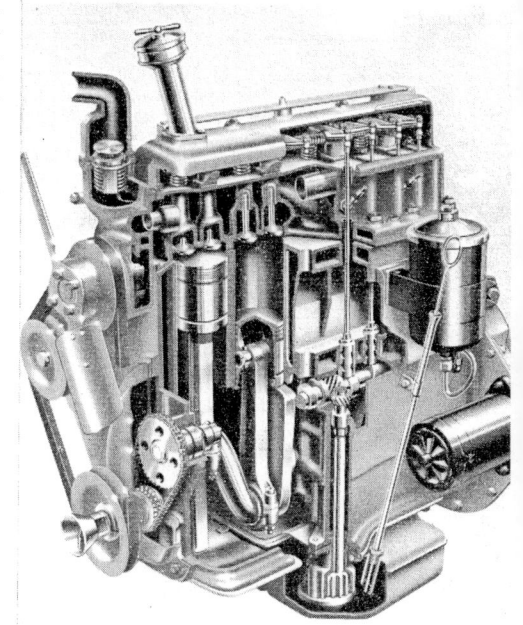

Bird's eye view of the high quality independent type seating. Note combined side-arm-hip rests, contributing to maximum riding comfort.

The power unit comprises many high-efficiency features—" cushioned power " engine mounting, polished inlet ports, specially tuned carburetter, sports type manifold, all contributing to high power and speed potentials.

least remarkable feature being the new and notably efficient hood design, permitting entire concealment within the bodywork yet brought into speedy service when conditions inspire the "raised" position.

In short, as well as giving typical Sunbeam-Talbot elegance related to an even more impressive performance (notably through its pronounced inter-gear acceleration), the new Sunbeam Alpine

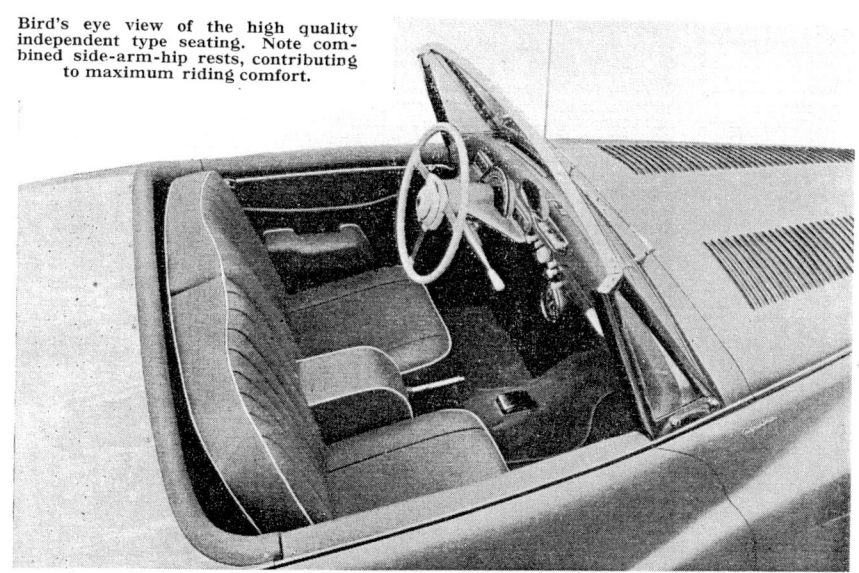

Depicting the commodious luggage locker with spring-assisted lid. Spare wheel has its own compartment.

Featuring the alternative racing type windscreen, available as optional extra.

Sunbeam Alpine Sports Roadster *(Concluded from page 31)*

Sports Roadster combines all proven mechanical features which have contributed so largely to the marque's success in the past.

For complete mechanical reliability, easy manœuvrability, simple, finger-light controls, impressive power surge, instantaneous gear-shift operation plus consistent and dependably smooth braking—the practical answer to all hazards in present-day competition requirements —no car is better designed or equipped.

Features at a glance:—
- Competition proved overhead valve power unit with high compression ratio.
- Chassis of immense rigidity and strength, meeting all strains and stresses of high speed motoring.
- Close ratio transmission, synchromatic finger-tip gear change control.
- Accurate precision steering.
- Lockheed hydraulic two leading shoe braking—light in operation, positive in action.
- Richly appointed interior—contour correct independent seating—combined padded arm and hip rests.
- Close-fitting, easily erected, waterproof hood, stowed neatly out of sight when not required.
- Spacious luggage locker, spring assisted lid—spare wheel in own compartment.

Engine features:—
- "Cushioned-power" engine mounting.
- Special high compression head.
- Peak output, sports type ignition coil.

Page 32   May, 1953

Suitable heating and air conditioning equipment can be easily installed.

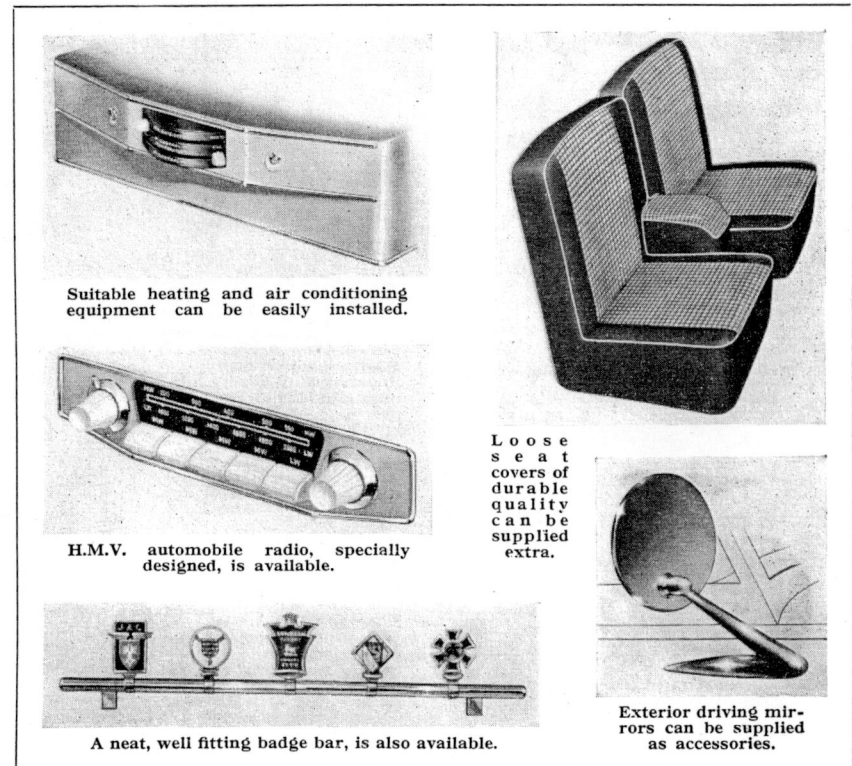

H.M.V. automobile radio, specially designed, is available.

A neat, well fitting badge bar, is also available.

Loose seat covers of durable quality can be supplied extra.

Exterior driving mirrors can be supplied as accessories.

- Enlarged and polished inlet ports.
- Hand-operated over-ride for automatic ignition.
- Specially tuned carburetter, with hand choke control.
- Air cleaner and silencer to carburetter.
- Special sports manifold for greater volumetric efficiency.
- Light alloy connecting rods.
- Selective cooling for exhaust ports.
- Fuel and oil filtration.

Additionally, a number of "optional accessories," as extras, are available, each conceived in the same applied competition experience—heating and ventilating installation, radio, tonneau cover, badge bar, cigarette lighter, external driving mirror, screen-washing equipment, racing windscreen, loose seat covers.

* * *

Export only!

AS with all good things, this new and fascinating sports model, initially for export only, is beyond immediate reach of the "home" sports car enthusiast. Meanwhile, it will surely bring back many welcome dollars, cashing in on the ever-growing demand in the Western Hemisphere for a distinctive, high-efficiency sports car, created in the first place by the Sunbeam-Talbot "90."

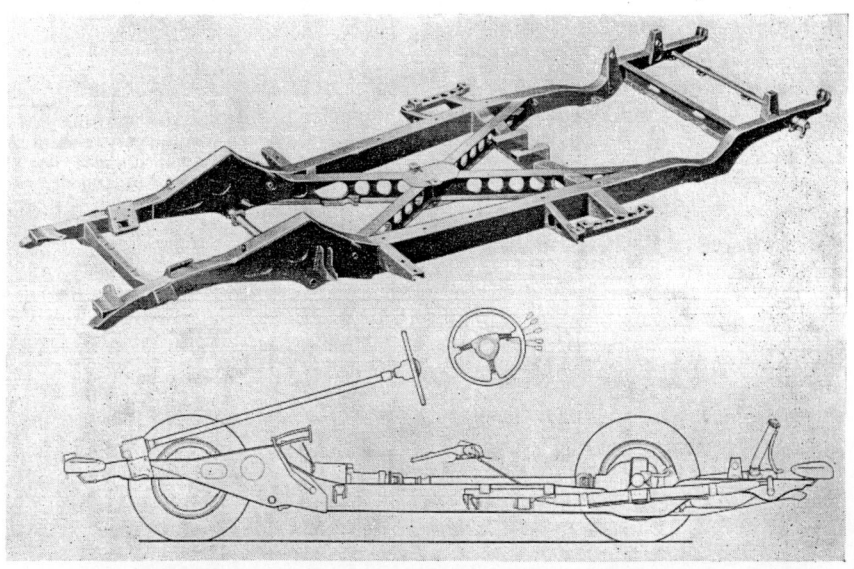

Diagrammatic sketch showing sturdy chassis design and high-efficiency mechanical linkage in relation to the dependable Lockheed two-leading-shoe braking system.

May, 1953

The Heritage of the New SUNBEAM ALPINE SPORTS ROADSTER

THE Sunbeam Alpine Sports Roadster has been developed, by the Rootes Group, from the world famous Sunbeam-Talbot.

This new model, brilliantly designed, incorporates many new features of special interest to the sports car enthusiast the while retaining all those outstanding qualities which have been proved by repeated successes over the years in international motoring events. The story of these awards bears witness to the mechanical excellence and quality of craftsmanship of this famous marque.

Driving day and night for over 2,000 miles—through every kind of weather, from tropical sun to arctic extremes; in dust, fog and rain—mercilessly punishing engine, gearbox, brakes and transmission; with the throttle often wide open for hours on end—nerves taut; the clock an ever present enemy, the map never closed; the twisting, tortuous roads of the mountains demanding continuous vigil; snatching only moments for sleep—forgetting all but the ultimate goal. Yes, this is the tempo of the International Alpine Rallies—toughest tests for man and machine in the world. It is thus that a car is really proved. Any weakness comes to light at once, only the best can survive the ordeal.

It is in the Alpine and Monte Carlo Rallies nevertheless, that the Sunbeam-Talbot has won such distinction. No better proof of mechanical excellence could be found. Awards have been gained consistently in almost every class.

In 1948 it won the highest of all distinctions—Coupe des Alpes—and in the same year recorded first in the acceleration and braking tests.

In 1949 a Sunbeam-Talbot team won the Manufacturers' Team Prize, and were again first in the acceleration and braking tests. They also won the Journalists' Cup.

In 1950 they came first and second in the 2-litre class; first for the timed climb of the Stelvio Pass, and of the Passo Tre Croce. They were also first in their class in the speed test and on the Autostrada, and first again in the acceleration and braking tests.

In 1952 the Team won three Coupe des Alpes, a most remarkable achievement. In addition they won the Manufacturers' Team Prize against all competitors, and were once again best in their class for the acceleration and braking tests.

More recently, in 1953, Sunbeam-Talbot merited supreme distinction, being awarded the coveted Dewar Trophy, given to the Manufacturer who, in the opinion of the Royal Automobile Club, contributed the most outstanding engineering and technical achievement during the previous year.

Our colour plate presents an impressive display of cups and other trophies awarded the Sunbeam-Talbot in open competition over the years.

THE **New** 21ˢᵀ ANNIVERSARY

* Completely new appearance
* All round increased economy
* More comfort
* Still greater refinement in every detail

Yes, it really is 21 years since the Hillman Minx made its first popu appearance! A fine car even in 1932, the Minx has been progressively veloped and improved ever since; and to-day, with well over 21,000 mill miles of happy family motoring to its credit, the Minx is part of the fabri life in almost every country in the world. To celebrate this great occasi here is the 21st Anniversary Minx . . . the most brilliant, the thrifti the most reliable family car of all time!

21 *years, and* ,000 MILLION MILE

HILLMAN MOTOR CAR CO. LIMITED COVENTRY · LONDON SHOWROOMS

Hillman Minx

SALOON

CALIFORNIAN HARDTOP

CONVERTIBLE COUPE · ESTATE CAR

- **NEW** attractive modern styling.
- 'Big Car' roominess and **NEW** comfort seating.
- All steel unitary construction.
- Independent front coil suspension.
- Lockheed hydraulic two leading shoe brakes.
- Exceptional luggage accommodation.
- **NEW** controlled 'air-flow' ventilation.
- Opticurve windscreen and rear window for all round visibility.

- Synchromatic finger tip gear change.
- Built-in 4-point jacking system.
- Wide opening bonnet for engine accessibility.
- Engine of **PROVED** performance and economy.
- **NEW** thermostatically heat controlled manifold for stop-start economy.
- **NEW** cylinder head—re-designed combustion chambers for exceptionally smooth running.

- 'Cushioned-power' engine mountings.
- Light and precise steering, re-styled steering wheel.
- **NEW** press button door handles.
- Double-dipping headlamps, foot operated.
- **NEW** attractively styled instrument panel including thermometer.
- **NEW** re-styled stop/tail lamps and rear number plate illumination.
- Comprehensive list of optional accessories.

A PRODUCT OF THE ROOTES GROUP

have perfected this car for you!

EXPORT DIVISION: ROOTES LIMITED · DEVONSHIRE HOUSE · PICCADILLY · W.1

TWO ATTRACTIVE CONTINENTAL RALLIES:

Sunny Riviera or Swiss and Italian Lakes

Arranged exclusively for members of the SUNBEAM-TALBOT OWNERS' CLUB

Late June or late August

IT can be problematical, we know, to decide upon a first-time Continental touring holiday.

All kinds of anxieties and doubts loom up in one's mind, even in the initial thought of crossing the Channel. How does one take one's car abroad; what about Customs regulations; passports, visas, the language problems, driving on the right of the road, choice of hotels, questions of petrol and oil costs, currency values?—all these and more seeming nightmares will whirl around in the most frightening manner.

* * *

BUT just one moment!
Each year tens of thousands of motorists do venture, you know, into these imaginary difficulties. And, for the most part, they return no less than thrilled with the experience.

Hours on end they will recite the delights of the trip—of new found enjoyment, new surroundings, of the warmth of welcome received everywhere, of the grandeur of the scenery, scenery that is different, even awe-inspiring, telling of the long poplar-flanked routes nationale of France, of the unforgettable pavé of Belgium — yes, maybe trying for a while—of roads of all kinds (after all, two world wars have raged across the countryside hereabouts), but really little worse than can be encountered in places at home.

They will tell of picturesque villages, interesting estaminets; they will extol Paris's gay boulevards, its shops and restaurants; surely, too, they will attempt to describe the great cathedral cities and their catholic shrines inspiring silent wonder, talk of happy peasants, smiling children, of colour and romance all over the place, perhaps of the oceans of golden corn, or fields of tulips literally dazzling with their brilliant hues and tones, breaking in here and there with mention of war cemeteries, equally impressive, not withstanding, with their living floral tributes to each and every epitaph and maintained thus by kindly local souls, or of rich vineyards, snow-capped mountains, fairy-like chalets, and, of course, the inevitable level crossings that halt one's progress and one's dreams only to permit eager continuity of travel and thought as their guard rails are relifted.

* * *

THERE is none so enthusiastic on the joys of Continental motoring as the first-timer—he, or she, on a second trip who will offer, in all good faith, the advantage of "experience" to the next newcomer! It is always thus: the pride of accomplishment in seeing and experiencing things for oneself is indestructible, a treasured recollection, a tale to be told and retold a thousand times and more.

Yet they doubted in the beginning as, perhaps, you are doing now!

* * *

WHAT would you wish, presuming the idea is, at least, attractive?
Would you like someone to arrange the whole thing, to leave all formalities and routine essentials to others? How nice, you feel, it would be to get across the Channel simply by driving to the port, seeing your car safely aboard, later to be lifted off at your feet. Would that your route also could be clearly detailed, your hotels—we know they will need to be good!—booked in advance, with someone to tell you what to see, how to get there, missing none of the items, you remind us, that your friends have never ceased to extol.

Would you like this and much else beside compiled in a sort of inclusive itinerary, a day-to-day programme full of all required information—mileages, routes, suggested excursions, recommended hotels costs and the like covering the entire trip?

Perhaps, also, you feel that while you would like to be near someone who could and would be a good Samaritan in moments of emergency, you have no desire for the "party" idea!

YOU see we know precisely what you have in mind : its condition of hope, hesitancy, expectation and unbalanced decision we had ourselves in the years long passed. But having read your mind, perhaps we can now but offer acceptable and agreeable answers, even solutions, to all the points we have raised.

As a member of the Sunbeam-Talbot Owners' Club or the owner of a Sunbeam-Talbot motor-car the gate of opportunity is wide open.

You simply select the particular Continental tour you prefer—and in the two itineraries we suggest there is abundant holiday interest—pay your deposit cheque and leave the rest, certainly the worry, to the organisers themselves.

* * *

YOU go as a party, i.e., all on the one ship, and set off on the great adventure either in the company of new-found friends and/or fellow Club members or slip quietly away on your own, each day to destinations selected especially for their comfort, cleanliness and good feeding, everything arranged for your convenience beforehand. In short, you please yourself from start to finish, to derive maximum holiday happiness in unique Continental atmosphere and style all the way.

Even were you so unlucky as to encounter unexpected mechanical trouble you need but call upon the qualified service mechanic attending your journey and, hey presto, you are on the move again.

* * *

IS it all true, this extraordinary offer? Every word, surely, factually, nor a trick of imagination, but a service tried and proved over many, many years.

(Continued on page 38)

S.T.O.C. COTSWOLD TRIAL:

"SPRINGTIME in the Cotswolds" would be a good holiday slogan for anyone interested in local publicity affairs, especially if the day of one's visit could be as was Sunday, March 8 last—the occasion of the Sunbeam-Talbot Owners' Club's Cotswold Trial starting at Gloucester and finishing at Cheltenham.

Under a blue sky, hedgerow, foliage, pastureland, even the live stock, all responding to spring's first sunny welcome, looked a picture of composite beauty and peace. Even the farm folk donned their Sunday best, strolled the lanes and offered a warm "Marning, sur" to each of their unexpected visitors, adding, almost without exception, "One of they moty-rallies?"

The drive was worth it—and competitors came from all parts of the country—if only to taste the fresh, sweet, if cold, air as it blew over the heights of Birdlip around which the course was routed.

Some 52 entrants faced the starters in the garage of Taylors (Crypt House) Motors, Ltd., by courtesy of Mrs. M. Taylor, and, once off, headed for Painswick, Pitchcombe, Randwick, Oxlinch, Stonehouse, Ebley and Sheepscombe—names all as delightful as their location—the way embodying a series of intriguing driving tests each for manœuvrability, braking and acceleration, "good manners at the farm gate" (and manners were, in fact, really commendable despite the infuriating reluctance of its security-stone to stay put!), a second braking test and, finally, a short regularity run to be covered at a set 16 m.p.h. average—a very elastic 16 m.p.h. with some—and so to the Irving Hotel, Cheltenham, for tea.

The occasion was notable in two other respects: it was Peter Miller's (the new Hon. Organising Secretary) first "official" appearance since his appointment—good luck, Peter—while almost the full committee of the new London Branch were in attendance, the preamble to its own first sectional trials' event, details of which will be announced in due course. The main committee was glad to welcome their co-officers, but of the result of their deliberations London members may have early opportunity of judging.

RESULTS:

Class A.—Sunbeam-Talbot, any capacity:—
1st, G. T. Lewis, of Sutton.. Marks lost 139.7
2nd, P. B. Booth, of Bradford „ „ 140.8

Class B.—Hillman cars:—
1st, R. A. Dando, of Manchester „ „ 147.4
2nd, E. A. Lloyd Davies, of Wolverhampton .. .. „ „ 149.4

Which Petrol should you use?

CLEVECOL SPECIAL
Very high Antiknock   Sparkling Performance

BENZOLE CLEVELAND MIXTURE
Smooth Running   Extra Mileage

CLEVELAND GUARANTEED
General Purpose   Superb Value

There are no better quality petrols than those supplied by

CLEVELAND

THE *SPECIALISTS* IN

MOTOR SPIRITS

Pre-war motorists well remember what CLEVELAND QUALITY means. Others have a real treat to enjoy. It was no secret that each of the Cleveland Brands supplied in the nineteen-thirties was the most popular in its price group. Cleveland premium grades pay by increased miles per gallon and add a pleasure to driving unknown for thirteen years.

Try them for yourself!

Continental Rallies:

(Continued from page 36)

The cost includes the lot, except, of course, personal spending and car running expenses, from Dover back to Dover.

We cannot decide for you, naturally, but we can guarantee your satisfaction in all things except the weather : which fact, incidentally, in these so-called enlightened times, is a very, very good thing !

* * *

WELL, now, is it to be late June or late August ; the Riviera or the Swiss and Italian lakes ?

You must choose soon, or miss the boat ! Reservations are limited in both instances.

Write to the Hon. Organising Secretary (F. J. Nutt), Sunbeam-Talbot Owners' Club, Ryton-on-Dunsmore, near Coventry, Warwickshire.

Better still, send also your deposit of £10 per person of your party and so secure accommodation now. An official application form will be forwarded with the receipt for your money, but you will know definitely, as you complete the entries, that you are already in on a very good thing.

Here are brief itineraries of the alternative schemes

★ ★ ★

RALLYE PORTOFINO

Saturday, June 20, to Sunday, July 5, 1953

A DELIGHTFUL itinerary embracing the Burgundy vineyards, lakes and mountains of Savoie, French Alps, French and Italian Rivieras, Italian lakes, Swiss Alps and Jura Mountains of France.

Saturday, June 20.—Cross the Channel from Dover to Calais in the car ferry and proceed via St. Omer, Arras and Peronne to spend the night at SOISSONS. Mileage 145.

Sunday, June 21.—Leave Soissons and proceed via Chateau Thierry, Troyes, Auxerre and Avallon, to spend the night in the Burgundy district at SAULIEU. Mileage 200.

Monday, June 22.—Continue through the vineyards to Chalon-sur-Saone and Bourg to spend the night beside the lake at AIX LES BAINS. Mileage 170.

Tuesday, June 23.—Continue southwards via Chambery and Grenoble to follow the Route Napoleon through the French Alps and spend the night at the mountain resort of DIGNE. Mileage 130.

Wednesday, June 24.—Leave Digne and continue through the mountains to Castellane and Grasse and then descend to the Mediterranean at Cannes. Follow the coast via Juan les Pins, Antibes, and Nice to spend two nights at MONTE CARLO. Mileage 120.

Thursday, June 25.—At leisure in Monte Carlo. Opportunity to sightsee in the Principality and to bathe at the summer beach, visit Beaulieu, Menton or La Turbie. Ample evening entertainment including the famous Casino and Sporting Club.

Friday, June 26.—Proceed to Menton to cross the Italian frontier for Bordighera and still following the coast proceed via San Remo, Alassio, Pia and Genoa to spend three nights at PORTOFINO. Mileage 125.

Saturday, June 27 ; Sunday June 28.—At leisure. The hotel is located at several hundred feet up overlooking the tiny yachting harbour, and is within a few miles of the large seaside resorts of Santa Margherita and Rapallo, which offer every conceivable holiday facility.

Monday, June 29.—Leave Portofino and return to Genoa, thence via the Autostrada proceed to Milan and again via Autostrada continue to Lake Maggiore to spend the night at STRESA. Mileage 170.

Tuesday, June 30.—Continue beside the lake via Baveno to Domodossola, to cross the Swiss Frontier and ascend the Simplon Pass to descend to the Swiss Rhone Valley and then climb to Gletsch to ascend the Grimsel Pass in the centre of the Alpine Range. Descend to Meiringen and Lake Brienz for Interlaken and Lake Thun, to spend two nights at BERNE, the capital of Switzerland. Mileage 160.

Wednesday, July 1.—At leisure. A specially arranged police motor cycle escorted sightseeing tour of the city in your own car. Excellent centre for shopping.

Thursday, July 2.—Leave Berne and proceed via the Lake of Neuchatel to cross the French frontier for Pontarlier, Dole, Dijon, Montbard and Tonnerre to spend the night at the city of SENS. Mileage 270.

Friday, July 3.—As Paris is only 70 miles away you can either leave after breakfast and lunch in Paris or take it more leisurely and visit the Palace at Fontainbleau to arrive in Paris at teatime. A visit can be arranged to the night spots. Mileage 70.

Saturday, July 4.—Either spend the morning sightseeing or shopping, or leave after breakfast and proceed leisurely via Beauvais and Abbeville to spend the night at HARDELOT near Boulogne. Mileage 155.

Sunday, July 5.—Leave Hardelot to cover the 30 miles to Calais by noon, to board the car ferry for Dover.

```
                              £   s.  d.
Cost: 4 persons, each ...   72  12   6
      3    ,,      ,,   ...   73  17   6
      2    ,,      ,,   ...   76   7   0
```

RALLYE DES LACS

Saturday, August 15, to Sunday, August 30, 1953

THIS itinerary embraces three places which proved to be very popular upon previous Rallies. The outward journey through the Vosges Mountains to Lake Lucerne then over the Swiss Alps to Lake Maggiore in Italy returning via the Swiss Rhone Valley to Lake Geneva and the Burgundy district of France.

Saturday, August 15.—Cross the channel from Dover to Calais in the car ferry and thence via St. Omer, Arras, Peronne, to spend the night at SOISSONS. Mileage 145.

Sunday, August 16.—Leave Soissons and proceed via Rheims and Bar le Duc to spend the night at the spa of VITTEL. Mileage 175.

Monday, August 17.—Continue through the Vosges Mountains via the Col du Bussang to cross the Swiss frontier at Basle and thence via Leistel and Olten to spend three nights at LUCERNE. Mileage 165.

Tuesday, August 18 ; Wednesday, August 19.—At leisure. Opportunity to explore the old town, ascend by Pilatus by mountain railway, boat on, or swim in, the lake. Shopping.

Thursday, August 20.—Leave Lucerne and follow the shore of the lake via Vitznau, Kussnacht and Brunnen, via the famous Axenstrasse for Altdorf and Andermatt, to cross the Alps, via the St. Gotthard pass for Bellinzona and Locarno and the Italian Frontier for Intra and Pallanza to spend three nights on Lake Maggiore at STRESA. Mileage 160.

Friday, August 21; Saturday, August 22.—At leisure. The hotel has its own Lido, rowing and motor boats are available to visit the Borromees Islands, an excursion can be made to Milan via the Autostrada.

Sunday, August 23.—Follow the lake shore via Baveno to Domodossola to cross the Swiss frontier and ascend the Simplon Pass. Thence via the Swiss Rhone Valley to arrive at Lake Geneva to spend three nights at MONTREUX. Mileage 125.

Monday, August 24 ; Tuesday, August 25.—At leisure. Opportunity to visit the Castle of Chillon, take a lake steamer across the lake to Evian in France, ascend by mountain railway to Les Pleiades or Les Avants, boat on, or swim in, the Lake. Excellent shopping facilities.

Wednesday, August 26.— Continue along the shore of the lake via Vevey and Lausanne to Nyon and thence ascend by the Col de St. Cerque, from which an excellent view of Mont Blanc can be obtained, to cross the French frontier for Lons le Saunier and Chalon-sur-Saone, to spend the night at SAULIEU. Mileage 190.

Thursday, August 27.—Continue on the fast road via Avallon, Auxerre and Sens, to the forest of Fontainebleu and thence past Orly Airport to enter Paris. An evening visit to a ' night spot ' can be arranged. Mileage 165.

Friday, August 28.—At leisure. Opportunity for sightseeing or shopping.

Saturday, August 29.—Leave Paris via Beauvais for Abbeville to spend the night at Hardelot near Boulogne. Mileage 155.

Sunday, August 30.—Leave Hardelot to cover the 30 miles to Calais by noon to board the car ferry for Dover.

```
                              £   s.  d.
Cost: 4 persons, each ...   73   2   6
      3    ,,      ,,   ...   74   7   6
      2    ,,      ,,   ...   76  17   0
```

Fuller information as to special facilities, private bath rooms, reserved " singles," and the like, from the organising Secretary, Sunbeam-Talbot Owners' Club, Ryton-on-Dunsmore, near Coventry, Warwickshire.

We are proud to announce that for style and dependability the new Humber Super Snipe incorporates Wilmot Breeden bumpers and over-riders, locks, handles, sun-visors, radiator mascot, wing motifs and arm-slings.

WILMOT BREEDEN

WILMOT BREEDEN LTD. · BIRMINGHAM · LONDON · MANCHESTER · GLASGOW.

LUCAS *Quality* WING MIRRORS

eliminate the "blind-spots" and provide a full and safe view of rearward traffic

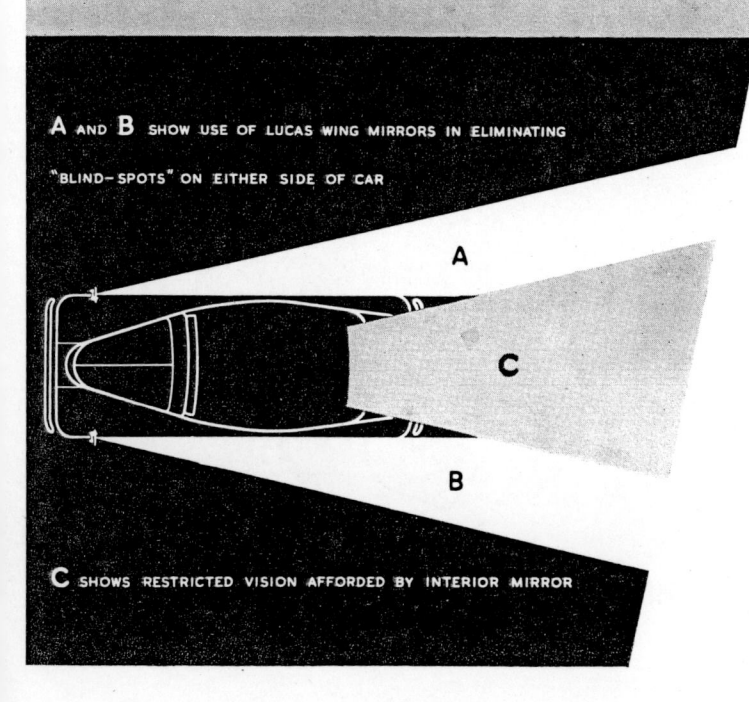

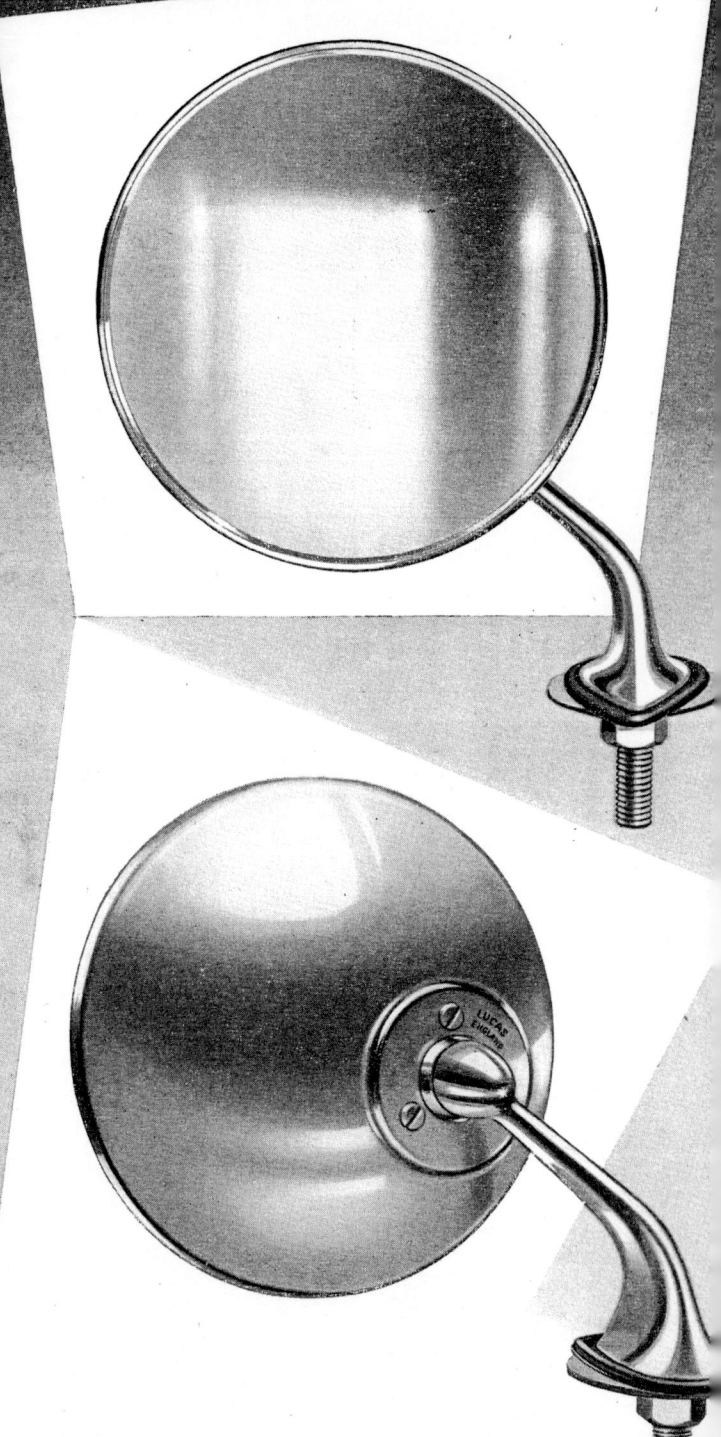

A AND **B** SHOW USE OF LUCAS WING MIRRORS IN ELIMINATING "BLIND-SPOTS" ON EITHER SIDE OF CAR

C SHOWS RESTRICTED VISION AFFORDED BY INTERIOR MIRROR

The stylish Lucas quality convex Wing Mirrors are designed for right and left hand fixing and provide an extra field of vision outside the limitations of the interior mirror and give unrestricted rearward view.
The universal ball joint, finally adjusted by three screws, gives a range of positions to suit every driver. A special rubber pad absorbs road shocks, protects the paintwork and prevents corrosion.
The brass mirror body and zinc based diecast bracket are both heavily chromium plated.
Fit two of these mirrors for all-round safety. They are ideal for seeing clearances when reversing, and can be very useful as width indicators. Model 406/29 for right hand fixing, and 406/41 for left hand fixing - - - - - - each **Price 19/6**

JOSEPH LUCAS LTD · BIRMINGHAM · ENGLAND

"I, too, am a Collector—but there is method in my madness"

says The Editor

EVERY tourist collects mementoes or souvenirs, if only picture postcards! Why not make the habit, as I do, a planned campaign?

I do not mean approach always to the local souvenir stores—the while many interesting novelties can be found in this way—but the careful collection of objects, old and new, which are mindful or characteristic, according to opportunity, of the occasion, the town, the county or the country.

* * *

I STARTED the pastime seriously some 33 years ago. Ever since, with each and every sojourn away from home, I have added one or more specific items.

Strangely enough, the habit with me was born unconsciously and in a peculiar manner. I suddenly discovered I had acquired no fewer than 47 sets of safety razors and a score of cigarette cases, all different, brought about by short-notice business journeys allowing no time for picking up the ever-ready hold-all from home.

* * *

TAKE any corner of the British Isles; North, South, East or West, and I have a souvenir which acts as a magic key to the past, as fresh to-day in all instances as at the time of acquisition.

* * *

Cornish marble, in the shape of the Longships Lighthouse, recalls a hair-raising descent of the rocks at Land's End.

* * *

"Erin go Bragh," carved on the base of a miniature armchair executed in Irish bog-oak, with its awesome companion piece, a shillelagh, bring back certain memorable days and nights in that fascinating emerald isle.

* * *

A glistening granite shines much brighter, believe me, than it did at the coal face of Ashington Pit, a mile or more below the earth's surface and nearly a level mile farther into the bowels of the earth. Each time I see it I am wriggling past bare-backed coal hewers in an approach " road " no more than 30 inches wide and 36 inches deep.

* * *

Antlers, white and dry, transport me to the summit of the Grotli mountains of Western Norway and recall, as a vivid nightmare, my descent in a cloudburst, blinded by the rain, expecting any moment to be washed over the boulders by the embroiled waters surging down the mountain tracks (they actually were water-sheds), later to be revived with a tumbler, repeat " tumbler " of Kirsch which, if it revived me in body-warmth, it expelled me into complete oblivion! It saved my life, then, but I hold the greatest respect for the stuff.

* * *

A wicker-straw hat lifts me across the Swiss and Italian Alps to Stresa, to my encounter with a beautiful Italian girl for whom I fell completely; that is, until she introduced me to her husband, no less handsome in figure and manner.

* * *

OF national hats, I have an enormous collection—Irish, Scottish, Welsh, French, Swiss, Tyrolean, Norwegian, Dutch, German and Danish—each with its particular history. The same with flags, tourist emblems, national badges, tie-pins, hotel labels; they all have treasured memories, the whole point of my narrative.

* * *

Photographs (my own), posters, picture postcards, maps (all route-marked as to the journeys undertaken), small and large novelty cabinets, clocks, drinking vessels, pipes, each in turn lift me to surroundings removed indeed from mundane thoughts.

* * *

Bedside lamp decorations carry my mind to Gruyere, Switzerland, to the Chedder Gorge, Somersetshire, or to Fossli (the great Vorringfoss waterfall), or to Norheimsund and the icy waters of the Hardanger Fjord, where, from the water bottom (14 ft. down) I picked up the pearl-like stone now resting on the mantelpiece of my sanctum.

* * *

Close by is a weird rock piece, also extracted from the bowels of the earth, this time from an hitherto unexplored part of Ingleton Cave, Yorkshire, at a point where further progress meant diving into the underground river, swimming underwater for 10 yards or so, to emerge into a wonderful "bejewelled" subterranean chamber. I wouldn't repeat the performance for a fortune! How comforting on the other hand, are these mementoes in times of irritating moments, always recalling much worse straits.

* * *

NEXT, for a change, I may peruse a volume or two of autographs and signed portraits—they are always fascinating—of pioneers of motoring, motor sport, aviation, of ships' captains, statesmen, even monarchs. The telegram from H.M. King Haakon of Norway greeting our motor rally in 1947 is a treasure indeed.

* * *

THESE are virile memories, never a dull moment when momentary leisure is at hand.

I can relax at any time, cast my eyes in any direction, fix upon an object, and the relative all-in detail of beauty, interest, pleasure and thrill comes surging back. If time is a healer of wounds, it can also be a destroyer of recollection—these souvenirs prevent undesirable obliteration.

* * *

A leather skull-cap, presented by Herr von Siebenthal, Mayor of Gstaad, brings to mind his 20-stone avoidupois against my 9 stone 7 pounds.

We changed jackets. He couldn't get his fist into my sleeve, his jacket wrapped me four times about with much to spare.

* * *

Another skull-cap recalls my adornment one-time in the costume of a Bernese fiddler. Espied by a visiting maiden of the mountains, as I tip-toed upon the open-air log-hewn dance floor, she invited me to a foursome reel.

When the band stopped, I couldn't! I continued solo, spinning out of control, the mountain peaks, great pines, and the green, translucent lake continuing to whirl about, with me as the axle piece, in the most sickening fashion.

* * *

Similarly, when a leader in a visit to Berne, young Toni Gauer, brother of the proprietor of the Schweizerhoff, invited me to " dress up " as a surprise for my party, using his magnificent Bernese costume, valued at over £300.

Because of our marked resemblance, they applauded spontaneously, expecting me to continue my repertoire (Toni's really) of Swiss folk songs offered our party the previous evening. I may be modestly versatile, but I just cannot sing. Yet I have only to pick up a lovely Swiss doll, dressed as of the same Canton, to recall the incident in meticulous detail.

* * *

ONE wouldn't, of course, consider a pair of Wellington boots the sort of souvenir for display in a glass-panelled cabinet. Yet by looking at my Dunlop's, size 8, I at once see myself behind that raging waterfall, Hardraw Force, Richmond, Yorkshire, where, in 1931, with the fall in full spate, I received the biggest drenching ever from millions of gallons of ice-cold water dropping 150 feet every second.

* * *

SO each memory brings forth another. Thinking of water, inspires me to tell my story of " beginner's luck," a fishing yarn of no ordinary character.

Way back in June, 1947, I was travelling from Fjaerland to Balestrand by motor speedboat, the mountains rising precipitously 1,000 feet or more either side, entering the water at perpendicular angles.

My Norwegian pilot spoke no word of English; I, then, no word of his native tongue. Yet his fish line and square, complete with spinner, worked miracles.

With eyes and actions I questioned him. He nodded. The line was spent out, the boat slowed down, and—bang!—I very nearly went overboard. Together we hauled in a giant salmon, my first-ever catch. Later, a second, third, fourth and fifth.

Would my companions believe me?

(Concluded on page 52)

"Glamour seems to have gone out of air racing" –

says Major Oliver Stewart

The Vickers Valiant in flight. It is equipped with four Rolls-Royce Avon turbojets.

WE are now fully informed about the entries for the England–New Zealand air race which is to take place in October. There are in all 19 entries, and 13 of these are in the speed section. Those 13, therefore, will all face the identical task of covering 12,155 miles (on a Great Circle reckoning), with one stop at Basra, in the shortest possible time. Now the point of interest is whether their efforts will attract wide public attention or not. Here is an attempt to stage another " great " air race—that is an air race which can be compared with the Schneider Trophy events and with the England–Australia air race.

First of all, there can be no doubt about the speed capabilities of the aircraft. They are the fastest jet-driven machines of their kind. The Vickers Valiant bomber's performance is not known, but its top speed must be somewhere between 500 and 600 miles an hour. Then there are the five English Electric Canberras, three of them entered by the Royal Air Force, the other two by the Royal Australian Air Force. These aircraft have demonstrated their speed capabilities on long journeys by their Atlantic and other flights. One of them did the England to Australia flight in 22 hours.

* * *

THERE can be no doubt, then, that the aircraft have the necessary speed capabilities to arouse interest. But there is one defect about them from the point of view of racing excitement; they are all British aircraft, they all have British engines, and they are all being handled by British crews. There is only one other jet-driven aircraft in the speed section; it is of American origin and will be flown by a Royal Danish Air Force crew. It is a Republic Thunderjet with Allison engine; not one of the latest types of machine.

On the face of it, then, the speed entries lack that important constituent, *international competitive interest*. It looks like a British victory even at this distance away. It is all the more sporting that there should have been additional entries of piston-engined aircraft, none of which stands a very good chance of winning or even of gaining a place. But good sportsmanship among the entrants is not enough to draw the attention of the crowds. They like to see different countries sending their best to compete with one another. That was what happened in the Schneider Trophy races. The United States, Italy and sometimes other countries as well as Great Britain all tried really hard with all the resources they could muster

* * *

THERE is much honour to be accorded to the British Government which, through the Royal Air Force, is entering the race. People are inclined to scoff at air racing and to ask why large organisations should bother about it. That is a completely wrong and ill-informed attitude. By entering the race with some of our latest jet aircraft we risk those failures that happen in racing even to the best prepared machines. But we also stand a chance of succeeding and of setting speed figures which will enhance the already high value of our aircraft. I applaud the government's and the Royal Air Force's action.

They have no worthy competitors. The United States Air Force has not entered. Few other air forces would have stood much chance; but it would have been pleasing to see them in the field.

My belief is that the Canberras will make a fine showing in this event, and will do much to prove how sound and practical are the British high performance jet-driven machines of to-day. But it may well be that the winner of the speed section will be the Valiant. And that would be a victory of supreme interest.

* * *

IN the design and construction of large bombers there is a certain amount of political wrangling. It has been suggested that the Americans ought to concentrate on these bombers while we concentrate on fighters. That view has been vigorously opposed by people in the British aircraft industry and also by officers of the Royal Air Force. And one of the reasons for opposing it has been that, if the Americans were to have a monopoly— as it were—of bomber work, they might not produce sufficiently advanced designs.

Nobody knows at the present time how the new American jet bombers would compare with British machines. The B47 has been put forward as one of the fastest bombers in existence, and the claim may well be true. But what of its operating qualities? There is no better way of demonstrating the operating-plus-speed qualities of an aircraft than by putting it into a long-distance race. But the B47 is not entered.

* * *

IN this year's race, K.L.M. crews will again—as in the Australia race— fly an American machine; but only in the handicap event. The aircraft will be a Douglas, and it will find itself faced with the Vickers Viscount turboprop aircraft. Here the chances on handicap formula are more difficult to determine. The Douglas, owing to its much greater all-up weight, might be favoured. But however good the showing on handicap, it is success in the speed event that counts most. And no United States jet bomber is there.

* * *

GLAMOUR seems to have gone out of air racing. In the days before the 1914–18 war the aircraft which used to race at Hendon were capable of speeds of about 100 miles an hour at most.

Some of them were only able to do about 60 miles an hour when at full throttle.

Yet they contrived in their round-the-pylons event to hold the crowds spellbound and to offer an exciting and satisfying spectacle. It was partly because they flew low and close to the spectators— which they could do by virtue of their lower speeds. But it was also partly because the speed capabilities of aircraft were then a new thing and that they attracted the attention of many people because of their novelty.

* * *

NOW we are accustomed to high aircraft speeds. We hear repeatedly of aircraft capable of penetrating the sonic barrier. The official world speed record is held by an American aircraft with an American pilot, and the figure is approximately 700 miles an hour. This is the speed recorded as an average of runs in opposite directions along a measured course. With speeds reaching these figures there is small wonder that the speeds set up in air races tend to be regarded with indifference. But the England–New Zealand air race may yet confound the pessimistic prophets and excite the public and popular imagination. No one can be sure until the starting flag falls at London Airport on October 8.

SUNBEAM-TALBOT

are proud to announce that the

ROYAL AUTOMOBILE CLUB

has awarded them

THE DEWAR TROPHY

for the most outstanding engineering and technical achievement during 1952 following the Sunbeam-Talbot successes in the Alpine Rally*

> * In the 1952 International Alpine Rally Sunbeam-Talbot won...
>
> • Three Coupes des Alpes
>
> • Manufacturers Team Prize
> (irrespective of size, class or nationality)
>
> • 1st, 2nd and 3rd places in the 2-3 litre class
>
> • Special cup for an outstanding performance

Accomplished under the competition rules of the RAC

The eight well-shaped ankles belong to lovely Barbara Thorson, Jean Lind, Lorraine Gale and Marjorie Walker, of R.K.O., that delightful dancing quartet of "If you knew Susie," in which Eddie Cantor and Joan Davis gave co-star lead.

O.K. FOR SOUND

Film Shorts and Starlights

UNIVERSAL-INTERNATIONAL will handle distribution in the United States of "A Queen is Crowned," the only Technicolor film to be made of the Coronation.

Hundreds of orders from film exhibitors wanting to show the hour-long feature, which will be produced by the Rank Organisation, have already reached the Company's head office in New York.

* * *

A SCIENCE-FICTION story, "It Came from Outer Space," will be the first three-dimensional film to be made by Universal-International.

The subject is said to be ideal for 3-D, and filming is being done entirely behind closed doors.

* * *

IN "The Day's Mischief," now in production at Pinewood Studios, a 17-year-old girl falls in love with a member of the teaching staff at a co-educational school. Then she disappears, and ugly rumours begin to spread.

Leo Genn plays the schoolmaster, who finds his career and his marriage are threatened. Gene Tierney plays his wife.

The small part of the schoolgirl is taken by Glynis Johns, who believes it is ridiculous that a star should be restricted to playing star roles. It is a brave decision.

* * *

TOUGHEST of all tough private-detective stories, Mickey Spillane's novels are to be brought to the screen in a series of films, and released through United Artists.

First two will be "I, the Jury" and "Kiss Me Deadly," both of which feature Spillane's leading character, Mike Hammer.

* * *

JAMES ("PICKWICK") HAYTER, filming at Pinewood in "Always a Bride," a new comedy with a Monte Carlo setting, has the role of "Cash" Dutton.

"Cash" is the richest man on the Riviera, with a yacht stuffed with banknotes.

His autobiography—"I was born in Watford. Get 'omesick sometimes. Can't go back. Income tax."

* * *

BEFORE the cameras in Naples recently was Errol Flynn for the colour film, "The Golden Blade," a swashbuckling romance of medieval Italy.

Playing the feminine role was Gina Lollobrigida, one of Italy's leading stars.

* * *

IN "Easy to Love," Van Johnson and Esther Williams are to share the star spotlight for the fourth time in their Hollywood careers.

Co-starring will be Tony Martin and John Bromfield.

* * *

FOR her role in "Turn the Key Softly," at Pinewood studios, Kathleen Harrison spent two hours every morning in the hands of the make-up man.

She plays a 70-year-old kleptomaniac who can't keep out of gaol.

Says Kathleen Harrison, "When producers see this film, word will get round that I'm too old to work!" Just for the record, she is 45.

* * *

STEWART GRANGER and Michael Wilding, who began their film careers together in London as extras, are to star together for the first time—in Hollywood.

The film, in colour, will be "The Scarlet Coat," telling the action-packed intrigue behind the defence of West Point in 1780.

Attractive Yolande Donlan in happy springtime mood during the location filming for the Technicolor comedy "Penny Princess," a Conquest production, near Montseny, a small mountain village north of Barcelona.

It will be Michael Wilding's first role under his M-G-M contract.

* * *

HOLLYWOOD'S two most travelled stars of late have been Robert Taylor and Stewart Granger.

Taylor has filmed in Italy ("Quo Vadis"), England ("Ivanhoe"), and Colorado ("Ride, Vaquero!"), and now comes to England again for "Knights of the Round Table."

Granger has been in Africa ("King Solomon's Mines"), Idaho ("The Wild North"), and Jamaica ("All the Brothers were Valiant").

* * *

THE screen play is now being written from the life story of Jackie Coogan.

New romantic team, John Fraser and Maureen Swanson, appearing in the new Associated British picture "Choir Practice." Cast as Welsh lovers, complete with dialect, actually they are both Scottish born.

Coogan's five-year-old daughter, Joann, is cast to play Jackie as a boy, the beloved "Kid."

* * *

FOR her role as a stage-struck daughter in M-G-M's "Fame and Fortune," Britain's Jean Simmons has three songs to sing. They are "Beautiful Lady," "By the Saskatchewan," and "When You Wore a Tulip."

Her "parents" in the film are Spencer Tracy and Teresa Wright.

* * *

GAY shouts from players 200 yards away on the Lakeside Golf Course in Hollywood kept interrupting scenes between Tyrone Power and Piper Laurie during the filming of "The Mississippi Gambler" at Universal-International.

After five attempted "takes," director Rudolph Mate called to an assistant: "Run over and offer those golfers five dollars apiece to keep quiet."

Five minutes later the assistant was back. "They all agreed except one guy who held out for 10 dollars," he reported.

"I couldn't get away with less—it was Bing Crosby."

"Hurry up dear, we'll be late for the dance!"

"It was our first night out in months. The wife had spent most of the day fiddling with her hair and one thing and another. We got into the car, and what do you think? It wouldn't start! For over an hour I tried everything, but no, it let me down—couldn't have picked a worse time!"

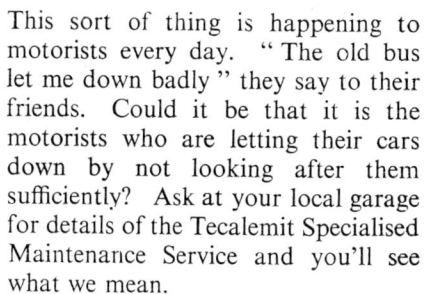

This sort of thing is happening to motorists every day. "The old bus let me down badly" they say to their friends. Could it be that it is the motorists who are letting their cars down by not looking after them sufficiently? Ask at your local garage for details of the Tecalemit Specialised Maintenance Service and you'll see what we mean.

The Tecalemit Specialised Maintenance Service entails the lubrication of each moving part and the checking of every component that contributes to the working of the vehicle.

THE AUTHORITY ON LUBRICATION — OFFICIAL TECALEMIT SERVICE — PLYMOUTH, ENGLAND

Springtime suggestions with a Coronation interest
by Brigid de Vine

"AS lovely as a lily" is pretty British star Barbara Murray. You can be beautiful, too, if you follow these hints.

Give your face a good "Spring clean" first by means of a thorough scrubbing with soapy lather and tiny rubber brush. Massage the skin, round and round, so that your face is pink and glowing. Then rinse . . . at least four times—preferably in rain water, or water softened by a pinch of borax.

Try a "pack" on your skin for special occasions. If you use a pack each week from now till June, for instance, you'll have a beautiful complexion in time for the Coronation. Packs help to remove Spring spots and blemishes, and good ones to use include those made of yeast and magnesia. A "Lemon-Magnesia" pack is specially good, and there is also a splendid "White Mask."

Powder-base should be changed if it does not suit you. See that it goes on smoothly using a very little, under your throat, your chin and on your cheeks, then on temples and forehead.

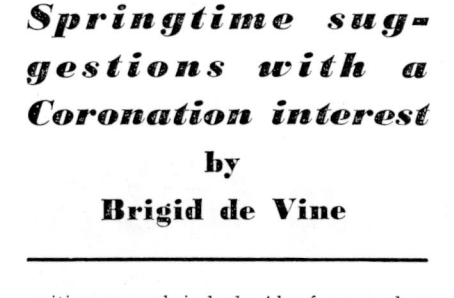

"BEAUTIFUL as a blossom" refers also to beautiful Muriel Pavlow.

That means—using perfume, the last word in good grooming . . . the essence of feminine charm. Muriel Pavlow, starring in "The Net," shows you the most effective way to use perfume is also the most economical. Muriel strokes it on her skin with the stopper. The warmth of the body releases the fragrance to the full, "wafting it round the room each time you turn your head," she says, "and no stale perfume next time you wear your nicest dress."

Now is the time for taking stock of your fragrance wardrobe for the Coronation celebrations. New outfits demand a careful checking-over of the perfume shelf. Choose a gay and sparkling perfume. Rise to the challenge, make your own contribution to a country *en fête* by surrounding yourself with a lovely evocative aura of fragrance. Take out the stopper, close your eyes, and let the spell of a new scent comfort you.—Ann M. Capell.

A KITCHEN cabinet which does the "wiping-up" for you is the newest item on the budget of Spring news to help the housewife.

Shown at the recent exhibition of British Furniture at Earls Court, it attracted a good deal of attention from both men and women.

All you have to do is to wash and rinse the dishes and then place them in specially built racks inside the cupboard, clean air is then passed through vents to dry them.

* * *

OTHER exhibits reflected the current need to save labour and overcome the shortage of space in modern living rooms.

There were many small dual-purpose pieces.

Coffee tables delicate and light in design for frail coffee cups yet sturdy enough to take a television set.

* * *

There was the Comfa-table, a small occasional table for drinks, reading, writing or meals in bed. Also for use when sitting in an armchair, the legs being attached only to one side of the table top, enabling it to stand close to the side of the chair with the top of the table protruding over the arm.

* * *

Another occasional table was fitted with two trays, each equipped with folding legs so that they, too, could be used as small tables.

An 18-inch square "pouffe" could be taken apart easily to provide FIVE separate upholstered stools, with folding legs, AND a coffee table. Very useful for occasional "television guests."

* * *

There was a tea trolley which could be turned into a small dining table by one easy movement, bringing the two shelves level. And a dining table which became smaller when a centre leaf was removed. the centre leaf then turned itself into a modern coffee table.

* * *

A sideboard of walnut had a "serving surface" covered in plastic which came into use when needed to avoid damage to the wooden top.

* * *

A bureau had its own strip light so that the user was independent of any other lighting in the room.

* * *

There was a chair with leg rest and table "entirely concealed when not in use" and a fireside chair "for the heavyweight," deceptively light-looking, it will "support 16 stone in comfort."

* * *

FOR teen-agers wanting to combine the facilities of a study with that of bedroom in one small space there was a wardrobe with a patent door opening device which enabled the wardrobe to be opened fully even if it was standing close up to a bed.

A modern two-level stepped coffee table concealed two drawers and a nest of little compartments for sewing equipment.

For mothers of small children there were folding play-pens, with *folding floors*, to store in a space measuring only 22 ins. by 9 ins.; play-pens made to fit across the *corner* of the room, and combined cot and play-pens which "do *not* raise the problem of what to do with the bedding."

There was a settee which actually s-t-r-e-t-c-h-e-s. Easily and silently whenever required, it "turns from a two-seater into a three-seater while retaining the same appearance." "More room for your guests, more space for your room."

It may take a little time for all the novelties shown at the recent Furniture Exhibition to reach shops in all parts of the country, but any furniture retailer should be able to make enquiries about possible delivery dates for customers who are interested.

* * *

AN idea from motor manufacturing was embodied in the kitchen of one of the houses shown at the wonderful
(Continued on page 48)

THESE two coiffures, inspired by the Coronation, are new among short styles.

RAYMOND'S "Angel Tiara" (left) possesses that unmistakable perfection of line achieved by skilful and precise cutting.

The hair is unparted, with a soft feather fringe, brushed forward on to the brow. The sides are dressed in a gentle waved-movement flowing back into flipped half-curls in the nape of the neck.

A glittering spiral headdress, specially designed by Raymond, can be worn either surmounting the smooth crown or at the back of the head, as shown. For this, quite ordinary materials are used to make an exciting Coronation-year accessory. A length of wire around which is bound white tape thickly sewn with gold and silver sequins, this idea can be adapted in many different materials.

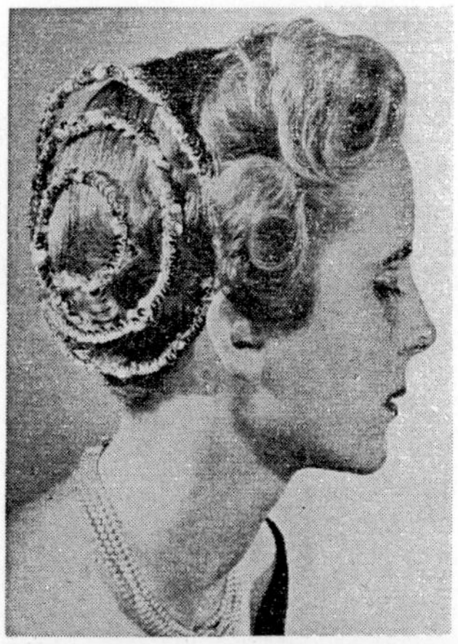

Coronation Style No. 2 (right) is from the salon of STEINER, another popular Mayfair hair stylist. Inspired by thoughts of crowns, this style features a halo of Coronet Ringlets in charming contrast to the smooth hair line at the front. The back hair is dressed in soft "cherub" curls.

Making the SUNBEAM-TALBOT body

By a succession of carefully planned operations, the flat sheets of high quality steel are pressed into beautifully shaped panels, in huge presses such as this, by the British Light Steel Pressing Co., at Acton.

Right: at the R.T.B. Steelworks at Ebbw Vale; teeming steel into ingot moulds.

When the steel is 'set', the moulds are lifted off, the ingots go to the soaking pits, where they are reheated, are then rolled down into slabs, and again into a long strip of sheet steel, which leaves the famous continuous strip mill at twenty miles an hour. It is then cold-reduced in other mills, until it has the required qualities for panel pressing, and is then cut up and sent to the customer.

RICHARD THOMAS & BALDWINS LTD.
47, PARK STREET, LONDON, W.1

CAN WE HELP YOU?

New Owner

SIR,—Having just taken delivery of a new Hillman Minx, I shall be grateful of advice on the following points:—
(1) Undersealing—whether advantageous or not.
(2) Any method of preserving body-paint, e.g., lacquer or other means.
(3) Ditto chromium parts in view of present-day poor quality.
With thanks in anticipation of your kind assistance, having only recently become a new reader.

(Sgd.) R. J.-G.,
LLANGOLLEN,
DENBIGHSHIRE.

(1) The undersurfaces of the Hillman Minx are already treated with a Bitumastic compound which should provide adequate protection.

(2) The synthetic enamel finish of the body-work of the car will need no special protection beyond a periodical cleaning with Humber Liquid Polish followed by treatment with Humber Wax Polish.

(3) Chrome parts should be cleaned with soap and water only.

* * *

Premium Fuel

SIR,—I would be grateful if you will please inform me as to the correct ignition and carburetter settings necessary for my Sunbeam-Talbot in view of the new petrols.
I presume the present settings were made at the factory to suit Pool petrol.

(Sgd.) H. B. G.,
COULSDON, SURREY.

All Rootes Group distributors and dealers have received advice from the manufacturers regarding any adjustments which may be necessary to obtain optimum results from Premium fuel.

Settings will be dependent upon engine condition.

* * *

Service in Canada

SIR,—I should like to purchase an A.C. oil filter, but I can't get it anywhere around here.

(Sgd.) R. B. (Hillman),
QUEBEC CITY, CANADA.

It is suggested you get in touch with the Rootes Group's concessionaires, Rootes Motors (Canada), Ltd., Box 174, Station "H," Toronto, 13. They will advise you, giving the names of recommended dealers in your area.

* * *

Towing Weight

SIR,—I am wondering if the tow-bar attachment available for use on the Hillman Minx Saloon would be suitable for towing a fire equipment trailer. Could you let me have further information on this item?

(Sgd.) D. H. C.,
MBEYA, TANGANYIKA.

If a satisfactory performance is to be maintained, the towing weight should not exceed 10 cwt. This can be slightly exceeded, but excess weight will tend to reduce the standard of reliability to a degree, dependent upon the load.

It is recommended that the maximum towing load should not exceed 15 cwt.

The Hillman tow-bar assembly is available through the International Motor Mart, Ltd., Rootes Group distributors of Dar-es-Salaam.

* * *

Hints on Travel Abroad

SIR,—We would like to know something of the holiday currency allowance, and whether it is necessary to join the A.A. or R.A.C.
If you could supply these details we could make some arrangements, but until the prices, etc., are known, we are unable to go any further with our plans.

(Sgd.) G. A. S.

The whole subject of going abroad was dealt with by our Touring Adviser in the last issue of this journal, and was intended to be of special assistance to those who go for the first time.

It is possible to take a car abroad without belonging to either the R.A.C. or A.A., but would-be Continental tourists are warned that in this event the procedure is most complicated.

* * *

In Spain

SIR,—In "Modern Motoring & Travel" was published your interesting article entitled "In Sunny Southern Spain," a part of the world which I know personally very well.

However, what particularly interested me was the framed "Horse's Address to his Master," the more so as I am the Honorary Secretary of the local Society of Prevention of Cruelty to Animals.

Calendar of Coming Events

MAY
- 2. Football Association Cup Final, Wembley, Middlesex.
- 9 (to Sept. 26) Pitlochry Drama Festival, Pitlochry, Perthshire.
- 13-23. The Bath Assembly (Festival of the Arts), Bath, Somerset.
- 14-16. The Royal Windsor Horse Show, Windsor, Berkshire.
- 20-22. Chelsea Flower Show, Chelsea, London.
- 22-29. Skye Week, Isle of Skye.
- 25-30. The Amateur Golf Championship, Liverpool.
- 27-30. Royal Ulster Agricultural Show, Belfast.
- 27 (to June 10) London Fashion Fortnight, London.
- 30, 31. S.T.O.C. Eastbourne Rally and Concours.

JUNE
- 2. Coronation of H.M. Queen Elizabeth II, London.
- 3-6. Bath and West and Southern Counties Agricultural Show, Somerset. Epsom Summer Race Meeting (The Oaks, 4th; the Derby, 6th), Epsom, Surrey.
- 8, 10, and 12. International Tourist Trophy Motor-Cycle Races, Isle of Man.
- 9-11. Three Counties Agricultural Show, Hereford.
- 10-27. The Royal Tournament, Earls Court, London.
- 10-25. Antique Dealers' Fair, Grosvenor House, London.
- 11. H.M. Queen Elizabeth's Official Birthday: Trooping the Colour Ceremony, Horse Guards Parade, London.
- 11-13. Richmond Royal Horse Show, Richmond, Surrey.
- 11-16. First Cricket Test Match: Australia v. England, Nottingham. (provisional)
- 13, 14. S.T.O.C. Scottish Rally, Turnberry.
- 16-19. Royal Ascot Race Meeting, Ascot, Berkshire.
- 22 (to July 5) All-England Lawn Tennis Championships, Wimbledon, Surrey.
- 25-30. Second Cricket Test Match: Australia v. England, Lord's, London. (provisional)

JULY
- 1-4. Henley Royal Regatta, Henley-on-Thames, Oxfordshire.

LIGHTING-UP TIMES THIS MONTH

	1st	9th	16th	23rd	31st
London	9.21	9.34	9.46	9.56	10.5
Bristol	9.31	9.44	9.56	10.6	10.15
Birmingham	9.33	9.46	9.56	10.8	10.17
Leeds	9.34	9.47	10.2	10.12	10.21
Manchester	9.37	9.50	10.4	10.14	10.23
Newcastle	9.39	9.52	10.8	10.18	10.27
Glasgow	9.54	10.7	10.23	10.33	10.42
Belfast	9.56	10.9	10.24	10.34	10.43

I am wondering whether by any chance you have the original of this address, that is, in the Spanish language, and if not, whether it would be possible for you to obtain it for me.

In passing, I would like to say how interesting I find your journal.

(Sgd.) R. L. H. J.,
MONTEVIDEO, URUGUAY.

Our Touring Adviser is endeavouring to provide the original wording for you.

* * *

Subscription List

SIR,—As I sometimes have difficulty in obtaining copies of your journal, could I possibly arrange to obtain it direct from you?

(Sgd.) J. D.,
TWICKENHAM, MDDX.

To avoid "taking a chance" with bookstalls and newsagents, you could receive regularly a subscriber's copy. Just send your full postal address, with a remittance for 11s. 6d. to The Manager, *Modern Motoring and Travel*, 53, Stratton Street, Piccadilly, London, W.1.

* * *

Coming to England

SIR,—I am the owner of a May 1951 Hillman Minx Saloon, Mark IV, bought second-hand from the Company I am employed with, in March, 1952.

I hope to go on three months' leave from here in June, 1953, and intend to take this Hillman with me to U.K.

If I feel inclined, will I be able to sell this car in U.K., and if I do, do I have to pay purchase tax, and how does customs' duty come into the matter?

When I take the car home, will I have to get it out again after a certain period?

What will be the arrangements regarding the road fund licence when I do take it home?

I am a regular subscriber to "Modern Motoring and Travel."

(Sgd.) T. R. T.,
LAGOS, NIGERIA.

(a) If you bring the car with you with the intention of returning to Nigeria with it, this is permissible up to 12 months under the ordinary Carnet or Triptique permit.

(b) If you bring the car in with the object of selling it while in the United Kingdom, you will be liable for import licence, customs dues and purchase tax. Some concession may be obtainable in regard to import licence and customs dues on British made vehicles; i.e., there may be some slight reduction in this connection. The purchase tax will be essential.

(c) On the question of Road Fund Licence—the unexpired portion thereof at the time of departure from the United Kingdom is returnable on prior application to the licensing authorities.

It is recommended that you contact your local licensing organisation who will be able to confirm, and possibly augment, this information.

The Dewar Trophy

Congratulations to Sunbeam-Talbot!

for winning the Dewar Trophy, which was awarded to them in recognition of their outstanding team successes in the Alpine Rally of 1952, using Shell X-100 Motor Oil. This is the third time in succession that the Dewar Trophy has been won on Shell X-100.

Shell X-100 is obtainable in the following grades:
SHELL X-100 GRADE 20/20W
SHELL X-100 GRADE 30
SHELL X-100 GRADE 40
SHELL X-100 GRADE 50

For your Sunbeam-Talbot:
Engine: Summer Shell X-100 Grade 30
Winter Shell X-100 Grade 20/20W
Gear Box: Shell X-100 Grade 30
Rear Axle: Bevel type: Shell Spirax 140 E.P.
Hypoid type: Shell Spirax 90 E.P.

SHELL X-100 MOTOR OIL

is exclusively recommended by the Rootes Group for all their models

fights acid action — main cause of engine wear

Springtime Suggestions:

(Concluded from page 48)

and looked dreadful. One ballet length evening dress in turquoise Terylene with a tiered full skirt finally appeared alone. It looked lovely, but our curiosity was aroused by the fact that Terylene in its *unfinished* state had apparently looked *too* "horrific" to be seen! Even the skill of the students had been unable to conjure it into crisp tiers.

It was most interesting to see so many new fabrics in the "loom state." One felt that the inventors must have been men of great faith to persevere. With the skilled aid of the Dyers' Group these new fabrics became materials of great beauty; and small expense.

The students of St. Martin's School of Art showed excellent workmanship; and the vivacity one would expect from a cosmopolitan centre where it is not unusual to find in one class students from 10 different countries. All the very chic hats worn with the models were created by a student with a name I find unpronounceable, raising Vudhijaya, who hails *from Thailand*.

* * *

ANOTHER event of the season, with the accent on youth, was the opening of "*Balcon*" in Piccadilly Arcade.

This is a fascinating place for all who share the new passion for growing plants indoors.

At least it is not *new*, cottagers have always had plants indoors in England, and the Victorians had their conservatories and aspidistras. But to-day plants are used as part of indoor decorative schemes and the two young men who run "*Balcon's*" have experience as architects and decorators as well as gardeners.

They will sell you an indoor ivy from 3s. 6d., or design a whole town garden. You can buy from them not only the plants but all the charming accessories for plant display.

For a few shillings you can buy modern white wire supports for plant pots to hang on a "plant wall"; or they will design you special window tables, or sell you woven squares or rectangles to hang on your wall as a background "frame" for a single special plant.

You can "floodlight" these from behind with a simple strip of lighting if you like, and they are *most* effective.

* * *

IF you are, like myself, an "indoor plant fiend" *do* visit "Balcon's of Piccadilly Arcade." It is a new, fascinating and friendly place, and they are just the people to advise you if you plan something rather special with plants as part of the indoor Coronation decoration in your own home.

They send their plants, safely packed, all over the country.

With our houses all nicely planned and furnished with labour-saving devices we *should* have a little more time to relax.

The newest electric oven, I am told, has an automatic time-switching device so that the business housewife can virtually be in two places at once and actually start the dinner an hour or more *before* she leaves the office.

* * *

WE should have more time for *recreation*, in the true sense, and now even those of us who dwell in flats will be able to stock up on indoor plants and settle down to take Candide's advice and—"*Cultivate our Garden.*"

I, too, am a Collector:

(Concluded from page 41)

They tried, but were still incredulous, when later we feasted upon the catch, appropriately dressed and garnished by the chef. The occasion, I remember, was the 21st birthday celebration of Mary Gilmour, daughter of Professor John Gilmour, M.S., F.R.C.S., of Newcastle, who will readily endorse my story.

The line and square I preserve to-day, Incidentally, three years after the incident, young Clement Gerhardsen, the boatman, was my welcome guest in London, with perfectly acquired English.

* * *

WERE space available one could continue indefinitely, but sufficient has been told already. I feel, to justify preference for objective collecting.

* * *

In all my discussions with interested visitors, there has been only one snag—they invariably ask my wife: "What do *you* think of his museum pieces?"

When that happens, I close my eyes and wait. Yes, here it comes: "Yes, all very interesting, I'm sure, so long as he keeps them clean and tidy. Personally, I wouldn't give them house room!"

To which, with a wink to my friends, I respond: "What about your workbaskets? Just tangled masses of cottons and silks, buttons galore, odd coins, aspirins, toffees, sewing machine parts, but never a needle!"

Then come, of course, the Captain's famous last words: "That's different!"

* * *

Well, cheerio! Good Luck, and good hunting!

Holidays Afloat:

(Concluded from page 22)

Should only two or three weeks be available, then there are frequent round sea tours from Rijeka-Fiume along the Dalmatian coast, taking 11 days and calling at about a dozen ports.

This latter tour, with good-grade ship and hotel accommodation, meals, etc., costs about £30.

* * *

A DIFFERENT, but very pleasant kind of holiday, is one which takes you along the inland waterways of Holland and Belgium, or up and down the Rhone. There are two British firms which specialise in such cruising holidays: Yacht Holidays, Ltd. (85, Buckingham Palace Road, London, S.W.1) and World Holidays Afloat, Ltd. (86, Strand, London, W.C.2).

* * *

Yacht Holidays, Ltd., offer cruises in Holland, Holland and Belgium, through the Rhineland, and on the River Seine to Paris.

* * *

World Holidays Afloat, Ltd., have a quite enticing tour on a luxury motor-ship through the waterways of Holland and Belgium, the all-in cost of the 10 days' holiday being 35 guineas.

Without a doubt, the ideal way of seeing and getting to know Holland is to travel by waterway. It is also about the most restful kind of change that anyone could wish for, especially for those who tend to get bored if they remain in place.

* * *

HAVE I given you some ideas for a holiday afloat? I hope so. But I still think that the keen enthusiast will want to peruse the brochures issued by the firms mentioned below. You may quite possibly find in one of them the offer of a journey to the land of your dreams—a holiday whose memories will last you a lifetime.

WHERE TO WRITE

Bowerman Bros., 28, Ely Place, Holborn Circus, London, E.C.1.

Bergen Line, Norway House, Cockspur Street, London, S.W.1.

Coast Lines, Ltd., Royal Liver Building, Liverpool 3, and at 227, Regent Street, London, W.1.

Thos. Cook & Son, Ltd., Berkeley Street, London, W.1.

Convoys, Ltd., 30, Bouverie Street, London, E.C.4.

Informal Travels, 45, Queensway, London, W.2.

Wakefield, Fortune & Co., Ltd., 32, Shaftesbury Avenue, London, W.1.

World Holidays Afloat, Ltd., 86, Strand, London, W.C.2.

Norway Travel Association, Cockspur Street, London, S.W.1.

Yacht Holidays, Ltd., 86, Buckingham Palace Road, London, S.W.1.

CAN WE HELP YOU?

Information Bureau

READERS are cordially invited to take full advantage of the facilities provided. The services of the "MODERN MOTORING & TRAVEL" Information Bureau (temporary address, 150 New Bond Street, London, W.1—Tel.: Mayfair 9761) with its team of Expert advisers, are entirely free. Correspondents are requested, if a reply direct is desired, to enclose a stamped and addressed envelope for this purpose.

Readers are also offered the free use of the Magazine's correspondence columns. All letters submitted for inclusion therein are subject, of course, to the Editor's approval, and all letters must bear the sender's signature and full address—not necessarily for publication—as an indication of good faith. Readers' criticisms and/or suggestions are welcome.

The Police have a word for it!

"COPROPHONIA" — or, the practice of swearing over the telephone

BUT, the police in many areas have a *good* word for "Apollo", the world-famous Car Polish, forerunner of every other liquid Car Polish, and although many users "swear *by*" it — no case is ever known of it being "sworn *at*" — telephonically or otherwise.

THAT'S WHY, against all comers, it is still used by Humber, Hillman, Sunbeam-Talbot, Renault, Morris, Wolseley, MG, Riley, Daimler, Lanchester, Singer, Standard, Triumph, Alvis, Allard, Jensen and other pedigree cars; leading motor-cycle and side-car makers; eminent coachbuilders, official, public and commercial transport.

Writing on 5th March, 1953 from Harrow, a regular user says: "I find it ('Apollo') to be EASILY THE BEST of many which I have tried over a number of years." (Ref. B/X/619.)

Sole Proprietors:

BERNARD J. ELLIS, LIMITED
EPSOM ROAD, LONDON, E.10, ENGLAND

who in case of local frustration will gladly send you a post-paid (full-size) tin against remittance 4/6.

"Apollo" CAR POLISH

What You Say, How You Say It, Can Make You More Popular And Successful

A well-known publisher reports there is a simple technique of everyday conversation which can pay you real dividends in both social and professional advancement and works like magic to give you added poise, self-confidence and greater popularity. The details of this method are described in a fascinating booklet, "Adventures in Conversation," sent free on request.

According to this publisher, many people do not realise how much they could influence others simply by what they say and how they say it. Whether in business, at social functions, or even in casual conversations with new acquaintances, there are ways in which you can make a good impression every time you talk.

To acquaint more readers of this paper with the easy-to-follow rules for developing skill in everyday conversation, the publishers have printed full details of their interesting self-training method in a 24-page booklet, which will be sent free to anyone who requests it. The address is: — Conversation Studies (Dept. MMT/CSI), Marple, Cheshire. *Enclose 2½d. stamp for postage.*

CAR HIRE

sponsored by the

world famous

ROOTES GROUP

with service

throughout the world

* *Phone* CUNningham 5141
* *Cable* ROOTESHIRE, LONDON

- Britain's finest cars
- Chauffeur Driven or Self Drive
- British & Continental Tours arranged
- Linguist Chauffeurs
- Clients met at Dock or Airport

ROOTES CAR HIRE

— ABBEY HALL ABBEY ROAD LONDON NW8 —

OVERSEAS BOOKING FACILITIES available through Rootes Group Regional Offices and Distributors in 119 countries

This handsome array of trophies (left) represents the golf and snooker achievements last season of Anchor Motors, Rootes Group distributors of Chester, Cheshire. They include the Ferguson Cup and the Liverpool, Manchester and Cheshire Trade Trophies.

Rootes Group enthusiasts are the Thomson family of West Calder, Scotland, who run Humber and Hillman cars (see above). From 1925 until recently the family operated a private car hire fleet as Messrs. Thomson & Son, with early Hillman " 14 " models.

IN A FEW WORDS:

News Items of Modern Motoring and Travel Interest

A STRONG Sunbeam-Talbot 90 team has been entered for the R.A.C.'s " Coronation Year " International Rally (March 23-28), to be contested over 1,500 miles of the most gruelling and varied terrain in the British Isles. The Rally—for which there were over 200 entries—is one of 10 events to count towards the International Touring Car Championship of Europe.

As we close for press, three Sunbeam-Talbot 90's have been entered for the men's team prize and one in the women's section.

Norman Garrad, the team manager, with co-driver John Cutts (both of Coventry), head the 2¼-litre Sunbeam-Talbots in the class " up to 2,500 c.c."

In car No. 2 will be two Bournemouth drivers, George Hartwell and Francis Scott. Hartwell and Scott drove together in this year's Monte Carlo Rally.

Car crew No. 3 will consist of John N. Pearman, of Kenilworth, Warwickshire, with R. J. Adams, of Belfast, both well-known trials' drivers.

Miss Sheila Van Damm, of Rustington, Sussex, with Mrs. Francoise V. Clarke, of Bitteswell Manor, near Rugby, will be out to set up the " best perfomance by an all-women's crew." Miss Van Damm and Mrs. Clarke, in a Sunbeam-Talbot 90, were Second in the Coupe des Dames in this year's " Monte."

With two starting points—Hastings and Blackpool—entries are divided between touring and sports cars. The route is via Silverstone, for special acceleration and braking tests; Blackpool (for an overnight stop and further special tests); the Lake District and Yorkshire (two more tests); Hastings (for an overnight halt), on then to Goodwood (more tests) and back to the Hastings finish where the 100 best-placed cars will compete for final general classification.

* * *

THE FULL RANGE of new Hillman cars—Anniversary Minx Saloon and Convertible Coupé, Californian Hard Top and Hillman Estate Car—were a feature of the Geneva Motor Show in March. The Humber Super Snipe, the Humber Hawk and the Sunbeam-Talbot " 90 " Sports Saloon and Sports Convertible Coupé, were also exhibited by the Rootes Group.

* * *

THE FAWLEY REFINERY of Esso Petroleum Company, Ltd. is to provide the Danish Esso Company with some 700,000 tons of petroleum products during 1953, to the value of more than £7 million.

* * *

MOTORISTS who intend licensing their cars for the first time this year are reminded that they must apply to the Local Taxation Office, and not to a Post Office. Whenever possible, applications to the Local Taxation Office should be made by post.

* * *

B.O.A.C.'s FOURTH Comet jet-liner passenger service, introduced in April between Britain and Japan, reduces the journey from 86 hours to 33 hours. The 10,000 miles' journey is through Rome, Beirut (or Cairo), Bahrain, Karachi, Delhi, Calcutta, Rangoon, Bangkok, Manila and Okinawa.

* * *

THE GOVERNMENT has decided that both types of motor-vehicle traffic indicator, the flashing light and the semaphore arm, are to be made optional.

Trico-Folberth, Ltd., of Great West Road, Brentford, have been manufacturing winking lights, for export, over the past four years.

* * *

OF SPECIAL INTEREST to motorists who tour abroad is the formation of the G.B. Car Club, with the chief aim of providing an inter-change of information on the many aspects of foreign touring. Mr. J. H. T. Fletcher is General Secretary, and the Club's offices are at 30, St. George Street, Hanover Square, London, W.1.

* * *

A PARTY of 63 Irish dealers flew from Dublin for a recent sales conference at the Rootes Group factories at Coventry, Warwickshire, where the Hillman " Anniversary " models were on view.

Headed by Mr. A. F. Buckley, Chairman and Managing Director of Buckley's Motors, Ltd., of Whitehall, Dublin, the visitors also saw films of the Humber Super Snipe's 90-hour run from Norway to Portugal and of the last Alpine Rally which led to Sunbeam-Talbot cars being awarded the R.A.C. Dewar Trophy.

* * *

OTHER VISITORS at the factories were executives of the Norwich Motor Company, Ltd., led by their Chairman, Mr. F. H. Olorenshaw and his son, Mr. J. F. Olorenshaw. They also toured the Rootes Group School.

(Continued on page 56)

Greaves & Thomas, Ltd., manufacturers of the Put-U-Up and other furniture, operate this 7-ton Commer and 3-ton Hands trailer overnight between London and Bolton. Delivery was made through Ray-Powell, Rootes Group dealers of Leytonstone, E.11, whose Commer Express Delivery Van is also shown.

May, 1953   Page 55   MODERN MOTORING & TRAVEL

it's a save money plan with
PRESTCOLD

The moment you put a Prestcold in your kitchen you start to save money, says Mr. Coolie. On good food kept good, on milk which never 'turns', on left-overs you can use again, on all waste curtailed. But more than that, a Prestcold saves still further money because it costs you less in the long run. Prestcold refrigerators are built by one of Britain's greatest engineering firms. Spend your money wisely on strength, dependability, service. Plan now to save with a Prestcold!

3 models to choose from

to keep good food good

PRESSED STEEL COMPANY LIMITED, COWLEY, OXFORD.   London Office & Showrooms: Sceptre House, 169 Regent St., W.1

Manufacturers also of Motor Car Bodies, Steel Railway Wagons, Agricultural Implements and Pressings of all types.

Keep your wheels smart . . .

with a set of these attractive Ace 'Rimbellishers'—they are well-made, well-plated and easily fitted. Have a look at your car and judge what a difference 'Rimbellishers' would make, not just to the wheels but to the entire appearance of the car. They will keep your wheels looking better for longer, and simplify wheel-cleaning too. Ask for them at your garage, or write to us for full details.

The name 'Rimbellisher' is a Registered Trade Mark of Cornercroft Ltd. and may not be used to describe any other wheel trim.

ACE RIMBELLISHERS
N.C.80

CORNERCROFT LTD
ACE WORKS, COVENTRY; Phone: COVENTRY 64123 and 32 CLARGES ST., PICCADILLY, LONDON, W.1; Phone: GROSVENOR 1646.

'A no-claim bonus on <u>home</u> insurance?'

Yes—the 'General' gives you a *free* year's insurance on your Householder's policy every sixth year—provided, of course, that you've had no claims in the meantime. If your house isn't covered already—or is insufficiently covered—why not let the 'General' insure it as well as your car? You can save yourself trouble, too, by making one cheque cover both premiums. Without trouble to yourself you can transfer any existing policy on renewal and start earning a bonus.

Peace of mind costs very little

General
ACCIDENT FIRE AND LIFE
ASSURANCE CORPORATION LIMITED
Send coupon to H.C. Dept., General Buildings, Perth, Scotland, or to nearest office (see Telephone Directory)

Please send full particulars of Household Insurance

Name ....

Address ....

M.M.

FAMOUS FOR ALL CLASSES OF INSURANCE

Stage illusionist Kalanag is now successfully touring Africa with his Magical and Musical Revue. Picture above shows the company with a fleet of Hillman Minx cars provided by Messrs. Coy & Coy Ltd., distributors of Port Elizabeth.

At Kuala Lumpur: Sir Reginald Rootes (fourth from left), deputy chairman, Rootes Group, meets local distributors of Rootes Group products during his extended overseas tour to further Britain's export drive. Left: Mr. J. L. Campbell, the Group's Far East representative; next, Mr. T. Graham, manager of Wearnes, Kuala Lumpur; extreme right, Mr. R. Jackson, manager of Lyons Motors, of Singapore.

Above, at a picnic spot near Rustenburg, in the Transvaal: see tribute by "G. C. S." on right.

In a Few Words:
(Continued from page 54)

THE SPEED LIMIT for motor vehicles through the Blackwall and Rotherhithe tunnels is to be increased from 15 to 20 m.p.h.

* * *

SPAIN last year showed the biggest percentage increase among British motorists holiday-making abroad of any country. Petrol is obtainable this year without coupons at 4s. 6d. per gallon.

* * *

BRITISH HOLIDAY-MAKERS are being offered special currency inducements to "Come to Yugoslavia." "We intend to see that the Britisher's £25 holiday allowance will go further than in any other country," states Mr. K. Novak, Director of the Yugoslav National Tourist Office.

* * *

THE MINISTER OF TRANSPORT, the Right Hon. Alan Lennox-Boyd, M.P., received a deputation to discuss the raising of the heavy goods vehicle speed limit from 20 to 30 m.p.h. The Minister undertook to give careful consideration to the case as stated.

* * *

SERVICE SHOW WEEKS arranged by Rootes Group dealers, include those of Manton Motors, Ltd., of Shirley Road, Croydon, Surrey, from April 13 to 18, and R. S. Mead (Sales), Ltd., of Queen Street, Maidenhead, Berks, from April 27 to May 2.

* * *

MR. GEORGE NOBLE, O.B.E., General Manager of Refining at the London head office of Esso Petroleum Company, Ltd., has been appointed a director. Mr. Noble was closely connected with the construction and the initial operations of the Fawley refinery.

MR. A. R. RODWAY, M.B.E., London Divisional Manager of Shell-Mex and B.P., Ltd., for over 20 years, has retired.

* * *

THE AUTOMOBILE ASSOCIATION has opened a branch office at 23, Frances Street, Truro, Cornwall.

* * *

THE MANCHESTER OFFICE of the Royal Automobile Club has removed to new and more commodious premises at 135, Dickenson Road, Manchester, 14.

SIR,—I have just returned after having spent a holiday touring with my 1951 Hillman Minx. During the month I completed 3,500 miles, and my speedometer reading is now almost 26,000 miles.

The Minx is as good as ever. . . . I completed my tour without having a puncture or mechanical trouble. I left Cape Town for Rustenburg in the Transvaal and most of my driving was during the heat of the day on the Highveld, yet the car behaved splendidly.

When one considers the fact that the engine of this car has not yet been decarbonised nor touched for any mechanical adjustment, it is an amazing performance for a 10 h.p. car to run so well after 26,000 miles.

Here are some facts of one of my trips: Kempton Park, Transvaal, to Cape Town in 20 hours. Distance, 956 miles. Cruising speed between 50 and 55 m.p.h. Average speed, 44 m.p.h. Petrol consumption for this trip was 36.7 m.p.g.

You can see, therefore, that I am "more than satisfied" with the general performance of my Minx.
(Sgd.) G. C. S.,
City Hall, Cape Town.

* * *

BRITISH RAILWAYS are to open a new booking and information office, to be known as the British Railways Travel Centre, at Rex House, at the corner of Lower Regent Street and Carlton Street, just off Piccadilly Circus in London's West End.

* * *

NEW FEATURES are included in the 1953 edition of the R.A.C. Continental Handbook, which is now available. A Customs (imports) section details articles which may, within specified limits, be brought back to this country without payment of duty. As before, all aspects of foreign touring are fully covered.

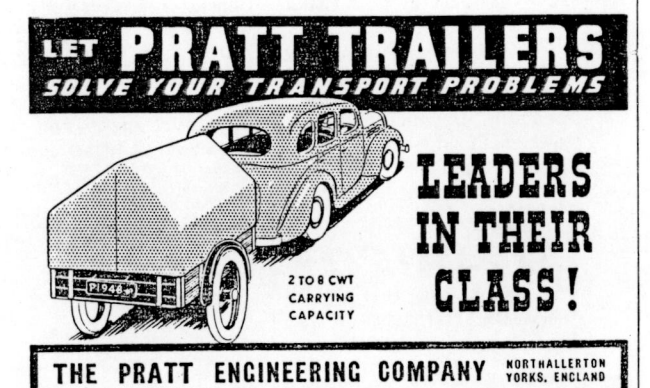

LET **PRATT TRAILERS** SOLVE YOUR TRANSPORT PROBLEMS

LEADERS IN THEIR CLASS!

2 TO 8 CWT CARRYING CAPACITY

THE PRATT ENGINEERING COMPANY — NORTHALLERTON, YORKS, ENGLAND

River Avon and Shakespeare Memorial Theatre.
Stratford-on-Avon :   Photo by Hugh Sibley.

> Soul of the age!
> The applause, delight, and wonder of our stage!
> My Shakespeare, rise! I will not lodge thee by
> Chaucer or Spenser, or bid Beaumont lie
> A little further off, to make thee room;
> Thou art a monument, without a tomb.
> *Ben Johnson.*

Sir Ambrose Dundas Flux Dundas, K.C.I.E., C.S.I., Lieut.-Governor of the Isle of Man and, until recently, Governor, North West Frontier Province of Pakistan, with his Humber Hawk Saloon now sharing honours with Sir Ambrose's new Hillman Minx.

The British Ambassador, His Excellency Sir Christopher Warner, K.C.M.G., visits the Humber stand at the recent Brussels Motor Show. Seen with the Ambassador are: Mr. B. B. Winter (left), Director of Engineering, Rootes Group, and Mr. H. P. Spencer, Director of Rootes (Belgique) S.A.

Sir Henry Hobson, K.B.E., (centre), H.M. Consul-General in New York, with Sir William Rootes, K.B.E., Chairman of the Rootes Group, and Mr. Brian Rootes, Regional Director, at the reception given in New York recently to announce the new Humber Super Snipe in the American markets.

Built expressly for the display of Rootes Group products, the new showrooms of London British Motors, Ltd., distributors, of York Street, London, Ontario, were recently opened to the public. Photo shows Mr. Roy Allison, sales manager; Mr. J. T. Panks, director of Rootes Motors (Canada) Ltd.; Mr. W. Thompson, President; Mr. Ian Garrard and Mr. McCoy, Secretary-Treasurer.

Editorial Comment

EDITORIAL AND ADVERTISING
53 STRATTON STREET,
LONDON, W.1
Telephone: GRO 3401

Conducted by E. D. O'BRIEN
Editor: THOMAS R. MULCASTER

BRITISH engineering skill has never stood so high in world acclaim as it does to-day. In this issue we take pride in demonstrating our part in the unchallenged triumph of British-built motor cars in global markets.

Firstly, we celebrate this month the twenty-first birthday anniversary of one of the most popular family cars of all times—the Hillman Minx.

This light car is outstanding by any standards. As we explain elsewhere, the car, during the past 21 years has been perfected through 21,000,000,000 miles of family motoring. This figure is no over-statement. The thousands of drivers of the Minx will together have greatly exceeded this figure.

On pages 22—27, you will find the wonderful story of the Minx, with full details of the new anniversary models.

* * *

THE second reason for a "pat-on-the-back" comes from the award by the Royal Automobile Club of Great Britain of its coveted Dewar Trophy, which is offered for "the most outstanding engineering and technical achievement of the year".

The Trophy goes to Sunbeam-Talbot cars for their classic performance in the 1952 International Alpine Rally.

Sunbeam-Talbots

Obtained three Coupes des Alpes out of a total of 10 only given

Were awarded the team prize for the best performance irrespective of size, class or nationality, and also the special team award offered by France for the best team performance by foreign cars

Occupied first, second and third places in the 2/3-litre class of the complete event, and

Were awarded the special cup for the most outstanding performance of the Rally.

Such achievements provide impetus to our export drive and keep the "Union Jack" proudly flying throughout the industrial world.

Congratulations to the designers, engineers and operatives who make these cars, and all praise to the Rally drivers whose team-work set the seal on success.

* * *

THE performances of the Hillman Minx and Sunbeam-Talbots will maintain the British flag proudly "wagging" in competitive export markets. Friend—and competitor alike—of British engineering products will note that there is to-day no slackening of effort.

June, 1953 — Page 1 — MODERN MOTORING & TRAVEL

ESSO EXTRA

LEAPS INTO THE LEAD!

Now you can give your car that Spring feeling with **Esso Extra,** star product of Britain's most modern refinery—*the great new petrol with six extras.*

The instant starting, unfaltering power, effortless acceleration, unique economy of this magnificent petrol has already established its clear lead in quality and in popularity.

Fill up today with **Esso Extra** and start on the road to **Extra** Happy Motoring.

TRY IT AND PROVE IT!

EXTRA ANTI-KNOCK · **EXTRA** MILES PER GALLON · **EXTRA** ACCELERATION
EXTRA EASY STARTING · **EXTRA** POWER · **EXTRA** ENGINE CLEANLINESS

Renew your oil filter regularly

- TRAPS CLOGGING SLUDGE → **AC**
- SAVES OIL AND PETROL → **AC**
- REDUCES REPAIRS → **AC**
- A BRITISH PRODUCT → **AC**
- MADE BY GENERAL MOTORS → **AC**

Correct Replacement elements to use :—

Humber, Super Snipe 1953, OHV	FF50
Humber, Pullman 1948-53 and Snipe 1948-52	K11
Humber, Hawk 1948 on	L11
Sunbeam-Talbot '90' and 2 Litre	L11
Sunbeam-Talbot '80' and 10 h.p.	L14

AC OIL FILTERS

AC-Delco, Division of General Motors Ltd., Dunstable, Beds., and Southampton, Hants.

Your Coronation Seat!

THE "RESTAWILE"

Patent applied for No. 3001/53

Why stand up for hours? The "Restawile" will provide a comfortable seat while you wait. It's light, portable, weighs only 7 lbs. folds to 16″ × 17″ × 1½″ and is so easy to carry.

Use it also in your caravan, in the garden or at the seaside. The backrest is easily adjustable to two positions. Fold it down and it can be used as a picnic table.

The metal frame is fitted with tubular legs and complete with high grade canvas fast colour gay stripes.

Price including Purchase Tax

£1 · 7 · 11

A **DESMO** PRODUCT fully guaranteed to give years of service.

DESMO LTD.
BIRMINGHAM 7
Telephone: Aston Cross 2831

London Showrooms:
220 SHAFTESBURY AVENUE, LONDON, W.C.1
Telephone: Temple Bar 1994/5.

In this Historic Year

Fabram REGD **PRODUCTS**

Remain — as ever
PROUD TO SERVE

- MINIMUFS AND RADIATOR MUFFS
- OVERALL CLOTHING FOR ALL TRADES
- LOOSE CAR SEAT COVERS

FAXALL PRODUCTS LTD.
BLACKLEDGE WORKS · HALIFAX
Telephone: Halifax 5208   Telegrams: FAXALL, Halifax

the Majority of
COMMER & KARRIER
vehicles are equipped with
BRAKES, HYDRAULIC EQUIPMENT and **DAMPERS**
by

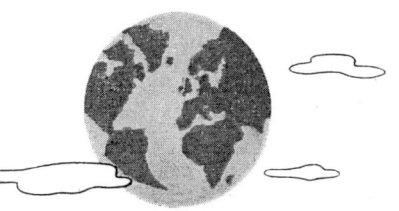

GIRLING
THE BEST BRAKES IN THE WORLD

Backed by a world wide **SERVICE** organisation that keeps them **WAY OUT AHEAD**

GIRLING LIMITED
KINGS ROAD · TYSELEY · BIRMINGHAM · 11

A CAR LOOKS AS NEW AS ITS CARPETS!

★

NEAT, PERFECT FITTING, LASTING.

Obtain complete car-interior cleanliness. Put into position or removed without fuss; design and finish in keeping with car's key-note of quality.

They are constructed of laminated rubberised cotton fabric, woven together on galvanised steel wires,
GUARANTEED FOR TEN YEARS.

FREE TRIAL OFFER

PRICES:

Humber Hawk and Snipe 1953 :	£ s. d.	Hillman Minx 1950/53 (Phase IV):	£ s. d.	Sunbeam-Talbot "90":	£ s. d.
Front Mats	1 19 4	Front Mats	2 3 10	Front Mats	1 16 7
Rear Mats	2 12 10	Rear Mats	1 18 5	Rear Mats	1 17 9
	4 12 2		4 2 3		3 14 4
Purchase Tax	0 17 4	Purchase Tax	0 15 5	Purchase Tax	0 13 11
	5 9 6		4 17 8		4 8 3

Fill in this coupon and post to The Universal Mat Co., Ltd., Tileyard Road, York Way, London, N.7.

Please send me on a week's free trial

Front pair mats .... ⎫ Please mark
Back pair mats .... ⎬ here set
Complete set mats .... ⎭ required.

I sign this coupon on the distinct understanding that I am at liberty to return the mats any time within one week of receipt. If retained, I undertake to pay for mats within thirty days net.

for.........h.p. Make............Year............

Signed (Name) ....

Address ....

Date...............

THIS OFFER APPLIES TO U.K. ONLY

Protect Your Carpets with UNIVERSAL CAR MATS

---

to AUSTRALIA and THE EAST

P&O

For Sailings and Fares apply:—
14/16 COCKSPUR ST. S.W.1.
9 KINGSWAY, W.C.2.
122 LEADENHALL ST. E.C.3.

Wilcot Loose Seat Covers

Tailor made in Tygan Woven Fabric, Felt and Cotton Duck. Send make, year and model of car for prices and patterns.

WILCOT (PARENT) CO. LTD.
FISHPONDS • • • BRISTOL

BIND YOUR "Modern Motoring and Travel"

★

"EASIBIND" Covers to hold twelve copies, or one full volume, now available; strongly made, steel reinforced.

Price 15s. post free.

★

Orders with remittances, to—

The Manager, "Modern Motoring & Travel," 53, Stratton Street, Piccadilly, W.1.

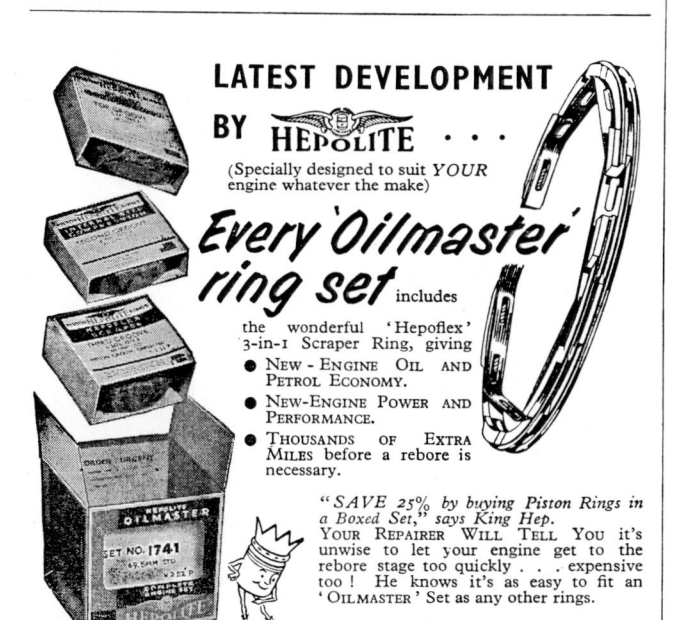

LATEST DEVELOPMENT BY HEPOLITE ...
(Specially designed to suit YOUR engine whatever the make)

Every 'Oilmaster' ring set includes
the wonderful 'Hepoflex' 3-in-1 Scraper Ring, giving
- NEW-ENGINE OIL AND PETROL ECONOMY.
- NEW-ENGINE POWER AND PERFORMANCE.
- THOUSANDS OF EXTRA MILES before a rebore is necessary.

"SAVE 25% by buying Piston Rings in a Boxed Set," says King Hep. YOUR REPAIRER WILL TELL YOU it's unwise to let your engine get to the rebore stage too quickly ... expensive too! He knows it's as easy to fit an 'OILMASTER' Set as any other rings.

HEPOLITE Oilmaster RING SETS SAVE YOU MONEY

Write Direct for fully descriptive folder on 'OILMASTER' to HEPWORTH & GRANDAGE LTD., DEPT. L, BRADFORD, YORKS. n.d.h. 1397.

---

the amber light gives you a warning

—fire never does

so always carry a

Pyrene TRADE MARK FIRE EXTINGUISHER

Pyrene "Pump" or "Pressure" type Fire Extinguishers are available at all good garages—or write for illustrated literature to Dept. M.M.6., The Pyrene Company Ltd., 9, Grosvenor Gardens, London, S.W.1. Telephone: VICtoria 3401.

SUCCESS!

"...MARKED ABSENCE OF PINKING"
"...THREE OR FOUR MILES PER HOUR BETTER"
"...NOTHING BUT PRAISE"
"...QUICKER AND BETTER ACCELERATION"

Delco-Remy OIL-FILLED COIL

is a better coil for ANY CAR!

—these are typical user reactions. All claims made for this remarkable coil have been confirmed by the sales figures and unstinted public praise. Now is the time to fit a Delco-Remy Oil-Filled Coil and ensure you get the best results from branded petrol. Hermetically sealed against moisture and oil-filled for permanent insulation, this coil carries a two-year guarantee.

Consult your local garage or write for descriptive leaflet.

DELCO-REMY-HYATT
DIVISION OF GENERAL MOTORS LTD.
GROSVENOR ROAD · LONDON · S·W·1

LIST PRICE **36/-** 6 AND 12 VOLT

ROOTES *Car Seat Covers*

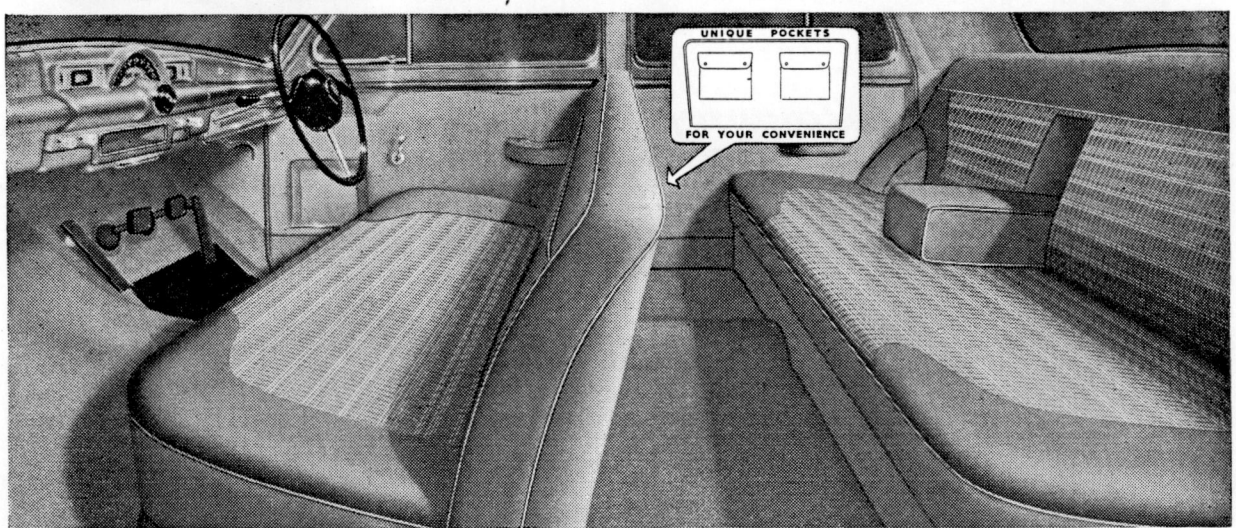

UNIQUE POCKETS FOR YOUR CONVENIENCE

Tailor-made from high quality materials for all car makes, they offer the following advantages:

ADDED COMFORT
GOOD LOOKS AND SHAPE
PREVENTION OF SHINE TO PERSONAL CLOTHING

A VARIETY OF COLOURS IN FELT OR TYGAN AND FELT
Patterns and prices available on application to Dept. M.M.

ROOTES LTD., LADBROKE HALL, BARLBY RD., LONDON, W.10
Tel. LADbroke 3232

BIRMINGHAM	90/94 Charlotte Street	Central 8411
MANCHESTER	Olympia, Chester Road	Blackfriars 6677
MAIDSTONE	Mill Street	Maidstone 3333
ROCHESTER	High Street	Chatham 2231
CANTERBURY	The Pavilion	Canterbury 3232
WROTHAM	Wrotham Heath	Borough Green 4
FOLKESTONE	86/92 Tontine Street	Folkestone 3156

and from all Rootes Group Distributors and Dealers

Is your carburetter too worn to be a good mixer?

PETROL IS WASTED AND PERFORMANCE IS LOST IF YOUR CARBURETTER CAN NO LONGER MIX THE RIGHT AMOUNTS OF AIR AND PETROL IN CORRECT RATIO

It's tough on a carburetter! It has an exacting job to do from the moment you press the starter until you switch off the ignition. Gradually over many, many miles, wear and tear begin to take their toll and before you may realise it performance deteriorates and petrol consumption goes up. No engine can give of its best when the carburetter is worn.

SERVICE EXCHANGE PLAN. Most cars on Britain's roads are Zenith equipped. Exchange your worn Zenith now for a new unit of the same type. A big cash allowance is made for the old carburetter which means that *for a few pounds you can restore economy and efficiency to your engine.*

ZENITH
CARBURETTERS

CONVERSION PLAN. If you have another make of carburetter or an early type Zenith fitted to your engine, this plan will give you latest Zenith carburation with *more power from less petrol.*

THE ZENITH CARBURETTER CO. LTD
HONEYPOT LANE, STANMORE, MIDDX

Please send me details of your Service Exchange/Conversion Plan and name and address of your nearest Service Station.

NAME ....

ADDRESS ....

....

MAKE OF ENGINE .... H.P. .... YEAR ....

MME

Most cars on Britain's roads are Zenith equipped

GO TO A ZENITH AGENT AND BE SURE OF GENUINE ZENITH SERVICE

AMERICA CABLES...

++ANNIVERSARY GREETINGS AND HEARTIEST CONGRATULATIONS STOP ITS NEW BEAUTY AND PERFORMANCE GUARANTEE BEST YEAR WE EVER HAD STOP THE USA WILL NEED MORE HILLMANS THAN EVER IN 1953 ++

Hillman Minx

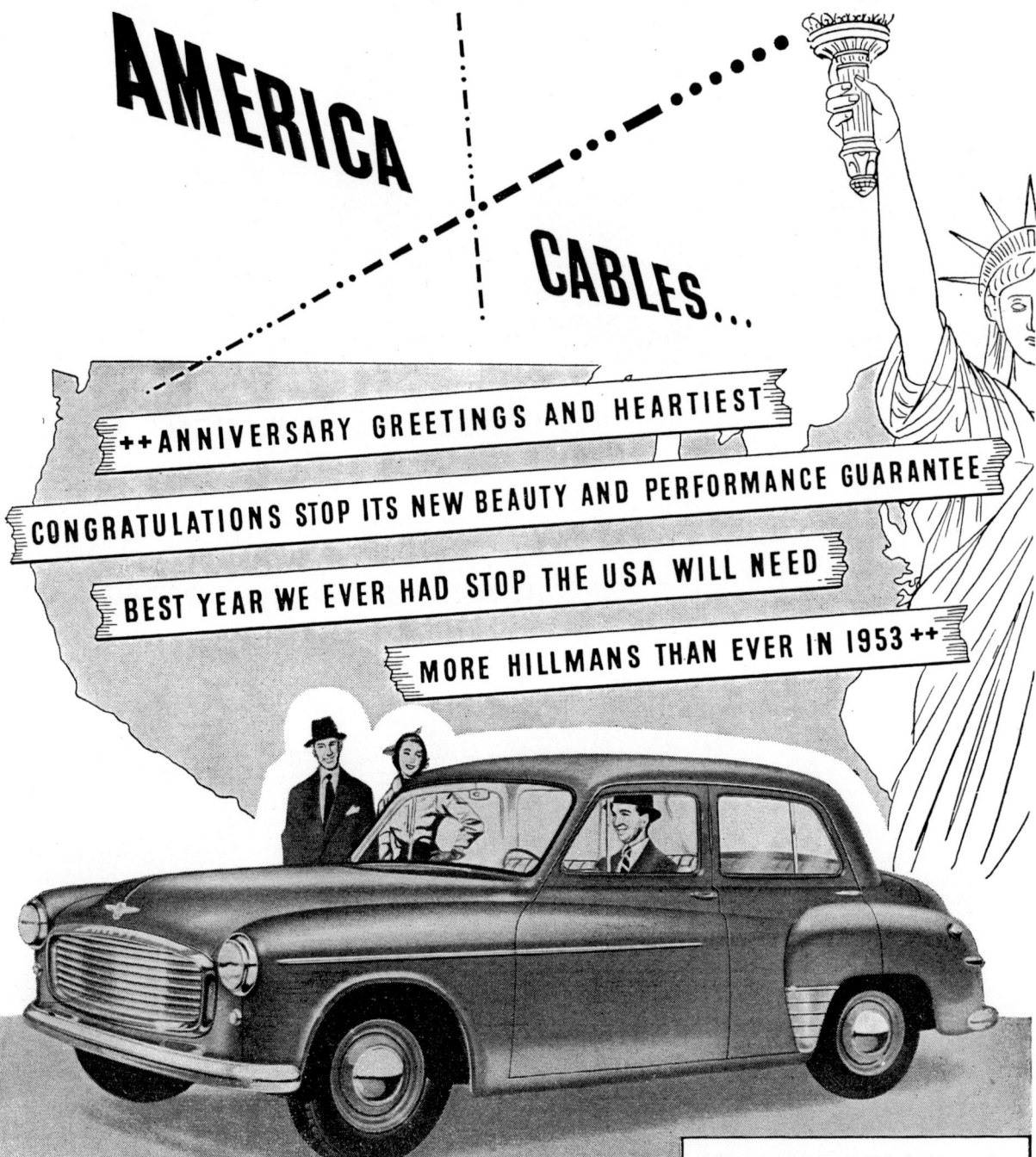

The new Anniversary Hillman Minx, perfection of 21 years' development, is the ideal family car. A roomy body, lively engine, low petrol consumption, durable construction and many detail refinements bring you more value than ever before.

The car which has won the heart of the world

EXPORT DIVISION ROOTES
DEVONSHIRE HOUSE
PICCADILLY LONDON W.1
Distributors throughout the World

ROOTES GROUP REGIONAL REPRESENTATIVES *located at:*

U.S.A. 505 Park Avenue, New York 22, N.Y. and 403 North Foothill Road, Beverly Hills, California.
CANADA 2019 Eglinton Avenue East, Toronto 13, Ontario.
AUSTRALIA & NEW ZEALAND Fishermen's Bend, Port Melbourne, Australia.
SOUTHERN AFRICA 750/2/4 Stuttaford's Buildings, St. George's St., Cape Town, S.A.
CENTRAL AFRICA Jackson Road, P.O. Box 5194, Nairobi, Kenya.
SOUTH EAST AFRICA Travlos House, Stanley Avenue, Salisbury, Southern Rhodesia.
BELGIUM Shell Building, 47, Cantersteen, Brussels.
FRANCE 6 Rond-Point des Champs Elysees, Paris, 8.
SWITZERLAND 3 Jenatschstrasse, Zurich.
FAR EAST Macdonald House, Orchard Road, Singapore, 9.
INDIA Agra Road, Bhandup, Bombay.
NEAR EAST 37 Kasr El Nil Street, Cairo, Egypt.
MIDDLE EAST & PAKISTAN Esseily Building, Assour, Beirut, Lebanon.
JAPAN Ol-Sakashita-Cho, Shinagawa-Ku, Tokyo.
ARGENTINA Casilla de Correo, 3478, Buenos Aires.
BRAZIL Av. Presidente Vargas 290 (S/1003), Rio de Janeiro.
CARIBBEAN P.O. Box 1479, Nassau, Bahamas.

To safeguard the in-built reliability of Rootes Group Cars you need

ROOTES GROUP CRAFTSMAN SERVICE

Guarantees:

Manufacturers' genuine parts protecting you against inferior quality.

Specialised tools and equipment essential to efficient service.

Factory trained mechanics, fully briefed on the latest technical developments.

Fully guaranteed factory-rebuilt units.

ROOTES

LONDON	Ladbroke Hall, Barlby Road	Ladbroke 3232
BIRMINGHAM	90/94 Charlotte Street	Central 8411
MANCHESTER	Olympia, Chester Road	Blackfriars 6677
MAIDSTONE	Mill Street	Maidstone 3333
CANTERBURY	The Pavilion	Canterbury 3232
ROCHESTER	High Street	Chatham 2231
FOLKESTONE	86/92 Tontine Street	Folkestone 3156
WROTHAM HEATH	Wrotham Heath	Borough Green 4

HEAD OFFICE & EXPORT DIVISION: DEVONSHIRE HOUSE, PICCADILLY LONDON W.1

June, 1953

If the wonderful Du Toit's Kloof impressed me by its majestic grandeur—so did the ruggedness of much else of the journey leave unforgettable memories.

Photo: Courtesy South African Railways

Unsolicited Tribute.

CAPE TOWN TO UMTALI—2,000 miles solo: By Brenda Scott Paine

IN the soft light of dawn the *Cape Town Castle* slipped quietly into Cape Town harbour, two weeks away from England's fog and intense cold.

Ahead of me lay 2,000 miles of motoring to my home at Umtali, in Southern Rhodesia.

Unfortunately, New Year's and Coon's holidays on January 1 and 2 caused some delay in the clearance of my new Hillman Minx, which I had on the ship with me, but everything was ready for me to start at mid-day on January 3.

I had called at the Cape Town office of the A.A. hoping to get a passenger-driver to accompany me, which is a usual procedure when travelling long distances, but without any luck.

* * *

THE weather was hot and gloriously sunny, and I travelled in extreme comfort on the perfect National road, which now extends from Cape Town for hundreds of miles.

I soon reached the Du Toit's Kloof and the Hex River Pass, two mountain passes about 56 miles from Cape Town, which the Minx took in perfect order.

The scenery of the country here is magnificent, and I travelled on my route steadily making the first two night stops at Touw's River and Hanover.

The only incident of note so far was driving through a swarm of young locusts!

During the afternoon of January 5, I was approaching Parys, holiday resort on the Vaal, which river forms the boundary of the Orange Free State and the Transvaal.

So I had traversed the Cape Province, the semi-desert countryside known as the Great Karroo and the Orange Free State, and had seen vineyards, desiduous farms, sheep ranches and lastly, the farming districts of the O.F.S.

* * *

NEARING Parys at six o'clock on the morning of January 6, I headed northwards into the Transvaal, the rich mineral province of the Union.

The weather was deteriorating, and after days of brilliant sunshine I now encountered thunder and lightning and rivers in spate.

At Paul Potgietersdorp I was held up by a cloud burst, when two inches of rain fell in half-an-hour.

That evening I gladly took refuge in the local hotel at Pietersburg, and left the following morning still in heavy rain.

I pushed on, over a ghastly road in the course of construction, to Louis Trichardt where the small but comfortable Mountain Inn is situated on the highest point of the Zoutspanberg and overlooking Wyllies' Poort, a natural pass through this lovely mountain area.

In spite of being so far north, there are large orchards of Citrus and sub-tropical fruits of all kinds.

The torrential rains forced me to spend three nights at the Mountain Inn, and the weather had not cleared properly when I left for Beit-Bridge, which crosses the Limpopo, the enormous river border between South Africa and the Rhodesias.

* * *

AT Beit-Bridge I was subjected to customs' formalities, and new registration plates were issued for the Minx.

I was told the usual route to Fort Victoria was impassable, all the bridges being submerged, in some places up to 12 ft.

This meant a diversion through West Nicholson and Bala-Bala, and some 150 extra miles. The road was shocking, with bridges under two feet of water, and low-gear was absolutely essential.

With new road works, the Minx frequently encountered conditions in the nature of a quagmire, but the car responded magnificently, in fact, the only trouble was the windscreen-wipers not operating properly, but then they had been in constant use for the past two days.

After varied difficulties of driving from Bala-Bala, a small mining Dorp, I reached the large asbestos mining centre of Shabani at 6 p.m. on January 10, a distance of 1,639 miles from Cape Town.

In spite of the trying circumstances, I was feeling surprisingly fresh, and this could only be put down to the unbelievable comfort of my small car.

Here at Shabani I was weather-bound, with other travellers, for the next five days. We were thankful to have the comfort of a hotel. as many motorists were held up on the edge of rivers with no food for days on end.

* * *

ON January 15, the A.A. reported that the Devuli River in the Sabi valley, always a doubtful proposition in the rainy season, could be crossed, and at 7 a.m. I set off on my last day's trek to Umtali.

This was a 280-mile journey, via Fort Victoria and Birchenough Bridge, and I carried sufficient food and drink to meet any reasonable eventuality.

I crossed two rivers in full spate, the fast-flowing M'Tokwe and the Lundi, and reached the wide and dangerous Deuuli river where lines of cars and lorries were waiting to cross. After waiting two hours and with the water still rising a foot high over the narrow bridge, I cautiously took the Minx across in second gear.

The upper side of the bridge was choked with trees and debris, threatening the frail structure, and it was a nerve-racking crossing.

When I regained the road I found the water had affected the brakes, but the last 100 miles of my journey were comparatively easy.

* * *

I ARRIVED home at Umtali at 5 p.m., the 2,000-mile journey having taken 12 days owing to the weather.

I had a great thrill in the achievements of the Hillman Minx, and I am sure that few cars with so small a horse-power have ever had a greater test of endurance,

June, 1953

Sporting Spotlights:

What it felt like doing 120 m.p.h. in the Sunbeam Alpine Sports—

Impressions by

Sheila Van Damm

With the new Sunbeam Alpine Sports Roadster: left to right—Norman Garrad, team manager, Leslie Johnson, Mr. Geoffrey Rootes, managing director, car manufacturing division, Sheila Van Damm, Stirling Moss and Sir William Rootes, chairman of Rootes Group.

Sir William Rootes makes an important triple announcement at a Press conference held in London—(a) the introduction of the new Sunbeam Alpine model; (b) the results of its remarkable officially observed speed trials at Jabbeke, Belgium, and (c) the award to the Sunbeam - Talbot of the coveted Dewar Trophy, presented by the R.A.C. for the most outstanding technical and engineering achievement of 1952.

MONDAY, MARCH 16 found me boarding the boat for Ostend in the company of Norman Garrad, Leslie Johnson, Raymond Baxter and several back-room boys.

My first glimpse of the new Sunbeam Alpine was when it was swung aboard the boat—a truly pretty and workmanlike car.

As we neared Ostend an Auster aircraft flew overhead, piloted by Stirling Moss, and so our team for operation Jabbeke was complete.

* * *

ON arrival we went immediately to the famous double-tracked road which runs in a straight line for 21 miles between Ostend and Ghent.

We spent the rest of the afternoon watching Leslie Johnson carrying out tests on the car and when he had to return to Ostend for some minor adjustments the rest of us went into Bruges and had hot chocolate and cream cakes. All very pleasant but so bad for the figure !

About 9 p.m. that evening I was told to climb aboard the car and with Leslie beside me I set off for my first drive—this was the first time I had ever driven a sports car, but I was given no time to wonder if I would like it as Leslie's instructions consisted of these words : " Keep your foot down ! "

He has the most amazing hearing as every time I tried to lift it even a fraction of an inch he caught me at it and shouted those four words even louder !

We went about five miles one way and then turned round and repeated the exercise—the car handled beautifully and held the road as well as her sister, the Sunbeam-Talbot saloon.

* * *

ON the way back Leslie informed me we had done 108 m.p.h. and on receipt of that information I nearly equalled the speed into the nearest bar for a brandy ! I must mention here that the speedometer had been disconnected so that I would not frighten myself more than necessary.

* * *

NORMAN GARRAD'S intention was for us to beat the existing class record of 106.8 m.p.h. held by the Austin Healey and he hoped we would do 110 m.p.h. My mind was much more at rest now because having driven over 100 m.p.h. at night I quite rightly thought it would be a lot easier when I could see where I was going !

So the great day dawned at 5.30 a.m. when 15 sleepy people assembled in the hall of the hotel—no breakfast to be had so we settled for a glass of Vichy water—funnily enough I wasn't hungry !

We drove through a heavy early morning mist to the timing area and there we sat waiting for it to clear.

When all was ready, the road was closed and policed all the way and the officials of the Belgium Automobile Club stood by.

Two runs have to be made for the mean average to be obtained—there are two chequered boards, one marking the end of the mile and the other the end of the kilometre and the time for both are taken on the same run.

* * *

STIRLING got in and set off. We were about 1¼ miles from the timing area and Norman Garrad and Leslie Johnson were waiting the same distance away at the other end of the run.

I stood around and waited and at long last Stirling returned giving the thumbs-up sign.

I jumped into the car but at that moment an official drove up to say the first of his runs had not been recorded correctly and he must do it again but he had done 119 m.p.h. on one run.

That was wonderful news, but I was finding the waiting a little tough !

Then it came to my turn and with a reassuring pat on the back from Stirling I set off.

My greatest impression was the screaming noise of the wind—obviously I was going very fast but exactly how fast I had no idea.

Suddenly I felt my helmet being lifted up—the wind was under my visor and my helmet was loose and the strap was strangling me. This was a most unpleasant situation, but I managed to hang on till the end of the run and when I stopped we found the canvas side of my helmet had split !

Leslie gave me his and I turned round and set off again—this time I was beginning to enjoy it. There was a slight hitch, however, on this run, so I was sent back to do it all over again.

* * *

THE next two runs were O.K. and on my return to the control box I was met by a highly delighted Norman Garrad and told I had done over 120 m.p.h.

We were all naturally very happy and agreed it was the best possible present we could have given Norman, this being his birthday !

The car literally went like a bomb and never gave me a second's worry—it is very comfortable as it has the standard upholstered seats, the only difference to its normal look being the cowling covering the passenger seat to reduce wind resistance.

* * *

STIRLING and I did the identical top speed of 120.459 m.p.h., but I was a fraction faster on my second run and, therefore, my average speed was higher than his.

He then did a thing that in my opinion you have to be one hell of a wonderful chap to do. He declined another run saying we had got what we came for and there was no need for him to repeat the effort.

That, in my humble opinion, entitles him to the name of the Sportsman of this or any other year, as undoubtedly he could have beaten my speed easily.

The R.A.C. Rally of Great Britain: By Mary Walker, runner-up in Ladies' Class.

AN innocent little telegram set me the most difficult of all sections of the R.A.C. Rally of Great Britain—but who could refuse Mr. Mulcaster, the Editor, and the friend of all members of the S.T.O.C. His message asked me for my personal impressions, and here they are:—

I thoroughly enjoyed every minute of the event. Quite definitely it is the best rally I have yet entered.

Looking back, one thinks of all the things one should have done, and blushes to think how much was left undone.

Still, that *is* rallying and we all hope for a next time.

Blackpool sent her competitors off in beautiful weather which held all the way to Silverstone where we joined the Hastings contingent.

The first test was run at a terrific pace, the braking area, 60 yards long and very wide, gave scope for all sorts of performances.

From Silverstone the Rally ran south to Ringwood, then north to Castle Combe for Test 2, a garaging test in which rear lights were an enormous advantage.

On next to Prescott for a timed hill-climb over the earlier parts of this very famous hill.

Here I think the co-drivers deserve an extra warm "Thank you" for sitting (more or less quietly) and being tossed about willy-nilly and wondering how can we possibly make the next corner!

At Haverfordwest everyone had different ideas about routes to Aberystwyth, Machynlleth and Dol Caradog.

After Dol Caradog we had a most beautiful run over the mountains and down into the valley before Llandrindod Wells. If it was really sacrilege to pass this Welsh scenery as we did the job in hand, of course, was getting to Llandrindod on time.

Rally H.Q. provided an excellent breakfast, for which we were grateful.

Now to Test 4. It must have been amusing to the spectators watching over various sprints to our cars.

Leaving beautiful Wales with her tongue-twister town titles (that in itself is not easy.—ED.), with glorious weather to Blackpool. About two miles short, chilly winds and sea mist took over.

Test 5 was held on the Promenade and was known as the "scissors" test.

It was quite incredible to watch Goff Imhof with his enormous Cadillac-Allard. Had his car had wings, then I think he would surely have become airborne.

Armed with our Route Books for the final section, at our friends' home we proceeded completely to disorganise the household with our maps and clobber.

More beautiful weather as we made our way to the Lake District; nothing could have been more pleasant with our Sunbeam-Talbot purring along in effortless style.

The first section of the Regularity Test was held at Ulpha, second part at Hard Knott Pass (well named, but Agnes insisted upon re-christening Hard Knock Pass), the third section on the Old Kirkstone Pass.

And so out of the Lake District and over to Corbridge-on-Tyne. This control was very busy and gave the impression that the entire village was out to see the Rallyists on their way.

With a straightforward run to Stranraer we then met a patch of fog which cleared after 20 or so miles. Turnberry was the setting for Test 6, which was a repetition of Castle Combe with garaging to the right instead of left.

Now the fun was really to begin with the fascinating control names of Crook Inn, Tushie Law, Fiddleton Toll, Deadwater Station and Kirkharle Cross Roads.

I believe that the marshals and spectators at Kirkharle had a very interesting time in guessing from which direction the next Rally car would appear.

From Turnberry the Rally became more and more furious and really got everyone worked up after Barnard Castle.

I must admit that I thoroughly enjoyed the Barnard Castle to Buxton section, but I have my doubts about my navigator's enjoyment here.

(Continued on page 40)

R. J. Adams (right) with co-driver John Pearman—winners of Second place in the general classification of the R.A.C. Rally of Great Britain—see story on p. 40.

Sporting Spotlights:

(Continued from page 37)

TRIUMPHANT we returned to Ostend to lunch and then off immediately to Paris.

The next morning we were all out at Montlhéry and there Leslie Johnson drove the same car for one hour at an average speed of 111.20 m.p.h.—a most impressive sight as the little pale blue car flashed round and round the track with monotonous regularity and once more I felt so very proud to be there to witness yet another British triumph.

When Leslie stopped, Stirling got in and lapped at 116 m.p.h. and then, as a reward for being a good girl, they let me have a go!

Have you ever driven round a goldfish bowl?—a very odd feeling indeed! The best way I can describe Montlhéry is the Wall of Death with two short straights on it.

I imagine after about six laps one might have some idea what is going on—I did three, and I leave the rest to your imagination! The extraordinary thing is they assured me I lapped at 114 m.p.h. Excuse me, please, if I leave you now. That's my cue for a large brandy!

Start of the recent S.T.O.C. Cotswold Trial at Taylors (Crypt House) Motors, Gloucester, and, left, Mr. G. Lewis going well—before he knew himself to be the winner! S.T.O.C. member's photographs.

Charles always picks a winner...

and he certainly picked a thoroughbred when he bought a Sunbeam-Talbot 90. It's so fast and yet so comfortable—the way it sticks to the road on corners gives me a nice feeling of safety... *and* we're always there first!

*Ask your dealer for a trial run today
—it will convince you*

The 90 m.p.h.
SUNBEAM-TALBOT 90
with <u>powers</u> of endurance proved by repeated International successes

AWARDED THE DEWAR TROPHY PRESENTED BY THE ROYAL AUTOMOBILE CLUB FOR THE MOST OUTSTANDING ENGINEERING AND TECHNICAL ACHIEVEMENT DURING 1952

A PRODUCT OF THE ROOTES GROUP

SUNBEAM-TALBOT LIMITED RYTON-ON-DUNSMORE COVENTRY.   LONDON SHOWROOMS AND EXPORT DIVISION: ROOTES LIMITED DEVONSHIRE HOUSE PICCADILLY, W.1

Sporting Spotlights:

(Continued from page 38)

The marshals were absolutely wonderful at all Controls, and a special tribute is due to all the noble people who sat for hours stamping our all-important Road Books.

Buxton-to-Hastings we chose our own routes and a very welcome bed.

Friday was very interesting. The run from Hastings to Goodwood being very deceptive—several competitors dropped marks for being late into Control.

I am quite sure, however, that on certain parts of the road many cars made faster times than on the Goodwood race track—no names! Friday evening brought us notice of the final 100 cars to compete in the tests next day.

Hastings, not to be outdone by Blackpool, put on drizzly rain to ensure complicating braking.

And so to the R.A.C. I say: "Thank you very much for a most interesting and exciting Rally."

To the Rootes Group: "Thank you also for manufacturing such a delightful car as my Sunbeam-Talbot '90' which gave me a most comfortable and absolutely trouble-free run."

The R.A.C. Rally as told by R. J. Adams, driver of the Sunbeam-Talbot which gained Second place in the general classification and First in the touring car classes.

THE Regulations for the R.A.C. Rally and for the Circuit of Ireland Trial were both waiting for me when I arrived home from the Monte Carlo Rally on January 31.

Although I had competed in every Circuit of Ireland Trial since it was inaugurated in 1936, I decided this time to have a go at the R.A.C. Rally instead, and selected Blackpool as my starting point.

* * *

HAVING entered my own car, it was only about 10 days before starting out that Norman Garrad 'phoned me to know if I would drive one of the team of three Works' Sunbeam-Talbots in place of Stirling Moss, who was unable to compete.

This necessitated cancelling my accommodation in Blackpool, as the team was to start from Hastings, but two days before I was due to leave home my co-driver, John Pearman, 'phoned me from Coventry to say that he had just received the Rally Number Plates, which indicated that we were starting from Blackpool!

We immediately had to scrap all our plans for meeting in London and had to re-arrange accommodation in Blackpool for the Saturday and Sunday nights prior to the start of the Rally.

On top of this last-minute excitement, it was only when we received our Road Book that we learnt the details of the various tests and the route.

* * *

JOHN and I then had some lengthy telephone chats about our preparations, and the day before my departure was spent in practising the tests in a Sunbeam-Talbot, which was very sportingly lent to me by a friend. Meanwhile John was pressing on with the procuring of maps and making our route sheets and time schedules.

John met me at Coventry Station, and we set off at once for Blackpool, arriving in good time for lunch, and probably the first competitors to reach this starting point.

That afternoon was spent in more practising of the tests and in the evening we went over all our plans, maps, route sheets, and checked our documents such as licences, insurance, etc., preparations vital if one wants to make sure of completing the Rally without a slip-up.

* * *

TEN-THIRTY on Monday morning saw us on the starting line feeling in fine fettle, each of us determined to see that the other did not exceed the permitted 40 m.p.h. average.

At Silverstone we were timed for a half-mile acceleration test and stop within 60 yards after the finishing line or incur a penalty of 100 marks. The thought of this penalty definitely decided us that this was not a test for fireworks, and, therefore, we made sure to start braking in good time; even so, we were doing about 80 m.p.h. when the brakes went on.

From here we had a long run down to Ringwood in Hampshire and on to Castle Combe by which time it was dark. Fog was encountered round the New Forest, but over Salisbury Plain it was as clear as crystal. We were in plenty of time at Castle Combe to watch some of the competitors doing the test before our turn came.

This consisted of driving forwards into a "garage," reversing out and into another one and then forwards over the finishing line.

* * *

IT was not far from here to the famous Prescott Hill, near Gloucester, where we arrived to find a delay of about half an hour while some car was being removed from the hill after having an argument with a bank half-way up. The timed dice up this narrow steep twisty hill amongst the trees at midnight was quite a thrill.

By 5 a.m. we had crossed Southern Wales and checked in at Haverfordwest, where we had an early breakfast of bacon and egg, and then on through a beautiful dawn to Machynlleth and thence to Llandrindod Wells, where we had another bacon-and-egg breakfast before tackling the tricky little manœuvring test which was held by the side of the lake in the most perfect sunny weather.

* * *

FROM here to Blackpool via a check at the "Three Cocks Inn," was an easy drive with the hot sun coming in through the windows and sunshine roof all the way to within sight of Blackpool, when we were met by a thick sea mist, the cold and damp of which was in great contrast to the sunshine which we had just left.

On arrival we went through the "scissors" test on the Promenade, where each competitor's time was announced over loud-speakers, and then the cars were impounded for the night.

At our hotel we met the other members of our team whom we had not seen so far during the Rally as they were early Hastings numbers.

AFTER a quick wash, change, and a good dinner, we settled down to nearly three hours of studying our route and time schedules for the next part of the Rally, which had only been disclosed to us on arrival. This lay through the Lake District, north-east through Northumberland to Corbridge, west to Stranraer and Turnberry, then back through the lowlands of Scotland with time controls at very short intervals to Barnard Castle.

Just before getting to bed we heard the results of the Rally up to and including the Blackpool test. Although we had not been able to gain any bonus marks either at Silverstone or Prescott against the more powerful saloon cars, the manœuvrability and liveliness of the Sunbeam-Talbot had paid off well in the tests at Castle Combe, Llandrindod Wells and Blackpool, and we found ourselves in second place in General Classification and well ahead of all other saloon cars, having made the best times of all saloon cars at Llandrindod Wells and Blackpool.

* * *

WEDNESDAY morning promised another fine day (after bacon-and-egg for breakfast) as we again took our departure from Blackpool, this time heading north for the Lake District, where the first consistency test was held.

This entailed three short-timed hill climbs from a standing start on the steepest part of each hill, these being Crosby Hill at Ulpha, Hard Knott Pass and Kirkstone Pass; the slowest time on any hill to count for marking.

Here, again, the Sunbeam-Talbot performed remarkably well for its size, especially considering that a large number of cars failed to get off the line at all on Hard Knott! Even so, we were unable to gain any bonus marks on this test. I should explain that the order of merit in General Classification was determined by averaging the best 10 performances in the Sports Car Group and in the Touring (saloon) car Group, and awarding bonus marks to each car according to their performance against the average of their respective group.

* * *

THE first control of the day was at the summit of Kirkstone Pass where, in bright sunshine, we were able to purchase coffee and sandwiches. The girl behind the counter was evidently quite unused to coping with such a volume of business, and we were almost late starting by the time she found that if one round of sandwiches cost 1s. 6d., then three half-rounds cost 2s. 3d.

By midnight we were at Turnberry airfield for a repeat of the Castle Combe test, but this time done in the opposite direction, and here we were again fastest of all the touring cars, being beaten by only six sports cars, and afterwards we learnt that, at this stage, we were leading the whole Rally on General Classification.

* * *

FROM here we now tackled the night navigation test, which took eight hours of concentrated navigation and driving.

On arrival at Barnard Castle for a one-hour breakfast halt, our plan was for John

(Continued on page 42)

June, 1953   Page 41   Modern Motoring & Travel

NUMBER FIVE OF A SERIES

The story of *the air you ride on*

Just as pneumatic bicycle tyres were introduced to America from England — so it was from Europe that the idea of applying pneumatics to the fledgling automobile first came. Production of the new tyres was immediately started in the United States, and the responsibility for making their valves fell to August Schrader.

This was not by chance, for Schrader had been closely associated with the young rubber industry. He had developed valves for air pillows, life belts and diving equipment, and his experience carried him automatically to the pneumatic tyre. Schrader produced his first tyre valve in 1891. From it, by 1898, had been developed the valve with the core replaceable in one unit. Construction and materials have been repeatedly improved, but today this basic design is still the keeper of the air you ride on.

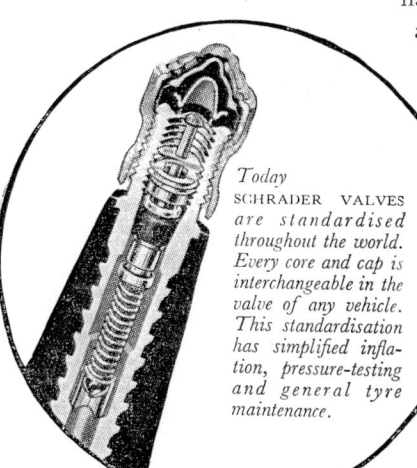

Today SCHRADER VALVES *are standardised throughout the world. Every core and cap is interchangeable in the valve of any vehicle. This standardisation has simplified inflation, pressure-testing and general tyre maintenance.*

Schrader
STANDARD TYRE VALVE
Keeper of the Air you ride on

A. SCHRADER'S SON • BIRMINGHAM • ENGLAND

Sporting Spotlights:
(Continued from page 40)

to take half an hour for his breakfast while I slept in the back of the car, and then for John to sleep for half an hour while I had my bacon-and-egg (same as John). By the way, we are both fond of meals of bacon-and-egg!

* * *

IN wet weather we now had to follow a written route which was to take us over the Yorkshire moors and through three more short hill-climbs, which constituted another consistency test similar to the Lake District one, and so on to Buxton.

It was when leaving Barnard Castle that we, in common with a good number of other competitors, could not make the written route agree with any of the roads in front of us, and by the time we eventually found ourselves on the right road we were over 20 minutes behind schedule, a quick calculation telling us that we now had to average 42 m.p.h. instead of 30 over third-class moorland roads to the next control.

We were relieved, indeed, to find ourselves there with still some time in hand.

* * *

FROM Buxton it was a long, tedious drive to Hastings, where we were due to clock in at 11.37 p.m.

On this journey we took turns sleeping in the back of the car, and were very glad to get to our hotel about midnight, where a cold supper had been arranged for us before getting to bed.

We woke refreshed, to find Friday a perfect summer day for our short run of 65 miles to Goodwood Circuit and back.

The test at Goodwood consisted of almost a complete lap of the course from a standing start, with twice on the way round having to stop and reverse over a line.

This day's run was notable for the number of police cars seen along the roads of the south coast; they were all out for blood but, with Rally cars going in both directions, they had difficulty in making up their minds who to chase.

In the test the road-holding and brakes of the Sunbeam-Talbot again showed up to advantage, and we found that we had beaten all but one car in the touring group.

* * *

IN the evening we learnt that we were again in second place in General Classification, and therefore it was a case of early to bed so as to be fresh for the two final tests on Saturday morning.

In these tests the Sunbeam-Talbot again showed that it is the ideal combination of the family saloon and sports car, and when the final results were published we found that we had ended First in all four classes of touring cars, and Second in the whole Rally, being the only saloon car in the first five places.

* * *

SO ended the third R.A.C. Rally in which the organisation had been carried out without a hitch, and which had been enjoyed by all taking part.

YORKSHIRE DALES' TRIAL

THAT the short duration trials arranged for S.T.O.C. members for week-end participation are generally popular is beyond dispute: the Yorkshire Dales' Trial, held on Sunday, March 29, being no exception.

As well as an intriguing 48 miles circuit, starting at Harrogate and finishing at Shipton—to be covered in 2 hrs. 24 mins.—tests en route included those for timed acceleration and braking, observed hill climbs and descents, reversing manœuvres, parking tactics and, a new one, for "agility" reactions, all making for enjoyable and healthy competitive endeavour, as well as, of course, good judgment and driving skill. And the enthusiasm with which members "have a go!" taking all in good spirit, is encouraging to say the least!

Nor do the "highlights" of the club have things simply without challenge—many new names should soon reach front rank merit.

Listen to the discussions which characterise any post-trial tea rally, this time at the Overdale Club. You will never be in any doubt as to the reason for the Club's rapid growth, now with well over 1,250 members.

Results:

Sunbeam-Talbot: 1st, R. Walshaw, of Halifax; 2nd, M. G. Briggs, of Leeds.

Hillman: 1st, R. J. Edmond, of York; 2nd, E.A. Lloyd Davies, of Wolverhampton

Stanley Gambles Trophy: R. Walshaw.

Prizes were presented by Mrs. J. Gibson, wife of the sales manager of the Thornton Engineering Co., Ltd., Sunbeam-Talbot distributors of Bradford, with Mr. Harold Cundall, donor of the "Harold Cundall" trophy (awarded annually) in support, and who congratulated the organisers upon a well-staged and supported occasion.

LONDON'S BIG OPENING NIGHT

SOME 150 Club members and friends helped, by really enthusiastic participation, in putting over the opening 1953 social event of the London branch of the S.T.O.C. in a really big way.

Held at the Berkeley Rooms, Zeeta House, Putney, on Friday, March 27, an excellent dinner was followed by dancing and cabaret entertainment of the highest order.

Among those present were Mr. R. G. Leaf (General Club Secretary) and Mrs. Leaf, and the full branch committee, headed by Mr. E. J. Rossiter (Chairman) and Mrs. Rossiter and Miss M. Tinckham, Hon. Branch Secretary, whose long associations with the Club were, and are, acknowledged as a valuable Branch asset.

For the "light fantastic," W. Grigg and his "Berkeley Orchestra" gave irresistible lead, the while none present attempted the terrific exposition of Barrie Manning, classic character—dancer—entertainer in "Dancing round the World," if many members and guests are still puzzling over the uncanny sleight of hand of popular David Nixon, a "name to conjure with!" A good evening in pleasant company and delightful conditions.

OUT FOR TREASURE!

A picture of Jane Russell's face,
Four hearts, Jack, Queen, King and Ace,
A dollar bill, a piece of rope,
A thimble and a telescope,
And just to prove you've really "caught on,"
A photograph of Tommy Lawton.

This was the "Treasure trove" to be gathered by competing members of the S.T.O.C. in the Northamptonshire Treasure Hunt, held on April 12 last, starting and finishing at the Old Elm Tree Hotel, Hoveringham Ferry, Notts. Some 32 cars and 150 club members and friends took part—with great enthusiasm and not a little ingenuity!

Clues also were in rhyme, while identification of landmarks and of wayside features had to be collated with great accuracy.

However, since it all comprises very good fun and pleasant competitive interest, no one really worries, least of all the losers! And the best of congratulations to the first three successful entrants:

1st, Mrs. Eve Dawson, of Gainsborough, Lincs.
2nd, Mr. G. P. Gummer, of Sheffield.
3rd, Mr. M. Milner, of Tolworth, Surrey.

Prizes were presented by Mrs. Stanley Matthews, wife of Mr. Stanley Matthews, co-director of R. Cripps and Sons, Ltd., distributors, of Nottingham, who entertained club members and friends to a delightful high-tea at the close of the rally.

Other motor sports reports on page 50.

Members and friends foregather for the first 1953 Social Event—see column three—arranged by the London Branch of the Sunbeam-Talbot Owners' Club.

Price for price India tyres are the best **value** because you're getting **better quality** without paying any more for it. Save with safety — fit long-mileage India tyres.

INDIA
"THE FINEST TYRES MADE"

Attractions of slimmed, simplified aircraft are now evident!
says Major Oliver Stewart

NOT many weeks ago details were announced of the Folland light fighter project, an aircraft called the Gnat, now building and expected to fly next year.

It is essentially a slimmed down, stripped aircraft which makes up by weight-saving what it loses in instrumentation and equipment.

I have been greatly impressed by the theoretical possibilities of the Gnat and aircraft like it. There seems little doubt that the light fighter, designed as such, could fly faster and farther and could climb more quickly than the standard type of heavy fighter to which we are committed to-day.

* * *

LIGHTER aircraft, it must be emphasised, have been getting exceedingly obese. They have been putting on fat at an alarming rate. They are becoming a bad surgical risk and—perhaps—a bad tactical risk.

Here is the picture: the fighter of the Second World War weighed five times as much as the fighters of the First World War; the fighters of the present day weigh three times as much as the fighters of the Second World War. And designs in being, but not yet built, indicate that the tendency to put on fat is continuing.

Nor is it only the weight that is increasing. The waistline is also going the way of all flesh.

The fuselages are thicker as well as heavier; the wings are bigger.

* * *

WHERE is this going to end? The two-ton Tessies of the Royal Air Force look as if they are going to become ten-ton Tessies. Actually some aircraft of the First World War weighed only about half a ton (the Sopwith Pup, for instance); now the ten-ton figure is within sight.

When human beings degenerate in this way they take a course of fruit juice. What can be done about aircraft? The answer has been given clearly enough by one of the greatest designers, no less a person than the designer of the Canberra bomber. He is W. E. W. Petter, and he has given the answer not in words but in one of the neatest, smallest and most ingenious fighters ever seen, the Gnat.

* * *

THE Gnat uses a smaller engine—that is the essential starting point of the lighter fighter.

It is no good imagining that a light fighter can be built round a couple of Avons. The engine must be absolutely smaller and absolutely lighter as well as specifically.

Its specific weight must be brought down to the lowest possible figure and it *can* be brought down sufficiently. The power-to-weight ratio of the entire machine is then better than the power-to-weight ratio of the larger machine. Power-to-weight means better acceleration and better climb.

* * *

I CANNOT here give all the figures which Mr. Petter has advanced in favour of his argument. But I can say that I am satisfied that the Gnat will perform better than the modern heavy fighters, cluttered up with vast quantities of equipment and so complex that they take enormous numbers of man-hours to make and to maintain.

But the Gnat will not be able to give all-weather, 24-hour service. It cannot take the radar and electronic equipment needed for closing with an enemy in cloud. It cannot carry elaborate batteries of rocket projectiles.

The Gnat—or any light fighter—is a fair-weather fighter. But most air fighting is done in fair weather, and if the

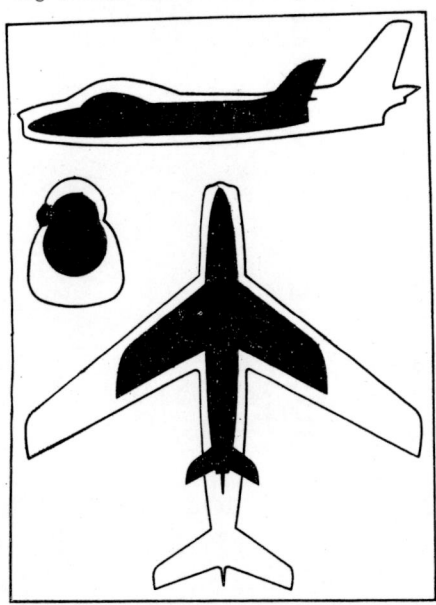

A pictorial comparison of the size and shape of the hypothetical light fighter compared with a North American Sabre fighter.

bombers of the future fly high—as many are expected to do—they will usually be flying " above the weather " where visual operations are possible.

* * *

MAINTENANCE and manufacturing advantages of the light fighter are immense.

The man-hours spent in building the machine and in keeping it serviceable in the field are a small fraction of those demanded by the complex heavy-weight machine. At least four and possibly six light fighters could be built to one heavy fighter, and they would be able to outperform it in speed, climb and manœuvre.

So the slimming operation, though unpleasant for all the specialists who wish to load down every military aeroplane with all their pet pieces of equipment, is rewarding in the end.

This does not mean that any essentials are sacrificed. There is full cabin pressurisation, for instance, and there is an ejection seat for the pilot.

In the Gnat there is an ordinary retractable undercarriage, although weight and bulk are saved by making this " double "—as the musicians say—the part of air brakes. In other words, the air brakes *are* the undercarriage and the undercarriage *is* the air brakes!

* * *

ALTHOUGH the Gnat has an ordinary undercarriage, however, it is obvious that the light fighter would be especially well suited to development in undercarriage-less form.

It would have in the first place enough thrust to enable it to climb vertically when near the ground; that is to say, the engine thrust measured in kilograms would be greater than the all-up weight of the aircraft.

So the light fighter could be launched from a steeply inclined ramp by catapult or with rocket assistance, and it could then make a rubber deck landing with belly-skid. There would be nothing particularly new in such a technique, and it would save further weight in the aircraft and offer a chance of further simplification.

* * *

SOME of the attractions of the slimmed, simplified fighter are now evident. And it is believed that, although the official view is at present unfavourable to this type of machine, some of the most experienced officers in the Royal Air Force believe it to be the only practical solution to the defence of these islands.

They do not believe that, under war conditions, we could produce enough of the heavy, complicated conventional fighters to offer an effective barrier to bomber attack.

They believe that the production lines for these heavy fighters would be too easily wrecked. There are so many processes and they are so delicately interlocked.

* * *

BRITAIN is not the only place where some attempt is being made to avoid piling on more weight in fighter aircraft.

A noted French company with a name running into dozens of capital letters which I shall abbreviate as the company of the *Sud Ouest* has built and flown a supersonic aircraft of small size and low weight and original conception.

It has two small turbojet engines which give enough thrust for cruising and do so at small cost in fuel consumption. But when battle is joined the pilot can plug in the enormous thrust of rockets mounted in the tail and go straight through Mach 1 to speeds of the order of 800 miles an hour.

* * *

IN brief, then, the light fighter deserves consideration. It offers so many advantages that it may well prove the right air defence solution for day time. And remember one thing: the light fighter will have greater speed, better manœuvrability and a higher rate of climb than the other, and the experienced fighter pilots of both wars are all agreed that performance is the one dominant factor which gives victory in air combat.

Benzole makes good petrol better

'National' is the ideal blend of both

However good petrol may be, blending Benzole with it makes it better for your car. *Better for starting*, because Benzole so very easily turns into a dry, easily-ignited vapour even on icy days. *Better for smooth, quiet running*, because Benzole is a fine anti-knock agent as well as a fuel, giving the piston a powerful shove in place of a harsh, hefty wallop. And best of all—*Benzole is better for more miles per gallon* because Nature herself has packed into every drop of Benzole more power—more energy —than she has packed into petrol.

NATIONAL BENZOLE MIXTURE

National Benzole Company Limited
Wellington House, Buckingham Gate
London, S.W.1
(*The distributing organisation owned and entirely controlled by the producers of British Benzole*)

O.K. FOR SOUND:

Film Shorts and Starlights

Six prize-winners from a Long Beach, California, bathing beauty contest who were given contracts for Tyrone Power's latest Technicolor film, "The Mississippi Gambler." Set in New Orleans of the 1850's, this is the era of grand dames and Creole belles.

THE first three-dimensional musical to go before the M-G-M cameras is to be "Kiss Me Kate," starring Kathryn Grayson and Ann Miller.

Ann Miller will put some of the year's most sensational dances before the 3-D cameras—the first dances ever planned expressly for the exacting new medium.

* * *

DIRK ("Appointment in London") Bogarde missed the London première of his latest film, "Desperate Moment," in which he stars with Mai Zetterling.

He had flown to Cyprus to start work on a new film, "The Rhodes Commando."

Bogarde has had six Hollywood offers in the past year—"but I'd rather stay here, as long as there is work for me in British films." Nothing is more certain than that there will be work here for Bogarde as long as he wants it.

* *

JOAN CRAWFORD and Michael Wilding are teamed in the forthcoming M-G-M picture, "Why Should I Cry."

With a setting of New York night-life, this is a romantic drama of a Broadway musical comedy star and a blind World War II veteran.

* * *

GLYNIS JOHNS, on the Pinewood set of "The Day's Mischief," received a telegram: *Cymru am Byth.*

It was from her father, actor Mervyn Johns, and, as every Welshman knows, it means Wales For Ever.

Hollywood's Gene Tierney and Britain's Leo Genn ("g" as in gamp), who co-star in the film, were asked to pose and kiss for a cameraman. Asked Genn hopefully, "Want any rehearsals?"

* * *

JIMMY DURANTE, who has been making night-club appearances in Miami and Las Vegas, returns to Hollywood for the top role in Universal-International's lavish Technicolor musical, "I've Got a Million of 'Em."

The title, of course, is one of Jimmy's own famed expressions. The story deals with a movie studio barber who also owns a theatrical boarding house, and assists four young people to film stardom and romance.

* * *

RONALD HOWARD, son of the late Leslie Howard, has established himself as a top-rung character actor in his own right in "Street Corner," London Independent Producers' screen salute to the policemen of Britain.

Ronald has several telling scenes in the picture with Rosamund John ... the same Rosamund who starred with Leslie Howard in some of his great successes.

* *

EDWARD G. ROBINSON will star in "The Glass Web," adapted from Max Ehrlich's novel of the same title.

He plays the dramatic role of an author trapped by his own writings after murdering a girl who spurned him.

A new heart-throb is Adele Mara (above), now appearing in Republic Pictures.

Right, off set during location shooting in Wales, are Clifford Evans, Maureen Swanson and John Fraser, stars of "Choir Practice," an Associated British picture.

PEGGY CUMMINS, now filming at Pinewood in the romantic comedy "Always a Bride," is lined up for yet another picture.

This will be "The Love Lottery," to be made at Ealing Studios, and she will co-star with David Niven and Herbert Lom. A Hollywood film idol finds himself involved in a world-wide lottery—with his hand in marriage as the prize!

* * *

JAMES STEWART will star in a gold-rush story, "Alder Gulch," as soon as he has completed Universal-International's Technicolor musical, "The Glenn Miller Story."

His last picture, "Thunder Bay," an oil-field drama, has not yet been released in Britain.

* * *

EDWARD EVERETT HORTON will return to the screen after an absence of five years in Hollywood's "Ma and Pa Kettle Hit the Road Home."

Horton, who has been touring, portrays the garden editor of a national magazine who has to spend a week on the old Kettle farm.

* * *

ESTHER WILLIAMS, Hollywood's swimming star actress, and her husband, Ben Gage, and their family, are to move into a new home in the autumn.

It is now being built, with a separate building for guests.

A feature of the new home will be a large swimming pool.

* * *

IT was a typical day for Peggy Cummins. She awoke, sat at her dressing-table, sat down to breakfast, then sat in her car for the journey to Pinewood Studios. There, on the set of the new comedy, "Always a Bride," she in turn sat in a Rolls-Royce, a French taxi, and an Italian Fiat.

Later, in a private telephone conversation, she was heard to say, "Sorry, dear, not to-night. I've been on my feet all day."

June, 1953
Page 27

NEW WITHIN THE WORLD—

or

Notes for a new Reign

By

Brigid de Vine

"NEW *Within the World*" is the official description for a new scarf designed by Mr. Oliver Messel to commemorate the Coronation of Queen Elizabeth.

The scarf is a triumph of British craftsmanship. A unique example of the printing of *pure gold leaf* on cloth.

Throughout the centuries experiments have been made with a view to using gold in connection with silks and textile fabrics. Hitherto, as in the case of the Indian sari, the gold leaf has had to be beaten on to the thread.

Now, as a result of collaboration with Mr. Tom Heron who founded the Cresta Silks business some 30 years ago, and whose name is famous for the fine art of the silk printer's craft, a *new* process has been evolved.

Pure gold leaf, pure solid metal, beaten to a thickness of *one quarter of a millionth of an inch*, is laid on screen-printed silk in such a manner that the design can range from arabesques of the utmost delicacy to, for instance, "a ball dress consisting of a sheath of shimmering pure gold of as high a carat as the wearer's bracelets or rings."

* * *

"DOLORES," Mr. Norman Hartnell's famous mannequin, recently wore at a party at the Ritz Hotel, a ball gown made from an experimental length of gold-printed grey organdie.

"In future I shall be a real snob," she said. "*I am the first woman in the world to wear Pure Gold*."

Mr. Eric Crabtree, Cresta's managing director, who achieved fame by selling English ready-made dresses to Paris a year or so ago, said: "This new printing process—of printing gold and precious metals on fabrics in such a way that they will last for thousands of years without tarnishing—opens up enormous possibilities for the British textile trade."

Fabric so printed can be dry cleaned—and even washed.

* * *

MANY dollar orders have already been received for the Coronation scarf. "At the same time," Mr. Crabtree explained, "owing to the extreme thinness of the metal, it should not cause Mr. Butler to worry by creating too heavy a drain on our gold reserves."

In the United Kingdom the delicately designed Coronation scarf—which almost deserves framing instead of wearing, is already on sale in the boutique of Mr. Norman Hartnell, the Royal Couturier, at Messrs. Fortnum and Mason, and at the Cresta shops in London and throughout Southern England.

* * *

OLIVER MESSEL'S delicate subtle designs were also seen for some embroideries used in the Coronation collection of John Cavanagh.

The theme of the lovely collection was "Cascade," the fulness drawn through and thrown down over the belt, and this theme was developed for evening into strapless bell-shapes, the cascade panels falling all round.

Last Season the famous cosmetic firm of Gala of London commented on the fact that the English women's "national" colour, according to national research, is "Baby Blue." John Cavanagh made this point using a great many *less usual* blues, almost always with white. This should appeal to the English women whose colouring the shades flatter so charmingly.

Gala of London have worked out the most suitable lipstick colours for this wider "blue" range:

Light intense turquoise and Nattier blue (greyer)   SEA CORAL
Periwinkle blue (more mauve)   HEAVENLY PINK
Intense royal and deep sapphire   RED SEQUIN

* * *

IN Gala's delightfully redecorated "Colour Room" in the Burlington Arcade you can experiment with a dozen different Lip Colours. Tiny lipsticks costing 1s. each are available or you can buy a set of the whole range of a dozen different colours for only 8s. 6d. These tiny lipsticks are excellent not only for test purposes but for use in small evening bags and for travelling.

You can pack a whole colour wardrobe in infinitesimal space. To make colour harmony as easy as possible there are 12

Ball gown, by Michael Sherard, in white rayon moiré from Courtaulds. Diamanté embroidery emphasises waist line. Worn with floor-length matching stole.

Court dress, also by Michael Sherard, in rayon lace of Coronation design by Birkin & Co. Floral motif emphasised on corsage with mother-of-pearl and gold thread embroidery. Worn with tulle boa.

CORONATION CHAPEAU
Left: Glittering cap from the "Otto Lucas" Coronation collection. Right: Another original model by the same designer, a draped crown-like cap in white satin with fascinating trail of pink camellias, trimming front and right side, to ear level.

Fabrics, fads, fashions—have you a Coronation Year problem? Let Brigid de Vine help you. Write her c/o this Journal, at 53 Stratton Street, Piccadilly, London, W.1., enclosing stamped and addressed envelope for the reply.

Above: Easy-to-wear jacket, in Krimmer Tescan embros lamb, with wide pointed collar, and cuffs turned back almost to elbow. Back falls into full flares—by Silverts.

Right: Charming jacket in dyed squirrel with becoming yoke shoulder line and deep turn back cuffs: Model by National Fur Co., price £265.

Below: Another National Fur Co. design in striking leopard, worn "belted" or "boxy" style. Note stand-up collar, ultra wide sleeves and tailored revers.

---

illuminated fabric panels on the walls of the Colour Room and more than 2,000 British Colour Council fabric shades are available. Gala encourages women to bring in their own new fabric samples or accessory colours so that the most becoming cosmetic colours may be chosen.

Other services available include a "Self Make-up," using Gala Fashion Cosmetics, for a nominal charge of 2s. 6d. Some women use it to experiment and "learn how," others to renew their make-up before a luncheon date, or after a hair appointment, or a long day in town. It is a service that should appeal particularly to Coronation visitors who want to "freshen up" before a cocktail party after a day's sightseeing.

The Gala "Pastel Rooms," in pink, blue and yellow, are also available for complete treatments or for the Gala Occasion Service.

* * *

VISITORS to London this summer will like to know that they can book an appointment for any time during the day, or even at 5.30 in the evening (if two days' notice is given) for a cleanse, make-up, manicure and change of dress before any important occasion, garden party, Ascot, wedding, dinner or dance.

Your dress can be brought in previously or on arrival it will be hung out and pressed if necessary. The make-up will be harmonised to the dress and nail colour matched to the lip colour. "Changing" comes last, and a miniature Gala lipstick is presented for re-touching. The "treatment" takes one and a half hours and this unique service costs only 15s. If you want somewhere to change in comfort after driving yourself up to town, do make a note of the Gala Salon address, 48, Burlington Arcade. It is wonderfully convenient.

They also stock a range of unusual accessories: cravats, Paris-inspired "roses" in various materials, many of which can be copied in your own colours.

* * *

INSTRUCTIONS for keeping *white* accessories really "white," come from the "Tide" Washing Clinic who have issued a special "direction" for dealing with the popular Coronation scarves, mostly white with brilliant coloured designs.

"Dip frequently in a mild lukewarm solution of weekly wash detergent and rinse quickly in clear water of the same temperature. Then spread the scarf out flat on a turkish towel, and roll it up firmly in the towel to remove excess moisture quickly. Be sure to keep the towel between the folds of the scarf, so that the dye has no chance of becoming transferred to another part of the design. Iron with a cool iron while still damp."

* * *

MORE than 1,000 different Coronation souvenirs, approved by the Council of Industrial Designs Coronation Souvenirs Committee, were shown recently at the Tea Centre in Regent Street.

In a short space of time, less than three weeks, 28,727 visitors, including the Duke of Edinburgh and the Duke and Duchess of Gloucester, visited the Exhibition.

Many of the exhibits are obviously designed to become heirloom pieces, beautiful examples from the English glass

(Concluded on page 32)

Restorap all-purpose rug—for every outdoor event! With waterproof zip carrier, fabric front to match, when full becomes a cushion. Various colours 70s., from all leading stores.

THE **New 21ˢᵀ** ANNIVERSARY
Hillman Minx

SALOON
CALIFORNIAN HARDTOP
CONVERTIBLE COUPÉ
ESTATE CAR

Completely new appearance

★

All round increased economy

★

More comfort

★

Still greater refinement in every detail

Yes, it really is 21 years since the Hillman Minx made its first popular appearance! A fine car even in 1932, the Minx has been progressively developed and improved ever since; and to-day, with well over 21,000 million miles of happy family motoring to its credit, the Minx is part of the fabric of life in almost every country in the world. To celebrate this great occasion, here is the 21st Anniversary Minx... the most brilliant, the thriftiest, the most reliable family car of all time!

21 years, and 21,000 MILLION MILES have perfected this car for you!

A PRODUCT OF THE ROOTES GROUP

HILLMAN MOTOR CAR CO. LTD. COVENTRY   LONDON SHOWROOMS AND EXPORT DIVISION: ROOTES LTD. DEVONSHIRE HOUSE PICCADILLY W.1

The Derby:
(Concluded from page 30)

and gunboats; some of them, I suppose, must win."

* * *

IN view of the condemnatory attitude which Queen Victoria exhibited towards the racing activities of her eldest son, it may come as a surprise to many to learn that in early life she was an enthusiastic racegoer.

Certainly it was Ascot rather than Epsom that the young Queen honoured by her presence. Just as her ancestor Queen Anne had founded a Gold Plate at the Ascot meeting, so Victoria, a year after accession, founded the Gold Vase, in addition to ordering the rebuilding of the grandstand.

The racing triumphs of Albert Edward, Prince of Wales, afterwards King Edward VII, have become so world-famous that it is superfluous to dwell upon them.

No royal figure in the history of the English Turf has attained the stature of that of the crowd's "Good Old Teddy." No victory was ever more widely acclaimed than that of the superb horse "Persimmon" over "St. Frusquin" in 1896, in what passed into the language as the "Prince's Derby."

Taken together with his subsequent successes, "Diamond Jubilee" in 1900 and "Minoru" in 1908, a double record was set up. Edward VII was the only royal owner to win the Derby three times, and the only one to win it whilst on the throne. Minoru's is the sole Derby won by a King of England.

* * *

IT was the misfortune of George V from a racing angle, to be called upon to follow so outstanding a Turf personality as his late father. He suffered from the penalty of all sons placed in a similar position.

There is no doubt that had George V stood in comparative isolation his unquestioned knowledge of form and thoroughbred breeding would have been more readily realised by the British public. As it was, his interest in racing was accepted as lukewarm, compared with that of his predecessor.

The truth was that it differed only in kind. His concern lay more with the breeding side of the sport than the wagering, which made little appeal to him. He was inordinately proud of the fact that within a period of 20 years the stock of his horse, "Friar Marcus," probably his best, won close on 370 races. He loved to ride over Newmarket Heath in the early morning to watch the strings exercising. Indeed, His Majesty seemed to get as much "kick" out of this as in watching the races themselves.

The thrill of winning the Blue Riband, however, was never vouchsafed to King George V, although on two occasions it appeared likely that he would achieve his ambition. In each case, unfortunately, to the disappointment of owner and public, the potential victor had to be scratched at the last moment.

* * *

THE same hard luck dogged the footsteps of our late beloved sovereign. In 1942 King George VI seemed to have the envied prize within his grasp, when the much-fancied "Big Game," who had outdistanced his field in the Two Thousand Guineas, gave a sorry display, failing to secure even a place.

His Majesty made no attempt to conceal his disappointment. One is inclined to wonder whether the fact that, during that particular year, the four other classics fell to the King was adequate compensation for the loss of the main event.

* * *

BUT the end is not yet. Our present Queen inherits to the full the sporting tendencies of her royal forbears. Who shall say that Her Majesty has not already cast a longing eye in the direction of Epsom Downs? The wishes of all Turf lovers will go with her.

"Tulyar," the 1952 Derby winner, being lead in by Prince Aly Khan, with C. Smirke up.

New within the world:
(Concluded from page 28)

and china industries were shown, and also much fine leather work.

But there were inexpensive little gifts also. Propelling pencils with crowns on top, table mats decorated with appropriate designs, lots of inexpensive and often quite charming brooches in the shape of crowns and Coronation coaches, Coronation horse brasses, a calendar with a picture of the Coronation coach which showed in turn *four* different sets of English Kings and Queens, ending with Queen Elizabeth and Prince Philip. Inexpensive red, white and blue paper lanterns from Hong Kong bearing a picture of the Queen, and patriotic electric light bulbs with a crown-shaped filament to glow when the lamp is lit.

* * *

BEFORE the day we shall probably see thousands of other "souvenirs," some well designed, others less so, but all showing a people's cheerful greeting to the New Reign.

There has been great regret that the dearly loved Queen Mary should not have lived to see her granddaughter actually crowned. Her death broke the last link with a more stable age. But there is a feeling in the air that with a new, young Queen, Britain and the Commonwealth face a new era of adventure.

The crowds who stand waving in the streets will feel themselves successors to those former Elizabethans who explored the unknown with courage and gusto. We have seen hard times, but we have won through them—as British cars continue to win through triumphantly in gruelling "trials."

We have even learned to cope with our weather if not to alter it.

* * *

ONE of the most interesting outfits shown in the Coronation Collection by Michael of Lachasse this year was a coat and suit in "BraDsyldA" proofed acetate rayon faille.

* * *

IT was the first time that a model has been commissioned from a member of the Incorporated Society of London Fashion Designers to show the fashion possibilities of a *finish*. This model was commissioned by the Bradford Dyers Association. The resulting outfit should see anyone through all the weather vagaries of Coronation summer.

The new process "gives a water-repellent finish which does not alter the colour lustre or handle of the fabric in any way." So you have an elegant silky suit, light and cool for a hot day, topped with a matching silky coat, lined with a fine black and white check wool to give protection against a sudden cold wind.

* * *

BUT if a summer shower comes, your clothes will come to no harm.
A perfect idea for an Ascot outfit.
Light, warm, waterproofed.
Perfect clothing for the new Elizabethan lady who may breakfast in one continent and lunch in another. And a very good outfit to wear on June 2 if you are coming to London to join the great crowds who will be thronging the streets to cry:
GOD BLESS THE QUEEN!

40,000 MILES IN VIGOROUS EXPORTS' DRIVE

SIR REGINALD ROOTES, deputy chairman of the Rootes Group, returned to London on April 14 last, at the conclusion of a four-months' tour of some of the Group's overseas manufacturing, assembling and distributing establishments, including Concessionaire companies, in an extended first-hand survey of current export marketing conditions.

First by air to Bombay, with visits to Ceylon and Singapore, his all-embracing tour included Melbourne, Sydney, Adelaide, Queensland and Brisbane, Australia; Wellington, New Zealand; Honolulu; San Francisco, Los Angeles, and Chicago, U.S.A.; Toronto, Canada, to terminate with his arrival in New York City for the launching of the new Sunbeam Alpine Sports Roadster (a model specially introduced for the dollar markets) by Sir William Rootes, chairman of the Rootes Group, attended by Mr. Brian Rootes, regional director for the Western Hemisphere, and Mr. Geoffrey Rootes, managing director, car manufacturing division, Coventry.

(The tour will be reported fuller in next issue.)

In Bombay—with executives of Automobile Products of India, Ltd., Concessionaires for Rootes Group products in India. L. to R.: Sir Reginald Rootes; Mr. A. J. M. Shepherd, general manager; Mr. N. Greenhalgh, works manager; and Mr. J. R. Mody.

Inspecting the uncrating of C. K. D. (completely knocked down) units exported from Great Britain for local assembly.

Sir Reginald Rootes is met at Eagle Farm airport by Mr. Gordon Wark, the Queensland, Australia, managing director of John McGrath, Ltd.

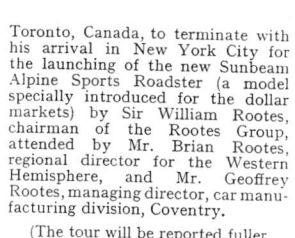

Left: Arrival at Sydney, Australia—with Mr. George Laird, director and general manager, Rootes Ltd., Australia, and Mr. Tony Shepherd.

Arrival in Delhi—Sir Reginald steps out of the private aeroplane of His Highness the Maharajah of Gwalior, at Willingdon airport.

Left:
While in Adelaide, Australia, Sir Reginald Rootes presented to Miss Mary Goldsmith, of Unley, the keys of the Hillman Minx she won in the recent "Australia's Hour of Song" radio mystery-melody contest.

Right:
With Sir William Rootes and Mr. Geoffrey Rootes and, centre, Mr. Gayelord Hauser, the celebrated American dietician—at the New York introduction of the Sunbeam Alpine.

Continental Touring "Emergency Service" Scheme: Exclusive to Rootes Group products

THE Rootes Group Continental Touring Scheme has been planned as an extra service for those touring in Europe with Rootes Group cars.

Developed with the permission of the Bank of England, the scheme—amongst other facilities—provides that in the event of breakdown or of bona-fide essential repairs being required whilst touring, payment for these can—subject to certain conditions—be made in Sterling in this country.

With the limited personal travel allowance, this scheme is of special value.

The following provisions constitute the basis on which the scheme operates:—

(a) The scheme can be used only in respect of a Rootes Group car.

(b) Participants must be residents of the United Kingdom.

(c) Arrangements are confined to the countries to which the basic travel allowance applies.

(d) Facilities are restricted to a maximum sum of £50 per car for any one tour.

(e) The facilities under the scheme are not transferable in any way.

(f) The scheme is limited in its application to payment for bona-fide essential repairs, and is not applicable to payment for petrol, oil, washing, lubrication, or other similar services.

(g) In the absence of credit facilities being available, it is necessary for a deposit in full to be made.

* * *

SUBJECT to these provisions, facilities for the carrying out of urgent bona-fide essential repairs will be available as follows:—

(a) Wherever possible the car should be taken to a Rootes Group Distributor or Dealer, and upon completion of the necessary Authorisation Form and submission of vouchers to a suitable value, the work which is required can be carried out without payment in local currency. This includes labour and material and any essential incidental charges such as towing.

(b) Where it is not possible for a car to be taken to a Rootes Group Distributor or Dealer, but where parts for repair purposes are urgently required, such parts may be cabled for from this country, being, if desired, despatched by air freight.

In these circumstances it is not possible for the labour charge involved in fitting the parts of any Customs charges involved, to be covered under the scheme.

In addition to the above, certain other facilities are also available—as later referred to.

The scheme will be operated by the Parts Department, Humber, Ltd., Stoke, Coventry, and all correspondence must be headed " Rootes Group Continental Touring Scheme."

How to Use the Scheme

ATTACHED to the descriptive booklet will be found a card which should be filled up in accordance with the details asked for, and handed either to a *Rootes Group Distributor or Dealer*, or—if necessary, sent direct to the Parts Department, Humber, Ltd., Stoke, Coventry.

It is important to note that the value of the facility required under the scheme must be stated—this being for any convenient amount, not exceeding a maximum of £50.

If arrangements have not been made through a *Rootes Group Distributor or Dealer*, the Application Card should be accompanied by a cheque, as a deposit to cover the sum for which the facilities are required.

Upon the necessary completion of the Application and Record Card having been made, there will be issued from the Factory, a " Continental Touring " wallet which will contain:—

(1) A list of Rootes Group Distributors and Dealers on the Continent.

(2) Authorisation Forms for use under the scheme.

(3) Vouchers up to the full amount for which the facilities have been covered.

(4) Full instructions for the completion of the Authorisation Forms, etc., in the event of these having to be used.

It is important that the utmost care should be taken of these documents—and in particular of the Authorisation Forms and Vouchers, which—except to the extent that they may have been used, must be returned to the Company upon termination of the tour.

Where a deposit has been made this will then be refunded in full if all vouchers are returned unused. Where vouchers have been used a refund of the remaining balance will be made.

* * *

Preparing the Car

BEFORE leaving for a Continental Tour, it is obviously wise to have the car thoroughly checked, and this will gladly be carried out by *Rootes Group Distributors or Dealers* in this country. For owners who desire, however, to carry out these preparations themselves, a detailed car preparation schedule will be supplied free of charge, if requested on the Application Card.

Touring Parts Kits

OWNERS sometimes wish to carry with them on tour, a small quantity of selected parts. To assist in the selection of such items, Recommendation Lists covering various models are available, and a free-of-charge copy may be requested, if required, when making out the Application Card. The parts may be obtained from *Rootes Group Distributors or Dealers*, and will be suitably packed, carrying on the outside of the package, a copy of the invoice for Customs declaration purposes.

Handbooks and Catalogues

IT is strongly recommended that to facilitate reference to any parts that may be required for repair or replacement —the appropriate Parts Catalogue should be carried on the car whilst touring. A copy of such Catalogue may be purchased from *Rootes Group Distributors and Dealers*. Additionally, it will frequently be found advantageous to have available an Owner's Handbook translated in the language of the country being toured. Owner's Handbooks translated into French, Portuguese, and German, are available for the majority of models.

Sporting Spotlights:

(Concluded from page 42)

S.T.O.C. CORONATION RALLY

THE " Coronation Rally, Eastbourne," is to be held on Saturday and Sunday, May 30 and 31: Road Section and driving tests on the Saturday, Concours d'Elegance on the Sunday.

The 15 starting points include Bedford, Nottingham, Bournemouth, Peterborough, Chester, Gloucester, Manchester, Leeds, Bury St. Edmunds, Norwich, London, Eastbourne, Birmingham, Maidstone and Plymouth. All routes will converge in High Wycombe.

Special hill test to be held at Willingdon, near Eastbourne; driving test on King Edward's Parade, Eastbourne.

Awards as follows: Special S.T.O.C. " Coronation Trophy " for best performance in Rally and Concours combined, to be won outright, trophy presented by Mr. Fred Senior.

Class awards to winner and runner-up in each class.

Novice's award for best performance by member not previously gaining an award in S.T.O.C. Trial or Rally.

Ladies' award (provided at least five entries are received).

Three route awards.

The Eastbourne Trophy (Perpetual Challenge) to be held for one year, for best performance in Rally.

Special award for best performance by competitor not connected with motor trade.

Twelve souvenir " Coronation " car badges for 12 best performances, irrespective of class.

There will be two classes: (A), Sunbeam Talbot, and (B), Hillman.

Rally Headquarters, Grand Hotel, Eastbourne.

Dinner-dance on Saturday, May 30.

Hotel accommodation limited; early booking essential.

* * *

THE Easter week-end provided a first-class collection of motor sporting events in great variety. Following on the R.A.C. Rally of the previous week, competitors, spectators and Press alike had a busy time keeping *au fait* with what happened.

The 1,000 miles Circuit of Ireland Trial, the Land's End Trial, hillclimbs at Lydstep and Trengwainton, race meetings at Goodwood, Castle Combe and Brands Hatch, a Scottish National Rally at Gleneagles—to mention the more important events—what more could the most enthusiastic sportsman want?

The 1,000 miles Circuit of Ireland Trial provided the usual strenuous motoring and here again Sunbeam-Talbots put up a fine performance by winning 1st prize (G. W. Houston) and 2nd prize (W. J. M. Glover) in the closed cars over 2000 c.c. class. Hillman Minx were again prominent in the event, winning the closed car Team Prize (J. E. Dowling, B. McCaldin and C. W. E. Maunsell) whilst J. Peile (Hillman Minx) was second in the closed car class for cars up to 2000 c.c.

* * *

The Land's End Trial attracted a post-war record of 426 entries of which 166 were cars. Weather conditions, alternating between snow, hail, rain and sunshine added somewhat to the difficulties of the route, although strangely enough those very old favourites, used for 20 years or more, Beggars' Roost and Bluehills Mine proved to be the most difficult. Probable and estimated number of 1st class awards is 40 motor-cycles and 30 cars.

* * *

Full illustrated report of the Sunbeam-Talbot Owners' Club's " Southport Motor Rally " will be published in the next issue: press dates prelude its coverage in this edition.

IN A FEW WORDS:

News Items of Modern Motoring and Travel Interest

COMMENTING on the January and February increases in road accident figures, the Parliamentary Secretary to the Ministry of Transport (Mr. Gurney Braithwaite, M.P.) called for "a very great improvement" in the standard of road conduct, particularly at night.

"I appeal especially to motor cyclists and drivers," he said, "to exercise the greatest possible care and so help us to turn back this disquieting rise in the tide of casualties."

* * *

ONE ROAD ACCIDENT in every seven which occurred last year involved a dog, states the R.A.C. The value of the proper training of dogs in traffic behaviour cannot be over-emphasised.

* * *

A NATIONAL ROAD SAFETY WEEK is to be held from October 17 to October 26. Details will be announced shortly.

* * *

B.O.A.C.'s NEW COMET SERVICE to Tokyo, which makes the 10,000-mile journey in 36 hours, operates twice weekly each way.

* * *

EXISTING Comet services to South Africa, to Ceylon and to Singapore have been accelerated by the speeding-up of the organisation at transit stops.

Sgt. J. R. Skeggs, Metropolitan Police Driving School, who drove President Tito in London.

BRITAIN'S CORONATION YEAR got off to a good start with tourist visitors, more than 25,000 arriving during January. A total of 800,000 overseas visitors can be expected during 1953, spending approximately £125 million in various currencies.

* * *

BY PERMISSION of H.R.H. the Princess Royal and the Earl and Countess of Harewood, Harewood House, on the Leeds–Harrogate road, is now open to visitors on Sundays (12 noon to 6 p.m.) and Wednesdays (10 a.m. to 6 p.m.) until September 30, and also on Whit Monday and August Bank Holiday Monday. Admission to the house, park and gardens is 2s. 6d.

* * *

ASHLEY COURTENAY'S "Let's Halt Awhile in Britain and Ireland" (20th edition), priced 8s. 6d., contains his personal impressions and recommendations of hotels, inns and guest houses, numbering about 660 in England, Scotland, Wales and Ireland.

* * *

ACCORDING to an analysis by the Automobile Association of motoring touring overseas, France again leads the list of countries visited by British motorists. Next comes Switzerland, Italy and Belgium with equal popularity, followed by Germany, Scandinavia, Holland and Austria in that order.

* * *

THE BELGIAN National Tourist Office in Brussels states that the 1953 holiday season will not be affected by the flooding along the Belgian coast. Entertainment programmes and attractions already fixed for the season will be carried out in full, and it is expected that 1952's record tourist figures will be exceeded.

* * *

CAPTAIN the Rt. Hon. Lord TEYNHAM, D.S.O., D.S.C., R.N. (Rtd.), has been elected chairman of the Automobile Association in succession to the late Canon F. W. Hassard-Short. Lord Teynham has been a member of the A.A.'s Executive Committee since March, 1950.

* * *

AT THE RECENT TURIN MOTOR SHOW, Humber, Hillman and Sunbeam-Talbot models were exhibited by the Rootes Group's Italian distributors, Autofamosa, of Rome, and Saigarage, of Milan.

* * *

SUBSTANTIAL ACCELERATIONS of long-distance passenger expresses are a feature of British Railways' summer timetables, which operate from June 8 to September 20. Routes affected include

Panel illustration of the Shell Oil Exhibition now touring museums in the provinces.

An old picture showing one of the first Commer trucks operating in New Zealand.

Humber Hawk chassis exhibited at the opening of new showrooms in Lisbon, Portugal, by Messrs. J. C. Pacheco, Ltd.

A Humber Super Snipe in the striking Imperial Palm Avenue at Kandy, Ceylon.

Door-to-door fish sales are made by this Commer Express Delivery Van, delivered through Messrs. A/B Auto, of Malmo, Sweden.

LET PRATT TRAILERS SOLVE YOUR TRANSPORT PROBLEMS

LEADERS IN THEIR CLASS!

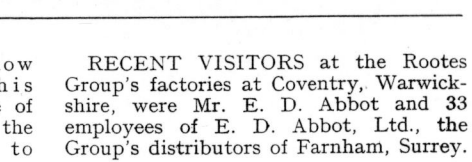

2 TO 8 CWT CARRYING CAPACITY

THE PRATT ENGINEERING COMPANY NORTHALLERTON YORKS, ENGLAND

In a Few Words:
(Continued from page 51)

London and Scotland, Birmingham, the West of England, South Wales, and East Anglia, and also Manchester-Liverpool.

* * *

TWO NEW AIR FERRY SERVICES for passengers, cars and cycles have been introduced by Silver City Airways between Gatwick and Le Touquet and Southampton and the Isle of Wight. The service to Le Touquet caters primarily for passengers.

* * *

A NEW CROSS-CHANNEL Steamer, the *Lisieux*, has been brought into service by the French Railways on the Newhaven/Dieppe route. She carries 1,450 passengers.

* * *

CAPTAIN O. P. JONES, C.V.O., O.B.E., who commands Stratocruiser airliners on B.O.A.C.'s North Atlantic routes, has now completed his 4,000,000th mile of flying. He is the first Briton to achieve such a remarkable total.

* * *

SIR,—It is now just over a year since I left England with my Humber Super Snipe Station Wagon and commenced to tour the Middle East.

The Humber has travelled throughout Lebanon, Syria, Turkey, Jordan and Iraq—apart from the Continent en route—and never once has there been a mechanical fault.

Despite the incredibly bad roads of most parts—roads which at home would never normally be attempted—and the great mountain passes, such as the Taurus, together with the long desert treks to Baghdad, never has the Humber faltered.

I have nothing but praise, and am indeed pleased that this was my selection.

(Signed) B.H.R.,
KYRENIA, Cyprus.

* * *

NEW HOTELS IN NORWAY are expected to open this year at Aalesund, Harstad, Henningsvag, Myrdal and in Kristiansund N.

RECENT VISITORS at the Rootes Group's factories at Coventry, Warwickshire, were Mr. E. D. Abbot and 33 employees of E. D. Abbot, Ltd., the Group's distributors of Farnham, Surrey.

* * *

A VIKING SERVICE to the Mediterranean island of Majorca has been introduced by British European Airways, leaving Northolt at 11.40 a.m. and reaching Palma, the capital, at 5.50 p.m. Tourist return costs £39 8s. 8d., including the "transportation tax" levied by the Spanish Government.

* * *

BY J. N. McHATTIE, A.M.I.Mech.E., M.S.A.E., the "Servicing Guide to British Motor Vehicles, Volume Two" brings the information of the first volume up to date with particulars of 1951 and 1952 models. The Hillman Minx is among the popular cars dealt with in the servicing information section.

* * *

WITH REGRET the death is recorded of Captain J. S. Irving, Technical Sales Manager of Girling, Ltd., on March 28, at Birmingham. Captain Irving played a prominent part in the design of the 1,500 h.p. Sunbeam, the first car to exceed 200 m.p.h., when he was Chief Engineer of the Sunbeam Motor Co. He later became Technical Director of the Rootes Group, leaving in 1931 to join Bendix, Ltd., one of the constituent companies of the present Girling Company.

* * *

MOORWELL MOTORS, LTD., of Cardiff, announce they have acquired the business of Sadler Bros., Windsor Road, Penarth. The business now comes into the South Wales group of Moorwell Companies which function as distributors for the Rootes Group.

* * *

ESSO PETROLEUM CO., LTD., have acquired Little Aston Hall, Streetly, near Birmingham, for the administrative headquarters of its Midland Division.

* * *

MR. P. R. SCUTT, Director and General Manager, has been appointed Managing Director of Tecalemit, Ltd. He was first appointed to the board in 1948.

A heavily laden Hillman Minx Saloon, bound for Kenya, makes a ferry-crossing of the Simiyu river in North Tanganyika : reader's photograph.